Macroeconomics

"Rossana has written a book that explains Macroeconomics very lucidly and in a very reader-friendly style. Covering Macroeconomics in a fair and balanced way with models from the major macroeconomic schools of thought and providing micro-foundations to the models, the book will be the text of choice for students who want to learn Intermediate Macroeconomics".

Tan Kim Heng, *Nanyang Technological University, Singapore.*

Research in macroeconomics in the last thirty years has featured, almost exclusively, two characteristics: an emphasis on the microfoundations of macroeconomics and secondly, intertemporal economics, that is, the behavior of economic actors over time. Curiously, textbooks in intermediate macroeconomics have been very slow to adopt these traits.

The aim of this book is to bring intermediate instruction in macroeconomics fully into line with the direction taken by the research community. Key hallmarks of the text include:

- a full introduction to the microfoundations of consumption and investment
- a complete model of the labor market with profit maximization for firms to determine labor demand and a utility maximization model to determine labor supply
- an analysis of the Baumol-Tobin model to determine money demand accompanied by a discussion of traditional money supply

Fully illustrated with figures and tables, and 'Doing Economics' boxes to bring the theory to life, this is an essential course book for modules in Intermediate Macroeconomics. Possessing a full range of additional learning features including a companion website and instructor's manual, the book takes an international view of macroeconomics with case studies and examples from the United States and beyond.

Robert J. Rossana is Professor of Economics, Department of Economics, Wayne State University, Detroit, USA.

Macroeconomics

Robert J. Rossana

Routledge
Taylor & Francis Group

LONDON AND NEW YORK

First published 2011
by Routledge
2 Park Square, Milton Park, Abingdon, Oxon, OX14 4RN

Simultaneously published in the USA and Canada
by Routledge
270 Madison Ave, New York, NY 10016

Routledge is an imprint of the Taylor & Francis Group,
an informa business

Typeset in Berling and Futura
by Keystroke, Station Road, Codsall, Wolverhampton
Printed and bound in the United States of America
by Edwards Brothers, Inc.

British Library Cataloguing in Publication Data
A catalogue record for this book is available from the British Library

Library of Congress Cataloging in Publication Data
Rossana, Robert J.
  Macroeconomics / Robert J. Rossana.
    p. cm.
  "First edition"—Pref.
  1. Macroeconomics. I. Title.
  HB172.5.R667 2011
  339—dc22   2010037443

ISBN: 978–0–415–77949–4 (hbk)
ISBN: 978–0–415–77950–0 (pbk)
ISBN: 978–0–203–82927–1 (ebk)

Contents

8 The Labor Market 224

PART III AGGREGATE ECONOMIC MODELS

9 Classical Models of the Aggregate Economy 267

10 Economic Growth 306

11 Aggregate Demand 340

List of "Doing Economics" Boxes

List of Tables

List of Figures

Guided Tour

LEARNING OBJECTIVES

This chapter introduces you to study in the social science of ecor asked by macroeconomists and (mathematical, graphical, and research. The objectives that v be presented, and we will di ome questions ansv

At the beginning of each chapter there is a box listing the learning objectives for the chapter. These give the student a quick summary of the chapter's subject matter and those questions answered by the material in the chapter.

These boxes highlight how the material covered in the chapter can be used to understand real world events. They also suggest additional reading that students might pursue to learn more about a topic.

Doing Economics:

The behavior of oil prices is faith (and sometimes downward) mov us to look at relative oil prices if behavior of the public. The figu Oil prices to the CPI. Now lo

Key Ideas

■ The basic insight of the the growth of inputs used in pro
■ Growth accounting is an em source of growth to the actu
■ A by-product of a growth growth of technology, kno
■ The basic one-sector mo parameters: the popu' anital stock.

At the end of each chapter, key words related to important chapter concepts are listed as well as the key ideas that the student should take away with them from reading the chapter. These relate directly to the learning objectives for the chapter.

Four types of questions are to be found at the end of chapters. Review Questions test students' ability to understand the basic concepts in the chapter. Thought Questions are more challenging and require the student to go beyond the material in the chapter. Numerical Questions allow the student to test their understanding of the economic models in a chapter. Data Questions ask the student to use the internet to find data that is related to the concepts in a chapter.

Questions for Study a

Review Exercises

1. Explain the concept of "double c
2. Gross Domestic Product (GDP) ' there are some non-market acti\ of a non-market production n'
3. Explain the difference betv

' Gross Domesti~ '

Preface to the first edition

This text grew out of lecture notes that I developed for teaching intermediate macroeconomics at the undergraduate level to students at Wayne State University. At the beginning, these notes filled in material that I wanted to teach, material that could not be found in existing textbooks. But as time passed, I found myself writing material because I enjoyed doing so and because I was not satisfied with the exposition found in many textbooks.

The material that I was adding to my course fell into two broad categories: microfoundations and intertemporal economic behavior. Microfoundations refers to the analysis of economic behavior by an individual firm or household, using these insights to understand the behavior of aggregate economies. Intertemporal economic behavior refers to the analysis of economic behavior over multiple time periods. If there were two trends to be found in macroeconomics research in the last forty years, it would be the increasing use of microfoundations and intertemporal analysis yet textbooks, for many years, never incorporated either of these methods of economic analysis. The absence from textbooks of these approaches to macroeconomics makes it impossible to present some of the most important insights offered by macroeconomic theory. Thus it seemed to me that any textbook presuming to represent the methods used by macroeconomists must invariably do the microfoundations of aggregate relationships and treat intertemporal topics.

In treating these and other topics, there is a strong emphasis in this book on using readily available data to test economic theories. Economic theory courses seem to me to be quite sterile if they are divorced from data on actual economies. For this reason, there is a recurring theme throughout the book that economic theories must be tested to see if they have relevance to the real world. This approach teaches the student the use of the scientific method to judge the merits of economic theories and it gives the student the chance to practice applying the theory they have learned. One of my goals is to convince the student that a great deal of what they observe around them and see in popular media can be understood and interpreted using the macroeconomics they will learn in this book. The ability to understand real world events is what I enjoy most about macroeconomics. I believe that students will find macroeconomics to be the fascinating subject that it is once they learn to use it to interpret actual events.

ANALYTICAL APPROACH

The theories that are discussed in this book will be the traditional workhorse models of macroeconomic analysis. They will be developed using graphical methods and algebraic derivations. It is my belief that most, if not all, of the important insights in macroeconomics can be derived in this way. However this approach requires that the student be able to manipulate and interpret graphs in order to learn the workings of macroeconomic models since graphical analysis will be used heavily throughout the book. Then the theories will be tested using macroeconomic data and this will typically involve time series or other types of charts to see if the implications of economic theories are apparent in actual macroeconomic data. The emphasis in presenting macroeconomic theories will be to develop economic intuition about economic models and to derive their testable predictions. Inspection of the data will serve to confirm that the theory is almost always evident in actual data but there will also be cases where the student will observe that the data does not support a theory that has been developed. Even when the implications of economic theory are evident in the data, the student will often see that there is more going on than just the predictions of the economic model being tested. In this way, students get a sense of how theories are developed, tested, and then refined when some or all of the parts of a theory fail testing. The constant interplay between theory and empirical testing is how advances in economic knowledge occur.

DOING ECONOMICS BOXES

It is important to convince students that the material they are learning can be used to understand real world events. Doing Economics boxes are contained in most chapters, accomplishing this and other objectives.

Some of these boxes will add some additional economic content to economic concepts. For example, the real interest rate and the marginal tax rate are defined and discussed in Chapter 2. In Chapter 4, a Doing Economics box points out that the return to saving actually depends upon the after-tax real interest rate and the box defines the after-tax real interest rate, showing how this new concept combines the marginal tax rate and real interest rate discussed previously.

Some boxes do real world applications of concepts discussed in the text. In Chapter 14 on Macroeconomic Policy, there are Doing Economics boxes dealing with macroeconomic policies were carried out to combat the most recent recession. There is also a discussion of policy rules in that chapter and there is a Doing Economics box describing the Taylor Rule for monetary policy, a monetary policy rule widely discussed by economists for carrying out monetary policy.

Chapter 13 provides a discussion of the Lucas Critique of economic policy evaluation, discussing the difficulty of evaluating the economic effects of policy rule changes. There is a Doing Economics box in this chapter describing the October 1979 policy rule change by the U.S. Federal Reserve, a real world example of a policy rule change relevant to the Lucas Critique.

Finally, some of the Doing Economics boxes suggest additional reading that students might pursue to learn more about a topic. For example, in Chapter 4, it is pointed out that bequests are ignored in the two-period model studied in the chapter. There is a Doing Economics box in that chapter that provides a brief discussion of actual bequest motives and gives references that might be read by students to learn more about the motivations for bequests.

UP TO DATE COVERAGE

The book contains quite a bit of material discussing the recession that originated in December 2007. This recession has origins that are unique in economic history and it generated policy responses that were also unique. There are Doing Economics boxes, as well as text discussion, describing these events in considerable detail.

UNIQUE FEATURES OF THE BOOK

This book has a number of features that distinguish it from other texts in the field.

- The book provides a complete set of chapters covering the microfoundations of each sector contained in aggregate macroeconomic models. For example, the labor market contained in aggregate models is developed in a chapter where the demand and supply for labor are derived and discussed. The aggregate model draws on the labor market microfoundations chapter to justify the properties of the labor market used in aggregate macroeconomic models.
- The microfoundation chapters frequently stress the intertemporal nature of economic decision-making. The chapter on household choice thoroughly describes the two-period model of consumption. Doing so allows the student to learn the Permanent Income Hypothesis and to use that theory to analyze policy questions such as Ricardian Equivalence and the effects of transitory tax cuts. The investment chapter provides a thorough treatment of the neoclassical investment model, derives the user cost of capital, and describes the forward-looking nature of investment decisions.
- Time series concepts are used to test the implications of aggregate economic models. As an example, Chapter 3 defines serial persistence in an economic time series. Then, in the business cycle chapter, each aggregate economic model is examined to see if it can explain serial persistence and, if it is present in the model, the student is given an explanation as to why serial persistence arises in the model.
- The chapter on the classical macroeconomic model contains the analysis of the Fisherian intertemporal production possibility schedule and develops the concepts of dynamic Pareto optimality. This part of the book describes the optimality criteria that must hold for an economy to have an optimal resource allocation over time while at the same time being consistent with household intertemporal utility maximization. The section establishes the relationship between the marginal rate of transformation and the real interest rate when an economy achieves intertemporal optimality.

BOOK ORGANIZATION

This book is comprised of the following three parts.

■ Part I consists of the first three chapters in the book covering preliminary concepts and measurement. What distinguishes this part of the book from many other texts is that the first chapter sets out the guiding principles of macroeconomic analysis, such as the implications of optimizing behavior by economic agents, that students must understand. Chapter 2 covers national income accounting. The chapter also defines and intuitively describes a number of important economic concepts such as the real interest rate and the marginal tax rate. The third chapter defines the time series properties of selected macroeconomic time series to be used in assessing the predictive abilities of aggregate macroeconomic models.

■ Part II contains five chapters covering the microfoundations of aggregate economic models. Three chapters cover intertemporal analyses of consumption, investment, and government. There is a chapter dealing with the financial markets (money and bond markets) and there is a chapter deriving the labor market to be used in aggregate macroeconomic models. These chapters are the motivation for the behavioral relationships in the aggregate models used later in the book.

■ Part III covers the workings of aggregate macroeconomic models. One chapter covers economic growth, including the important topic of technical progress as an engine for growth. The closed-economy models, used for business cycle analysis, provide a balanced view of the aggregate macroeconomic models used by macroeconomists. There will be discussions of New Classical, New Keynesian, Menu Cost, and Real Business Cycle models. Each model will be assessed regarding its ability to match the time series characteristics of macroeconomic data. It will be observed that each model has strengths and weaknesses regarding the model's ability to match the actual time series behavior of selected macroeconomic time series. The open economy model establishes the linkages, through goods and financial markets, permitting business cycle shocks, originating in a country, to be transmitted to other countries.

LEARNING AIDS

This book has a number of features designed to help students identify and learn the important concepts in each chapter. Below is a list of these features.

■ At the beginning of each chapter there is a box listing the goals to be achieved in the chapter. The information in the box gives the student a quick summary of the chapter's subject matter and the box lists a few questions answered by the material in the chapter.

■ Graphs are done in two colors. Black is used to portray initial positions in a diagram and a second color is used to show shifts of the curves in a diagram.

■ Important ideas are isolated from adjacent text and set out as propositions to make clear to the student that a crucial idea has just been presented.

■ Throughout the text, new concepts are in bold to alert the student that a new concept is being discussed.

- The results of a section are frequently summarized in a table to give the student a handy reference for the implications of an economic model.
- Key ideas are listed at the end of each chapter.
- At the end of each chapter, key words related to important chapter concepts are listed.
- Four types of problems are to be found in nearly every chapter. Review Questions are ones that are straightforward and test the student's ability to understand the basic concepts in the chapter. Thought Questions are more challenging; they ask the student to do more than just apply a chapter concept by asking questions that require the student to go beyond the material in the chapter. Numerical Questions are present to give the student an alternative way to test their understanding of the economic models in a chapter. Data Questions ask the student to use the internet to find data that is related to the concepts in a chapter. Finding and using data also gives the student the chance to see, in the data, the economic content of the chapter.
- The first chapter has an appendix that covers the mathematical concepts used in the book.
- There are appendices in several chapters containing the derivations of economic relationships used in the chapter containing the appendix.

FINAL THOUGHTS

It astonishes me to think of how much more knowledge is contained in a course based upon this book as compared to the macroeconomic theory course that I took as an undergraduate (although I prefer not to discuss how many years ago my undergraduate macroeconomics course was taken). One might conclude from this fact that the modern-day undergraduate student of macroeconomics must work much harder than students in the same course decades ago. While this is undoubtedly true, it is my hope that a student taking a course using this book will conclude that the course was well worth the effort because of how much the student has learned about how the world around her actually behaves. To use the jargon of economists, I hope that the extra benefits of doing macroeconomics using this book are at least as great as the extra costs of learning the contents of this book. At least this was my intent in writing this text. Students will ultimately decide if I have successfully achieved this goal.

Acknowledgments

A text results from the efforts of many individuals. On the list of people causing this book to happen, the name at the top must be that of Rob Langham, the sponsoring editor, who was willing to take the chance of allowing an economist, inexperienced at textbook-writing, to develop the first macroeconomics text offered by Routledge. I am very grateful to Rob for his confidence in me. My development editor at Routledge, Katy Hamilton, has made the development process as free of pain as it can be because of her competence and her ability to work amiably with an author.

A number of students at the undergraduate and graduate levels, too many to list here, read parts of the manuscript and made many useful suggestions. However I owe a special debt of gratitude to Susanne Buesselmann for the many hours she spent developing presentation slides and for reading and commenting upon earlier drafts of this book. Her impact on this book is everywhere to be seen.

Thanks are due to a number of anonymous reviewers who constructively commented on parts of this book. Many of their suggestions found their way into the final product. I also wish to thank two economists for their impact upon my thinking about economics and how to apply it. Louis J. Maccini has been a dissertation supervisor, mentor, and friend for many years. My development as an economist owes much to his training and his approach to doing economics. John J. Seater, a friend and colleague, has spent much time with me over the years discussing economics and using it to explain events around us. My enthusiasm for economics stems importantly from these conversations.

Finally, my wife Eileen and sons Matthew, Brian, and Thomas deserve my thanks for their support over all these years. My career in academia involved positions at a number of universities and they all went along for the ride with a minimum of fuss. Their presence in my life has made it all worthwhile.

The author and publisher would like to thank the following for permission to use copyright material:

Part I

Preliminary Topics

Chapter 1

An Introduction to Macroeconomics

LEARNING OBJECTIVES

This chapter introduces you to macroeconomics, one of the many areas of study in the social science of economics. We will discuss the types of questions asked by macroeconomists and you will be introduced to the sorts of tools (mathematical, graphical, and statistical) that are used in macroeconomics research. The objectives that we will assume for households and firms will also be presented, and we will discuss how we can assess economic policies. Below are some questions answered in this chapter.

- What topics are studied in macroeconomics?

- What is an economic model?

- How can economic policies be assessed in an economic model?

- What do households and firms try to maximize?

- What conditions hold when households and firms optimize?

- How do economists test economic theories?

- What is the best way to learn macroeconomics?

Economics is a social science containing specialized areas of study within it. Macroeconomics is one of those specialties and it is the branch of economics concerned with the behavior of aggregate economic systems (macro means "large in scale"). This means that in macroeconomics, economists try to determine, for example, the behavior of aggregate output in the economy rather than trying to explain the output produced by an individual firm studied in the branch known as microeconomics (micro means "small in scale"). Thus a crucial difference between microeconomics and macroeconomics is **aggregation**; macroeconomics focuses on behavior aggregated over households and firms, whereas microeconomics studies the behavior of economic agents at a disaggregated level.

Our purpose in this chapter is to explain the issues studied in macroeconomics, to describe how macroeconomists go about their study of these issues, and to present general principles of analysis and methods used in macroeconomics.

1.1 METHODS OF ANALYSIS IN MACROECONOMICS

Modern macroeconomics can be divided into two broad areas of study. These areas are: **microfoundations** and models of aggregate economies.

Microfoundations

Even though it was stated above that studying individual firms was the province of microeconomics, you will see that macroeconomists frequently study the behavior of individual households and firms. They do so because it is possible to obtain important insights into the behavior of aggregate economies by trying to understand the choices made by individual households and firms at the individual level. So later in the book, you will see chapters devoted to the consumption choices by households, the investment decisions by firms, and the determinants of money holdings by households. These analyses will shed light on how aggregate consumption and investment, and the aggregate demand for money, are determined.

Static and Intertemporal Behavior

In studying the behavior of the household and firm, it is possible to do so in a single period or multiple periods of time. If a single period is chosen for analysis, the economic theory developed is called **static**; if multiple periods of time are chosen, the analysis is said to be **intertemporal** or **dynamic**. There are situations where static and intertemporal analyses have economic implications that are about the same but there are important classes of problems where an issue must be examined in a multi-period framework. For example, if we are interested in learning about what determines saving by households, it is essential to use an analysis that applies to more than one period of time. After all, a saving decision is really a process involving the choice of future consumption by consumers since saving today can be used to finance future consumption. So our study of consumer behavior in Chapter 4 will require us to develop an economic framework applied to more than one period of time in the life of the household.

Aggregate Economic Models

Once the microfoundations of the economy have been established, aggregate economic models of the entire economy are developed which draw upon the results from the study of individual households and firms. The components of these models will be ones aggregated over households and firms. These aggregate models will have sectors corresponding to the major economic variables whose behavior we wish to understand. Thus there will be a market for goods where we try to determine the behavior of aggregate output. There will be a labor market where we can learn what determines the aggregate amount of labor used in production and the wage rates paid to labor. There will be a money market where we can learn about the way in which money is supplied to the economy and what determines the money the public wishes to hold. All of these markets, and possibly others, will be connected and as a group they will constitute a complete model of the aggregate economy. Such a model is sometimes called a **general equilibrium system** for the entire economy.

Economic Policy Evaluation

Economies are made up of households and firms pursuing their objectives but the economy also contains policymakers whose actions affect the performance of the economy. The government makes spending and taxation decisions that will affect the choices made by the public. There is also a central bank that supervises the monetary system and whose policy actions, affecting the supply of money, will also affect the economy. Part of the subject matter of macroeconomics is to study how the actions of these policymakers affect aggregate economic activity. In evaluating the effects of economic policies, two types of analyses will be conducted: positive and normative policy assessment.

Positive and Normative Policy Evaluation

One way to study the effects of economic policy is simply to study its effects on the economy without making any judgments about the efficacy or desirability of that policy. A **positive policy** assessment is one where we simply determine the effects of a policy without judging the desirability of that policy. As an example, you will learn later in this book that if the central bank reduces the growth rate of the stock of money, the inflation rate (the rate at which all prices in the economy rise) will decline. We will not be concerned with whether or not this is a good or a bad policy. We will only care about the economic effects of the reduced money growth rate.

A **normative policy assessment** is one where we try to decide if a particular policy intervention is desirable for an economy. So if we are studying a change in the distribution of income in the economy, we will want to know if giving one person more income, at the expense of others, is a desirable policy to implement. To do so will mean that we must have some way of evaluating the efficacy of changes in the income distribution.

1.2 WHAT MACROECONOMISTS DO: BUILDING AND TESTING MODELS

Knowledge in macroeconomics evolves in much the same way that it does in any scientific discipline. Economic models are built by economists. Then these models are tested to see if the predictions of economic models can be verified empirically, that is, verified with actual data.

The behavior of households, firms, and aggregate economies is represented in macroeconomics by **economic models**, abstractions that are meant to represent the structure of actual economies or to represent the behavior of households and firms. Graphs and/or equations will be used to illustrate the implications of economic models. These models produce predictions about economic behavior. So, as an example, our model of the household in Chapter 4 will generate a prediction about how consumption by the household responds to a change in its current income. A model of the business cycle, discussed in Chapter 12, will provide a prediction about how wages behave when economic activity declines.

These predictions must then be tested with **empirical research** to see if the predictions of these economic models can be found in actual economic data. This testing can take several forms. It can be as simple as looking at the behavior over time of economic data to see if the series behaves in a way predicted by economic theory. Sometimes testing requires the use of formal statistical methods which provide a way of rejecting the hypotheses implied by economic models.

To see how statistical testing can be done, imagine that an economic theory of the household predicts that household consumption obeys the following relationship.

$$C = a + b \cdot Y$$

where C is household consumption and Y is household income. Suppose that our theory implies that $a > 0$ and $b > 0$. Statistical testing of this relationship requires finding data on consumption and income and using this data to develop statistical estimates of the two parameters, a and b. If this statistical test verifies the predictions made by the model about the two parameters, an economist would conclude that the equation is a reasonable description of the relationship between consumption and income. If the parameters were found to be negative, say, an economist would conclude that the equation is not a good description of the consumption–income relationship.

Whatever method of empirical testing is used, the scientific method involves first developing economic theories, followed by the testing of economic theories, and then refining the theories if they fail economic testing. Equivalently, economic theory provides testable hypotheses about economic behavior. Empirical testing is then used to see if the hypotheses are false. The process is then usually repeated since, very often, some aspect of an economic theory does not hold up in the data. Economic theory is then refined and the testing process again occurs. In this way there is a constant interplay between theory and empirical work with the goal of enhancing our understanding of the economy.

Events Studied by Macroeconomists

Now that we have listed the tools used by macroeconomists, we can list some of the events studied by macroeconomists using the tools just described. A partial list is given below.

- What causes the level of output in the economy to rise or fall?
- What determines how many people are out of work and looking for a job?
- What determines the level of prices in the economy?
- Why does an economy grow over long periods of time?

Note that all of these questions, as well as others that we will ask, are "big picture stuff." They involve questions affecting all the members of a society and they are questions that involve the welfare of everyone in a society. The answers to these questions, if we can find them, have the potential for the application of economic policies improving economic welfare for the members of a society.

1.3 PRINCIPLES OF MACROECONOMIC ANALYSIS

Modern macroeconomic research uses a number of principles to develop an understanding of the workings of economic systems. Here we state a number of these guiding principles and discuss each one below. It is essential that you understand each of these concepts; they will be used repeatedly in this book as we study economic behavior. Partly you will be getting familiar with jargon used by economists. But you will also be learning the reasoning used by economists when they study economic systems.

Principles and Methods of Macroeconomic Analysis

- Households and firms optimize **intertemporally**.
- Households and firms may need to form **expectations** about economic magnitudes when they optimize.
- Households and firms face **constraints** when they optimize.
- A consequence of optimizing behavior is that **marginal benefits and costs are equal**.
- Macroeconomists use the device of a **representative household or firm** to describe the behavior of all households and firms.
- **Economic models** are made up of one or more equations and graphs.

- Economic models use the concept of a **market** to describe how prices and quantities are determined by the interactions of buyers and sellers.
- An **excess demand** in a market is a situation where the quantity demanded by economic agents exceeds the quantity of it supplied.
- An **excess supply** in a market is a situation where the quantity demanded by economic agents is less than the quantity of it supplied.
- The economy as a whole will be described by a **general equilibrium system**, a system of interconnected markets.
- General equilibrium systems contain **endogenous** and **exogenous** economic variables. Endogenous economic variables are determined within the general equilibrium system. Exogenous economic variables are determined outside of the general equilibrium system.
- A market and an economy can be in one of two sorts of equilibria: a **temporary equilibrium** or a **general equilibrium**.
- An economy is in a **temporary equilibrium** when excess demands and supplies for goods and financial assets in the economy are zero and when expectations are incorrect.
- An economy is in **general equilibrium** when there are no excess demands or supplies for goods and financial assets in the economy and when expectations are correct.

We now discuss each of these principles individually.

Households and Firms Optimize Intertemporally

If we are to understand why households and firms make the decisions that they make, we will need to understand their motivation. What objectives are they trying to achieve by their actions? Economists always take it to be the case that **economic agents** (a phrase used to describe both households and firms) try to maximize something. In the case of households, we will assume that they are trying to maximize their economic welfare. Regarding firms, we will assume they are trying to maximize their profits.

But if households and firms optimize, they could do so for a single period of time or for multiple periods of time. We will usually assume that optimization is done **intertemporally**, that is, over multiple periods of time. The reason for this assumption is simple; as stated above, many issues cannot be studied sensibly in a single period. Households have no reason to save if they were to live for only a single period of time. Similarly, firms make investment decisions over multiple periods of time since the equipment they use will provide services over more than one time period. Thus it is realistic to study households and firms optimizing over time in most, but not all, situations of interest to us.

Households and Firms May Form Expectations When They Optimize

When households maximize their welfare over time, they will need to use information about various economic magnitudes, such as their present and future income. Present income is likely to be known by the household but future income is unknown at the time that economic decisions are made. Sometimes we will assume, for simplicity, that the household acts as if it knows future income but, more realistically, households must somehow form an **expectation** about future income. These expectations may or may not be correct and it can be crucial to the household's welfare that they correctly forecast economic magnitudes. Later in the book, we will explore alternative ways that households and firms may form their expectations and we will see that the implications of economic models can be remarkably different depending upon how those expectations are made.

Households and Firms Optimize Subject to Constraints

We usually assume that household welfare is tied to a household's consumption of goods and services. Just as you can't have all of the things you want because you are constrained by your own income, so too will the households we study be constrained, in a static context, by their incomes; when they optimize over time, we will assume that there is an **intertemporal budget constraint** or **wealth constraint** that binds consumer choices over time. Similarly firms will have a technology, known as a **production function**, which represents the technical relationship between inputs in production, such as labor and raw materials, and the output that these inputs can produce. This technological constraint will bind the firm's choices when it attempts to maximize its profits. Thus we will always assume that economic actors optimize subject to constraints on their choices.

Optimization Causes Marginal Benefits and Costs to be Equalized

When an optimizing firm decides to use more or less of an input in production, such as labor services, it will choose what to do on the basis of how the decision will affect its profits. If using more labor raises profits, the firm will hire more labor. If profits rise by using less labor, the firm will choose to use less labor in production. As the firm continues to add labor, it decides if the extra or marginal benefit exceeds or is equal to the marginal cost of adding labor. This manner of decision-making leads to the following conclusion: marginal benefits and costs are equalized when the firm has maximized profits. We will see that similar reasoning applies when households make their expenditure decisions.

When agents optimize over time, a similar condition will arise. The **present value of marginal benefits will equal marginal costs** when agents make decisions for multiple periods of time. A **present value**, discussed later in the book, is a method of translating future benefits into their present equivalent. In this way, a household or firm can compute the benefit today of benefits arising in the future.

The Representative Household and Firm

Our analysis of household and firm behavior will provide what are called the **microeconomic foundations** of aggregate economies. Once these microeconomic foundations are developed, they will be used to represent components of aggregate economic models describing the behavior of households and firms. To do so, we will use the idea of a **representative household or firm**. This will mean that an aggregate relationship, describing the behavior of all households, is exactly like the relationship obtained from the analysis of an individual household. This is a simplifying assumption that makes it much easier to do macroeconomics.[1] As a result, the implications of our study of a household or a firm will carry over to an aggregate relationship involving all households and firms in the economy.

Economic Models Are Comprised of Equations and Graphs

Actual aggregate economies are very complex systems, too complex for economists to study them in all of their detail. As a result, economists construct simplified versions of actual economies that are hoped to be tractable (or manageable) approximations of reality. While some realism is lost by this approach, the hope is that these simplified models provide reliable descriptions of how actual economies function. An additional purpose of this model-building is that these models will provide insight into the workings of the economic system, helping us to develop economic intuition about how the economy as a whole operates.

The development of this economic intuition is aided by the use of equations and graphs. These tools are useful for they compactly describe the workings of an economic model and the implications of economic theory. So if we were to describe the demand for money, the graph we draw of it displays the implications of a theory of the household deciding how much money to hold. We can then use such a graph to organize our thoughts about how money demand varies with other economic magnitudes. Equations have a similar purpose; for example, they can embody the results of optimizing behavior by firms or households, helping us develop intuition for why households and firms behave as they do. The equations and graphs implied by these simplified abstractions of reality describe the testable implications of economic models.

Markets Are Components of Economic Models

In any aggregate economic model, there must be some device that can be used to describe how prices and quantities are determined by the buyers and sellers of products produced by the firms in the economy. Economists use the concept of a **market** to describe how prices and quantities are determined. A market arises due to the optimizing behavior of firms and households so that the microeconomic foundations described above provide the framework that allows a market to arise. A market is where buyers and sellers come together pursuing their self-interest (i.e., maximizing their welfare and profits) and their attempts to buy and sell goods will set the prices of goods and the quantities of goods that are traded in the market.

---

1 Aggregation over agents is not a trivial operation. It can happen that the properties of an aggregate relationship can be very different from the properties of an individual relationship. We follow the customary procedure in macroeconomics of ignoring these difficulties in our analyses.

The exact details of how a model of a market works can vary in different economic theories. Sometimes we will assume that prices and quantities change in accordance with market forces and sometimes we will assume that, at least temporarily, market forces are impeded in their effects upon prices and quantities. Whatever the details of how the market operates, a market framework will be frequently used to examine the consequences of optimizing behavior by economic agents.

Markets May Have Excess Demands or Supplies

In establishing how prices and quantities are determined in markets, we will need to know what forces drive prices and quantities towards their equilibria. We will use the concepts of market excess demands and supplies to establish how prices and quantities change in markets not in equilibrium. So in a market where there is an **excess demand** (defined to be quantity demanded exceeding quantity supplied), we will argue that this causes price in the market to rise. When there is an **excess supply** (defined to be a case where quantity supplied exceeds quantity demanded), we will argue that the price in the market will fall. This reasoning describes how equilibrium is reached in the market. In excess demand or supply situations, price and quantity will change in the market until the excess demand or supply has been eliminated.

Aggregate Economic Models Are General Equilibrium Systems

Aggregate economies contain a number of markets where buyers and sellers interact. For example, there is a labor market where households offer labor supply and where firms demand labor to be used in production. There will also be a money market where households demand money to be used in exchange for goods and services and where money is supplied to households through the banking system. All of these markets are interconnected and the complete set of these markets is referred to as a **general equilibrium system**. These abstractions of aggregate economies built by economists contain a set of interconnected markets, represented by equations and/or graphs, and part of the challenge of understanding the operation of an economy is to learn how changes in one market can affect other markets in the economy. Thus when there is a change in the supply of money to households, this can have implications for goods, labor, and other markets. A complete understanding of the effect of economic policy will require an understanding of how all markets in an economy are affected by a policy change.

General Equilibrium Systems Have Endogenous and Exogenous Variables

In any general equilibrium system, there will be variables that are determined outside of the economic model. One example of such a magnitude is government spending where we will usually assume that the value of this variable is determined by the government and set independently of the economic system.

An endogenous variable is determined within an economic model, given the values of the exogenous variables contained in the economic model. So when we study the economic properties of a general equilibrium system, one question we will ask is how output is determined, given the values of all the exogenous variables in the economy. A standard exercise that we will do is to determine how endogenous variables in an economic model change in response to variations in individual exogenous variables. In this way we can study the economic effects of economic policies set by the government and central bank.

A Temporary Equilibrium Has Incorrect Expectations

There will be markets in some economic models where the expectations of economic agents will partly determine the behavior of price and quantity in the market. For example, we will study a labor market in Chapter 8 where labor suppliers do not know the price level and so must form an expectation of it. The possibility will exist in such models that, although there is no excess supply or demand in the market, expectations could be incorrect or they may be correct. When they are incorrect, we will expect economic actors to discover their error and then form new expectations. Doing so will change price and quantity in labor and other markets. For this reason, we refer to the situation where there are no excess supplies or demands for goods and services with incorrect expectations as a **temporary equilibrium** in the market or the economy as a whole.

General Equilibrium Requires Correct Expectations

When agents have correct expectations, they will observe this to be the case and so will not change their expectations; market prices and quantities will not change in this case. As a result, we refer to the situation where there is no excess demand or supply in any market and correct expectations as a **general equilibrium** in the economy.

1.4 LEARNING MACROECONOMICS

To learn macroeconomics is to learn how to think like an economist and this means developing the economic intuition of a macroeconomist. You develop this intuition by using the tools employed in macroeconomics, equations and graphs. The use of these tools to represent economic behavior imposes a logical discipline on your thinking about an economic problem. It is the learning of this logic that can sometimes cause students to struggle in understanding the implications of economic models. This difficulty can be avoided in the following way.

Macroeconomics is a subject best learned by doing it. By this is meant that the material is learned most effectively by applying what you learn in problem-solving, sometimes called by economists **learning-by-doing**. That is, working through economic models is essential to learn how these models work. That may mean solving problems given to you by your instructor or found at the end of each chapter. It may also mean working through economic models on your own, doing exercises designed to illustrate how those models work in a Study Guide or on a web site. But it is essential that you do the stuff; do not just sit back in class and listen, trying to memorize what you are told. You must be engaged as a student in class but that must be supplemented outside the classroom with learning-by-doing (or problem-solving).

1.5 CHAPTER ORGANIZATION

This book is divided into three parts. Part I is concerned with economic measurement. In these chapters, we define and explain the construction of the economic data series (Chapter 2) that we will use in our analysis of the economy. We will also discuss important economic concepts used later in the book. In addition, we will illustrate how the business cycle (Chapter 3) is defined and measured since business cycle analysis will be an important element of our study of aggregate economic systems.

Part II comprises the microfoundations of macroeconomics. Here you will find a chapter discussing the theory of the household (Chapter 4) where you will study how individuals make buying and saving decisions over time. There is then a chapter dealing with the investment decisions by firms (Chapter 5) where you will learn what determines the amounts of plant and equipment that firms will want to use in production. Chapter 6 deals with government, listing the various ways in which the government can affect economic life and how government finances its activities. Chapter 7 deals with the monetary system. In this chapter, there will be a discussion of why households hold money, we study the money supply process and thus the banking system, and we will discuss the role of the central bank in the monetary system. Chapter 8 deals with the labor market. This chapter contains a model of the demand for and supply of labor, a model that will be used to determine the quantity of labor used in the economy and the wage rates paid to workers. This analysis will be part of the foundation for the supply side of our aggregate economic models.

Part III contains economic models of the aggregate economy and an examination of economic policy. Chapter 9 provides an analysis of a classical model of the economy, one where there is no business cycle. Chapter 10 covers the important subject of economic growth where you will learn why living standards grow over long stretches of time. In Chapters 11 and 12, we build a model of cyclical fluctuations which we will use to explain why economies can depart from the analysis we saw in the classical model of the economy. Chapter 13 will have a discussion of the relationship between inflation and unemployment, how the public's expectations may be formed, and how those expectations can affect the economy. Chapter 14 contains a discussion of economic policy. Here we will ask how changes in government spending, tax rates, and the money supply will affect economic activity. Finally, Chapter 15 extends our aggregate models of the closed economy by adding an international sector to our analysis, and asking how trade in goods and financial capital will affect the functioning of the economy.

We attempt to evaluate the predictions of economic models throughout all of these chapters to give students a real sense of how the implications of economic models can be observed in the world around them. So when we discuss aggregate economic models of the business cycle, we will compare the predictions of these models with the measurement of the business cycle in Chapter 3. The purpose of these exercises will be to give students the chance to practice applying economics to the world around them and to illustrate how economic theories are tested. Students will see that, as in most disciplines, there are some aspects of economic theory that hold up in the data and some aspects do not. This explains why economic research continues.

The issues arising in macroeconomics are discussed in the media nearly every day. If you master the material in this book, you will have a better understanding of the world around you, and you will be better able to make sense of these media discussions.

Key Ideas

- Macroeconomics is that branch of economics that studies the behavior of aggregate economic systems.
- The microfoundations of macroeconomics is that part of macroeconomics where the behavior of individual economic agents is studied.
- Aggregate macroeconomic models are sets of relationships describing the behavior of an entire macroeconomic economy.
- Analysis of economic behavior confined to a single period of time is called static analysis.
- The analysis of economic behavior over multiple periods of time is known as intertemporal analysis.
- The relationships in aggregate economic models are assumed to be behaviorally similar to relationships obtained from the behavior of individual households and firms.
- Positive economic policy evaluation is a method of economic analysis where the effects of economic policies are described but not judged regarding their efficacy or desirability.
- Normative economic analysis is a method of economic analysis where we attempt to determine the desirability of economic policies.
- An economic model is a set of equations and/or graphs that represent all sectors of an aggregate economy.
- Empirical research attempts to establish the correctness of the economic implications of an economic theory using actual economic data. The predictions of a model are compared to actual data to see if they are evident in economic data.
- Households and firms will be assumed to maximize their objectives (economic welfare or profits) over multiple periods of time.
- Households and firms optimize subject to constraints on their choices.
- Optimization in a static context causes marginal benefits and costs to be equal.
- Optimization in an intertemporal context causes the present value of marginal benefits to equal marginal costs.
- Prices and quantities will be set in markets where households and firms maximize utility and profits.
- An excess demand is a situation where the quantity demanded by the public exceeds the quantity supplied by firms.
- An excess supply is the situation where the quantity demanded by the public is less than the quantity supplied by firms.

■ A temporary equilibrium is one where excess demands and supplies are zero and the expectations of economic agents are incorrect.

■ A general equilibrium is one where excess demands and supplies are zero and the expectations of economic agents are correct.

■ The representative household or firm is a device for representing the actions of all households or firms in the economy.

■ An aggregate economic model is a general equilibrium system representing all sectors of an aggregate economy.

■ Economic models contain exogenous variables, determined outside of the economic model, and endogenous variables, determined by or within the economic model.

Key Words

Microfoundations	Intertemporal Budget	Present Value of	Market
General Equilibrium	Constraint	Marginal Benefits	Wealth Constraint
System	Temporary Equilibrium	Dynamic	General Equilibrium
Normative Policy	Aggregation	Exogenous Variables	Endogenous Variables
Assessment	Positive Policy Evaluation	Static	Intertemporal
Excess Supply	Optimization	Expectations	Excess Demand
Learning-by-Doing	Economic Model	Constraints	Representative Firm
Marginal Cost	Representative Household	Empirical Research	Marginal Benefit

Questions for Study and Review

Review Exercises

1. What are the main assumptions economists make about household and firm behavior?
2. What is the difference between static and intertemporal economic behavior?
3. Explain the difference between normative and positive policy evaluation.
4. Explain how economists test the implications of economic theory.
5. Which institutions take part in economic policy making?
6. What condition arises as a result of optimizing behavior by firms and households?
7. Explain how price and quantity are set in a market context.

Thought Question

1. Consider the following system of equations for x and y: $a{\cdot}x + b{\cdot}y + c{\cdot}z = 0$, $d{\cdot}x + e{\cdot}y + f{\cdot}z = 0$. Find two equations that show how y and x are determined by z.

Numerical Question

1. Suppose a nonlinear function is given by $y = 2 \cdot x^2 + 8$. What is the value of the y-intercept? What is the value of the slope at $x = 5$? Draw the function into a coordinate system.
2. Suppose output, Y, is produced by the following production technology: $Y = 100 \cdot L^{0.5} + 20 \cdot K^{0.8}$, where L is labor, and K is physical capital. Calculate the change in Y given a change in x, denoted by $\Delta Y/\Delta L$. Also calculate the change in Y with respect to a change in capital, denoted by $\Delta Y/\Delta K$.
3. Repeat Numerical Question 2 except now use the equation $Y = 100 \cdot L^{0.5} \cdot K^{0.8}$.
4. Assume again that the production function is given by $Y = 2 \cdot L \cdot K$, where Y is output, L is labor, and K is capital. The growth rate of labor, $\Delta L/L$, is 1.5 percent, whereas the growth rate of capital, $\Delta K/K$, is 2 percent.

   a) Calculate the growth rate of output.
   b) What is the growth rate of capital if labor grows at 1.5 percent and output grows at 5 percent?

5. Solve the following equations for L and K: $2 \cdot L + 4 \cdot K = 48$, $17 = K + L$.
6. Assume that $y = 15 \cdot x - 3$ and $x + y = 13$. Find the values for x and y where the two curves intersect by drawing the functions into a coordinate system. Verify your graphical solution numerically.
7. A production function is given by $Y = 2 \cdot L \cdot K$, where Y is output, L is labor, and K is capital. Find $\Delta Y/\Delta L$.
8. What is the slope ($\Delta y/\Delta x$) of the line $y = 10 + .3 \cdot x + .7 \cdot z$? By how much will y change due to a one-unit change in z?

Data Exercises

1. Visit the web site of the Federal Reserve (www.federalreserve.gov). List four policy tools for monetary policy. Check out the data available at this site.
2. Visit the following web sites that provide economic data: The Bureau of Labor Statistics (www.bls.gov), the Bureau of Economic Analysis (www.bea.gov), and the Council of Economic Advisors (www.whitehouse.gov/cea). Make a list of the economic series and other information that you find at these sites that you can use later in the course.

For further questions, multiple choice quizzes, and weblinks related to this chapter, visit www.routledge.com/textbooks/rossana

MATHEMATICAL APPENDIX: ANALYTICAL METHODS

In this appendix, there is a discussion about the use of equations, graphs, and other analytical methods used in this book. In the discussion below, the symbol Δ denotes the change in a variable.

Functions of Two or More Variables

The economic models that you will study in this book provide predictions about relationships between two or more economic magnitudes. The content of the theory is that it will determine the particular economic variables to be contained in an economic relationship and the theory will also predict how changes in one variable will change another variable in the relationship.

As an example, the demand for money that we discuss in Chapter 7 predicts that the money held by an individual will depend upon the individual's level of real consumption and the interest rate, among other things. Equivalently, the demand for money is a function of (depends upon) real consumption and the interest rate. The theory will also predict that when the interest rate rises, money held by the individual will fall and that money demand rises if consumption rises. In mathematical notation, we will describe this money demand relationship as $M^D = L(C, i)$ where M^D refers to the demand for money, C is real consumption, and i denotes the interest rate. The notation $L(C, i)$ shows that there is a functional relationship relating the two magnitudes, C and i, to the demand for money. If there were more than two variables that determine money demand, the additional magnitudes would be listed within the function $L(\ )$. If there is an inverse relationship between the interest rate and money demand implied by economic theory, we will denote this fact with the notation $\Delta M^D/\Delta i < 0$. The response of money demand to a change in consumption would be denoted by $\Delta M^D/\Delta C > 0$. Notice the structure of the notation $M^D = L(C, i)$ used to describe the money demand relationship; it describes the causality implied by economic theory. The variable chosen by the individual or household is on the left side of the equal sign with the determinants of this variable on the right hand side of the expression embedded within the functional relationship $L(\ )$.

These economic relationships can take the form of an explicit equation that embodies the predictions of an economic theory or it could take the form of a graph illustrating the implications of economic theory. The two approaches are typically equivalent but offer differing perspectives on economic theory, each of which has its own uses. It is important that you develop the skills needed to understand the economic implications of both equations and graphs since they will both figure heavily in the presentation of the topics studied in this book.

Equations

Consider the two-variable equation

$$y = 10 + .75 \cdot x.$$

The intercept of this equation (the value of y when x is equal to zero) is 10. As the value of x ranges over different values, the value of y will change in a manner consistent with the equation that relates y and x. So imagine that x takes the discrete values x = 0, 1, 2, 3, and 4, the table below reports the values of y consistent with the equation above. In the equations that will be used in this book, there will be a unique value of y associated with each value of x, although this need not always be the case.

Value of y	Value of x
10	0
10.75	1
11.50	2
12.25	3
13.00	4

The Slope of an Equation

The slope of a line is defined to be

$$\text{Slope} = \frac{\Delta y}{\Delta x}.$$

The slope of a line measures, by definition, the change in y associated with a change in x. We can infer the slope of the line from the tabular data above. Note that in the table, a one unit increase in x is always associated with a change in y of .75.

In the equation specified above, the slope is positive and its value is observed to be .75 by applying the change operator to the equation. That is, $\Delta y/\Delta x = .75$. This implies that an increase in x will cause an increase in y. This describes the **qualitative** response of y to a change in x. But because we have an explicit function given to us, the slope also measures the **quantitative** change in y associated with the change in x. In this equation, a one-unit change in x results in a change in y of .75. The slope of this line is always .75, irrespective of the values taken by the variable x. The slope is quantitatively the same everywhere (for any value of x) because the equation is **linear**. This constant slope value is also evident in the tabular data above.

In Figure 1.1 below, we plot a linear equation with positive slope and one with a negative slope. Economic models will lead to both positive and negative relationships between pairs of variables and one task for you in studying economic models will be to understand the economic intuition for the relationships between pairs of economic magnitudes that are implied by economic theory.

In Figure 1.2, we plot an example of a **nonlinear** function at two points, x_1 and x_2. The important characteristic of such a function in this book is that its slope is qualitatively the same everywhere (but this is not always true) but the magnitude of the slope varies with changes in the value of x. The figure displays these features by showing that the slope is everywhere positive but the slope clearly declines as x rises. Economic models will usually have an explanation for the slope of nonlinear functions and they also will explain why the slope declines or rises with x.

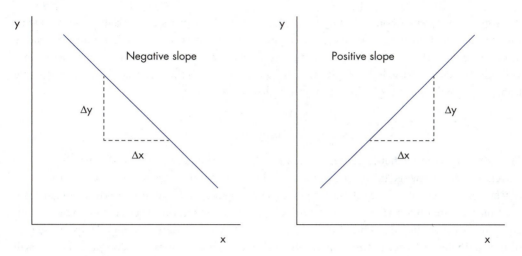

FIGURE 1.1 Linear Functions

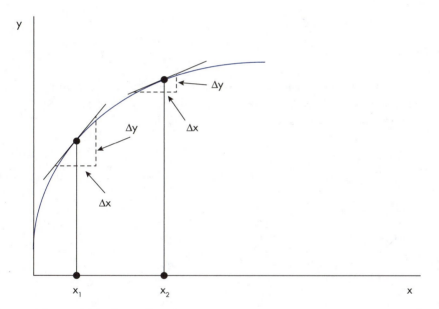

FIGURE 1.2 A Nonlinear Function

Shifts in Equations

An equation may only involve two economic variables of interest to us but usually there will be more than two variables in the equations with which we will work. As an example, consider the three variable equation given below.

$$y = 10 - .25 \cdot x - .75 \cdot z$$

If we graph this expression in the xy plane, the variable z appears as a variable that will shift the equation that we have. Now consider Figure 1.3. The equation above has a negative slope in the xy plane (the coefficient preceding x is a negative number). But now an increase in z will shift the curve to the left. Why to the left? Because the coefficient preceding z is a negative number, we will denote this shift using the following notation.

$$\left.\frac{\Delta y}{\Delta z}\right|_{\Delta x=0} < 0$$

In words, for given x (that is, for the situation where x is constant so $\Delta x = 0$), the change in y associated with a change in z is negative. So in the figure, an increase in z will reduce the value of y at a given value of x. A decline in z will raise y at a given x. Economic models will generate relationships involving two or more variables and the economic model will explain why equations shift as they do. The direction in which the curve will shift depends upon the sign of the coefficient preceding the variable that changes its value. Because economic models will suggest economic relationships with more than one shift variable, your challenge will be to understand the economic reasoning for why the change in each variable shifts an equation in the way that it does.

Differentials

In applying the change operator to linear equations above, we were using examples of computing the differential of equations. Here we give several rules, without proof, for the computation of the differentials of an equation.

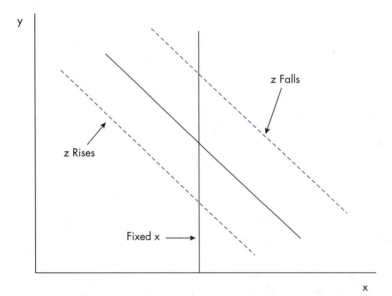

FIGURE 1.3 Shifts in Equations

Given a fixed value for x, an increase in z will reduce the value of y if z has a negative coefficient preceding it. A decline in z will therefore increase the value of y. The equation in the text, illustrated here, is y = 10 −.25·x−.75·z

Constant Rule: If $y = c$ with c a constant, $\Delta y = \Delta c = 0$
Sum (Difference) Rule: If $y = x \pm z$, $\Delta y = \Delta x \pm \Delta z$
Product Rule: If $y = x \cdot z$, $\Delta y = z \cdot \Delta x + x \cdot \Delta z$
Ratio Rule: If $y = x/z$, $\Delta y = (z \cdot \Delta x - x \cdot \Delta z)/z^2$
Power Rule: $y = x^n$, $\Delta y = n \cdot x^{n-1} \cdot \Delta x$

So given the equation $y = 100 \cdot x^{.5}$, $\Delta y = 100 \cdot .5 \cdot x^{.5-1} \cdot \Delta x = 50 \cdot x^{-.5} \cdot \Delta x$. This example illustrates the use of the Constant Rule (the differential of a constant, 100, is zero), the Product Rule, and the Power Rule. Finally, consider $y = 2x/3z$. Then this equation implies $\Delta y = (3 \cdot z \cdot 2 \cdot \Delta x - 2 \cdot x \cdot 3 \cdot \Delta z)/(3z)^2 = 2 \cdot \Delta x/3 \cdot z - 2 \cdot x \cdot \Delta z/3 \cdot z^2$.

Chart Types

We will need to use several sorts of charts or graphs when we are working with actual economic data. One type is a time series chart where we measure an economic magnitude at several points in time and plot the series in a chart. On the horizontal axis are the time periods at which we measure the data and, on the vertical axis, we measure the series values at each point in time. The chart below, Figure 1.4, provides an example of this sort of chart using a measure of output produced in the U.S., Gross Domestic Product.

An alternative way to display the data on GDP is to display it in a **bar chart**, given in Figure 1.5. Here the horizontal axis again is the year to which the data applies. The vertical axis measures GDP at each date but a bar is used to display the data. The height of each bar corresponds to the size of each data point.

The final chart type that we will use is a **scatter diagram**, shown in Figure 1.6. Here we will be interested in observing what kind of a relationship exists between a pair of economic series.

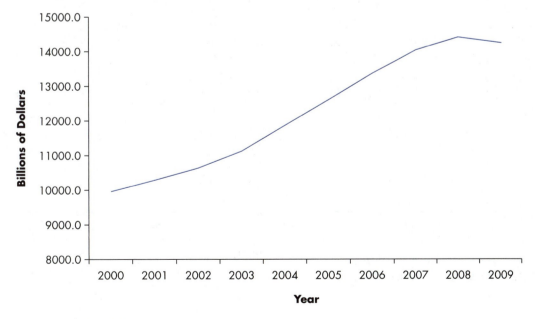

FIGURE 1.4 U.S. GDP

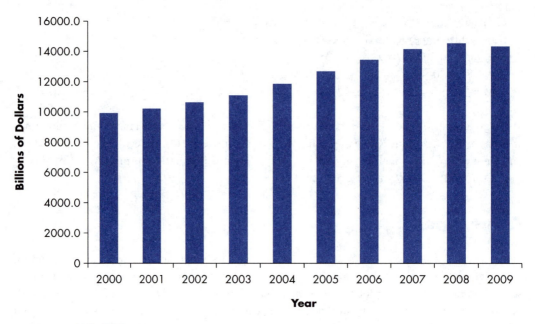

FIGURE 1.5 U.S. GDP

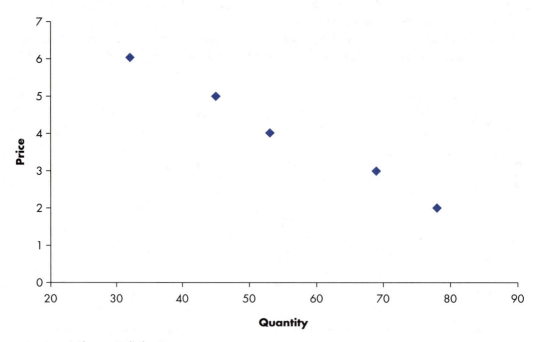

FIGURE 1.6 Plotting Tabular Data

To illustrate this type of chart, suppose first that we have data on price and quantity for a product, data that is displayed in the table below. This tabular data describes some sort of relationship between price and quantity for some commodity.

Quantity	Price
78	2
69	3
53	4
45	5
32	6

In Figure 1.6, quantity is measured on the horizontal axis with price measured on the vertical axis. The diagram reveals what appears to be a negative relationship between price and quantity. And so by plotting price and quantity, we get information on how price and quantity are related to each other.

Growth Rates

It will be useful to be able to compute the growth rate of the product and ratio of variables. To see how to do this, consider the equation

$$y = x \cdot z.$$

To compute the growth rate of y, apply the change operator to the product of x and z in the following way, using the rules for differentials given above.

$$\Delta y = \Delta x \cdot z + x \cdot \Delta z$$
$$\Delta y = \frac{\Delta x \cdot x \cdot z}{x} + \frac{x \cdot z \cdot \Delta z}{z}$$
$$\frac{\Delta y}{xz} = \frac{\Delta x}{x} + \frac{\Delta z}{z}$$
$$\frac{\Delta y}{y} = \frac{\Delta x}{x} + \frac{\Delta z}{z}$$

Sensibly enough, the growth rate of y is the sum of the growth rates of x and z.

Suppose we have the ratio given below.

$$y = \frac{x}{z} \cdot$$

The growth rate of y can be derived in the following way.

$$\Delta y = \frac{\Delta x}{z} - \frac{x}{z^2} \cdot \Delta z$$

$$\Delta y = \frac{x}{z} \cdot \frac{\Delta x}{x} - \frac{x}{z} \cdot \frac{\Delta z}{z}$$

$$\Delta y = \frac{x}{z} \cdot \left[\frac{\Delta x}{x} - \frac{\Delta z}{z} \right]$$

$$\frac{\Delta y}{y} y = \frac{x}{z} \cdot \left[\frac{\Delta x}{x} - \frac{\Delta z}{z} \right]$$

$$\frac{\Delta y}{y} \frac{x}{z} = \frac{x}{z} \cdot \left[\frac{\Delta x}{x} - \frac{\Delta z}{z} \right]$$

$$\frac{\Delta y}{y} = \frac{\Delta x}{x} - \frac{\Delta z}{z}$$

And so the growth rate of a ratio is the difference between the growth rates of the numerator and the denominator.

As a final example, consider a case that is a combination of the two preceding examples. Suppose you are given the ratio

$$v = \frac{p \cdot y}{m} .$$

To compute the growth rate of v, do the following.

$$\Delta v = \frac{\Delta p \cdot y}{m} + \frac{\Delta y \cdot p}{m} - \frac{p \cdot y}{m^2} \cdot \Delta m$$

$$\Delta v = \frac{\Delta p}{p} \cdot \frac{y \cdot p}{m} + \frac{\Delta y}{y} \cdot \frac{p \cdot y}{m} - \frac{p \cdot y}{m} \cdot \frac{\Delta m}{m}$$

$$\Delta v \cdot \frac{m}{p \cdot y} = \frac{\Delta p}{p} + \frac{\Delta y}{y} - \frac{\Delta m}{m}$$

$$\frac{\Delta v}{v} = \frac{\Delta p}{p} + \frac{\Delta y}{y} - \frac{\Delta m}{m}$$

The growth rate of the ratio is again the difference between the growth rates of numerator and denominator; the only difference from what we did above is that, now, the growth rate of the numerator is the sum of two growth rates.

Solving Systems of Equations

Economic models will sometimes be written as numerical problems to be solved. Here we illustrate a quick method of solving a two-equation system of equations involving two unknown variables, Y and X.

Suppose you were given the two equations below.

$$.75 \cdot Y = 5000 - 1000 \cdot X$$

$$4000 = 250 + .5 \cdot Y - 100 \cdot X$$

Rewrite these equations as

$$1000 \cdot X = 5000 - .75 \cdot Y$$

$$100 \cdot X = 250 + .5 \cdot Y - 4000$$

Multiply the second equation by 10 to get

$$1000 \cdot X = 5000 - .75 \cdot Y$$

$$1000 \cdot X = 2500 + 5 \cdot Y - 40000$$

Now subtract the second equation from the first and solve the result to get

$$0 = 5000 - 2500 - .75 \cdot Y - 5 \cdot Y + 40000$$

$$5.75 \cdot Y = 42500$$

$$Y = 7391.3$$

which is the solution for one of the variables in the model. The solution for the other variable, X, may be obtained by taking the value of Y just computed and substituting this value into either equation in the model, solving the resulting equation for X.

Logarithms

Economists use logarithms when they study economic models because they can be very convenient when manipulating equations describing economic behavior. By definition, a logarithm is the power to which a base number must be raised to generate a particular number. So in the case where $5 \cdot 5 = 5^2 = 25$, then $\log_5 25 = 2$. The base used can be any number but, in practice, two base numbers are used. One is the base ten (called a common logarithm and denoted by $\log_{10}$ or just log) and the other is the base e (called a natural logarithm and denoted by ln). The number e is approximately equal to 2.71828.

The number e is actually the limiting value of a particular mathematical expression. That particular expression leads to the following examples illustrating the use of natural logs.

$$\ln e^5 = 5 \qquad \ln e^1 = 1 \qquad \ln 1 = 0 \qquad \ln 1/e = \ln e^{-1} = -1,$$

The examples show that, for a given expression e^a with exponent a, a is the natural log of e^a. Additionally, logarithms obey mathematical rules illustrated by the following examples.

$$\ln (a \cdot b) = \ln a + \ln b, \ln (e^2 \cdot e^3) = 2 + 3, \ln (a/b) = \ln a - \ln b, \ln (A \cdot e^r) = \ln A + r$$

As these examples show, taking the natural log of a product or ratio can simplify an expression by converting a product or ratio into a sum or difference; a sum or difference can often be simpler to handle in mathematical expressions.

Finally it is useful to apply the results that we just discussed for logarithms to operations with growth rates illustrated earlier in this appendix. Consider the following examples.

$$y = x \cdot z, \ \ln y = \ln (x \cdot z) = \ln x + \ln z, \ \Delta\ln y = \Delta\ln x + \Delta\ln z$$

$$\Delta y/y = \Delta x/x + \Delta z/z$$

$$y = x/z, \ \ln y = \ln(x/z) = \ln x - \ln z, \ \Delta\ln y = \Delta\ln x - \Delta\ln z$$

$$\Delta y/y = \Delta x/x - \Delta z/z$$

$$v = p \cdot y/m, \ \ln v = \ln(p \cdot y/m) = \ln p + \ln y - \ln m, \ \Delta\ln v = \Delta\ln p + \Delta\ln y - \Delta\ln m$$

$$\Delta v/v = \Delta p/p + \Delta y/y - \Delta m/m$$

To prove that $\Delta\ln y = \Delta y/y$ requires some tools from calculus which are not provided here.

Chapter 2

Concepts and Measurement

LEARNING OBJECTIVES

This chapter has two goals. One is to explain the accounting system that is used to measure economic activity in aggregate economies. The second goal is to present and explain a series of important economic concepts that will be crucial to your understanding of the economic models used later in the book. Here are a few of the questions that we seek to answer in this chapter.

- How do we measure the amount of output produced and income earned in a society?
- What is the difference between final and intermediate goods?
- What is meant by **private** and **government** saving?
- How do we measure the level of prices in the economy?
- What is the difference between nominal and real economic magnitudes?
- What is meant by the real interest rate?
- How are payments occurring in the future translated into their present equivalents?

Macroeconomics could not exist as a functional social science without macroeconomic data. The existence of this data is necessary for economists to learn how the economy functions and to test theories of economic behavior. The most important source of macroeconomic data is the National Income and Product Accounts (NIPA) data compiled by the Bureau of Economic Analysis, an agency of the U.S. government. One purpose of this chapter is to introduce you to this crucial source of data and to study the information that it provides.

The second objective of this chapter is to discuss a series of economic concepts that will be used repeatedly throughout this book. These concepts will be needed as you work through the economic models discussed later in this book. Part of what you must do in a course like this is to learn how to think about economic problems in much the same way that a professional economist thinks about them. By learning these economics concepts, you will have a foundation for applying economic analysis, as an economist would, to the many sorts of economic problems that you will study in this book.

The first part of the chapter provides a discussion of the NIPA data where you will see that there are three ways to measure output and related measures of economic activity. Two of these arise because the NIPA accounts are a double-entry accounting system tracking the aggregate purchases in the economy as well as the incomes arising from these transactions. You will see what data is provided by this system and you will learn how the various sectors of the economy are related.

Next we will discuss a series of important economic relationships implied by the NIPA system. For example, the aggregate level of saving by the public and the government will be derived. These are important concepts for understanding the budgetary positions of households and the government as well as the connection between saving and the international transactions in the economy.

Then we take up a discussion of a series of important economic concepts that you will need to understand in order to apply macroeconomic theory. For example, we discuss how real output can be measured in the economy, a crucial concept for business cycle analysis. There will also be a discussion of index numbers, showing what information they reveal and how they can be used to measure prices in the economy. The marginal tax rate will be defined; this magnitude has an important impact upon the incentives faced by households and firms. We will also discuss interest rates and show how to use them in making present value calculations. Present values will be important in understanding how households and firms make decisions over time.

Sometimes it is felt by students (and economists!) that the material in this chapter is tedious and unimportant. Nothing could be further from the truth. Without the existence and knowledge of macroeconomic data, and without an understanding of important economic concepts, no understanding of an economy is possible. Hopefully by the time you have mastered the material in this chapter, you will realize just how important it is to know the data and to know the concepts needed for you to think like an economist.

2.1 NATIONAL INCOME ACCOUNTING

The National Income and Product Accounts is an accounting system that was started in the 1930s. The construction of this system was perhaps the most important development in economic history. The Department of Commerce retained economist Simon Kuznets of the National Bureau of Economic Research to develop a system of economic accounts for measuring national income. The results of these efforts were first published as a complete accounting system in the July 1947 issue of the *Survey of Current Business*, a publication of the Department of Commerce that is still regularly published. The original estimates were limited; for example, they were only available in current dollars and only a few series were available quarterly. But they have been expanded and refined since that time and now provide a comprehensive set of accounts used for economic analysis by professional economists and other members of the public.

The key statistic contained in this system is **Gross Domestic Product (GDP)**.

Gross Domestic Product

Gross Domestic Product is the most comprehensive and well-known measure of the flow of output produced in an economy. Here is its definition.

Definition of Gross Domestic Product

■   Gross Domestic Product measures the market value in current dollars of final goods and services produced within a given time period by labor and property located within the borders of the U.S.

It is important to carefully examine each part of this definition.

1. *GDP Includes Market and Non-Market Production.* Economists describe goods and services as being sold in a market where they are purchased voluntarily at market-determined prices. GDP contains goods traded in this way. But there are goods and services that are provided to the public that do not get traded in a market. For example, governments provide defense and education services to the public and these services are not sold in a market; measures of these non-market services, valued at the cost of producing them, are contained in GDP. In addition, there are non-market productive activities that are not included in GDP because it is hard to measure them properly. A parent staying home to care for a child provides child-care services that are not included in GDP. Similarly there are transactions that are carried out "off the books" (part of the **underground economy**) because they are illegal or because people are trying to avoid taxes on these transactions. These activities are not measured in GDP.

2. *GDP Uses Market and Imputed Prices.* Wherever possible, GDP contains the prices of goods and services sold in markets. But there are services produced that do not have market prices available. For example, owner-occupiers of housing are receiving the services of the houses they own. What is the price of these services and how can the value

of these services be included in GDP? To answer these questions, BEA uses rental price information for housing and imputes this rental income to those owning their own homes.

3. *GDP Measures Production, Not Sales*. GDP records the value of goods when they are produced, not when the goods are sold. So if a toaster is produced by a manufacturer and placed into its inventories of finished toasters, the production of the toaster is recorded as a change in inventories, part of investment. When the toaster is later sold, the sale is recorded in household **consumption** and as a reduction in inventories.

4. *GDP Includes the Production of "Final" Goods and Services*. Final goods and services are those that are consumed by households, firms, domestic and foreign residents. They are not used in the production of other goods and services. **Intermediate goods and services** are used in the production of other products. To count these in GDP would result in double counting because the value of intermediate goods is already included in the prices of the goods produced by using these intermediate goods and services.

5. *GDP Measures Output Produced in the U.S.* Output produced is included in GDP if it was produced within the U.S. So the foreign office of a U.S. corporation will not have its production included in GDP but the U.S. office of a foreign corporation will have its output included in GDP. A related measure, GNP, does not require that output be produced within the borders of the U.S.

6. *GDP Does Not Deduct the Value of Depreciation*. Equipment and structures depreciate or wear out over time. Some of the output produced in the economy replaces these worn-out capital goods. GDP makes no adjustment for depreciation but **Net Domestic Product** deducts the value of **depreciation** from GDP. Thus Net Domestic Product measures goods and services produced which may be consumed or added to the stock of physical assets in the economy.

There are three methods of measuring GDP. Two of these methods arise because these accounts are a double-entry bookkeeping system. For every dollar of output sold in the market, there is an entry on the expenditure (revenue) side of the ledger and an entry on the income side of the ledger. The revenues of firms are used to pay the factors of production (labor and capital) that produced the goods sold; so each side of the ledger sums to the same number. The third way of measuring GDP uses information on the stages of production within firms to produce output. Each of these methods is discussed below.

The Expenditure Approach to GDP Measurement

One method of measuring GDP uses the expenditures by households, firms, the government, and foreign residents to measure GDP. Table 2.1 provides these expenditures for 2006.

Personal consumption expenditures are the goods and services purchased and consumed by households. The table gives a breakdown of these expenditures into three categories. Consumers purchase durable goods that provide their services over time. They buy nondurable goods such as food and they purchase services. Households are the final consumers of these goods and services.

Firms are the final consumers of investment goods used to augment their capital stocks. **Gross investment** measures additions to the stock of capital goods held by firms. Note that

TABLE 2.1 Gross Domestic Product – Expenditure Approach, Billions of Dollars

	2008
Gross domestic product	14441.4
Personal consumption expenditures	10129.9
Durable goods	1095.2
Nondurable goods	2308
Services	6726.8
Gross private domestic investment	2136.1
Fixed investment	2170.8
Nonresidential	1693.6
Structures	609.5
Equipment and software	1084.1
Residential	477.2
Change in private inventories	–34.8
Net exports of goods and services	–707.8
Exports	1831.1
Goods	1266.9
Services	564.2
Imports	2538.9
Goods	2126.4
Services	412.4
Government consumption expenditures and gross investment	2883.2
Federal	1082.6
National defense	737.9
Nondefense	344.7
State and local	1800.6

Source: Bureau of Economic Analysis, www.bea.gov, Table 1.1.5

investment refers to goods used to add to the stock of capital, not the purchase of stocks and bonds. Firms build structures and buy equipment to be used in the production of their output. Computer software is durable and is used to produce output and so is now included in gross investment. Residential investment refers to the purchase of newly built housing by households. Firms sometimes hold inventories of finished goods rather than producing for final sale directly to consumers. Any additions to the stock of finished goods held by firms are included in gross investment. Finally gross investment measures the additions to the stock of capital without regard to how much of this investment just replaces worn-out goods due to depreciation. **Net investment** deducts from gross investment the amount of investment needed to replace worn-out capital goods so it measures net additions to the stock of capital.

Exports measure goods and services produced domestically that are consumed by foreign residents. Domestic residents consume goods produced domestically and abroad. **Imports** measure foreign-produced goods consumed by U.S. households. **Net exports** are the difference between exports and imports. A **closed economy** is one where there is no trade in goods and services or financial transactions between countries. An **open economy** is one where there is trade in goods and services and financial assets between countries.

Governments buy goods and services and they provide services that are not sold in markets and so are valued at the cost of producing these services. **Government purchases** refer to the goods and services purchased by governments at all levels. Governments also buy durable capital goods and these are regarded as being **government investment**. Table 2.1 gives some additional detail regarding defense and nondefense spending at the federal level. Note also that the government also makes **transfer payments** to individuals, such as Social Security payments, and these are not included in the NIPA government figures. Transfers are not goods and services produced in the economy.

An important expression arises from these expenditures accounts that will be used many times in this book. This expression is

$$Y = C + I + G + NX$$

where Y is GDP, C refers to consumption, I is gross investment, G is government purchases, and NX denotes net exports. We will use this equation later to develop other important relationships that hold in the economy.

The Income Approach to GDP Measurement

When a firm sells goods to final consumers, the revenues they receive are used to pay the factors of production that produced the goods sold. The income approach to GDP measurement looks at the income side of these transactions. Tables 2.2 and 2.3 provide data on the income approach to GDP measurement for the year 2008, showing how one can derive a measure of personal income and personal saving starting from GDP.

Recall that GDP restricts attention to goods produced within the borders of the U.S. whereas GNP does not impose this restriction. To arrive at GNP requires adding payments to U.S. residents received from abroad and subtracting payments by U.S. residents to foreign residents. Consumption of fixed capital is a measure of the depreciation of fixed capital goods in the economy because capital goods wear out and must be replaced; subtracting this leads to Net National Product, the amount of revenue available for consumption and wealth accumulation. National income is obtained by applying a statistical discrepancy in the table as a "fudge factor" needed to make the expenditures and income accounts sum to the same number. BEA gets data on income and expenditures from different sources and believes that

TABLE 2.2 Gross Domestic Product – Income Approach, Billions of Dollars

	2008
Gross domestic product	14441.4
Plus: Income receipts from the rest of the world	809.2
Less: Income payments to the rest of the world	667.3
Equals: Gross national product	14583.3
Less: Consumption of fixed capital	1847.1
Equals: Net national product	12736.2
Less: Statistical discrepancy	101.0
Equals: National income	12635.2
Less: Corporate profits with inventory valuation and capital consumption adjustments	1360.4
Taxes on production and imports less subsidies	993.8
Contributions for government social insurance	990.6
Net interest and miscellaneous payments on assets	815.1
Business current transfer payments (net)	118.8
Current surplus of government enterprises	–6.9
Wage accruals less disbursements	–5.0
Plus: Personal income receipts on assets	1994.4
Personal current transfer receipts	1875.9
Equals: Personal income	12238.8

Source: Bureau of Economic Analysis, www.bea.gov, Table 1.7.5

the expenditure data is higher in quality. Thus the statistical discrepancy is added to the income accounts to cause the two accounts to balance.

To arrive at personal income, a series of adjustments are made. Corporations retain earnings that are not paid to households. Tax payments, net of subsidies received, are made to governments and thus do not appear in personal income. Payments are made for social insurance such as Social Security that must be deducted. Interest payments are made by firms and they also make transfers that must be deducted. The current surplus of government enterprises is the difference between the revenues and subsidies of government enterprises, such as the Post Office, net of expenses. Wage accruals, net of disbursements, measure net wage payments to employees. To finally arrive at personal income, payments for interest and dividends must be added as well as transfers received from the government.

Table 2.3 gives the sources and uses of personal income in the economy for 2008. The largest component of personal income is the compensation of employees for their labor supply.

TABLE 2.3 Sources and Uses of Personal Income, Billions of Dollars

	2008
Personal income	12238.8
Compensation of employees, received	8042.4
Proprietors' income with inventory valuation and capital consumption adjustments	1106.3
Rental income of persons with capital consumption adjustment	210.4
Personal income receipts on assets	1994.4
Personal current transfer receipts	1875.9
Less: Contributions for government social insurance	990.6
Less: Personal current taxes	1432.4
Equals: Disposable personal income	10806.4
Less: Personal outlays	10520.0
Personal consumption expenditures	10129.9
Personal interest payments	237.8
Personal current transfer payments	152.3
Equals: Personal saving	286.4

Source: Bureau of Economic Analysis, www.bea.gov, Table 2.1

Proprietors' income is the income received by individuals for their labor and capital such as for farmers. Rental income is income received from the rental of property. Receipts on assets include interest earnings and dividends. Personal current transfers less contributions to social insurance such as Social Security provide a measure of net transfers to the public, thereby generating a measure of personal income. Subtracting taxes from personal income yields **disposable** or **after-tax income**.

The uses of personal after-tax income include consumption, interest payments, and transfer payments. Subtracting these from disposable income yields personal saving.

Value Added

The third way to measure GDP is to measure the **value-added** by firms at each stage of their production processes. Firms buy **intermediate goods** that they use along with labor and capital to produce their output. Intermediate goods are products produced by other firms in the economy. Value-added is defined below.

Definition of Value-Added

■ The value-added of a firm is the difference between the value of a firm's output and its purchases of intermediate goods used in production.

Table 2.4 gives a traditional example of how to measure value added in the production of a loaf of bread. The table lists transactions through three stages in the production of bread.

TABLE 2.4 Measuring Value-Added in Production

Firm	Intermediate Goods	Value-Added	Sales
Farmer, Wheat	$0	$100	$100
Miller, Flour	$100	$150	$250
Baker, Bread	$250	$150	$400
Total	$350	$400	$750

The production of bread requires the purchase of wheat from a farmer assumed to use no intermediate inputs in the production of wheat. We suppose that the farmer sells $100 worth of wheat to a miller who uses the wheat to produce flour. The farmer's sales are $100 and value-added for the farmer is the same since we assume that the farmer uses no intermediate inputs in production.[1] The miller buys wheat from the farmer, using it to produce flour that is sold to a baker for $250. The baker purchases the flour for $250, using it to produce bread that is sold for $400. The baker's value-added is $150. Notice that if we were to simply sum the sales of each producer, $750, we would be **double-counting** the value of intermediate goods produced in the economy. The value of the flour, $250, would be counted in the sales of the miller and it would also be counted in the value of the bread sold. So the value-added approach to GDP measurement leads to a value of $400.

Finally, note that the table actually illustrates all three approaches to GDP measurement. Using the expenditure approach, GDP is the value of the bread sold to final consumers (households), $400. Using the income approach, we add up the incomes earned at each stage of production which is also value-added in production. Incomes for the three producers sum to $400, the sum of value-added at each production stage.

Now we examine relationships implied by the NIPA accounts.

2.2 RELATIONSHIPS IMPLIED BY NIPA ACCOUNTING

The NIPA accounts can be used to derive a number of very important relationships that must be obeyed in the aggregate economy. To see these expressions, begin with the definition of disposable income for the private sector which can be written as

---

[1] Note that sales and output are identical in this example because we assume that there are no inventories of finished goods being held.

$$YD^p = Y + NIRW + TR + INT - T.$$

Definitions of the variables in this expression are as follows.

$$YD^p = \text{Private Disposable Income}$$

$$Y = GDP$$

$$NIRW = \text{Net Income Receipts from the Rest of the World}$$

$$TR = \text{Net Government Transfer Payments}$$

$$INT = \text{Interest Payments on Government Debt}$$

$$T = \text{Tax Payments to the Government}$$

Disposable income is, by definition, the income available to consumers to finance their consumption and saving. Thus if we start with GDP we must add net payments from abroad received by the public (recall that GDP plus net payments from abroad is GNP). If the public receives net transfer payments from the government, these must be added to pre-tax income along with any interest payments received by the public for holding government bonds. Finally tax payments must be subtracted to give us a measure of disposable income.

There is a similar relationship for the government given below.

$$YD^g = T - TR - INT$$

In this equation, YD^g is the disposable income of the government which is equal to tax revenues less net transfer and interest payments made to the public. If we add together the disposable incomes of the private sector and the government we obtain GNP.

Aggregate Savings

Households save by not consuming all of their disposable income. The difference between the public's consumption and disposable income is saving by the private sector, defined below.

$$S^p = Y + NIRW + TR + INT - T - C$$

The source of private saving, S^p, is thus the difference between the resources available to the public, disposable income, and the amount of consumption by households.

There is a similar measure for government saving which is

$$S^g = T - TR - INT - G.$$

This relationship has been simplified because, for simplicity, we will not make any distinction between government consumption and government investment. You will recall from our discussion of the NIPA accounts above that government spending is broken down into government consumption, purchases of goods and services by governments, and government investment. The latter refers to purchases of long-lived durable assets, such as roads and structures, by governments. In the NIPA accounts, government saving is the difference between government disposable income and government consumption, analogous to our definition of private saving above. For simplicity, we will use the expression for government saving above by making no distinction between government consumption and investment.

There is another definition of government saving that is likely to be more familiar to you. The sum of net transfers (TR), interest payments on government bonds (INT), and government spending (G) is defined as **government outlays**. If tax receipts exceed government outlays, there is a government **budget surplus**. If outlays exceed tax revenues, the government is running a **budget deficit**. So our definition of government saving is really a measure of the government's budget position, be it positive or negative.

Aggregate saving is the sum of private and government saving given below.

$$S = S^p + S^g$$

$$S = Y + NIRW + TR + INT - T - C + T - TR - INT - G$$

$$S = Y + NIRW - C - G$$

This expression describes the source of saving in the aggregate economy. Saving is aggregate income, GDP, plus net income from the rest of the world, less current consumption and government spending.

The uses of private saving can be obtained by using the NIPA expenditures relationship

$$Y = C + I + G + NX$$

and substituting this into the equation for aggregate saving. The results of this exercise follow.

$$S = C + I + G + NX + NIRW - C - G$$

$$S = I + NX + NIRW$$

The last equation states that aggregate saving must equal aggregate investment, I, plus the sum of net exports, NX, and net income from the rest of the world. The **current account balance**, CA, is defined as

$$CA = NX + NIRW$$

giving us

$$S = I + CA.$$

Finally, using our definition of aggregate saving as the sum of private and government saving, we have

$$S^p = I - S^g + CA$$

This expression is important because it defines the sources and uses of private saving in the economy. Private saving is used in three ways.

1. Firms borrow from households because they wish to add to their stock of capital goods (plant and equipment). Part of private saving can be used to finance investment by firms.
2. The government can use up a portion of private saving if it is running a deficit (its outlays exceed its tax receipts). In this case, $S^g < 0$ using our definition of government saving. The government issues bonds to borrow from the public when it runs a deficit. If the government runs a surplus, it will use this surplus to retire some of its outstanding debt.
3. The current account balance, CA, can also use up a part of private saving. To see why, imagine that $CA < 0$ as it has been in the U.S. in recent years. In this case, there is a current account deficit meaning that our payments to foreign residents exceed the funds foreign residents pay to U.S. residents. In this case, U.S. residents must borrow from foreign residents or sell some assets to foreigners to finance part of our consumption of goods produced abroad. If we are running a current account surplus, our payments to foreigners are less than what foreigners pay to U.S. residents. So foreigners must either borrow from U.S. residents or sell assets (financial or physical) to U.S. residents.

All of the relationships just discussed are contained in a summary box (See **Doing Economics**: Aggregate Macroeconomic Relationships). Finally, now that you know about the important macroeconomic relationships in an aggregate economy, it is useful to know where to find data on these magnitudes. The internet has now made data acquisition enormously easy compared to the pre-internet age. See **Doing Economics**: Where to Find Macroeconomic Data.

Doing Economics: Aggregate Macroeconomic Relationships

Here we summarize the economic relationships just discussed regarding the measurement of important macroeconomic data.

Private Sector Disposable Income: $YD^p = Y + NIRW + TR + INT - T$

Government Disposable Income: $YD^g = T - TR - INT$

Private Saving: $S^p = Y + NIRW + TR + INT - T - C$

Government Saving: $S^g = T - TR - INT - G$

Aggregate Saving: $S = S^p + S^g = Y + NIRW + TR + INT - T - C + T - TR - INT - G$

Aggregate Saving: $S = Y + NIRW - C - G$

Expenditures Definition of GDP: $Y = C + I + G + NX$

Aggregate Saving: $S = C + I + G + NX + NIRW - C - G = I + NX + NIRW$

(continued)

Current Account: $CA = NX + NIRW$

Aggregate Saving: $S = I + CA$

Private Saving: $S^p = I - S^g + CA$

Definitions:

Y = GDP, C = Consumption, I = Investment, G = Government Expenditures, NIRW = Net Income Receipts from the Rest of the World, NX = Net Exports, TR = Net Government Transfer Payments, INT = Interest Payments on Government Debt, T = Tax Payments to the Government, CA = Current Account

Doing Economics: Where to Find Macroeconomic Data

U.S. Government

> Bureau of Economic Analysis (BEA): www.bea.gov
> Bureau of Labor Statistics (BLS): www.bls.gov
> Census Bureau: www.census.gov
> Congressional Budget Office (CBO): www.cbo.gov
> Council of Economic Advisors (CEA): www.whitehouse.gov/cea
> Office of Management and Budget (OMB): www.whitehouse.gov/omb
> U.S. Department of the Treasury: www.treasury.gov
> Social Security Administration: www.ssa.gov

Federal Reserve System

> Board of Governors: www.federalreserve.gov
> St. Louis Federal Reserve Bank (FRED Database): research.stlouisfed.org/fred2/

> Also be aware that there are twelve regional district banks in the Federal Reserve System, each of which maintains web sites with considerable amounts of economic information.

International Macroeconomic Data

> The Organization of Economic Cooperation and Development (OECD): www.oecd.org
> The International Monetary Fund (IMF): www.imf.org

Other Data Sources

> Economagic: www.economagic.com
> Resources for Economists: rfe.org

The St. Louis Federal Reserve FRED database, an excellent data source available without charge, will be frequently used in this book. We will also have occasion to use OECD data. Resources for Economists is a web site designed for finding many types of economic information, including data.

This completes our discussion of measurement of economic variables. Now we discuss a number of economic concepts, crucial to your understanding of the economic analysis that we will do subsequently.

2.3 ESSENTIAL ECONOMIC CONCEPTS

In this section we discuss a number of important economic concepts that are necessary for you to understand the economic models that we will later develop.

Stocks vs. Flows

An important distinction in economic analysis is the distinction between stocks and flows. **Stocks** are economic variables measured at a point in time; **flows** are measured relative to a time period. So we will use the phrase "stock of capital" to refer to the quantity of plant and equipment used by a firm at a point in time. The stock of money is the quantity of money in an economy at a point in time. Income and output are flow measures; these will be measured relative to a time period such as a year. The NIPA data, discussed earlier in the chapter, are flows since they are measured with a time dimension. An accounting relationship, drawn from the theory of investment, illustrates the connection between stocks and flows.

Firms buy capital goods to augment their stocks of capital goods. The activity of buying new capital goods is called gross investment and capital goods wear out due to wear and tear. The net change in the capital stock, net investment, obeys the relationship

$$K - K_{-1} = I - \delta \cdot K_{-1}, \ 0 < \delta < 1$$

where K is the capital stock today and K_{-1} is the capital stock at the end of last period. Net investment, or the net change in the capital stock, is measured by $K - K_{-1}$. Gross investment, I, is a flow and so is depreciation, $\delta \cdot K_{-1}$. The depreciation rate is the parameter δ (the Greek parameter delta) and it is a fraction between zero and unity. So a fraction of the capital stock wears out each period. The change in a stock, net investment, is therefore a flow. Each side of this accounting relationship consists of flow measures so that the equation is consistent in what it measures on either side of the equal sign.

Nominal and Constant-Dollar GDP

There are two measures of Gross Domestic Product available to the public. **Nominal GDP** measures the output produced in the economy in current-dollar units; **constant-dollar GDP** or **real GDP** measures output in base year prices. The difference between these two measures of GDP is the prices that are used in the computation of each. Table 2.5 displays this difference for an economy producing just two goods, computers and bags of potato

TABLE 2.5 Computing Nominal and Constant-Dollar GDP

	Bags of Potato Chips		Computers	
Year	Price	Quantity	Price	Quantity
2003	$2.00	10,000	$10,000	1
2004	$2.50	11,000	$5,000	2
2005	$3.00	12,000	$2,500	4
2006	$3.50	13,000	$1,250	8
	Nominal GDP	Real GDP Base 2004	Real GDP Base 2005	Real GDP Base 2006
2003	$30,000.00	$30,000.00	$32,500.00	$36,250.00
2004	$37,500.00	$37,500.00	$38,000.00	$41,000.00
2005	$46,000.00	$50,000.00	$46,000.00	$47,000.00
2006	$55,500.00	$72,500.00	$59,000.00	$55,500.00

chips.[2] The top section of the table gives you the information on prices and quantities produced in four years. The bottom section gives you nominal and real GDP measures using this data.

To compute nominal GDP for 2003, use the price and quantity data for that year giving

$$\$2.00 \cdot 10,000 + \$10,000.00 \cdot 1 = \$30,000.00.$$

Nominal GDP in each year is measured in dollars using current-year prices and quantities.

Nominal GDP can change because prices change, quantities change, or because both prices and quantities change. Changes in nominal GDP are not useful if we are interested only in quantity changes as we would be for business cycle analysis where we want to measure changes in physical units of goods produced in the economy. For this reason, constant-dollar GDP has traditionally been used and this magnitude can change only if quantities change as you will see by observing the following expression where constant-dollar GDP is computed for the year 2006 using 2004 prices.

$$\$2.50 \cdot 13,000 + \$5,000.00 \cdot 8 = \$72,500.00$$

Nominal and constant-dollar GDP are both measured in dollar units but the difference is the year in which prices are measured. Constant-dollar GDP uses prices from 2004 and that year

---

[2] Data in this table is drawn from the article by Charles Steindel, "Chain-Weighting: The New Approach to Measuring Real GDP," *Current Issues in Economics and Finance* 1, No. 9, New York Federal Reserve Bank (December 1995).

is called the **base year** and the base year is an arbitrary choice. If you were to compute real GDP for the other years in the table, base year prices are always used and current year quantities are used. From one year to the next, real GDP changes only because quantities change.

One problem with the computation of real GDP is that the growth rate of the economy, implied by real GDP, can change dramatically depending upon the base year that is chosen. Indeed the numbers in the table are chosen to illustrate this problem because it arises in economies that are rapidly changing. The potato chips sector has prices and quantities changing modestly each year in the table; the computer industry has rapidly falling prices and rapidly rising quantities. Some sort of compromise is needed to deal with this disparity. The method chosen by BEA is known as **chain-weighted real (or constant-dollar) GDP growth** (see **Doing Economics**: Constructing Chain-Weighted Real GDP Growth).

Doing Economics: Constructing Chain-Weighted Real GDP Growth

The choice of base year used in computing real GDP can make a big difference in the implied growth rate of real GDP. To see this, use the real GDP data in Table 2.5 for base years 2005 and 2006, reproduced below.

Real GDP

	Base Year 2005	Base Year 2006
2003	$32,500.00	$36,250.00
2004	$38,000.00	$41,000.00
2005	$46,000.00	$47,000.00
2006	$59,000.00	$55,500.00

Now use this data to construct the growth rates in real GDP for 2004–2006. The results are given below.

Real GDP Growth Rates

	Base Year 2005	Base Year 2006
2004	0.17	0.13
2005	0.21	0.15
2006	0.28	0.18

The growth rates in real GDP are quite different, particularly in 2006. Some type of compromise is needed to prevent the choice of base year from creating a distorted view of the economy's growth rate.

The compromise that has been chosen is to make two growth rate calculations. One uses the year itself and the preceding year as base years averaging the resulting two growth rates. So the real GDP growth rate for 2006 will be the average of the growth rates obtained with 2006 and 2005 base years. The average of those two years will be about 23 percent (the average of 28 percent and 18 percent).

A slightly simplified version of how to compute the real GDP growth rate using this method is that it is an average of real GDP growth using current year and preceding year prices. So to compute real GDP growth for 2006, compute the growth rate using 2006 prices as the base year; then compute the growth rate using 2005 prices as the base year, averaging the two calculated growth rates. This growth rate can then be used to generate **chain-weighted constant-dollar GDP** by using the growth rate for each year along with the base year value of nominal GDP (nominal and real GDP are the same in the base year).

Index Numbers

Index numbers are widely reported by the media and they are used for many reasons by the public and government. To see what information is revealed by these numbers, a simple example of an index number can be constructed by using only a single price for a good. Suppose that we measure the price of this good for five years and use it to construct an index number for the price of that commodity. Table 2.6 illustrates how this can be done.

The index numbers in the third column of the table are constructed by first choosing a base year. In the table, the base year is chosen to be year three and we compute the value of the index in the base year from ($260.00/$260.00)*100 = 100. As this calculation shows, an index number is a pure number without a unit of measurement (the dollar units cancel out of the calculation). The remaining entries in the third column are computed by taking each dollar price and dividing it by the base year price. So, for year one, the index is ($230.00/$260.00)*100 = 88.46. Doing this simple calculation for each year, you immediately realize that an index number reveals the direction of change in a series in an easily understood fashion. The price of this good in year 5 is just over 15 percent more than in the base year and somewhat less than 12 percent in year one compared to the base year.

The base year is the reference point for the comparison of price changes in the example and it was chosen arbitrarily. It could have been set to any period in the example but, no matter what base year is chosen, the index will still reveal the direction of change in the series in a simple way.

TABLE 2.6 Constructing an Index Number

	Dollar Price	Index Number
Year 1	$230.00	88.46
Year 2	$275.00	105.77
Year 3	$260.00	100.00
Year 4	$280.00	107.69
Year 5	$300.00	115.39

Index numbers wouldn't be of much use if this were all that could be done with them. In fact, index numbers are far more useful than this example shows because they can provide the same information when there are many goods and services produced as in a modern economy. This can be understood by considering the **Consumer Price Index** (CPI).

The CPI is an important statistic in our society because so many decisions are tied to its value. For example, wage rates and Social Security payments are frequently tied to the CPI and, if this price index goes up, so too will the wages of many workers and payments to retired workers. The Bureau of Labor Statistics (BLS) publishes the CPI after it surveys households about their buying patterns. There are hundreds of items included in the CPI but we can illustrate its construction by using the two goods contained in Table 2.5 above. The CPI is a **Laspeyres** price index, defined below, that includes the prices of many goods and services consumed by households.

Definition of a Laspeyres Index

■   A Laspeyres price index measures the current cost of a fixed market basket of goods and services relative to the cost of the market basket in a base year.

Suppose that the base year is the year 2003 and that we want to construct the CPI for the year 2006 using the data in Table 2.5. This may be accomplished by the following calculation.

$$\left[\frac{\$3.50 \cdot 10,000 + \$1,250 \cdot 1}{\$2.00 \cdot 10,000 + \$10,000 \cdot 1} \right] \cdot 100 = 120.83$$

The denominator of this expression uses base year prices and quantities and measures expenditures in the base year for the basket of goods in the index (potato chip bags and computers) while the numerator measures the current cost of the base year basket of goods. Thus the market basket costs about 121 percent more in 2006 than it did in 2003. For each year, the index is calculated using the same base year quantities and prices; only the current year prices change from one period to the next.

The BLS surveys the buying patterns of households and uses the survey results to arrive at the basket of commodities to include in CPI calculations. Since expenditure patterns change over time, BLS periodically revises the base year (currently the base year is 1982 to 1984) and market basket of goods and services to reflect these changes in household behavior.

There are some problems that arise in measuring inflation with the CPI (see **Doing Economics**: The Boskin Commission and the CPI for a more complete discussion of these measurement problems). We mention three here that are relevant.

1. *Treatment of Durable Goods*. The market basket of goods in our example contains a perishable item (potato chips no longer provide any consumption or utility value once the chips are consumed) and a durable item (computers provides their services to their owners for more than one period of time). Our CPI price index captures the services of newly produced computers but what about the services of computers produced last year as well as earlier years still in use? They are not counted in the example yet it is clear that there are used durable goods in the economy whose services should be counted as well as those

just produced. For this reason, the proper way to measure the services of durable goods is to use **rental prices** for new and used durable goods presumably taken from samples of rental goods market prices that could be used to value the services of durable goods of all vintages. But there is little rental price data for anything other than housing and so BLS uses rental price information only for housing services. For all other durable goods, purchase prices of newly produced goods are used.

2. *Fixed Baskets of Goods.* The CPI is known to overstate inflation because consumers do not consume constant quantities of goods. As the prices of goods and services change, so will the quantities of goods purchased by consumers. This problem is sometimes called **substitution bias** in the CPI. When the price of one commodity rises relative to other goods and services, economists refer to this as a change in **relative prices**. When these price changes occur, households will change their buying patterns, buying less of the good that is more expensive, and more of other goods. Because of these changes in the goods bought by households, the CPI, because it uses a fixed basket of goods and services, makes it look as though the cost of living has risen by more than it really has. This is one reason why base years change over time.

3. *Quality Changes.* Over time, quality changes occur in the production of goods and services in an economy, distorting the information provided by the CPI. An obvious example is found in computers. Computers today provide much higher quality than they did a decade ago. Thus a computer costing $1000 ten years ago is far lower in quality than one purchased today costing the same amount. The CPI takes no account of this when it uses a fixed basket of goods and services in its construction. So if the price of a computer rises by 10 percent but also provides far more computing power at this higher price, the CPI overstates the effects of the price increase because it assumes that quality is constant. This problem is referred to as **quality adjustment bias**. This is another reason why it may be sensible to periodically change the base year used in CPI calculations.

Doing Economics: The Boskin Commission and the CPI

The Advisory Commission to Study the Consumer Price Index (also called the Boskin Commission because economist Michael Boskin served on this commission) was charged with studying the problems in the CPI. This commission concluded that the CPI was not a correct measure of the cost of living and that it overstated inflation by about 1.1 percent per year. The commission identified a number of biases in the CPI. In addition to those mentioned in the text, the commission mentioned New Product and Outlet Substitution biases as measurement problems in the CPI.

New Product bias refers to the fact that new products are introduced into dynamically changing economies and these new products are omitted from the CPI until changes in the base year are made and new market baskets are set by the BLS (Bureau of Labor Statistics). Outlet Substitution bias refers to the fact that the BLS did not adequately account for the emergence of discount retailers, firms frequented by consumers that charge prices below those charged by traditional retailers.

(continued)

> The commission made a substantial number of specific recommendations to the President and Congress. Among other things, they suggested that the CPI should move towards measuring the cost of living and they suggested changing the type of index number used to measure the price level.
>
> For further details, see www.ssa.gov/history/reports/boskinrpt.html.

While the CPI is a very well-known measure of the price level, it is not the only one used by economists. The **implicit GDP deflator** is another measure of prices in the economy that can be useful because it is a broader measure of prices in the economy compared to the CPI. Its construction is quite easy, given our discussion of nominal and real GDP. The formula below shows how to construct this measure of the price level.

$$\text{Implicit GDP Deflator} = (\text{Nominal GDP/Real GDP}) \cdot 100$$

So this price level measure arises by simply taking the ratio of nominal to real GDP and multiplying the result by 100.

However you will recall that real GDP has limitations when an economy is undergoing rapid structural change so the price level derived from real GDP will also be distorted as well. This problem can be corrected by using a **chain-weighted GDP deflator**. In the formula above, if real GDP is replaced by chain-weighted real GDP, you obtain this alternative measure of the overall price level.

Inflation

The rate of price inflation between any two years is simply measured by

$$[(P - P_{-1})/P_{-1}] \cdot 100$$

so price inflation is measured by the percentage change in a price index between two periods of time: P stands for the current price level and P_{-1} is the price level last period. The index used could be the CPI or another price index. But this is not the operative definition of inflation used by economists. For the purposes of economic analysis, it is important to distinguish between changes in the price level and inflation. The reason is that there are events that could cause either type of change in the price level. The economist's definition of inflation is given below.

Definition of Inflation

■ Inflation is an increase in the level of all prices in the economy, an ongoing or continuing process that can last indefinitely.

Notice what our definition does not say. It does not involve relative price changes, referring only to all prices, even though relative price changes occur frequently in modern economies. Further, inflation is not a one-time increase in the price level because it is possible for all prices to rise indefinitely when inflation occurs. A one-time change in the price level means that prices stop rising eventually. There are forces that can cause a one-time increase in the price level and we will discuss these later in the book. But inflation is conceptually different because the price increases occurring during inflation need not end.

As a matter of actual observation, it can be difficult to make the distinction between inflation and one-time changes in the price level and no distinction is usually made in the popular media. This is easy to understand; after all, prices don't change at exactly the same time when there is ongoing inflation and so inflation can easily be mistaken for one-time changes in the price level or even relative price changes. Even if it is difficult to know the difference in actual practice, it is important to keep this distinction in mind when working through economic models later in the book. We will work through exercises in aggregate economic models where all prices change continuously and where they do not change continuously.

Real vs. Nominal Magnitudes

Economists usually assume that economic agents (households and firms) are free of **money illusion**, meaning that they know the difference between real and nominal magnitudes. Nominal magnitudes are measured in dollar units (units of money), such as the hourly wage rate that you earn at your job. The nominal wage rate is stated by your employer as dollars per unit of labor (usually an hour). But your nominal wage rate does not tell you what you can buy with your hourly wage; this is really what you want to know if you are free of money illusion. It is what you can buy with your nominal wage that tells you the welfare you achieve by working. To find out how well off you are by working, the nominal wage must be converted into a magnitude telling you what you can buy with your nominal wage. This is easily accomplished by **deflating** the money wage by the prices of goods somehow measured.

Imagine that there is only one good in the world, apples, having the price P^{Apples}. Then the ratio W/P^{Apples} is the **real wage** rate and it is measured in units of goods. So if your wage rate is $10 per hour and the price of apples is $2.00, then your real wage rate is 5 apples per hour ($10 per hour divided by $2 per apple); that is, you earn five apples by working one hour. If an individual is free of money illusion, the decision to work will be determined in part by the real wage rate since, ultimately, the welfare of individuals is tied to their consumption of goods and services. This example also explains why wages are tied to the CPI. Since the purchasing power of money wages declines when the CPI rises, wages are sometimes automatically increased to try and maintain the same welfare level for workers.

Since there is more than one price in the world, the price used to deflate a nominal magnitude will be a price index (like the CPI discussed above), rather than an individual price. So we will speak of the real wage as the nominal wage deflated by the price level; as another example, the stock of real money balances will be the ratio of the nominal stock of money deflated (divided) by the price level; it measures the quantity of goods that may be purchased by the nominal stock of money.

Nominal and Real Interest Rates

Just as we assume that households are free of money illusion by knowing the difference between the real and nominal wage rate, so we will also assume that lenders and borrowers know the difference between the real and nominal interest rate. Loan contracts are written using the nominal interest rate; the lender agrees to lend an amount, called the *principal*, and requires the payment of a dollar amount each year expressed as a fraction of the principal. Thus a one-period loan of $100, at a nominal interest rate of 5 percent, results in a repayment to the lender after one year of $105. But the real interest rate is the important magnitude for decisions by lenders as the following example will illustrate.

Imagine that a household chooses to lend funds to a borrower for one year. Saving is the decision not to consume part of the household's disposable income and so if our household has made the decision to forego consumption, it must expect to be compensated for waiting to consume the loaned-out part of its disposable income until next period. So the welfare loss of not consuming, say an apple today, must be offset by the welfare gain of eating the apple next period plus some additional consumption next period to compensate the household for waiting to consume the apple. The real interest rate is that extra compensation which compensates the household for waiting.

We can now define the real interest rate in the following way.

Definition of the Real Interest Rate

- The real interest rate is the nominal interest rate minus the expected rate of inflation.
- Our notation for the real interest rate will be as follows: $r = i - \Delta P^e/P$ where the superscript "e" denotes an expectation.

To understand this definition, consider an example of a one-year loan of a dollar by an individual. The price of apples is currently assumed to be $1.00 so the household is foregoing the consumption of one apple when it chooses to lend. A borrower is willing to borrow from our household and it is agreed that the nominal interest rate on this one-period loan will be 5 percent. That means in one year, the lender will get back the principal loaned out, $1.00, and will get an additional amount of interest, in this case $.05. Is the lender made better off by lending?

We can't tell if the lender is better off unless we know the price of apples a year from now. To see why, suppose that apples cost $1.00 next year, just as they do now. Then our lender gets to consume more than one apple next year by lending; she gets back her principal, $1.00, plus interest earnings, a fraction of an apple, $.05. So by lending, the lender gives up the consumption of an apple today but gets in return to eat more than one apple after a year.[3]

---

[3] Using a bit of algebra and the definition of inflation, the real interest rate can be written as the ratio $[(1 + i) \cdot P - P_{+1}]/P$. Here P is the money price of goods today and P_{+1} is the money price of goods next period. The quantity $(1 + i) \cdot P$ is what the lender gets next period by lending today so if $(1 + i) \cdot P > P_{+1}$, then lending today allows the lender to buy more goods next period than he/she could by not making the loan.

In the example, the real interest rate is positive. If it is negative, the lender is made worse off by lending. Work through the example where the price of apples rises by ten percent with our lender still getting a five percent interest rate. After one year, the lender can buy less than one apple.

If you look at the definition of the real interest rate, you will notice that the definition includes the expected, not the actual, rate of inflation. The reason is that when lenders initiate loans, they do not know what the inflation rate will be over the life of the loan so they must somehow form an expectation about the rate of inflation when they decide to undertake a loan. They will only want to make loans when the real interest rate is expected to be positive but, as the example above illustrates, the real interest rate can turn out to be negative. The lender's expectations need not be correct. The example shows that lenders have an incentive to forecast inflation correctly; with incorrect expectations, lending can make them worse off. More will be said about expectations in Chapter 13 where we discuss an optimal way of forming expectations.

The Marginal Tax Rate

We omitted an important consideration in our discussion above about real wages. The government will take a fraction of your earnings because of the personal income tax. This fact leads us to consider the **marginal tax rate** (MTR), defined below.

Definition of the Marginal Tax Rate

■ If you earn an extra dollar of income, the additional tax that you pay on this extra income is called the marginal tax rate.

There is more than one marginal tax rate in many countries because income tax codes are frequently *progressive*, meaning that the higher your income, the higher is your marginal tax rate. We will not be concerned with progressivity since this is unimportant for our purposes. So we will assume that there is only one tax rate denoted by t; it is a fraction bounded between zero and unity ($0 < t < 1$). When we discuss labor supply and saving decisions, we need to adjust the returns from work and saving by the MTR to reflect the returns that labor suppliers and savers actually get after taxes.

Present Values

When we study decision-making over time by firms and households, it will be necessary to compute the present value of payments that accrue to economic agents. The important distinction to be made here is that these payments will occur in the present and the future. We will need a way for households and firms to translate future payments into their equivalents in the present. Computing the present value of a payment stream will do just this.

Suppose that you have an amount today denoted by $A(0)$. You put this in the bank in a savings account paying the nominal annual interest rate interest rate, i ($0 < i < 1$). After one year, your money is worth an amount we denote by A(1). Your funds grew because they obey the following equation.

$$A(0)\cdot(1 + i) = A(1)$$

In this expression, A(1) is the sum of your original funds (or principal), A(0), plus your interest earnings on your funds, the product i·A(0). Rewrite this equation in the equivalent way

$$A(0) = \frac{A(1)}{(1+i)}$$

and this is a simple example of a present value formula. The value A(1) is an amount you will have in the future (one year from now) so, by dividing this future amount by one plus the interest rate, you compute the value today of an amount accruing to you in the future.

Now suppose that you leave this amount in the bank for two years, earning the nominal annual interest rate, i, in each period. Your funds at the end of two years will obey the following expression.

$$[A(0)\cdot(1 + i)]\cdot(1 + i) = A(2)$$

In this equation, A(2) is the amount you will have two years from now. At the end of one year, you will have A(0)·(1 + i) just as before but now you leave these funds in the bank (your original principal and interest will now earn interest), giving you [A(0)·(1 + i)]·(1 + i) at the end of two years. Rewrite this last equation in the equivalent way

$$A(0) = \frac{A(2)}{(1+i)^2}$$

a second present value formula translating an amount two years from now into its present value.

As a final example, suppose someone plans to pay you A(1) a year from now and A(2) two years in the future. The present value of this payments stream is

$$A(0) = \frac{A(1)}{(1+i)} + \frac{A(2)}{(1+i)^2}$$

You should be able to generalize this expression to the case where there are more than two years of annual payments.

There are other uses for these present values formulae although, in measuring the salaries over time of some individuals, discounting is usually ignored (see **Doing Economics**: Star Athlete Salaries and Discounting). And they can be used to explain the pricing of bonds (see **Doing Economics**: Bond Pricing). They may also be used to compute growth rates for economic time series over multiple time periods (see the appendix to this chapter).

Doing Economics: Star Athlete Salaries and Discounting

Anyone who follows professional sports will read news stories from time to time about the contracts signed by professional athletes. Contracts often involve payments accruing to athletes in the future. Press reports rarely, if ever, discount the salaries of athletes to adjust for payments occurring in the future, thus exaggerating the economic value of these athletes' contracts.

Suppose that an athlete signs a contract for a 5year period. The payment stream for this athlete is listed in the following table.

Contract Year	Dollar Amount	Discounted Amount
Signing Bonus	$1 million	$1 million
Year 1	$2 million	$1.8 million
Year 2	$3 million	$2.5 million
Year 3	$4 million	$3.0 million
Year 4	$2 million	$1.4 million
Year 5	$2 million	$1.2 million
Total	$14 million	$10.9 million

Assume a nominal interest rate of 10 percent (i = .10), and recall that if we want to find the present value of an amount n periods in the future we use the formula

$$\text{Discounted Value} = \text{Dollar Amount}/(1 + i)^n$$

Our athlete gets a signing bonus now so we don't need to discount that amount but all other payments occur in the future and so must be appropriately discounted. The table contains the payments and their discounted values. Totals are provided at the bottom of the table.

Discounting substantially reduces the payments in all but the first year and the athlete has a contract with a present value that is about $3.1 million less than the figure you get by just adding up the payments each year. So adding up the payments overstates the worth of the contract by about 20 percent.

Finally, many states in the U.S. run lottery systems where the winners get a stream of payments out into the future. These payments are regularly reported in the press by simply summing the payments without discounting any of the future payments received by the winners. Payments to lottery winners are thus overstated because payments are not discounted.

Time Preference

Economists usually assume that households would prefer to consume now rather than later. This seems reasonable; all else the same, if you were offered the chance to use the services of an Ipod now or one year from now, you would choose to use the Ipod now. To get you to wait for consumption, you would need to be compensated for waiting. **Time preference** is the amount that you must be offered to get you to wait for consumption. Sometimes it is said that time preference is the "rate of impatience." The definition of time preference is given below.

Definition of Time Preference

■ Time preference is the extra consumption you must be offered to make you indifferent between consumption today and next period.

■ Put differently, one unit of consumption today provides more welfare to an individual than one unit of consumption next period.

Doing Economics: Bond Pricing

Bonds are issued by governments and firms when they wish to borrow funds from lenders for investment purposes, among other reasons. When a bond is used, a *term to maturity* is chosen; the loan will be outstanding for this length of time. The term can be as short as a few months or it can cover many years. The *face value* of the bond is the amount that will be paid to the bondholder when the loan ends. The *coupon* is the interest payment to the bondholder each year as a condition for making the loan. Thus issuing a bond provides a present value stream to the lender consisting of periodic interest payments and a face value payment. Bonds are bought and sold in bond markets.

Let P_{Bond} denote the price of a bond, FV denote face value, C refers to interest (the coupon payment), and let i denote the nominal interest rate. Bond pricing can be done in the following way.

One Year Bond: $P_{Bond} = \dfrac{C}{1+i} + \dfrac{FV}{1+i}$

Two Year Bond: $P_{Bond} = \dfrac{C}{1+i} + \dfrac{C}{(1+i)^2} + \dfrac{FV}{(1+i)^2}$

To see why these formulae must hold, imagine what would be true if the price of a bond were less than the present value of the payment stream. Such a situation is a very good deal, making individuals want to buy such a security. The more people who see this situation, the more will want to buy it, driving up the price of the bond until the expressions above hold.

There is also another type of bond that is sometimes used in economic analysis. This bond is one with an infinite term to maturity, known as a *consol*. The bondholder gets periodic interest payments but there will never be a repayment of face value. This type of bond has a particularly simple pricing formula as you will see below.

Consol Bond: $P_{Bond} = \dfrac{C}{1+i} + \dfrac{C}{(1+i)^2} + \dfrac{C}{(1+i)^3} + \cdots = C \cdot \left[\dfrac{1}{1+i} + \dfrac{1}{(1+i)^2} + \dfrac{1}{(1+i)^3} \cdots \right] = \dfrac{C}{i}$

(continued)

The term within the brackets can be shown to be $1/i$. Thus the pricing formula for a consol is very simple and it illustrates an important fact (although the other bond pricing formulae show this as well); there is an inverse relationship between bond prices and the interest rate, given a fixed coupon (and face value) payment.

You may be wondering why interest payments are called coupon payments. The reason is that, in the past, interest payments were made when a bondholder would clip a coupon and turn it in to the borrower in order to be paid their interest payment. Coupon-clipping is no longer necessary for holding bonds and receiving interest payments.

Time preference will be an important idea when you study how aggregate consumption can change over time. Further, when you study the theory of the neoclassical economy in Chapter 9, you will see that there is a close connection between time preference and the real rate of interest.

2.4 CONCLUDING REMARKS

This chapter has been concerned with the economic data that is the primary source of information used by economists to study the U.S. economy. In addition the chapter covers a series of topics designed to give you the foundation for learning to apply economic analysis to a variety of economic problems.

The first part of our discussion concerned the NIPA accounts, an accounting system that constructs estimates of GDP and related measures of economic activity. We discussed three approaches to GDP measurement (the expenditures approach, the income approach, and the value-added approach), and showed how they reveal different aspects of economic activity in the economy. We then discussed several important relationships implicit in the NIPA accounts involving private and aggregate saving.

The next section of this chapter examined a number of important concepts that will be needed when you begin to apply economic analysis to economic models later in the book. We discussed how to measure real GDP, index numbers, and alternative measures of prices. Interest rates were defined including the crucial idea of the real interest rate. The marginal tax rate was defined, a variable that will have an important impact upon the incentives faced by households when they make labor supply and saving decisions. We discussed the computation of the present value of payment streams occurring in the future, showing how to convert a future payment stream into its value in the present. Finally we defined the idea of time preference, the idea that households prefer to consume now rather than later and that they must be compensated to wait for consumption in the future.

The material in this chapter provides the foundation for doing economic analysis later in the book. Once you have mastered the material in this chapter, you can begin to think like an economist which you will need to do to work through the economic models that we will discuss.

Key Ideas

■ Gross Domestic Product measures the market value in current dollars of final goods and services produced in a given time period by labor and property located within the borders of the U.S.

■ The underground economy refers to transactions that are done secretly because they are illegal or to avoid taxation.

■ The government imputes rental income to owner-occupiers of houses.

■ GDP measures the value of goods and services sold to final consumers.

■ Intermediate goods and services are used in the production of other products.

■ Intermediate goods are not included in GDP to avoid double counting.

■ The expenditure approach measures GDP by adding up the expenditures on goods and services by households, firms, the government, and net exports.

■ The income approach measures GDP by adding up payments to the factors of production used to produce the goods and services in GDP.

■ The value-added approach to GDP measurement measures GDP by subtracting the value of intermediate goods used in production from the revenues of firms.

■ The current account is the difference between exports and imports.

■ The government runs a deficit if its expenditures on goods and services, net transfer and interest payments, exceed its tax revenues.

■ The government runs a surplus if its expenditures on goods and services, net transfer and interest payments, are less than its tax revenues.

■ Stocks are economic variables measured at a point in time.

■ Flows are economic variables measured relative to a time period.

■ Nominal GDP measures the output produced in the economy in current-dollar units.

■ Constant-dollar GDP or real GDP measures output in base year prices.

■ Index numbers reveal the direction of change in a series relative to a base year.

■ The CPI measures the cost in current prices of base year quantities relative to the cost of base year quantities using base year prices.

■ The GDP deflator is the ratio of nominal to constant-dollar GDP times 100.

■ Inflation is an increase in the level of all prices in the economy. It is an ongoing or continuing process that can last indefinitely.

■ The real interest rate is the nominal interest rate minus the expected rate of inflation.

■ If you earn an extra dollar of income, the extra tax you pay on this extra income is called the marginal tax rate.

■ A present value converts a stream of future payments into their present equivalent.

■ Time preference is the extra consumption you must be offered to make you indifferent between consumption today and next period.

Key Words

GDP	Inflation	GDP Deflator	Index Number
Net Domestic Product	Present Value	Nominal Interest Rate	Substitution Bias
	Underground Economy	Time Preference	Real Interest Rate

Value-Added	Expenditure Approach	Intermediate Goods	Deflating
Consumption	Exports	and Services	Depreciation
Private Saving	Gross Investment	Income Approach	Net Exports
Budget Deficit	Government Saving	Imports	Transfer Payments
Constant-Dollar	Stock	Government Purchases	Nominal GDP
(Real) GDP	Chain-Weighted	Budget Surplus	Quality-Adjustment Bias
CPI	Real GDP	Flow	Marginal Tax Rate

Questions for Study and Review

Review Exercises

1. Explain the concept of "double counting" in the context of intermediate and final goods.
2. Gross Domestic Product (GDP) includes market and non-market production. However, there are some non-market activities not included in the GDP. Give at least two examples of a non-market production not in GDP.
3. Explain the difference between

   a) Gross Domestic Product and Net Domestic Product.
   b) Nominal Gross Domestic Product and Real Gross Domestic Product.
   c) Gross Domestic Product and Gross National Product.

4. Below are transactions that may or may not affect GDP in the United States. If it affects GDP, state to which NIPA categories it would belong.

   a) Chrysler sells a truck to a Canadian business owner for his private use.
   b) Chrysler sells a truck to the U.S. government.
   c) Chrysler sells a truck to your parents for personal use.
   d) Alcoa Co. sells aluminum to Chrysler to produce cars.
   e) Toyota sells a truck to your neighbor.
   f) Chrysler builds an S.U.V. to be sold next year.

5. List and describe the four major components of GDP in the expenditure approach.
6. Explain why real GDP in years before the base year is likely to exceed nominal GDP.

Thought Exercises

1. How does the price of a bond change, as implied by bond pricing formulae, if the nominal interest rate changes?
2. A two-year bond has a coupon of $100 each year and pays no face value at the end of the second year. If the price of the bond is $173.55, compute the interest rate on this bond. (Hint: You need to use the quadratic formula to solve this problem.)
3. The State of California considers legalizing marijuana to increase its tax revenues. Discuss the impact on GDP of legalizing the drug.

Numerical Exercises

1. Suppose a two-year bond pays a $50 coupon in each year and repays $1000 in Face Value at the end of the second year. Compute the price of the bond if the interest rate is 10 percent.

2. Assume Lisa wins $1,000,000 in the lottery. She has the following options to receive her money: (1) An immediate one-time payment of $900,000; or (2) ten annual payments of $100,000 with the first $100,000 received immediately.

    a)   Which option will Lisa choose if her personal discount rate is 2 percent?
    b)   Which option will Lisa choose if her personal discount rate is 6 percent?
    c)   Is Lisa more impatient in part a) or part b)? Explain.

3. Calculate real GDP for the years 2007 through 2009 from the information in the table below. Assume that the GDP deflator in 2007 equals 100.

Year	Price of Video Games	Quantity of Video Games	Price of Milk	Quantity of Milk	Price of T-Shirts	Quantity of T-Shirts
2007	$33	320	$2.50	4,500	$23.00	600
2008	$34	315	$2.80	4,600	$25.00	800
2009	$39	300	$3.00	6,000	$22.00	900

4. Consider the following data for an economy.

Year	Price of CDs	Quantity of CDs	Price of Corn	Quantity of Corn
2004	$15.00	170	$2.00	4500
2005	$15.30	160	$2.10	4500
2006	$16.00	180	$2.40	3800
2007	$15.80	185	$2.60	3900

    a)   Compute nominal GDP for each year.
    b)   Compute real GDP for each year when the base year is 2005. Compute the GDP deflator for each year using the results from this and the previous question a).
    c)   Compute the CPI for this economy for each year using 2005 as the base year.
    d)   Compute and compare the rate of price inflation for each year using both the GDP deflator and the CPI.
    e)   Compute the chain-weighted real GDP growth rates for 2006 and 2007.

5. The table below shows the Euro/Dollar Exchange rate from November 2007 to April 2008. Construct index numbers for this series using a base period of January 2008.

Month	Exchange Rate
Nov-07	0.683107 EUR/$
Dec-07	0.692857 EUR/$
Jan-08	0.673764 EUR/$
Feb-08	0.681477 EUR/$
Mar-08	0.640861 EUR/$
Apr-08	0.632871 EUR/$

Data Exercises

1. Go to the web site of the Bureau of Economic Analysis (www.bea.gov) and find data on the nominal GDP expenditure components for the year 2008.
2. Go to the Bureau of Labor Statistics web site (www.bls.gov) and collect monthly data for the CPI and average hourly earnings in Manufacturing for 2008.
3. Find latest data on the website of the Bureau of Economic Analysis for

    a) Table 2.1
    b) Table 2.2
    c) Table 2.3

For further questions, multiple choice quizzes, and weblinks related to this chapter, visit www.routledge.com/textbooks/rossana

Reference

Steindel, C. (1995) "Chain-Weighting: The New Approach to Measuring Real GDP," *Current Issues in Economics and Finance* 1 (9), New York Federal Reserve Bank (December).

APPENDIX: COMPOUND GROWTH RATE FORMULAE

The present value formulae may be used to compute compound rates of growth for economic time series. In this appendix, we illustrate how this may be done.

Suppose you have the initial value of an economic time series and you know that in the next period of time, called period one, that variable grew by 5 percent. At the end of that next period, the value of the series would be

$$\text{Initial Value} \cdot (1 + .05) = \text{Value After One Period}$$

Thus if we begin with $10 and we earn 5 percent interest, our initial sum would grow to $10 \cdot (1 + .05) = \$10.50$.

If we take our initial amount and want to know its worth after two periods, earning 5 percent in each period, we can find out by computing

$$[\text{Initial Value} \cdot (1 + .05)] \cdot (1 + .05) = \text{Value After Two Periods}$$

or

$$\text{Initial Value} \cdot (1 + .05)^2 = \text{Value After Two Periods}$$

Now you can see the pattern that emerges. If we want to compute the value of an initial amount after an arbitrary number of periods, denoted by n, we would have

$$\text{Initial Value} \cdot (1 + .05)^n = \text{Value After n Periods.}$$

So if we begin with $10 and earn 5 percent for ten years, we would eventually have

$$\$10 \cdot (1 + .05)^{10} = \$16.29.$$

This formula may now be used to compute the growth rate of a series between two points in time.

To see how, rewrite the our formula as

$$(1 + g)^n = \text{Value After n Periods/Initial Value}$$

where we have replaced the value .05 by the letter g which stands for "growth rate."

Chapter 3

Business Cycle Measurement

LEARNING OBJECTIVES

Business cycles have a number of key characteristics manifested by economic time series. It is the purpose of this chapter to discuss those characteristics and to show how we can use them to test the implications of economic models. In some cases those properties pertain to an individual economic time series; in other cases, the properties apply to pairs of economic time series. But in every case, we will use these properties as a form of testing for economic models of aggregate economies. Here are a few of the questions that we address in this chapter.

- How do we define the business cycle?
- Do all economies experience cyclical fluctuations in economic activity?
- What is a recession?
- What does it mean for a time series to be nonstationary?
- Is there any way to know if an economy is headed for a recession?

Any economic theory must be tested for its ability to match up with actual economic data. One way to assess the predictions of aggregate economic models requires that we first measure the time series behavior of macroeconomic data over the **business cycle**, then compare those time series patterns with the time series characteristics predicted by an aggregate economic model. In this chapter, we describe the key time series characteristics of macroeconomic data over the course of the business cycle. We later use those characteristics to assess the predictive ability of aggregate economic models.

The first concept that we will discuss is what we mean by a business cycle. Here we present the traditional view of a business cycle as a departure from the trend or general direction of change in an economy. In this section, you will learn how business cycles are measured and we look at the historical record of business cycles in the U.S. In the next section, we discuss two possible sources of trends that can be present in macroeconomic data. These trend types will later be important as we assess the ability of aggregate economic models to explain the behavior over time of macroeconomic data because the type of trend in the data can determine the type of economic model consistent with that data. Then we discuss the time series characteristics of individual and pairs of economic time series. These properties describe how economic time series behave over the business cycle. Our final topic is a discussion of cyclical indicators, indexes of time series that can be useful for forecasting a coming recession or to asses the current state of the economy. A final section summarizes the topics addressed in this chapter.

Once you have mastered the material in this chapter, you should have a solid understanding of how business cycles are defined, how economic variables behave over the course of the business cycle, and how to use various indicators of the state (as well as the future state) of the economy.

3.1 THE BUSINESS CYCLE: A DEFINITION

All industrialized economies experience economic fluctuations. Aggregate economic output, the unemployment rate, and many other economic magnitudes rise or fall over time. These swings in economic activity vary in size and duration and these fluctuations in economic activity are the characteristics of the business cycle. Figure 3.1 provides a graphical description of these events.

Business cycles are defined in relation to the behavior of real output. The figure gives an illustration of the conventional view about business cycles. Output (real GDP) has a general direction of change, described by a **trend line**. Output will fluctuate about this trend line and it is these fluctuations that are what we mean by the business cycle. The fluctuations in economic activity involve **turning points**; a **peak** is when real output stops rising and begins to decline and a **trough** is when output stops declining and begins to rise. An **expansion** (sometimes called a **boom**) is the period of time where real output is expanding, rising from a trough to a peak. A **recession** (or a **contraction**) is the time period where real output is

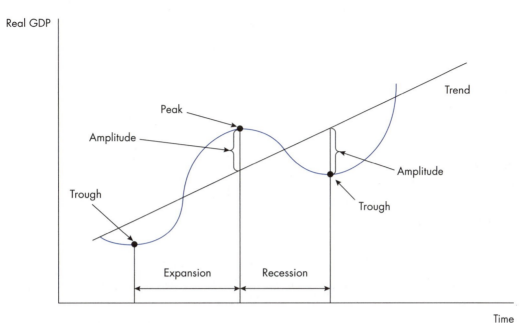

FIGURE 3.1 The Business Cycle

Business cycles involve fluctuations in real output (real GDP) around a trend. An expansion occurs when output increases from a trough to a peak and a contraction is when output declines from a peak to a trough. The amplitude of the cycle measures the distance between a peak or a trough from the trend.

declining, falling from a peak to a trough in real output. The **amplitude** of the business cycle measures the distance between a peak or a trough and the trend in real GDP.

Figure 3.2 provides a times series graph of U.S. real GDP for two decades, the 1970s and 1980s. The data on the trend level of real GDP (the straight line in Figure 3.1) is constructed by the Congressional Budget Office (CBO). The data in the graph cover two decades where recessions (two are marked in the graph) occurred as defined by the National Bureau of Economic Research (see below). The graph shows that real GDP was above and below trend GDP during these years. The graph also shows that the actual behavior of the business cycle is typically not as smooth as Figure 3.1 would lead us to believe. Real GDP actually increased by a small amount (an annual growth rate of 1.4 percent) between 1974:1 and 1974:2 (see Table 3.1 below) yet the trough in the cycle was dated to be March 1975. Further, there was positive growth in real GDP between 1977:3 and 1977:4. Also the strength of the expansion was quite variable, with growth rates of less than one percent to a high of over 15 percent (at annual rates) during the expansion.

The Historical Record

In the U.S., a nonprofit corporation called the **National Bureau of Economic Research (NBER)** is an organization of economists that, among other things, dates business cycles. Table 3.2,

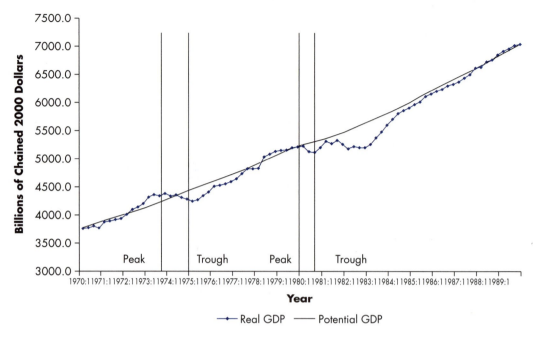

FIGURE 3.2 U.S. Real and Potential GDP

Source: St. Louis Federal Reserve Bank FRED Database

TABLE 3.1 Annual Real GDP Growth Rates in the 1970s

	Recession		Expansion
1973:4	3.83	1975:1	−4.78
1974:1	−3.47	1975:2	2.93
1974:2	1.15	1975:3	6.78
1974:3	−3.87	1975:4	5.24
1974:4	−1.57	1976:1	9.01
1975:1	−4.78	1976:2	2.98
		1976:3	1.92
		1976:4	2.87
		1977:1	4.83
		1977:2	7.85
		1977:3	7.16
		1977:4	−0.04

1978:1	1.29
1978:2	15.77
1978:3	3.94
1978:4	5.26
1979:1	0.78
1979:2	0.38
1979:3	2.88
1979:4	1.18
1980:1	1.28

TABLE 3.2 The U.S. Business Cycle Record

BUSINESS CYCLE REFERENCE DATES		DURATION IN MONTHS		
Peak	**Trough**	**Contraction**	**Expansion**	**Cycle**
Quarterly dates are in parentheses		*Peak to Trough*	*Previous Trough to this Peak*	*Trough from Previous Trough*	*Peak from Previous Peak*
	December 1854 (IV)	–	–	–	–
June 1857(II)	December 1858 (IV)	18	30	48	–
October 1860(III)	June 1861 (III)	8	22	30	40
April 1865(I)	December 1867 (I)	32	46	78	54
June 1869(II)	December 1870 (IV)	18	18	36	50
October 1873(III)	March 1879 (I)	65	34	99	52
March 1882(I)	May 1885 (II)	38	36	74	101
March 1887(II)	April 1888 (I)	13	22	35	60
July 1890(III)	May 1891 (II)	10	27	37	40
January 1893(I)	June 1894 (II)	17	20	37	30
December 1895(IV)	June 1897 (II)	18	18	36	35
June 1899(III)	December 1900 (IV)	18	24	42	42
September 1902(IV)	August 1904 (III)	23	21	44	39
May 1907(II)	June 1908 (II)	13	33	46	56
January 1910(I)	January 1912 (IV)	24	19	43	32
January 1913(I)	December 1914 (IV)	23	12	35	36
August 1918(III)	March 1919 (I)	7	44	51	67
January 1920(I)	July 1921 (III)	18	10	28	17

TABLE 3.2 Continued.

BUSINESS CYCLE REFERENCE DATES		DURATION IN MONTHS			
Peak	**Trough**	**Contraction**	**Expansion**	**Cycle**	
	Quarterly dates are in parentheses	Peak to Trough	Previous Trough to this Peak	Trough from Previous Trough	Peak from Previous Peak
May 1923(II)	July 1924 (III)	14	22	36	40
October 1926(III)	November 1927 (IV)	13	27	40	41
August 1929(III)	March 1933 (I)	43	21	64	34
May 1937(II)	June 1938 (II)	13	50	63	93
February 1945(I)	October 1945 (IV)	8	80	88	93
November 1948(IV)	October 1949 (IV)	11	37	48	45
July 1953(II)	May 1954 (II)	10	45	55	56
August 1957(III)	April 1958 (II)	8	39	47	49
April 1960(II)	February 1961 (I)	10	24	34	32
December 1969(IV)	November 1970 (IV)	11	106	117	116
November 1973(IV)	March 1975(I)	16	36	52	47
January 1980(I)	July 1980 (III)	6	58	64	74
July 1981(III)	November 1982 (IV)	16	12	28	18
July 1990(III)	March 1991(I)	8	92	100	108
March 2001(I)	November 2001 (IV)	8	120	128	128
December 2007 (IV)			73		81
Average, all cycles:					
1854–2001 (32 cycles)			17	38	55 56*
1854–1919 (16 cycles)			22	27	48 49**
1919–1945 (6 cycles)			18	35	53 53
1945–2001 (10 cycles)			10	57	67 67
* 31 cycles					
** 15 cycles					

Source: National Bureau of Economic Research (www.nber.org)

taken from the NBER web site (www.nber.org), provides the official business cycle record for the U.S. from the middle of the nineteenth century. Several facts stand out in this table.

1. *Business Cycles Are Not a Recent Phenomenon.* The first important fact shown in the table is simply that business cycles are not a recent phenomenon, always having been a part of recorded economic history. Business cycles were present in the nineteenth century just as they have been more recently.

2. *Duration Is Not Constant.* The table also reveals that the **duration** of recessions and expansions varies over time. The duration of a cycle just refers to the length of time that the economy experiences an expansion or contraction in economic activity. The table shows that the length of contractions has varied from 6 to 65 months. Expansions have been as short as 10 months and as long as 120 months.

3. *The Amplitude of the Cycle Is Not Constant.* The severity of recessions or the strengths of booms have varied throughout economic history. To give an extreme example, consider the contraction known as the Great Depression. The peak of the expansion at the start of this contraction was in August 1929, with the trough occurring in March 1933. There was a contraction in output of about 33 percent between 1929 and 1933. The unemployment rate rose to about 25 percent of the labor force at the height of the Great Depression. This was the most extreme contraction in U.S. economic history. Most recessions, fortunately, are nowhere near as severe as this and, if you were to look at other cyclical episodes in Table 3.2, you would see differences in the amplitude of the business cycle.

4. *Business Cycles Are Not Specific to the U.S.* Figure 3.3 provides a graph of industrial production in the G7 countries. This series is an index number for each country measuring production of goods and services; using this index allows us to observe output produced over time in different countries with a common unit of measurement. The graph covers the same time period contained in Figure 3.2. The figure clearly shows that each country experienced a decline in output in the recession that began in the fourth quarter of 1973. Thus the business cycle exists in all industrialized countries, not just the U.S. The fact that cycles occur in all of these countries suggests the possibility that there is a common explanation for the business cycle, one that is not country-specific.

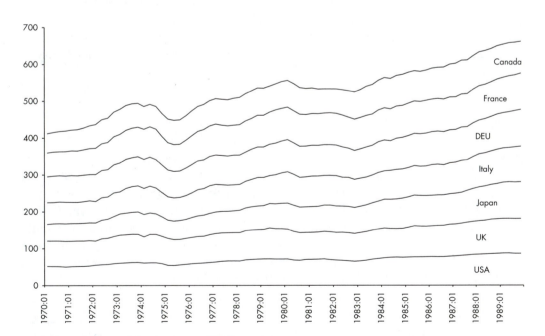

FIGURE 3.3 Industrial Production in G7 Countries

Source: OECD

The fact that business cycles occur in all industrialized economies has caused economists to study the properties of macroeconomic data in these economies. The view has developed that there is enough commonality in the behavior of the data from these economies to suggest that an explanation of the causes of business cycles may be found which would apply to all industrialized economies.[1]

Some of the cyclical episodes listed in Table 3.2 are noteworthy and merit some comment because they are associated with events important in U.S. economic history. In our later analysis, each of the four cases below provide much of the motivation for our analysis of models of the business cycle, although not every example below is associated with cyclical changes in real output. For example, there are events such as technical progress that are really changes in trend GDP; such changes do not involve cyclical changes in real output. However it is easy to see why we study the sources of cyclical fluctuations as we do once you understand the four cases below.

The Great Depression

No cyclical economic event in the history of the U.S. has had more impact upon the thinking of economists than the Great Depression. Indeed the emergence of macroeconomics as a separate specialty within the economics profession can be traced to this traumatic event. Beginning in August 1929, this major contraction was larger than any other recession in recorded history, an event involving an enormous loss in output and a correspondingly large increase in unemployment. Policy changes, still in effect today, grew out of this cyclical episode. For example, many of the banking regulations in use today were implemented as a direct result of the Great Depression because one feature of that contraction was that many banks failed, causing depositors to lose their deposited funds. U.S. policymakers set monetary and regulatory policies in part to prevent the recurrence of such a large contraction in economic activity.

Supply-Side Shocks

The formation of the Organization of Petroleum Exporting Countries (OPEC) is an event that brought supply-side shocks into prominence in business cycle analysis. OPEC formed a cartel that restricted the supply of oil, driving up oil's relative price and causing contractions in 1973 and in 1981. Supply-side shocks have very different effects in an economy as compared to shocks arising on the demand side of the economy. Policymakers face a considerably more difficult task in dealing with these types of disturbances as compared to other types of shocks as you will see but, nonetheless, supply-side shocks have caused policy changes in the U.S. and other countries and we will wish to study the effects of those policies.

---

1 See the article by Robert E. Lucas Jr. entitled "Methods and Problems in Business Cycle Theory," *Journal of Money, Credit, and Banking* 12, No. 4 (November 1980), pp. 696–715.

Policy-Induced Recessions

Economic policy can be a source of booms or recessions. One important example of this possibility is the recession that began in early 1980. When this recession occurred, the U.S. economy was experiencing a historically high inflation rate and the Fed (the U.S. central bank) decided to pursue a restrictive monetary policy with the aim of reducing inflation. In addition, policymakers at the Fed felt that they needed to change the way in which they carried out their monetary policies to give them a better chance of achieving their policy goal of reducing inflation. A recession followed the implementation of this new form of monetary policy in October 1979. The Fed pursued a restrictive monetary policy with its new policy methods and this tight-money policy caused a recession. Fiscal policy can also cause cyclical changes in the economy, as you will learn.

The Booming 90s

The U.S. economy experienced its longest cyclical expansion covering most of the 1990s. The duration of this expansion was 120 months with a cyclical peak occurring in March 2001. The cause of this remarkable expansion has been a subject of great research interest for economists. Evidence will be presented in a later chapter that this period was one of unprecedented technical progress, some of which was associated with the personal computer. Strictly speaking, technical progress is not a cyclical phenomenon although it can look like a cyclical event when looking at macroeconomic data; rather technical progress raises the non-cyclical level of real GDP. It will be important to separate cyclical from non-cyclical changes in real output when we study business cycles.

3.2 PROPERTIES OF MACROECONOMIC DATA

In this section, we discuss a number of the business cycle characteristics of individual and pairs of macroeconomic time series. Models of the economy have been developed to explain the existence of these properties. As it turns out, there is some disagreement among economists about some of these statistical properties; there are competing explanations for the source of the trends apparent in macroeconomic data. This difference of professional opinion has caused the development of alternative aggregative models of the economy, consistent with each type of trend in the data. We begin by studying the trends that can be present in macroeconomic data.

Stationarity and Nonstationarity

Some economic time series appear to have trends in them, that is, they seem to have a general tendency to rise or fall over time. Macroeconomic data fall into this category as almost all macro data seem to be rising over time. But other series have no such tendency to rise or fall. Rather they seem to be fluctuating about a constant value. These patterns give rise to the following two definitions.

Definitions of Stationary and Nonstationary Time Series

■ An economic time series is **stationary** if its average (or **mean**) value is constant over time.
■ An economic time series is **nonstationary** if its average value is not constant over time.

The formal statistical definitions of these concepts, used in actual practice by macroeconomists, are somewhat more complicated than the definitions above but the conditions given here are sufficient for our purposes. These properties of macroeconomic data can easily be seen by looking at a graph of two hypothetical time series. Figure 3.4 has a graph of each type of time series.

In the left panel of this figure, an example of a stationary time series is drawn. Notice that it is fluctuating about a value that is unchanging over time. So if something causes this time series to move away from this constant value, the series will return to it over time. This constant value is the long-run average (mean) of the series and so it is often said that a stationary time series is **mean-reverting**, meaning that if something were to cause this series to deviate from its mean, it will return to its mean if enough time passes.

Now consider the right panel of Figure 3.4 and observe that there is no tendency for this time series to return to a fixed value over time. The series is trending down (a series might also trend up as you will shortly see) and so, no matter how long we wait, this series will not settle down to a constant value if the series were to move away from its downward trend. A nonstationary time series does not revert to a fixed average value over time. Figure 3.5 displays the actual time path of quarterly U.S. real GDP over the period 1947 to 2008 and just by inspection it is clear that real GDP is a nonstationary time series. To confirm this, compute the average for this data in two ways; use the first half and the second half of the data and compare the resulting values. For the data in the figure, in billions of chained 2000 dollars, these

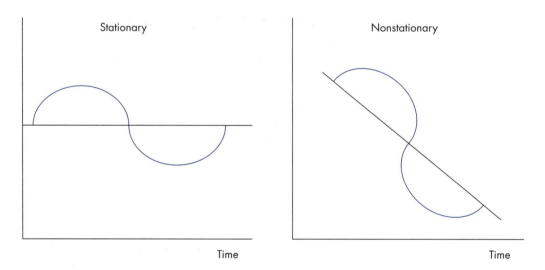

FIGURE 3.4 Stationary and Nonstationary Time Series

A stationary time series fluctuates about a fixed value. A nonstationary time series fluctuates as well but does not do so around a constant value.

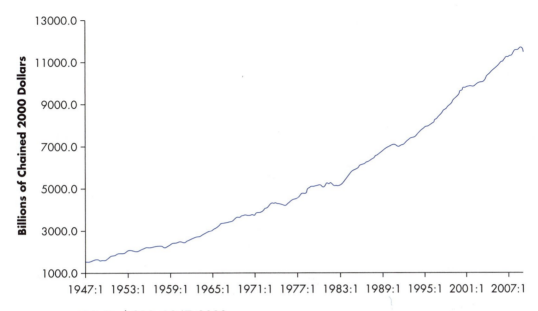

FIGURE 3.5 U.S. Real GDP, 1947–2008

Source: St. Louis Federal Reserve Bank FRED Database

averages are 3328.6 in the first half of the sample data and 7346.3 in billions in the second half. The average for the second half is considerably higher (it is more than two times as large) and so the mean of real GDP is evidently not constant. Real GDP is therefore nonstationary and the same can be said for almost all other macroeconomic data. This rising mean will also be the concern of the theory of economic growth (see Chapter 10), a theory designed to explain long-run trends in the economy.

Now consider a macroeconomic time series that may be stationary. Figure 3.6 shows a plot of the quarterly U.S. unemployment rate for the period 1948 to 2008. Inspection of this diagram reveals no clear-cut positive (or negative) trend in the mean of the series over time. The average unemployment rate for the first half of the sample is 5.1 percent and the average for the second half is 6.1 percent; these two averages are much closer, in percentage terms, than they were for real GDP. Over this time period, it appears that the unemployment rate is stationary.

Each of the aggregate models, developed later in the book, will provide an explanation rationalizing stationarity or nonstationarity in economic time series. Economic models will differ regarding their explanations for these trends in macroeconomic data because there is more than one way that an economic time series can be nonstationary. There are two ways that nonstationarity can arise.

Trends in Macroeconomic Data

Once we have established that the mean of a time series is changing over time, the next step is to identify the source of that nonstationarity. Here are the definitions of two possible sources of trends in macroeconomic data.

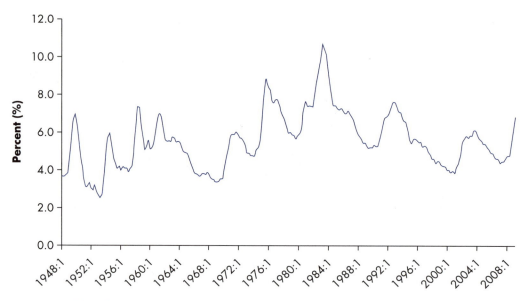

FIGURE 3.6 The U.S. Unemployment Rate

Source: St. Louis Federal Reserve FRED Database

Definitions of Possible Trends

■ An economic time series may contain a deterministic time trend.

■ An economic time series can appear to contain a trend because there are unpredictable permanent changes in its level.

We can describe the differences in these two definitions as follows.

When looking at real GDP data as in Figure 3.4, it seems natural to think that there is a **deterministic trend** in the data. A deterministic trend is one that can be represented in the following way.

$$\text{Trend} = a_0 + a_1 \cdot \text{Time}$$

So a trend in this case is just a linear function of time. Figure 3.7 contains a plot of part of the real U.S. GDP data used above to discuss nonstationarity and a dotted trend line has been imposed upon this data. Real GDP is never zero and it is rising over time. Therefore both parameters in the deterministic trend must be positive ($a_0 > 0$ and $a_1 > 0$). Suppose that we were to use statistical methods to estimate the parameters a_0 and a_1. Using these parameter estimates, the difference between the trend and the actual real GDP series can also be plotted and this is done in Figure 3.8. The series in this figure is stationary, fluctuating about zero.

It may well be the case that there is no trend in the data – the data may simply mislead us about the presence of a trend – and this is exactly what some economists believe on the basis

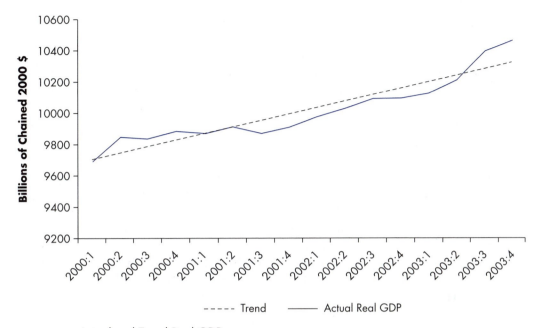

FIGURE 3.7 Actual and Trend Real GDP

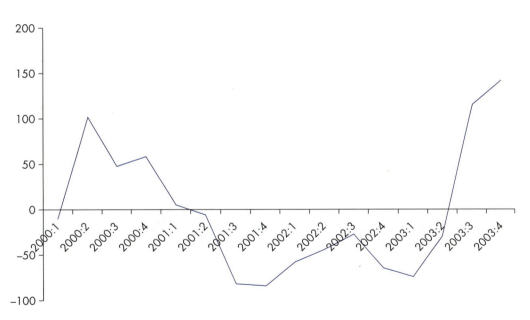

FIGURE 3.8 Real GDP Minus Trend

of statistical tests applied to macroeconomic data.[2] Rather there could be events occurring that simply change the level of the series permanently, up or down. These events may cause the data to look as if it contains a deterministic trend but these economists would argue that this is an illusion; in actual fact, there is no such trend in the data. If a time series experiences permanent changes to its level, we will describe this by saying that the series is subject to **permanent shocks**. As you will learn later, there are important issues, related to business cycles, which heavily depend upon the sources of the nonstationarity in macroeconomic time series. Here is a brief introduction to these issues.

Suppose that real GDP does contain a deterministic trend. Then it is natural to regard a model of the business cycle as one explaining deviations from that trend. Since those deviations are stationary, then the business cycle is best viewed as a transitory phenomenon and the causes of it must be transitory as well. These observations have led economists to attribute the business cycle to shifts in aggregate demand; as you will see later, shifts in aggregate demand only temporarily cause real output and other economic magnitudes to deviate from their general equilibrium values. There is also scope for demand-management by policymakers in this case since a deviation from equilibrium presumably involves welfare losses to firms and households. Thus it is desirable for policymakers to try to manage aggregate demand to keep it close to trend GDP. This is the traditional view of business cycles.

On the other hand, if the fluctuations in real output are manifestations of permanent shocks in the economy, there is no scope for aggregate demand management because the economy is simply moving from one equilibrium to another and thus policymakers would have no reason to use economic policies to change the level of real output. Real output (trend GDP) is shifting permanently up or down and, if output declines, the economy may still be in a position where households and firms are maximizing their welfare and profits. Thus there would be no reason for changes in economic policy because the public cannot be made better off even when output declines.

These two competing views thus have very different implications for how we view fluctuations in output and how those fluctuations are related to economic policy. We will return to these issues when we discuss business cycle models of the economy.

There are additional properties of economic data that we will use in business cycle analysis. These involve the behavior over time of individual time series as well as the behavior of pairs of macroeconomic series. We now turn to a discussion of these properties of macroeconomic data.

3.3 SERIAL PERSISTENCE AND COMOVEMENT

Macroeconomic data often tend to be high or low relative to trend for some period of time. Real GDP and other economic time series seem to move together in certain patterns over time. There are two time series concepts that are related to these properties and these are defined below.

---

2 This position is taken by Charles R. Nelson and Charles I. Plosser in their very provocative study "Trends and Random Walks in Macroeconomic Time Series," *Journal of Monetary Economics* 10, No. 2, pp. 139–62.

Definition of Serial Persistence

■ An economic time series displays **serial persistence** if the series tends to be above or below trend for more than one period of time.

Look back at Figure 3.8 and notice that detrended real GDP (that is, real GDP with its time trend removed) is frequently positive or negative for more than one period. This is precisely what is meant by serial persistence; output persists above or below trend for a time. Put differently, expansions and contractions in economic activity last for more than one time period as we observed above in Table 3.1.

A second time series concept refers to the **comovements** between pairs of economic time series.

Definitions of Comovements in Economic Time Series

■ An economic time series is **procyclical** if it tends to be above trend when real GDP is above trend.
■ An economic time series is **countercyclical** if it tends to be below trend when real GDP is above trend.
■ An economic time series is **acyclical** if it is neither procyclical nor countercyclical.

Note that in each of these comovement definitions, one time series is always real GDP so, in each definition, we are comparing the pattern in one economic time series to the pattern in real GDP. To apply these concepts in judging the predictive ability of aggregate economic models, it is useful to focus on a few key time series that we can use to assess an economic model. Table 3.3 provides these concepts and documents their comovements.

As you can see from the table, most of the series are procyclical with the notable exception of the unemployment rate. To see why the unemployment rate is considered to be countercyclical, consider Figure 3.9. In this figure, we plot a subset of the data in Figure 3.5 to enable us to see clearly how the unemployment rate behaves during a recession.

TABLE 3.3 Cyclical Characteristics of Selected Macroeconomic Data

Time Series	Comovement	Timing
Employment	Procyclical	Coincident
Unemployment	Countercyclical	Unclassified
Real Wages	Procyclical	Unclassified
Money Stock	Procyclical	Leading
Nominal Interest Rates	Procyclical	Lagging
Inflation	Procyclical	Lagging

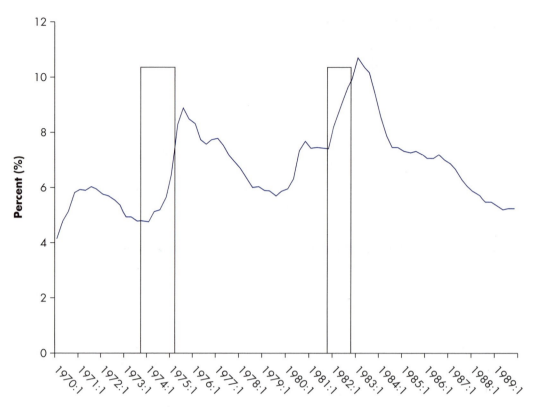

FIGURE 3.9 The U.S. Unemployment Rate

The figure contains data for the 20-year period beginning in 1970 and this period contains three recessions (see Table 3.1), two of which are marked in the figure. Notice that in both of these episodes, the unemployment rate was rising while the economy was in recession (when output is declining), indicating why it is classified as a countercyclical time series.

As a second example, consider Figure 3.10 which gives a graph of the annual growth rate of the money stock (M2) from 1970 to 1989. Two recessions are marked in the diagram and, in each recession, the growth rate declined. This indicates why the money stock is considered to be procyclical. But as each figure shows, the behavior of each series is imperfect in the sense that the behavior of a series is not exact. The money growth rate was rising for part of each recession, not falling, as would be true if there were an exact relationship between money and real GDP. For this reason, economists look at many series to learn about the cyclical state of the economy since any one series is an imperfect indicator of the business cycle.

Table 3.3 also contains information on the timing of each time series relative to real output. These definitions are given below.

Definitions of the Timing of Economic Time Series

■ A **coincident series** is one that moves above or below trend at the same time that real output moves above or below trend.

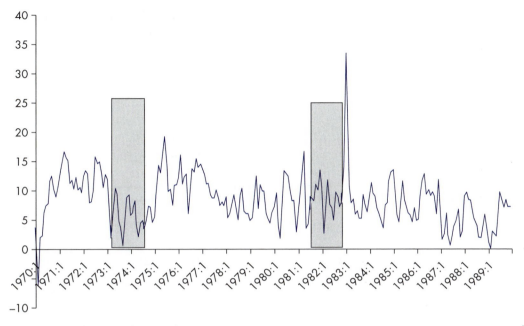

FIGURE 3.10 The Growth Rate of U.S. M2

- A **leading series** is one that moves above or below trend prior to the time that real output moves above or below trend
- A **lagging series** is one that moves above or below trend after the time that real output moves above or below trend

These definitions are self-explanatory, although more will be said below about timing. But we should also note that a series may be unclassified as to its timing relative to real output.

The public learns about the state of the economy with a lag and, for this reason, they are interested in indicators of the state of the economy. To provide this information, economists use index numbers known as cyclical indicators.

3.4 CYCLICAL INDICATORS

How do we know when we are in a recession? Is there any way to predict that a recession will soon occur? The NIPA data comes out with a lag after the end of a quarter and the NBER certifies recessions after turning points occur. These two sources of information are thus not going to be useful for learning about the current and future states of the economy. In addition, an index number can be useful to policymakers if it reliably predicts the onset of a recession in the near future. The central bank could adjust its monetary policy in a timely way if one or more economic time series indicators, along with other information, indicate a coming recession. Therefore the timing of an economic time series can be useful for assessing the current and future prospects of the economy.

In 1938, two economists at the NBER, Wesley C. Mitchell and Arthur F. Burns, published research on the cyclical behavior of economic time series.[3] Their work was used by the U.S. Department of Commerce which published indexes of cyclical indicators in the publication *Business Conditions Digest*. These index numbers are summary measures of the turning points in real output implied by many economic time series, collected together in the index number, building upon the information contained in Table 3.3 about the timing of individual macroeconomic time series. The Commerce Department no longer publishes these index numbers. But they are now constructed by the Organization for Economic Cooperation and Development (OECD). There are three types of cyclical indicators historically available.

Definitions of Cyclical Indicators

- **A leading indicator** is an index number whose behavior suggests a future recession or boom.
- **A coincident indicator** is an index number whose behavior suggests a current recession or boom.
- **A lagging indicator** is an index number whose behavior suggests a past recession or boom.

Just as in the case of individual time series, the difference in the three concepts hinges on the timing of changes in each index number relative to a recession or boom. So a leading indicator will decline (increase), say, in advance of a recession (boom). A coincident indicator will decline (increase) during a recession (boom). A lagging indicator will decline (increase) after a recession (boom) has begun. The index of leading indicators therefore contains time series thought to lead changes in real GDP. The coincident indicator contains series whose behavior mirrors current changes in real GDP while the lagging indicator contains series whose changes lag behind changes in real GDP

Table 3.3 provides an historical classification of each individual series as to its timing relative to real GDP. Changes in the nominal money stock occur prior to recessions whereas changes in the inflation rate lag behind the onset of a recession.[4] Look back at Figure 3.9 and notice that prior to the two recessions marked in the figure, the growth rate of money was flat or falling, suggesting why money is considered a leading indicator. Table 3.3 above lists only a few economic time series that can be useful as forecasting devices but it would be informative to look at indexes of cyclical indicators, which include many economic time series, to see how they track the business cycle. Table 3.4 provides data on leading indicators published by the OECD for G7 countries. The table contains data preceding and during the onset of the most recent recession. This shows clearly that the index leads changes in real GDP.

The final time series that we discuss gives us a direct measure of consumer expectations, useful for predicting a future recession.

---

3 This publication is *Statistical Indicators of Cyclical Revivals*, National Bureau of Economic Research, New York (1938).

4 Real wages and the unemployment rate do not have well-defined behavior relative to the business cycle and so their timing is unclassified.

TABLE 3.4 Index of Leading Indicators for G7 Countries

Month	Index Value
2007:8	102.90
2007:9	102.74
2007:10	102.62
2007:11	102.51
2007:12	102.40
2008:1	102.31
2008:2	102.20
2008:3	102.06
2008:4	101.84
2008:5	101.51
2008:6	100.98
2008:7	100.17
2008:8	99.08
2008:9	97.72
2008:10	96.19
2008:11	94.70
2008:12	93.45

Source: OECD

The Index of Consumer Sentiment

The University of Michigan, in conjunction with Reuters News, interviews households and publishes an index of consumer sentiment. The U.S. news media regularly report the latest data from this telephone survey because this index is thought to reveal the attitudes of consumers about the current and future state of the economy. Figure 3.11 provides a graph of this data. Vertical lines are drawn in 1990 and 2007 at the beginning of each year.

The graph has the most recent recession in it because it covers December 2007, the beginning of the current recession. Notice that the index tends to decline in the recession as seems reasonable. Households become more pessimistic as a recession proceeds and become more optimistic as an expansion continues. But note also that the index tends to change its direction prior to the beginning of the recession, declining throughout 2007 even before the recession had begun. There is a similar pattern in 1990. The recession in that year began in July and the index was declining before that point. The index thus leads economic turning points because it begins to rise before a trough in economic activity and it starts to fall before a peak is reached. But there is another aspect of this index that is interesting to economists.

As you will learn later in the book, economic theory will often indicate that households and firms make their decisions in a forward-looking manner, meaning that they form an

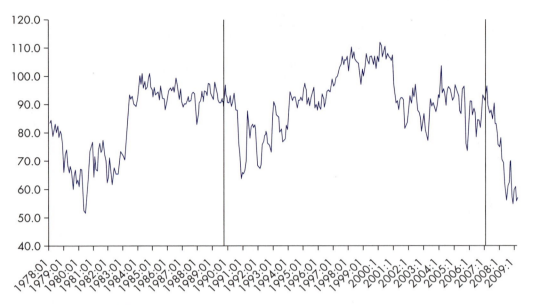

FIGURE 3.11 Index of Consumer Sentiment

expectation about the future determinants of their economic decisions. So, for example, the theory of household choice (see Chapter 4) will show that households make current and future consumption choices partly on the basis of their expectations about future disposable income. If consumers decide that their future incomes will be lower than they had expected, they will reduce their planned consumption now and in the future. That decline in household consumption can cause a recession in the economy. The Index of Consumer Sentiment reveals information on consumer expectations about the future, one reason why the index is of interest to economists. When the index declines, this suggests that there may be a recession occurring in the near future. Because this index is a direct measure of expectations, there is great attention paid to any changes in the index.

Testing Economic Models of the Economy

Now that we have concluded our discussion of the properties of macroeconomic data, we can state how an economic model of the economy can be judged using these concepts. Our discussion leads us to conclude that an economic model must explain what causes contractions or expansions in economic activity (that is, why does output fluctuate), and it must explain why they last as long as they do (that is, it must explain duration). Further, an economic model must explain the trends that appear in macroeconomic data; it must explain why economic variables display serial persistence and why they have the comovements that they do. As you will see, economic models are capable of explaining some of these facts. But there is no economic model that is capable of explaining all of these characteristics in an entirely satisfactory way.

3.5 CONCLUDING REMARKS

The macroeconomic models that we will develop to explain the existence of business cycles must be tested for their abilities to explain the cyclical characteristics of macroeconomic data. This chapter has established those properties of aggregate macroeconomic data over the business cycle that you will need to assess the economic models discussed later in the book.

We began by defining the business cycle in the traditional way, as a deviation in real output from its trend. We showed that business cycles have occurred in the nineteenth century as well as more recently, the duration and amplitude of cycles are not constant, and cycles occur in all industrialized economies. We defined the statistical properties of macroeconomic data that will be useful to us in studying models of the business cycle. We established the two types of trends that can be present in aggregate economic data, suggesting that the source of these trends will have an important influence on the types of economic models used to study the business cycle. We then defined two properties of economic data useful in studying the business cycle. Expansions and recessions last for more than one time period, a property defined as serial persistence. We discussed the comovements of pairs of economic data series over the cycle, showing that output and other macroeconomic data have a consistent relationship to trend. We looked at cyclical indicators that can be used by the public to learn whether the economy is currently or soon will be in recession. Finally the Index of Consumer Sentiment was shown to be, among other things, a direct measure of the expectations of the public and a leading indicator of economic activity.

With the tools developed in this chapter, you will be in position to decide for yourself if economists have devised models of economic fluctuations that do a good job of explaining the origins and characteristics of business cycles.

Key Ideas

- The traditional view of the business cycle is that output deviates from a trend line.
- An alternative view of the business cycle is that there is no trend in the data. The economy, in this view, is simply subject to permanent shocks.
- Business cycles have existed for all of recorded economic history.
- The duration of the cycle, the length of time that expansions and contractions occur, has varied over time.
- The amplitude of the cycle is the distance of peaks and troughs from trend and these have varied over time.
- A stationary time series fluctuates around a fixed average value.
- A nonstationary series fluctuates around a value changing average over time.
- A trend in macroeconomic data can be caused by a deterministic trend or by permanent shocks to macroeconomic variables.
- Serial persistence is the statistical property meaning that a variable tends to be above or below trend for more than one time period.
- Comovement refers to the relationship between a variable, relative to its trend, and real GDP relative to its trend.
- A series is procyclical if it is above trend when real GDP is above trend.

- A series is countercyclical if it is above trend when real GDP is below trend.
- A series is acyclical if it is neither procyclical or countercyclical.
- A leading indicator is an index made up of a number of macroeconomic variables whose movements tend to occur prior to cyclical turning points.
- A coincident indicator is an index made up of a number of macroeconomic variables whose movements tend to occur coincident to cyclical turning points.
- A lagging indicator is an index made up of a number of macroeconomic variables whose movements tend to occur after cyclical turning points.

Key Terms

Business Cycle	Lagging Indicators	Coincident	Acyclical	Comovement
Trend Line	Turning Point	Indicators	Index of Consumer	Leading
NBER	Expansion	Peak	Sentiment	Indicators
Deterministic	Mean	Contraction	Trough	Amplitude
Trend	Permanent Shock	Mean-Reverting	Boom	Recession
Procyclical	Countercyclical	Serial Persistence	Stationary	Nonstationary

Questions for Study and Review

Review Exercises

1. Provide a definition for each of the following concepts.

    a) Stationarity and Nonstationarity
    b) Procyclical, Countercyclical, Acyclical
    c) Serial Persistence

2. Comment on the following statement: "In the past, economic business cycles were similar in size and duration; they only varied across different countries."
3. Define the following business cycle concepts: peak, trough, expansion, recession.
4. Provide two reasons why a time series may be nonstationary.
5. Explain leading, lagging, and coincident indicators.

Thought Exercises

1. Download the Consumer Price Index, U.S. City Average, All Items (1982–84=100) available at the web site of the Bureau of Labor Statistics for the years 1998 through 2008.

    a) Plot the CPI into a time series diagram. Is the series stationary?
    b) Calculate the rate of inflation for each year of the 10-year period and plot the series in a time series diagram. Is the series stationary?
    c) Repeat Thought Exercise 1 above using data on real GDP.

Data Exercises

1. Go to the Bureau of Labor Statistics. Find data on real wages by finding data on the nominal wage rate for Manufacturing (average hourly earnings) and the CPI price index. Using data on real GDP, determine the comovement of real wages and real GDP.
2. Repeat Data Exercise 1 using the unemployment rate.
3. Go to the St. Louis FRED Database. Find data on the Industrial Production Index for Manufacturing covering 2000 to 2008. Is the data stationary?

For further questions, multiple choice quizzes, and weblinks related to this chapter, visit www.routledge.com/textbooks/rossana

References and Suggestions for Further Reading

Lucas, R.E. Jr. (1980) "Methods and Problems in Business Cycle Theory," *Journal of Money, Credit, and Banking* 12 (4) (November): 696–715.

Mitchell, W.C. and Burns, A.F. (1938) *Statistical Indicators of Cyclical Revivals*, New York: National Bureau of Economic Research.

Nelson, C.R. and Plosser, C.I. "Trends and Random Walks in Macroeconomic Time Series," *Journal of Monetary Economics* 10 (2): 139–62.

Part II

Microfoundations

Chapter 4

Consumption

LEARNING OBJECTIVES

Household spending is a large component of the demand for goods in the aggregate economy. Any model of the business cycle will need to contain a sector where household spending is determined. Thus we will need to understand how it is that households make their spending and savings choices so that we can use this information in constructing models of the business cycle later in the book. Towards this end, here are some questions that we will answer in this chapter.

- What determines the consumption and saving choices made by households?

- How will household spending respond to a tax cut?

- How do expectations of future income impact consumer spending decisions?

- What form of the consumption function will be used in aggregate economic models?

Households consume a large fraction of the total output produced in the economy. Figure 4.1 provides a graph of quarterly U.S. Personal Consumption Expenditures (PCE) as a share of Gross Domestic Product (GDP). As the figure shows, from 1947 through 2008, the average share of the economy's output consumed by households was about 65 percent. If we have any hope of constructing a model of an entire economy that will explain how output in that economy is produced, it is crucial that we develop a model of household choice that we can use to understand the buying decisions of households since the household sector is such a big part of the total demand for goods and services. But there are other reasons that require that we know what motivates households.

People save by not consuming all of their income and those **savings** are channeled, through the financial system, to firms who use these borrowed funds for plant and equipment expenditures. These additions to the stock of capital are used in the future to produce output. The stock of capital is thus an important determinant of future living standards in our economy. Saving is the starting point for our understanding of how we can get the right amount of capital in the future. Therefore it is important that we know what determines the savings of households. Figure 4.2 illustrates why the savings rate has sometimes been a concern to policymakers.

The graph plots gross personal savings as a fraction of disposable personal income, covering the period 1959 to 2008 at monthly frequency. Notice how this fraction has been declining recently. It averages about 6.9 percent over the entire period but it has been very low near the

FIGURE 4.1 U.S. Consumption as a Share of GDP

Source: St. Louis Federal Reserve Bank FRED Database

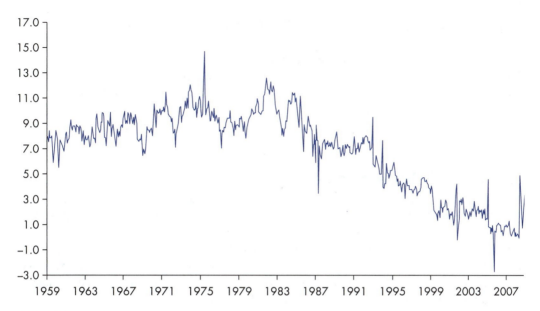

FIGURE 4.2 U.S. Personal Saving Rate

Source: St. Louis Federal Reserve Bank FRED Database

end of the sample period. It is even negative in two months, suggesting that households were dissaving. Since saving has been declining as a share of income in recent years, this fact has motivated discussions among policymakers about policies to stimulate household saving

Our model of the household will also be used to understand how tax policies affect household decisions. If there is a tax cut passed by our government, how will consumers react? Will they spend the tax cut or save it? If the tax cut is a one-shot deal, lasting for just one year, will it have an important impact on consumption? These are just some of the questions we will try to answer using our household model regarding the impact of taxes on consumer choice.

We can also use our model of household choice to understand a controversial theory of government finance called Ricardian Equivalence. Traditional views about the methods of financing government suggest that how we finance government matters for the economy as a whole. Using taxes to finance government expenditures, so it is often said, has a fundamentally different impact upon the economy than using bonds (borrowing from the public) to finance the activities of government. A new theory of government finance, first discussed by the classical English economist David Ricardo and revived by Harvard economist Robert J. Barro, asserts that it really doesn't matter how we finance the expenditures of government. The use of either method will have equivalent effects on the economy. As you will see, our model of consumer choice will enable us to see under what conditions the Ricardian proposition is true.

Finally, a recurring theme of all intertemporal economic models is that current decisions by households and firms will respond to future changes in income, taxes, and other economic magnitudes. Thus we will see that how much is consumed today by households will depend upon their perceived incomes in the future, as well as any tax changes expected to occur in the future. Thus it is possible that the current levels of household consumption will change in response to events that have not yet occurred.

4.1 A MODEL OF HOUSEHOLD BEHAVIOR

In this section we will describe a model of how consumers make their consumption choices over two periods of life. They will earn after-tax income in each period which is given (labor supply is assumed constant for simplicity). And they will have access to a loan market where they can borrow or lend in the first period of their lives. The real interest rate, determined in this loan market, is initially fixed and is unaffected by the actions of the household.

Household Preferences

In order to understand how individuals make their decisions about the goods and services that they will consume, we will first need a way to represent a consumer's preferences over commodities. These preferences will be used by consumers to guide their purchasing decisions. Consumer preferences will be represented by a concept called an **indifference map** which is simply a collection of **indifference curves**. This will describe the way that consumers rank bundles of commodities in terms of the welfare provided to them by these goods and services.

A number of assumptions will be made to simplify our analysis. Consumers will be assumed to make their choices over just two periods. They consume a **composite commodity** in each period. A composite commodity is a device for aggregating all of the goods consumed by a household into one quantity, an assumption that will allow us to use graphical analysis to represent household decision-making. Consumption in the current period is denoted by C_0; future consumption is represented by C_1. Figure 4.3 provides our description of household preferences over these dated consumption bundles.

On the horizontal axis we have current consumption, and future consumption is on the vertical axis. Three fundamental assumptions that we will make about consumer preferences, in addition to the assumptions discussed above, are summarized in the following propositions.

Propositions About Household Preferences

- Consumers will always prefer more of a commodity to less of it, all else equal.
- If a household consumes less of one commodity, it can be compensated for this loss in welfare by consuming more of another commodity. This is referred to as the **indifference principle**.
- Consumer preferences have the property of **diminishing marginal utility**; as consumption of a commodity increases, the consumption of all other goods fixed, the extra utility given to the household from consuming the commodity declines.

These assumptions seem reasonable and roughly in accordance with actual consumer behavior. Consider the first of these assumptions.

It is possible that a consumer could be satiated with a commodity, having so much of it that consuming more of the commodity could actually make her worse off. But if we are discussing a collection of goods, which is what we mean by a composite commodity, it seems inappropriate to regard consumers as being satiated with goods and so we assume that

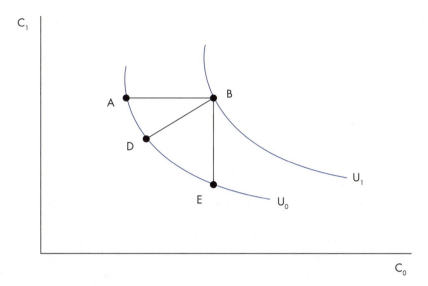

FIGURE 4.3 Household Preferences

Households prefer commodity bundle B to the bundle at A since B has more of C_0 but the same amount of C_1. B is preferred to E since B has more of C_1 but the same amount of C_0. B is preferred to D because B has more of both goods than the bundle at D. The household is indifferent between all points along a given indifference curve. All points along U_1 yield higher utility or welfare compared to the points on U_0.

consumers prefer more to less of the commodities they buy. Now consider Figure 4.3 to see how this assumption is represented in our indifference map.

Compare points A and B in Figure 4.3. Point B contains the same amount of future consumption, C_1, as there is at point A, but it has more of C_0, present consumption. As a result of our assumptions, we would conclude that the commodity bundle at B is preferred to the bundle at A (more is always preferred to less). Similarly, we would conclude that point B is preferred to point E; B has more future consumption but the same amount of current consumption as there is at E. Finally, point B is preferred to point D because B has more of both commodity bundles when compared to D.

Now consider our second assumption, the indifference principle. If we compare points A and D in Figure 4.3, we observe that A contains more future consumption but less present consumption when compared to D. The indifference principle asserts that the household can be indifferent between these two points. Put differently, the household achieves the same level of economic welfare by consuming at either of these two points. Finally, the points along the line containing points A, D, and E provide lower economic welfare when compared to the points on the line containing point B. All points along the indifference curve U_1 confer a higher level of welfare compared to the points along the curve U_0.[1]

Our final assumption is the principle of diminishing marginal utility. To explain this concept, we first require the definition of marginal utility, given below.

---

1 Also one consumption bundle cannot confer more than one level of utility.

Definition of Marginal Utility

■ The marginal utility of a good measures the change in welfare associated with a change in the consumption of that good, the quantities of all other goods held constant.

We will denote the marginal utility of current consumption as

$$MU_{\text{Current Consumption}} = \Delta U / \Delta C_0$$

and a similar definition holds for the marginal utility of future consumption. Recall that diminishing marginal utility means that, as we increase the consumption of one commodity, its marginal utility declines, the quantities of all other commodities held constant. To illustrate this idea requires that we look at the slope of a tangent line at two points along a given indifference curve. Two such tangent lines are drawn in Figure 4.4; one is tangent at point A, and the other is drawn as a tangent to point B and we want to compare the slope of the tangent lines at each point. These slopes measure a ratio of two changes: the change in C_1 over the change in C_0. This slope is negative at each point along a given indifference curve; the slope will therefore be denoted by $(\Delta C_1 / \Delta C_0) < 0$. Related to this is the concept of the **Marginal Rate of Substitution** (MRS) between present and future consumption. Two equivalent definitions of this are given below.

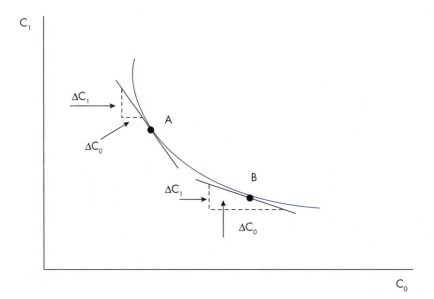

FIGURE 4.4 Diminishing Marginal Utility

As consumption changes along a given indifference curve, moving between points A and B, the marginal utility of future consumption rises and the marginal utility of current consumption falls. Thus the marginal rate of substitution (MRS = $MU_{\text{Current Consumption}} / MU_{\text{Future Consumption}}$) falls as we move from A to B in the diagram. The slope of the line is given by $-$MRS.

Definitions of the Marginal Rate of Substitution

■ The marginal rate of substitution (MRS) between present and future consumption measures the extra current consumption that must be consumed by the household to compensate it for the loss of a given amount of future consumption.

■ The marginal rate of substitution (MRS) between present and future consumption is given by the ratio $MU_{Current\ Consumption}/MU_{Future\ Consumption}$.

■ The slope of an indifference curve is given by –MRS.

To see why the slope of an indifference curve is given by –MRS, imagine that we are at point A in Figure 4.4. As we move between points A and B, we give up future consumption in return for more present consumption, maintaining the same level of welfare. Using the principle of diminishing marginal utility, as we give up some future consumption, the marginal utility of future consumption rises; as we consume more currently, the marginal utility of current consumption falls. Both of these facts imply that the marginal rate of substitution falls as we move between points A and B. This explains why an indifference curve has the curvature that it does. That is,

$$MRS_{Point\ A} > MRS_{Point\ B}.$$

Put differently, the loss of C_1 results in a welfare gain to the household given by the marginal benefit $MU_{Current\ Consumption}$ while the additional C_0 comes at the cost of foregone C_1 whose marginal welfare loss to the household is given by $-MU_{Future\ Consumption}$. As shown in Figure 4.4, a given loss of C_1 requires more C_0 to compensate the household at point B as compared to point A. Because the household has more C_0 at B than at A, the marginal utility of current consumption is lower at point B than it is at point A (alternatively, the marginal utility of C_0 is higher at point A than it is at point B), requiring more C_0 to compensate the household for the loss of C_1.

The Household's Intertemporal Budget Constraint

Our previous discussion explains the preferences of the household over goods and services but all households are constrained by their financial resources and this constraint limits the bundles of goods that households may buy. This constraint will be called the **intertemporal budget constraint** faced by the household.

A household will consume over two periods and it may choose to borrow or lend in the first period of life. If the household borrows, it will consume more than its current income $(C_0 > Y_0)$; if it saves, it will consume less than its current income $(C_0 < Y_0)$. Therefore in the first period we have

$$S = Y_0 - C_0$$

where S denotes saving which may be positive or negative. It is important to think of Y_0 as measuring **after-tax income** (or **disposable income**), the resources that can be spent by the household once taxes have been paid. Saving is simply the difference between after-tax income and consumption.

In the second period, the household has an income that it can consume plus, if the household saved in the first period, it can consume the principle it saved (loaned out) plus the interest earnings on the amount loaned out $(C_1 > Y_1)$. If the household borrowed in the first period, it must repay the amount borrowed (the principle) and pay interest to the lender from whom it borrowed $(C_1 < Y_1)$. In the second period then, the following expression must hold.

$$C_1 = (1+r) \cdot S + Y_1$$

In this equation, r is the real interest rate and $r \cdot S$ measure interest payments received (paid out).

To derive the intertemporal budget constraint, eliminate saving S from this last expression by using the first-period relationship between income, consumption, and saving. This leads to

$$C_1 = (1 + r) \cdot (Y_0 - C_0) + Y_1.$$

A bit of algebra applied to this last equation gives us

$$C_0 + \frac{C_1}{1+r} = Y_0 + \frac{Y_1}{1+r}.$$

This is the constraint that faces the household. The constraint simply states that the present value of the household's consumption must equal the present value of household income. The latter present value is defined as **household wealth**.

Definition of Household Wealth

■ Household wealth is defined to be the present value of household income.

$$Y_0 + \frac{Y_1}{1+r}$$

Consumers may borrow or lend in the first period of life as long as they satisfy the constraint that the present value of consumption is equal to wealth. This wealth definition is an example of a present value formula, which provides a way to translate future values into their current equivalents. Future payments, such as Y_1, must be "discounted" at the real interest rate r and so are worth less now since these payments will occur in the future.

Figure 4.5 illustrates the constraint we've just obtained. At point D, second period consumption, C_1, is zero so the consumer's consumption is equal to first-period income plus the amount borrowed out of future income. At point B, first-period consumption is zero so that second-period consumption is equal to income in the second period of life, plus first-period income and interest earnings obtained by lending out first-period income. The triangle contained in Figure 4.5, marked by the origin and points B and D, determines the **feasible set** of consumption combinations available to the household. At points outside the feasible set,

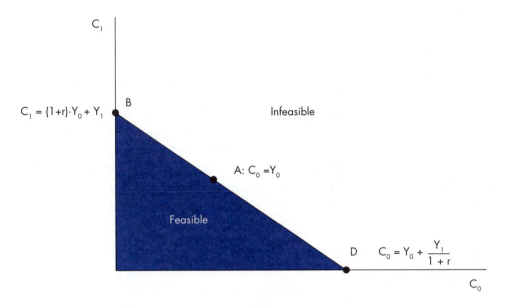

FIGURE 4.5 The Constraint on Household Choices

The household is constrained by the line from point B to point D. The feasible set is the triangle given by these points and the origin.

the household cannot consume because it is exceeding its intertemporal budget constraint. At points inside the frontier of the feasible set, the household is consuming amounts less than what they can consume in accordance with their intertemporal budget constraint. Along the boundary between points B and D, they are consuming amounts of current and future consumption such that the intertemporal budget constraint holds exactly. We will see momentarily that the household will never wish to consume anywhere but along the frontier of this feasible set of consumption points.

There is a point along this present value line that will be important for later discussion. This point is the one where the consumer neither borrows nor lends, thus consuming exactly their first-period income. To see that such a point exists, start at point D in Figure 4.5 and imagine moving along the wealth line towards point A. At the starting point, the consumer consumes nothing in the second period and so is maximizing first-period consumption. As you move along the curve, first-period consumption declines as does borrowing and second-period consumption rises. At point A, we reach the point where $C_0 = Y_0$. Thus somewhere along the line the consumer no longer borrows and we denote this point as point A.

Finally, the slope of this intertemporal budget constraint will be useful to us later in understanding the consumer choice problem and so we can apply the change operator to this constraint (remember that income in each period is constant in this exercise) to get

$$\Delta C_0 + \Delta C_1/(1 + r) = 0$$

which can be rearranged to give

$$\Delta C_1 / \Delta C_0 = -(1 + r) < 0$$

To interpret this last expression, remember that our consumer can borrow or lend in the first period and the capital market (the market where funds are traded between borrowers or lenders) determines the real interest rate. The slope tells our consumer that if he/she foregoes one unit of consumption today (the first period of life), they will receive $1 + r$ units of consumption next period in return for saving today. Or if they borrow today they give up $1 + r$ units of consumption in the future. Thus the slope of the constraint confronts the household with the terms of trade between present and future consumption as determined in the capital market where households borrow and lend.

Household Optimization

Now that we have learned how households rank commodities in terms of their preferences and how they are constrained by their wealth, we can combine these two analyses to determine the actual consumption choices of the household. Before doing this however, we need to spell out one more assumption about the household that defines its overall motivation. We do this in the following proposition.

Proposition About Household Objectives

■ The household wishes to reach the highest indifference curve that it can reach, given its intertemporal budget constraint. That is, the household wishes to maximize intertemporal utility in making its constrained consumption choices.

Figure 4.6 combines our previous two diagrams and illustrates the proposition just stated about the objectives of consumers.

This figure displays the intertemporal budget constraint and preferences of the household. We have also labeled indifference curves from lowest to highest; U_0 has lower welfare associated with it when compared to U_1 which has lower welfare compared to U_2. The consumer's choices can be explained as follows.

The critical assumption that determines the outcome of this optimization is that the household wishes to be on the highest indifference curve that it can reach, given its intertemporal budget constraint. The indifference curve, U_2, cannot be achieved by the household; it is outside the feasible set constraining the household and so the household can't reach this level of welfare. Indifference curve U_0 can be achieved by the household but most of the points on this curve are inside the feasible set. You might at first think that the household would choose one of the points where the intertemporal budget constraint and indifference curve cross. But the household can do better than this.

Notice the tangency point E. At this point the household has achieved the highest level of welfare that it can, given its intertemporal budget constraint. This tangency point satisfies this constraint (point E is in the feasible set) and U_1 is a higher level of welfare than U_0 (remember

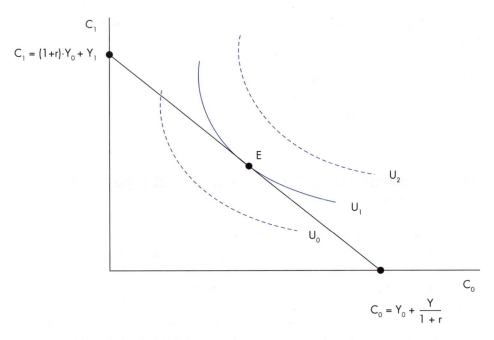

FIGURE 4.6 Household Optimization

The household will consume at point E which allows it to attain the highest indifference curve that it can achieve, given its intertemporal budget constraint.

that the indifference curve U_2 isn't feasible). We conclude that the solution of this optimization by the household is at point E.

There is an important property of this solution that illustrates the "marginal benefit equals marginal cost" principle that arises from optimizing behavior. At the equilibrium point E, the slope of the indifference curve U_1 (–MRS) is just equal to the slope of the intertemporal budget constraint (–(1 + r)). So the solution of the optimization problem by the household results in the condition

$$MRS = (1+r).$$

To interpret this condition, imagine that the household is a saver in the first period. Recall that the capital market determines the returns to saving (the real interest rate r) so 1 + r measures the benefit of saving one unit of current consumption. The marginal rate of substitution MRS measures the level of indifference between present and future consumption. If MRS > 1 + r, the household should rearrange its consumption over time by consuming more now and less next period (the foregone interest income resulting from more current consumption is less than the benefit in terms of marginal utility) whereas, if MRS < 1 + r, the household should consume more in the future and less now since the benefits of saving more now exceed the costs in terms of the foregone marginal utility. But at point E, the household will not be better off by choosing a different pair of consumption points because these marginal benefits and costs are just equal. Thus the solution to the household choice problem occurs at point E.

4.2 HOW CONSUMPTION RESPONDS TO CHANGES IN ITS DETERMINANTS

Households change their consumption choices when the determinants of their consumption choices (current income, future income, and the real interest rate) change. We will take each of these determinants in turn and study how changes in each will have an impact on household consumption choices.

The Intertemporal Budget Constraint and Changes in the Real Interest Rate

There are important policy questions attached to the issue of what determines saving by households. According to our model of the household, one of those determinants is the real interest rate. This means that we want to understand how first-period consumption will change when the real interest rate changes. Once we can answer that question, we will know how savings are affected because, using the definition $S = Y_0 - C_0$, changes in C_0, given first-period income Y_0, tell us how saving is changing. But we must first learn how the intertemporal budget constraint will be affected by changes in the real interest rate.

   Figure 4.7 illustrates how the constraint is affected by changing the real interest rate. Two real interest rates are used in the figure. The initial real interest rate is r_0 while the new real interest rate is r_1. We assume that $r_1 > r_0$. Begin by looking at point A, the point where there is no borrowing or lending. If the consumer neither borrows nor lends, then point A is feasible no matter what the interest rate. Thus the constraint under either real interest rate must pass through point A. If the consumer is maximizing second-period consumption by setting first-period consumption, C_0, equal to zero, then the consumer will have higher second-period consumption when the real interest rate rises (it will have higher interest earnings) so the new wealth line associated with a higher real interest rate must intersect the vertical axis at a higher point compared to the original intertemporal budget constraint. Similarly, if the consumer maximizes first-period consumption by consuming Y_0 and borrowing its second-period income, it will be able to borrow less with a higher real interest rate. Therefore, the point where the new wealth constraint intersects the horizontal axis must intersect the axis to the left of the point where the original wealth constraint intersected this axis. So we conclude that a higher real interest rate rotates the wealth line through the point A, the point where there is no lending or borrowing.

Saving and the Real Interest Rate

We now can determine how saving responds to a change in the real interest rate and it will turn out that the answer we obtain depends upon whether the consumer is a borrower or a lender in the first period. The lender case will be discussed first. Figure 4.8 illustrates how changing the interest rate affects this consumer. There are two constraints in the diagram corresponding to the initial real interest rate, r_0, and the new higher one, r_1. The consumer's

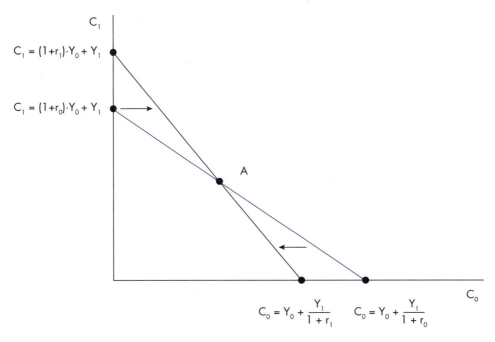

FIGURE 4.7 Changing the Real Interest Rate and the Intertemporal Budget Constraint

The real interest rate rises to r_1 from r_0, rotating the wealth constraint through the noborrowing-or-lending point A which is feasible under either real interest rate.

initial consumption choices are denoted by point B and the new consumption bundles, chosen by the household at the new real interest rate, are denoted by point E. Notice that the initial consumption choices are to the left of the no-lending-or-borrowing point A because the consumer is assumed to lend in the first period.

The figure indicates that when the real interest rate rises, first-period consumption falls. However, for a household saving when the real interest rate rises, it need not be the case that saving will increase, a fact that will now be demonstrated.

To understand why this is true, we need to decompose the movement from point B to point E into two parts. The first part is known as the **substitution effect** and the second is known as the **wealth effect**. Here is the definition of the substitution effect.

Definition of the Substitution Effect

■   The substitution effect measures the response of consumption in each period to a shift in the real interest rate measured along the original indifference curve.

The substitution effect is measured by the movement from points B to D. The dotted line has the same slope as the constraint with the new, higher real interest rate. Thus where this dotted line is tangent to the original indifference curve is the end-point we need to measure the substitution effect. The substitution effect is *always* negative, given the shape of the indifference curves. The substitution effect implies that saving rises with the real interest rate.

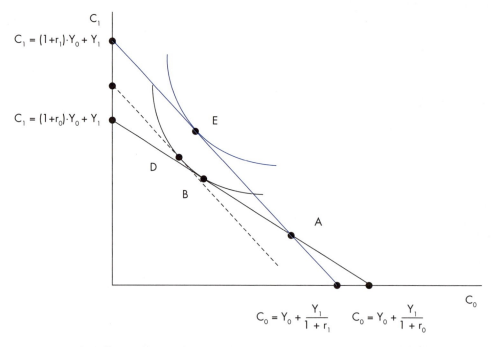

FIGURE 4.8 The Effects of Changing the Real Interest Rate on a Household that Saves

The real interest rate rises to r_1 from r_0, rotating the wealth constraint through point A, the point where there is no lending or borrowing. The substitution effect causes consumption to change from B to D, reducing C_0 and raising C_1. The wealth effect causes consumption to change from D to E. The total effect on C_0, and thus saving, is ambiguous, but C_1 will rise.

The second part of the total response of saving to the real interest rate is given by the wealth effect, defined below.

Definition of the Wealth Effect

◼ The wealth effect measures the change in consumption associated with a change in wealth at the new real interest rate.

The wealth effect is given by the movement from point D to point E in Figure 4.8. With composite commodities, it is reasonable to assume that higher wealth will raise consumption in both periods (they are said to be **normal goods** in this case) so the wealth effect, measured by the shift from the dotted line to the new intertemporal budget constraint, is positive. So the total response of saving to the real interest rate is the sum of conflicting forces: a negative substitution effect, tending to raise saving, and a positive wealth effect, tending to reduce saving. Thus our theory cannot guide us about the relationship between saving and the real interest rate for savers because the answer depends upon the magnitudes of the substitution and wealth effects. Equivalently, the response of saving to changes in the real interest rate would be an empirical question that needs answering for the case of households that are savers.

For a household that is a borrower in the first period, the connection between saving and the real interest rate is unambiguous. Figure 4.9 illustrates this case and note that the initial consumption choices, at point B, are to the right of the no-lending-or-borrowing point A. The ultimate consumption choices are at point E and, once again, we decompose this movement from B to E into its two constituent parts.

The movement from B to D is the measure of the substitution effect and, as before, saving rises with the rise in the real interest rate. However, remember that the household was initially borrowing so, more precisely, borrowing falls with the higher real interest rate, using just the substitution effect.

The wealth effect is measured by the movement from D to E in the figure. With normal goods, we said that wealth effects would be positive which means, in this case, that as we slide the dotted line towards the new constraint, consumption of both goods will fall. Therefore, in the borrower case, the wealth effect reinforces the substitution effect so that we can state that first-period consumption will fall (or borrowing declines) with the rise in the real interest rate.

In an aggregate economy, where there are both borrowers and lenders, the aggregate response of saving to a shift in the real interest rate will be uncertain, depending in part on how many households are in each group. Ultimately, for an entire economy with heterogeneous households (both lenders and borrowers), the relationship between saving and the real interest rate is thus an empirical question. But, despite this uncertainty, there is often a desire by those who set economic policy to try to stimulate saving and it is possible for tax

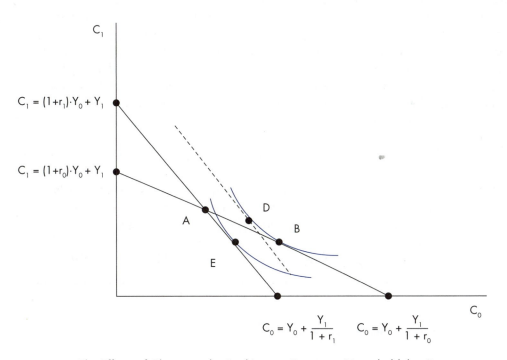

FIGURE 4.9 The Effects of Changing the Real Interest Rate on a Household that Borrows

For a household that borrows, a rise in the real interest rate from r_0 to r_1 causes C_0 to fall; the substitution effect moves consumption from B to D. The wealth effect causes consumption to move from D to E. Both effects reduce C_0 but the effect on C_1 is uncertain.

policies to have an impact on household saving (see **Doing Economics**: Tax Rates and Household Saving).

The connection between second-period consumption and the real interest rate also depends upon whether the household saves or borrows. For a household saving in the first period, the substitution effect raises second-period consumption, C_1, (see Figure 4.6) and the wealth effect raises C_1 as well. The end-result is that second-period consumption rises with the real interest rate. For the household borrowing in the first period, the substitution effect works in the same way: C_1 will rise with r. But the wealth effect tends to reduce second-period consumption (see Figure 4.9) so the total effect, the sum of the substitution and wealth effects, is uncertain.

Doing Economics: Tax Rates and Household Saving

The President and Congress jointly determine how to change the tax code in part to achieve economic objectives that they regard to be important. These officials often express concern that the level of saving in our economy is not high enough and then try to implement tax policy changes designed to stimulate saving. The recent cut in U.S. tax rates on dividends is an example of this sort of concern. Here we will illustrate how tax rates, set by these policymakers, can influence the returns to saving.

An important concept for this discussion is the idea of the marginal tax rate (MTR), a concept introduced in Chapter 2. The marginal tax rate measures the extra tax paid by a household on an additional dollar of before-tax income. Let t denote the MTR ($0 < t < 1$). Suppose that the government taxes part of the nominal returns that households get from saving. Now there is a difference between what the household earns on its savings and what it gets to keep. The household earns the pre-tax real interest rate on its saving (measured by r) but it only gets to keep the after-tax real interest rate, defined as

$$\text{After-Tax Real Interest Rate} = (1 - t)\cdot i - (\Delta P/P)^e.$$

In this definition, i is the nominal interest rate on savings and $(\Delta P/P)^e$ is the expected inflation rate. So we see that by reducing the MTR, the government can act to increase the returns to saving. Recall, however, that our analysis of the relationship between the real interest rate and saving indicates an ambiguous relationship between the two for those who save. Thus the effect on saving of this tax policy in an aggregate economy must be established empirically.

Consumption and Income

Consumption will vary with the level of income. We will now look at the effects on consumption of changes in both present and future income and an important finding from these exercises will be that consumption in the present responds to a change in future income, illustrating the important property that, in intertemporal economic models, current decisions by households (and firms as we will see in the next chapter) will be affected by future economic magnitudes.

Let's begin by considering how current income will affect the household's consumption choices. Figure 4.10 illustrates the effects of an increase in current income for a household that is currently saving. Current income is initially at Y_0, rising to Y_0'. If current income rises, the household's intertemporal budget constraint will shift out, reflecting the effects of higher current income. The household's feasible set has now expanded, reflecting its higher income. Since the composite commodity is assumed to be a normal good, consumption in both periods will rise with wealth and present (and future) consumption is increasing in the level of first-period income.

But this diagram shows more than just the effects of an increase in current income. If future income rises, the diagram will look much the same, with the constraint shifting out just as it does when current income rises. So this establishes the fact that current and future consumption will rise with an increase in future income as well.

This discussion illustrates the idea mentioned earlier about an important property of economic models involving economic decisions made over time. Current decisions (here measured by how much to consume in the current period) are determined in part by future economic magnitudes (in this case future income). Recall that we are interpreting Y_1 to be future disposable income, the difference between pre-tax income and taxes. Thus the model predicts that current consumption rises in response to an increase in future pre-tax income or

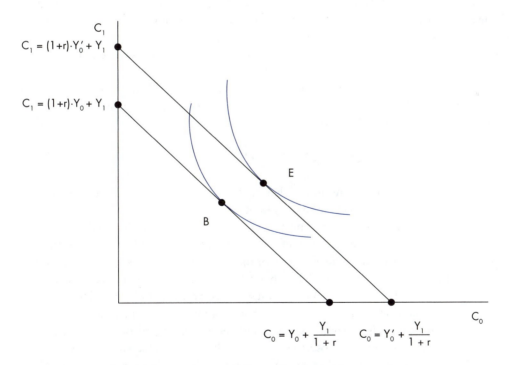

FIGURE 4.10 Household Consumption and Rising First-Period Income

First-period income rises from Y_0 to Y_0'. The wealth constraint shifts out, expanding the household's feasible set and the household moves from B to E. Consumption in each period rises.

TABLE 4.1 The Relationship Between Consumption and Its Determinants

Real Interest Rate for Lenders	$r \uparrow$ causing C_0 ? and $C_1 \uparrow$
Real Interest Rate for Borrowers	$r \uparrow$ causing $C_0 \downarrow$ and C_1 ?
Current Income: Y_0	$Y_0 \uparrow$ causing $C_0 \uparrow$ and $C_1 \uparrow$
Future Income: Y_1	$Y_1 \uparrow$ causing $C_0 \uparrow$ and $C_1 \uparrow$

Note: C refers to consumption and Y denotes income. The subscript 0 indicates the present period and the subscript 1 denotes the future period.

---

a decline in future taxes (since both changes imply higher disposable income in the future). Table 4.1 summarizes the results established for the household model.

4.3 THE PERMANENT INCOME HYPOTHESIS

Milton Friedman was a Nobel laureate in economics who developed a very important theory of consumer behavior known as the **Permanent Income Hypothesis**.[2] In this section, this theory will be developed because it will be useful to us in understanding the effects on consumers of tax changes and it will be helpful in explaining the idea of **consumption smoothing**. Smoothing consumption refers to the idea that consumers find it in their interest to have their consumption spending be less variable than their income over time. The reasons for this household behavior will be discussed later.

Friedman's thinking about consumer behavior revolves around a distinction between two types of income that a household receives. Actual real income can be broken up into two parts: **transitory income** and **permanent income**. We then have

$$Y = Y^P + Y^T$$

where Y^P refers to permanent income and Y^T denotes transitory income. An example will serve to clarify the distinction between these two types of income.

Imagine a factory worker, earning an hourly wage of $10.00 per hour for a 40-hour work-week. His or her income before taxes is therefore $400.00 per week but it is also possible that this individual will work overtime if the demand for the company's products is unusually strong. So when overtime is worked, income is higher than $400.00. In this example, overtime income is less predictable than the regular weekly earnings of this worker because the demand for a firm's products is somewhat unpredictable. The amount of overtime worked thus depends on factors that are unpredictable to some extent. Friedman would regard predictable earnings streams to be permanent income; those that are much less predictable would be transitory income. Friedman's intuition was that households would be likely to save most of their

---

2 See Milton Friedman, *A Theory of the Consumption Function*, Princeton University Press, 1957.

transitory income, spreading out this income over time into the future. As a result, he argued that real consumption was primarily determined by permanent income, obeying the relationship

$$C = k \cdot Y^P, \ 0 < k < 1.$$

In this equation above, k is called the **marginal propensity to consume out of permanent income** and it is defined as follows.

Definition of the MPC Out of Permanent Income

■ The marginal propensity to consume (MPC) out of permanent income measures the additional consumption that occurs in response to a one unit increase in permanent income.

Later, a way of measuring permanent income will be discussed. What we do now is provide one possible interpretation (a second similar one follows later) of Friedman's theory using our two-period model of household choice.

First let's define what will be meant by a change in transitory income as opposed to a change in permanent income. A change in transitory income will mean a change in only Y_0 (first-period income) with Y_1 (second-period income) constant. If permanent income changes, it will be mean that both Y_0 and Y_1 will change.

Figure 4.11 illustrates the effects upon consumption of changes in transitory and permanent income. This diagram is the same as Figure 4.10 with the exception that there is a further shift

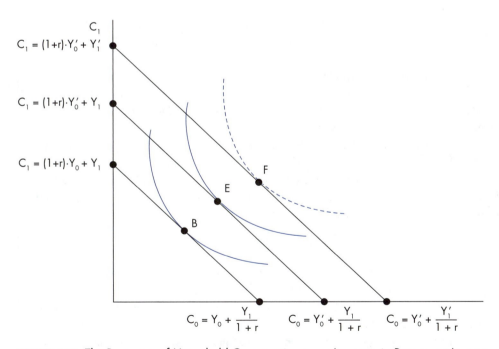

FIGURE 4.11 The Response of Household Consumption to an Increase in Permanent Income

An increase in transitory income, that is an increase in Y_0, causes the consumer to move from B to E. An increase in permanent income, that is Y_0 and Y_1 rising, moves the consumer from B to F.

in the intertemporal budget constraint beyond what was present in Figure 4.10. The initial consumption choices of the household occur at point B for a household that is saving. The shift in the constraint associated with a rise in just Y_0 is represented by the constraint that leads to the consumption choices at point E. This is just a repetition of the analysis in Figure 4.10. But now there is an additional shift in the constraint beyond the one going through point E. The reason is that now Y_1 is rising as well as Y_0, leading to new consumption choices at point F. The implication is that a transitory increase in income (Y_0 rising only) will lead to a smaller increase in consumption than will be the case when there has been an increase in permanent income (Y_0 and Y_1 rising). Thus Friedman's intuition seems to be correct in our two-period model of consumer choice.

Since this two-period model suggests that first-period consumption does not respond by much to variations in transitory income, it follows that anything causing a shift in transitory income will have relatively little effect upon current consumption. This implies that transitory tax cuts, like ones previously implemented in the U.S., have little impact upon household spending (see **Doing Economics**: Temporary Tax Cuts and Consumer Spending). But there is reason to be skeptical of this finding.

Doing Economics: Temporary Tax Cuts and Consumer Spending

On a number of occasions, the U.S. government has passed temporary tax cuts designed to raise economic activity by stimulating consumer spending. The thinking behind this is that consumers will spend the extra funds they receive from the tax cut, thereby raising production and incomes in the economy.

But the Permanent Income Hypothesis makes clear that transitory or temporary tax cuts will have a negligible effect upon consumer spending simply because a transitory tax cut has almost no effect upon the permanent income of households. Numerical and empirical examples will serve to make this point.

Consider a household with ten years of income remaining, earning $75,000 per year and this income is expected to remain constant. Using a discount rate of 2 percent (r = .02), the present value of their remaining lifetime earnings is about $687,000. Permanent income is $75,000 because income is assumed constant; so a tax rebate of, say, $500 is much less than one percent of permanent income. If consumers follow Friedman's consumption function, then

$$C = kY^P \Rightarrow \Delta C/C = \Delta Y^P/Y^P,$$

so the percentage increase in consumption will be equal to the percentage increase in permanent income, a number well below one percent. So a tax rebate on the order of $500 generates an increase in consumer spending that is very small. If income were expected to rise over time, a reasonable assumption for many households, then the tax rebate would be an even smaller percentage of permanent income, thereby leading to an even smaller percentage increase in consumer spending.

(continued)

In 2008, U.S. households received a tax rebate from their government. The graph below illustrates the response of consumption to this tax rebate

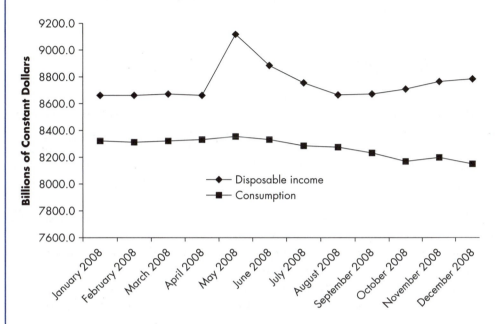

U.S. Constant-Dollar Consumption and Income

It is evident in the graph that there was an increase in real disposable income in the months of May and June as households received their rebate checks. What is also evident is that there was a very small response in real consumption expenditures associated with the increase in real disposable income. Friedman's Permanent Income Hypothesis would classify the income increase as transitory, implying a small response in consumption expenditures because household permanent income was largely unaffected by the tax rebates. The data in the chart supports the predictions of the Permanent Income Hypothesis.

Most of the predictions of the Permanent Income model hold up well, but there is one aspect of the theory's implications that seems not to fare so well in applied research studies. And that is the implication that current consumption should be only weakly related to current income. Our two-period model suggests that this is true but research studies have found that consumption is "excessively sensitive" to current income.[3] These findings set off a search by economists for explanations of what might account for the fact that current consumption is so heavily affected by current income. One possible explanation that has been suggested is that

3 See Marjorie A. Flavin, "The Adjustment of Consumption to Changing Expectations About Future Income," *Journal of Political Economy* 89, No. 5 (October 1981), pp. 974–1009.

one of the fundamental assumptions of our two-period model, namely the assumption of a perfect capital market (meaning that households can borrow or lend as they choose) may be inappropriate, at least for some households. We now pursue this possibility in our two-period model of the household.

Borrowing Constraints

We assumed in the consumer optimization problem that households could borrow or lend as they wished in the first period of life. But it may be the case, particularly for low-income households, that borrowing is not feasible; this means that the restriction $C_0 \leq Y_0$ holds in the first period. This fundamentally alters the analysis of household choice (at least for borrowers as you will soon see) and so we now study how consumer behavior might change with this constraint on its behavior. Figure 4.12 lays out the graphical details when the constraint is imposed upon the household.

This figure illustrates the effects of the **borrowing restriction** on the intertemporal budget constraint facing the household. As we move along the constraint towards the horizontal axis, we eventually reach the no-borrowing-or-lending point A. With the borrowing restriction in place, the points to the right of A along the constraint are no longer in the feasible set because the consumer can't borrow. The constraint effectively eliminates this portion of the intertemporal budget constraint and so this is illustrated with a dotted line. But the borrowing

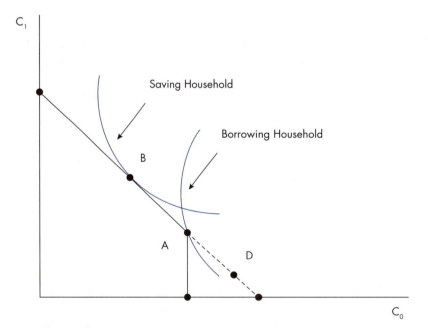

FIGURE 4.12 Borrowing Constraints and the Household

A borrowing constraint has no effect on a household that saves as its equilibrium is at point B as it would be with no borrowing constraint. For the household that wishes to borrow, the constraint does bind, changing the equilibrium from point D to point A.

restriction doesn't bind in this case; the household is a lender in the first period and so the borrowing restriction has no effect. For this new restriction to matter, we must look at the case of a household wishing to borrow. Figure 4.12 also illustrates this case, using an indifference curve for each of two different households: a saver and a borrower.

Point A is once again the no-borrowing-or-lending point and note that the household is consuming at this point where it is consuming all of its first-period income. The household would like to borrow if it could (the consumption choice for the household without the borrowing restriction is given at point D) but, because of this borrowing restriction, it cannot. This point is no longer in the feasible set. It will consume all of its income and now the MRS is not equal to $1 + r$. The implication of this analysis is that if something raises current income (say a tax cut passed by the government), then the household's consumption could rise by more than it would if it were not constrained by the restriction $C_0 \leq Y_0$.

The moral of this story is that economic theories need not hold exactly in real-world economies. While there is reason to believe that this model, without the borrowing restriction, is broadly consistent with the facts, there are some details of the story that may not match up in quite the way that the theory says they should. But there is another aspect of the model that does seem to be evident in actual economies. Namely, intertemporal models of the household imply that consumers smooth their consumption, an issue to which we now turn.

Consumption Smoothing

Most individuals have a hump-shaped earnings stream over their lifetimes. Typically incomes are relatively low when people are young. They may be in school, working only infrequently or at part-time jobs, but as they age and move into the workforce full-time, their incomes rise, rising further as they move up the corporate ladder. Late in life, incomes fall, in part because people retire. If a household could not borrow in the capital market while young, its living standard could be quite low because its income is low early in life. If these households face a perfect capital market where they can borrow or lend in line with their preferences, they could enjoy a higher standard of living early in life by borrowing against future earnings; that is, they can borrow or lend in such a way that their consumption path is smoother than the path followed by their income. This fact is illustrated in Figure 4.13.

We can also illustrate this idea using Friedman's permanent income model of consumption but it will be necessary to use a method of measuring permanent income. We begin with a definition of permanent income.

Definition of Permanent Income

■ Permanent income is the constant amount of income with the property that the household's wealth is the same whether it is measured by permanent or actual income.

The present value formulae that you have already seen can be used to compute permanent income. From our two-period wealth definition used previously, permanent income can be formalized as follows.

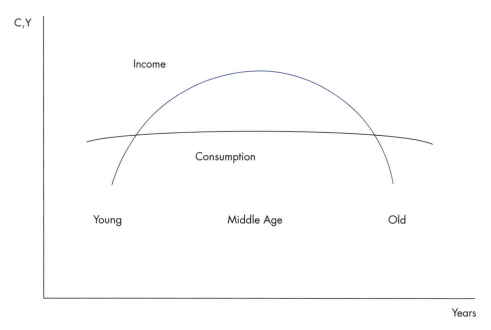

FIGURE 4.13 Life Cycle Income and Consumption

Lifetime earnings typically follow a hump-shaped pattern. Consumption can be smoother than income if consumers can borrow in a perfect capital market.

$$Y^P \cdot \left[1 + \frac{1}{1+r}\right] = Y_0 + \frac{Y_1}{1+r}$$

It is important to realize that it is not necessarily the case that $Y_0 = Y_1$ but permanent income, Y^P, *is* the same each period. This makes sense because the intuition behind the word "permanent" is that it persists or is predictable, even though actual income may rise or fall with the business cycle or for other reasons. A numerical example may help to clarify this.

Suppose that we interpret period 0 as the first half of a person's working life and period one as the second half. Consistent with this, suppose that a person will work for 40 years. For the first half of this time, assume that they average \$50,000 per year so that $Y_0 = \$1$ million. In the last 20 years of their working life, assume that they average \$70,000 per year, giving $Y_1 = \$1.4$ million. Then at a real interest rate of 2 percent, we can compute wealth and permanent income using the formula above. The results are displayed in Table 4.2. Notice that the household's permanent income is above actual income in the first period but less than income in the second period. Permanent income doesn't fluctuate as much as actual income since it is constant. Put differently, permanent income is smoother than actual income.

Now we want to compute household consumption. Friedman's consumption equation was

$$C = k \cdot Y^P, \ 0 < k < 1.$$

To find consumption, we will need a value for the marginal propensity to consume out of permanent income and suppose for the sake of illustration that $k = .9$. This gives,

TABLE 4.2 Computing Wealth and Permanent Income

Income	Wealth	Permanent Income
Y_0 = $1 million Y_1 = $1.4 million	$2.372 million	$1.2 million

approximately, $C_0 = C_1 = \$1.1$ million. Note that consumption is *very* smooth; it is the same each period. It is also smoother than the actual income of the household. The household borrows in the first period (there are no borrowing restrictions in this example) so the perfect capital market assumption is crucial for the ability of the household to generate a smooth consumption path over time when consumption is compared to income.

This example illustrates how important it is for the household to be able to look ahead, see its higher earnings in the future, and borrow out of these earnings to improve its welfare while young. This same ability to see into the future has implications for the theory of government finance, an issue that we now take up in the context of our two-period model of the consumer.

4.4 RICARDIAN EQUIVALENCE

Government expenditures are financed by levying taxes upon the public and/or the government may borrow from the public. If the government borrows, it issues a bond, promising to pay interest to the bondholder and then repaying the principal in the future. David Ricardo, a classical English economist, suggested the idea that the methods used to finance government, taxation or borrowing, would have equivalent effects upon the economy. Robert J. Barro, a Harvard University economist, revived interest in this idea, known as **Ricardian Equivalence**.[4] Here we will do a simple example illustrating the basic ideas behind this theory of government finance. This is a controversial idea among many economists because it challenges long-held views about the impact of government deficits.

The conventional wisdom has been that if the government decides to run a deficit with its spending exceeding its tax receipts, this will lead to an increase in real interest rates in the economy, crowding out or reducing private investment expenditures (you will learn more about crowding out later in the book). But what lies behind this scenario is the idea that if this deficit is caused by a tax cut, consumers will spend the proceeds of the tax cut. In the Ricardian story, consumers save the tax cut, spending none of it. The reason is that they recognize the future tax increases associated with deficits and save in anticipation of these tax increases. That is, they look ahead and see that taxes must rise in the future and take account of this fact in their behavior. An example illustrates these ideas.

---

4 See Robert J. Barro, "Are Government Bonds Net Wealth?" *Journal of Political Economy* 82, No. 6 (November–December 1974), pp. 1095–117.

Imagine that the government is running a balanced budget with its tax receipts just equal to its expenditures. Taxes are of the lump-sum variety, not depending upon income. Over a 2-year period, the government decides to run a transitory deficit for the first year, eliminating the deficit in the second year. The government's expenditures are fixed in each period. Taxes are cut in the current period, causing the income of our representative household to rise by the lump-sum amount $\Delta T > 0$. In the second period, the government will close its deficit by raising taxes by the amount ΔT, causing the household's income to fall by this amount, and taxes will rise further to cover the interest payments on the bonds it must issue (remember that government expenditures are fixed in this example). Taxes must therefore rise by $r\Delta T$ to cover these interest payments so the household's income will fall by this amount in the second period. To see if the consumption choices of a representative household will change as a result of this temporary tax cut and the resulting transitory government deficit, let's look at the wealth of the household before and after the change in policy by the government.

Household Wealth

$$\text{Wealth Before the Policy Change: } W = Y_0 + \frac{Y_1}{1+r}$$

$$\text{Wealth After the Policy Change: } W = Y_0 + \Delta T + \frac{Y_1 - \Delta T - r \cdot \Delta T}{1+r}$$

The disposable income of the household rises in the fist period but then declines in the second period. Has the wealth position of the household really changed? If not, the consumption choices of the household will be unaffected by this change in the government's behavior.

In fact, the household's wealth is unchanged by the temporary deficit of the government. To see this, take the new intertemporal budget constraint written above and do a bit of manipulation as follows.

After the Policy Change:

$$W = Y_0 + \Delta T + \frac{Y_1 - \Delta T - r \cdot \Delta T}{1+r} = Y_0 + \Delta T + \frac{Y_1}{1+r} - \frac{\Delta T + r \cdot \Delta T}{1+r}$$

$$= Y_0 + \Delta T + \frac{Y_1}{1+r} - \frac{(1+r) \cdot \Delta T}{1+r} = Y_0 + \frac{Y_1}{1+r}$$

As these steps show, household wealth is unchanged by the government's transitory deficit; the household's consumption choices are unchanged as well. Consumers save the tax cut, rather than spend it.

This example may seem artificial in the sense that there are reasons why it may not correctly represent the response of consumers to a tax cut. Economists have developed a number of possible objections to this example because this story has many "hidden" assumptions and if any of these assumptions are relaxed, the Ricardian proposition fails. A complete accounting of these qualifications will be postponed until the chapter discussing government economic policy activities in more detail, but one of these assumptions can be easily relaxed here in order to illustrate one reason why the Ricardian position may not hold. That assumption concerns the time horizons of the public and the government.

Time horizons for each of us are finite, with men having a life-expectancy of about 73 years and women having a longer life-expectancy of approximately 81 years. The government has a time horizon far greater than its citizens; indeed it is often assumed that the government has an infinite time horizon in economic models since there seems to be no good way to decide what finite time horizon would be appropriate for a government. If we return to our illustrative example of the effects of a temporary tax cut, we can examine how the story changes if the government has a longer time horizon than does the representative household.

Now imagine that the government runs a temporary deficit but it now plans to raise taxes to cover its interest payments and close the deficit in a time period beyond the second period of our household's existence. Then the constraint on the household would be

$$W = Y_0 + \Delta T + \frac{Y_1}{1+r}$$

and, in this case, the Ricardian proposition fails. Lifetime resources for the household have expanded and so it will consume more in each period just as we described above in Figure 4.10.

Due to differing time horizons for the public and the government, and for other reasons as well, Ricardian Equivalence may not be an accurate representation of the effects of government financing choices. As with many ideas in economics, empirical evidence needs to be brought to bear if theory is inadequate to the task of establishing the correctness of an idea. There has been a considerable amount of research on this topic and there is some evidence favoring the Ricardian position as a description of the effects of government deficits.[5] Despite the evidence in support of the Ricardian position, many economists are still unwilling to believe that Ricardian Equivalence holds and so it is still a subject of lively debate.

4.5 A SIMPLIFIED CONSUMPTION MODEL

Many of the models that will be used later in the book to study aggregate economies will have a consumption function as one of their building-blocks. However those models will often use a consumption equation seemingly different from, and simpler than, the model described earlier in this chapter. We now show how the consumption theory above is related to the simpler one later in this book.

The simple version of the consumption equation that will appear later, sometimes called a Keynesian consumption function, can be written as

$$C = a + b \cdot Y, \, a > 0, \, 0 < b < 1.$$

---

5 See John J. Seater, "Ricardian Equivalence," *Journal of Economic Literature* 31, No. 1 (March 1993), pp. 142–90.

These later models will be static; that is, they will be unconcerned with the behavior of households over more than one period, being concerned only with current-period decisions by the household. In the consumption equation above, C refers to current consumption (called C_0 in the two-period model) and Y corresponds to current income, Y_0, in that earlier model.

This consumption function has a positive intercept given by the parameter a. This component of the simplified model accounts for that part of consumption that is unrelated to current income. The parameter b is an important part of many economic models and is defined as the **marginal propensity to consume** (MPC) out of current income. Here is its definition.

Definition of the MPC Out of Current Income

■ The marginal propensity to consume (MPC) out of current income measures the change in current consumption associated with a one unit increase in current household disposable income, Y.

Since this parameter is assumed to be between zero and unity, an extra dollar of income is partly consumed and partly saved by the household. There is an analogous definition for saving that is related to this consumption equation. The **marginal propensity to save** (MPS) is given by $s = 1 - b$. Its formal definition is as follows.

Definition of the MPS Out of Current Income

■ The marginal propensity to save (MPS) out of current income measures the change in current saving associated with a one unit increase in current household disposable income, Y.

Note that $0 < s < 1$, given our restriction on the MPC.

A diagram containing this consumption equation is given in Figure 4.14. The diagram has current income Y on the horizontal axis and consumption, C, on the vertical axis. It has a positive slope, given by the MPC, so this slope measures $b = \Delta C/\Delta Y$. Now compare this diagram to the next one, Figure 4.15.

The latter figure illustrates the effect of an increase in current income using the two-period apparatus we developed earlier in the chapter. In the figure, consumption rises by the amount $\Delta Y > 0$. Inspection of the figure shows that, because consumption is a normal good, consumers will consume more of it as their incomes rise so $\Delta C/\Delta Y > 0$ which is essentially what we have assumed about the relationship between C and Y in the previous two-period model of the household. Viewed from this perspective, the two consumption models are quite comparable. But they differ in other ways.

The two-period model also brings in future income and the real interest rate as determinants of consumption in the current period. The simplified model in Figure 4.14 seems to omit these other aspects of household behavior. This is where we can use the intercept term in the simplified model to good advantage. The intercept, a, can be used as a "catch-all" variable. We can imagine that this intercept shifts and use this as a way of capturing the effects of economic forces omitted from the simplified model. Consider the effects of an increase in future income, Y_1, in the two-period model described earlier.

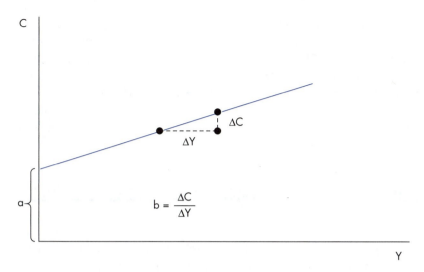

FIGURE 4.14 A Simplified Consumption Function

Aggregate models often use a simplified consumption function like the one displayed here. The marginal propensity to consume, is given by the slope of the line.

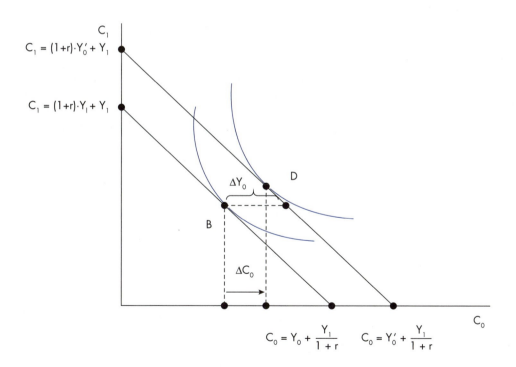

FIGURE 4.15 Household Consumption and Rising First-Period Income

The two-period model implies that current consumption rises with current income which is consistent with the simplified consumption model where the MPC is positive.

We studied this case earlier in the chapter, establishing that the effects of a rise in future income would produce a diagram much like Figure 4.10, showing that higher future income raises current consumption. Here we illustrate that effect in Figure 4.16 which shows that current consumption rises with an increase in the intercept so we associate a larger intercept with more future income. Thus while the simplified model does formally omit other economic determinants of consumption, there is a way to make the simpler consumption function incorporate these omitted factors. We can thus shift the intercept term to describe the effects of changes in the real interest rate or future income.

4.6 CONSUMPTION AND SAVING OVER THE LIFE CYCLE

Economists doing applied studies of consumption behavior discovered conflicting evidence of the parameters that were found in a variety of applied studies. For example, suppose we take the simplified consumption equation $C = a + b \cdot Y$ and use statistical methods to come up with estimated values for the parameters, a and b, in this simplified equation. The values found for these parameters varied from study to study, leading to a search by economists for an explanation for these research findings.

Franco Modigliani, a Nobel laureate in economics, and Richard Brumberg developed a theory of consumption behavior called the **Life Cycle Hypothesis**. This theory has much in common with the Permanent Income Hypothesis already discussed but it stresses the fact that demographic factors, such as the age of the workers in households, should be important in explaining the consumption and saving behavior observed in aggregate economies. As the age distribution of families in the economy changes over time, so too will the aggregate consumption and saving behavior observed in an economy. Here is how these effects arise.

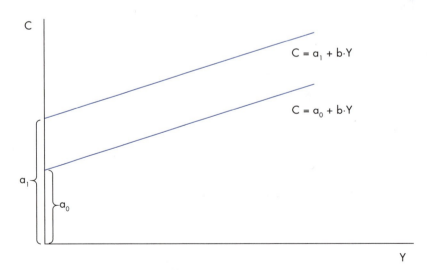

FIGURE 4.16 Using the Intercept to Capture Omitted Effects on Consumption

Shifts in the intercept of the simplified consumption function can capture omitted effects on consumption. Here an increase in the intercept can capture the effect on consumption of a rise in future income.

Previously we noted the fact that workers frequently have a time path for their income that is hump-shaped; early in the life cycle when workers are young, incomes are low. As workers gain experience in the workforce, incomes rise, then incomes fall in retirement. This view can be illustrated in the following figures. In Figure 4.17, the income path is drawn and it is assumed that the household wants to smooth consumption exactly. That is, consumption is constant over the life cycle. The household is borrowing when young (consumption exceeding income), saving in the next phase of the life cycle (income now exceeding consumption), then again consuming more than its income in retirement. If we were to graph the assets of this household, we get a diagram such as Figure 4.18. Early in life, assets are negative (the consumer is borrowing), they then become positive, and then assets (wealth) decline in retirement, reaching zero at the end of life.[6] As these diagrams show, a country with a young population will have relatively less saving compared to a country with a middle-aged population. A country that has an old population saves less than one which has middle-aged consumers. In fact, the elderly should be running down their financial assets to finance consumption but it has been observed that the elderly do not dissave to the extent suggested by this model (see **Doing Economics**: Saving, Bequests, and the Elderly).

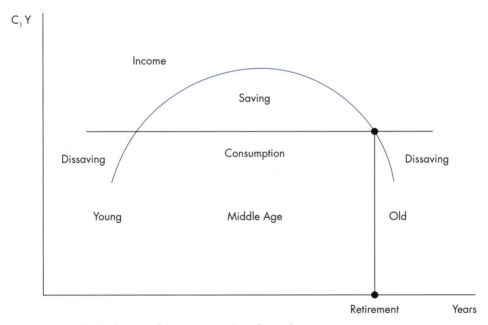

FIGURE 4.17 The Behavior of Saving over the Life Cycle

Life cycle models of the household predict dissaving early in life and in retirement. The household accumulates assets in the middle of the life cycle.

---

6 For now, we assume that households do not leave behind assets to be passed on to their descendents in the form of bequests nor is there any Social Security system available. So the household must save in order to finance consumption during its retirement years.

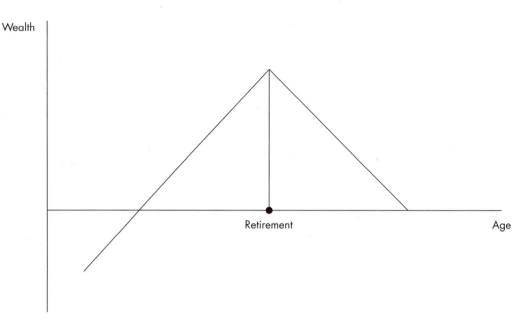

FIGURE 4.18 The Behavior of Assets over the Life Cycle

Households borrow early in life, thereby holding negative assets, save in the middle of their life cycle, and run down their assets in retirement.

Doing Economics: Saving, Bequests, and the Elderly

We have worked with a model in this chapter that ignores a very important aspect of consumer behavior regarding bequest motives. We have assumed that there are no bequest motives, implying that the elderly reduce their assets to zero at the end of their lives. But it has been observed that the elderly do not dissave to this extent and one possible explanation for this fact is that they plan to leave assets behind to their descendents. Indeed there is a substantial body of evidence showing that the accumulation of capital is very closely tied to bequests. Bequests can be motivated by altruism; parents may wish to leave assets to their children simply to raise the children's welfare. But there may be strategic motives behind bequests. For example, parents may wish to use bequests as a way of changing their children's behavior. Or the absence of a bequest can be used to punish perceived misbehavior by children. To learn more about bequests and household behavior, the following two references will be useful.

Laurence J. Kotlikoff and Lawrence H. Summers, "The Role of Intergenerational Transfers in Aggregate Capital Accumulation," *Journal of Political Economy* 89, No. 4 (August 1981), pp. 706–32

B. Douglas Bernheim, Andrei Shleifer, and Lawrence H. Summers, "The Strategic Bequest Motive," *Journal of Political Economy* 93, No. 6 (December 1985), pp. 1045–76.

How does this relate to empirical estimates of the simplified consumption function? To answer that question, think about what must be true about the intercept term, a, in the equation C = A +bY. Our discussion about age and saving suggests that the value of this intercept will vary with the age distribution in a country. As the population moves from being young to middle-aged, the intercept falls (consumption declines and saving grows) whereas, if the population ages beyond middle-age status, the intercept rises (consumption rises and saving falls). That is, we can regard this intercept as being dependent upon the level of the population's wealth or age.

It is also instructive to look at the present value constraint facing a household making its consumption choices. This will allow us to build retirement into the permanent income model used previously. This present value constraint is

$$C_0 + \frac{C_1}{1+r} = Y_0 + \frac{Y_1}{1+r}$$

where it was pointed out previously that Y_0 need not be equal to Y_1. We could imagine that this equation builds in retirement with the relationship $Y_0 > Y_1$ since income falls in retirement. But a better way would be to imagine that the household will be alive for three periods and obeys

$$C_0 + \frac{C_1}{1+r} + \frac{C_2}{(1+r)^2} = Y_0 + \frac{Y_1}{1+r}$$

This makes it very clear that retirement occurs in period two, the last period of life (recall that discounting an amount two years into the future requires squaring the term in the denominator for second-period consumption). Since income is zero in this period, the household must spend its assets to finance consumption (by assumption, there is no Social Security system). Now suppose we have a household that wants constant consumption over the life cycle and uses permanent income to guide its consumption choices. Then we have

$$C \cdot \left[1 + \frac{1}{1+r} + \frac{1}{(1+r)^2} \right] = Y^P \cdot \left[1 + \frac{1}{1+r} \right]$$

Suppose we pick a value for the real interest rate of r = .02. Evaluating the terms in the brackets gives

$$2.94 \cdot C = 1.98 \cdot Y^P, \implies C = .67 \cdot Y^P$$

So the factor of proportionality, k, is equal to .67 in this example; it does indeed lie between zero and unity as Friedman suggested.[7] We can thus derive Friedman's consumption function precisely when we allow for a retirement period. What we also discover along the way, again as Friedman suggested, is that the factor of proportionality, k, is not really constant. Rather it varies with the real interest rate. The simplified consumption equation has an intercept that is not constant either, as we said earlier in the chapter.

---

7 The factor of proportionality is equal to unity with no retirement period. You should be able to look at the two bracketed terms in the equation above to convince yourself that $0 < k < 1$ for any value of the real interest rate such that $0 < r < 1$.

4.7 CONCLUDING REMARKS

This chapter has been devoted to the study of an intertemporal model of the household. The model examines how a consumer would choose consumption of a composite (aggregate) commodity in each of two periods while being constrained by a relationship that requires that the present value of household consumption is equal to the present value of the household's income. The model was used to study the response of consumption to changes in the real interest rate and income; the real interest rate has an uncertain impact upon aggregate consumption but income, present or future, raises consumption in each period. The permanent income hypothesis was developed where we found that transitory income had a smaller impact on present consumption than permanent income would have. Consumers were shown to choose a smooth consumption path if they could borrow or lend in a capital market. The role of borrowing constraints was illustrated, showing that consumption might be quite sensitive to current income when households are unable to borrow. We also found that demographic factors, such as age, would have a role to play in explaining consumption fluctuations.

This completes our discussion of one of the crucial building-blocks of aggregate macroeconomic models. Much of what we say about how the economy behaves will depend importantly on a solid understanding of this model of consumer choice.

Key Ideas

- The substitution effect measures the response of consumption to a change in the real interest rate while the household is constrained to its original indifference curve.
- The wealth effect measures the response of consumption to a change in wealth rate measured at the new real interest rate.
- Saving responds ambiguously to the real interest rate in a household that saves because of conflicting substitution and wealth effects. For households that borrow, saving rises (borrowing declines) when the real interest rate rises.
- Current consumption is positively related to current and future income.
- Future consumption is positively related to current and future income.
- The Permanent Income Hypothesis implies that transitory income has a smaller impact upon current consumption as compared to the impact of permanent income.
- A perfect capital market permits consumers to borrow or lend so as to produce a consumption stream smoother than their income stream.
- Current consumption responds little to changes in current income according to the Permanent Income Hypothesis but this may not be true for households facing borrowing constraints.
- A controversial theory of government finance, known as Ricardian Equivalence, implies that if consumers foresee the future tax liabilities associated with transitory tax cuts, they will save, rather than spend, any tax cuts they receive.
- A simple form of consumption function relates changes in current income to changes in current consumption. The intercept term can be used to capture the influence of other determinants contained in the two-period model of consumption.

■ Demographic factors, such as age, may have a role to play in explaining the level of saving in the economy. The elderly may draw down assets to finance retirement consumption but they may not draw down their assets to zero at the end of life if they plan to leave bequests to their descendents.

Key Terms

Indifference Map	Indifference Curve	Ricardian	Substitution Effect
Diminishing Marginal	Composite	Equivalence	Transitory Income
Utility	Commodity	Indifference	Marginal Propensity
Intertemporal Budget	Feasible Set	Principle	to Save
Constraint	Wealth	Disposable	Normal Good
Saving	Permanent Income	Income	Wealth Effect
Borrowing Restriction	Marginal Propensity	Marginal Rate of	Consumption
Life Cycle Hypothesis	to Consume	Substitution	Smoothing

Questions for Study and Review

Review Exercises

1. Describe the assumptions that were made in this chapter about the preferences of households over present and future consumption.
2. Describe substitution and wealth effects in the model of household choice.
3. Describe how the household's feasible set is affected by an increase in either current or future income.
4. Describe how saving will respond to a fall in the real interest rate for two classes of households: borrowers and lenders.
5. What is the difference between the marginal propensity to consume out of permanent income and the marginal propensity to consume out of current income?

Thought Exercises

1. Draw a diagram of the intertemporal budget constraint facing a household when the real interest rate at which the household can borrow exceeds the real interest rate at which the household may lend. What type of household (lender, borrower, no lending or borrowing) will make different consumption choices when real interest rates differ in this way as compared to the case where lending and borrowing rates are the same?
2. Explain why current consumption responds more to a permanent tax cut than to a transitory one.

3. What will happen to the size of the MPC out of permanent income when the real interest rate rises?
4. Suppose that the interest rate at which the government borrows is lower than the rate at which households may borrow. Does Ricardian Equivalence hold in such a situation?
5. Explain how the existence of a borrowing constraint affects consumption smoothing by the household.

Numerical Exercises

1. Assume that current and future income are both $1,000 and that current consumption equals $800. If the real interest rate is 5 percent, what is the level of future consumption?
2. Consider an individual who plans to retire in the year 2011. The real interest rate is 3 percent. She has the following after-tax income stream.

Year	After-Tax Income
2007	$27,000
2008	$65,000
2009	$80,000
2010	$75,000

   a) Compute the individual's lifetime wealth.
   b) Compute the individual's permanent income.
   c) Assume that the individual wants to keep consumption constant each year. Calculate how much she can consume each year.
   d) Compute the level of the individual's assets for each year.
   e) Calculate the marginal propensity to consume out of permanent income.

3. Consider a three-period model of household choice. The real interest rate is 4 percent. A household wants to have $10,000 available for consumption during last period of life (retirement). How much does it have to save in the second period when its income is $65,000 and it saves $5,000 in the first (current) period?
4. Suppose that the household's preferences are represented by the utility function $U(C_0, C_1) = 100C_0^{0.5}C_1^{0.25}$. If the real interest rate is 5 percent, what is the value of the MRS of this household when it has maximized its two-period welfare?
5. Assume that the real interest rate in an economy is 4 percent and that the marginal income tax rate is 10 percent. Further assume that the household plans to retire in the year 2012. Its before-tax income stream is as follows

Year	Income
2009	$24,444
2010	$50,000
2011	$60,000
2012	$0

a) Verify that the household's after-tax wealth is $115,195.
b) If the household has a smooth consumption stream of $30,515 each year and a marginal propensity to consume out of permanent income of .7645, what is the household's level of permanent income?
c) Assume that the net income in the year 2010 rises surprisingly by $5,000. What happens to consumption in the year 2010? What will happen to the level of permanent income?

Data Exercise

1. Visit the Consumer Expenditure Survey on the website of the Bureau of Labor Statistics. Starting in 1997, the agency collected data on the buying habits of Americans. Calculate the percentage of total annual expenditures that American households spent on food and gasoline from 1997 to 2007 and plot the data in a time series graph.
2. Go to the website of the Bureau of Economic Analysis. Collect annual data on total household consumption and services consumption from the NIPA accounts. Draw a times series graph of services consumption as a share of total consumption annually for the 30-year period ending in 2005. What does the graph reveal about spending habits in the U.S. over this 30-year period?

For further questions, multiple choice quizzes, and weblinks related to this chapter, visit www.routledge.com/textbooks/rossana

References and Suggestions for Further Reading

Barro, R.J. (1974) "Are Government Bonds Net Wealth?" *Journal of Political Economy* 82 (6) (November–December): 1095–117.

Bernheim, B.D., Shleifer, A. and Summers, L.H. (1985) "The Strategic Bequest Motive," *Journal of Political Economy* 93 (6) (December): 1045–76.

Flavin, M.A. (1981) "The Adjustment of Consumption to Changing Expectations About Future Income," *Journal of Political Economy*, 89 (5) (October): 974–1009.

Friedman, M. (1957) *A Theory of the Consumption Function*, Princeton: Princeton University Press.

Kotlikoff, L.J. and Summers, L.H. (1981) "The Role of Intergenerational Transfers in Aggregate Capital Accumulation," *Journal of Political Economy* 89 (4) (August): 706–32.

John J. Seater, (1993) "Ricardian Equivalence," *Journal of Economic Literature* 31 (1) (March): 142–90.

Chapter 5

Investment

LEARNING OBJECTIVES

This chapter is concerned with the decision by firms to carry out new investment in plant and equipment and to hold inventories. We want to understand how a firm determines the size of its capital stock and we will study how the firm determines when it is profitable to add to its stocks of plant and equipment and inventories. We will learn how to measure the costs of investment and we will study how government policies can affect the investment decisions of firms. Here are a few of the questions that we will answer in this chapter.

■ How does a firm determine how much plant and equipment to hold?

■ How do we measure the cost of new capital goods?

■ How does the real interest rate affect investment?

■ How does the **corporate tax rate** affect investment spending?

■ Why do firms hold inventories?

Capital formation, the activity of building more plant and equipment in the economy, is an important part of the process helping to maintain our living standards in the future. The level of output produced in the economic system depends in part upon the stock of plant and equipment that is available for production. In the previous chapter, we looked at the first part of the linkage between saving and capital formation. Households provide loanable funds (savings) to the financial system by not consuming all of their income. In this chapter, we look at the second part of this linkage: investment. Firms borrow from households, through financial intermediaries like banks, and use these borrowed funds to add to the stock of plant and equipment that they have, using these capital goods to produce output in the future. The primary goal of this chapter is to understand what determines the investment decisions of firms.

Figure 5.1 provides a graph of the quarterly share of investment in Gross Domestic Product (GDP). Since 1947, investment has averaged about 16 percent of GDP and so, compared to consumption, it is a much smaller share of GDP. Investment is important, not because of its size in a given time period, but because the accumulated amount of investment determines the stock of capital in the economy and the capital stock is an important determinant of Potential GDP, the full-employment level of output in the economy. In Chapter 9, we will show how Potential GDP is determined.

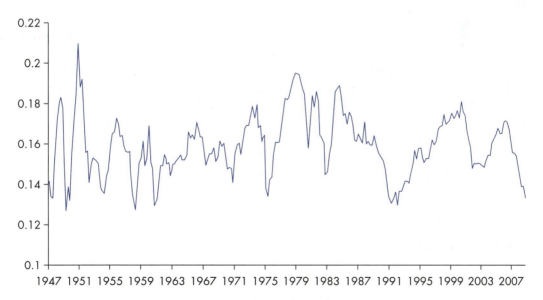

FIGURE 5.1 Gross Private Domestic Investment as a Share of GDP

Source: St. Louis Federal Reserve Bank FRED Database

In order to understand the investment process leading to this stock of capital, the first step will be to understand what is meant by the **desired stock of capital** that a firm wants to hold. We will see that this desired capital stock is determined from the solution of a profit maximization problem solved by the firm. Labor will be adjusted rapidly (relative to capital) but there are **adjustment costs** attached to the installation of new capital goods. As a result, firms will adjust their stock of capital slowly towards its desired level. This gradual adjustment process will be what we mean by investment.

In solving this profit-maximization problem, the firm will pay factor input prices for its inputs in production. The factor price associated with the stock of capital is known as the **user cost of capital**. This is the factor input price that is one of the determinants of the firm's investment policies and, from our discussion of the firm's behavior, you will learn how to measure this important factor price. This factor price measures the cost of ownership of durable goods, not just for firms, but for anyone owning durable goods, and it will be observed that the user cost of capital is one mechanism permitting tax policies to affect the investment decisions of firms. For example, we will show that the corporate income tax rate can affect the user cost of capital, thereby influencing the investment decisions of firms. We will also show how investment by the firm is related to the firm's stock market value.

Our final topic in this chapter will be about inventory investment where we will discuss the **production-smoothing** model of inventories. That analysis will explain why firms hold inventories and we will draw out the implications from this model for the inventory investment policies set by firms. Our discussions of investment in plant and equipment and inventories will reveal how the real interest rate affects the investment decisions of firms.

5.1 THE BEHAVIOR OF A FIRM

Our discussion of investment begins with an analysis of an individual firm, sometimes known as a representative firm, because we will assume that what we say about this firm represents the actions of all other firms in the economy. The theory we discuss has been called the **neoclassical theory of investment** because it is built upon optimizing (or profit-maximizing) behavior by the firm. We will assume that the firm wants to maximize its profits regarding how much labor and capital to use in the production of its output. In order to solve this profit maximization problem, we first need to illustrate the production process available to the firm where these inputs in production are used. For this purpose, we will use the concept of a **production function**, a device that represents the production technology possessed by the firm.

The Production Function

The firm uses two inputs in production, capital and labor, to produce a single output that cannot be stored (inventories are discussed later in the chapter). These inputs are measured as flows per unit of time (their measurement involves a time dimension) because output is a flow, measured with a time dimension. For labor, a reasonable measure of labor services in production would be man-hours (the product of the number of workers and hours worked per worker); for capital, we might mean machine-hours (the product of the number of machines and the hours of usage per machine). We will pay little attention from here on as to how these inputs are measured but, for simplicity, we will associate capital services in production with the stock of physical capital (measured at a point in time) used by the firm, thereby ignoring the amount of time (or utilization) that plant and equipment is used.

These inputs are used in a production function drawn in Figure 5.2. This is a representation of the technology that the firm has at its disposal to be used in producing its output. In the diagram, K refers to the stock of capital and L denotes labor services. On the horizontal axis we measure capital and output, Y, is on the vertical axis. L_0 is a given quantity of labor. The diagram illustrates a number of important assumptions that we will make regarding the firm's technology. These assumptions may be summarized as follows.

Propositions About the Production Function

- Output is increasing in the level of each input in production.
- There are diminishing returns in production associated with each factor input.
- A higher level of labor input increases the amount of output that may be produced at any level of the capital stock.

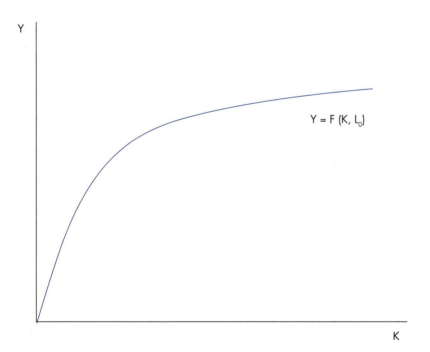

FIGURE 5.2 The Production Function of a Firm

The output, Y, of a firm depends upon the level of capital, K, used in production where L_0 is a given quantity of labor. Output rises with the level of inputs in production and there are diminishing returns to each input in production.

The first assumption is what produces a diagram with a positive slope; if the quantity of capital rises, so too does the quantity of output. That is, $\Delta Y/\Delta K > 0$. If we were to draw the same diagram with labor services on the horizontal axis, the shape of the production function would be the same.

The quantity $\Delta Y/\Delta K$ is an important concept in this model of the firm. It is referred to as the **Marginal Product of Capital** (denoted MP_K). Here is its definition.

Definition of the Marginal Product of Capital

■ The Marginal Product of Capital (MP_K) measures the extra output produced by an additional unit of capital used in production when the quantities of all other inputs are held fixed.

There is an analogous measure for the labor force, $\Delta Y/\Delta L$, which we will denote by MP_L. The MP is always positive for both inputs in production.

The second assumption about the production function is important for many of the results obtained later in this chapter. Diminishing returns is a crucial assumption about the technology and its definition is provided below.

Definition of Diminishing Returns in Production

■ A production function displays diminishing returns in production when the Marginal Product (MP) of an input declines as the level of the input increases, the quantities of all other inputs held fixed.

This property is illustrated by the slope of the production function. Figure 5.3 shows how the slope of the production function declines as the level of capital input rises. The slope is positive at both points in the diagram but the slope at point A is larger than the slope at point B. The MP of labor also declines as the level of labor rises, given the level of capital.

The final assumption described above concerns how the production function shifts with the level of labor. Figure 5.4 illustrates how the level of L will affect the production function. The production function shifts up with a higher level of L, raising the MP of capital. This is plausible because we are in effect saying that the availability of more labor in production raises the productivity of the capital stock. So the production function still starts at the origin but has a higher slope everywhere along the line, compared to the initial production function. That is, the production function rotates up from its original position. Similarly, a higher level of the capital stock raises the productivity of the labor force.

However, later in the book we will have reasons to use a production function that incorporates other inputs in production. Technical progress can occur which can change the production function that a firm has, allowing it to produce more with given levels of capital and labor. Energy inputs, and other intermediate inputs, are also used in production. To understand a number of important issues that affect aggregate economies, such as economic growth or the effects of oil cartels, it will be necessary to use these additional inputs in production. For now, we omit them for simplicity.

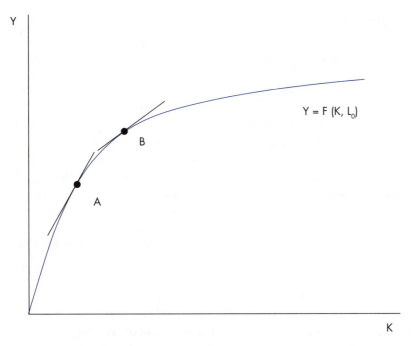

FIGURE 5.3 Diminishing Returns in Production

The Marginal Product of Capital, MP_K, is given by the slope of the production function and it declines as K rises. Points A and B both have positive slopes but the slope at B is smaller than the one at A.

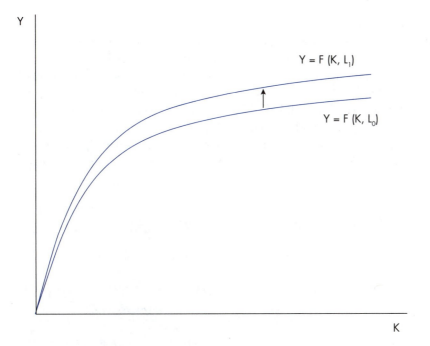

FIGURE 5.4 The Effect of an Increase in Labor

The production function shifts up with an increase in labor L ($L_1 > L_0$). This raises the MP_K.

Profit Maximization

The firm will choose its labor and capital inputs to maximize its profit. Profit can be written as

$$\text{Profit} = P{\cdot}Y - W{\cdot}L - U_K{\cdot}K$$

where P is the selling price of the firm's output (the product P·Y is thus the firm's revenue). Payments for labor are the product of the nominal wage rate, W, and the quantity of labor, L (sometimes called the wage bill). Payments for capital are given by the **nominal user cost of capital**, U_K, and the quantity of capital K. For now we will not say much about how U_K is measured; simply think of it as a factor price, just like the nominal wage rate. Later we will have a good deal more to say about how the nominal user cost of capital is measured.

Solving this maximization problem shows how the firm chooses its inputs in production and, to illustrate this process, substitute the production function into the profit expression above.

$$\text{Profit} = P{\cdot}F(K,L) - W{\cdot}L - U_K{\cdot}K$$

It will be assumed that the firm is a **price-taker** in output and input markets. This means that the price of the firm's output, P, and the nominal factor input prices (W and U_K) that it pays for its productive inputs are fixed and unaffected by the firm's actions. This is sometimes known as the assumption of **perfect markets**: prices are simply fixed parameters faced by the firm. The solution of this problem leads to two optimality criteria that guide the input choices of the firm.

To obtain these guiding principles, the firm compares the marginal benefits and marginal costs attached to its use of inputs. For capital, what is the marginal benefit of another unit of capital? If the firm uses one more unit of K, it will produce some additional output and this output can be sold in the output market at price P. The extra output it produces is measured by the MP_K (the Marginal Product of Capital). The extra cost of an additional unit of capital is given by the nominal user cost of capital, U_K. Table 5.1 summarizes the comparisons that confront the firm and how the firm should proceed in each case.

To understand why the firm will take the actions indicated, remember that the firm wants to maximize its profits so, whatever it chooses to do, that action must raise profits. If the

TABLE 5.1 Choosing the Profit-Maximizing Capital Stock

Comparison of Marginal Benefit and Cost	Action Taken by the Firm
$P{\cdot}\Delta Y/\Delta K < U_K$	Firm Must Use Less K
$P{\cdot}\Delta Y/\Delta K > U_K$	Firm Must Use More K
$P{\cdot}\Delta Y/\Delta K = U_K$	Firm Has the Optimal K

N.B. P is the firm's output price, K is the stock of capital, and U_K is the nominal user cost of capital. The MP_K is denoted by $\Delta Y/\Delta K$.

product $P \cdot MP_K > U_K$, profits will rise with a higher capital stock; a higher capital stock raises revenues by more than it raises costs, implying that profits rise. If $P \cdot MP_K < U_K$, profits will rise with a lower capital stock; as K declines, marginal costs fall faster than marginal revenue. Finally at the position where $P \cdot MP_K = U_K$, the firm has the profit-maximizing capital stock. It should keep K at its current level. The extra revenue obtained by the firm, $P \cdot MP_K$, is called the **value of the marginal product of capital** or **marginal revenue**. So when marginal benefit and marginal cost are just equal, the firm has determined the optimal level of the capital stock.

A similar analysis applies to the choice of labor, L. Choosing the quantity of labor to maximize profits will lead the firm to the profit-maximization condition $P \cdot MP_L = W$ (more will be said about the labor input decision in Chapter 8 when we explicitly consider the demand for labor by firms). The following propositions summarize the results of solving this problem.

Propositions About Choosing Factor Inputs to Maximize Profits

- The firm has the profit-maximizing quantity of capital when the value of the marginal product of capital is equal to the nominal user cost of capital.
- The firm has the profit-maximizing quantity of labor when the value of the **marginal product of labor** is equal to the nominal wage rate.

These results simply apply the principle of marginal benefit equals marginal cost that we have said is a consequence of optimizing behavior by households and firms. The benefit is marginal revenue; the marginal cost is the nominal factor input price associated with each input.

An important definition can now be provided regarding the **desired capital stock** that the firm wants to hold.

Definition of the Desired Stock of Capital

The desired capital stock of the firm is that level of the capital stock consistent with profit maximization by the firm.

This desired level of the capital stock will be denoted by K^*.

The Demand for Capital

The firm has solved the problem of how much capital to use to maximize its profits, leading to the condition that the value of the marginal product of capital is equal to the marginal cost of capital. This condition can be written in two equivalent ways: nominal terms (dollar units) or in physical units (units of output). Both conditions are given below.

$$\text{Nominal Units: } P \cdot MP_K = U_K$$

$$\text{Physical Units: } MP_K = U_K/P$$

Thus U_K/P is the **real user cost of capital** since it is measured in units of physical output.[1] The long-run demand for capital will now be obtained using the real factor input price for capital.

Figure 5.5 illustrates the demand for capital that we will obtain as a result of this profit-seeking behavior by the firm. The figure has two values on the vertical axis: the real user cost of capital that is initially facing the firm, $(U_K/P)_0$, and a second one that is lower than the initial real user cost of capital: i.e., $(U_K/P)_0 > (U_K/P)_1$. We want to determine how a change in the real user cost of capital will change the choice of K by the firm. So at the initial real user cost, the firm chooses the profit-maximizing capital stock, K_0, by comparing marginal benefits and costs. Then if the real user cost falls, the firm will find itself in the position where the following is true.

$$MP_K > (U_K/P)_1.$$

It was shown earlier that when this condition is true, the firm will find it profitable to use more capital since revenues rise by more than costs at the margin. So the firm will want

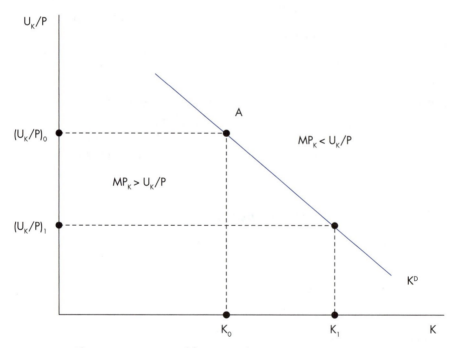

FIGURE 5.5 The Long-Run Demand for Capital

At the initial value of the real user cost of capital, $(U_K/P)_0$, the firm chooses K_0 as the optimal level of capital. When the real user cost falls to $(U_K/P)_1$, the firm will want more capital, choosing K_1 as the profit-maximizing quantity of capital. The area to the right of the K^D schedule is where $MP_K < U_K/P$. The area to the left is where $MP_K > U_K/P$. Along the K^D schedule, $MP_K = U_K/P$.

---

1 When in doubt about units of measurement, just do an exercise to figure out how something is measured. For example, W is measured in dollars per unit of labor and P is measured in dollars per unit of output. Form the ratio W/P and you will see that the real wage is measured in units of output per unit of labor.

more capital and, because we assume that there are diminishing returns in production, the MP_K will fall until we reach the profit-maximizing position $MP_K = (U_K/P)_1$. The conclusion that we reach is that the demand for capital is inversely related to the real user cost of capital: $\Delta K^D/\Delta(U_K/P) < 0$. At all points on the line giving the demand schedule for capital, the firm is maximizing its profits with respect to its choice of capital stock. At all points off this line, the firm is not maximizing its profits by its choice of the capital stock. At each point along the demand curve for capital, we see the desired stock of capital associated with each value of the real user cost of capital. We refer to this as the long-run demand for capital.

A similar analysis could be done for the choice of labor in production. That analysis will show that the demand for labor is inversely related to the real wage, W/P (see Chapter 8). You should be able to use the reasoning illustrated above for capital to convince yourself that the demand for labor will have this inverse relationship to real wages.

It is also true that the demands for productive inputs will have cross-factor price effects; that is, the demand for capital will also depend upon the real wage and the demand for labor will also depend upon the real user cost of capital. However, for the sake of simplicity, we will suppress these effects, focusing instead upon own-factor price responses. Our findings are summarized in the following propositions.

Propositions About the Long-Run Demand for Capital

■ Given a real user cost of capital, the desired capital stock is the profit-maximizing capital stock.
■ The demand for capital is inversely related to the real user cost of capital, U_K/P.

This completes our discussion of how profit-seeking behavior pins down the quantities of capital in production that the firm wants to use. We can now turn our attention to the problem of investment, what the firm does when it doesn't have the level of the capital stock consistent with profit maximization.

5.2 INVESTMENT IN PLANT AND EQUIPMENT

When the firm does not have the profit-maximizing quantity of capital goods, it accumulates (or reduces) its stock of capital to reach the optimal stock of capital goods. This process obeys the relationship

$$\Delta K = I - \delta \cdot K, \ 0 < \delta < 1.$$

This accounting identity expresses the connection between net investment, ΔK, gross investment, I, and replacement investment, $\delta \cdot K$.

Net investment measures the net change in the capital stock between two points in time. **Gross investment** refers to the quantity of plant and equipment that the firm purchases in the marketplace. This quantity can be positive or negative; the firm could be buying new capital goods (I > 0) or it could be selling them off in the second-hand market

$(I < 0)$.[2] Investment is a flow because it has a time dimension (it is measured by purchases of capital goods per unit of time).

But it is also true that these capital goods wear out. This fact is referred to as **depreciation** and, while it is true that the usage of a unit of capital has an effect on how rapidly it depreciates, we usually assume for simplicity that capital wears out at a fixed rate, given by δ (the Greek symbol delta). We restrict the **depreciation rate**, δ, to be between zero and unity because it is reasonable to suppose that only a fraction of the firm's capital will be wearing out in each time period (see **Doing Economics**: How Rapidly Do Capital Goods Depreciate?). We refer to the activity of replacing worn-out capital goods as **replacement investment**. This type of investment is also a flow because it is measured relative to a period of time.

Doing Economics: How Rapidly Do Capital Goods Depreciate?

In macroeconomics, it is customary to aggregate to very high levels so that, for example, there is only one type of capital good in an economic model. At such a high level of aggregation, there is only one depreciation rate but, in reality, there are many kinds of capital goods and they can depreciate at rates that differ considerably.

To get a sense of how diverse these depreciation rates can be, the following table presents a number of annual depreciation rates for capital assets. There are two classes of assets in the table: producer durable equipment and nonresidential structures. Structures depreciate much more slowly than does equipment. Autos and trucks depreciate particularly rapidly. It is evident that aggregation over asset classes masks a considerable amount of heterogeneity in economic depreciation rates.

Producer Durable Equipment	Depreciation Rate
Furniture and Fixtures	.1100
Agricultural Machinery	.0971
Electrical Machinery	.1179
Trucks, Buses, and Truck Trailers	.2537
Autos	.3333
Nonresidential Structures	
Industrial Buildings	.0361
Commercial Buildings	.0247
Educational Buildings	.0188
Railroad Structures	.0176
Farm Structures	.0237

Source: Dale W. Jorgenson, "Empirical Studies of Depreciation," *Economic Inquiry* 34, No. 1 (January 1996), pp. 24–42.

---

2 Investment can be irreversible. That is, it could be true that the firm is unable to sell off capital goods in the second-hand market. This assumption would complicate our analysis of investment and is thus ignored for simplicity.

Finally net investment, also a flow concept, measures net changes in the firm's capital stock. The sign of net investment (that is, whether it is positive or negative) depends upon the difference between gross and replacement investment. If gross investment exceeds replacement investment, the capital stock rises. If gross investment is less than replacement investment, the capital stock falls. The capital stock is constant when gross investment equals replacement investment. Table 5.2 summarizes these relationships. The firm is in equilibrium when it only does replacement investment, implying that its capital stock is constant at its desired level K* (I = $\delta \cdot$K*). This makes good sense; if the firm has its profit-maximizing stock of capital, it wants to keep it and so it just replaces the capital goods that wear out.

But what if the firm doesn't have this optimal capital stock? If this is the case, the firm undertakes net investment to achieve it. It could do this very rapidly but, for reasons that we will now discuss, the firm will be inclined to move slowly towards its optimal capital stock because there are additional costs attached to the investment process. We now discuss these costs.

Costs of Adjustment

The firm must pay for any new capital goods that it buys in the market for capital goods and this is one component of the costs of investment. But there are other costs that the firm will incur and these costs are referred to as **adjustment costs**.

If a firm wants to augment its capital stock, it must devote resources to the planning and installation of these new types of equipment. Engineers and managers must jointly decide what types of machinery to buy and where to place the new equipment in the plant when it arrives. It may be necessary to shut down a plant when the new equipment is installed, meaning that the firm can't produce any output while installation occurs, losing revenue in the process. Thus there are **planning and installation costs** attached to changing the capital stock. Economists often embody these ideas by writing the firm's technology in the following way.

$$Y = F(K, L) - C(\Delta K)$$

TABLE 5.2 The Connection Between Gross and Net Investment

I > $\delta \cdot$K	ΔK > 0
I < $\delta \cdot$K	ΔK < 0
I = $\delta \cdot$K	ΔK = 0

N.B. I is gross investment, K is the capital stock, ΔK is net investment, and δ is the depreciation rate (0 < δ < 1).

The production function that we have used previously has now been augmented by a term that captures the costs attached to net investment.[3] The first term in the expression, F(K, L), is familiar from earlier discussion and is now referred to as the **gross production function** because it takes no account of the planning and installation costs attached to net investment. The expression as a whole is now referred to as the **net production function** because it describes the ability of the firm to produce output net of the planning and installation costs associated with net investment. For reasons to be discussed shortly, these costs provide an incentive for the firm to gradually adjust its capital stock, rather than bear all of these costs immediately. That is, the firm will find it sensible to bear only a portion of these costs in the short run, pushing off some of these costs into the future. Figure 5.6 illustrates the properties of these costs. There are several features of this figure that must be stressed.

The firm will incur costs attached to net changes in the capital stock that occur; that is, the firm bears such costs, not only when there is a net increase in the capital stock, but also when there is a net reduction in the stock of capital. Thus we are assuming that there are costs associated with disposing of capital goods, say if the firm decides to sell off capital goods in second-hand markets. And these would be the same sort of costs that we discussed above. The firm must devote internal resources to the activity of eliminating capital. Further, there are no

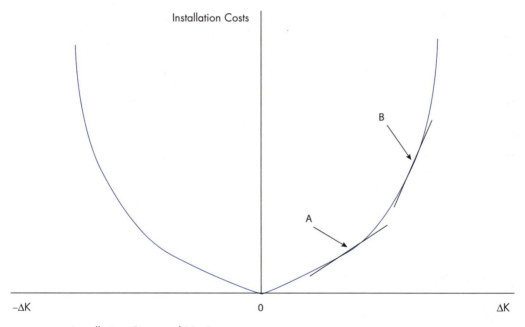

Installation Costs

$-\Delta K$ 0 ΔK

FIGURE 5.6 Installation Costs and Net Investment

The slope of the line at point A is less than the slope at B. Marginal installation costs therefore rise with net investment which is the reason why firms gradually adjust their stock of capital goods.

---

3 We could specify these costs in terms of gross, rather than net, investment but the advantage of using net investment is that the standard form of the technology, used elsewhere in the text, will arise when the firm is in equilibrium; that is, it will arise when $\Delta K = 0$.

planning costs that the firm will bear in equilibrium ($\Delta K = 0$) since the firm can presumably anticipate these costs and avoid them since it is just replacing worn-out capital goods. When the firm has its long-run desired level of capital, adjustment costs disappear.

But the crucial feature of these planning and installation costs is that *marginal installation costs rise with net investment*. This fact is also illustrated in Figure 5.6. This is the crucial assumption causing firms to gradually change their capital stocks, rather than jumping as quickly as they can, to the desired stock of capital. Because it becomes increasingly expensive as more investment is carried out, the firm will want to avoid rapid investment, preferring to slowly change its stock of capital. This leads to an investment process displaying **partial adjustment** which means that the firm will only adjust its capital stock part of the way towards its desired level in each period of time. These characteristics are summarized below.

Propositions About Net Investment and Costs of Adjustment

■ The marginal costs of installing or disposing of capital goods rise with the size of net investment.

■ Because marginal installation costs rise with net investment, the firm will gradually adjust its capital stock towards its desired or equilibrium level. Net investment displays partial adjustment.

Net Investment

The firm obeys an investment policy that moves it slowly towards its desired stock of capital, K^*. The net investment demand equation, displaying partial adjustment to equilibrium, is

$$\Delta K = \lambda \cdot (K^* - K), \ 0 < \lambda < 1.$$

The parameter λ (the Greek character lambda) has an important interpretation. This parameter determines the **speed of adjustment** of the capital stock. It measures the fraction of the gap between actual and desired capital stocks that is made up each period. So this net investment expression shows that the firm will move only part of the way to its desired capital stock, K^*, in each time period. This is the effect of the assumptions illustrated in Figure 5.6; because installation costs rise at the margin, the investment displays partial adjustment to K^*. Net investment is determined by the capital stock that the firm has in place, K, and the determinants of the desired stock of capital, K^*.

The firm will build up its capital stock slowly when it has less capital than it wants to have in equilibrium. That is, $\Delta K > 0$ if $K^* - K > 0$. Similarly, the firm reduces the capital stock when it has more than it wants to have in the long run ($\Delta K < 0$ when $K^* - K < 0$). Net investment is zero when the firm is at its desired level ($\Delta K = 0$ when $K^* - K = 0$). In this last case, the firm will only do replacement investment ($I = \delta \cdot K^*$). These relationships are summarized in Table 5.3.

Panel (A) of Figure 5.7 illustrates this gradual adjustment process of the capital stock and its relation to net investment; panel (B) displays the behavior of the capital stock. The initial capital stock is K_0 and the firm wishes to build up its capital stock to K^*. It does so gradually over time with net investment declining until K^* is reached, at which point net investment is

TABLE 5.3 Net Investment

$K^* - K > 0$	$\Delta K > 0$
$K^* - K < 0$	$\Delta K < 0$
$K^* - K = 0$	$\Delta K = 0$

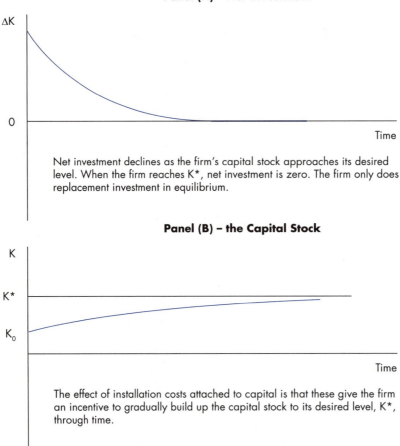

Panel (A) – Net Investment

Net investment declines as the firm's capital stock approaches its desired level. When the firm reaches K^*, net investment is zero. The firm only does replacement investment in equilibrium.

Panel (B) – the Capital Stock

The effect of installation costs attached to capital is that these give the firm an incentive to gradually build up the capital stock to its desired level, K^*, through time.

FIGURE 5.7 Net Investment and the Capital Stock over Time

zero. Figure 5.8 provides another perspective; this figure shows the firm moving towards its long-run demand for capital from arbitrary initial levels of capital.

We are now in a position to establish the investment demand equation that will be used in our aggregate models of the economy. We will look first at net investment; gross

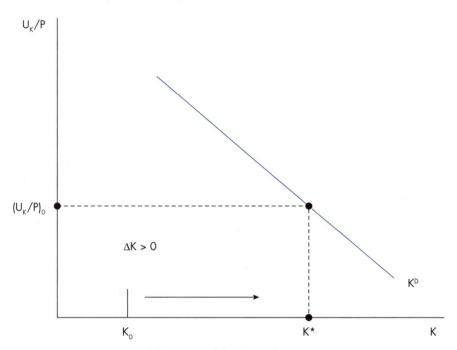

FIGURE 5.8 Investment and the Demand for Capital

Given the user cost of capital $(U_K/P)_0$, profit-maximizing behavior by the firm leads the firm to want the capital stock K*. If the firm has an initial level of capital given by K_0, net investment will be positive.

investment will turn out to be quite similar. Net investment has just two determinants: the actual capital stock and the real user cost of capital. The partial adjustment rule, given above, shows that if K rises, net investment ΔK falls (a one unit increase in K reduces ΔK by – λ). The reason is that the more capital the firm has relative to the desired stock of capital, the less investment the firm must do to reach the optimal capital stock. Investment is the activity of reaching an equilibrium capital stock; the closer it is to that equilibrium, the less investment the firm will do. Investment declines as the firm gets closer to the optimal capital stock.

The net investment demand for capital depends upon the real user cost of capital because this magnitude determines the desired stock of capital. A lower real user cost of capital raises the desired stock of capital (see Figure 5.5) and, when the gap between K* and K rises, the firm will do more net investment.

To establish the determinants of gross investment, use the accounting relationship that ties together gross and net investment, using the determinants of net investment. Doing so yields

$$I = \lambda \cdot (K^* - K) + \delta \cdot K = \lambda \cdot K^* + (\delta - \lambda) \cdot K.$$

We find that a higher user cost of capital reduces the desired stock of capital; it reduces net investment and gross investment as well. But the response of investment to variations in the actual capital stock is ambiguous, depending upon the difference δ – λ. If δ – λ < 0, then both gross and net investment would be inversely related to the actual capital stock held by the firm.[4]

Serial Persistence

You may recall from our discussion of business cycle measurement in Chapter 3 that one feature of aggregate economies is that they display serial persistence, the characteristic that if output is above trend this period, it tends to be above trend next period as well. Partial adjustment is one possible reason, developed by economists, which provides an explanation for this persistence as may be seen from the following expressions.

$$\Delta K = K - K_{-1} = \lambda \cdot (K^* - K_{-1})$$

$$K = (1 - \lambda) \cdot K_{-1} + \lambda \cdot K^*$$

The first equation is just the partial adjustment rule we discussed above that describes the net investment behavior of the firm except that we now show that ΔK measures the difference between capital stocks at two points in time: last period, and this period. In the equation, K refers to the capital stock this period while K_{-1} is last period's capital stock, so that ΔK gives us the net change in the capital stock between two periods. The next equation collects terms and illustrates how partial adjustment can provide an explanation of the serial persistence in aggregate output. Notice that $1 > 1 - \lambda > 0$, thereby implying that there is a positive relationship between today's capital stock and the one in place last period. Thus anything that caused an increase in the capital stock last period will increase the capital stock today and, because capital goods are being used in producing output, this means that output is positively related to the level of output last period. So the assumption of adjustment costs (or planning and installation costs) attached to the capital stock is one possible mechanism that induces serial persistence in the output produced by firms and, therefore, in the aggregate economy.

To summarize our findings, gross and net investment are inversely related to the real user cost of capital and to the actual stock of capital. While these relationships form the basis for the investment equations used in our models of the macro economy, one aspect of the investment decision has been put aside and that is the forward-looking nature of investment decisions. This is the subject of the next section.

5.3 THE FORWARD-LOOKING NATURE OF INVESTMENT

When the firm finds that it does not have the optimal capital stock, it makes a present value calculation that was lying behind the scenes of the discussion above about investment. It is important to make this calculation clear to you so that you realize that, as a result of this

---

4 We are effectively assuming that the depreciation rate is very small, as it is for structures. See the data on the depreciation rates for structures in **Doing Economics**: How Rapidly Do Capital Goods Depreciate?

present value calculation, the firm makes investment decisions that are forward-looking, in much the same way that the household did when we studied household behavior in the previous chapter.

Capital goods are durable. They last for more than one period of time and can therefore be used to produce output for more than one period of time in the future. Firms take account of this fact when they plan their investment decisions by computing the present value of the benefits of adding capital to their existing stock of plant and equipment. For now, assume for simplicity that the rate of depreciation, δ, is zero. Then the firm must compare the discounted benefits of adding capital to the costs of investment. As we discussed above, those costs include the purchase prices of capital and the marginal planning and installation costs that must be incurred. Thus if the firm decides to invest in an additional unit of new capital, it must be true that

$$P_K + MC(\Delta K) = \frac{P \cdot MP_K}{(1+r)} + \frac{P \cdot MP_K}{(1+r)^2} + \dots$$

for new capital goods put in place one year ahead. In this expression, P_K is the purchase price of new capital goods, and $MC(\Delta K)$ measures the marginal planning and installation costs attached to adding capital. As before, MP_K is the marginal product of capital, $P \cdot MP_K$ is the value of the marginal product of capital (the product of the firm's output price and the marginal product of capital), and r is the real interest rate. The present value goes on into the indefinite future because there is no reason for the firm to stop this calculation at some arbitrary point in the future (capital goods last forever because they do not depreciate). Maximizing profits will lead the firm to this comparison and we can use earlier reasoning to see that this will be true.

Suppose the firm is considering the acquisition of another unit of capital. It computes the present value of the extra revenue it will receive by using this new machine to produce output. Since the capital good is durable, these benefits last for many time periods and thus must be discounted from the future in order to determine their present value to the firm. The firm compares these discounted benefits to their costs; if the discounted benefits exceed the costs, the firm will purchase the new machine. The firm will go through the same calculation for the next unit of capital and if the discounted benefits exceed the costs, it buys that one as well. As more and more capital is added, the MP_K falls (remember that we have diminishing returns to capital) so, eventually, the equality above will hold. So once again, we compare marginal costs and benefits to determine what the firm will do but, in this case, we use discounted benefits in making this comparison. In this way the firm makes forward-looking decisions when it makes an investment decision.

Now suppose that the firm is in equilibrium so that there are no net changes in the capital stock (the firm is only doing replacement investment in this situation). Marginal planning and installation costs no longer occur in this case (see Figure 5.6).[5] Now take the expression above where we compared discounted benefits and marginal costs and, using the fact that marginal planning costs are zero, we get

---

5 Recall that we have assumed that planning costs apply to net, as oppose to gross, investment. Since net investment is zero in equilibrium, so too are planning and installation costs.

$$P_K = \frac{P \cdot MP_K}{(1+r)} + \frac{P \cdot MP_K}{(1+r)^2} + \ldots$$

which can be rewritten as

$$P_K = P \cdot MP_K \cdot \left[\frac{1}{(1+r)} + \frac{1}{(1+r)^2} + \ldots \right]$$

The term in the brackets simplifies to the ratio 1/r (it is a geometric sum). The expression can now be written as

$$P_K = \frac{P \cdot MP_K}{r}$$

or, equivalently,

$$\frac{r \cdot P_K}{P} = MP_K.$$

We have now developed a concept that is extremely important in the theory of investment. Recall that we used U_K/P to denote the real user cost of capital, saying that we would have more to say about how to measure U_K at a later point in the chapter. Now we can see how U_K is measured; it is the product of the real interest rate, r, and the relative purchase price of capital goods, P_K/P. We have obtained a simple form of the real user cost of capital, first devised by Harvard University economist Dale W. Jorgenson.[6] The intuition behind this relationship is quite natural.

Imagine that the firm has computed the value of the marginal product of capital (the product of the firm's output price and the MP_K of capital). The costs of investment are really the **opportunity costs** of investing funds into the stock of plant and equipment. What are these alternative costs? Well, the firm could be investing in the bond market, earning a real return, measured by the real interest rate r, on a dollar of its invested funds. Since one unit of capital can be purchased for P_K, this amount could be invested in the bond market, generating interest receipts of $r \cdot P_K$. The funds that it could earn in the bond market are thus given by $r \cdot P_K$. This measures the foregone interest earnings on one unit of capital goods. Thus the nominal user cost of capital can be interpreted as an opportunity cost of investment. The ratio U_K/P, contained in our profit maximization discussion earlier in the chapter, actually measures the real opportunity cost of investment.

This version of the user cost of capital is somewhat simplified because it omits the effects of depreciation and taxes. These issues are addressed in the next section where you will see that, once we incorporate the corporate income tax rate into the user cost of capital, a government-controlled policy variable can directly affect the investment decisions of firms.

---

6 See Dale W. Jorgenson, "Capital Theory and Investment Behavior," American Economic Association *Papers and Proceedings* 53, No. 3 (June 1963), pp. 247–59.

Before doing so, we first take up the question of expectations and the investment decisions of firms.

Expectations and Investment

Previously in this section, we stressed that the decision to invest in new capital goods was a forward-looking one because the firm's managers know that capital goods are durable; the durability of capital goods means that the benefits of owning a new unit of machinery will last for some period of time into the future. As a result, we argued that firms would make a present value calculation when deciding upon the purchase of a new capital good. That calculation, rewritten here for convenience, is

$$P_K + MC(\Delta K) = \frac{P \cdot MP_K}{(1+r)} + \frac{P \cdot MP_K}{(1+r)^2} + \dots$$

and this is how the firm decides if it is profitable to own an additional unit of capital. But the firm does not know the future values of prices, P, at which it can sell output in the future (remember that we assume that the firm is in a competitive output market). Thus the firm must somehow form an expectation about prices and the other magnitudes that bear on the profitability of new units of capital. And it is easy to see that incorrect expectations can be very costly to the firm.

For example, imagine that the firm decides to install new capital, believing that the prices it can get for its output will be rising in the future. As the firm carries out its investment plans over time, it will observe whether its expectations were correct. If they were correct, then the firm will find that it was worth bearing the planning and installation costs attached to the installation of new capital because its profits will be rising through time. But if its expectations are wrong, say that prices are found to fall, rather than rise, over time, the firm will come to realize that the resources invested into the installation of new capital were wasted as it was not profitable to add new capital goods into production. Thus expectations are of crucial importance in making investment decisions. Firms (and households) have strong incentives to forecast the values of future economic magnitudes correctly because forecasting mistakes can lead to reduced profits and economic welfare.

Later in the book we will have more to say about expectation formation by households and firms. For now, we leave unspecified how economic actors form their expectations but you should remember that these expectations need not be correct. When we return to this topic later in the book, we will observe the implications of the optimal forecasting schemes that may be used by the public.

5.4 MORE ON THE USER COST OF CAPITAL

We obtained a measure of the user cost of capital using the simplification that the depreciation rate was zero. Now we need to reintroduce the depreciation rate so that we can get a more realistic measure of the user cost of durable goods.

When the depreciation rate, δ, is no longer zero, the real user cost of capital becomes

$$\frac{P_K \cdot (r+\delta)}{P}.$$

This expression is only slightly different from what we had before. Now we have an additional component of nominal user costs: the product $\delta \cdot P_K$. To see why this term appears, recall that the capital goods of the firm wear out at the rate δ. This means that because a fraction of a capital good will wear out in each period of time, the firm bears the cost $\delta \cdot P_K$. Put differently, that part of a unit of capital which "evaporates" at the rate δ can't be sold off by the firm in the future so that this is a part of the cost of a new machine. Thus the firm has two components of the nominal user cost of capital: foregone earnings from the bond market and the loss of the purchase price P_K covering that part of the machine wearing out. While you may think that the user cost of capital applies only to a firm making an investment decision, it applies equally well to any purchase of a durable good, including those durable goods that you buy as a consumer (see **Doing Economics**: The User Cost of A New Car).

Doing Economics: The User Cost of A New Car

In casual conversation, you often hear people say that a durable good, such as a car, is expensive based upon the purchase price of the good. Superficially this seems sensible; a BMW or Mercedes-Benz car will have a sticker price far exceeding the sticker on comparably-sized cars produced by other manufacturers. But are these cars really so expensive when we compute the user cost of owning them? Surprisingly, they may in fact be cheaper to own as an example will serve to demonstrate.

The key part of the example is the depreciation rate on a durable good. Cars which sell at prices higher than the prices of other cars often have depreciation rates far smaller than cars selling at lower purchase prices. And there is empirical evidence that this is the case. So consider the following example.

If the real interest rate is two percent ($r = .02$), compute the nominal user cost of a car using the formula $U_K = P_K \cdot (r + \delta)$. The results are displayed below for two cars: one that costs \$40,000 to buy and another that costs \$25,000. The results of this computation are given below.

	Depreciation Rate	Nominal User Cost
Expensive Car: \$40,000	.10	\$4,800
Cheap Car: \$25,000	.20	\$5,500

The car with the higher price tag certainly looks more expensive than the one with the lower purchase price if we only look at purchase prices. But if the expensive car depreciates much more slowly than the cheaper car (in fact it is assumed that it depreciates at half the rate of the cheaper car), then despite a much higher opportunity cost due to its higher purchase price, the car with the higher purchase price turns out to have a lower user cost of capital compared to the car with the lower purchase price. Thus the car with the higher purchase price is cheaper to own because of its low depreciation rate. The sticker (or purchase) price is clearly a very misleading measure of the true cost of owning durable goods.

One further point must be addressed here, and that is the measure of the user cost of capital, that will be used later in the book when we discuss aggregate models of the economy. The real interest rate will later be used as the measure of the user cost of capital and here is how that emerges from the user cost we have used in this chapter. For simplicity, we will be working with a one-good model of the economy (there is only one type of output produced in the economy) so that $P_K = P$ in this circumstance. As a result, the user cost of capital becomes $r + \delta$ and, if the depreciation rate is taken to be fixed as will be the case, then we can simply ignore it and treat the user cost of capital as equivalent to the real interest rate.

Taxes and the User Cost of Capital

Firms pay taxes on the profits they earn through the corporate income tax. This fact turns out to change the user cost of capital that the firm faces, providing an avenue for tax policies to affect the investment decisions of firms. We now turn to a discussion of how taxes influence the user cost of capital.

Corporations pay a fraction of their taxable income in taxes to the government through the corporate income tax code. We assumed in our previous discussion of the user cost of capital that the firm got to keep all of the returns that it earns from the installation of new capital goods but, because of the effects of taxes, this is not true. The firm has to pay a part of these extra returns to the government in the form of taxes. So we need to determine how the firm can compute the **after-tax** return on an additional unit of capital. Here is how this is computed.

The firm earns, *before* taxes, the marginal revenue attached to using an additional unit of capital in production, measured previously as the product of the firm's output price, P, and the MP_K. It is now the case that the firm gets to keep only a fraction of this amount. If we use t_c to denote the marginal corporate income tax rate $(0 < t_c < 1)$, then after-tax marginal revenue is

$$(1 - t_c) \cdot P \cdot MP_K.$$

If the firm solves a profit maximization problem to determine its desired stock of capital, this magnitude now gets compared to the nominal user cost of capital, leading to the condition

$$P_K \cdot (r + \delta) = (1 - t_c) \cdot P \cdot MP_K.$$

This last condition leads us to a definition of the **after-tax user cost of capital** given below.

$$\frac{P_K \cdot (r+\delta)}{(1-t_c) \cdot P}$$

Using this definition, we can see that a policy variable now affects the real user cost of capital, namely the corporate income tax rate appears in this expression and an increase in this tax rate reduces the after-tax marginal revenue from an additional unit of capital, thus effectively raising the after-tax real user cost of capital. This explains why cutting the corporate income tax rate is often suggested as a way to increase investment in the economy because a lower tax rate reduces the user cost of capital, thus raising the desired stock of capital and net investment.

But this is not the only way in which tax policies can influence investment spending. Tax credits for the purchase of new capital goods (see **Doing Economics**: The Investment Tax

Credit and the User Cost of Capital) have historically been given to firms and the ability to reduce taxable income by writing off the depreciation of capital goods is also a policy choice determined in the corporate income tax code.[7] These considerations suggest that the user cost of capital, and thus investment spending, is heavily influenced by the corporate tax code.

Doing Economics: The Investment Tax Credit and the User Cost of Capital

In the past, corporations were able to deduct a fraction of the purchase price of capital goods directly from their tax bill, a provision of the tax code known as the Investment Tax Credit. This past feature of the tax code changes the after-tax real user cost of capital, introducing another policy variable into the mix of possible avenues for tax policy to stimulate investment. Let the investment tax credit rate be denoted by ITC $(0 < ITC < 1)$, then the after-tax purchase price of a capital good is no longer given by P_K; it is now $(1 - ITC) \cdot P_K$. So we now have a new definition of the after-tax real cost of capital, given below.

$$\text{After-Tax Real User Cost of Capital:} \quad \frac{(1-ITC) \cdot P_K \cdot (r + \delta)}{(1 - t_c) \cdot P}$$

As we did before, we use t_c to indicate the corporate income tax rate. The implication of this new feature of a tax code is that, if the government were to decide to allow firms to deduct a larger fraction of the purchase price of capital (ITC rises), then the effect would be to lower the net cost of a new machine, reducing the after-tax real cost of capital. Thus we have another policy parameter influencing the investment decision of the firm.

5.5 THE STOCK MARKET AND INVESTMENT

James Tobin, a Nobel laureate in economics, offered a theory of investment by the firm which appears, superficially at least, to be an alternative to the theory just described.[8] Tobin suggested that the stock market value of the firm, relative to the replacement cost of the firm, was the driving force behind the investment behavior of firms, and he dubbed this measure "q." A number of years passed before this theory of investment was integrated into the neoclassical theory of investment described earlier in the chapter and we discuss here Tobin's theory in a neoclassical framework as developed by the economist Fumio Hayashi.[9]

---

7 A more complete accounting of the relationships between taxes and the user cost of capital can be found in Robert E. Hall and Dale W. Jorgenson, "Tax Policy and Investment Behavior," *American Economic Review* 57, No. 3 (June 1967), pp. 391–414.

8 See James Tobin, "A General Equilibrium Approach to Monetary Theory," *Journal of Money, Credit, and Banking* 1, No. 1 (February 1969), pp. 15–29.

9 See Fumio Hayashi, "Tobin's Marginal q and Average q: A Neoclassical Interpretation," *Econometrica* 50, No. 1 (January 1982), pp. 213–24.

We first need a definition of **Marginal q**. It can be defined in the following way.

$$\text{Marginal q} = 1 + MC(\Delta K)$$

The second term in the definition of marginal q is the marginal installation cost of net changes in the capital stock. This is one of the components of the cost of new investment that we described previously. Go back to Figure 5.6 and recall that marginal installation costs (the slope of the planning cost relationship), $MC(\Delta K)$, are positive when the firm is building up its capital stock; they are negative when the firm reduces the stock of capital and zero in equilibrium when net investment is zero. The implication of this is that marginal q exceeds unity when the firm is expanding its capacity and it lies below unity when the firm is contracting. Marginal q equals unity in equilibrium. These findings are summarized in Table 5.4.

Marginal q is not observable because to measure it requires that we have data on marginal installation costs and this data is generally not available. But there is another measure of Tobin's q that can be measured and, under certain conditions, this new measure is equivalent to marginal q.[10] This new measure is called **Average q** and it is defined below.

$$\frac{\dfrac{Pr\,ofit}{(1+r)} + \dfrac{Pr\,ofit}{(1+r)^2} + K}{P_K \cdot K}$$

The numerator of the ratio is the discounted profits of the firm and here is where the stock market appears. The stock market value of the firm is measured by the nominal value of the firm's outstanding shares, and it is a measure of the expectations of investors regarding the profits that the firm will make now and in the future. The denominator of this expression is the replacement cost of the firm: that is, it is the product of the quantity of capital owned by the firm and the purchase price of those capital goods. Thus to replace the firm's capital stock requires that $P_K \cdot K$ be spent.

The implication of this theory of the firm is that when the market value of the firm exceeds its replacement cost, the firm will be expanding (raising its capital stock) and, when the market

TABLE 5.4 The Relationship Between Marginal q and Net Investment	
q > 1	$\Delta K > 0$
q < 1	$\Delta K < 0$
q = 1	$\Delta K = 0$

N.B. Marginal q is denoted by q and net investment is ΔK.

10 The conditions required are that the firm's technology and installation costs be homogeneous of degree one. For the production function, this restriction will be called constant returns to scale, a condition that you will learn about later in the book.

value lies below the replacement cost, the firm will contract. This implies that it is possible to infer the investment behavior of firms by measuring the value of the firm's outstanding shares of stock and by measuring the replacement costs of the firm's physical assets, an exercise that Hayashi carried out in his study of this theory of investment.

This completes our discussion of investment in plant and equipment. We now turn to another component of investment that is of particular significance for the business cycle. That component is inventory investment.

5.6 INVENTORY INVESTMENT

Macroeconomic models frequently omit any explicit consideration of inventory investment but, as a matter of fact, part of the investment that a firm can undertake is inventory investment. Firms may hold three types of inventories: **finished goods, materials and supplies**, and **work-in-process**.[11]

Finished goods are products ready for sale to the public. The electronics store where you buy your music CDs holds an inventory of these CDs on its shelves, out of which customers make their purchases. Manufacturing firms hold inventories of materials and supplies which they use in the production of their own products. These inventories are intermediate goods, produced by other firms. Automobile manufacturers may hold a stock of radios, made by another firm, which they install in the cars that they produce. Finally, firms may not complete the production of a product in a given time period and so hold a stock of semi-finished goods, referred to as work-in-process. That same automobile manufacturer, using the radios that it holds in inventory, may not complete the production of the car in which the radio was installed. That unfinished car is an example of work-in-process. Firms that hold inventories of finished goods are described as **producing to stock**.[12]

There are a number of reasons why firms find it in their interest to hold stocks of inventories. Each one reflects a balancing by the firm of the marginal benefits and costs attached to holding inventories.

Motives for Holding Inventories

The reason for holding inventories that has been given the most attention by economists is the **production-smoothing** motive. Firms face a demand for their output which is unpredictable, at least to some extent. When demand is unexpectedly high, firms could increase production to meet this higher level of demand but this is costly. This is so because producing more output leads to higher marginal costs of production. For example, the workforce may need to be put

---

11 For a survey of research on inventories, see Louis J. Maccini and Alan S. Blinder, "The Resurgence of Inventory Research: What Have We Learned?" *Journal of Economic Surveys* 5, No. 4 (1991), pp. 291–328.

12 Firms sometimes do not hold inventories of finished goods. Rather they produce goods in response to customer orders, producing output and delivering it to their customers with a substantial delay from the time that a new order is placed. Firms of this type are said to **produce to order**.

on overtime pay, earning a higher-than-normal wage rate in order for production to increase. Or the firm may have to pay a premium to its suppliers of materials if it wants to take delivery of additional intermediate materials to rapidly produce more output. In order to avoid these higher costs, the firm can hold a stock of finished goods and service this unexpectedly higher demand from inventory, avoiding the higher costs of increasing production.

A second reason for holding inventories is simply that they are **factors of production**, required for the production of a firm's output. Stocks of intermediate materials and goods-in-process fall into this category as these are goods used in the production of final output. A firm may thus hold stocks of these goods, produced and purchased from an outside supplier, until they are installed into products being built for final sale.

A final reason for holding inventories is that firms want to avoid **stock-outs** by holding inventories. The electronics store where you go to buy music CDs may not have the particular CD that you want because it is temporarily out of stock. Perhaps the demand for this CD was unexpectedly high so that the firm sold all of its initial holdings very quickly after they were put on the shelf. In this case, the firm that stocks-out loses customer goodwill (you aren't happy to be unable to buy what you want) and customers who can't buy what they wish will turn to the firm's competitors, perhaps not returning again to the store where the stock-out occurred. So to avoid these costs, the firm can hold inventories of finished goods.

We now draw out the implications of the production-smoothing model of inventories in order to learn what determines the inventory investment policies set by firms.

The Production-Smoothing Model of Inventories

For simplicity, the firm is assumed to hold only finished goods inventories. There is a basic accounting identity that describes changes in the stock of finished goods inventories which is

$$\Delta F = Y - S.$$

Here, F refers to finished goods, Y is production, and S denotes sales. In a model with inventories of finished goods, production and sales are no longer identical. This relation shows that when production exceeds sales, inventories rise (if $Y - S > 0$, $\Delta F > 0$) and when sales exceed production, inventories fall (if $Y - S < 0$, $\Delta F < 0$). When inventories are constant, production and sales are just equal ($Y - S = 0$, $\Delta F = 0$). Table 5.5 summarizes these relationships.

A crucial part of the model is that the firm is assumed to want to maintain an optimal relationship between the level of inventories and sales, holding a **buffer stock** of finished goods because demand for the firm's output fluctuates unpredictably (see Figure 5.9). The relationship between optimal inventories and sales is

$$F^* = \alpha \cdot S, \; \alpha > 0$$

where F^* refers to the optimal (or desired) level of finished goods. The optimal level of inventories rises with the level of sales (the Greek parameter α is assumed to be positive). And, if there is a deviation of inventories from this optimal relationship, the firm will incur costs.

TABLE 5.5 The Relationship Between Finished Goods Inventories, Production, and Sales

$Y > S$	$\Delta F > 0$
$Y < S$	$\Delta F < 0$
$Y = S$	$\Delta F = 0$

N.B. Y is output, S denotes sales, and ΔF refers to inventory investment.

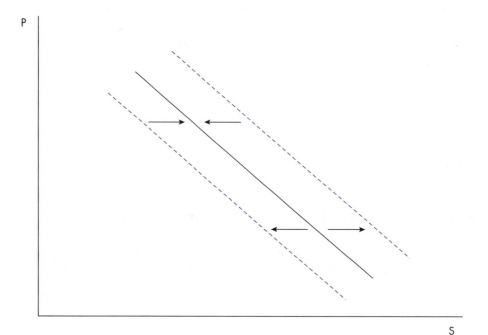

FIGURE 5.9 The Demand Curve Facing the Firm

The firm's demand curve shifts randomly between the dotted lines and these shocks to demand are unpredictable. P is the firm's output price and S refers to sales.

These costs are the stock-out costs that were mentioned above that will induce the firm to try to maintain this optimal relationship between inventories and sales.

The firm can produce more output with its existing factors of production, labor and capital, but doing so leads to higher marginal costs of production. This feature of the model is illustrated in Figure 5.10. In addition, there are costs attached to holding inventories. These are insurance, storage, interest, maintenance costs, and the like that must be borne by the firm if it holds inventories. These costs rise at the margin just as production costs do. A diagram of inventory holding costs would be just like Figure 5.10 except that holding costs would be on the vertical axis and inventories would be on the horizontal axis.

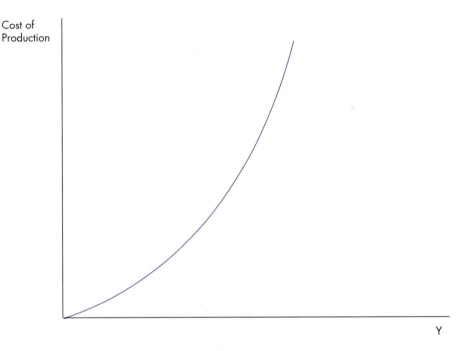

Y

FIGURE 5.10 The Production Costs of the Firm

The costs of producing output rise at the margin in the production-smoothing model of inventories. The slope of the curve rises as output, Y, increases.

The firm is presumed to maximize its profits in choosing the level of inventories to hold. The results of this profit maximization lead to an inventory investment relationship of the form

$$\Delta F = \lambda \cdot (F^* - F),\ 0 < \lambda < 1$$

which is called the **flexible accelerator** model of inventory investment. The model implies that $0 < \lambda < 1$ (the Greek character λ is bounded between zero and unity). This parameter measures the fraction of the gap between desired inventories and the actual level of inventories held by the firm; it determines the **speed of adjustment** of inventories because this parameter measures how rapidly the firm closes the gap between desired and actual inventories. Inventories display partial adjustment because of the restriction on the size of the speed of adjustment (because it is between zero and unity). Inventories adjust slowly because there are costs of adjusting inventories. This is true because of the costs attached to production (see Figure 5.10). Since increasing output raises the stock of inventories, and since the costs of increasing output rise at the margin, then the marginal costs of changing inventories rise. Thus the firm will adjust its finished goods slowly, just as it does for the stock of plant and equipment. If the firm has fewer inventories than it wants to hold in equilibrium, it accumulates them (if $F^* - F > 0$, then $\Delta F > 0$). If the firm holds excess inventories, it reduces its stock (if $F^* - F < 0$, then $\Delta F < 0$). If the firm holds a stock of inventories equal to the desired stock, inventory investment is zero.

The desired stock of inventories, F^*, is determined by two magnitudes: planned sales and the real interest rate. An increase in sales causes the firm to want a higher level of inventories

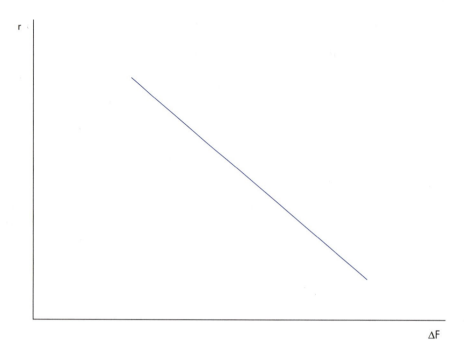

FIGURE 5.11 The Real Interest Rate and Inventory Investment

The diagram illustrates the inverse relationship between the real interest rate, r, and inventory investment, ΔF.

to guard against the costs of stock-outs; thus inventory investment rises. If the real interest rate rises, the opportunity cost of holding inventories rises. The firm foregoes more interest by holding inventories rather than bonds and so will hold a smaller desired stock of inventories. This implies that inventory investment falls when the real interest rate rises.

Figures 5.11 and 5.12 summarize the relationships between sales, the real interest rate, and inventory investment. What should be stressed is that there is a negative relationship between inventory investment and the real interest rate, just as there is between the real interest rate and plant and equipment investment. The real interest rate measures the opportunity cost of investing in inventories of finished goods rather than investing these funds in alternative interest-bearing assets. Equivalently, the real interest rate is the user cost of finished goods inventories.

Thus when we discuss the connection between investment and the real interest rate, we need not distinguish between the two types of investment because the relationships between each type of investment and the real interest rate are qualitatively the same. We will therefore aggregate investment in plant and equipment with inventory investment when we discuss aggregate models of the economy.

How Well Does the Inventory Model Fit the Facts?

The production-smoothing model of inventories has been a popular vehicle for the analysis of inventory behavior but it has been criticized for having implications that do not match up well

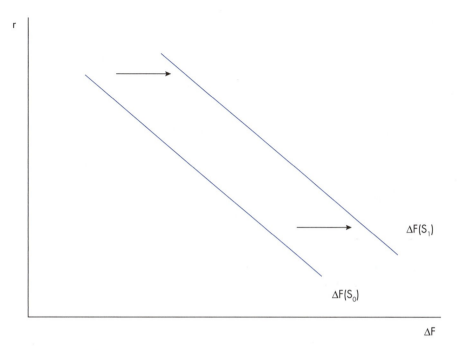

FIGURE 5.12 Sales and Inventory Investment

The diagram illustrates the fact that if sales rise ($S_1 > S_0$), inventory investment, ΔF, will increase.

with empirical evidence. We focus on just one aspect of this criticism: the relationship between the variability of sales and production.

The production-smoothing model implies that sales should be more variable than production is for the firm. The intuition for this finding is easy; it is costly to change production because production costs rise at the margin. So the firm should want to avoid large changes in production that would greatly reduce its profits and this should result in the finding that sales are more variable than production. Thus it should be true that

$$\text{Production Variability} < \text{Sales Variability.}$$

Princeton University economist Alan S. Blinder has suggested that the empirical facts do not support the production-smoothing model of inventories.[13] He constructed measures of sales and production variability, finding that the data often are just the opposite of what is predicted by the production-smoothing model of the inventories (see **Doing Economics**: The Variability of Production and Sales). As a result, a considerable amount of research effort has been put into explaining these departures from the predictions of the model. While there is now some skepticism about the suitability of this model as a description of the actual inventory policies pursued by firms, it still remains the standard framework for the analysis of inventory behavior.

---

13 See Alan S. Blinder, "Can the Production Smoothing Model of Inventory Behavior Be Saved?" *Quarterly Journal of Economics* 101, No. 2 (May 1986), pp. 431–54.

5.7 CONCLUDING REMARKS

Investment is a critical component of macroeconomic models and there has been a great deal of effort devoted to the development of models of the firm that specify the determinants of investment. These models have used the assumption that firms engage in profit maximization over time in making their investment decisions and that firms make their investment decisions in a forward-looking manner. We first examined the behavior of a firm that incurs planning and installation costs attached to investment in plant and equipment, obtaining the important result from this analysis that firms will adjust their capital stocks slowly towards their desired levels. The desired capital stock is that which maximizes the firm's profits. It was found that investment is inversely related to the real user cost of capital. This real user cost reduces to the real interest rate in aggregate models of the economy. We also showed how tax rates and the stock market can affect the investment choices of firms. In our study of inventory investment, the firm was assumed to hold a buffer stock of inventories in the face of fluctuations in output demand. In this model it was found that the real interest rate is the relevant measure of real user cost, and inventory investment is inversely related to the real interest rate. Inventories also are increasing in the level of sales because the firm wants to maintain an optimal relationship between inventories and sales. It does so to avoid the costs of being caught out of stock with no output that can be sold to potential customers. This model predicts that production should be less variable than sales, an implication challenged in applied research.

Doing Economics: The Variability of Production and Sales

The production smoothing model can be tested in various ways. One possibility would be to use statistical methods to test the relationship between the real interest rate and inventory investment. Another way would be to test the implications for the variability of production and sales. This second manner of testing has received a great deal of attention so here we present the numbers that have cast some doubt on the suitability of the production smoothing model of inventories.

The variability of production should be found to be less than the variability of sales if the production-smoothing model is a good approximation to industry data. Below are some actual measures of this variability.

Industry	Production Variability	Sales variability
All Manufacturing	10.22	8.90
Durable Goods	6.23	5.21
Primary Metals	.244	.257
Fabricated Metals	.146	.131
Electrical Machinery	.197	.163
Non-Electrical Machinery	.230	.154
Transportation Equipment	.802	.657

(continued)

Lumber and Wood Products	.0146	.013
Furniture and Fixtures	.0046	.0036
Stone, Clay, and Glass Products	.0098	.0086

Source: Alan S. Blinder, "Can the Production Smoothing Model of Inventory Behavior Be Saved?" *Quarterly Journal of Economics* 101, No. 2 (May 1986), pp. 431–54.

In all but one case, the variability of production exceeds the variability of sales, thus contradicting the implications of the production-smoothing model.

There have been a number of responses to these findings. Some argue that the data used to construct these numbers are low in quality, producing unreliable estimates of these variability measures. Aggregation over firms may also distort tests of this model. But whatever the explanation, some doubt has been cast on the production-smoothing model as a description of actual inventory behavior.

These are the two models of investment that will be part of the foundation for the aggregate models that we study later in the book. They both imply a negative relationship between investment and the real interest rate. This will be a characteristic of the investment relationships found in our aggregate models of the economy.

Key Ideas

- Profit maximization by the firm results in the marginal product of each input in production being set equal to the real factor price of each input.
- Long-run demands for inputs are inversely related to their own real factor input prices.
- Firms bear installation and planning costs attached to acquiring new capital. As a result, they will move slowly towards their desired stock of capital. Net investment in each period is thus a fraction of the gap between desired and actual levels of capital.
- Net capital investment is inversely related to the real user cost of capital.
- The real user cost of capital is $P_K \cdot (r + \delta)/P$ where P_K is the purchase price of capital, r is the real interest rate, δ is the depreciation rate, and P is the price of the firm's output.
- If the firm pays a corporate income tax rate, this tax rate will be a component of the user cost of capital.
- Investment can also be viewed as dependent upon Tobin's q, the stock market value of the firm relative to its replacement cost. q is above unity when the firm expands, it is less than unity when it contracts, and it equals unity when the firm is in equilibrium.
- The production-smoothing model of inventories assumes that firms want to avoid changing production because it is costly to do so. As a result, they move slowly towards their desired stock of inventories.
- The production-smoothing model implies that production should be less variable than sales, a prediction at variance with empirical evidence.

Key Terms

Desired Stock of
Capital

Production Function

Diminishing
Returns

Gross Investment

Gross Production
Function

Speed of
Adjustment

Average q

Work-in-Process
Inventories

Stock-Out

Production to Stock
Adjustment Costs

Marginal Product
of Capital

Marginal Revenue

Net Investment

Net Production
Function

Depreciation Rate

Finished Goods
Inventories

Production
Smoothing

Flexible Accelerator

Production to Order

User Cost of Capital

Price-Taker

Value of the Marginal
Product of Capital

Replacement
Investment

Partial Adjustment

Corporate Tax Rate

Materials
Inventories

Buffer Stock

Speed of Adjustment

Marginal Product
of Labor

Marginal q

Questions for Study and Review

Review Exercises

1. What determines the desired stock of capital held by the firm?
2. What is it about the firm's technology that induces a stock-producing firm to smooth production?
3. Why doesn't the firm immediately increase its capital stock to its desired level when it holds less capital than it wishes to hold in equilibrium?
4. Why does inventory investment depend upon the real interest rate?
5. Suppose that the marginal physical product of capital exceeds the real user cost of capital. Will net investment be positive or negative? Explain.

Thought Exercises

1. Suppose that the firm's marginal adjustment costs increase. What will happen to the parameter measuring the speed of adjustment of the firm's capital stock towards the desired stock of capital?
2. Suppose that the marginal cost of production rises for a firm producing to stock. What will happen to the speed of adjustment of the firm's finished goods to its desired level?
3. How does serial persistence in the production of output arise in the neoclassical model of investment by the firm?
4. How does a change in the marginal corporate income tax rate affect Tobin's q?

Suppose that the stock-producing firm experiences fluctuations in factor input prices. How does this fact affect the relationship between the variability of production and sales for a stock-producing firm?

Numerical Exercises

1. A production function is given by $Y = F(K, L) = 200 \cdot K^{0.5} \cdot L^{0.5}$, where L is the current level of employment and K measures the current stock of capital. Let $L = 100$ workers. Verify numerically that the marginal product of capital (MP_K) increases when employment increases to 150 workers, keeping the capital stock constant at 50 units.

2. Suppose that the marginal product of capital (MP_K) is given by $552 \cdot K^{-0.8} \cdot L^{0.6}$. The price of the firm's output is $100. If the real interest rate and depreciation rate are each 2 percent, and if the purchase price of capital goods is $1,250, find the desired stock of capital when the firm uses 250 units of labor.

3. Suppose that the real interest rate and depreciation rate are each 3 percent. If the purchase price of capital goods is $5,000, compute the nominal user cost of capital. Now using the same information, assume that the corporate tax rate is 25 percent and compute the real user cost of capital when the price of the firm's output is $100.

4. Let the marginal product of capital (MP_K) be $10 \cdot K^{-0.6} \cdot L^{0.6}$. The price of the firm's output is $5. If the real interest rate and the depreciation rate are each 2 percent and if the price of capital goods is $3,000, find the desired stock of capital when the firm uses 2,500 units of labor.

5. Solve for a firm's long-run equilibrium values of labor and capital using the following information.

   MP_K: $150 \cdot K^{-0.7} \cdot L^{0.4}$ MP_L: $200K^{0.3} \cdot L^{-0.6}$ Money Wage Rate: $50
   Purchase Price of Capital: $75,000   Output Price: $20
   Real Interest Rate: .02   Depreciation Rate: .01

6. Suppose that the firm currently has 200,000 units of capital and that the desired stock of capital is 300,000 units. If the speed of adjustment is 10 percent per period, compute net investment for five periods.

7. Assume a firm that sells 1,000 units of output at a price of $1,000 per unit, facing a real interest rate of 5 percent, and a depreciation rate of 0 percent. The purchase price of capital goods is $500 and the marginal adjustment costs are estimated to be $5 \cdot (\Delta K)^{0.2}$. If the marginal physical product of capital (MP_K) is equal to $5 \cdot K^{-0.5}$, should the firm add another unit of capital to its existing capital stock of 35,000 units? How would your answer change if the firm has a depreciation rate of 10 percent?

Data Exercise

1. Go to the St. Louis Federal Reserve Bank FRED database and collect data on constant-dollar gross investment for the U.S. covering the period 1955 to 2008. Also collect data from the same source on the real interest rate for this same time period using the Bank Prime Loan Rate and the GDP deflator. Describe the behavior of each time series over the business cycle. Do the two series seem to be related in the way that the theory of investment suggests?

For further questions, multiple choice quizzes, and weblinks related to this chapter, visit www.routledge.com/textbooks/rossana

References and Suggestions for Further Reading

Blinder, A.S. (1986) "Can the Production Smoothing Model of Inventory Behavior Be Saved?" *Quarterly Journal of Economics* 101 (2) (May): 431–54.

Hall, R.E. and Jorgenson, D.W. (1967) "Tax Policy and Investment Behavior," *American Economic Review* 57 (3) (June): 391–414.

Hayashi, F. (1982) "Tobin's Marginal q and Average q: A Neoclassical Interpretation," *Econometrica* 50 (1) (January): 213–24.

Jorgenson, D.W. (1963) "Capital Theory and Investment Behavior," *American Economic Association Papers and Proceedings* 53 (3) (June): 247–59.

Jorgenson, D.W. (1996) "Empirical Studies of Depreciation," *Economic Inquiry* 34 (1) (January): 24–42.

Maccini, L.J. and Blinder, A.S. (1991) "The Resurgence of Inventory Research: What Have We Learned?" *Journal of Economic Surveys* 5 (4): 291–328.

Tobin, J. (1969) "A General Equilibrium Approach to Monetary Theory," *Journal of Money, Credit, and Banking* 1 (1) (February): 15–29.

Chapter 6

Government

LEARNING OBJECTIVES

This chapter considers the role of government in the market economy. We begin our discussion by considering some basic reasons why there is a role for government in the economic system. We will then have a look at some data to get a sense of how large the government sector is in the U.S. economy. There will be a discussion of the tax code and we will examine the budget constraint that the government must obey. Finally we will look at the difference between the deficit and the stock of government debt and we will discuss the possible connection between government deficits and inflation. Here are some specific questions that we will ask.

- How big is government spending relative to the entire economy?

- What aspect of the income tax code affects economic incentives?

- What is the constraint on its activities that the government must obey?

- Is there any connection between government spending and inflation?

Almost every facet of economic life is affected by the government and no capitalistic society could function without a government. The task of this chapter is to describe why this is the case and to describe the framework through which the government affects the functioning of the macroeconomic system.

We begin the chapter with a brief discussion of the reasons why there is a need for government in a capitalistic society. These reasons are really related to microeconomics but we will also discuss those aspects of government activities that are of interest for macroeconomics. An important topic in this discussion will be the tax code where we discuss how tax payments are tied to income and what is meant by a progressive tax. You will also learn about the tax rates contained in the tax code and how these tax rates can affect your behavior. We then move on to a discussion about **government expenditures** and tax receipts, looking at actual measures of government expenditures and receipts and observing their behavior over time.

An important topic follows this discussion. The constraint that must be obeyed by the government, describing the sources and uses of the government's funds, will be the next item on our agenda. This constraint will also be written in present value form that we can use to describe two different types of government spending that have very different effects upon households. We then will discuss the manner in which the government finances its activities (taxes or bonds) and whether these two alternatives are equivalent in their effects upon households. We also examine an important idea about the way in which taxes are set that we can use to determine how a government might choose to finance its spending. Our final topic for discussion is the relationship between the **stock of government debt** and deficits and we will indicate why there may be a relationship between deficits and the rate of price inflation in the economy.

When you have mastered the material in this chapter, you should have a clear understanding of why a government is essential to a capitalistic society and how the government finances its activities, and be prepared to use the material in this chapter to study how the government can affect the aggregate economy when it changes its spending and tax policies.

6.1 THE ROLE OF GOVERNMENT

Public Finance is the branch of economics where the role of government is studied in much more detail than is typically done in macroeconomics. But here we want to sketch the most important reasons why a government is essential to a modern society and what aspects of government behavior are of interest for macroeconomics.

No capitalistic economic system could function without a *legal system*. A crucial role of government is therefore to enforce the elements of a legal system, protecting the lives and property of its citizens by maintaining a criminal justice system and enforcing individual property rights. This is a fundamental reason why a government is necessary to the existence of capitalism. But there is an additional role for government that is due to the peculiar nature of certain kinds of goods, requiring that these goods be provided by government.

Goods known as **public goods** may not be provided at the appropriate levels in a market economy by private firms because these goods have certain characteristics that involve the problem of **free riders**. National defense is the classic example of a service involving the problem of free riders, resulting in the under-provision of a system of defense, if defense were provided by the private sector. If your neighbor signs up for defense services, you would have an incentive to understate your preferences for defense and not buy defense services. The reason is that, because of your proximity to your neighbor, you would get the benefits of a defense system simply because your neighbor has them (you are a free rider). Since there almost certainly will be individuals who will understate their preferences for defense in this way, a market economy will not produce socially optimal amounts of public goods, requiring that the government provide such goods.

An additional reason for governmental provision of certain goods is **externalities**. An externality refers to the activity of one individual that affects the welfare of others. Smoking can damage the health of one who smokes but the second-hand smoke inhaled by others can damage their health. As another example, government will provide (or hire a firm to provide) the collection of trash even though the private sector could provide the service by contracting directly with the public. The reason the government collects the trash is easy to establish; if a person does not have their trash removed, public health will deteriorate and so the government provides the service. Thus governments provide services that involve significant externalities when those goods are consumed (or not consumed) by the public.

Finally the government may **redistribute income** to those at the lower end of the income distribution. This can take the form of lower (or even no) taxes for some individuals or perhaps the direct provision of goods. Food stamps are an example of a poverty program where goods are given to low-income households. In many countries, there is a **progressive tax system** where the tax rate on before-tax income rises with the level of before-tax income.

In macroeconomics, we are concerned with the effects of government expenditures upon the aggregate economy, the economic impact of alternative ways in which the government finances its spending, and the incentive effects of government taxation in the aggregate economy.

Government expenditures are a component of Gross Domestic Product and variations in these expenditures can have an impact upon the level of output produced in the economy. These expenditures can be used as a stabilization tool, being manipulated by policymakers to respond to the economy's cyclical fluctuations. Thus we will be interested in knowing how variations in government expenditures will affect the level of output produced and how these expenditures might be used in stabilizing the economy.

Government expenditures must be financed and there are two ways in which this may be accomplished: **tax revenues** and bond issue.[1] The government levies taxes on households and

---

1 Strictly speaking, this is not quite correct because it is possible for the central bank to buy up the bonds issued by the government such that, in effect, money is used to finance part of the government deficit. We will say more about this issue when we discuss economic policy later in this chapter.

firms, using these receipts to finance its spending. But it often happens that the government spends more than its tax receipts and so it will also issue bonds (government debt), selling these bonds to the public and then using these borrowed funds to pay for some of its expenditures. Changes in tax rates or the stock of bonds may have very different effects upon the economy. We will study the economic effects of using either of these financing methods.

Finally, government taxation affects the incentives that households and firms face in making their economic decisions. The government sets the **marginal tax rate** (MTR) on wage income and the returns to saving.[2] The definition of the MTR was given in Chapter 2 and is given below for convenience.

Definition of the Marginal Tax Rate (MTR)

■ The marginal tax rate is the additional tax collected by the government on an additional dollar of income before taxes (or pre-tax income).

The MTR could be applied to nominal or real incomes (this is discussed further below). As you saw in Chapter 4, this tax rate affects the returns from savings; in Chapter 8, you will see that this tax rate affects the labor supply choices of households. You will also discover that the level of Potential GDP, the level of output produced when the aggregate economy is in equilibrium, is affected by this tax rate. The economic effects of changes in the MTR are often at the heart of debates about the efficacy of cutting the MTR paid by households.

Average and Marginal Tax Rates

If we wish to use an income tax code that incorporates an MTR, we will represent the tax code using the simple formula

$$\text{Tax receipts: } T = T_0 + t{\cdot}Y, \, 0 < t < 1$$

where T denotes tax receipts, t is the marginal tax rate (MTR), T_0 is an intercept term interpreted below, and Y is pre-tax (or before-tax) real income. There is a concept, related to the MTR, that we will have occasion to use. The **average tax rate** is defined below.

Definition of the Average Tax

■ The average tax is the ratio of tax payments to before-tax real income.

Using the tax schedule above gives us

$$\text{Average Tax: } T/Y = T_0/Y + t.$$

---

2 The government could also tax household wealth and/or consumption but we will focus on income taxes since they are the most important type of tax revenue for our purposes in this book.

Notice that the average tax rate can vary while the marginal tax rate, t, is fixed. This is going to be a very convenient property when we discuss a number of issues that will interest us. For example, when we discuss the effects of taxes on labor supply, it will turn out that the response of labor supply to a change in a tax rate is quite different depending upon whether the average or marginal tax rate changes. We will also refer to variations in T_0 as changes in **lump-sum taxes**, or taxes independent of income.

The U.S. income tax code (and that in most industrialized economies) is of course much more complicated than the simple schedule described above. The tax code that we will use has just one tax bracket and a tax code like this is called a **flat tax** (see **Doing Economics**: The Flat Tax). The tax code actually in use in the U.S. has more than one MTR based upon the taxable income of an individual or household because the tax code is progressive. Further, the intercept T_0 can, in principle, be positive or negative. If it is negative, we would have a simple example of a **negative income tax**. In such a tax code, if taxable income is below a certain level, the household receives a payment from the government rather than making a payment to the government (See **Doing Economics**: The Progressive Tax and Indexation).

Doing Economics: The Flat Tax

Industrialized economies have tax codes that usually tax both household and corporate income. These tax codes are usually anything but simple. Regarding personal taxes, it is often the case that certain types of income are taxed differently than other sources of income. There may be reductions in taxable income for certain kinds of expenditures. A complete description of a tax code may require many volumes of books sitting on library shelves to be completely described.

A flat tax has been proposed as a replacement for these complicated tax structures. In such a tax scheme, there would be only one tax rate applied equally to all individual taxpayers. There would be no special preferences for certain types of economic behavior or activities. The tax schedule would be simple enough to be filed using a postcard.

Proponents of such a system argue that the system saves substantial amounts of time and money for households, improving their welfare. Such a system removes the double taxation of saving and investment, thus increasing economic growth. And it would be an inherently fair system since it would treat all taxpayers equally. Finally, the system would be easy to administer since a simple tax system is easy to enforce, improving tax compliance by individuals.

However others might argue that the flat tax is undesirable because is not progressive and so does not require those with higher incomes to shoulder a greater burden for financing government. Further there are those who would argue that it is a proper role for government to encourage or discourage economic activities through the tax code for political or social reasons.

Clearly such an extreme overhaul of a tax code remains controversial. For further discussion, see Robert E. Hall and Alvin Rabushka, *The Flat Tax*, 1995 Second Edition, Hoover Institution Press and Stanford University Press.

Now we will have a look at some data on government expenditures and tax receipts. This will allow you to learn about the sources and uses of the government's funds. You will also see some interesting patterns in time series graphs of this data.

6.2 GOVERNMENT EXPENDITURES AND TAX RECEIPTS

Government has an impact upon the economic system partly through its spending and tax schedule and its implied tax payments. In this section, we examine these budgetary items at the federal, as well as state and local, levels. We begin with government expenditures in the National Income and Product Accounts (NIPA) and then discuss measures more comprehensive than those in the NIPA accounts.

Government Expenditures in the NIPA Accounts

Table 6.1 provides data for **government consumption** and investment appearing in the National Income and Product Accounts (NIPA). The data are in billions of dollars and include data for federal and state and local governments. Government consumption expenditures refer to the nondurable goods and services produced by the government and consumed by the general public. Gross investment expenditures by the government refers to the durable capital goods that the government provides to the public whose services are consumed by them; these are services such as those from highways, schools, and military equipment.

Underlying this data is the view that government is a producer of goods and services that are consumed by the public. But unlike goods produced by the private sector, there are no

TABLE 6.1 Government NIPA Expenditures, Billions of Dollars, 2008

		Share of GDP
Government Consumption and Gross Investment	2882.4	20.2
Federal	1071.9	7.5
National Defense	734.9	5.2
Consumption Expenditures	639.7	
Gross Investment	95.2	
Nondefense	337.0	2.4
Consumption Expenditures	292.2	
Gross Investment	44.8	
State and Local	1810.4	12.7
Consumption Expenditures	1454.4	
Gross investment	356.0	

Source: Bureau of Economic Analysis Table 3.9.5 (www.bea.gov)

markets for these goods, raising the problem of how one might measure the market value of these goods and services. The government's solution to this problem is to measure the market value of these goods by the cost of producing them and so the compensation of employees, the value of any intermediate goods purchased, and the consumption of durable capital goods are used as the basis for these measures of government-provided goods and services.

The table provides U.S. data in nominal terms for the year 2008 and it also provides some information on government spending as a share of GDP. About 20 percent of GDP is made up of the services provided by government. State and Local spending is considerably larger as a share of GDP (12.7 percent) than is Federal spending (7.5 percent). Defense spending at the federal level is a smaller share of GDP as compared to nondefense spending. Using this data in time series graphs also reveals some interesting trends. Figure 6.1 provides a time series plot of government spending shares of U.S. GDP. Panel A of the figure reveals a downward trend in the total government (the sum of federal and state and local) share of GDP over most of the time period in the graph. There is a mild positive trend in State and Local spending over this time period and a declining share at the Federal level. Over the entire 1947–2008 period, total government spending averaged 20 percent as a share of GDP, with Federal and State and Local spending each averaging about 10 percent of GDP.

Doing Economics: The Progressive Tax and Indexation

We will always assume there is only one MTR whenever we allow taxes to depend on income. We will also assume that taxes are levied on real, as opposed to nominal, income before taxes. As a matter of fact, there is more than one tax rate at which income is taxed and the tax code currently does not quite tax real income. Consider the diagram overleaf.

The intercept term for this tax schedule is negative, which illustrates the idea of a negative income tax. Once taxable income is below point A, a household receives a payment from the government rather than pay any tax to the government.

A progressive tax code is one where the tax rate on pre-tax income rises with pre-tax income. This tax code embodies the notion that the richer the household, the more it should pay to support government activities. The diagram illustrates a tax code with two brackets (15 percent and 25 percent). Thus income in the range between points A and B is taxed at an MTR of 15 percent and income above point B is taxed at a 25 percent MTR.

When the tax code taxes nominal income (PY), it is said that taxes are not **indexed** to the price level. In such a tax code, inflation causes tax payments to rise faster than inflation. Imagine that your income before taxes puts you in the region between points A and B so that your MTR is .15. Now suppose that the price level doubles and that your nominal income doubles. You can't buy any more goods than you could before prices doubled but your MTR could rise to .25 if your new nominal taxable income puts you into the 25 percent tax bracket. Part of your income is now being taxed at the rate of 25 percent. This phenomenon is known as **bracket-creep**. Thus your tax payments rise by more than the rate of inflation because inflation has pushed you into a higher tax bracket. One aspect of the tax changes enacted

(continued)

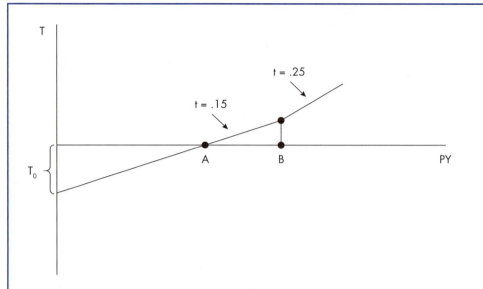

Under President Reagan in 1981 was that the tax code stopped taxing nominal income in large part, bringing the U.S. closer to an indexed tax code. Capital gains are still not adjusted for inflation, one reason why the tax code is not completely indexed to the price level.

Panel B of the figure describes changes in the composition of federal spending. Regarding the federal government, there has been a distinct shift in the mix between defense and nondefense expenditures; defense has declined while nondefense has increased. Finally, there has been an evident shift in the mix between federal and state and local spending; as a share of total government spending, federal spending has been declining while state and local spending has been increasing.

Although this data reveals interesting information, it is not suitable for a discussion about the federal government's deficit as you will see shortly. For this reason, broader measures of government activities are required; government outlays and receipts are necessary and the data are contained in Table 6.2. The table also contains shares of total expenditures and receipts.

Government Receipts

The sources of funds supporting government expenditures are listed at the top of the table. Governments receive revenue through personal and corporate income taxes. At the federal level, personal taxes are 43 percent of total receipts but are only 17 percent of receipts at the state and local level. Corporate tax payments are much smaller shares of total receipts. The federal government levies taxes on currently produced goods such as excise taxes and it taxes imported commodities; these amount to 4 percent of revenues. Sales taxes on goods consumed by households are almost half of the revenues received by state and local governments. The federal government receives a small amount of tax revenue from

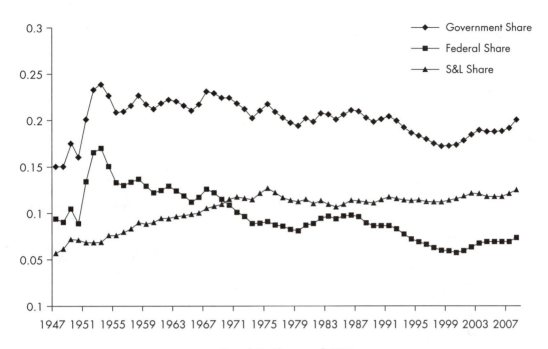

Panel A: Shares of GDP
Source: Bureau of Economic Analysis Tables 1.1.5 and 3.9.5

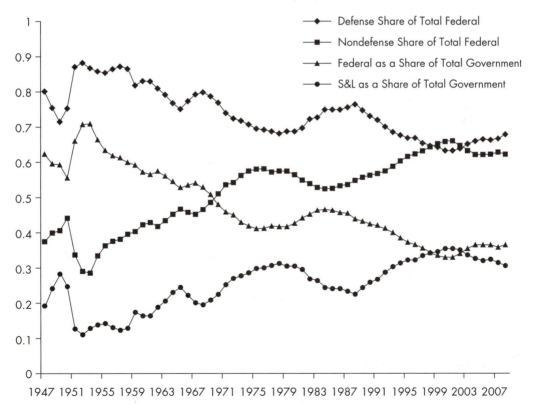

Panel B: Shares of Government Spending
Source: Bureau of Economic Analysis Tables 1.1.5 and 3.9.5

FIGURE 6.1 Government Expenditure Shares

TABLE 6.2 Government Total Receipts and Outlays, 2008

	Federal		State & Local	
	Billions of $	Share	Billions of $	Share
Receipts				
Personal Taxes	1127.2	.43	333.4	.17
Corporate Income Taxes	291.1	.11	47.6	.02
Taxes on Production and Imports	96.2	.04	937.6	.47
Taxes from the Rest of the World	15.5	.01	NA	NA
Contributions for Government Social Insurance	972.2	.37	23.7	.01
Income Receipts on Assets	31.8	.01	103.7	.05
Current Transfer Receipts	39.3	.02	496.7	.25
Current Surplus of Government Enterprises	–0.5	.00	–7.6	0.0
Outlays				
Consumption	931.9	.29	1454.4	.72
Transfer Payments	1806.4	.56	455.8	.23
Gross Investment	140.0		356.0	
Interest Payments	308.2	.10	102.0	.05
Subsidies	47.7	.02	3.0	.00

Sources: Bureau of Economic Analysis (www.bea.gov) Tables 3.2 and 3.3.

foreign residents but it receives a substantial amount of its receipts in the form of social insurance payments, such as payments for **social security**, hospital insurance, and unemployment insurance. There are receipts in the form of interest, dividends, and rents. State and Local governments receive grants-in-aid from the federal government, called transfer receipts. Finally, government enterprises may generate a net profit (or loss) from their activities.

Government Outlays

Outlays measure all uses of government revenues. It is thus a broader measure than government NIPA spending since it includes, for example, transfer payments made by the government. Data on the components of government expenditures are given in the bottom part of Table 6.2. Government consumption (29 percent of total expenditures at the federal level and 72 percent at the state and local levels) is the same as the government consumption listed in the NIPA accounts above. Governments make transfer payments to individuals, such as Social Security payments and, in the case of the federal government, grants-in-aid are made to state and local governments (56 percent of total expenditures at the federal level and 23 percent at the state and local levels). Governments make interest payments to individuals holding the bonds they have issued. Governments also make direct subsidy payments to firms.

Figure 6.2 provides some time series graphs of total U.S. government outlays and its components as shares of GDP during the post-World War II period. The figure shows that total outlays and transfers have been rising as shares of GDP. Interest payments by the government seem to be fluctuating about a mild positive trend over this period. NIPA spending (consumption plus investment) appears to have a mild downward trend.

Now that we have discussed the revenues and spending of the government, we can move on to consider the constraint that these expenditures and revenues must obey, a topic of great importance in understanding the behavior of government since this constraint determines what will happen to the stock of government debt over time.

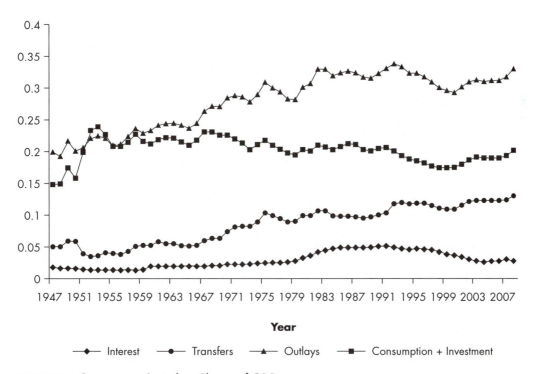

FIGURE 6.2 Government Spending Shares of GDP

Source: Bureau of Economic Analysis (www.bea.gov) Table 3.1

6.3 THE GOVERNMENT BUDGET CONSTRAINT (GBC)

An important concept associated with government activity is the **Government Budget Constraint** (GBC), an accounting relationship listing, in tabular or equation form, the sources and uses of funds by the government. Table 6.3 lists each of these items.

The uses of government revenues are NIPA spending (G), interest payments on outstanding government bonds ($i \cdot B_{-1}$), the product of the interest rate (i) and the stock of government bonds at the end of last period (B_{-1}), and **net transfers** (TR) made to individuals by the government. If the government does pure redistribution (for every dollar it takes from one taxpayer it pays out a dollar to another), then TR = 0. If the government makes payments in excess of what it gets from some of its taxpayers, TR > 0. This is a simplified version of the outlays and receipts discussion above. G here corresponds to government consumption plus investment from the NIPA accounts, and we carry along interest payments as we did earlier in the chapter, but TR consolidates everything else, including all of the government's transfer payments, into one concept. Government outlays are the sum of NIPA spending, interest payments, and net transfers, and are the uses of government funds.

The sources of the government's revenues are tax receipts (T) plus any bonds that the government issues to borrow funds. The term $B - B_{-1}$ gives the change in the stock of government bonds outstanding between the current and last period. The stock of bonds can either rise or fall for reasons described below.

We can write the GBC as an equation, consolidating all of the spending and revenues of the government into one expression. This is given below.

$$G + i \cdot B_{-1} + TR = T + B - B_{-1}$$

The left side of this equation lists the uses of the government's revenues (spending, interest payments, and net transfers) while the right side lists the sources of the government's expenditures (tax revenues and bond issue). Using this expression, the government's surplus or deficit can be defined simply by moving tax revenues to the left side of the equation above. This gives us the following definitions.

$$\text{Deficit: } G + i \cdot B_{-1} + TR - T > 0, \Rightarrow B - B_{-1} > 0$$

$$\text{Surplus: } G + i \cdot B_{-1} + TR - T < 0, \Rightarrow B - B_{-1} < 0$$

TABLE 6.3 The Government Budget Constraint

	Uses of Funds		Sources of Funds
G	Government NIPA Expenditures	T	Tax Receipts
TR	Net Transfers	$B - B_{-1}$	Bond Issue (Retirement)
$i \cdot B_{-1}$	Interest Payments		

Note: In the table, G is government NIPA expenditures, TR is net transfers, i refers to the interest rate on government debt, B is the stock of government debt, and T denotes tax revenues.

If the government finds that its spending exceeds its tax revenues, it is running a deficit. Then if it wishes to avoid reducing its spending or raising taxes, it will need to issue bonds to the public, borrowing funds to maintain its current spending and tax policies. In this case, $B - B_{-1} > 0$. If it issues bonds, it must pay interest to induce people to hold its bonds. Thus the term $i \cdot B_{-1}$ (the product of the interest rate and the stock of debt last period) measures the interest payments that the government must pay on its outstanding stock of bonds. If the government is spending less than its revenues, it is running a surplus and it will retire debt (buy back bonds issued in the past). In this case, $B - B_{-1} < 0$.

Who holds this debt? It can be private individuals, either domestic or foreign, foreign governments, and **central banks** can also hold this debt. When we discuss the Federal Reserve Board (the Fed), the U.S. central bank, you will see that the Fed will buy or sell government bonds when it carries out its monetary policies. Why the Fed would want to buy or sell government debt is an important subject that we will discuss extensively when we study economic policy.

This measure of the deficit contains what are known as on-budget and **off-budget** items. An off-budget item is one that is listed separately from the rest of the government budget. The best-known, but not the only, off-budget program is the Social Security system. The actual size of the government's surplus or deficit (or, equivalently, the amount of borrowing that the government must do) is importantly affected by including off-budget items (see **Doing Economics**: Social Security and the Federal Government Budget).

Doing Economics: Social Security and the Federal Government Budget

The government budget treats the Social Security System as an off-budget item, meaning that it is listed separately in the government's budget. To determine the need of the federal government to borrow from the public, the Social Security System must be combined with the remainder of the government's spending and tax revenues (both on-budget and other off-budget items) to arrive at the *unified budget surplus or deficit*.

The Social Security System generates both off-budget revenues and expenditures. The revenues comprise payments from workers and firms equal to 12.4 percent of earnings, split evenly between workers and firms. There are additional, and much smaller, revenues that arise from income tax payments on the Social Security earnings of some individuals receiving Social Security payments. The expenditures arise from making payments to Social Security recipients. The government maintains an accounting mechanism called the Social Security Trust Fund, using it to keep track of payments and expenditures in the program. There are no assets in the trust fund, only bookkeeping entries. The government spends the excess of payments into the Social Security System over payments made to Social Security recipients, promising to repay the funds that have been spent. The size of the trust fund at a given instant of time is determined by the whole history of payments received from workers and firms plus credited interest less the payments made to Social Security recipients. The government also maintains other trust funds, such as one associated with the Medicare System.

(continued)

The **unified budget** contains all of the on-budget and off-budget revenues and expenditures of the federal government. The extent to which the size of the reported deficit or surplus is affected by the off-budget items can be seen from the data below for 1995–2004.

Surplus (+) or Deficit (–) Millions of Dollars

	Unified	On-Budget	Off-Budget
1995	–146274	–205829	61298
1996	–110891	–182517	71084
1997	–2446	–91667	89427
1998	53932	–21360	76089
1999	155644	–6680	162325
2000	255008	136376	118633
2001	92123	–101564	195418
2002	–231885	–397845	167176
2003	–396680	–556332	157274
2004	–400745	–559333	158590

Source: U.S. Department of treasury, Monthly Treasury Statement

The unified budget was in surplus for four years (1998–2001); if we remove off-budget items and look only at the on-budget deficit or surplus, only in 2000 was there a budget surplus.

The Social Security Trust Fund has an important role in determining future benefits paid out of the system. The Congressional Budget Office (CBO) currently expects that around the year 2016, payments into the Social Security Trust Fund will be below expenditures out of the fund with this deficit growing into the future. All else the same, the government's deficit will be rising (or its surplus declining) as the Social Security deficit grows (or its surplus declines) and the government repays the borrowings from the Social Security Trust Fund. As the trust fund declines and is finally exhausted in the future, payments from the Social Security System will need to fall to match the payments into the system.

Having defined the government's budget, we now want to ask how it can be affected by the business cycle.

The Budget and the Business Cycle

One useful insight into the behavior of the government's budget is that it is affected by the state of the economy. The reason is that the government's revenues (tax receipts) and spending depend upon the level of output or income in the economy. To see this, consider a simplified government budget expression given below.

$$G - T_0 - t \cdot Y$$

Here we ignore net transfers and bond interest (or, equivalently, we include them in G) and portray the tax code using a flat tax with just one MTR. Suppose that the government is running a balanced budget $(G - T_0 - t \cdot Y = 0)$. Then if the economy enters a recession, output (income) will fall. As a result, the government's tax revenues decline and, for a given level of government spending, the government runs a deficit $(G - T_0 - t \cdot Y > 0)$. An economic boom would generate a surplus $(G - T_0 - t \cdot Y < 0)$ because incomes and tax receipts would rise. Thus the government's surplus or deficit is affected by the cyclical state of the economy. In addition, government spending is affected by the business cycle. For example, a recession will result in worker layoffs and the government's expenditures for unemployment compensation will rise. Thus both spending and tax revenues depend upon the state of the business cycle.

For these reasons, the actual surplus or deficit does not necessarily provide an accurate picture of the government's intentions. The President and Congress may be trying to balance the budget but may not be able to do so because of the business cycle. For this reason, there is another definition of the government's deficit or surplus that removes the effects of the business cycle, presumably giving a more accurate picture of the government's intentions.

The **full-employment deficit (surplus)** is defined as

$$(G + i \cdot B_{-1} + TR - T)^{FE}.$$

In this definition, all measures of government spending and tax receipts are constructed assuming that real GDP is at its potential level; this is what is meant by the superscript, FE, in the above expression. Potential GDP is the level of output occurring when the economy is at full employment equilibrium. By definition, in equilibrium, the economy is not in a boom or recession and so the government's budget is being measured without any of the effects of the business cycle.

Figure 6.3 provides a graph of the actual and full employment surplus (deficit) covering the period 1962 to 2008 provided by the Congressional Budget Office (CBO). With the exceptions of 1998 through 2001, deficits in nominal dollars have occurred since 1962 whether these are measured by the actual or full-employment measures of the deficit. Note also that the graph illustrates the relative difference between the two budget measures in one recession and a boom period.

In the graph, a recession is denoted by the two vertical lines, marking the recession beginning in July 1981 and ending in November 1982 as determined by the National Bureau of Economic Research (NBER). Using these NBER reference dates, the cyclically adjusted (or full employment) deficit was smaller than the actual deficit, reflecting the effects of the recession. During the period spanning 1998 through 2001 denoted by two vertical lines, the economy was booming and the reverse was the case; there was a budget surplus and the actual deficit was smaller than the deficit at full employment (see Figure 6.3). Figure 6.4 provides a somewhat different perspective on the actual and full-employment deficits. This figure plots the same two budget concepts but now it is done relative to GDP. Thus the figure measures the deficit relative to the size of the overall economy. The reason for looking at this alternative measure is that most economists would argue that if the deficit has an impact upon the economy, it will be if it is large relative to the economy as a whole. Thus a $10 billion deficit has effects in a $20 billion economy that may be quite different than a $10 billion deficit would have in a trillion-dollar economy. A deficit is measured as a negative ratio in the figure.

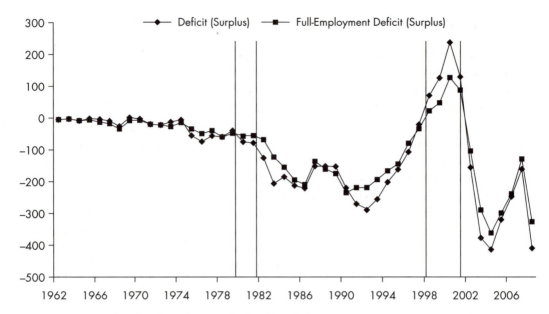

FIGURE 6.3 Actual and Full-Employment Deficit (Surplus)

Source: The Cyclically-Adjusted and Standardized Budget Measures," October 20008, Congressional Budget Office

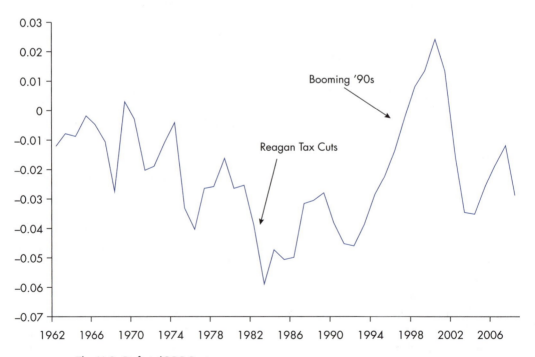

FIGURE 6.4 The U.S. Deficit/GDP Ratio

Source: St. Louis Federal Reserve Bank FRED Database

The deficit measured in this way reveals two interesting patterns. The deficit was rising both in dollar terms and relative to the economy as a whole during the 1980s, reflecting the tax cuts instituted under President Reagan. In the 1990s, a decade of above-average economic growth, the deficit was declining relative to the economy as a whole, as well as in dollar terms.

In view of the fact that the U.S. has been running nominal deficits for such a long time, there are individuals who call for a balanced-budget amendment to the U.S. Constitution. Many economists oppose a balanced-budget restriction, believing that such an amendment would exacerbate business cycle fluctuations (see **Doing Economics**: A Balanced Budget Amendment).

The Present-Value Form of the GBC

Any economic model must include some sort of constraint upon government expenditures that describes the choices over time of government spending, taxes, and debt issue. For the purposes of the economic models that we build later in the book, we can write an alternative form of the government budget constraint, implied by the GBC above, illustrating the overall constraint on government spending in a form useful for economic analysis. Here is this definition.

Doing Economics: A Balanced Budget Amendment

There are individuals who believe that the government should run a balanced budget whereas most economists would argue that the government should run deficits in recessions and surpluses in boom periods, thereby running a balanced budget when measured over the business cycle. The reasons that economists take this position are easily seen by looking at the government's likely budget positions in recessions and boom periods.

$$\text{Recession: } G + i \cdot B_{-1} + TR - T > 0, \Rightarrow B - B_{-1} > 0$$
$$\text{Boom: } G + i \cdot B_{-1} + TR - T < 0, \Rightarrow B - B_{-1} < 0$$

Now ask what the government would need to do when it finds itself in either of these situations. In recessions, the government would be required to cut spending or raise tax rates. You will see later in the book that these actions are likely to make a recession worse than it would otherwise be. The government's actions in a recession would cause output to decline further below Potential GDP. In a boom, the government would need to cut tax rates and/or raise spending, actions likely to make output rise even more above Potential GDP. Thus the swings in the business cycle would be enlarged by a balanced budget amendment (the depth of the decline in real GDP during a recession and the size of the increase in real GDP during a boom) and so economists often recommend surpluses during booms, deficits during recessions, and balanced budgets when output is at its potential level.

Definition

■ The government budget constraint in present value form states that the present value of spending must equal the present value of taxes.

This formula for this definition is

$$\frac{G_1}{1+r} + \frac{G_2}{(1+r)^2} + \frac{G_3}{(1+r)^3} + \cdots = \frac{T_1}{1+r} + \frac{T_2}{(1+r)^2} + \frac{T_3}{(1+r)^3} + \cdots$$

where G refers to real government expenditures, T denotes real tax revenues, and r is the **real interest rate**. We will refer to this formula as the **intertemporal GBC**. In this present value formula, we are assuming that there is an infinite horizon that is appropriate for discounting the government's spending and tax revenues because there is no good reason to assume a finite horizon for the government's existence. Written in this form, it is evident that the government is under no requirement to balance its budget period by period. It can run deficits for a time as long as they are offset by surpluses in such a way that the present values of spending and tax revenues are equal. Equivalently, deficits now must be offset by surpluses later. To see this, simply take a two-period version of the present value formula above, given below.

$$\frac{G_1 - T_1}{1+r} = \frac{T_2 - G_2}{(1+r)^2}$$

For the equality in this expression to hold, if there is a deficit in period one ($G_1 > T_1$), there must be a surplus in period two ($T_2 > G_2$).

This is the form of the GBC that is the most useful for studying economic policy because it is reasonable to think of the government as running periodic deficits and surpluses for many reasons, such as to stabilize aggregate economic activity over the business cycle. But there is an additional advantage to using this form of the GBC useful for analyzing economic policy.

We can use this present value expression to draw a distinction between permanent and **transitory government spending**, a distinction important when we investigate the effects on aggregate output of government spending and tax policies.

Permanent and Transitory Government Spending

In Chapter 4, we studied the theory of the household and there we used a distinction between permanent and transitory income when the Permanent Income Hypothesis was presented. Here we will develop an analogous distinction applied to government expenditures. This decomposition of government spending was introduced by economist Robert J. Barro of Harvard University.[3]

---

3 See "Output Effects of Government Purchases," *Journal of Political Economy* 89, No. 6 (December 1981), pp. 1086–121.

Our theory of the household stressed that there were two types of income accruing to households: permanent and transitory income. Permanent income is predictable whereas transitory income is not. We will assume that there are analogous types of government expenditures. Transitory government expenditures are expenditures implemented during extraordinary or unpredictable circumstances. The standard example of transitory spending is that occurring during wars but it is not hard to imagine other forms of emergency spending such as the spending that occurs in the wake of natural disasters. Wars are presumably impossible to foresee and so this seems to match up well with our notions about transitory income in the theory of the household since transitory income was assumed to be unpredictable in advance to households. All other spending will be presumed predictable by the government and so will be lumped into the permanent category. Transitory spending is defined below.

Definition

■   Transitory government spending has the property that the present value of transitory government spending is zero.

We defined permanent income as the constant amount of income with the property that household wealth was the same using either permanent income or actual income. Here we will define permanent government expenditures in a similar manner; it is the constant amount of spending with the property that the present value of government spending is the same using actual or **permanent government spending**. However, unlike our household analysis, here we will use an infinite horizon for government for the reasons given above.

Government expenditures are thus the sum of permanent and transitory expenditures

$$G = G^P + G^T$$

and, for each component, there is a present value relationship that must be considered.

Our assumptions about transitory government expenditures can be illustrated using the following formula:

$$\frac{G_1^T}{1+r} + \frac{G_2^T}{(1+r)^2} + \cdots = 0$$

So we imagine that if the government needs to carry out emergency spending, there will be later reductions in spending that will cause this present value restriction to hold.

Now substitute this assumption about transitory spending into the overall present value relationship, making the distinction between permanent and transitory spending, to get

$$\frac{G_1^P}{1+r} + \frac{G_2^P}{(1+r)^2} + \cdots + \frac{G_1^T}{1+r} + \frac{G_2^T}{(1+r)^2} + \cdots = \frac{T_1}{1+r} + \frac{T_2}{(1+r)^2} + \cdots$$

and now we interpret G^P (as opposed to G^T) as spending apart from the transitory variety. Now use our familiar definition of Permanent Income from Chapter 4 and apply it to non-transitory spending to give

$$\frac{G_1^P}{1+r} + \frac{G_2^P}{(1+r)^2} + \cdots = G^P\left[\frac{1}{1+r} + \frac{1}{(1+r)^2} + \cdots\right] = \frac{G^P}{r}$$

and substitute this into the previous expression to arrive at the intertemporal GBC for the government.

$$\frac{G^P}{r} + \frac{G_1^T}{1+r} + \frac{G_2^T}{(1+r)^2} + \cdots = \frac{T_1}{1+r} + \frac{T_2}{(1+r)^2} + \cdots$$

This intertemporal GBC will be used to make an important distinction about how the present value of taxes must change depending upon whether permanent or transitory government spending changes. This distinction is summarized in the following propositions.

Propositions About Taxes and Government Spending

- If there is an increase in permanent government expenditures, G^P, there must also be an increase in the present value of taxes paid by households.
- If there is an increase in transitory government expenditures, there will be no increase in the present value of taxes.

In Chapter 8, you will see that changes in tax rates (either average or marginal) will affect the labor supply decisions of households. Given our definition of transitory government spending, labor supply will be unaffected by variations in transitory government spending because a change in transitory spending does not change the present value of taxes. The wealth of households is thereby unaffected. The difference between transitory and permanent government expenditures is that transitory spending is thought to be temporary spending that eventually disappears and there will be future reductions in spending to offset any increases in transitory spending that occur. Permanent government expenditures will affect labor supply because changes in permanent expenditures imply a change in the wealth of households (because it changes the present value of taxes) and so changes in permanent government expenditures do affect labor supply by households.

There is thus an important distinction about the effect on labor supply of an increase in either transitory or permanent expenditures. These labor supply effects will be important when we discuss the economic effects of fiscal policy. Whenever we discuss the effects of a change in government expenditures, we will need to exercise care in stating whether spending changes are permanent or transitory.

6.4 FINANCING GOVERNMENT EXPENDITURES

In explaining the economic effects of government expenditures, our discussion in the previous section made clear that we need to distinguish between permanent and transitory expenditures. Now we need to ask how these two forms of spending can be financed. We begin by revisiting our discussion from Chapter 4 on this issue which suggested that the choice of finance is irrelevant but then we move on to consider additional reasons why a government might want to choose either bond or tax finance.

Ricardian Equivalence Once Again

In Chapter 4, we considered a thought experiment where we wanted to know how the wealth of a household would be affected by a transitory (temporary) deficit run by the government. Our aim was to discover if the wealth of the household would be affected by a transitory shift from tax to bond finance by the government for a given level of government spending. Here are the details of that experiment.

The government gives a tax cut to the representative household in the first period of life and issues bonds to cover the cost of the tax cut (remember that the government's spending is constant throughout). In the second period of life, the household experiences a tax increase as the government has now decided to eliminate its deficit. But in addition, the household's taxes rise by an additional amount needed to cover the interest that the government paid on the bonds that it issued.

We found that that the household's wealth would not be affected by this switch in expenditure methods and so we concluded that the consumption and saving decisions of the household would be unaffected because household wealth was unchanged. From the household's point of view, tax and bond finance were equivalent in that the household's behavior was the same using either method to finance government spending. This is the essence of the **Ricardian Equivalence Proposition**. Now we need to suggest some of the reasons why the Ricardian proposition may not be valid.

1. *Differing Time Horizons.* The government and households do not have identical time horizons. Households obviously have finite horizons but governments do not. Recall that in our previous discussion of the government's intertemporal GBC, we used the assumption of an infinite horizon, arguing that there did not seem to be any compelling reason why we would want to assume a finite horizon for the government. If this is the case, then the Ricardian Proposition will fail if the government were to raise taxes after the household's second period of life. In this case, the current period tax cut increases household wealth, causing the household to change its spending and savings choices.

2. *Differing Discount Rates.* The experiment that we conducted assumed that the interest rate paid by the government on its debt was the same as the discount rate used by the household to discount its income. Clearly this is not the case. Governments borrow at rates far below the rates at which households borrow (governments have lower default risk).[4] Thus the Ricardian Proposition fails when there are differing discount rates for the government and households.

---

4 Governments are safer borrowers than households because they can raise taxes to repay their debts. They may even be able to print money to repay debt. As a result, governments can borrow more cheaply (at lower interest rates) than households.

3. **Myopia**. In our thought experiment, the government raised taxes in the second period of the household's life, cutting them in the first period. We implicitly assumed that the household was forward-looking in its behavior, recognizing the future tax liabilities associated with the tax cut that it received in the first period. If the household does not see these future tax implications (and thus is said to be myopic), it will perceive the tax cut in the first period as an increase in its wealth, changing its consumption choices when it receives the tax cut.

4. **Operative Bequests**. Let's recognize now that the government has a longer time horizon than households. As noted by economist Robert J. Barro, the Ricardian Proposition may still hold if there are operative bequests.[5] If households care about the welfare of their descendants, then they may leave a bequest to their descendants to allow them to achieve a given level of welfare. If they recognize the future tax increases attached to a tax cut (that is, as long as they are not myopic), they may therefore leave an additional bequest to their descendants to compensate them for the future tax increases implied by a tax cut. With an operative bequest motive, households once again save the tax cut, passing it on as an asset to their descendants to be used to pay future tax increases. As a result, the consumption choices of the household are unchanged.

5. **MTR Effects**. Ricardian Equivalence may fail if taxes are not of the lump-sum variety. When the government varies marginal tax rates, labor supply decisions by households will be affected, as you will see in Chapter 8. As one possibility, a decline in marginal tax rates today and a corresponding increase in these rates in the future could cause households to rearrange their consumption, labor supply, and saving decisions over time. Thus the economic choices made by households will differ from what would otherwise occur.

This is not an exhaustive list of all of the reasons why the Ricardian Proposition may not be valid. But the implication of all of the possible reasons above is clear; the validity of Ricardian Equivalence is an empirical issue that cannot be settled purely on theoretical grounds.[6]

There is an additional interesting aspect of the Ricardian position. If it does hold, why would a government choose to use one method of finance or another? Clearly it does not matter to the households in the economy; households behave in exactly the same way whether either method of finance is used. If the Ricardian position is correct, there would be no way to explain why a government would choose to use tax or bond finance. Barro has provided an explanation for this choice that involves tax smoothing.

Tax Smoothing

Any student of the political arena knows that it is difficult for tax rates to be increased by politicians. Either because of the administrative costs of doing so or because of the hostility of

---

5 See "Are Government Bonds Net Wealth," *Journal of Political Economy* 82, No. 6 (November–December 1974), pp. 1095–117.

6 John J. Seater reviews this empirical evidence in "Ricardian Equivalence," *Journal of Economic Literature* 31, No. 1 (March 1993), pp. 142–90.

voters to the idea of paying higher taxes, it is likely that tax increases, if they occur, are likely to be infrequent and small. This leads us to ask how a government would finance transitory spending in such an environment. Expenditures to wage a war are regarded by economists to be the standard example of transitory government expenditures. If the government must wage war, how will it be financed? **Tax smoothing** provides the following answer.

If it is costly to raise taxes, then bonds would be the preferred method of financing transitory government spending. Taxes will perhaps be raised by a small amount to avoid the wrath of the taxpayers or to keep additional administrative costs low but a small tax increase could be used to slowly pay off the debt and to pay interest on the debt that is issued to finance transitory spending. This theory leads us to expect that governments will primarily use debt to finance transitory spending; taxes will be used mainly to finance permanent spending, except that a small portion of tax receipts is used to pay interest on the debt and repay the debt over time.

This discussion leads us to expect that debt will be used when a government wages war. As you will see below, there is such a connection. This is how the U.S. financed World War II (see Figure 6.6 below) and England behaved in this way during the seventeenth and eighteenth centuries (see **Doing Economics**: British War Finance Prior to the French Revolution).

Debt and the Deficit

Our discussion about the intertemporal GBC and the financing of government expenditures can be used to understand the behavior of the stock of government debt over time. Figures 6.5 and 6.6 provide two perspectives on the connection between **government deficits** (surpluses) and the stock of government debt.

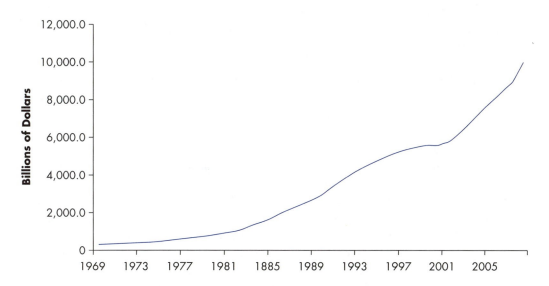

FIGURE 6.5 Stock of Federal Debt

Source: Council of Economic Advisors Table B87

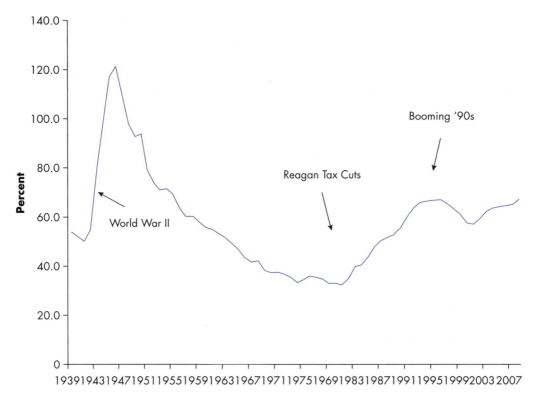

FIGURE 6.6 Federal Debt/GDP Ratio

Source: Council of Economic Advisors Table B79

Doing Economics: British War Finance Prior to the French Revolution

Economists Thomas J. Sargent and François R. Velde have provided historical evidence that the British government financed its war expenditures in the period prior to the French Revolution using the tax-smoothing ideas advanced by Robert J. Barro of Harvard University.

During 1688–1788, the British fought four wars. Using data that covers this period, Sargent and Velde provide data on the level of government expenditures broken out into three components: civil spending, debt service, and military expenditures. Comparing these time series with government revenues, they look for evidence of how the British and French governments chose to finance their spending. Figure 2, taken from their study, shows the behavior of the British government. This data provides evidence of tax smoothing by the British government. Civil expenditures are roughly constant but, in several periods, total government expenditures rise by much more than tax receipts. Thus whenever government spending exceeded revenues, as would be true during wars, the British government was clearly using debt to finance the transitory spending needed to wage war. The data appear to support

(continued)

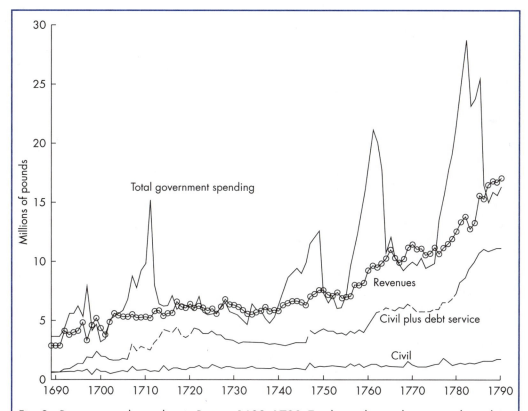

Fig. 2. Revenues and spending in Britain, 1689–1790. Total spending is decomposed into three components: civil, debt service, and military expenditures. The three lines recorded for expenditures pertain to civil expenditures, civil plus debt service, and then total expenditures, so that the vertical distances between these lines represent, respectively, civil expenses, debt service, and military expenditures. Total revenues are depicted with small circles. *Source*: Mitchell (1988).

the view that taxes were raised to cover interest payments on the debt that was issued and to gradually repay the bonds issued to wage war. Interestingly, the French did not pursue tax smoothing.

See Thomas J. Sargent and François R. Velde, "Macroeconomic Features of the French Revolution," *Journal of Political Economy* 103, No. 3 (June 1995), pp. 474–518 and Brian R. Mitchell, *British Historical Statistics*, Cambridge: Cambridge University Press (1988).

At any point in time, the stock of government debt reflects the entire history of the government's deficits and surpluses. To see this, examine the GBC that we discussed earlier, reproduced here for convenience.

$$\text{Deficit: } G + i \cdot B_{-1} + TR - T > 0, \Rightarrow B - B_{-1} > 0$$
$$\text{Surplus: } G + i \cdot B_{-1} + TR - T < 0, \Rightarrow B - B_{-1} < 0$$

The GBC shows that government deficits or surpluses increase or reduce the existing stock of government debt. Thus whenever we measure the stock of debt, what we are observing is whether the government, on a net basis over time, has been running deficits or surpluses. We can also observe the circumstances in which the government has chosen to issue debt to finance its activities; specifically, we may find some evidence of debt issue to finance transitory government expenditures.

Figure 6.5 provides a time series graph of the stock of government debt outstanding at the end of each fiscal year in billions of dollars. The graph conveys the impression that, while the stock was steadily rising over the entire time period, it was not until 1970 and beyond that the government's deficits and surpluses might have had a substantial impact upon the economy. However, Figure 6.6 conveys a very different impression.

Figure 6.6 adjusts the debt data using the size of the economy. This figure provides a graph of the **debt-to-GDP ratio** and also reveals much more about the government's behavior over time. The financing of World War II is clearly evident with a substantial increase in the debt ratio during the war. It is also interesting to see the ratio decline consistently after the war until the tax cuts under the Reagan presidency. The debt ratio (and deficits) rose substantially during this time and then declined during the latter part of the 1990s when, as we will see in a later chapter, there was an unprecedented increase in technical progress and thus incomes and output. We have argued that debts and deficits should be adjusted by the size of the economy to discover the impact of government debt and deficits. This last figure shows how much more economic information is revealed by making an economic scale adjustment.

Figure 6.6 suggests that tax smoothing was used during World War II and Figure 6.7 confirms this and shows further that tax smoothing was also used during World War I. The figure provides outlays and receipts data in a time series graph covering the fiscal years between 1901 and 1950. It is clear that during both wars, government outlays rose relative to government receipts. The government was also running fiscal year deficits during the Great Depression. Our explanation for the deficits during this great contraction in economic activity will not be about tax smoothing. Rather this is a business cycle phenomenon. In both of the world wars in the twentieth century, governments did not exclusively use taxes to finance wartime expenditures, instead using debt to finance a substantial part of these transitory expenditures.

The Economic Effects of the Deficit

While measuring the actual deficits run by the government is informative, a more important issue is to determine the economic effects, if there are any, of the government's deficit. Here we sketch the answer to this question of how the government's actions can affect economic activity, leaving a more detailed discussion to later chapters that discuss the implications of aggregate economic models of the economy.

In a Ricardian world, the manner of financing government spending is irrelevant. Households foresee the future tax implications associated with government deficits and so it will not matter to their consumption choices how the government chooses to finance its spending. What does matter in such a world is the level of government spending and, in

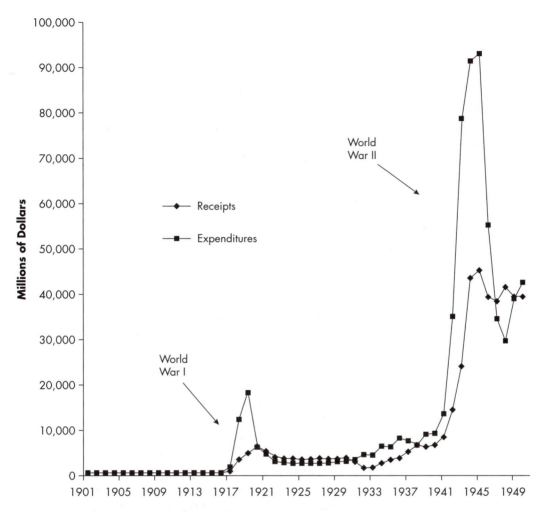

FIGURE 6.7 Federal Receipts and Expenditures, 1901–1950

Source: Office of Management and Budget, Historical Table 1.1

particular, whether that spending is permanent or transitory. If there is a transitory increase in government spending, households will not see an increase in the present value of their tax payments; the present value of transitory government spending is zero. A permanent increase in government spending does imply an increase in the present value of household tax payments. If there is no change in the present value of tax payments, there will be no change in the labor supply of households. If labor supply is fixed, there will be an increase in the real interest rate associated with a rise in transitory government spending and that increase in the real interest rate can reduce the economy's capital stock. You saw in the last chapter that investment, and thus the capital stock, is inversely related to the real interest rate and so one important concern is that Potential GDP, determined in part by the level of the capital stock, will decline if there is an increase in transitory spending by the government. A permanent increase in government spending may result in a higher level of Potential GDP if households offer increased labor supply in response to a higher stream of tax payments over time.

In a non-Ricardian world, it does matter how the government chooses to finance its spending. If it uses bonds to finance spending, and so runs a deficit, one implication would be that the government will drive up the real interest rate, and thus reduces Potential GDP, because the capital stock will fall in the face of a higher real interest rate. This is the conventional wisdom often expressed by politicians and others who argue that government deficits have adverse economic consequences, although these critics of deficits usually do not distinguish between real and nominal interest rates when they discuss the effects of government deficits. This is a distinction that we must always be careful to make because nominal interest rates can behave quite differently than real interest rates because of inflation, among other reasons.

Deficits and Inflation

There can be a connection between government deficits and the rate of price inflation. Economists have found some statistical evidence supporting this linkage.[7] Figure 6.8 provides a scatter diagram for U.S. deficits (a deficit is a positive number), and the annual rate of inflation in the CPI at annual frequency over the period 1962 to 2008. The diagram shows a possibly positive relationship (note the dotted line) between deficits and inflation but the relationship is not a very tight one. In this section we briefly explain why there may be a positive relationship between government deficits and inflation. A more complete understanding of this issue requires that you understand the activities of the Federal Reserve System (the Fed), the U.S. central bank. This discussion will occur in the next chapter.

Our discussion about the government budget constraint (GBC) showed that the government will issue government bonds to borrow funds from the public when it finds that its spending exceeds its tax revenues, assuming that the government does not wish to raise taxes and/or cut its spending to eliminate the deficit. We also pointed out that while private individuals may hold these new securities, the central bank could also buy them up. If the Fed does so, this action can cause inflation to occur. Here is why.

The Fed has the ability to buy or sell government bonds to manage the U.S. money supply. It does this as part of its monetary policy. When it buys government bonds, the U.S. money supply expands and the money supply increase will cause an excess demand for goods in the aggregate economy, thereby causing the price level to rise. You will learn the exact details of this process later in the book. Indeed we will argue later that inflation (defined as a continuing increase in all prices in the economy) is entirely a monetary phenomenon. Thus the activity of buying the newly issued government bonds can cause inflation if the bond issue causes a central bank to expand the money supply.

But it is important to stress that the Fed is under no obligation to buy these government bonds. The Fed is a creature of Congress but with a substantial degree of autonomy. It is often

---

7 For some empirical evidence on this issue, see Luis A. V. Catao and Marco E. Terrones, "Fiscal Deficits and Inflation," *Journal of Monetary Economics* 52, No. 3 (April 2005), pp. 529–54.

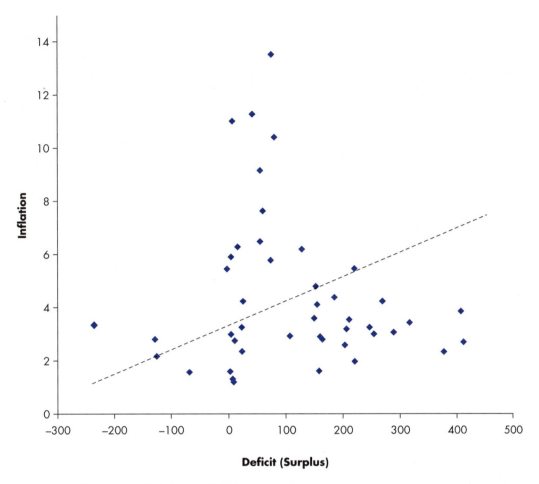

FIGURE 6.8 Government Deficits and Inflation

Source: St. Louis Fed FRED Database, CBO The Cyclically Adjusted and Standardized Budget Measures, October 2008 Table 3

described as a quasi-independent organization. It may choose to buy government debt as a conscious policy decision perhaps because those in charge of monetary policy do not like the consequences to the economy of the government's deficit. Whatever the reasons for the bond purchase, this action increasing the money supply will raise the price level. But it is important to realize that the increase in the money supply is the cause of inflation, *not* the deficit run by the government.

6.5 CONCLUDING REMARKS

This chapter concerns the role of government in the aggregate economy. We began our discussion with a number of microeconomic issues that make government an essential component of any capitalistic society. We looked at some data on government expenditures, in the NIPA, as well as broader measures of expenditures and receipts, to get a complete picture of the revenue and outlays of the government. We looked at the Government Budget Constraint (GBC) that lists the sources and uses of funds by the government that determines the need to issue or retire government debt. An intertemporal version of the GBC was also examined, a version showing that deficits must be offset by surpluses in the future if the present value of spending will equal the present value of tax receipts.

The next set of topics concerned how the government financed its spending and we listed reasons why it may or may not matter how the government finances its actions. We also provided some reasons why it makes sense for the government to use bonds to finance transitory spending, avoiding a tax increase that would otherwise be necessary to finance this spending. The chapter concluded by providing a discussion of why deficits may have adverse consequences to the aggregate economy and why there may be a connection between deficits and inflation.

The ideas discussed in this chapter will be used later in the book when we take up issues related to economic policy. As you will learn when we discuss economic policy, the government may have a useful role to play in stabilizing economic activity.

Key Ideas

- Governments must enforce a legal system, maintaining a criminal justice system and establishing the property rights of its citizens.
- Public Goods are goods involving the problem of free riders. Government provides public goods because the private sector will not produce these goods in socially optimal amounts.
- Externalities refer to situations where the actions of one economic agent affect the welfare of another.
- Governments often provide goods that involve significant externalities.
- The NIPA contains a measure of government consumption and investment, the goods and services consumed by the public provided by the government.
- Government outlays contain, among other things, transfer payments made by the government to households.
- The Government Budget Constraint (GBC) lists all of the sources and uses of funds by the government.
- If the government has a deficit, its outlays exceed its tax receipts, requiring that the government issue bonds.
- If the government has a surplus, its outlays are less than its tax receipts, requiring that the government retire (buy back) bonds outstanding.
- The intertemporal GBC states that the present value of spending must equal the present value of tax revenues.
- If Ricardian Equivalence holds, tax and bond finance of a given government expenditure stream are equivalent to households.
- Transitory government spending has a present value of zero.

■ Permanent government spending is the constant amount such that the present value of non-transitory spending is equal to the present value of taxes.

■ A change in transitory government spending implies no change in the present value of tax receipts.

■ A change in permanent government spending implies a change in the present value of tax receipts.

■ Deficits add to the stock of debt. At any point in time, the stock of debt outstanding reflects the entire history of surpluses and deficits run by the government.

■ The real interest rate can be affected, in a non-Ricardian world, by the existence of a government deficit.

■ Deficits can be associated with inflation if the government runs a deficit, issues bonds, and the central bank decides to buy these new securities, increasing the money stock and the price level.

Key Terms

Free Rider

Marginal Tax Rate

Indexation

Government
    Expenditures

Net Transfers

Central Bank

Full-Employment
    Deficit

Permanent Government
    Spending

Ricardian
    Equivalence

Tax Smoothing

Real Interest Rate

Public Goods

Average Tax

Bracket-Creep

Tax Revenues

Government
    Deficit

Social Security

Intertemporal
    Government
    Budget Constraint

Transitory Government
    Spending

Myopia

Stock of Government
    Debt

Deficits and Inflation

Externalities

Flat Tax

Government
    Consumption

Government
    Budget Constraint

Unified Budget

Operative Bequests

Debt-GDP Ratio

Progressive Tax
    System

Negative Income Tax

Off-Budget

Questions for Study and Review

Review Exercises

1. What does tax-smoothing mean, and what is its implication for government financing?
2. Discuss whether or not the U.S. Constitution should be amended to require the federal government to have a balanced budget.
3. What is the difference between a progressive tax schedule and a flat tax?
4. Why does the government need to supply public goods?
5. List three reasons why Ricardian Equivalence may not hold.
6. What is the government's budget constraint?
7. What is the difference between permanent and transitory government expenditures?

Thought Exercises

1. Suppose that the economy has a progressive income tax on household income. What will happen to the aggregate marginal tax rate as GDP fluctuates around its trend over the business cycle?
2. Suppose that households are not myopic and do not plan to leave bequests to their descendents. Does Ricardian Equivalence hold in such an economy?

Numerical Exercises

1. Consider the following information describing a government's projected budget position:

Year	Govt. Spending	Transfer Payments	Nominal GDP
2010	$600	$1,200	$11,000
2011	$400	$1,500	$11,505
2012	$150	$2,100	$11,700
2013	$145	$2,500	$12,000
2014	$175	$3,200	$12,500

Assume that the tax schedule is given by $T = -500 + 0.2Y$ and that the interest rate on debt is 5 percent. Also assume that the government has zero debt at the beginning of 2010.

a) Compute the government deficit/surplus for each year.
b) Compute the projected stock of government debt at the end of 2014.
c) The government realizes that the large amount of debt at the end of the year 2014 is not acceptable and decides to raise the marginal tax rate by two percentage points. What is the change in the stock of government debt in 2014?

2) Consider the following stream of permanent government expenditures for three periods: $G_1^P = \$20,000$, $G_2^P = \$21,000$, $G_3^P = \$21,500$.

a) Calculate the present value of government expenditures, assuming that the present value of transitory government spending is zero and that the interest rate is 5 percent.
b) Find the annuity-equivalent amount of permanent government expenditures using this data.
c) Assume that the policymakers want to pursue perfect tax-smoothing. What is the tax revenue collected by the government in each period to cover the above expenses?

3) Suppose federal tax receipts and net transfer payments depend on the level of nominal output in the economy, Y_{nom}, and are given by $T = 0.25Y_{nom}$ and $TR = 0.075Y_{nom}$. Nominal government expenditures are assumed to be exogenous, $G = \$2,000$. The outstanding nominal debt in the beginning of the year 2004 is $6,000. Assume that real GDP in 2004 is $10,000 and that the deflator in 2004 is .98. Finally, assume that the nominal interest rate is 2 percent.

a) Calculate the nominal actual budget deficit and the nominal full-employment budget deficit for the year 2004 assuming that potential output is $11,000 and that the government does not have to make interest payments on the outstanding debt.

b) Calculate the nominal actual budget deficit in 2004 and consider the fact that the government has to make interest payments on outstanding debt.

c) What is the federal nominal debt at the start of 2005?

d) Calculate real government debt at the beginning of 2004.

e) Calculate real government debt in 2005 if the inflation rate during 2004 is (i) 4 percent, (ii) 1 percent.

Data Exercises

1) Download Table 3.1 from the U.S. Government Printing Office for the years 1940 through 2014: http://www.gpoaccess.gov/usbudget/fy10/sheets/hist03z1.xls. What items are listed under "Human resources" and "Physical Resources"?

a) Plot the time series of outlays on national defense, human resources, physical resources, and net interest payments from 1940 through 2014 (projected). Which of the four series experiences the greatest increase? Why?

b) Plot the time series for national defense, human resources, physical resources, and net interest payments from 1940 through 2014 (projected) as a percentage of outlays.

c) Plot the growth rates of total outlays and net interest payments from 1950 through 2014 (projected). Describe the development over time of these time series.

For further questions, multiple choice quizzes, and weblinks related to this chapter, visit www.routledge.com/textbooks/rossana

References and Suggestions for Further Reading

Barro, R.J. (1974) "Are Government Bonds Net Wealth," *Journal of Political Economy* 82 (6) (November–December): 1095–117.

__(1981) "Output Effects of Government Purchases," *Journal of Political Economy* 89 (6) (December): 1086–121.

Catao, L.A. and Terrones, M.E. (2005) "Fiscal Deficits and Inflation," *Journal of Monetary Economics* 52 (3) (April): 529–54.

Hall, R.E. and Rabushka, A. (1995) *The Flat Tax*, Second Ed., Hoover Institution Press and Stanford University Press.

Mitchell, B.R. (1988) *British Historical Statistics*, Cambridge: Cambridge University Press.

Sargent, T.J. and Velde, F.R. (1995) "Macroeconomic Features of the French Revolution," *Journal of Political Economy* 103 (3) (June): 474–518.

Seater, J.J. (1993) "Ricardian Equivalence," *Journal of Economic Literature* 31 (1) (March): 142–90.

Chapter 7

Money

LEARNING OBJECTIVES

This chapter develops a money and bond market model to be used in our aggregate economic models of the economy in subsequent chapters. We begin with a discussion of the uses of money, developing a transaction cost model of money demand. We then turn to a discussion of the money supply process, introducing you to the interaction of the central bank with the banking system in determining the supply of money available to the public. The money and bond markets will be discussed and we will show how to use money to control **inflation**, one of the most important insights offered by macroeconomics. Here are some questions that we answer in this chapter.

- ■ Why do people hold money?
- ■ What determines the demand for money?
- ■ How does the central bank control the supply of money?
- ■ What determines the rate of inflation in the aggregate economy?

One of the great events in economic history is the discovery of the benefits of using money in the ordinary activities of daily life. By recognizing these benefits, the members of a society experience substantial gains in their economic welfare. The task of this chapter is to explain these benefits, to discuss how households decide on their money holdings, and to explain how that money is supplied to the public.

We begin this chapter by listing the benefits to a society of using money. We need not use money to conduct our economic activities but there are good reasons why we have chosen to do so. Next we provide a formal discussion of the demand for money. This economic model is the foundation for the money demand relationship that we will use in our aggregate economic models so it is important to understand the microeconomic foundation for the financial sector of these economic models. The model concerns a representative household and its decision to hold money in connection with its plans to carry out a given level of consumption. The model will explain the connection between the money holdings of the household and its determinants, the price level, real income, and the bond yield. The analysis will make it clear what features of an economy are crucial in explaining why we use money to trade goods and services.

Next we turn to a discussion of the money supply. Money supplied to the members of an economy requires actions by the Federal Reserve System (the Fed), the central bank of the U.S., and the banking system. Here you will be introduced to the activities of the Fed. This organization has a critical policy role in the economy because it is charged with supervising and regulating banks, and because it carries out monetary policies that have an important impact upon the state of the economy. You will learn how **monetary policy** is carried out and how the Fed regulates the activities of banks. You will also learn about the role of banks in providing money to households and how they meet the regulatory requirements imposed upon them by law.

We then construct the markets for money and bonds that will make up the financial sector of our aggregate economic models. We illustrate how the interest rate will be set in the money and bond markets, showing how variations in real income will affect both markets. Finally, we discuss the implications of our analysis for the origins of inflation, using the concepts of this chapter to explain how inflation can occur. Empirical evidence will be provided verifying the connection between the rate of inflation in an economy and the rate at which the money stock grows. The cause of inflation is perhaps the single most important insight offered by macroeconomics.

7.1 DEFINITIONS AND USES OF MONEY

Economies become **monetized** (use money) precisely because the members of a society recognize that there are benefits to them of using items that we call money. Here is a list of the economic functions of money providing these benefits.

The Economic Functions of Money

- Money is used as a medium of exchange.
- Money is used as a **unit of account**.
- Money is a **store of value**.
- Money is used as a standard of deferred payment.

The first use of money, its **medium of exchange** function, means that people trade items called money for the goods and services that they want to consume. This need not be so. In a **barter system**, individuals acquire goods by trading goods that they own or by offering to perform services in return for goods. As an example, a plumber could offer to repair an accountant's faucet in return for having the accountant fill out his or her tax return. It is easy to see that such a system is very inefficient.

When people trade goods for other goods, they must find others who are willing to trade. This is known as the **double coincidence of wants**. As you can imagine, this can be a very time-consuming process and it may well be that an individual cannot find another with whom to make a trade. In a barter system, therefore, many trades may not occur because the transactions costs of trading are very high. The notion of **transactions costs** generally refers to the costs of carrying out a transaction. Sometimes these can be the fees charged by an individual such as when a real estate agent charges a fee for selling a house. But these costs more generally refer to the time and other costs of carrying out transactions (these are sometimes called **shoe-leather costs**). By using money, households reduce these costs and have more time available for work and leisure.

Money is also used as a **unit of account**, meaning that we measure prices in terms of money. Suppose that money is not in use so barter must be used to make trades. You would need to find the best trade by looking at the price of the good you wish to trade in terms of other goods in the economy. If there were just three goods in the economy, you would need to measure three relative prices but imagine that there were a thousand commodities (far less than there are in well-developed industrialized economies). It turns out that there are 499,500 such relative prices in this economy so that shopping for the best trade would be very difficult and time-intensive.[1] By measuring prices in units of money, we simplify our lives by reducing the number of prices that we need to know in order to carry out our transactions under the best terms available to us.

Money is also a **store of value**. If you plan to buy a product but do not wish to do so now, you can hold money for a time until you are ready to buy. But note that this function is not unique to money. Other financial **assets**, such as bonds, can provide the same services.

Finally, money is a **standard of deferred payment**. Loans are carried out by measuring their terms in units of money. Thus the principal borrowed and repayments by the borrower, including interest, are stipulated in units of money.

These benefits can be provided by forms of money having very different physical characteristics. A **commodity money** standard is a system where commodities, such as gold or silver, circulate as exchange media. The intrinsic value of these commodities in non-monetary uses is nontrivial. In contrast, the paper **currency** that we use each day is an example of a **fiat**

---

1 In an economy with N prices, there would be $N(N-1)/2$ relative prices that one could compute.

money; it is money because of government decree or fiat. The cost of producing this currency is negligible, far less than its value in exchange. An essential difference between these two systems is how the supply of these monetary forms is controlled. In a commodity money system, an industry supplies money to society and the supply of money (and the economic consequences of this supply) is affected by production conditions in the industry supplying the commodity. For example, a strike by workers in the gold-mining industry restricts the addition of gold to the stock of monetary gold. In a fiat money system, the money supply is controlled by a country's government or its central bank.[2]

Measuring Money

The considerations discussed above about the benefits of using money are what are used to guide us in deciding what financial assets to include in measuring the quantity of money. It turns out that there are several definitions of money that are compiled because it is not altogether clear just how we should measure money.

The Federal Reserve Board, the central bank of the U.S., calculates and publishes measures of the money stock (more will be said about the Fed later in the chapter). Table 7.1 provides data on these measures. Each of the components of **M1** (currency, demand and **checkable deposits**, and travelers' checks) clearly qualifies as an item providing the medium of exchange services of money. Currency refers to the coin and paper money used in day-to-day transactions by the public. Travelers' checks are like currency and are used in exchange for goods and services.[3] Demand and other checkable deposits are deposits owned by households that may be used to purchase goods and services by writing a check drawing down these deposits.

TABLE 7.1 Measures of Monetary Aggregates, February 2009

M1	1556.1	M2	8238.4
Currency	834.3	M1	1556.1
Travelers' Checks	5.5	Savings Deposits	4291.4
Demand Deposits	395.6	Small Time Deposits	1354.3
Other Checkable Deposits	320.7	Retail Money Market Funds	1036.6

Note: Data are in billions of seasonally-adjusted dollars.
Source: Federal Reserve Statistical Release H.6

---

2 Further reading on commodity money as well as other issues in monetary economics can be done by reading two classic references in the field. See *A Monetary History of the United States, 1867–1960*, Princeton University Press for the National Bureau of Economic Research (1963) by Milton Friedman and Anna J. Schwartz, and *Monetary Economics: Theory and Policy*, Macmillan Publishing (1989) by Bennett T. McCallum.

3 They are purchased by individuals because, unlike currency, they will be replaced by the issuing company if lost by the holder.

M2 is a more comprehensive measure of money since it includes M1 but with three additional components. Some, but perhaps not all, of the additional items in M2 may also be used as exchange media by the public. Time and savings deposits are deposits held at banks and the funds in these accounts can be withdrawn sometimes with restrictions. Money market accounts are offered by non-bank institutions and have check-writing privileges. These assets are thought to be less liquid as compared to the assets in M1. **Liquidity** generally refers to the ease with which an asset can be converted into another asset or into goods and services. Alternatively, there are low (or zero) transactions costs associated with liquid assets, making it easy to exchange them for other assets. It is reasonable to ask why it might be sensible to look at more than one measure of the money stock and the answer, in part, lies with the monetary policy activities of the central bank. Here we sketch one policy issue that bears on the choice of monetary aggregate to be used for policy purposes, leaving a more thorough discussion of monetary policy issues for later in this chapter and elsewhere in the book.

Structural change occurs in financial markets just as it does elsewhere in the economy. Innovations in financial markets can occur which might cause a policymaker to prefer to use one monetary aggregate over another when setting monetary policy. As an example, interest payments on checkable deposits were prohibited by law for many years.[4] Depositors would like to earn interest on their funds and profit-seeking firms have an incentive to find a way to meet the desires of the public to earn interest on their deposits. Suppose a depositor moves funds out of a checkable deposit that pays no interest to a money market account that does pay interest. Checkable deposits, and thus M1, decline but M2 is unaffected (both checkable deposits and money market accounts are in M2). Thus this structural change is hidden by M2, making it a more reliable guide for policymakers.

Now that we have covered the descriptive details of the financial markets, it is possible to start building up the components of an economic framework that we can use to analyze the functioning of these markets. We begin with the demand for money, the basic framework describing how households decide how much money to hold for transaction purposes. The goal of the analysis is to be precise about those features of an economy that make it sensible for money to be used in exchange for goods and services.

7.2 THE DEMAND FOR MONEY

In this section, we describe the **transactions demand for money** as devised by the economists William J. Baumol and Nobel laureate James Tobin. The setting for the analysis is that of a household making a decision about how much money to hold for transaction purposes. Thus the medium of exchange motive lies behind the demand for money in this theory. The consumption decision has already been made; that is, the household already knows how much it will consume in the period but it must decide how much money to hold to finance these consumption purchases. We further assume that money must be used to purchase these goods and expenditures will occur evenly throughout the period.

---

4 The Banking Acts of 1933 and 1935 prohibited the payment of interest on checking accounts and Regulation Q regulated the payment of interest on time and savings deposits.

The Sawtooth Pattern of Money Balances

The household will plan to purchase the nominal amount of goods denoted by P·c where P is the price of the goods to be purchased and c is the real bundle of goods (c is a composite commodity) it wishes to consume. To fix ideas, imagine that the household decides to deposit the entire amount that it needs to purchase all of the goods it wishes to buy into a cash balance by withdrawing these funds from an interest-bearing account. Figure 7.1 displays the money holdings of the household through the period. Initial holdings are the entire amount P·c and then this cash balance is drawn down smoothly through the period. Next period, the cash balance begins again at the amount P·c and is drawn down in the same way. The average cash balance for each period is P·c/2.

But note that the household does not need to begin the period with the entire amount P·c; rather it could start with P·c/2 and, in the middle of the period, make a second withdrawal of the same amount (we assume that the household will withdraw the same amount each time). Figure 7.2 illustrates this situation by taking the previous figure, using this additional possible choice by the household. Now the cash balance starts at P·c/2, is drawn down, and then, halfway through the period, the cash balance is replenished. We could repeat the same exercise for additional withdrawals but it should be clear by now that the more withdrawals that are made, the smaller will be the average cash balance that is held by the household. What we need now is a way of determining how many withdrawals the household will want to make. This requires that we solve an optimizing model that we next discuss.

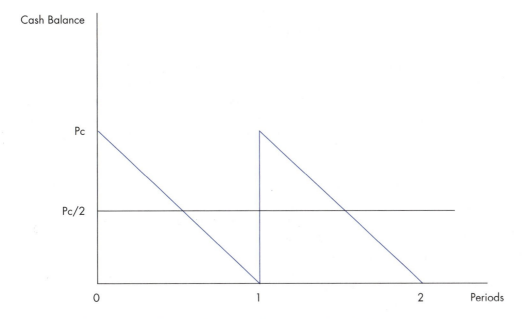

FIGURE 7.1 The Sawtooth Pattern of Money Balances with One Withdrawal

The household wishes to spend the nominal amount Pc and makes one withdrawal from an interest-bearing account, depositing the proceeds into a cash balance. Funds are spent at an even rate through the period, drawing down the cash balance to zero at the end of the period. The average cash balance is Pc/2.

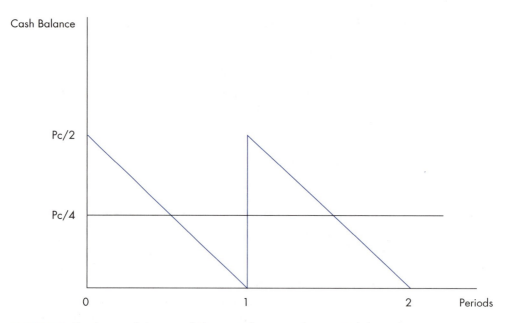

FIGURE 7.2 The Sawtooth Pattern of Money Balances with Two Withdrawals

If the household makes two withdrawals per period, its beginning cash balance is Pc/2. The average cash balance in this case is Pc/4.

An Optimizing Model of the Household

The first step in determining how many withdrawals of the same amount the household would make is to establish the costs and benefits attached to each withdrawal that is made. It was stated above that the motive for holding money in this model is that associated with the medium of exchange and, earlier in the chapter, it was argued that transactions costs are the underlying reason for the need to hold money as an exchange medium. Thus it is reasonable to assume that there will be a cost of making each withdrawal from the interest-bearing account and this will be denoted by P·w where w is the real cost of each "trip to the bank." But there is a corresponding benefit to each withdrawal.

The household initially has its funds in an interest-bearing form, bonds or an interest-bearing bank account. As the number of withdrawals rises, the average cash balance declines (the same amount is withdrawn each time) and, therefore, the more the household has in the interest-bearing form that is earning interest. Thus as more withdrawals are made, the foregone interest of holding money declines (we assume, for simplicity, that money pays no interest as would be true for currency). This establishes the nature of the tradeoff faced by the household. As the number of withdrawals increases, transactions costs rise but foregone interest declines. The solution of the optimization problem solved by the household will determine the number of withdrawals that balances these costs and benefits at the margin.

We need to develop the objective to be maximized by the household and doing so requires that we define the average cash balance of the household to be

$$M = \frac{P \cdot c / n}{2}$$

where n is the number of withdrawals that are made by the household. The numerator of this expression is the initial cash balance of the household. The household's foregone interest is $i \cdot M$ where i is the interest rate and its nominal transactions costs are given by the product $n \cdot P \cdot w$. Using the definition of the average cash balance above, we can eliminate the parameter n from the measure of transactions costs as follows.

$$n \cdot P \cdot w = \left[\frac{P \cdot c}{2 \cdot M} \right] \cdot P \cdot w = \frac{c \cdot P^2 \cdot w}{2 \cdot M}$$

The household wishes to choose the number of withdrawals, n, to minimize its costs which are the sum of its transactions costs and foregone interest earnings. These costs are

$$i \cdot M + \frac{c \cdot P^2 \cdot w}{2 \cdot M}$$

In this formulation, the household is choosing its average money holdings, M, to minimize these costs, equivalent to choosing the number of withdrawals (trips to the bank). The following condition must hold for these costs to be at a minimum.[5]

$$i = \frac{c \cdot w \cdot P^2}{2 \cdot M^2}$$

This expression once again uses the marginal benefit equals marginal cost principle that is always a consequence of optimizing behavior. The interest rate measures the optimal benefit of an additional withdrawal since one more withdrawal generates additional interest earnings measured by the interest rate. The right side of this expression is the marginal cost of an additional withdrawal given by the additional transactions costs of that withdrawal. Optimizing behavior balances these marginal benefits and costs. We want to solve this last expression for M, giving us the demand for money by the household. Some algebra leads to the following expression.

$$\frac{M}{P} = \sqrt{\frac{c \cdot w}{2 \cdot i}}$$

This is known as the **square-root rule** of money demand. We want to look closely at the implications of this money demand rule because its characteristics will be important for our macroeconomic models of the aggregate economy.

Note first that nominal money demand, M, is proportional to the price level, P. The factor of proportionality is given by the square root term in the expression. Thus a doubling of the

---

5 We are setting the first derivative of this expression, with respect to the choice of M, equal to zero which is a necessary, but not sufficient, condition for minimizing a function.

price level will double holdings of money by the household for the simple reason that, to buy the same real quantity of goods, c, it will now be necessary to hold twice as much money. This means that $\Delta M/M = \Delta P/P$.

Second, note that if there are no withdrawal costs facing the household (w = 0), money demand will be zero. The intuition for this is clear; money is held because there are transactions costs incurred by individuals and, if we eliminate these costs, people will simply withdraw funds from their interest-bearing account at the instant that they wish to buy goods. There is no need to carry around an inventory of money that does not pay interest. The higher are these transactions costs, the fewer withdrawals will be made and, therefore, the higher will be the average cash balance of the household.

The demand for money implies that there is a positive relationship between money demand and the quantity of goods that the household plans to buy. The more goods that are bought, the more money is needed to finance these purchases. In addition, the theory predicts an inverse relationship between the interest rate and money demand. The higher the interest rate, the greater the foregone interest earnings attached to holding money and the less money will be held as a result. Using the implications of the model, Table 7.2 summarizes our findings regarding the determinants of the demand for money. Figure 7.3 graphically summarizes our findings about money demand.

In our aggregate economic models, we will write our money demand relationship as

$$M^D/P = L(Y, i)$$

where the demand for real cash balances is increasing in real income and inversely related to the interest rate. Thus we will replace consumption with real income; the reason for doing so is just that it simplifies our aggregate economic models by using this substitution.

Regarding the consumption and interest rate effects upon money demand, however, the Baumol-Tobin model is actually more precise than we have indicated. Typically, economic theories provide **qualitative** predictions about the relationships between economic magnitudes. So they may imply positive or negative relationships but they will usually not provide **quantitative** (magnitude) predictions about these relationships. The Baumol-Tobin model of money demand actually provides quantitative predictions about the consumption and interest

TABLE 7.2 The Determinants of the Demand for Money

Determinant	Nominal Money Demand
Price Level: P	$\Delta M^d/M^d = \Delta P/P$
Transaction Cost: w	$w \uparrow \Rightarrow M^d \uparrow$
Consumption: c	$c \uparrow \Rightarrow M^d \uparrow$
Interest Rate: i	$i \uparrow \Rightarrow M^d \downarrow$

Note: In the table, M^d is the nominal demand for money, P refers to the price level, w denotes real transactions costs, c is real consumption, and i is the interest rate.

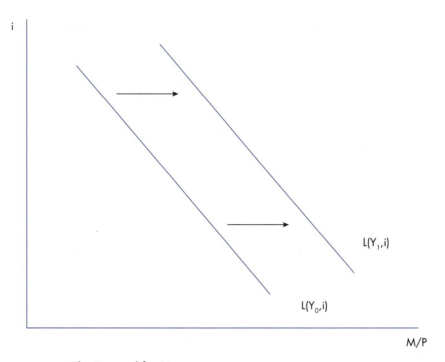

FIGURE 7.3 The Demand for Money

Money demand is inversely related to the interest rate, i. An increase in real income, $Y_0 < Y_1$, shifts money demand to the right.

rate effects on money demand. These predictions regard **elasticities** of money demand with respect to consumption and the interest rate. The definition of an elasticity is given below.

Definition of Elasticity

■ The elasticity of a variable y with respect to another variable x is given by the percentage change in y with respect to a percentage change in x. That is, the elasticity between y and x is measured by the ratio $(\Delta y/y)/(\Delta x/x)$.

The Baumol-Tobin model predicts that the elasticity of money demand with respect to consumption is $1/2$. Thus for every one percent increase in consumption, there will be a $1/2$ percent increase in money demand. Regarding the interest rate, the theory predicts an elasticity of $-1/2$; a one per cent increase in the interest rate will cause a $1/2$ percent reduction in money holdings. Regarding this latter effect, it is useful to say a bit more about exactly what is meant by foregone interest.

A Closer Look at Foregone Interest

The opportunity cost of holding money is actually a real interest differential, the difference between the real return on money and the real return on the financial asset that is the alternative to holding money. In the Baumol-Tobin theory, this real interest differential reduced to the nominal bond yield because a number of simplifying assumptions were made causing this to be true. For example, it was assumed that money paid no interest; it was therefore useful to think of money as currency. We also made no mention of inflation in the analysis. And there was only one interest-bearing asset (bonds or another financial asset) from which funds were withdrawn to be deposited into a cash balance so that the interest rate relevant to money demand was the interest rate on this account. More generally, money can pay interest; checkable deposits have this feature and we would certainly regard a checking account as a form of money providing medium of exchange services to its owner. Here we illustrate how to measure the opportunity cost of money where money pays interest and when there is inflation in the economy. But, for simplicity, we retain the assumption that there is only one financial asset that is an alternative to holding money.

To understand how to measure opportunity cost involves using the real interest differential

$$(i^b - \Delta P^e/P) - (i^m - \Delta P^e/P)$$

where i^m is the nominal return on money, i^b is the nominal return on bonds, and $\Delta P^e/P$ is the expected rate of inflation. We always assume that economic agents are not subject to money illusion so it is the real return on assets, and thus the real opportunity cost of money, that will be relevant to the money demand decision since this is a demand for real cash balances. The expression above simplifies to

$$i^b - i^m$$

so you can see that when money pays no interest ($i^m = 0$), the real interest differential reduces to the nominal bond yield which is essentially what was used in the derivation of the Baumol-Tobin model. But when money *does* pay interest, then the nominal return on money would also appear as a shift parameter in the demand for money.[6]

This completes our discussion of the demand side of the money market. We now take up the supply side which will introduce you to the role of the central bank and the banking system in supplying money to households and firms.

7.3 THE SUPPLY OF MONEY

Money is supplied to the economic system through the interactions of the central bank and the banking system. To understand how money is supplied to the economy, we need to discuss each of these two components.

---

6 In some studies of money demand, it is assumed that the expected rate of inflation is the cost of holding real money balances. We can state the assumptions that would cause this to be the case; when money pays no interest and when there is no alternative financial asset, the cost of holding money reduces to the expected rate of inflation.

The Federal Reserve System

The Federal Reserve System was created by Congress in 1913. The Fed is headquartered in Washington, D.C. and the United States is divided into twelve Federal Reserve districts, each of which contains a regional Federal Reserve bank.[7] The Federal Reserve Board consists of seven governors, appointed by the President and confirmed by the Senate, each serving a 14-year term. One of these governors is appointed by the President to serve as Chairman for a 4-year term. Each regional bank is supervised by the Federal Reserve Board and has a president chosen by its nine-member board of directors. The Federal Reserve supervises and regulates financial institutions in the U.S. financial system and it has responsibilities for carrying out monetary policy. It is a quasi-independent agency; while it does report to Congress on its activities, it is structured so that it can carry out its responsibilities without any direct influence by elected politicians.

Regarding its regulatory activities, financial institutions are subject to a variety of laws that regulate their activities and the Fed is charged with ensuring that financial institutions are in compliance with some of these regulations. As an example, banks are subject to **reserve requirements** and the Fed ensures that banks meet these obligations. Banks are required to hold reserves against deposits on their books in the form of **vault cash** (cash held by the bank) or in the form of a **deposit**, owned by the bank, and held with the Fed. A fraction of every dollar of the checkable deposits, owned by the bank's depositors, must be held as reserves and this fraction is set by law and/or by the Fed.

A second area of responsibility for the Fed is the conduct of monetary policy. The seven governors, and five regional bank presidents on a rotating basis, carry out monetary policy by their participation as members of the **Federal Open Market Committee** (FOMC). The FOMC makes decisions regarding open market operations carried out by the Fed. An open market operation is a financial transaction whereby the Fed buys or sells government bonds in financial markets. These transactions are designed to change the money supply or possibly an interest rate in order to meet the Fed's ultimate policy goals. These policy objectives may involve reducing inflation, combating a recession, or perhaps meeting other objectives for the aggregate economy.

Table 7.3 contains selected items from the **balance sheet** of the Federal Reserve System. As you may recall, a balance sheet lists the assets and liabilities of an individual or organization.

Assets

On the asset side, gold refers to the value of the official U.S. stock of gold. Special Drawing Rights (SDRs) are collections of foreign exchange held by the Fed. Central banks can buy or sell foreign exchange just as they buy other assets such as government bonds. Coin refers to the coin held by Federal Reserve Banks. Securities and Loans refers to government

---

7 These districts are Atlanta, Boston, Chicago, Cleveland, Dallas, Kansas City, Minneapolis, New York, Philadelphia, Richmond, San Francisco, and St. Louis.

TABLE 7.3 Federal Reserve Balance Sheet, Selected Items, June 2009

Assets		Liabilities	
Gold	11,037	Federal Reserve Notes	867,521
Special Drawing Rights	2,200	Reverse Repurchase Agreements	70,166
Coin	1781	Deposits	1,079,880
Securities and Loans	1,643,934	Deferred Availability Cash Items	2,683
Items in Process of Collection	719		
Bank Premises	2,200		
Total Assets	2,074,239	Total Liabilities	2,026,910

Note: Data are in millions of dollars.

Source: Federal Reserve Statistical Release H.4.1

securities that the Fed purchases when it conducts open market operations; loans are made to banks and other institutions through the Discount Window. These loans are an asset of the Fed and a **liability** of the banks that borrow. Items in Process of Collection are assets related to checks written and cleared by the Fed. Bank premises are physical assets owned by the Fed.

Liabilities

On the liability side, Federal Reserve Notes is the amount of currency outstanding net of any quantities held by the Federal Reserve. Reverse Repurchase Agreements are borrowings using securities as collateral (that is, selling securities), under an agreement to buy them back at a stipulated date in the future. Deposits refer to the accounts with the Federal Reserve of banks, the U.S. Treasury, and other institutions. Deferred Availability Cash Items is a liability arising from check clearing carried out by the Fed.[8] If you were to look at the balance sheet of the Fed and compare it in periods before and after the recession beginning in December 2007, you would see new assets on the balance sheet because the recession was an unprecedented one in economic history (see **Doing Economics:** The Fed's Balance Sheet Before and After December 2007).

---

8 When a check is drawn on a bank, the amount of the check must be added to the account of one bank (say a merchant receives a check from a buyer and deposits it into a bank account) and subtracted from the account of another bank (the buyer's account must have the amount of the check deducted from it). The difference between Items in Process of Collection and Deferred Availability Cash is called float. Once the check has cleared completely, float is zero but it can be nonzero during the process of collection.

Doing Economics: The Fed's Balance Sheet Before and After December 2007

The most recent recession experienced by industrialized economies began in December 2007 according to the National Bureau of Economic Research (www.nber.org). This contraction was unique in the sense that it originated in U.S. housing markets. Homeowners began to default on their home mortgages to an unprecedented extent. A mortgage is a liability of the borrowing homeowner and an asset to the financial institution, say a bank, originating the loan made to the homeowner. When these defaults occur, the value of the mortgage on the bank's books declines, reducing the **net worth** of the bank. This in turn can cause a bank to be rendered insolvent (or bankrupt) if these defaults occur to a sufficient extent. But there was an additional aspect to these defaults causing the Fed to behave differently than it did in previous recessions.

Mortgages were used in the U.S. financial system to create a new financial asset called mortgage-backed securities. Such a security is tied to a collection of mortgages with the property that if one or more of the underlying mortgages goes into default, the mortgage-backed security declines in value. More seriously, market participants cannot easily determine the value of a mortgage-backed security when the mortgages underlying the security cannot be determined accurately to be in default. As a result, an institution such as a bank holding a mortgage-backed security may find that the security is worthless, reducing the bank's net worth and thus pushing the bank towards insolvency.

These unique features of the recession caused the Federal Reserve to behave quite differently than it did in previous recessions with respect to the types of actions that it took in the financial system. The standard response of any central bank to a recession would be to carry out open market operations designed to increase the money supply (we discuss this further in this chapter and in Chapter 14) and the U.S. central bank did indeed operate in this way. But the Fed also bought mortgage-backed securities in the financial system. To see how the Fed responded to the recession, we can look at the Fed's balance sheet just before the recession began and then again when the recession was well under way or possibly ended. Below you will see selected balance sheet items for the Fed in late November 2007 and items from the balance sheet measured two years later. In the table, a repurchase agreement is a collateralized loan using securities offered by the borrower.

Selected Federal Reserve Balance Sheet Items

	November 29, 2007	November 27, 2009
Assets		
Securities, Repurchase Agreements, and Loans	825,747	1,994,313
Securities Held Outright	779,693	1,783,726
US Treasury	779,693	776,535
Federal Agency	0	155,066
Mortgage-Backed Securities	0	852,124
Repurchase Agreements	46,000	0
Loans	54	210,587

Source: Federal Reserve Statistical Release H.4.1. Data are in millions of dollars.

(continued)

There are several noteworthy entries in the table. Notice first that the securities held by the Fed more than doubled over the two points in time. As you will see later in this chapter, the enormous increase in the security holdings of the Fed increased the money supply substantially. Note also that the Fed began to hold mortgage-backed securities and Federal agency securities, U.S. government agencies associated with housing markets. Thus not only did the Fed engineer an enormous increase in the assets that they held, they also changed the composition of their assets due to the peculiar nature of the recession.

In understanding the money supply process, an important point to recognize is that whenever the Fed engages in an action that changes the size of an asset, there will be a corresponding change on the liability side of its balance sheet. So if the Fed carries out an open market operation designed to increase its holdings of government securities, thus increasing one of its assets, there will be a corresponding increase in the reserve balances of banks, an item on the liability side of the balance sheet. As you will see shortly, this is how an open market operation affects the supply of money.

Finally, in carrying out its monetary policy, there are a number of tools used by the Fed. The Fed sets the **discount rate**, the interest rate paid by banks that borrow from the Fed through the **discount window**. The Fed may also carry out open market operations designed to set the **Federal Funds rate**. If a bank does not have adequate reserves to meet its reserve requirements, it can borrow reserves from the Fed, paying the discount rate on the borrowed funds, or it can borrow reserves from another bank having **excess reserves** (reserves in excess of what is required by law). If reserves are borrowed in the federal funds market, the borrowing bank pays the federal funds rate on the borrowed funds. Finally, the Fed can change reserve requirements as part of its monetary policies.

The Banking System

The earliest banks were storage facilities for the safe-keeping of money. In return for a fee, the bank would place a depositor's funds in a safe storage facility and would not lend out any of the funds that were deposited. Because they did not lend out any funds, these banks were said to operate with **one hundred percent reserves**. If a depositor returned and wished to withdraw all of her funds on deposit, the bank would have no trouble in meeting this demand. Modern-day banks are part of a **fractional reserve banking system**. In such a system, banks lend out part of their depositor's funds. Fractional reserve banking is attractive to bankers because there are profit opportunities available that the bank can exploit when it needs to keep only a fraction of its depositor's funds in reserve. Think about the bank holding one hundred percent reserves. It is in no danger of failing because it has all of the funds that were deposited. But its profits are lower than they would be if some of its depositor's money were loaned out, earning the bank some interest income. But a bank with fractional reserves is riskier than one with one hundred percent reserves because there is a danger that it will not be able to meet the demands of customers for funds. A bank is obligated to convert customer deposits into currency. If a bank fails to do so, this can trigger a **bank run** (or bank panic). In this situation, information spreads among depositors that the bank is having trouble meeting currency demands, causing even more depositors to show up on the bank's doorstep demanding currency. This explains the need to hold reserves and why laws require that reserves be held. The stability of the financial system is one objective of the Federal Reserve and the discount window is the "lender of last resort" function of the Fed that can be and has been used to prevent bank runs.

Modern-day banks are **financial intermediaries**. An intermediary brings parties together to facilitate a transaction. In the case of a financial intermediary, lenders and borrowers are brought together by banks to facilitate loan transactions. Thus a bank pools together the deposits of individuals, screens loan applicants for their credit-worthiness, and then makes loans to borrowers (firms or individuals) that it deems capable of repaying the loan with interest. Table 7.4 provides selected balance sheet items for a bank. The items appearing on each side of the statement reflect the actions of bank management to earn an income for their stockholders (the bank's owners); in addition, there may be regulations that dictate the assets that the bank may have and so the items appearing on the asset and liability sides must generally be consistent with any applicable laws. The bank has assets consisting of loans, holdings of government securities, and the reserves that it needs to meet reserve requirements on its checkable deposit liabilities (an asset to the owners of the deposits). Satisfying these reserve requirements works as follows.

Define the **required reserve ratio** to be rr; the law sets this so that $0 < rr < 1$. Then if the bank is meeting its reserve requirements, it must be true that

$$\text{Reserves} = \text{rr} \cdot \text{Deposits.}$$

Thus if the law requires that 10 percent of checkable deposit liabilities be kept as reserves, then with $100 million of checkable deposits, the bank must have $10 million held as reserves, either in the form of vault cash and/or its deposit at the Fed. If the bank does not have adequate reserves, it can borrow reserves in the Federal Funds market, paying the Federal Funds interest rate. Or it can borrow the reserves from the Fed, paying the discount rate. For the banking system as a whole, this same equation must hold if all banks in the aggregate are meeting their reserve requirements.

TABLE 7.4 Bank Balance Sheet	
Assets	*Liabilities*
Loans	Checkable Deposits
Government Securities	
Fed Deposit	
Vault Cash	

Money Supply Determination

The money stock rises and falls through the interaction of the banking system and the Fed when the Fed carries out **Open Market Operations**. We illustrate this process by imagining that the Fed decides to buy government securities directly from a bank, although you will see that the Fed could simply buy these securities in the open market with the same result. Tables 7.5 and 7.6 provide the initial balance sheets for the bank and the Fed where we have listed only those assets and liabilities that are needed for our analysis. With a required reserve ratio of 10 percent, the bank is satisfying its reserve requirements because its vault cash and Fed deposit are 10 percent of its checkable deposits, the only bank deposit liability requiring the holding of reserves.

Now suppose that the Fed decides to increase its holdings of government bonds by 10. It arranges to buy the bonds from the bank and pays for them by simply adding the appropriate amount to the bank's Fed deposit. The resulting balance sheets are given below. Notice that the net worth of each organization is unchanged (net worth is the difference between assets and liabilities) because assets and liabilities changed by the same amount. But now the bank has excess reserves because the sum of its Fed deposit and vault cash are now 20 but it only requires 10 (checkable deposits are unchanged) to satisfy reserve requirements. The bank now has an incentive to loan out these excess reserves and it will do so to raise its earnings. The end result of these actions will raise the money supply by more than 10 as you will see below in Tables 7.7 and 7.8.

The example above may seem artificial in the sense that the Fed is buying directly from an individual bank rather than in the open financial market that is in fact what it does. This makes no important difference. Suppose that the Fed bought the securities in much the same way that ordinary individuals and firms buy them. All the Fed would need to do is send a check to a bond dealer, the bond dealer deposits the check into a checkable deposit (unlike our previous

TABLE 7.5 Initial Bank Balance Sheet

Assets		Liabilities	
Government Securities	200	Checkable Deposits	100
Fed Deposit	8		
Vault Cash	2		

TABLE 7.6 Initial Fed Balance Sheet

Assets		Liabilities	
Government Securities	500	Bank Deposits	300

TABLE 7.7 Final Bank Balance Sheet

Assets		Liabilities	
Government Securities	190	Checkable Deposits	100
Fed Deposit	18		
Vault Cash	2		

TABLE 7.8 Final Fed Balance Sheet

Assets		Liabilities	
Government Securities	510	Bank Deposits	310

example, checkable deposits initially change in this case), and the bank would then present the check to the Fed which would add the amount of the check to the Fed deposit of the bank. **Bank reserves** still rise by the amount of the open market purchase. The important point to be made about these transactions is given below.

Proposition About Open Market Operations

■ Open market operations change the quantity of bank reserves in the banking system.

The example above does not show how much the money supply will change in response to an open market operation. For that, we need to derive a formal money supply function. But before doing so, it is useful to point out that buying bonds is not the only action by the Fed that causes bank reserves to change.

Look back at Table 7.3 and notice the asset listed as Special Drawing Rights. This is just a collection of foreign currencies owned by the Fed. Central banks can buy or sell foreign currencies just as they buy or sell bonds. We will not discuss their reasons for doing so here (this issue will be taken up in Chapter 14) but it is important to note that buying foreign currency affects bank reserves in the same way as an open market bond purchase. If the Fed wishes to add to its holdings of euros, it would purchase them from dealers making the market for foreign exchange. The Fed sends a check to those dealers who deposit them in their bank accounts. The banks' reserve accounts are increased by the amount of the foreign currency purchase. Just as for the bond purchase, the money supply and bank reserves rise.

Now we can construct a formal money supply equation. In our analysis, we assume that money consists of currency plus checkable deposits. So

$$\text{Money} = \text{Currency} + \text{Checkable Deposits}$$

$$M = C + D$$

We will also need a definition of the **Monetary Base**, given below.

$$\text{Monetary Base} = \text{Currency} + \text{Bank Reserves}$$

$$MB = C + R$$

We will also need the reserves relationship described earlier.

$$R = rr \cdot D, \ 0 < rr < 1$$

The money supply function is a relationship between the monetary base and money used by economic agents. To obtain this we also use an assumption regarding currency holding by the public. Namely, we will assume that there is a simple proportionality relationship between currency and checkable deposits given by

$$C = k \cdot D, \ k > 0.$$

In the above expression, k is the **currency-checkable deposit ratio**. We assume, for now, that it is fixed although, at a later point, we will suggest some possible determinants of this ratio. The money supply equation that we seek is found by using this assumption and our previous relationships to yield the money supply equation.

$$MB = k \cdot D + rr \cdot D$$

$$MB = (k + rr) \cdot D$$

$$M = C + D = k \cdot D + D$$

$$M = (1 + k) \cdot D$$

$$M = \left[\frac{1+k}{k+rr} \right] \cdot MB$$

The bracketed term in the last expression is called the **money multiplier**. Given our assumptions about the required reserve ratio, this magnitude is greater than unity. Note the implication of this fact; if the Fed increases the monetary base through an open market operation, the money supply will rise by more than the increase in the monetary base. For this reason, the monetary base is sometimes called **high-powered money**. The fundamental reason for this is that we have a fractional reserve system of banking. Set the reserve ratio, rr, equal to unity, and you will see that the money multiplier is also equal to unity. The monetary base is no longer "high-powered" in a system where banks hold one hundred percent reserves.[9]

---

9 There are economists who have advocated a one hundred percent reserves banking system because it removes the possibility of bank runs, thus causing the banking system to be immune to this instability.

In addition to the monetary base, the required reserve ratio is also a policy variable affecting the money supply. The higher this fraction, the lower will be the money supply. To see why, go back to our example above using bank and Fed balance sheets. If banks have excess reserves, how much they can lend out depends upon the required reserve ratio. The higher this ratio, the less of these excess reserves they can lend out, and thus the smaller the increase in the money supply.

Finally, the currency to checkable deposit ratio is also a determinant of the money supply. Figure 7.4 shows that this was slowly rising in the economy up until the middle of the 1990s after which the currency-checkable deposit ratio began to rise sharply. In extreme circumstances, there have been even larger changes in this magnitude.[10] It can be shown that there is an inverse relationship between the money multiplier and the parameter k. Thus a higher currency to checkable deposit ratio will reduce the supply of money. We can suggest some reasons why the parameter k might change.

One factor that can cause the public to desire more currency relative to its checkable deposits is the marginal tax rate. As this tax rate rises, it is possible that people will try to conduct their economic affairs by using currency to an increasing extent. By using currency, they can try to avoid some of the taxation of their income by understating their income for tax

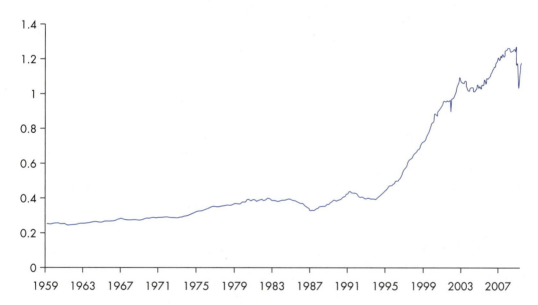

FIGURE 7.4 Currency-Checkable Deposit Ratio

Source: St. Louis Federal Reserve Bank FRED Database

---

10 During the Great Depression, there was a substantial increase in the ratio of currency to checkable deposits. The reason was that banks were failing which caused households to hold more currency to avoid losing their deposits in a failed bank. See Chapter 12 for data on the ratio of currency to checkable deposits during the Great Depression.

purposes. This phenomenon is often called the **underground economy**, that is, the economic transactions that are "off the books."[11]

A second reason for the size of k is related to the risk of holding deposits in the banking system. If the public comes to believe that banks are unsafe and in danger of failing, they will choose to convert their deposits into currency (see fn. 8 above). Table 7.9 summarizes our findings about the determinants of the money supply.

Finally, new assets can emerge in the market that are substitutes for checkable deposits, causing households to shift out of checkable deposits and into these new assets. Firms in financial markets offered money market funds in the 1980s that acted as checking accounts that paid interest, often at interest rates higher than what was offered by banks. Thus households moved funds into these new assets and out of checkable deposits.

This completes our discussion of money supply determination. We now combine our analyses of the demand and supply sides of the market. This will enable us to analyze the properties of the financial markets that will be contained in our aggregate economic models.

7.4 THE MONEY MARKET

Now that we have developed each side of the market for money, we can combine them in order to understand the market for money. Figure 7.5 illustrates this market. The figure combines the analysis of the demand for money with the supply of money as determined by the interaction of the Federal Reserve and the banking system. The real supply of money is denoted in the figure as M_0/P. The money supply equation that was developed above did not depend upon the interest rate and so the money supply is drawn as a vertical line in Figure 7.5. It is important to understand the forces causing the nominal interest rate to achieve the level i^* in the figure.

Suppose that the nominal interest rate is initially at the level i_1. At this interest rate, there is an excess supply of money. This situation sets forces in motion that will eliminate this excess supply of money. These forces involve both the money and bond markets because we imagine that people are making a portfolio decision involving their holdings of each financial asset. If households hold more money than they wish at this interest rate, they will begin to reshuffle

---

TABLE 7.9 Determinants of the Money Supply

Causal Factor	Response of the Money Supply
R ↑	MB ↑ ⇒ M ↑
rr ↑	M ↓
k ↑	M ↓

Note: In the table, R refers to bank reserves, rr is the required reserve ratio, k is the ratio of currency to checkable deposits, MB is the monetary base, and M is the money supply.

---

11 The underground economy can also involve illegal activities, such as trade in illegal drugs, which are carried out in cash to avoid detection by law enforcement agencies.

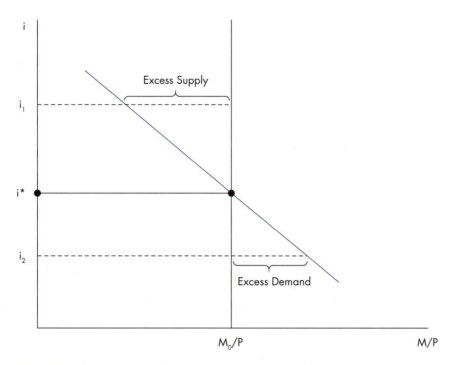

FIGURE 7.5 The Money Market

The money market is in equilibrium at the nominal interest rate i*.
At i₁ (i₂), there is an excess supply (demand) for money.

their holdings of money and bonds to arrange their holdings of these assets into optimal amounts. This connection between the money and bond markets can be explained more fully if we consider an idea known as **Walras' Law** which is stated below.

Walras' Law of Markets

■ In an economy with an arbitrary number of markets, the sum of all the excess demands in the economy must be zero.

Leon Walras was a nineteenth-century economist who proved that this proposition must hold. Suppose we apply this to the money and bond markets. We assume that all other markets in the economy are in equilibrium. Then Walras' Law implies that

$$(M^d - M_0) + (B^d - B_0) = 0.$$

In this expression, M^d is the nominal demand for money, B^d is the nominal demand for bonds, while M_0 and B_0 are, respectively, the nominal supplies of money and bonds. The excess demand for each asset is measured by the difference between nominal demand and nominal supply. Now return to Figure 7.5 and ask what is true in the bond market when there is an excess supply of money in the money market at the interest rate i_1. Using Walras' Law, an excess supply of money must be matched by an excess demand for bonds (a negative excess demand is, by definition, an excess supply). So people will buy up bonds with this excess supply of money, driving up bond prices and thus driving down the nominal bond interest rate.[12] This is the mechanism that will eliminate the excess supply of money. Using the same type of reasoning, you should be able to work out the case where the initial interest rate is i_2.

The Effects of Changing Income

We can use the money market diagram to establish the reaction of the interest rate to a change in real income, Y. Recall from our discussion of money demand that an increase in real income will cause households to wish to increase their consumption and, as a result, they will wish to hold more money to pay for these purchases. Figure 7.6 illustrates this situation.

The increase in real income causes a rightward shift in the demand for money. At the original interest rate, i_0, there is now an excess demand for money and, by use of Walras' Law, an excess supply of bonds. Thus people begin to sell off the bonds they no longer wish to hold and this causes a decline in bond prices and a corresponding increase in the interest rate. The interest rate keeps rising until the excess demand for money is eliminated.

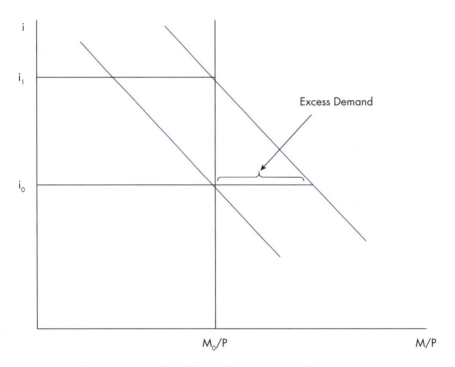

FIGURE 7.6 The Money Market Effects of Increasing Real Income

When real income rises from Y_0 to Y_1, there will be an increase in the demand for money, causing an excess demand for money at the original interest rate i_0. This will cause the nominal interest rate to rise to the level i_1.

---

12 As was shown in Chapter 2, there is an inverse relationship between bond prices and bond yields

The Financial Sector

Walras' Law effectively determines the properties of the bond demand schedule that is consistent with our money demand model. These two financial markets constitute the financial sector that will be embedded in the aggregate economic models discussed later in the book. These markets are illustrated in Figure 7.7 where their connections are made explicit. Both markets are initially in equilibrium at the interest rate i_0. The discussion earlier in the chapter indicated that at an interest rate above i_0, there would be an excess demand (supply) for bonds (money) so the bond demand schedule must be increasing in the interest rate, a reasonable finding since lenders would be more inclined to lend if the bond yield rises. If income rises, there would be an increase in money demand in the Baumol-Tobin model and so there must be a corresponding decline in the demand for bonds as households sell bonds to acquire additional money for transaction purposes.

The Effects of Increasing the Money Supply

Figure 7.8 provides the graphical details describing the economic events that follow from an increase in the money supply by the Fed. When the Fed engages in an open market purchase of government securities, the supply of money increases because banks initially have excess reserves which they then lend out. These actions cause a rightward shift in the supply of money generating, at the original equilibrium interest rate, an excess supply of money. The corresponding excess demand for bonds causes an increase in bond prices and a decline in the interest rate. The interest rate falls until the excess supply of money has been eliminated. This is the source of the conventional wisdom that is frequently stated in the press; a "loose money" policy causes interest rates to decline. But there is an important qualification that must be offered here.

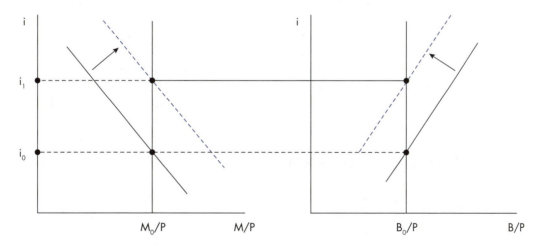

FIGURE 7.7 The Money and Bond Markets

The initial nominal supplies of money and bonds are M_0 and B_0 and the equilibrium interest rate is i_0. Walras' Law implies that bond demand (B^d) is increasing in the interest rate and that, if income rises, there will be an increase (decrease) in the demand for money (bonds).

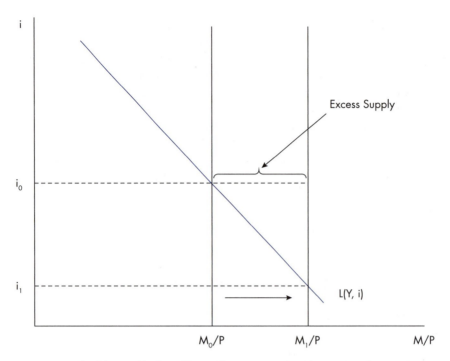

FIGURE 7.8 The Money Market Effects of Increasing the Money Supply

When nominal money supply rises from M_0 to M_1, there will be an excess supply of money, and an excess demand for bonds, at the original interest rate i_0. This will cause the nominal interest rate to fall to the level i_1.

We will observe later that sustained increases in the money supply will actually raise, rather than lower, nominal interest rates because sustained increases in the money stock generate inflation and that will cause nominal interest rates to rise. What is illustrated in Figure 7.8 is a very short-run story about the initial effects of an open market purchase of government securities but it is a misleading guide as to the ultimate effects of increasing the money supply.

Finally, this money market diagram can be used to illustrate issues related to the manner in which a central bank should carry out its monetary policies. One application of this framework deals with the consequences of pegging interest rates in conducting monetary policy. This exercise introduces you to policy topics that will be discussed later in the book (see **Doing Economics**: Pegging the Interest Rate by the Central Bank).

7.5 THE VELOCITY OF MONEY

The concept of the **velocity of money** is used in connection with monetary policy. Here is its definition.

Definition of the Velocity of Money

■   The velocity of money is defined as the ratio of nominal income to the money stock.

Using v to denote velocity, we have

Doing Economics: Pegging the Interest Rate by the Central Bank

In carrying out monetary policy, one issue that must be decided by central bankers is how to carry out their policies in the financial markets. Among other things, they will need to decide whether it is appropriate to peg the interest rate or the money stock as the best way of meeting the ultimate objectives of their policies. Here we use the money market diagram to illustrate these policy alternatives.

We imagine that there are transitory shifts in the demand for money. The Fed does not know the origin of these shifts; these shifts are assumed unpredictable. They may merely reflect temporary changes in the demand for money by households but, whatever their origin, we illustrate their existence by the dotted lines in the diagram that are parallel to the demand for money. Now observe what will happen when the Fed fixes the money stock or the interest rate.

The Fed could simply keep the supply of money fixed at the level M_0/P in which case the interest rate will fluctuate between the levels i_1 and i_2 but the money stock remains constant in the face of these disturbances to the demand for money. Now consider what will happen if the Fed pegs (fixes) the interest rate at the level i_0.

To keep the interest rate constant, the Fed must move the supply of money in whatever

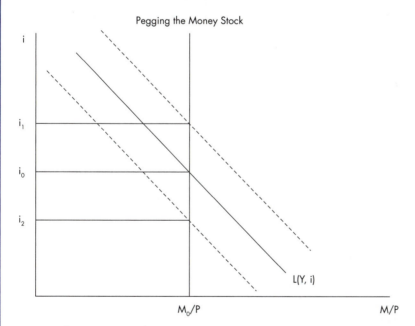

Pegging the Money Stock

When there are unpredictable shifts in the demand for money, only the interest rate will change, fluctuating between i_1 and i_2, in response to shifts in money demand. The money stock remains constant as long as the Fed fixes the money supply.

(continued)

manner is necessary to prevent the interest rate from changing. So if there is a rightward shift in money demand, the Fed must increase the money supply; if it does not do so, the interest rate will increase. Similarly, the money stock must fall if there is a leftward shift in money demand.

The implications of the analysis are clear. Either the interest rate or the money stock fluctuates but not both. Fixing the interest rate results in larger swings in the money stock than would occur if the money stock were fixed. Thus there is a clear tradeoff between stability of the money stock or the interest rate. We will revisit this issue later in the book when we look more closely at the conduct of monetary policy.

$$v = \frac{P \cdot Y}{M}$$

where P is the price level, Y is real GDP, and M is the money stock. Velocity is sometimes described as a turnover rate for the money stock since it measures the dollar value of transactions in the economy per dollar of money in use in the economy. Figure 7.9 plots monetary velocity under two definitions of the money stock, M1 and M2. We can use the concept of velocity to explain why a central banker might prefer one definition of money over another.

The figure shows very clearly that velocity is much more stable over time if we use M2 rather than M1. M2 velocity seems to be roughly constant over time whereas M1 velocity has been consistently trending up. To see why this is important, our expression for velocity above can be manipulated to give

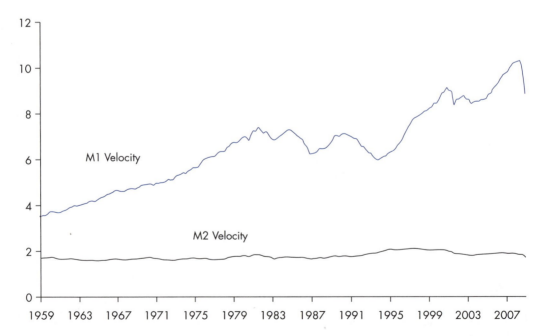

FIGURE 7.9 M1 and M2 Velocity

Source: St. Louis Federal Reserve Bank FRED Database

$$\frac{\Delta v}{v} = \frac{\Delta P}{P} + \frac{\Delta Y}{Y} - \frac{\Delta M}{M}.$$

Now suppose that velocity is constant. Then the equation above simplifies to

$$\frac{\Delta M}{M} = \frac{\Delta P}{P} + \frac{\Delta Y}{Y}.$$

If a central banker is interested in achieving an inflation target of, say, 2 percent per year, then knowledge of the growth in real output gives the policymaker a rough guide as to how much the money stock should grow to achieve the desired rate of price inflation. So if we were to use a long-run growth rate for real output of 2.5 percent, not far from its actual long-term value in the U.S., then money can grow at 4.5 percent to achieve an inflation rate at the target level. This analysis suggests that a policymaker would prefer to use M2 as the monetary aggregate best suited to making monetary policy.

As a matter of fact, our analysis of the transactions demand for money predicts that velocity will not be constant. Notice that we can rewrite the definition of velocity as

$$v = \frac{P \cdot Y}{M} = \frac{Y}{M/P} = \frac{Y}{L(Y,i)}$$

The denominator of this expression is the implication of the demand for money analysis that we carried out earlier in the chapter. Using real income in place of consumption, our analysis predicts that velocity will rise with the level of the nominal interest rate (because the demand for money will fall) and with the level of real income (this latter point follows from using some algebra to prove this to be true). Thus we could use empirical estimates of money demand to predict the movements over time in velocity. Using actual data on real income, the nominal interest rate, and the estimates of the impacts of these magnitudes on money demand, predicted velocity could be compared to actual velocity. This exercise has been carried out and it was found that, using M1, velocity increased much more rapidly than predicted by estimated money demand equations after 1974. This has been interpreted to mean that there were structural changes in money markets causing unexpected reductions in the demand for M1, further evidence that M2 may be the preferred monetary aggregate for monetary policy purposes.[13]

The Origin of Inflation

The velocity of money also can be used to illustrate one of the fundamental insights of macroeconomics. This will be illustrated more thoroughly when we analyze aggregate models of the economy later in the book but here we can observe the causes of inflation quite simply if we use the assumption that velocity is constant. Recall our definition of inflation, given previously.

---

13 Rather mysteriously, Stephen Goldfeld referred to this evidence as "The Case of the Missing Money," in the *Brookings Papers on Economic Activity* 3 (1976), pp. 683–730.

Definition of Inflation

■ Inflation is a sustained increase in the prices of all goods and services in an economy.

The definition excludes relative price changes, referring only to a situation where all prices are rising. Relative prices do change but this is not what we mean by inflation. Finally, inflation refers to continual, as opposed to one-time, changes in the prices of all goods and services. There are economic explanations for one-time changes in the price level, discussed elsewhere in this book, but these do not have a monetary origin. The monetary cause of inflation can now be explained.

Earlier we used the expression

$$\frac{\Delta M}{M} = \frac{\Delta P}{P} + \frac{\Delta Y}{Y}$$

to explain how constant velocity can be useful in monetary policymaking. But the expression can also be used to provide the justification for the famous statement by Milton Friedman that "Inflation is always and everywhere a monetary phenomenon."[14] The expression indicates that, in a stationary economy (one where equilibrium output growth is zero), price stability requires a constant money supply whereas, in a growing economy, money growth can be non-inflationary if it is equal to the long-run growth rate of the economy. Figure 7.10 provides some empirical evidence on the relationship between money growth and the inflation rate for European OECD

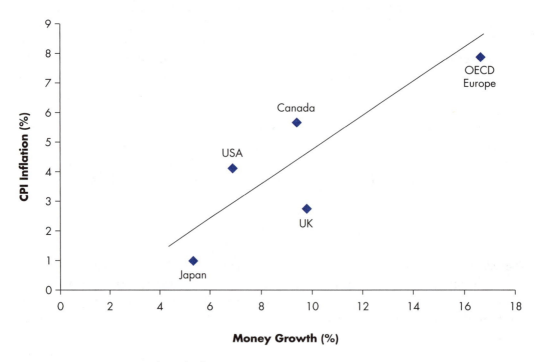

FIGURE 7.10 Money Growth and Inflation

14 See "Inflation: Causes and Consequences" in *Dollars and Deficits*, Prentice-Hall (1968), p. 29.

countries, Canada, Japan, the United States, and the United Kingdom. The figure shows the growth rate of the money stock and the inflation rate for each country and there is an evident positive relationship between these two magnitudes. Thus the greater the growth rate of the money stock, the higher the inflation rate in these countries. But the figure also suggests that the relationship between money growth and inflation is not one-to-one, meaning that a one percent increase in the money growth rate seems not to be associated with a one percent increase in inflation. One possible reason for this fact, discussed later in the book, is that there are many other factors that can affect the price level, such as disturbances emanating from the supply-side of the economy, which can cause changes in the price level. But the diagram leaves little doubt that Friedman's statement about the monetary cause of inflation does receive considerable support from the actual performance of aggregate economies. The cause of inflation is arguably the most important insight offered by macroeconomics.

7.6 CONCLUDING REMARKS

The use of money is a feature of all developed economies and the task of this chapter has been to explain why money is used, and what determines its demand and supply, and to provide an analysis of the financial markets that will be one component of our aggregate macroeconomic models developed later in the book.

Money provides a number of benefits to society but its most important one is that its use reduces the transactions costs of carrying out economic trades. For this reason, money is used as the medium of exchange in economic transactions. The basic model of money demand is built upon the existence of these transactions costs. That model presumes that households want to minimize the costs of holding money and those costs comprise foregone interest and the transactions costs of making a withdrawal from an interest-bearing account into a cash balance. The economic implications of this model are that money demand is proportional to the price level, increasing in transactions costs and real consumption volume, and decreasing in the interest rate.

The money supply process involves both the central bank and the banking system. Banks are required by law to hold reserves against certain deposit liabilities. The Fed can affect the overall supply of these reserves by the purchase or sale of government bonds. In addition, the Fed can change the fraction of a dollar in deposits that must be held as reserves by banks. The supply of money relationship that was derived above revealed that the supply of money rises with the purchase of government bonds by the Fed, falls with a rise in the required reserve ratio, and falls with an increase in the currency-checkable deposit ratio chosen by households.

The money market is built using this demand and supply analysis. The interest rate is set by the interaction of the money and bond markets and it was shown how to obtain a bond demand curve consistent with the demand for money. This financial sector reveals that an increase in real income raises the interest rate clearing the financial markets and it shows that an increase in the supply of money, generated by an open market purchase of bonds by the Fed, will reduce the interest rate clearing the financial markets.

This chapter introduces the concept of the velocity of money, showing how it can be used as a rough guide for central bankers wanting to achieve a desired inflation target. It was also shown that this concept is useful in understanding the origin of inflation in the economy. The velocity of money clearly shows that inflation, defined as a sustained increase in the prices of all goods and services in the economy, must have a monetary origin.

The analysis in this chapter provides the microfoundations of the financial sector used in almost all aggregate economic models. Many of the results in this chapter, most importantly those regarding the origins of inflation, carry over into the aggregate models discussed later in the book so that many of the results of this chapter are actually more general than they appear.

Key Ideas

- Money is used as a medium of exchange because it reduces the transactions costs of carrying out the exchange of goods and services between individuals.
- The prices of goods and services are measured in terms of money, reducing the number of prices that need to be computed to determine the most advantageous trade by individuals.
- Money is a place to store purchasing power over goods and so it is a store of value.
- Money is used as the means of repaying debts so it is a standard of deferred payment.
- In a barter system, people do not use money, instead trading goods and services.
- Transactions costs are the time and direct expenses of carrying out transactions.
- The Baumol-Tobin model of money demand explains the holding of an inventory of money as due to the transactions costs of trade.
- In the Baumol-Tobin theory of money demand, money demand is proportional to the price level, increasing in transactions costs and real consumption volume, and decreasing in the interest rate.
- The Federal Reserve System controls the overall supply of bank reserves through the purchase or sale of government bonds.
- The Federal Reserve also controls the fraction of reserves that banks must hold against certain deposit liabilities.
- Banks are required by law to hold these reserves as a way of avoiding bank failures that may lead to bank runs or bank panics.
- Reserves may be held by banks as cash in the vault or a deposit at the Fed.
- The supply of money is increasing in the quantity of bank reserves, and decreasing in the required reserve ratio and the currency-checkable deposit ratio.
- The currency-checkable deposit ratio can be affected by the marginal tax rate and the riskiness of holding deposits in banks.
- Walras' Law may be used to derive the bond demand schedule consistent with the demand for money, showing that bond demand is increasing in the interest rate, and decreasing in real income.
- The money market shows that an increase in real income raises the equilibrium interest rate and an increase in the money supply reduces the equilibrium interest rate.
- The velocity of money is defined as the ratio of nominal income to the money stock.
- Inflation is a sustained increase in the prices of all goods and services in an economy.
- If the velocity of money is constant, then the growth rate of the money stock must equal the sum of the inflation rate and the growth rate of output.
- Inflation is caused by money growth in excess of the equilibrium growth rate of output.

Key Terms

Monetize
Standard of
   Deferred
   Payment
Transactions
   Costs
Currency
Square-Root Rule
Reserve
   Requirements
Federal Open
   Market
   Committee
Asset
Federal Funds
   Rate

Bank Run
Bank Reserves
High-Powered
   Money
Underground
   Economy
Medium of
   Exchange
Barter System
Shoe-Leather Costs
Checkable
   Deposits
Qualitative
Vault Cash
Open Market
   Operations

Liability
One Hundred
   Percent
   Reserves
Financial
   Intermediary
Monetary Base
Currency-Checkable
   Deposit Ratio
Velocity of
   Money
Unit of
   Account
Double
   Coincidence
   of Wants

Commodity
   Money
M1
Quantitative
Monetary
   Policy
Balance Sheet
Net Worth
Fractional
   Reserves
Required
   Reserve
   Ratio
Excess
   Reserves
Walras' Law

Inflation
Store of
   Value
Fiat Money
M2
Transactions
   Demand for
   Money
Discount
   Window
Money
   Multiplier
Liquidity
Elasticity
Discount
   Rate

Questions for Study and Review

Review Questions

1. Explain why the demand for money is inversely related to the nominal interest rate.
2. Why is the money multiplier greater than unity?
3. What happens to the money supply if there is an increase in required reserve ratio?
4. During a recent recession more people began to barter, that is, they exchanged goods for other goods without using money (see *Merchants Barter Exchange Fighting Recession* on http://www.free-press-release.com/news/200801/1200679762.html). What are the advantages and disadvantages of a barter system?
5. Why is demand for money increasing in the planned consumption by households?
6. What are the economic functions of money?

Thought Questions

1. Using the money market and the money demand framework by Baumol and Tobin, explain why interest rates are procyclical.
2. What will happen to the money supply if there is an increase in the currency-checkable deposit ratio of households?
3. What will happen to the money supply if laws are changed making it legal to use certain currently-illegal drugs?
4. Suppose that the Fed decides to buy apartment houses instead of government bonds when it carries out monetary policy. What happens to the stock of bank reserves when the Fed makes these purchases?

Numerical Questions

1. The Fed decides to increase the money supply by $100 million. The current money supply is $300 billion, out of which $260 billion are deposited as checkable deposits at commercial banks. The required reserve ratio is 10 percent. What is the appropriate monetary policy action to achieve an increase in money supply by the desired amount?

2. Suppose Joe, a small business owner, is worried about the banking system and decides to keep this week's revenue of $1,000 in his safe instead of depositing it in his bank account. Assume that, on average, people hold 5 percent of their money in currency and that the required reserve ratio is 3 percent. How much money could Joe's bank give out in loans if he had deposited the money in his bank account?

3. The demand for money is given as $M^D / P = 200 + 0.7Y - 1,500i$. In addition, consider the following information: monetary base (MB): $2,000 billion; required reserve ratio (rr): 0.1; currency/checkable deposit ratio (k): 0.3.

   a) Compute the money supply.
   b) If the price level is 1.2 and real GDP is $7,800 billion, what is the level of the nominal interest rate?

4. Suppose that the velocity of money is constant, real GDP grows by 6 percent per year each year, the money stock grows by 9 percent per year, and the nominal interest rate is 7 percent.

   a) What are the inflation rate and the real interest rate?
   b) Suppose the central bank decides to target the inflation rate at 2 percent. What is the corresponding growth rate of the money stock?

Data Questions

1. Visit the website of the Federal Reserve Bank of St. Louis http://research.stlouisfed.org/fred2/. Under the category "Monetary Aggregates" you find the monetary aggregates M1, M2, and M3.

   a) For each of those monetary aggregates, plot a seasonally adjusted, monthly time series covering the last five years. Also, plot the currency component of M1. Discuss your findings.
   b) For M1, plot the percentage change from a year ago.
   c) In the category "Interest Rates," the effective Federal Funds rate is displayed at daily, weekly, and monthly frequency. Looking at either graph, what can you say about the relationship between the Federal Funds rate and the money supply over the last two years?

2. Go the St. Louis Federal Reserve Bank FRED database and retrieve data on the Federal Funds interest rate during the years 2007–2008. What does the time pattern of this data tell you about the Fed's monetary policy intentions?

For further questions, multiple choice quizzes, and weblinks related to this chapter, visit www.routledge.com/textbooks/rossana

References and Suggestions for Further Reading

Baumol, William J. (1952) "The Transaction Demand for Cash: An Inventory Theoretic Approach," *Quarterly Journal of Economics* 66, No. 4 (November), pp. 545–66.

Friedman, M. (1968) "Inflation: Causes and Consequences" in *Dollars and Deficits*, Englewood Cliffs, NJ: Prentice-Hall.

Friedman, M. and Schwartz, A.J. (1963) *A Monetary History of the United States, 1867–1960*, Princeton University Press for the National Bureau of Economic Research.

Goldfield, S. (1976) "The Case of the Missing Money," *Brookings Papers on Economic Activity* 3: 683–730.

McCallum, B.T. (1989) *Monetary Economics: Theory and Policy*, New York: Macmillan.

Tobin, James (1956) "The Interest-Elasticity of the Transactions Demand for Cash," *Review of Economics and Statistics* 38, No. 3 (August), pp. 241–7.

Chapter 8

The Labor Market

LEARNING OBJECTIVES

This chapter develops the economic theory of the labor market, one of the components of the supply-side of aggregate economic models of the economy. This labor market model requires that we study how firms decide upon the amount of labor to be used in production and we will need to know how it is that households choose their labor supply, including how taxes affect their labor supply decisions. We will also establish the important idea of the equilibrium unemployment rate and we will study variants of the labor market model that will be used in our models of the business cycle. Here are a few of the questions that we will answer in this chapter.

■ What determines the equilibrium unemployment rate in an economy?

■ How do firms choose the level of labor to use in production?

■ How do taxes and real wages affect the labor supply decisions of households?

■ How does the labor market determine the level of employment and real wages?

■ What labor market assumptions will be used in models of the business cycle?

The labor market is a component of the supply-side of aggregate macroeconomic models. The level of output in an economy is produced using the quantity of labor services set in the labor market where firms and households interact to determine how much labor will be used by firms to produce output and the actions of households and firms determine the return to labor services (the real wage) received by households. This chapter is designed to illustrate how labor markets function.

To understand economic processes, it is important to understand the data that emerges from those processes, so your first task in learning about the labor market is that you must become familiar with data compiled by the U.S. government, data that reveals the activities of the participants in the labor market. Inspection of this data will show interesting trends in the economy and will help us understand something about the nature of business cycles. In addition, the critical concept of the natural rate of unemployment will be discussed. When you understand this economic magnitude, you will know why a modern industrialized economy will always have a portion of its labor force that is seeking employment.

Once you understand the data, the next task is to develop a model of the labor market that can be used to explain the movements in this data. The demand-side of the market will be straightforward; using a simple profit maximization framework that should be familiar to you by now, the demand for labor will be derived. On the supply-side, we will study utility maximization by households, sorting out how individuals decide upon how much labor to provide in the labor market. You will use tools that you saw in Chapter 4 regarding substitution and income effects to establish how labor supply responds to changes in real wages. This discussion will also establish how households respond to tax incentives because the analysis will reveal how tax rates can have an impact upon the labor supply decisions of households.

Once we have analyzed the decisions of firms and households on both sides of the market, we can combine these analyses to study how the market determines employment and real wages. We will look at several variants of the basic model, asking how the labor market functions depending upon the degree of flexibility manifested by money wages. It turns out that labor and goods markets can behave quite differently if money wages are flexible as compared to when they are not. Therefore we look at a classical version of the labor market model using the assumption that labor markets are characterized by flexible money wages. This section will also look at the relationships between the demographic characteristics of the public (race, gender, and age) and the unemployment rate. You will see that the unemployment experience of individuals varies with these demographic traits. We then examine a version of the labor market called the "New Classical" version, a model where money wages are flexible but where there is incomplete information about the price level at the time that labor suppliers make their decisions. This discussion will introduce the critical idea of expectation formation and show how important it is for economic agents to correctly forecast economic magnitudes.

Then we move to a "New Keynesian" version of the labor market where money wages are inflexible. This will introduce you to one of the main assumptions of Keynesian economics, the economics of price and wage rigidity, showing how money wage inflexibility affects the allocation of labor. Finally, you will be introduced to economic theories of real wage inflexibility, ideas introduced to explain why real wages may not clear the labor market.

Once you have completed your study of this chapter, you will be in a better position to understand the economic content of labor market statistics, statistics often appearing in the news media. You will also have mastered one of the critical building blocks of aggregate macroeconomic models.

8.1 LABOR MARKET CONCEPTS AND DATA

The Bureau of Labor Statistics (BLS), an agency within the U.S. Department of Commerce, compiles data on U.S. labor markets. The unemployment rate is probably the best-known labor market statistic that they construct since it is widely reported in the news media each month but this agency releases many more statistics of interest to economists. We want to discuss the most important of these statistics because they will provide us with a wealth of insights into the activities of households and firms in the economy. All of the data that we discuss is available on the web using an outstanding web site maintained by the BLS (www.bls.gov).

Recall that our definition of the **unemployment rate** was

Unemployment Rate = Stock of Unemployed Workers/Labor Force

expressed as a percentage. The labor force is the sum of the stocks of employed and unemployed workers. To understand what information the unemployment rate conveys, it is crucial to look at how its components are measured and to understand the determinants of these components.

To be counted in unemployment rate calculations, a person must be a labor force participant, defined as someone who is either working or unemployed. The **labor force** participation rate is the ratio of the labor force to the **civilian population**. To be unemployed, a person must be without work and actively seeking employment. That is, he or she must be a **job searcher**. The **duration of unemployment** is the time in weeks that the individual has been without work and looking for a job. If a person is not actively searching for work, they are considered to have withdrawn from the labor force. Sometimes these individuals are referred to as **discouraged workers** since people may give up looking for work if they have been unsuccessful in finding work after a substantial period of job search. Thus published unemployment rates do not account for these workers. If a person is employed, it makes no difference if their hours have been reduced for any reason. It only matters that they are working. The productivity of employed workers is measured by **output per unit of labor**. Labor used in production is measured by the hours worked by the employees of the firm and these hours are given by the product of hours per worker and the number of workers. Table 8.1 summarizes these labor market concepts.

Labor market time series, such as the labor force participation data, can often reveal interesting trends in the labor market. As you are no doubt aware, one of the most striking

TABLE 8.1 Labor Market Concepts

Labor Force	Employed Workers + Unemployed Workers (Job Searchers)
Unemployment Rate	Unemployed Workers/Labor Force as a %
Labor Force Participation	Labor Force/Civilian Population as a %
Labor Productivity	Output per Unit of Labor Services (Hour)
Duration of Unemployment	Time in Weeks Unemployed and Job Searching
Labor Services	Total Hours Worked by Employees

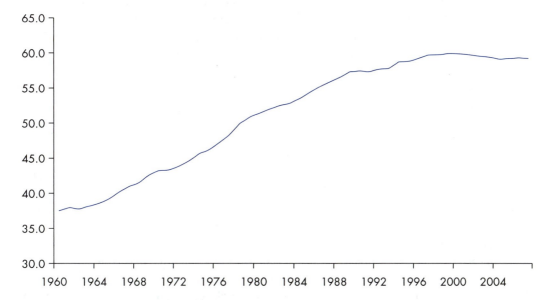

FIGURE 8.1 U.S. Female Labor Force Participation

Source: 2009 Economic Report of the President, Table B39

changes in the U.S. workplace in the last thirty years is the increasing presence of women. This trend is evident in published female labor force participation rate data (see Figure 8.1). The figure shows that, for women aged 16 and over, labor force participation has risen from 38 percent in 1965 to 59.3 percent in 2007. But some women and men are unemployed and, for the purposes of economic analysis, it is important that we ask how these unemployed individuals became unemployed. It turns out that there are a number of ways that unemployment can occur.

One possible reason for unemployment is related to the business cycle and that is **layoff unemployment**. When demand declines for the goods produced by firms, they will often cut the size of their workforce, planning to re-employ laid-off workers when output demand increases in the future. This type of unemployment occurs when the economy is not in equilibrium and is below its long-run growth path (this path will be defined more precisely below). But there are other reasons why individuals may be unemployed, reasons unrelated to the business cycle.

One characteristic of industrialized economies is that firms cease operation and new ones form to produce new goods and services. These activities can cause **structural unemployment** and an example will serve to illustrate this process. Engineers now do their computations on calculators and personal computers but, before these products had been invented, they used slide rules (these looked like large rulers) for their calculations. The inventions of the calculator and personal computer eventually caused the demise of firms producing slide rules because calculators and computers are far superior to slide rules for making calculations. Workers, employed by the firms producing slide rules, lost their jobs. This type of unemployment is structural; that is, it results from the changing structure of the economy. Unemployment of this form is inevitable in any dynamic economy where competition between firms often results in new and improved products that replace products invented in the past. The workers who lost their jobs presumably had skills specific to the production of slide rules, skills that may not have been useful in other industries. Such workers may need to accept entry-level jobs in other industries, acquiring the skills on-the-job that are appropriate to these industries. Or they may remain unemployed while they acquire new skills through retraining programs.

Another form of unemployment, again unrelated to the business cycle, is known as **frictional unemployment**. This refers to the fact that firms and workers operate in labor markets under incomplete information about the characteristics of jobs and workers, and so it takes time for appropriate job matches to occur. Workers must find out about job vacancies and apply for them, a process that takes time. Firms must find workers and determine their qualifications, screening them for their suitability to vacant jobs. Thus matching workers to jobs takes time and this type of unemployment will always exist in an economy. Firms may **fire** workers if they are judged unsuitable for a particular job and these individuals may be searching for work. People could be searching for work because they have voluntarily quit a job, so **quits** are a reason for people to be unemployed. Others may be **new entrants** into the labor market, as would be true for young people searching for their first job after leaving school. People can be **re-entrants** into the labor market as would be the case for individuals who chose to withdraw from the workforce for a time and then return to work at a later point in life. As should be clear from this discussion, the unemployment rate itself conveys very little information about economic welfare because there are so many reasons why people become unemployed. If the unemployment rate rises due to layoffs, this fact has very different implications for the economic welfare of households than would be the case if the unemployment rate were to rise because of a substantial inflow of young people entering the labor market for the first time. Table 8.2 summarizes the reasons that individuals become unemployed.

For the purposes of economic analysis, it is important to distinguish between unemployment that is related to the business cycle and that which is not. The **natural unemployment rate** is a crucial concept for understanding the nature of unemployment over the business cycle. If we can measure the natural rate of unemployment, then using this series along with the actual unemployment rate, it is possible to disentangle cyclical and non-cyclical unemployment rates.

TABLE 8.2 Reasons for Unemployment

Type	Reason Unemployed
Layoffs	Firms Experience a Temporary Decline in Output Demand
Quits	People Quit a Job
Fires	People Are Dismissed Due to a Bad Match with a Job
New Entrants	People Enter the Labor Force for the First Time
Re-Entrants	People Go Back to the Labor Force After Leaving It For a While
Structural	Firms Cease Operation

The Natural Unemployment Rate

Milton Friedman provided the most popular definition of the natural unemployment rate in his address to the American Economic Association in 1968. The relevant passage from that address is given below.

> The 'natural rate of unemployment,' in other words, is the level that would be ground out by the Walrasian system of general equilibrium equations, provided there is embedded in them the actual structural characteristics of the labor and commodity markets, including market imperfections, stochastic variability in demands and supplies, the cost of gathering information about job vacancies and labor availabilities, the costs of mobility, and so on.
> (*American Economic Review* 58, No. 1 (March 1968), p. 7)

Evidently Friedman's definition of the natural unemployment rate has nothing to do with business cycle concerns but it does refer to the incomplete information arguments given above that relate to frictional and structural unemployment.[1] This leads us to define the natural unemployment rate in the following equivalent ways.

Proposition Regarding the Natural Unemployment Rate

- The natural unemployment rate is the sum of frictional and structural unemployment.
- The natural unemployment rate is that unemployment rate occurring when cyclical unemployment is zero or when the economy is operating at full employment.

The natural rate is also referred to as the Non-Accelerating Inflation Rate of Unemployment (**NAIRU**). It is important to estimate the NAIRU as one way of establishing whether the

---

1 The word "natural" has no normative implications here. It only refers to the unemployment rate that emerges from the economic system at full employment. Nothing is meant to be implied that this unemployment rate is associated with a welfare maximum for households.

economy is operating at full employment or whether it is in a recession or boom. The Congressional Budget Office (CBO) is a federal agency created in 1974 to provide economic analysis to Congress. It has produced estimates of the NAIRU and these are shown in Figure 8.2. The CBO uses statistical methods to arrive at estimates of the NAIRU and, as is clear by inspection of the chart, the NAIRU is changing over time and is now thought by the CBO to be approximately 5 percent of the labor force. The chart also shows the behavior of the actual unemployment rate over the business cycle; in recessions, it rises above the NAIRU (the dark areas in the chart correspond to recessions) and it falls below the NAIRU in boom periods. However it should be kept in mind that this is only an estimate of the NAIRU and there is reason to believe that economists can only estimate this important magnitude very imprecisely.[2] Later in this chapter, there will be a discussion of the determinants of the NAIRU and you will see that this equilibrium unemployment rate is driven by factors outside the scope of macroeconomics.

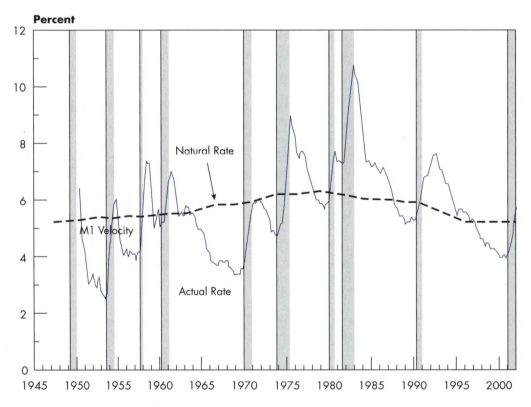

FIGURE 8.2 The Natural and Actual Rates of Unemployment

Source: Congressional Budget Office

---

2 See "How Precise are Estimates of the Natural Rate of Unemployment" by Douglas Staiger, James H. Stock, and Mark W. Watson, in *Reducing Inflation: Motivation and Strategy*, edited by C. Romer and D. Romer, University of Chicago Press (Chicago 1997).

There is a level of real GDP associated with the natural rate of unemployment. That level of output is defined below.

Definition of Potential GDP

■ When the economy is at full employment, the level of output produced by the economy is known as Potential GDP.

■ When the unemployment rate is at its natural level, the economy produces a level of output known as Potential GDP.

Thus when there is no cyclical unemployment in the economy, the output produced in the economy is on its trend or long-run path. Equivalently, output is at its potential or full-employment level. This level of output will be derived more formally later in the book.

While the unemployment rate mirrors the business cycle, so too does the duration of unemployment. In recessions, the duration of unemployment rises as there is an increasing number of unemployed workers searching for work and there are fewer vacant jobs available because the economy is in recession. In boom periods, the duration of unemployment declines as there are more vacant jobs available to be filled by unemployed workers.

This completes our discussion of labor market concepts and data. The next task is to develop economic models of the labor market that can provide a framework for understanding the determinants of these magnitudes.

8.2 THE DEMAND FOR LABOR

The demand side of the labor market reflects the activities of firms producing output for sale in the economy. Our standard approach to the analysis of firms is that they are profit-seeking entities when they make factor input decisions and so we will derive the demand for labor using profit maximization by the firm. The firm's profits are simply

$$\text{Profits} = P \cdot F(L) - W \cdot L$$

where P is the price of the firm's output, Y. The term F(L) is the technology (production function) possessed by the firm, L refers to labor services used in production, and W is the money wage rate. The capital stock is assumed fixed for now (recall that Chapter 5 dealt with the capital stock decisions of the firm) and, for this reason, the labor demand schedule that we derive here is often referred to as the short-run demand for labor. The firm is a price-taker in output and input markets (the firm's price and the nominal wage are independent of the firm's actions). The firm's output is nonstorable (goods are not produced into a stock of finished goods inventories). In Chapter 5, you saw that profit maximization leads the firm to choose input levels so that the **value of the marginal product** (or **marginal revenue**) of an input equals the nominal factor price of the input. Profit maximization therefore leads to the condition

$$P \cdot \frac{\Delta Y}{\Delta L} = P \cdot MP_L = W.$$

When the firm possesses a labor force satisfying this condition, the marginal benefit of an additional unit of labor (marginal revenue) just equals the **marginal cost** of an additional unit (the nominal wage rate), ensuring that labor is chosen to maximize the firm's profits. **Marginal revenue** is the product of the firm's output price, P, and the **Marginal Product of Labor**, MP_L.

The labor demand curve displays an inverse relationship between the real wage and the demand for labor services (see Figure 8.3) and the slope of this schedule can be established with the following reasoning. Suppose that the real wage initially has the value $(W/P)_0$ and that the firm has maximized profits by choosing the labor force so that

$$MP_L = \left(\frac{W}{P}\right)_0$$

where L_0 is the profit-maximizing quantity of labor given the real wage. Now imagine that the real wage were to fall to a new lower level $(W/P)_1 < (W/P)_0$ and, as a result, the firm would find that $MP_L > (W/P)_1$; i.e., the marginal product of labor exceeds the new lower real wage rate. The firm would conclude that its profits rise by hiring more labor and it would continue to increase its labor force until $MP_L = (W/P)_1$. By adding labor, the MP_L of labor declines (it is assumed that there are diminishing returns in production).[3] Thus when the real wage falls, labor input in production rises. There is an inverse relationship between the real wage and labor input in production because the firm uses more of an input in production when that input becomes cheaper because its profits rise by doing so.

The labor demand curve will shift if factors affecting the productivity of labor change. We now address how shifts in the capital stock affect labor demand since this case will be important in understanding the impact of shocks to the supply-side of the economy. Technical progress can also affect labor demand. This issue will be taken up later in the book.

The Capital Stock and Labor Demand

The firm maximizes profits when it chooses the flow of labor services in production for a given stock of capital. This will lead to the profit maximization condition

$$P \cdot MP_L(L, K) = W$$

where we now write the marginal product of labor, MP_L, in such a way that we make clear that the capital stock as well as the quantity of labor affects the size of the MP_L. How will a higher capital stock affect the productivity of labor? It seems reasonable to suppose that a higher capital stock will raise labor's productivity and, if so, we can trace out how a shift in the capital stock affects labor demand.[4]

---

3 Remember that diminishing returns in production means that the marginal product of an input declines as more of the input is used to produce output, holding constant all other inputs in production.
4 Mathematically, we are assuming that $F_{KL} > 0$ or that the MP_L rises with an increase in K.

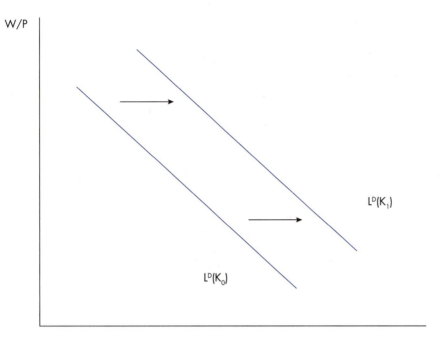

W/P

$L^D(K_1)$

$L^D(K_0)$

FIGURE 8.3 The Demand for Labor

The firm maximizes its profits by choosing a labor force along the labor demand schedule. For a given real wage, if the firm finds itself to the right of this curve, it should reduce the labor force. Points to the left of the curve are positions such that the firm should use more labor. A higher capital stock $(K_1 > K_0)$, raises the productivity of the labor force and causes the firm to demand more labor at any value of the real wage.

Imagine that, for a given real wage denoted by W_0/P_0 and an initial capital stock K_0, the firm has chosen the profit-maximizing quantity of labor, L_0, from the condition

$$MP_L(K_0, L_0) = W_0/P_0$$

and now observe that if the capital stock were to rise $(K_1 > K_0)$, it will now be true that

$$MP_L(K_1, L_0) > W_0/P_0.$$

Figure 8.3 illustrates the case of a rising capital stock and its effect on labor demand. With more capital, the marginal product of labor rises, all else the same. Firms will now want more labor at any level of real wages and so labor demand shifts. In this situation, we have argued that the firm will want to hire more labor because its profits will rise. This implies that the firm will want more labor at any value of the real wage. The bottom line is that labor demand shifts to the right as is shown in Figure 8.3.

This completes our discussion of labor demand. To construct a model of the labor market requires an analysis of labor supply. We now discuss the supply-side of the labor market.

8.3 LABOR SUPPLY

Labor supply decisions are made as one of the outcomes of utility maximization by households. That is, household welfare depends upon goods and services consumed (represented as before by a composite commodity) but also on how much leisure is taken. We imagine that the household has only two uses for its time: time spent working and time spent taking leisure (not working). With a fixed amount of time available per period, labor supplied to the labor market and leisure sum up to the total amount of time that is available to households. That is $L_T = L + L_e$ where L_T denotes the total time available to the household, L is labor supplied to the market, and L_e is leisure. Figure 8.4 illustrates the solution of the welfare maximization problem that the household solves.

Utility depends upon consumption and leisure and so is given by the expression $U(C, L_e)$. The marginal utilities of consumption and leisure are assumed positive ($MU_C > 0$, $MU_{L_e} > 0$) and diminishing. Figure 8.4 displays the preferences of the household, defined over consumption goods and leisure, and the indifference curve has the familiar appearance that we get when there is diminishing marginal utility associated with the determinants of utility, goods consumption, and leisure.[5]

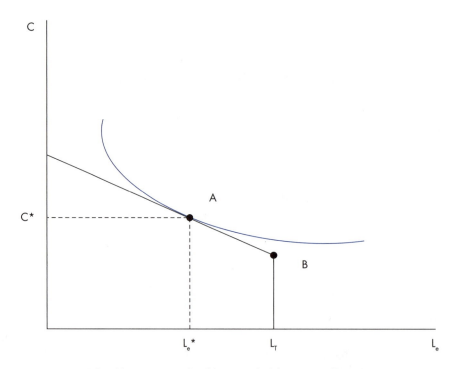

FIGURE 8.4 Utility Maximization by the Household

If the individual's utility is maximized by working, equilibrium will be at a point such as A. If the individual does not work, equilibrium will be at a point such as B.

---

5 Analogous to our definition of diminishing returns in production, diminishing marginal utility means that the marginal utility of a commodity declines as its consumption increases, holding constant the consumption of all other goods.

To determine how consumption and leisure are chosen by the household, preferences must be confronted with the budget constraint facing the household. This constraint is given by

$$(1 - t) \cdot W \cdot L + D = (1 - t) \cdot W \cdot (L_T - L_e) + D = P \cdot C.$$

In this budget constraint, W is the money wage rate for labor services, t is the **marginal tax rate** $(0 < t < 1)$ on labor income (and so $(1 - t)W$ is the after-tax money wage rate), P is the price level for the composite commodity C, and D is an exogenous source of after-tax nominal income, say from financial assets such as stocks and bonds paying dividends and interest. The sources of household income are thus after-tax nominal labor income, $(1 - t) \cdot W \cdot L$, and any exogenous income received by the household, given by the magnitude D. The household uses its income to purchase the composite commodity C, bought at prices given by P. Variation in D can capture two forces that we will want to study. D can vary because asset earnings (or other exogenous earnings streams) change, allowing us to trace out the effects of variations in D on the supply of labor and consumption. But D may also vary because taxes, independent of income (called **lump-sum taxes**), change and this may also affect consumption and labor supply. We assume that $D > 0$.[6]

Figure 8.4 illustrates the solution of the maximization problem by a household choosing to participate in the labor force by working. The budget line confronting the household defines the feasible set of consumption-leisure choices. The slope of this budget line is negative. This can be established by first solving the budget constraint to give

$$C = \frac{(1-t) \cdot W}{P} \cdot (L_T - L_e) + \frac{D}{P}$$

which implies that

$$\frac{\Delta C}{\Delta L_e} = -\frac{(1-t) \cdot W}{P} < 0.$$

In the first of the two lines above, the budget constraint has been rearranged to solve for consumption in terms of its real determinants (**after-tax real wages** and real after-tax dividends). Note that the budget line is truncated past the point L_T. The reason is that, at this point, the household is not working ($L_e = L_T$) and so labor income is zero. If the household chooses not to work, consumption must equal the amount of real after-tax exogenous income, D/P. Two equilibrium positions are in the diagram; point A is an outcome where the household chooses to work (it is a labor force participant) and, if an indifference curve were tangent to the budget line at point B, this would be an equilibrium where the household has withdrawn from the labor force and so is not a labor force participant.

---

6 As will be evident below, if $D > 0$, this permits the household to withdraw from the labor force ($L = 0$) yet continue to consume a positive amount of the composite commodity C.

As argued before, if the household intends to maximize its welfare, it wants to reach the highest indifference curve that it can, given the constraint that it faces regarding the sources and uses of the its resources. This occurs at the tangency point A in Figure 8.4 where the following condition holds.

$$MRS = \frac{\text{Marginal Utility of Leisure}}{\text{Marginal Utility of Consumption}} = (1-t) \cdot \frac{W}{P}$$

The **marginal rate of substitution** (MRS) is defined as the ratio of the marginal utilities of leisure and consumption (the slope of an indifference curve is given by –MRS). When the household maximizes its welfare, the MRS between consumption and leisure is just equal to the marginal cost of leisure. The cost of another unit of leisure is the loss of after-tax real wages, given by $(1-t) \cdot W/P$ and the associated loss of consumption. Equivalently, at the optimum, the household is at the point where the benefit of another unit of labor supply, given by the product of the after-tax real wage and the marginal utility of consumption, is just equal to the "cost" of another unit of labor supply, measured by the loss of marginal utility from reduced leisure.

With this optimization problem set up, we can now examine how the household responds to changes in its sources of income.

Changes in the Pre-Tax Real Wage

The market for labor that we want to develop will determine the real wage and labor input used in production by firms and, to build this model, we will require a relationship between the labor supply offered by households and the real wage. Figure 8.5 illustrates how an increase in the pre-tax real wage, W/P, caused by a change in money wages W (the price of the composite commodity P is assumed fixed), will change the labor supply of the household under a particular set of restrictions discussed below.[7]

If the pre-tax real wage increases, the budget line will rotate around the point B where labor supply is zero. The reason is simply that consumption must equal after-tax dividends if the household chooses not to work and so point B is part of the feasible set at any value of real wages. The new equilibrium is at point D in the figure. Comparing this point to the original equilibrium at point A, leisure has declined (and therefore labor supply has risen) and, with higher labor income, the household may also increase its consumption of the composite commodity C. Thus the new equilibrium has higher consumption, less leisure, and more labor services supplied to the market. Figure 8.6 sets out the result of this exercise in a diagram showing the relationship between real wages and labor supply. The supply curve has a positive slope, consistent with our discussion above.[8]

---

7 The price level is assumed fixed throughout our discussion of labor supply decisions so that real wages change because of a change in W and, below, real exogenous income changes because of a change in D.

8 It is possible for a labor supply schedule to be "backward-bending" over some region. So in Figure 8.6, labor supply could be increasing in real wages over some portion of the x-axis, say 0 to $(W/P)_0$ and, beyond $(W/P)_0$, labor supply could begin to decline as real wages increase further. We ignore this possibility for simplicity.

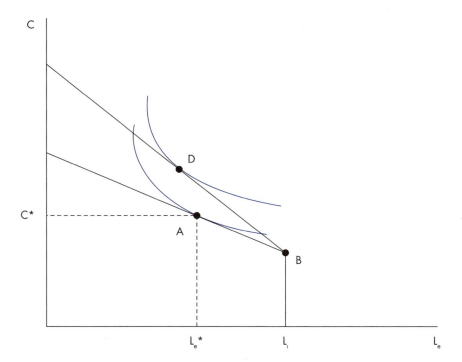

FIGURE 8.5 Utility Maximization When Real Wages Change

If the household is initially working, equilibrium will occur at point A. If the real wage rises, labor supply will rise, and leisure will fall, if the substitution effect dominates the income effect, leading to a new equilibrium at point D.

However, there are some assumptions implicit in this analysis that must be made clear; it turns out that labor supply need not rise with the real wage for reasons that we will now discuss.

Substitution and Income Effects

The real wage rate is sometimes called the price of leisure. The reason is that if the household chooses to consume another unit of leisure, it gives up (ignoring the tax rate for the moment) the real wage, W/P. In our analysis of the relationship between saving and the real interest rate in Chapter 4, there were substitution and wealth effects that were present in our explanation of how choice variables in an optimizing framework respond to incentives and such is the case here. Now we investigate how substitution and income effects arise in our labor supply model above to show exactly what must be true so that there will be a positive relationship between real wages and labor supply.

We begin by noting that it is reasonable to assume that consumption and leisure are **normal goods**, meaning that if income rises, households would choose to consume more consumption and leisure. As we have stated in earlier chapters, this amounts to ruling out satiation; that is,

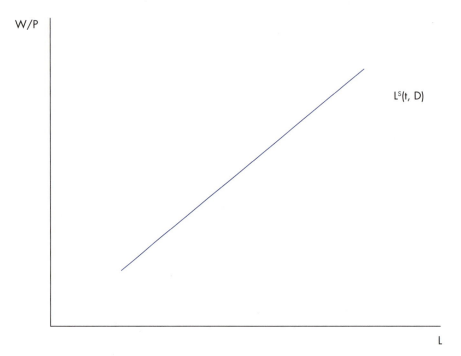

W/P

L^S(t, D)

L

FIGURE 8.6 Labor Supply and Real Wages

Labor supply rises with real wages if the substitution effect dominates the income effect. The marginal tax rate, t, and exogenous after-tax exogenous income, D, can shift the labor supply curve.

if consumers were satiated with goods, they would not consume more of them as income rises but this seems an unlikely case so we exclude it from our analysis. If the composite commodity and leisure are normal goods, then we will see that the response of labor supply to the real wage depends upon the relative magnitude of the **income** and **substitution effects** that are associated with changes in the real wage rate.

Substitution effects are measured along the indifference curve where the original equilibrium occurs in an optimization problem. So in analyzing the effects of changing the real wage, we ask how the consumer would change his/her choices of leisure and consumption while constrained to the original indifference curve. Figure 8.7 lays out the details regarding these substitution effects. This diagram is identical to Figure 8.5 except that an additional dotted line is in the figure and this line is parallel to the budget line associated with the higher real wage. The substitution effect is measured from the original equilibrium point, A, and the tangent point on the dotted line along the original indifference curve, point E. Moving from A to E, we observe that a higher real wage raises consumption and reduces leisure. The substitution effect is always negative when the utility function has the curvature properties we've assumed, implying an inverse relationship between the real wage (the "price" of leisure) and the quantity of leisure chosen by the household. These results are summarized in the following propositions.

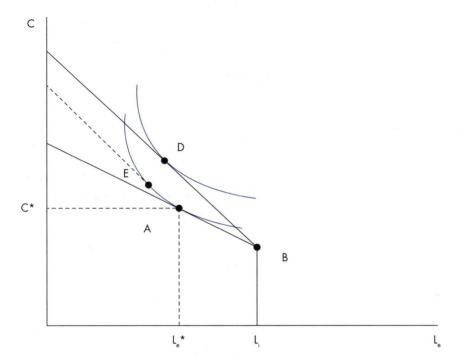

FIGURE 8.7 Substitution and Income Effects When Real Wages Change

The initial household equilibrium is at point A. If the real wage rises, the substitution effect is measured as the movement from point A to E and is always negative. The income effect is positive and given by the movement from E to D, leading to a new equilibrium at point D.

Propositions About Substitution Effects

■ The substitution effect is always negative which implies that, along the original indifference curve, leisure declines when the real wage increases.

■ Along the original indifference curve, if leisure declines, labor supply rises as does consumption when the pre-tax real wage rises.

The **income effect** is measured by asking how consumption and leisure would change if income were to rise at the new pre-tax real wage as we move from the original indifference curve to the new one where the ultimate equilibrium will occur. The income effect is measured in Figure 8.7 by the movement from points E to D. As is evident in this figure, both consumption and leisure rise as income rises (remember that we are assuming that they are normal goods). This finding is summarized in the following proposition.

Proposition About Income Effects

■ Since consumption and leisure are normal goods by assumption, the income effect in this consumer optimization problem is positive, implying that consumption and leisure rise (and labor supply falls) with an increase in income at the new higher real wage rate.

The complete effect of a change in the pre-tax real wage is the sum of the substitution and income effects. Clearly these forces conflict (one is negative and one is positive) and so, if labor supply is increasing in the real wage, then it must be the case that the substitution effect dominates (is larger in magnitude than) the income effect. This is the implicit assumption in Figure 8.6 and this will be maintained whenever we discuss the market for labor (see the empirical evidence below).

As you will see by inspecting Figure 8.6, the marginal tax rate is listed as a shift parameter of the labor supply curve. To establish this, we could repeat the exercise we carried out for changing the real wage but now we imagine that the slope of the budget line shifts as in Figure 8.6 because the tax rate, t, has declined. Cutting the marginal tax rate will therefore change the labor supply and consumption choices of the household and you should be able to work through this case just as we did for the change in the pre-tax real wage rate. The end result of that exercise will depend upon the magnitude of the substitution and income effects attached to changing the tax rate. For this reason, Figure 8.6 shows the tax rate as a shift parameter in the labor supply curve because the pre-tax real wage rate is on the vertical axis of the diagram. As a result, variations in the tax rate will change labor supply at any pre-tax real wage. So a lower tax rate shifts the curve to the right if the substitution effect dominates the income effect. There is empirical evidence that labor supply will vary with the marginal tax rate to an extent sufficient to explain the difference between hours worked in the U.S. and European countries (see **Doing Economics**: Tax Rates and Hours Worked).

Doing Economics: Tax Rates and Hours Worked

The effect of tax rates upon economic behavior is important to an understanding of how tax policies affect the aggregate economy. Some evidence on the effects of marginal tax rates on hours worked has been provided by Edward C. Prescott, a Nobel laureate in economics, who has argued that relative marginal tax rates (MTR) can explain why hours worked per worker are higher in the U.S. than they are in many European countries. He calculated hours worked per individual aged 15 to 64 and computed a measure of the marginal tax rate on labor income in the U.S. and a number of other countries. Some of his results are given below.

Period	Country	Labor Supply	Marginal Tax Rate
1993–1996	Germany	19.3	.59
	France	17.5	.59
	Italy	16.5	.64
	Canada	22.9	.52
	United Kingdom	22.8	.44
	Japan	27	.37
	United States	25.9	.40

As you can see in the table, there is an apparent inverse relationship between hours worked and the marginal tax rate. For example, the U.S. MTR is below that in Germany, France, and Italy and hours worked are higher in the U.S. than in these other countries. For further discussion of these findings, see "Why Do Americans Work So Much More Than Europeans?" *Federal Reserve Bank of Minneapolis Quarterly Review* 28, No. 1 (July 2004), pp. 2–13.

Pure Income Effects on Labor Supply

Figure 8.6 lists an additional magnitude that may change and thus affect labor supply and leisure choices and that is the exogenous income parameter, D. This variable can capture changes in taxes that are independent of the marginal tax rate (described as lump-sum taxes) or changes in exogenous income from financial assets. Figure 8.8 illustrates the effect of changing this parameter on the consumption and leisure choices of the household.

The feasible set confronting the household shifts out as a result of an increase in D. However, the slope of the budget line does not change because the slope is determined by the after-tax real wage rate and this is unchanged. As a result, it is easy to predict the outcome of an increase in D. Since consumption and leisure are normal goods, they both rise with income, and labor supply falls. Thus Figure 8.6 shows D as a shift parameter in the labor supply curve, shifting the curve to the left if there is an increase in D.[9] Table 8.3 summarizes our findings about the determinants of labor supply, consumption and leisure.

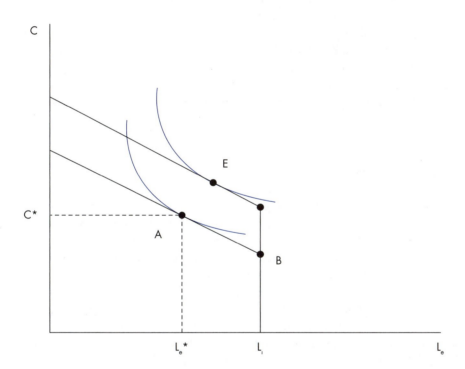

FIGURE 8.8 The Response of Consumption and Leisure to a Change in After-Tax Exogenous Income

If the household chooses to participate in the labor market by working, equilibrium will occur at points A and E. Consumption and leisure rise with increases in D because consumption and leisure are assumed to be normal goods.

---

9 Note that both an increase in D and a cut in the tax rate t could induce households to withdraw from the labor force, choosing to consume their exogenous income stream D. This possibility will generally be ignored in our analyses as we will assume that consumers choose interior solutions where L > 0.

TABLE 8.3 The Determinants of Consumption, Leisure, and Labor Supply

Exogenous Factor	Household Response
Real Wage W/P ↑	L_e ↓, L ↑, C ↑
Marginal Tax Rate t ↓	L_e ↓, L ↑, C ↑
Exogenous Income ↑	L_e ↑, L ↓, C ↑

Note: Results in the table assume that the substitution effect dominates the income effect.

Now we can compare the effects of a tax increase on labor supply. If the tax increase comes in the form of a higher marginal tax rate, generally the effect on labor supply is uncertain but, if the substitution effect dominates the income effect, labor supply will fall. If the tax increase comes in the form of a decline in exogenous income (the average tax has increased but not the marginal tax), labor supply will rise because there are only income effects. Clearly the effect of a tax increase on labor supply differs depending upon the form of the tax increase.

This completes our discussion of the supply of labor. It is now possible to combine the theory of the firm and household into a model of the market for labor where firms and households jointly determine real wages and employment in production. Our next task is to study this important market component of macroeconomic models.

8.4 THE MARKET FOR LABOR

The operating characteristics of the labor market depend importantly on a number of critical assumptions that we might make. There may or may not be flexible money wages in the market for labor and it is possible to build macroeconomic models with either assumption about money wages. Further, economic agents may not have complete information about the price level when they make decisions about how much labor to demand or supply in the market. As you will see, the labor market will behave quite differently as we change our assumptions about the information available to households and firms. In this section, we will work through several variants of labor market models because these models will be components of aggregate macroeconomic models that we study later in the book. As always, optimizing behavior will be an important part of our story describing the behavior of economic agents.

A Classical Labor Market

As we have stressed many times in the book, classical models assume market clearing in asset and goods markets and so it should be no surprise that a classical model of the labor market will use the assumption that money wages are flexible. But there is another aspect of economic behavior that we will also use; there are correct expectations held by the public regarding the price level. In classical models where there is market clearing, it is natural to assume that expectations are correct since we are (implicitly or explicitly) taking a long-run view of economic behavior. Assuming correct expectations seems a sensible approach in such a long-run equilibrium. In subsequent models, we will relax this assumption and see how the labor market will function under incomplete information about the price level.

Figure 8.9 displays a classical labor market where there is a flexible money wage rate that eliminates any excess supply or demand in the market for labor. As a result, real wages are flexible. The unemployment rate is at its equilibrium or natural level and, for the moment, there are no forces at work that will disturb this equilibrium. To see how this equilibrium is reached, imagine for the moment that real wages were at a level below the equilibrium level of W_0/P_0. At this real wage, there is an excess demand for labor and firms will bid up the nominal wage, raising real wages towards their equilibrium level. A similar story may be told if the real wage were above its equilibrium (and you should work through this mental exercise), resulting in an excess supply of labor and, ultimately, a reduction in real wages.

We may also assume that there are shifts in exogenous variables, observing how the labor market reacts. Figure 8.9 also illustrates how the market will respond to a shift in the capital stock.[10] If the capital stock were to rise, our analysis of the behavior of the firm indicated that there will be an increase in labor productivity associated with a higher capital stock, inducing firms to demand more labor at any real wage rate. This causes an excess demand for labor at the original real wage rate, W_0/P_0, and this excess demand will cause firms to bid up money wages. The end result is that a higher capital stock raises the equilibrium real wage and employment.

The Natural Rate of Unemployment

The classical labor market model can be used to illustrate the equilibrium (or natural) rate of unemployment in the economy. Recall that there are job searchers at all times in the labor market and that the definition of the labor force is that it is the sum of the stocks of unemployed and employed workers. We can take the classical labor market model and interpret labor supply as the supply of effort by employed individuals and add to that the stock of job searchers. The result is displayed in Figure 8.10.

Milton Friedman provided a statement indicating the connection between the natural unemployment rate, real wages, and employment. That statement is given below.

> At any moment of time, there is some level of unemployment which has the property that it is consistent with equilibrium in the structure of real wage rates.
>
> (*American Economic Review* 58, No. 1 (March 1968), p. 8)

In Figure 8.10, the labor market is in equilibrium at real wage W_0/P_0. At this point, there is no excess supply or demand for labor and thus firms have no incentive to adjust the wage they pay workers. But at this real wage, there is unemployment because there are job searchers

---

10 A good exercise for you to do would be to work out the case where there is an increase in labor supply.

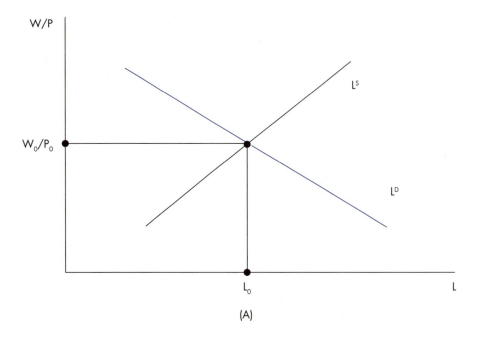

(A)

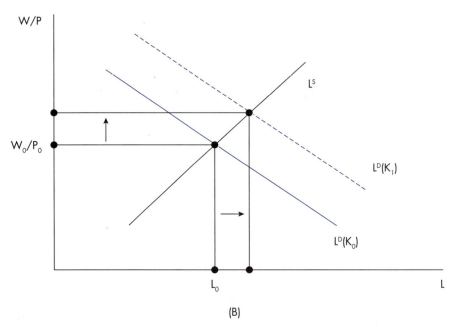

(B)

FIGURE 8.9 A Classical Labor Market Model

Panel A shows labor market equilibrium. If the real wage is above (below) W_0/P_0, there is an excess supply (demand) for labor and the nominal wage adjusts to eliminate the disequilibrium. In Panel B, a higher capital stock ($K_1 > K_0$) will increase labor demand at any real wage, causing real wages and employment to rise.

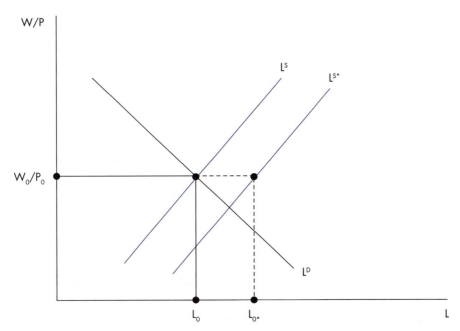

FIGURE 8.10 The Labor Market and the Natural Unemployment Rate

In the diagram, L^S is the supply of employed labor and L^{S*} is L^S plus the stock of job searchers. The market is in equilibrium at real wage W_0/P_0 and employed labor level L_0. The stock of job searchers is given by the distance $L^*_0{-}L_0$. The ratio of this distance to the labor force, L_0*, is the natural or equilibrium unemployment rate.

seeking work and the stock of these unemployed workers is given by the distance $L^*_0 - L_0$ which is the difference between the labor force and the stock of employed labor. The precise size of this distance depends upon the demographic characteristics of the workforce and does not contain any cyclical unemployment; the business cycle can generate a level of unemployment in the economy that differs from the natural rate of unemployment. But the natural unemployment rate is an equilibrium phenomenon and so does not contain any unemployment associated with the business cycle. This is the level of unemployment that occurs when the economy is on its long-run growth path.

In our analyses of macroeconomic models, we will often abstract from job search unemployment because it will not be necessary to carry it along to address the issues that we want to study. However, it should always be recognized that the economy will have unemployment beyond the unemployment that is associated with the business cycle; job search unemployment is a characteristic of modern economies, although in practice it may be difficult to distinguish between cyclical and non-cyclical unemployment. And estimating the natural rate is an imprecise art.[11]

What determines the size of the natural unemployment rate? The answer to that question depends on factors outside the scope of macroeconomics but we can enumerate some of them here for completeness. Part of the explanation lies with demographic factors. Unemployment

---

11 See fn. 2 above regarding the precision of estimates of the natural unemployment rate.

rates vary by gender, age, race, and by educational attainment. The CEA (Council of Economic Advisors) report provides data on the relationship between unemployment rates and demographic factors. Figure 8.11 provides a graph of unemployment rates for selected demographic groups. It is clearly evident that young people have higher unemployment rates than older people. Gender has little effect upon unemployment among white individuals, but minorities have higher unemployment rates than whites.

Finally, there are government policies that can have an impact on the natural rate of unemployment. **Minimum wage** rates can create unemployment if they keep real wages above their equilibrium level (see Section 8.5 below). And an unemployment compensation system that replaces a high fraction of lost income due to a temporary layoff can also raise unemployment because it can make unemployment too attractive to workers to remain unemployed, thereby raising the natural rate of unemployment.[12] Indeed it has been argued that unemployment compensation was one factor inducing John Maynard Keynes to develop his macroeconomic theories. A generous unemployment compensation system during the 1920s increased unemployment but Keynes interpreted this evidence as being caused by a deficient aggregate demand for goods, not realizing that unemployment was rising in interwar

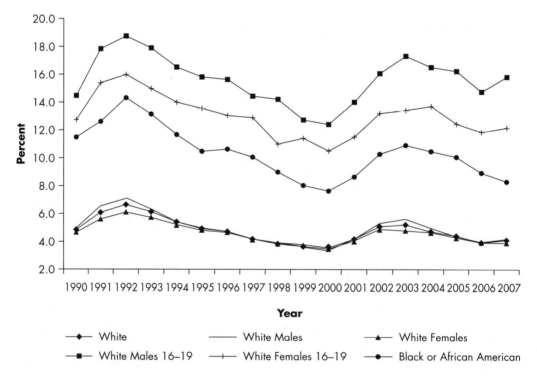

FIGURE 8.11 Unemployment Rates by Demographic Characteristic

Source: 2009 Economic Report of the President, Table B43

---

12 See "The Effect of Unemployment Insurance on Temporary Layoff Unemployment," by Martin S. Feldstein in the *American Economic Review* 68, No. 5 (December 1978), pp. 834–46.

Britain because of generous unemployment compensation programs (see **Doing Economics**: Unemployment Compensation in Interwar Britain).

Thus if the actual unemployment rate is judged to be unacceptably high by policymakers and the public, it is important to distinguish between unemployment in equilibrium, which may call for changing economic policies at the microeconomic level, and unemployment related to the business cycle which can be addressed using traditional monetary and fiscal policies that are the province of macroeconomics.

Doing Economics: Unemployment Compensation in Interwar Britain

Daniel K. Benjamin and Levis A. Kochin studied unemployment in the United Kingdom in the period between the first and second world wars, discovering some remarkable evidence regarding the effects of unemployment compensation programs on the unemployment rate.

Benjamin and Kochin establish that interwar Britain had a higher unemployment rate than had ever been observed prior to Word War I despite the fact that the economy had experienced very rapid real growth over a comparable time period. As you will learn in more detail later in the book when you study aggregate economic models, this is a paradox; an economy that grows rapidly is thought by economists to be one with low unemployment. Firms hire more labor when they increase production, thereby reducing the stock of unemployed workers. Why was the unemployment rate in interwar Britain so high?

The answer provided by Benjamin and Kochin is that, beginning in 1920, unemployment compensation programs became increasingly generous in three ways: the size of the payments received by workers, the ease with which individuals could qualify for unemployment payments, and the length of time during which they could receive payments. By 1931, a qualified unemployed worker could receive weekly payments exceeding 50 percent of the average weekly wage and some could receive benefits for an unlimited length of time.

Benjamin and Kochin then go on to estimate the effect of the high unemployment insurance payment program on the unemployment rate and provide the following estimates.

Unemployment With and Without High Unemployment Compensation:

Year	Actual	Unemployment Rate with 1913 Replacement Rate	
		Upper Limit	Lower Limit
1926	12.5	8.0	5.4
1927	9.7	5.3	2.9
1928	10.8	6.1	3.4
1929	10.4	5.5	2.8
1930	16.1	10.6	7.1
1931	21.3	15.5	11.5
1932	22.1	17.1	13.4
1933	19.9	14.8	11.4
1934	16.7	11.2	7.8
1935	15.5	9.5	5.9

(continued)

The 1913 Replacement Rate was the rate at which lost wages were replaced before replacement rates were raised in the 1920s. Benjamin and Kochin provide a range of estimates but, no matter which estimate is used, the effect of the increasingly generous unemployment programs was to raise the unemployment rate from what it would otherwise have been.

Source: Daniel K. Benjamin and Levis A. Kochin, "Searching for an Explanation of Unemployment in Interwar Britain," *Journal of Political Economy* 87, No. 3 (June 1979), pp. 441–78.

A "New Classical" Labor Market

The distinguishing characteristic of the modern version of the classical labor market, sometimes referred to as the "New Classical" model, is that there is incomplete information about the price level on the part of labor suppliers when they make labor supply decisions. This approach is sometimes referred to as the Friedman-Phelps **island paradigm**, named after economists Milton Friedman and Edmund Phelps, who introduced the idea of incomplete information into macroeconomic models.[13] Here is what we assume in this paradigm.

We imagine that the economy is made up of informationally distinct islands. Within each island, economic agents have complete information about the prices of the goods that are sold and bought. But individuals on a given island do not know the prices of goods on other islands and they consume these goods as well as those produced on their own island. As a result, the price level, a measure including the prices of goods on all islands, is not known with certainty when labor supply decisions are made. Therefore the expected real wage (the ratio of the observed money wage and the expected price level) is the relevant variable driving labor supply decisions and how households form their expectations about the price level will be very important for the implications of macroeconomic models. Firms, assumed to be competitive, need only know the price of their own output on their own island and are thus assumed to know this magnitude.

The mechanics of this labor market are displayed in Figure 8.12. Note first that we have nominal wages on the vertical axis, rather than real wages. You will soon see that this is convenient for our purposes. This implies that the price level, or the expected price level, appear as shift variables in labor demand and supply.[14] The diagram illustrates the properties of the market in equilibrium and it also shows how changes in the price level and expected

13 This view of labor markets under incomplete information is presented in the volume *Microeconomic Foundations of Employment and Inflation Theory*, edited by Edmund S. Phelps, W. W. Norton and Company (New York 1970).

14 To see how this arises, recall the profit maximization condition $P_0 MPP_L = W_0$, the condition guiding the firm facing the price level P_0 and money wage rate W_0, leading it to choose labor input level L_0. Then if the price level rises, it would be true that $P_1 MPP_L > W_0$ and the firm would hire more labor in production. You should be able to work out a similar analysis showing that labor supply will shift left if there is an increase in the expected price level.

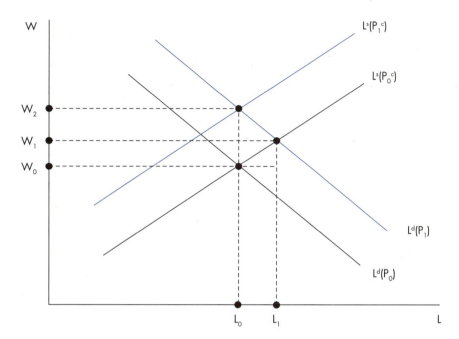

FIGURE 8.12 The "New Classical" Labor Market

The market is in equilibrium when price expectations are correct and there is no excess demand or supply for labor. This occurs at W_0 and L_0. If the price level rises unexpectedly, labor demand shifts and wages rise to W_1 and labor input rises to L_1. If a price increase is anticipated, there is a coincident shift in labor demand and supply. Labor input remains fixed at L_0 but wages rise to W_2.

price level will affect the equilibrium in this market. Now consider the properties of equilibrium in the market for labor.

The concept of equilibrium has a new dimension when we introduce expectations into an economic model. Previously we defined equilibrium to be a situation where there is no excess supply or demand in a market and this remains true here. But now we require that expectations be correct in the labor market if there is an equilibrium that prevails. The reason for this is simple; if expectations were incorrect, labor suppliers would eventually learn that their expectations are wrong and shift labor supply as they adjust price expectations. So for a wage-labor input combination to persist over time, expectations must be correct.

Equilibrium occurs in the labor market in Figure 8.12 when the nominal wage is at W_0 and labor input is at L_0. There is no excess supply or demand for labor and price expectations are correct ($P_0 = P^e_0$). The actual real wage rate equals the expected real wage ($W_0/P_0 = W_0/P^e_0$). If the money wage were below W_0, firms would experience an excess demand for labor and bid up nominal wages as they try to hire more workers. At a money wage above W_0, there would be an excess supply of workers who would drive money wages down as they seek employment.

The figure illustrates two comparative static exercises. The figure traces out the effects of **unanticipated and anticipated price changes**, concepts that are defined below.

Definitions of Price Changes

■ An unanticipated price change is a change in the price level that is not recognized by labor suppliers.

■ An anticipated price change is a change in the price level that is recognized by labor suppliers.

The crucial distinction between the two types of price changes is whether or not labor suppliers recognize what is happening to the price level. For the case where the price change is not recognized (and so is unanticipated), there will be no change in the expectations of labor suppliers. If the price change is recognized (and is thus anticipated), labor suppliers adjust their expectations accordingly. The effects of these two price changes are quite different.

First consider the case where a price increase is unanticipated by labor suppliers. The labor demand curve shifts as firms demand more labor at any money wage but the labor supply curve is unchanged because labor suppliers do not recognize the increase in prices that has occurred. These actions set off an excess demand for labor, driving up the money wage to the level W_1. What has happened to real wages? We know from our classical analysis that real wages must decline if firms will want to hire more labor. In fact, the real wage has declined, inducing firms to use more labor in production. This may be established in the following way.

Look in the figure and realize that, along a vertical line extending up from L_0, the real wage is constant (since labor input is constant). The distance measured by W_0–W_1 is the amount that money wages increase but the distance given by W_0–W_2 is the distance that money wages must rise to keep real wages constant (that is, so that $\Delta W/W = \Delta P/P$). Since money wages rise by less than the increase in prices, real wages must fall and so labor use in production rises. But there is another interesting implication of this experiment.

Labor suppliers have been fooled into working more because they think that real wages have risen whereas they have not. They see the increase in money wages but they have not yet recognized that prices have risen so that $W/P < W/P^e$. This divergence between actual and expected magnitudes will be a recurring theme in the macroeconomic models that we discuss later in the book. What we can say here is that an unanticipated increase in prices has real effects. That is, if prices rise unexpectedly, real wages will fall, employment will rise, and actual and expected real wages will diverge. These properties of the **new classical labor market** are summarized in the following propositions.

Propositions Regarding the Effects of an Unanticipated Price Change

■ An unanticipated increase in the price level will cause the real wage to fall, labor input in production will rise, and the expected real wage will be above the actual real wage.

■ Labor suppliers have been fooled into working more because they have not correctly recognized the increase in the price level that has occurred but firms are not fooled by the increase in prices.

The market pair (W_1, L_1) is a **temporary equilibrium**. The reason is that while there is no excess supply or demand for labor at this point, there will be forces in the economy that will cause wages and employment to move away from this position. Those forces involve adjustments in price expectations. At some future time, labor suppliers will become aware that their price expectations are incorrect and they will change their expectations in some manner. As a result there will be a shift in labor supply associated with these new expectations and thus wages and employment will change. So this position in the market is temporary, only applying to the time period when labor suppliers remain unaware of the new price level that prevails in the economy.

Now we consider an anticipated increase in the price level. The distinguishing characteristic of this exercise is that, unlike the unanticipated price change example, labor suppliers now recognize the increase in the price level as it occurs and shift their expectations coincidently with the increase in prices. The outcome here is quite unlike the unanticipated price change case; there are no real effects associated with the increase in the price level. Money wages rise from W_0 to W_2, employment remains fixed at L_0, and there is no difference between actual and expected real wages ($W/P = W/P^e$). Money wages rise by just enough to offset the increase in the price level. An anticipated price increase has no effect on real wages, the expected real wage, or labor input in production. These implications are summarized below.

Propositions Regarding the Effects of an Anticipated Price Change

■ An anticipated increase in the price level has no impact upon the real wage, the expected real wage, or the level of labor input in production. The money wage rises in such a way that real wages and expected real wages are constant ($\Delta W/W = \Delta P/P = \Delta P^e/P^e$).

■ Labor suppliers are not fooled into thinking that real wages have fallen because they recognize the increase in the price level that has occurred.

The implication of these exercises is that it makes a great deal of difference whether price level changes are anticipated or not. This same finding will carry over into macroeconomic models built with the new classical labor market as one of their components. This suggests that it will be very important to specify how expectations are formed because, as we saw in the unanticipated price change example, labor suppliers do not want to be fooled by price changes and will have an incentive to find forecasting schemes that will help them to avoid expectational errors. This insight is the main motivation for the assumption of rational expectations, used later in the book; a rational expectation of the price level is one where systematic mistakes are not made by economic agents and so are optimal forecasting mechanisms.

A "New Keynesian" Labor Market

One cogent criticism of the assumption of the classical model of the labor market is that we simply do not see money wages change as rapidly as suggested by the foregoing models of the labor market. You yourself have seen empirical evidence suggesting this skepticism. In jobs that you have had, your employer could have told you that your money wage will be decided at the instant that you arrive for work. This is sometimes called a **spot market**; wages are set "on the spot" when firms and workers come together in the labor market. Labor markets don't work this way; your money wage remains fixed for some period of time and is constant throughout the working day (although overtime is often paid for working beyond the normal length of the work day). This empirical evidence has led Keynesian economists to develop models of the labor market where there is inflexibility in money wages.[15]

Keynesian economics is a label attributed to economic models developed in the tradition of John Maynard Keynes, a British economist who wrote a very influential book stressing that aggregate economies are characterized by wages and prices that are "sticky" for some periods of time.[16] This Keynesian argument led economists to develop economic models that are often thought to describe the "short run," that period of time of unspecified length where prices and wages are fixed. We can illustrate a "New Keynesian" labor market in the following way.

Imagine that firms and workers engage in a bargaining process where a wage bargain is struck that will prevail for some period of time. The money wage that is set is thought to be mutually beneficial, meaning that it will be consistent with both profit maximization by firms and utility maximization by households. But because the money wage will prevail for some period of time, the price level, prevailing over this period, is not known with certainty by either firms or workers. We assume, for simplicity, that the contract wage that is set once all market participants reach agreement about the expected price level. Figure 8.13 shows this initial bargaining outcome where the contracted money wage, W^c, is set in the market. The dotted line in the figure is the labor supply curve and it is presented this way because we will suspend its relevance to the market in the following way.

The hallmark of Keynesian labor market models is that they are "demand-determined." By this is meant that the amount of employment that we observe in the market for labor, under any and all circumstances, is the amount that is implied by the labor demand schedule for firms.[17] As a result, if the price level were to change, shifting out the demand for labor, only the labor demand schedule will determine the quantity of employment set in the market and used in production. So in Figure 8.13, if the price level rises to P_1 ($P_1 > P^e_0$), the labor demand curve shifts out and employment rises from L_0 to L_1. We might imagine that firms get the additional labor input by requiring their workers to work longer hours (agreed to as part of the initial bargaining process) or by hiring workers out of the pool of unemployed who are searching for work. But however the increase occurs, the employment outcome is consistent with the labor demand schedule. The results from this exercise are summarized in the following proposition.

---

15 There is survey evidence on the degree of money wage flexibility. See "Rigid Wages?" by Kenneth J. McLaughlin, *Journal of Monetary Economics* 34, No. 3 (December 1994), pp. 383–414.

16 Keynes wrote the extraordinarily influential treatise *The General Theory of Employment, Interest, and Money*, published by Macmillan and Company, Ltd. (London 1936).

17 Representative examples of this style of labor market model may be found in "Long-term Contracts, Rational Expectations, and the Optimal Money Supply Rule," by Stanley Fischer (*Journal of Political Economy* 85, No. 1, February 1977, pp. 191–205) and "Aggregate Dynamics and Staggered Contracts," by John B. Taylor (*Journal of Political Economy* 88, No. 1, February 1980, pp. 1–23).

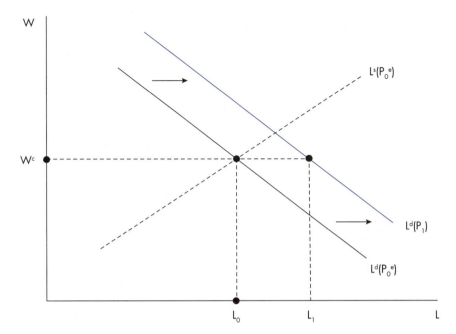

FIGURE 8.13 The "New Keynesian" Labor Market

The market begins in equilibrium when price expectations are identical for all participants in the labor market. This equilibrium occurs at W^c and employment level L_0. If the price level rises, labor demand shifts and employment in the market is determined by the labor demand schedule. The result is that while money wages remain fixed at W^c, employment rises to L_1.

Proposition Regarding the Effects of Price Changes in the New Keynesian Model

■ In the "New Keynesian" theory of the labor market, if the price level rises above the level assumed to hold during the bargaining process, real wages fall, employment in production rises to the level implied by the labor demand curve, and output produced increases.

The foregoing discussion about bargaining and money wages seems fine in a setting where unions represent employees, but union membership has been declining in the U.S. for many years. Less than 25 percent of the workforce is represented formally by unions in the U.S. and so it is somewhat difficult to believe that money or real wage stickiness for the entire U.S. economy can be justified by the actions of such a small fraction of the workforce. Economists have therefore searched for other reasons why the labor market might not clear and these reasons involve policies set by the government or the incentives of firms and workers that would prevent real wages from being flexible. We discuss these issues in the next section.

8.5 INFLEXIBLE REAL WAGES

Here we discuss additional reasons why real wages may not adjust to clear the market for labor. None of these theories is completely satisfying in the sense that there are reasons, given below, to be skeptical that any one of these theories is important enough to explain why the labor market may not be in equilibrium for sustained periods of time. But each theory has an element of truth to it, so it is worthwhile to describe each of these ideas because, as a group, they might provide some insights into the existence of disequilibrium in the market for labor. We begin with the minimum wage, an example of a government program that can prevent the real wage from clearing the labor market.

The Minimum Wage

The federal government sets a minimum wage rate that must be paid to many, though not all, workers in the economy. This wage rate is adjusted periodically and is stated in dollar units but, at any point in time, this minimum wage rate has the effect of fixing the real wage that can be paid to the affected employees of firms. For many workers, the minimum wage is irrelevant; their wage rates are far in excess of the minimum wage rate set by the government so the minimum wage has no effect on their employment.[18] But for other workers, the minimum wage has an effect on their earnings and employment. So we want to analyze the effects of the minimum wage as it applies to workers of this sort.

Figure 8.14 sets out a classical labor market where the real wage is kept above its equilibrium level by government mandate. Observe that in this case, there is a persistent excess supply of labor that cannot be eliminated by a reduction in the real wage. The end result is that employment is reduced from what would occur in the absence of the minimum wage and there is more permanent unemployment in the economy. There are now more job searchers looking for work as compared to the case where the economy is in equilibrium and therefore has persistent unemployment beyond the level of the natural rate of unemployment that would occur without the minimum wage. But it is also true that some workers do benefit from the minimum wage because those that do not lose their jobs will experience higher real wages. The reduction in employment, and resulting unemployment, that results from the minimum wage can be estimated empirically and there is a large empirical literature, developed by labor economists, testing for the effects of the minimum wage.[19] In particular, there is evidence that the minimum wage reduces teenage employment (See **Doing Economics**: The Minimum Wage and Teenage Unemployment).

---

18 It should also be obvious that a minimum wage is irrelevant in the case where the resulting real wage is below its equilibrium level. For in this case, nothing prevents firms from bidding up nominal wages, thus raising real wages to eliminate the excess demand for labor. So the minimum wage would have no effect on employment or real wages. The minimum wage matters only when it causes real wages to be above their equilibrium level.

19 For a survey of empirical evidence on the effect of the minimum wage, see "The Effect of the Minimum Wage on Employment and Unemployment," by Charles Brown, Curtis Gilroy, and Andrew Kohen, in *Labor Economics, Volume 1, Labor Supply and Labor Demand*, Elgar Reference Collection. International Library of Critical Writings in Economics, Vol. 47. Aldershot, United Kingdom (1995), pp. 444–485.

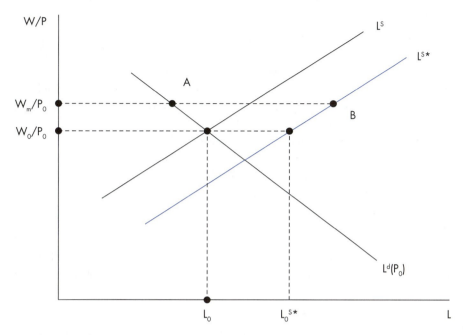

FIGURE 8.14 The Minimum Wage in a Classical Labor Market

In the diagram, L^S is the supply of employed labor and L^{S*} is L^S plus the stock of job searchers. When the market is in equilibrium at real wage W_0/P_0, the stock of job searchers is given by the distance $L_0^{S*}-L_0$. With a real minimum wage of W_m/P_0, the stock of unemployed job searchers is given by the distance between points A and B.

The analysis above indicates why economists generally do not support the imposition of minimum wages in the labor market. Either it is irrelevant if the policy results in a real wage below equilibrium, or the policy creates persistent unemployment. Further, it creates two classes of individuals: the winners who benefit since they don't lose their jobs, and the losers who become unemployed. It is hard to see how this can be viewed as the best way to raise the incomes of workers (presumably the reason for imposing the minimum wage) when there are other ways to raise incomes, say through the tax code, which will not result in increased unemployment. In addition, it is hard to believe that the minimum wage alone can be used to rationalize any observed real wage inflexibility in the entire economy because the minimum seems to apply to a small enough group of workers that its effects can't be important enough to explain real wage rigidity in the economy as a whole.

Doing Economics: The Minimum Wage and Teenage Unemployment

One demographic group that would seem to be particularly vulnerable to the employment effects of the minimum wage would be teenage workers who frequently work in entry-level jobs paying wages at or near the minimum wage. Economists Richard V. Burkhauser, Kenneth

(continued)

A. Couch, and David C. Wittenburg have provided empirical evidence on the effects of the minimum wage on teenage employment.*

There are two aspects of this evidence that are provided in this study. We pointed out that the minimum wage could be irrelevant to employment in the labor market if the minimum wage is set below the market-clearing wage. Burkhauser et al. first provide empirical evidence that teenage wage rates are significantly increased by the minimum wage so that it is therefore possible that teenage employment is also affected by minimum wages. They then provide a battery of empirical tests, finding that the elasticity of teenage employment with respect to the minimum wage lies between −.2 and −.6. Thus they conclude that the minimum wage does indeed reduce the employment of teenagers.

Finally minimum wages have been imposed at the local level in cities as small as Ann Arbor, MI and as large as Chicago, IL but using the description "The Living Wage."

* See Richard V. Burkhauser, Kenneth A. Couch, and David C. Wittenburg, "A Reassessment of the New Economics of the Minimum Wage Literature with Monthly Data from the Current Population Survey," *Journal of Labor Economics* 18, No. 4 (October 2000), pp. 653–80.

But even without an institutional restriction such as the minimum wage, there are other reasons why it may be in the interests of firms and workers for the labor market to remain out of equilibrium. We now turn to these additional theories of the labor market.

Risk Aversion

One theory of the labor market suggests that workers might prefer a stable real wage because they are **risk averse**.[20] Risk aversion refers to a characteristic of the utility functions possessed by individuals. Risk-averse individuals generally dislike variability in the magnitudes affecting their welfare and, if possible, would prefer to make arrangements to eliminate or reduce this unpredictability. So in the case of the labor market, workers would be attracted to work for firms where, as part of the wage-employment bargains made implicitly or explicitly with workers, firms agree to stabilize the real wage in the presence of shocks to the labor market that might otherwise induce them to cut real wages. Therefore a disturbance in the labor market, generating an excess supply of labor, will create persistent unemployment in the economy beyond the level of the natural rate of unemployment because firms will not cut real wages as part of their implicit wage bargain with workers.

20 See "Implicit Contracts and Underemployment Equilibria," by Costas Azariardis, *Journal of Political Economy* 83, No. 6 (December 1975), pp. 1183–202.

Efficiency Wage Models of the Labor Market

There are classes of labor market models that introduce limited information into the labor markets in ways that we have not addressed up to now. These are known as efficiency wage models of the labor market and all of these theories suggest that firms might find it profitable to keep real wages above their equilibrium levels for reasons related to their inability to observe certain aspects of workforce behavior.[21] Two possible explanations for this follow.

1. ***Adverse Selection***. One such theory is based on the idea that firms can experience adverse selection, reducing the quality of applicants for job vacancies in the firm. The theory is predicated on the idea that, unlike the models we've seen so far, workers differ in terms of their productivity (they are not homogeneous as we have assumed previously). Second, firms are unable to completely observe the productivity of workers and it is further assumed that productivity is positively correlated with real wages (the higher the real wage, the higher the productivity of employees). If firms cut the real wage when it is above its equilibrium, the pool of applicants for the firm's vacant jobs will be adversely affected. It will become increasingly dominated by potential workers low in productivity (equivalently, low-quality workers will increasingly apply for a job with the firm) and so it can be profitable for the firm to keep real wages above their equilibrium so as to attract higher quality workers into its applicant pool and, ultimately, into its workforce.
2. *Shirking*. It is possible that workers may shirk while on the job and, in this style of model, firms can only imperfectly monitor worker performance. As a result, one possible reason for rigid real wages may be that it is in the interest of the firm to avoid reducing real wages when they are above their equilibrium level because there will be less shirking on the job by workers. Workers will shirk less because getting fired is more costly to workers (who would be forced to look for a job when there is unemployment in the economy above the natural rate). If the real wage is lower, there will be less unemployment in the economy and so getting fired is less costly to workers who will be more likely to shirk and lose a job. Thus keeping real wages above equilibrium is a way for firms to discipline workers to reduce on-the-job shirking.

Labor Turnover

A final possible explanation for rigid real wages is based upon the idea that new workers must be trained when they are hired by the firm. If the firm cuts real wages, they may find that they lose employees and, to replace them, the firm will need to hire workers who require training before they will be productive. To avoid the costs of training new hires, the firm may find it in its interest to simply avoid cutting the real wage, thereby avoiding having to bear these training costs. For this theory to work, quit rates must be sensitive to real wages, rising when the real wage falls.

---

21 Further details on this literature may be found in *Efficiency Wage Models of the Labor Market*, edited by George A. Akerlof and Janet L. Yellen, Cambridge University Press, Cambridge (1987).

All of these stories have some plausibility but it would be useful to obtain some empirical evidence that might indicate which, if any, of these theories actually represents the behavior of firms and workers in labor markets. Economists usually use statistical methods to test economic hypotheses with actual data, but these alternative theories of the labor market do not lend themselves to the task of being tested. Alan S. Blinder and Don H. Choi used an alternative approach, surveying firms to find out which of these theories was true for firms in the survey.[22] They found evidence providing support for the labor turnover model of the labor market (there seems little doubt that new hires must be trained by their employers) but there was no evidence found to support the adverse selection theory of the market. Evidence on the remaining theories was indecisive but, interestingly, fairness seemed to have an important role in explaining wage rigidity according to the managers surveyed, an idea rarely used in economic models.[23]

8.6 CONCLUDING REMARKS

The labor market is an important building-block of any aggregate economic model. To understand the fluctuations in output produced in the economy, it is necessary to understand how employment decisions are made in the labor market. This chapter explains how those decisions are made by the interaction of firms and households.

The chapter began with a discussion of the data that economists use to measure activity in the labor market. Studying the data tells you how to interpret unemployment statistics because fluctuations in this statistic can be caused in very different ways with welfare implications that are quite different. The crucial idea of the natural rate of unemployment was introduced, a concept that shows why economies will always experience unemployment.

Once the data was examined, we then developed theoretical models pertaining to both sides of the labor market. Firms obey a labor demand curve that arises from choosing a labor force to maximize profits. Households decide on their consumption and labor supply (leisure) by maximizing their welfare subject to a household budget constraint. The labor supply and demand schedules illustrate the response of household and firm decisions to incentives, in this case given by the after-tax real wage and exogenous income.

Several variants of this labor market model were examined, models that will appear later in the aggregate macroeconomic models that you will study. The classical version applies to long-run equilibrium, the state where all prices and wages are free to adjust to eliminate any excess demand or supply for labor. The "New Classical" version introduced the idea of incomplete information into the classical labor market on the part of labor suppliers, illustrating how important it is for labor suppliers to correctly forecast the price level to avoid being fooled about the true value of the real wage rate. The "New Keynesian" version illustrated how a labor

---

22 See "A Shred of Evidence on Theories of Wage Stickiness," by Alan S. Blinder and Don H. Choi, *Quarterly Journal of Economics* 105, No. 4 (November 1990), pp. 1003–15.

23 Wage reductions were found to have occurred more frequently than expected but the managers interviewed said that wage reductions must be viewed by their workers as fair, interpreted to mean that they are necessary to save the firm or to align wages with those paid by competitors.

market can function when money wages are set for some period of time. This was an example of Keynesian economics, a style of economic analysis predicated on sticky wages and prices. Finally, we discussed several ideas that may explain why real wages may not fall to clear the labor market, ideas that may explain why unemployment is persistently above its natural level.

This chapter has described the microfoundations of the labor market and shown how firms and workers operate in the labor market to determine the quantity of labor used in the production of output. This will be part of the foundation of the "supply-side" of the aggregate economic models seen in later chapters of the book.

Key Ideas

- The unemployment that occurs because there is incomplete information in the economy regarding worker and job characteristics is known as frictional unemployment.
- The unemployment that occurs because of the changing structure of the economy is called structural unemployment.
- The unemployment that occurs due to a recession in the economy is known as cyclical unemployment.
- The natural unemployment rate can be defined as the sum of structural and frictional unemployment.
- The natural unemployment rate is the unemployment rate that occurs when cyclical unemployment is zero.
- The profit-maximizing level of labor input in production is chosen when the value of the marginal product of labor (marginal revenue) is just equal to the money wage rate (marginal cost).
- The profit-maximizing level of labor input in production is chosen when the marginal product of labor is just equal to the real wage rate.
- There is an inverse relationship between the real wage and labor input in production because there are diminishing returns in production associated with labor.
- An increase in the capital stock increases labor demand at any real wage if a higher capital stock increases the productivity of the labor force.
- Utility maximization by the household results in the marginal rate of substitution between consumption and leisure being equal to the after-tax real wage.
- The substitution effect implies that a higher after-tax real wage reduces leisure and raises goods consumption by the household.
- Normal goods are ones where more of these goods are consumed by households when income rises.
- The income effect of a higher after-tax real wage causes consumption and leisure to increase.
- The responses of consumption and leisure (labor supply) to a change in the after-tax real wage are generally ambiguous because of conflicting substitution and income effects.
- Consumption will rise and leisure fall when the after tax real wage rises if the substitution effect dominates the income effect.
- Higher exogenous after-tax real income raises household consumption and leisure.

- A classical labor market has flexible wages and prices that cause excess demands and supplies for labor to be eliminated.
- A higher capital stock raises real wages for labor.
- A "New Classical" labor market has the property that labor suppliers have incomplete information about the price level.
- In a "New Classical" labor market, unanticipated price increases reduce real wages, increase labor used in production, and cause expected real wages to be more than actual real wages.
- In a "New Classical" labor market, an anticipated price increase causes no changes in real wages, expected real wages, or employment used in production.
- In a "New Keynesian" labor market, money wages are fixed for some time and employment is determined by labor demand.
- In a "New Keynesian" labor market, an unexpected price change reduces real wages and increases employment.
- Real wages may not decline to eliminate an excess demand for labor for the following reasons: real wage stability may be a part of the wage bargains between firms and risk-averse workers, lower real wages may cause workers to shirk on the job, lower real wages can cause lower productivity workers to dominate the applicant pool facing the firm, or quits may rise with falling real wages, causing the firm to incur training costs for new workers.

Key Terms

Unemployment Rate
Civilian Population
Discouraged Worker
Structural Unemployment
New Entrants
Marginal Product of Labor
Marginal Cost
Income Effect
Lump-Sum Taxes
Unanticipated Price Change

New Keynesian Labor Market
Minimum Wage
Risk Averse
Labor Force
Job Searcher
Output per Unit of Labor
Frictional Unemployment
Fires
Value of the Marginal Product
Marginal Rate of Substitution

After-Tax Real Wage
Normal Goods
New Classical Labor Market
Anticipated Price Change
Efficiency Wage
Spot Market
Adverse Selection
Duration of Unemployment
Layoff Unemployment
Quits
Natural Unemployment Rate

Marginal Revenue
Substitution Effect
After-Tax Money Wage
Marginal Tax Rate
Island Paradigm
Temporary Equilibrium
Labor Turnover
Re-Entrants
NAIRU
Classical Labor Market

Questions for Study and Review

Review Questions

1. Discuss the relationship between the natural rate of unemployment and Potential GDP.
2. Describe the adjustment process towards the labor market equilibrium when the marginal physical product of labor (MP_L) exceeds the real wage (W/P).
3. Explain why labor supply responds differently to an increase in either the marginal tax rate or lump sum taxes.
4. Explain how a shift in the capital stock affects the demand for labor.
5. Explain the difference between cyclical unemployment and the natural rate of unemployment.
6. In the New Classical model of the labor market, explain the response of labor to an unexpected change in the price level. How would your answer differ if the change in the price level was expected by the public?
7. For a given unexpected increase in the price level, why does labor input in production rise by more in a **New Keynesian labor market** as compared to a New Classical labor market?

Thought Questions

1. During the 1980s, labor economists observed higher real wages and found that "computerization" played a significant role in explaining the change in real wages. Explain this relationship.
2. Business owners are often concerned when Congress passes a law raising the nominal minimum wage. What happens to employment and output if the increase of the nominal minimum wage exceeds the increase in the price level?
3. Proponents of so-called "Supply-Side Economics" often argue that a reduction in marginal income tax rates will raise Potential GDP. Is this true? If so, explain how this might occur.

Numerical Questions

1. Suppose that the supply of labor is given by $L^S = 10 + 5 \cdot (W - P^e)$ and labor demand is given by $L^D = 25 + 0.75 \cdot K - 2.5 \cdot (W - P)$.

   a) Assume a classical labor market. Compute the nominal wage, W, the real wage, here denoted by ($W - P$), and the quantity of labor in equilibrium when K equals 100 and the price level is 2.
   b) Draw the labor market equilibrium into a diagram with nominal wages on the y-axis and the quantity of labor on the x-axis.
   c) Assume a neoclassical labor market where the price expectations of the labor suppliers remain at $P^e = 2$ (part a) but where the actual price level rises to $P = 4$. Draw the change into the diagram. How many workers would the firm hire if the nominal wage rate remained the same? What is the resulting nominal wage rate?

2. Consider the following information for a classical labor market. Marginal Physical Product of Labor: $300 - 2 \cdot L$, Labor Supply: $L^S = 20 + 5.5 \cdot w + 2 \cdot T$. *Definitions*: L = labor, T = lump-sum taxes, w = real wage rate.

    a) Explain why an increase in lump-sum taxes will raise labor supply.
    b) Suppose that $T = 35$. What are the equilibrium values of w and L?
    c) Suppose that T remains at 35. If the government imposes a minimum wage requiring that the real wage must be at least 7 what are the resulting values of w and L?

3. Consider the following "New Classical" model of the labor market. Labor Demand: $L^D = 100 - 5 \cdot (W - P) + 14 \cdot K$, Labor supply: $L^S = 20 + 4 \cdot (W - P^e) + 2 \cdot T$, Labor Market Equilibrium: $L^D = L^S$. *Definitions*: L = Labor, P = Price Level, P^e = Expected Price Level, K = Capital Stock, T = Lump-sum Taxes, W = Money Wage. Note: The real wage in this model is given by $W - P$ (the model is "log linear").

    a) Compute the equilibrium money wage, the real wage, and employment when $P = P^e = 100$, $K = 25$, and $T = 50$.
    b) Compute the equilibrium money wage, the real wage, and employment when $P = 120$, $P^e = 100$, $K = 25$, and $T = 50$.

4. Consider the following economy with a classical labor market. Production function: $Y = 9 \cdot K^{0.5} \cdot L^{0.5}$, $MP_L = 4.5 \cdot (K/L)^{0.5}$, Labor supply: $L^S = 10 \cdot [(1 - t)w]^2$. *Definitions*: Y = output, L = labor, K = capital stock, t = Marginal Tax Rate, w = real wage rate.

    a) Find the labor demand schedule.
    b) Calculate the equilibrium levels of w and L, and the total after-tax income of workers. Assume that $t = 0$ and $K = 100$.
    c) Repeat part b) under the assumption that $t = 0.6$.
    d) Suppose that a minimum wage of $w = 4$ is imposed. If $t = 0$, what are the resulting values of w and L? Does the introduction of the minimum wage raise the incomes of workers, taken as a group?

Data Questions

1. Unions, like the UAW, have been covered extensively in the media, and they play a major role in negotiations between the automakers and their employees. Visit the website of the Bureau of Labor Statistics (*www.bls.gov*) to answer the following questions.

    a. For the years 2000 to 2008, plot the percentage of employed workers that are members of unions by age category (age 16–24, 25–34, 35–44, 45–54, 55–64, and older than 65 years). Which group has the highest percentage of union members?
    b. Compare the percentage of employed union members to the percentage of workers represented by a union.

2. The Bureau of Labor Statistics publishes unemployment rates based on educational attainment (*www.bls.gov*). Compare the unemployment rate for high school graduates and college graduates during the last decade.

3. While the unemployment rate rises during recessions, one can also look at the duration of unemployment to analyze the severity of unemployment. Using data from the BLS, plot the average number of weeks of unemployment for the last 50 years (1959–2009). Discuss the time series development of this variable.

 For further questions, multiple choice quizzes, and weblinks related to this chapter, visit www.routledge.com/textbooks/rossana

References and Suggestions for Further Reading

Akerlof, G.A. and Yellen, J.L. (eds) (1987) *Efficiency Wage Models of the Labor Market*, Cambridge: Cambridge University Press.

Azariardis, C. (1975) "Implicit Contracts and Underemployment Equilibria," *Journal of Political Economy* 83, (6) (December): 1183–202.

Benjamin, D.K. and Kochin, L.A. (1979) "Searching for an Explanation of Unemployment in Interwar Britain," *Journal of Political Economy* 87 (3) (June): 441–78.

Blinder, A.S. and Choi, D.H. (1990) "A Shred of Evidence on Theories of Wage Stickiness," *Quarterly Journal of Economics* 105 (4) (November): 1003–15.

Brown, C., Gilroy, C. and Kohen, A. (1995) "The Effect of the Minimum Wage on Employment and Unemployment," in *Labor Economics, Volume 1, Labor Supply and Labor Demand,* Elgar Reference Collection. International Library of Critical Writings in Economics, Vol. 47. Aldershot, UK: Edward Elgar, pp. 444–85.

Burkhauser, R.V., Couch,K.A. and Wittenburg, D.C. (2000) "A Reassessment of the New Economics of the Minimum Wage Literature with Monthly Data from the Current Population Survey," *Journal of Labor Economics* 18 (4) (October): 653–80.

Feldstein, M.S. (1978) "The Effect of Unemployment Insurance on Temporary Layoff Unemployment," *American Economic Review* 68 (5) (December): 834–46.

Fischer, S. (1977) "Long-term Contracts, Rational Expectations, and the Optimal Money Supply Rule," *Journal of Political Economy* 85 (1) (February): 191–205.

Friedman, M. (1968) "The Role of Monetary Policy," *American Economic Review*, 58 (1) (March): 1–17.

Keynes, J.M. (1936) *The General Theory of Employment, Interest, and Money*, London: Macmillan and Company.

McLaughlin, K.J. (1994) "Rigid Wages?" *Journal of Monetary Economics* 34 (3) (December): 383–414.

Microeconomic Foundations of Employment and Inflation Theory (1970) edited by Edmund S. Phelps, New York: W. W. Norton and Company.

Prescott, E.C. (2004) "Why Do Americans Work So Much More Than Europeans?" *Federal Reserve Bank of Minneapolis Quarterly Review* 28 (1) (July): 2–13.

Staiger, D., Stock, J.H. and Watson, M.W. (1997) "How Precise are Estimates of the Natural Rate of Unemployment," in *Reducing Inflation: Motivation and Strategy*, edited by C. Romer and D. Romer, University of Chicago Press.

Taylor, J.B. (1980) "Aggregate Dynamics and Staggered Contracts," *Journal of Political Economy* 88 (1) (February): 1–23.

Part III

Aggregate Economic Models

Chapter 9

Classical Models of the Aggregate Economy

LEARNING OBJECTIVES

In this chapter we begin our study of aggregate economies by considering the features of a classical model of the economy. The model abstracts from business cycles and focuses on the behavior of the economy in equilibrium, leaving the business cycle for later study. We first derive the level of full-employment output in the economy and the demand for goods schedule. The model is used to investigate the effects upon the economy of economic policy and supply disturbances. We also examine the properties that the economy must obey to achieve intertemporal efficiency, allocating resources efficiently over time and achieving welfare maxima. The chapter is closed by a brief introduction to the theory of economic growth. Here are a few of the questions that we investigate.

- What determines the level of **Potential GDP**?
- How do shifts in the demand for goods affect the allocation of goods across the sectors of the economy?
- How do supply-side shocks affect the aggregate economy?
- What is meant by intertemporal efficiency?
- Why does an economy grow?

In this chapter, we begin our study of aggregate economies by examining a classical model of a **stationary economy**. To say that the economy is stationary implies that the level of full-employment equilibrium (the level of output when the unemployment rate is at its natural level) is constant over time, an assumption that is clearly at variance with economic reality. But we will initially abstract from this trend in full-employment output to simplify our analysis. The theory of economic growth, introduced at the end of this chapter and discussed more thoroughly in Chapter 10, will address the sources of this evident trend increase in real GDP.

The crucial feature of classical models is that they are based upon the assumption that wages, prices, and interest rates are flexible and thus capable of eliminating any excess supplies or demands in goods, labor, and asset markets. On the basis of empirical observation, economists are well aware that this need not be the case over short periods of time. But over long enough time horizons, economic forces will eliminate excess demands or supplies in markets and so you should view these models as applying to the long term. Models applying to shorter time periods, where markets are not yet in equilibrium, will be developed later in the book.

In this chapter, we begin our study of the classical model by first establishing what is meant by the notion of Potential GDP and how it is determined. This is a crucial benchmark for our understanding of the economy's economic performance. It will be seen that Potential GDP is reached when the labor market is in equilibrium, a condition that arises when there are flexible money wages and prices in the economy. Once this has been developed, we then can determine what causes Potential GDP to change over time and here we will discover that technical progress, capital accumulation, and changes in labor supply will change the level of Potential GDP. Having determined the level of Potential GDP, we will then draw upon our analyses of household, firm, and government behavior from earlier chapters, using these economic models to derive the **goods demand schedule**, a relationship between the **real interest rate** and the level of output in the economy. We will then combine the demand schedule with the analysis of Potential GDP to study the classical model of the aggregate economy, a model that shows how the real interest rate and Potential GDP are jointly determined. This model will then be used to study how supply-side disturbances occurring in the economy affect the real interest rate and potential output and how variations in goods demand will affect the economy.

Having completed our discussion of the classical model, we then discuss intertemporal optimality in the economy. The classical model offers many useful insights about the long-run properties of the economy but we must have some way of judging the performance of the economy from a welfare perspective, not just from the point of view of market equilibrium. The classical model really does not address this concern and so we will develop the tools needed to determine how we know if an economy has desirable intertemporal optimality properties. To do so we first discuss the intertemporal production possibilities curve, a dynamic generalization of the static production possibility frontier used in microeconomic analysis. This concept is used to determine productive over time efficiency that then will be combined with the household utility function from Chapter 4 to permit us to develop the important concept of Pareto Optimality; the latter concept will be how we determine if the economy has desirable welfare properties from the perspective of the households in the economy. We will use this idea to learn how the existence of capital markets can improve economic welfare. The framework will be used to discuss the important concept of **time preference**, a measure of an individual's impatience to consume. This idea will be useful in learning why consumers smooth their consumption over time. Finally, we will use this intertemporal welfare analysis to introduce the important topic of economic growth, discussed more thoroughly in Chapter 10. Economic growth can be represented by a shift in the intertemporal production possibilities frontier, representing the increased production that occurs due to expanding levels of resources in the economy. Combining this insight with the household utility function clearly illustrates how a growing economy generates higher levels of economic welfare over time.

When you have completed this chapter, you will understand the characteristics of aggregate economies when they are in equilibrium and will have an appreciation of the ability of an economic system to achieve a welfare optimum for households. This will be a useful benchmark for your study of economies in disequilibrium, later in the book, because business cycles involve a departure from the classical equilibrium seen in this chapter.

9.1 POTENTIAL GDP

It is important to have a precise definition of Potential GDP, a definition that is given below.

Definition of Potential GDP

■ Potential GDP is the level of real output produced in the economy when there is equilibrium in the labor market.

Equilibrium in a market context, as discussed in earlier chapters, means that there is no excess supply or demand in the labor market, these conditions having been eliminated because wages and prices are flexible; wages and prices adjust, in classical economic models, to eliminate disequilibrium conditions. There is unemployment in the economy but the unemployment rate is at its natural or equilibrium level.

Figure 9.1 illustrates how equilibrium output is determined. In the figure, the **production function** is shown with a fixed capital stock. This technology has a familiar shape because we assume that there are diminishing returns to labor, just as there are for capital.[1] For now, there is no possibility of technical progress although we take up this matter later in the chapter. The demand for labor has a negative slope as a result of the diminishing returns to labor in production. The labor supply curve has a positive slope, reflecting the fact that substitution effects are assumed to dominate the income effects of an increase in real wages. The figures

---

1 Recall that diminishing returns in production is defined to be the case where the marginal product of an input declines as its usage increases, given all other inputs in production.

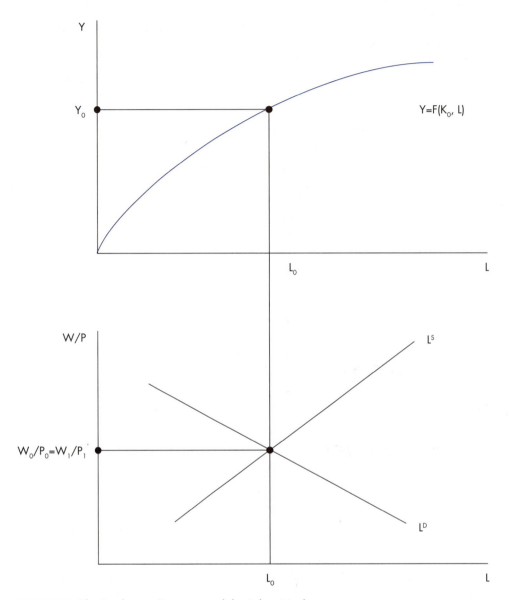

FIGURE 9.1 The Production Function and the Labor Market

Labor market equilibrium occurs when there is no excess supply or demand for labor and this occurs where real wages are W_0/P_0 or W_1/P_1. Labor input is L_0 producing output Y_0.

illustrate labor market equilibrium; there is no excess supply or demand for labor in the labor market. The labor market has determined the amount of labor employed in production and, using the production function, we can then determine how much output that quantity of labor produces. In the figures, L_0 is the equilibrium quantity of labor and Y_0 is the corresponding level of output produced. The real wage prevailing in the labor market is given by the ratio W_0/P_0. Now we need to determine how output varies with the price level. To see this, and to learn how Potential GDP is determined, carry out the following thought experiment.

With a price level at P_0, the economy produces output level Y_0 and both of these points are given in Figure 9.2, the figure where we will obtain the full-employment level of output. Now imagine what would happen in the labor market if the price level were to rise and, temporarily, keep money wages fixed at the level W_0. A higher price level reduces real wages, creating an excess demand for labor in the labor market. What would happen to the money wage in this case? Your intuition should be that firms will bid up money wages as they attempt to hire more labor and, as money wages rise, this reduces the excess demand for labor at any level of prices. Where will the process end? Clearly it will end when there is no longer a reason for firms to bid up money wages and this happens when the excess demand for labor has been eliminated. This position is given by the original level of the real wage except that now, money wages and prices are higher than they were previously. That is, $W_0/P_0 = W_1/P_1$ but $W_1 > W_0$ and $P_1 > P_0$. The level of labor input in production is just the same as it was at the start of this mental exercise, as is the level of output. Thus the level of full-employment output, which we will call Potential GDP, is independent of the price level in the economy. It is crucial that you remember that this finding, namely that Potential GDP is fixed and independent of the price level, is a consequence of our assumption that money wages can adjust to eliminate any excess supplies or demands in the market for labor. If money wages are inflexible, GDP will not be independent of the price level. Later in the book, we will investigate economic models where output supply varies with the price level because markets are not in equilibrium.

Finally, Potential GDP is also independent of the real interest rate because neither labor demand nor supply is affected by variations in the real interest rate. This is a consequence of our assumption that labor supply and demand decisions are carried out statically, that is,

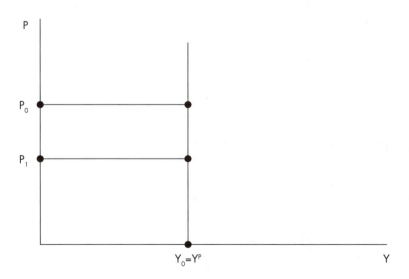

FIGURE 9.2 The Classical Aggregate Supply Curve

without regard for the future.[2] This omission seems harmless as there is relatively little evidence that labor market choices are affected by the real interest rate.

The Capital Stock and Potential GDP

Having learned how Potential GDP is determined, we might now ask how this level of full-employment output changes over time. We will discuss three possible reasons why Potential GDP changes: capital accumulation, technological progress, and shifts in labor supply. The first two cases are very similar and so we will discuss changes in the capital stock only, leaving it to you to carry out a parallel analysis for the case of technical progress. Consider what would happen if the capital stock were to rise in the economy.

Our analysis from Chapter 8 showed how a higher capital stock affects both the labor market and the production function and is illustrated in Figure 9.3. A higher capital stock causes more output to be produced from a given labor force, shifting up the production function. This higher capital stock raises the marginal product of the labor force, thereby increasing the demand for labor at any real wage rate. For a given supply of labor, the higher demand for labor generates a higher equilibrium real wage when the labor market is in equilibrium. Notice that there will now be a higher level of labor used in production and, as a result, there will be more output produced in the economy.

How does this affect the full-employment supply curve for this classical economy? Recall that the crucial assumption in the classical model is that wages and prices are flexible so that variations in the price level result in no changes in the level of output produced. Thus our analysis of the labor market shows that there will be more output produced at any level of prices, meaning that the supply curve has shifted to the right. This is shown in Figure 9.4. A similar analysis applies to increases in the level of technology. (Hint: If the economy has a production function of the form $Y = T \cdot F(K, L)$ where T refers to the level of technology, how does a higher level of T affect the production function and the labor market?)

Our analysis shows that capital accumulation, financed by household saving as discussed in Chapter 4, raises Potential GDP as firms use these savings to finance higher levels of the capital stock used in production, an important insight that we will revisit in the theory of economic growth in the next chapter. Next we examine how an increase in labor supply can affect the full-employment level of output.

Shifts in Labor Supply and Potential GDP

Households may choose to offer increased levels of labor supply for a number of reasons. One possible reason may be that the marginal tax rate on labor income has declined (see **Doing**

---

2 Strictly speaking, what we are assuming is that the implications of intertemporal models are equivalent to those of static economic models. For this to occur requires that the objectives of firms and households can be maximized in each time period independently of adjacent periods of time. This is assumed true for labor market decisions but it is not true for other decisions, such as the saving and investment decisions, discussed in earlier chapters.

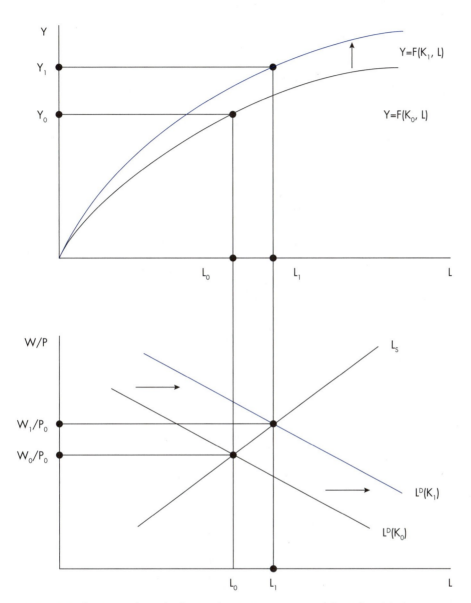

FIGURE 9.3 The Capital Stock, the Production Function, and the Labor Market

When the capital stock rises ($K_1 > K_0$), labor market equilibrium occurs at a higher real wage because the labor force is more productive. Labor input and output are higher as well.

Economics: Supply-Side Economics and the Reagan Tax Cuts). Or perhaps changes in perceived lifetime resources may induce households to work more; we will discuss this issue further when we analyze the effects of **permanent changes in government expenditures**. Figure 9.5 shows how an increase in labor supply affects **labor market equilibrium** and Potential GDP.

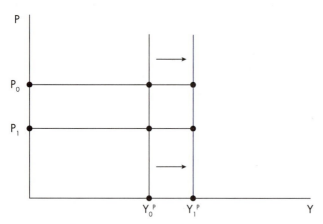

FIGURE 9.4 The Capital Stock and the Classical Aggregate Supply Curve

Potential GDP rises as the capital stock increases.

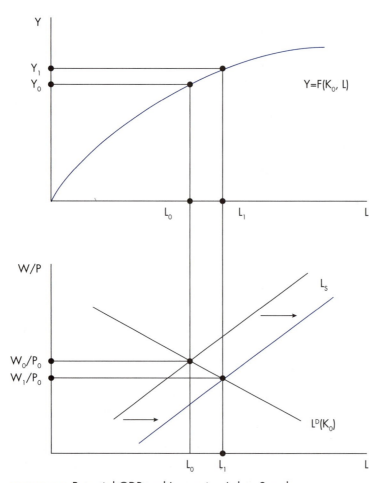

FIGURE 9.5 Potential GDP and Increasing Labor Supply

An increase in labor supply at any real wage causes an increase in the level of labor input in production. Output produced rises as well at any level of prices.

Doing Economics: Supply-Side Economics and the Reagan Tax Cuts

In 1981, President Ronald Reagan signed a bill that reduced marginal tax rates on household income. The President's support for this cut in marginal tax rates was due in part to his belief that these reduced tax rates would raise real GDP and our analysis shows that, purely as a matter of theory, it is possible to show that, under the right circumstances, this assertion is correct.

Households do not get to keep their nominal wage, W; rather the government taxes away a part of this wage through the personal income tax code and so households get to keep $(1 - t)W$, known as the after-tax money wage rate. Here t refers to the marginal tax rate (MTR) and $0 < t < 1$. Labor suppliers do not make their labor supply decisions using nominal magnitudes so, in the presence of this marginal tax rate, households use the after-tax real wage, defined as $(1 - t)W/P$, to determine how much labor supply to offer. At any pre-tax real wage W/P, a change in the MTR changes the after-tax real wage and thus labor supply. Therefore the MTR now appears as a parameter which can shift the labor supply curve. A decline in the marginal tax rate will therefore increase labor supply (that is, as long as substitution effects dominate income effects) at any level of pre-tax real wages. This is illustrated in the following labor market diagram showing the effects of a reduction in the marginal tax rate ($t_1 < t_0$).

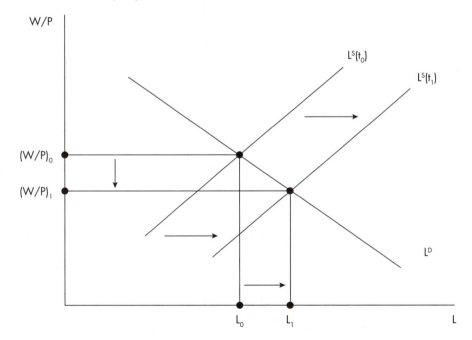

But it is more than just a matter of theory; economists want to know if these tax cuts would have a substantial impact upon labor supply and thus Potential GDP. So the policy must be judged, not just by theoretical arguments, but also by empirical evidence that the labor supply

(continued)

and other effects of these tax cuts are large enough to be evident in the aggregate economic system. For a somewhat skeptical view of the empirical evidence on the impact of these tax cuts, see "Supply-Side Economics: Old Truths and New Claims," by Martin Feldstein appearing in the *American Economic Association Papers and Proceedings* 76, No. 2 (May 1986), pp. 26–30.

An interesting aspect of the discussion surrounding these tax cuts is that policy discussions in the press and elsewhere, at the time that this tax bill was under consideration, focused almost exclusively on the efficacy of the tax cuts, paying little or no attention to the component of the tax cut bill changing the tax code from one taxing nominal income to one taxing, almost entirely, real income. This is referred to as indexing the tax code and this has important implications for the economy (see the discussion in Chapter 6 on this subject).

TABLE 9.1 The Relationship Between Potential GDP and Its Determinants

Capital Stock	$K \uparrow$ causing $Y^P \uparrow$
Technology	$T \uparrow$ causing $Y^P \uparrow$
Labor Supply	$L^s \uparrow$ causing $Y^P \uparrow$

Note: K refers to the capital stock, T is the level of technology, L^s is labor supply, and Y^P denotes Potential GDP.

The analysis shows that as labor supply rises, the real wage falls compared to the original real wage; the increase in labor supply creates an excess supply of labor, causing real wages to decline. But labor input in production and output rise. A diagram like that in Figure 9.4 illustrates the impact upon Potential GDP. Thus an increased willingness to work will result in a higher level of full-employment output in the economy.

This completes our discussion of Potential GDP. Table 9.1 summarizes the results from our discussion of Potential GDP and its determinants. In short, the analysis has shown that Potential GDP is supply-side determined. That is, the labor market and the characteristics of the economy's technology generate the level of Potential GDP.

9.2 THE DEMAND FOR GOODS AND THE CLASSICAL MODEL OF THE ECONOMY

In this section we complete the task of building a classical model of the economy. To accomplish this, we need a representation of the demand for goods that we can use in combination with our analysis of Potential GDP.

The Demand for Goods

Consider the national income accounting identity that we have used relating real GDP to its expenditure components. For a closed economy (one with no international trade), this is

$$Y = C + I + G$$

where C is consumption by households, I is gross investment by firms, and G refers to government expenditures. We now must make behavioral assumptions about each of these components; for this purpose, we can draw upon the microfoundations that we discussed earlier in the book (Chapters 4, 5, and 6). For consumption, we analyzed a two-period model of the household to establish that, if substitution effects dominate wealth effects, then

$$C = C(r) = C_0 - C_r r, \ C_r > 0.$$

Consumption is thus inversely related to the real interest rate, r (equivalently, saving rises with the real interest rate). The intercept term can be thought of as capturing the effects of other possible determinants of consumption in addition to the real interest rate. This will represent household behavior in the goods demand schedule.

For firms, we will use the relationship

$$I = I(r) = I_0 - I_r r, \ I_r > 0.$$

You may recall that when we discussed the theory of investment by the firm, we argued that the demand for net investment was driven by the user cost of capital. Here this user cost is given by the real interest rate. Investment is inversely related to the real user cost of capital because the firm will use less capital as its opportunity cost rises and so investment in capital is inversely related to the real user cost of capital or the real interest rate.

Finally, we will treat government expenditures as exogenous (that is, determined outside of our economic model). For now, we will make no distinction between permanent and transitory government expenditures although we will do so at a later point in the chapter. So the demand for goods, denoted by Y^d, will be given by the following expression.

$$\text{Goods Demand: } Y^d = C_0 - C_r r + I_0 - I_r r + G = C_0 + I_0 + G - (C_r + I_r)r$$

As shown by this expression, the demand for goods is a relationship between the real interest rate and output that can be defined formally as follows.

Definition of the Demand for Goods

■ The demand for goods is a relationship between real output and the real interest rate showing how much output will be demanded by households, firms, and the government at any level of the real interest rate.

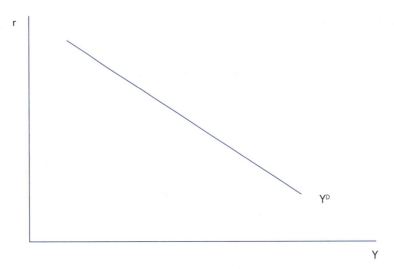

FIGURE 9.6 The Demand for Goods

The demand schedule has a negative slope because, as the real interest rate falls, households save less because the returns to saving have declined and thus consume more. Firms want to use more capital goods as their user cost declines, thus raising planned investment.

Figure 9.6 shows the relationship between the real interest rate and the demand for goods. The figure shows that this demand schedule has a negative slope because, as the real interest rate declines, households want to reduce their saving (substitution effects dominate wealth effects) because the return to saving has fallen, thus they wish to consume more. Firms will want to increase investment because capital goods become cheaper inputs in production as the user cost of capital falls so that firms will plan to do more investment in order to build up their capital stocks. We can get an explicit measure of this slope from the demand schedule as follows.

$$\Delta r / \Delta Y^d = -1/(C_r + I_r) < 0$$

The slope of this schedule therefore depends upon how elastic (responsive) consumption and investment are with respect to variations in the real interest rate. The more elastic are consumption and investment with respect to the real interest rate, the larger will be the increase in demand for goods when the real interest rate falls. We now describe what can cause shifts in the demand schedule.

Factors That Shift the Demand for Goods

There are three magnitudes in the demand schedule that can cause a shift in the demand for goods at any level of the real interest rate. These are the components of consumption and investment that are unrelated to the real interest rate (sometimes referred to as **autonomous** components), denoted by C_0 and I_0, and the level of government expenditures, G (either transitory or permanent). The government expenditures case will be discussed now but it should be easy for you to work through exercises where the other two magnitudes shift the curve.

A change in government expenditures will shift the demand curve in a way that can be determined from the equation for goods demand as

$$\left.\frac{\Delta Y^d}{\Delta G}\right|_{\Delta r=0} = 1$$

This expression is very simple; it merely says that at a given real interest rate, a one unit increase in government expenditures raises the demand for goods by one unit. An increase in government expenditures therefore shifts the demand curve to the right as illustrated in Figure 9.7. Similar results arise regarding the autonomous components of consumption and investment.

This completes our discussion of demand for goods. The classical model emerges once we combine the demand schedule with our model of Potential GDP.

The Classical Model of an Aggregate Economy

The classical model is given in Figure 9.8 where the output demand schedule and Potential GDP are brought together. At first, it might seem odd that the diagram shows the real interest rate and Potential GDP whereas our earlier discussion of the supply schedule included the price level and real output. But it was pointed out earlier in the chapter that, in our theory of the labor market, the labor demand and supply schedules are independent of the real interest

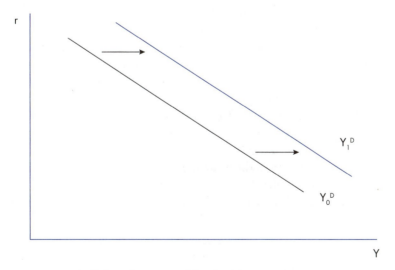

FIGURE 9.7 A Shift in the Demand for Goods

An increase in government expenditures, or in the autonomous components of consumption and investment, will increase the demand for goods at any level of the real interest rate.

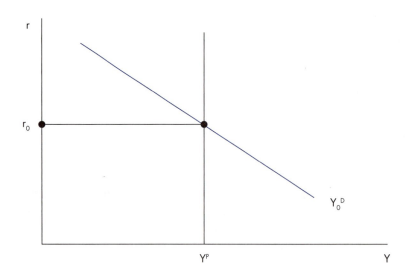

FIGURE 9.8 The Classical Model of the Economy

The classical model is a model of long-run equilibrium where there are flexible wages, prices, and interest rates. Thus the equilibrium real interest rate is r_0 with output produced at the level of potential GDP, Y^P.

rate.[3] That means that labor input in production, and output, are also independent of the real interest rate. Thus we can say that the aggregate supply schedule in the classical model, with the real interest rate on the vertical axis, is vertical just as it was when we had the price level on the vertical axis.

In Figure 9.8, the economy is in long-run equilibrium when the real interest rate is at the level r_0 and when output in the economy is at the level of Potential GDP, denoted by Y^P. If the real interest rate were not at the level r_0, economic forces would come into play driving the real interest rate to its equilibrium level. At a level above r_0, firms and households would be unwilling to buy all of the output being produced in the economy; the real interest rate would need to fall to induce them to buy more goods (saving would decline and consumption demand would increase). If the real interest rate were below r_0, firms and households would be unable to consume all of the goods that they wish. If the real interest rate were to rise in this situation, saving would rise and consumption fall, eliminating the excess demand for goods. At r_0, there is no excess demand or supply for goods in the economy. At this position, a stationary economy has achieved its long-run equilibrium.

Having established the equilibrium position of the economy, we can now observe how that equilibrium changes in response to a number of exogenous events. These are known as exercises in **comparative statics**. That is, we compare equilibrium positions in the economy as a result of changes in **exogenous variables**. The new equilibrium positions are constant over

---

3 We have treated the labor market in a static fashion for simplicity so that real interest rate effects in the labor market can be ignored (also see fn. 2 earlier in this chapter). There are theories of the labor market that would result in a relationship between the real interest rate and labor demand and supply but there is little evidence that real interest rates have a substantial impact on labor supply or demand so it seems safe to ignore these effects.

time assuming that there are no further changes in exogenous variables. These exercises are to be the subject of the next section.

9.3 EXERCISES USING THE CLASSICAL MODEL

To understand how an economic model works, it is always a good idea to do exercises in which exogenous variables change. Then we can observe how the **endogenous variables** (those determined within the model) respond to these exogenous events. This section carries out such exercises for the classical model.

Supply-Side Shock I: Energy Prices and the OPEC Cartel

In the early 1970s, the OPEC cartel restricted their production of crude oil, substantially reducing world supplies of oil. The actions of the cartel raised the relative price of oil throughout the world. Figure 9.9 provides monthly data on crude oil prices beginning in 1970. Prices increased sharply in early 1974 and again spiked dramatically in late 1979. At the end of 1973, crude oil sold for $4.30 per barrel and one month later it was selling for just over $10 per barrel. In January of 1979, crude sold for $14.85 per barrel and, by December of that year, a barrel of oil was selling for $32.50. The economy entered a recession as a reaction to these price increases (return to our discussion of business cycles in Chapter 3 to look at business cycle dates). The question we might now ask is this: in our classical model of the economy, how can we represent the effects of these spikes in energy prices?

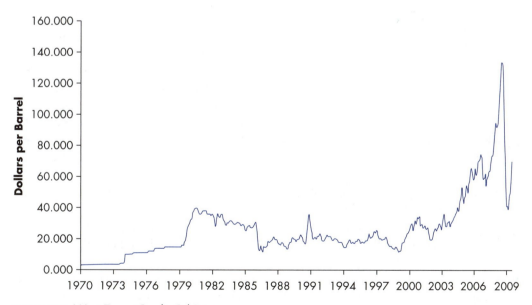

FIGURE 9.9 West Texas Crude Oil Prices

Source: St. Louis Federal Reserve Bank FRED Database

Before going further, it is important to note that economic theory instructs us to look at relative, as opposed to absolute, oil prices, in trying to discern the effects of oil prices upon the aggregate economy even though the data in Figure 9.9 is the sort of data reported in the media. Some interesting differences can be observed when looking at absolute and relative oil prices (see **Doing Economics**: The Relative Price of Crude Oil). In the analysis below, we are assuming that it is relative oil prices that have increased due to the efforts of OPEC.

One possible effect of these relative oil price increases is that the effective quantity of capital in production declined. The reason is that many capital goods were no longer profitable to operate in production because they used energy intensively. So firms would no longer be willing to use these inefficient capital goods in production. The economy's effective capital stock would therefore have declined as a result of the increase in the relative price of oil and the products derived from it. The full-employment equilibrium in the economy will change as a result of the decline in the capital stock. Figures 9.10 and 9.11 trace out the economic effects.

A reduction in the capital stock causes a downward shift in the production function, reducing the productivity of the labor force at any level of labor input. This decline in productivity results in a decline in the demand for labor; at any real wage rate, firms would now want to use less labor in production since their workers are less productive due to the decline in the stock of capital. Real wages decline and less labor is used in production. As a result, Potential GDP declines and the real interest rate rises. With less output being produced, there must be a decline in the quantity of goods demanded by the private sector. The government's share of total output rises as we assume that government expenditures are fixed. The private sector (households and firms) now has a smaller share of the economy's output as the higher real interest rate reduces the demand for goods by households and firms. But note that the implication of the classical model is that the economy has not experienced a disequilibrium in the sense of goods markets manifesting excess demands or supplies. All markets are in equilibrium; the economy has experienced a permanent reduction in Potential GDP. Other endogenous variables (real wages, employment, the real interest rate, and the shares of output going to the private and public sectors) have changed permanently as well.

Our analysis of the effects of the formation of the OPEC cartel has two implications that we might test with economic data: real wages are predicted to fall and the real interest rate should be observed to rise. Remember that the real interest rate is the equivalent of the marginal product of capital so, with a smaller capital stock, the marginal product of capital is higher (due to the assumption that we have made of diminishing returns in production). Figures 9.12 and 9.13 provide some empirical evidence on these implications of our classical model.

Figure 9.12 contains a measure of the real wage rate in manufacturing, computed by forming the ratio of Average Hourly Earnings in Manufacturing to the CPI (Consumer Price Index). Notice that there is a distinct downward trend in real wages, a pattern that is consistent with our classical model. But the timing of this decline lags behind the first OPEC oil price shock; real wages begin their decline about three years after the increase in the price of oil. What might account for this lagged effect? One possible explanation is that the decline in capital stocks was gradual (recall our discussion from Chapter 5 about the installation costs attached to capital goods) so that the effect of reduced labor productivity on real wages may not have occurred until some time after the increase in oil prices.

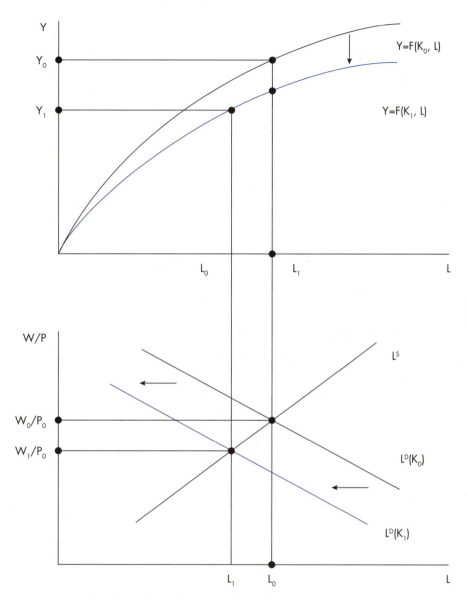

FIGURE 9.10 The Effects of a Lower Capital Stock

When the capital stock falls ($K_0 > K_1$), labor market equilibrium occurs at a lower real wage because the labor force is less productive. Labor input and output are lower as well.

Now consider Figure 9.13 where we again see that the implication of the classical model has some support in the data but the timing is once again different from what we might have expected. The data in the figure is a measure of the real interest rate computed using a high quality corporate bond yield and subtracting from it the rate of inflation using the GDP (Gross Domestic Product) deflator. Clearly there is a sharp increase in the real interest rate in the early 1970s and 1980s but the increases are somewhat later than the sharp increases in oil prices. A reasonable conclusion to draw from this empirical evidence, as well as the evidence from real

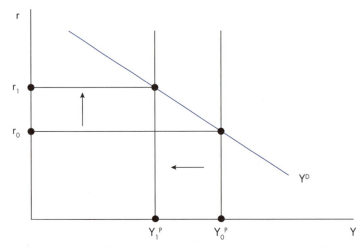

FIGURE 9.11 The Effects of a Reduced Capital Stock in the Classical Model

Potential GDP, Y^P, declines when the capital stock used in production declines. The level of the real interest rate increases. The private sector share of output falls while the government's share of output rises.

Doing Economics: The Relative Price of Crude Oil

The behavior of oil prices is faithfully reported in the media whenever there is a sharp upward (and sometimes downward) movement in the per barrel price of oil. But economic theory tells us to look at relative oil prices if we want to observe how changes in the price of oil affect the behavior of the public. The figure below is a time series graph of the ratio of West Texas Crude Oil prices to the CPI. Now look back at Figure 9.9 and compare that figure to the one below.

The Relative Price of Crude Oil

Source: St. Louis Federal Reserve Bank FRED Database

(continued)

These two figures are certainly similar in some respects. For example, the relative price chart reveals the 1973 and 1981 spikes in oil prices that are also evident in Figure 9.9. And the two charts also show the sharp upward increase in absolute and relative oil prices starting around 2003. But there are also some important differences in these two graphs.

Figure 9.9 leads one to believe that oil prices were increasing steadily from 1973 and were always higher than they were in 1973. But the graph of relative prices paints a different picture. Relative oil prices rose sharply between 1973 and 1981 but notice that after 1981, the relative price of oil steadily declined throughout the next two decades. In fact, by the end of 1998, the price of West Texas Crude oil was lower than it was in 1973!

This explains what seemed to be so puzzling to many observers of the economic scene during the 1990s. Cars grew in size and weight during much of the 1990s and a look at absolute oil prices makes it hard to understand why cars would grow in size while oil prices would seem to dictate that cars should get smaller in size and weight. But once we look at relative oil prices, the puzzle disappears. It seems quite sensible that cars grew in size because it was relatively cheaper to operate cars because oil was relatively cheaper than it had been in 1973.

The moral of the story is that absolute prices do not convey useful information regarding the effects of oil prices upon the public's behavior. It is the relative price of oil that is the meaningful measure of oil prices that we need to use in understanding the public's behavior.

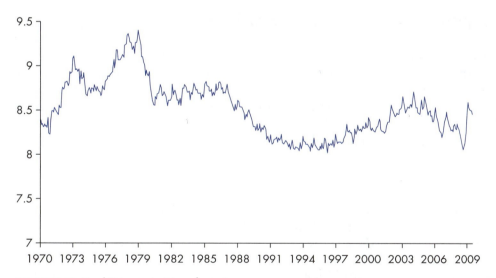

FIGURE 9.12 Real Wages in Manufacturing

Source: St. Louis Federal Reserve Bank FRED Database

wages, is that the data provide some support for the predictions of the classical model but there are some important aspects of the evidence, namely the timing of the changes in real wages and the real interest rate, that don't match up quite as well as we might have hoped, perhaps reflecting the influence of economic forces that our models have not addressed.

FIGURE 9.13 The U.S. Real Interest Rate

Source: St. Louis Federal Reserve Bank FRED Database

Supply-Side Shock II: Technical Progress

The production function that we used earlier in this chapter did not incorporate technical progress. This is a serious omission because it is hard to believe that our standard of living today could be as high as it is without any improvement in our technology. We will use one type of technical progress in this section, leaving a more complete account of it until the next chapter on economic growth.

Consider a production function of the form

$$Y = T \cdot F(K, L)$$

where we have now introduced a parameter preceding the production function used earlier. That parameter, T, will be a measure of the level of technology available for use in production. The eminent economist Sir John Hicks introduced this manner of placing technical progress into the production function but we will see in the next chapter that there are other ways of doing so. This parameter is a particularly easy way to represent technological progress. This can be shown by a shift in the production function and labor demand using reasoning very much like the arguments illustrated in Figures 9.3 and 9.4. Due to improved technology, the productivity of labor rises and so there will be a shift out in the demand for labor at any level of the real wage.

An analysis of the labor market leads us to conclude that there will be an increase in the level of Potential GDP. Now, because of improved methods of using inputs in production, more output is forthcoming at any level of resource use in the economy. The reason is that the MP

TABLE 9.2 Supply Shocks in the Classical Model	
Exogenous Event	*Response of Economic Data*
OPEC Shock: $K \downarrow$	$W/P \downarrow, L \downarrow, Y^P \downarrow, r \uparrow$
Technological Progress: $T \uparrow$	$W/P \uparrow, L \uparrow, Y^P \uparrow, r \downarrow$

Note: In the table, K is the capital stock, T is the level of technology, W/P is the real wage, L is labor input in production, Y^P is Potential GDP, and r is the real interest rate.

(Marginal Product) of labor increases due to technological progress. Real wages rise and more labor is used in production, thus increasing output produced in the economy. The government's share of the economy's output declines (recall that we are assuming that there is no change in government expenditures) and the private sector (households and firms) consumes a larger share since the real interest rate has declined. Table 9.2 provides a summary of our findings about the effects of supply shocks on economic magnitudes in the classical model.

Demand Shock I: A Transitory Increase in Government Expenditures

As a first example of using the classical model to study shifts in goods demand, consider a transitory increase in government expenditures. You may recall from our discussion in Chapter 6 that a transitory increase in government expenditures is different from a change in the permanent level of expenditures; the increase will last for a relatively short time period in the transitory case and then expenditures will eventually fall back to their permanent level. A good example of such an increase is that occurring during wartime. Figure 9.14 illustrates the effects of this transitory increase in the classical model.

The transitory increase in government expenditures shifts the goods demand curve to the right because there is now a higher demand for goods at any level of the real interest rate. Since Potential GDP is fixed, the real interest rate must rise to reduce private sector demands for goods. The private sector's share of the economy's output falls while the government's share rises. In looking for empirical evidence about these effects, we would need to look for evidence from time periods when there have been transitory changes in government expenditures, checking to see if real interest rates move during these periods as predicted by the classical model. World War II is a good choice for this purpose because there clearly were large and transitory increases in government expenditures needed to prosecute it. Economists have looked at this time period as a test of these implications and have found that the evidence is poor (see **Doing Economics**: The Real Interest Rate in World War II). Thus this implication of the effects of a transitory increase in government expenditures on the real interest rate has yet to be convincingly established.

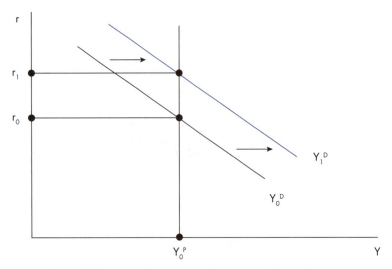

FIGURE 9.14 A Transitory Increase in Government Expenditures

The real interest rate rises when there is a transitory rise in the level of government expenditures. The private sector share of output falls while the government's share of output rises.

Demand Shock II: A Permanent Increase in Government Expenditures

If there is an increase in government expenditures that is permanent, then there will be a shift in the demand for goods as illustrated in Figure 9.15. But there is an important difference in this case; there will be a response in labor supply that was not present in the transitory case. Specifically, labor suppliers will now recognize that the present value of their taxes has risen, implying that their lifetime resources, available for consumption, have diminished. Remember that we have an intertemporal budget constraint for government that is

$$\frac{G^P}{r} = \frac{T_1}{1+r} + \frac{T_2}{(1+r)^2} + \cdots$$

where the left side of this expression is the present value of permanent government expenditures (G^P indicates permanent government expenditures) and transitory government spending is ignored. Further, T refers to lump-sum taxes and we assume that the only tax changes involve lump-sum taxes. Marginal tax rates are fixed. Since expenditures have permanently risen, so must the present value of government tax receipts, and those receipts come from households. As a result, there will be an increase in labor supply at any real wage, reducing real wages, implying more labor input in production and hence an increase in Potential GDP. Figure 9.15 illustrates this case. As you can see from the figure, real GDP will rise and the real interest rate need not increase. Thus the shares of the economy's output going to the private sector may not fall because of a rising real interest rate. The government's share of output will almost certainly rise (although this is not necessarily the case). Table 9.3 summarizes our findings from analyzing the economic effects of shifts in government expenditures.

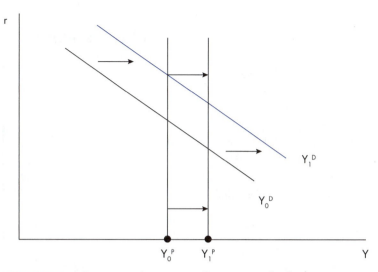

FIGURE 9.15 A Permanent Increase in Government Expenditures

The real interest rate may not rise when there is a permanent increase in the level of government expenditures. Labor supply rises, raising the level of Potential GDP.

TABLE 9.3 Demand Shocks in the Classical Model

Transitory Case: $G \uparrow$	$Y^P \rightarrow$, $r \uparrow$, $W/P \rightarrow$, $C/Y^P \downarrow$, $I/Y^P \downarrow$, $G/Y^P \uparrow$
Permanent Case: $G \uparrow$	$Y^P \uparrow$, r ?, $W/P \downarrow$, C/Y^P ?, I/Y^P ?, $G/Y^P \uparrow$

Demand Shock III: The Money Stock and Monetary Neutrality

The classical model that we have analyzed is a **barter economy**; that is, households and firms trade goods but they do not trade pieces of paper, called money, in exchange for goods and services. An economy is monetized if money is used in exchange for goods and services. While it may seem unrealistic to study a barter economy since this is not how modern industrialized economies are structured, it turns out to be instructive to think about how the classical economy fits into a more realistic economy that does have economic agents exchanging goods for money.

The classical model determines an array of real economic magnitudes, that is, endogenous variables measured in units of output. These are real wages, output, employment (unemployment is at the natural or equilibrium rate), and the real interest rate. These quantities are independent of the money stock for the obvious reason that money is not used in this model. But imagine that we had an economy where the elements of the classical model were embedded in that economy but where we also have a form of money used in trade by economic agents. How would the overall supply of that money, say it was controlled by an

Doing Economics: The Real Interest Rate in World War II

Transitory government expenditures should cause a rise in the real interest rate according to our classical model of the economy. This prediction can be tested if we can find data on a time period when government expenditures rose temporarily. Wartime data is a good choice for this purpose as there was a substantial increase in government expenditures during World War II. Data on the nominal interest rate and inflation can be obtained for the decade of the 1940s. The nominal interest rate is the 30-year corporate bond yield and the rate of inflation is calculated using either the GNP deflator or the CPI. Below are two measures of the real interest rate for this period using either measure of inflation.

Year	Bond Yield	Inflation GNP Deflator	Inflation CPI	Real Interest Rate (GNP)	Real Interest Rate (CPI)
1940	2.70	1.62	0.96	1.08	1.74
1941	2.65	7.52	5.00	–4.87	–2.35
1941	2.65	12.29	10.66	–9.64	–8.01
1943	2.65	7.17	6.15	–4.52	–3.50
1944	2.6	2.47	1.74	0.14	0.86
1945	2.55	2.58	2.28	–0.027	0.27
1946	2.43	11.73	8.53	–9.30	–6.10
1947	2.50	11.84	14.36	–9.34	–11.86
1948	2.80	6.70	7.77	–3.90	–4.97
1949	2.74	–0.63	–0.97	3.37	3.71

Inspection of this data reveals that, under either definition of the real interest rate, there is not much evidence of the rise in the real interest rate as implied by the classical model. Real interest rates declined at the onset of the war and remained below their pre-war level during the entire war period.

Source: Charles R. Nelson and Charles I. Plosser, "Trends and Random Walks in Macroeconomic Time Series: Some Evidence and Implications," *Journal of Monetary Economics* 10, No. 2 (September 1982), pp. 139–62.

agency of the government, affect the real equilibrium observed in the economy if that supply were changed? The answer to this question comprises one of the fundamental insights, and perhaps the most important insight, of macroeconomics. That answer is summarized in the following propositions.

Propositions: The Neutrality of Money

■ The real equilibrium of an economy will not be affected by a one-time increase in the stock of money.
■ The real equilibrium of the economy is independent of the money stock.

Thus if money is neutral, then the equilibrium that you studied in the classical model will be the same as the real equilibrium in an economy where money is in use if money is neutral. The classical model, then, is a description of equilibrium in a **monetized economy** where money is neutral. Studying the classical model reveals insights on the workings of monetized economies.

Is money actually neutral? We will see later that there are theoretical reasons to believe that money is not neutral depending upon certain details of the economic system to be explained in later chapters.[4] But the question then will turn on empirical evidence; there are empirical studies testing neutrality, finding that money is indeed neutral with respect to its impact upon real economic magnitudes.[5,6]

This completes our discussion of the classical model. The next subject of our attention will be how we can judge the efficiency and welfare properties of an aggregate economy, giving us a way of judging performance of our economy from an intertemporal welfare perspective.

9.4 INTERTEMPORAL PRODUCTIVE EFFICIENCY

The first step in judging the performance of the economy over time is to temporarily ignore the welfare of consumers and first focus on the efficient use of resources in the economy. An economy cannot be at a welfare optimum if it does not use its resources efficiently for the simple reason that if the economy wastes resources, a reallocation of resources would result in the production of more output from the same resource base, raising the economic welfare of the households in society who can consume this additional output. Thus, a necessary, but not sufficient, requirement for maximal economic welfare is that resources must be efficiently used in production.

But what does it mean to use resources efficiently over time? To answer this question requires that we develop a device for measuring productive efficiency and macroeconomists use the idea of an **intertemporal transformation surface**, a generalization of the concept of the **production possibility frontier (PPF)**, used in microeconomic theory.[7]

Imagine that the economy produces just two goods, with the quantities of these two goods denoted by C_0 (present consumption) and C_1 (future consumption). Within a given time period, there is a fixed resource base (labor, capital goods, and other productive inputs) available to produce these two goods. All these resources could be devoted to the production of one good or the other and, in addition, a combination of the two could be produced. A production possibility frontier represents the output combinations available to the economy as a result of its technology and supply of productive resources. Figure 9.16 presents these

---

4 For example, we will show later in the book that if marginal tax rates in the economy are affected by inflation, then if the Federal Reserve permits ongoing inflation to occur, as a result of increases in the money stock, then the real equilibrium in the economy will not be invariant to the behavior of the money stock.

5 For some empirical evidence on the neutrality of money see Mark E. Fisher and John J. Seater, "Long-Run Neutrality and Superneutrality in an ARIMA Framework," *American Economic Review* 83, No. 3 (June, 1993), pp. 402–15.

6 There is a related neutrality concept regarding the effects of changes in the growth rate of the money stock upon real economic magnitudes. If the real equilibrium is independent of variations in the growth rate of the money stock, the money stock is said to be **superneutral**.

7 The classic reference on the material in this section is *Investment, Interest, and Capital* by J. Hirshleifer (Prentice-Hall Inc. 1970), Chapter 2.

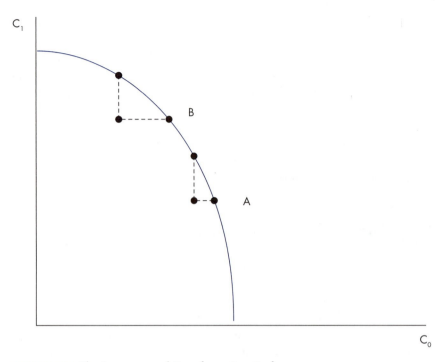

FIGURE 9.16 The Intertemporal Transformation Surface

Moving resources from present to future consumption requires increasing losses of present consumption, illustrating the idea of increasing opportunity cost.

technological possibilities. The crucial feature of this figure is its shape; the shape represents the principle of increasing opportunity cost, a concept that is summarized below.

The Principle of Increasing Opportunity Cost

■ As resources are transferred from the production of one good to another, the opportunity cost of producing more of one good rises.

Opportunity cost is an important concept in this definition; the opportunity cost of producing more consumption tomorrow is that we must give up consumption today and that cost rises as we continue to produce more future output. Why should this be the case? The reason is that as we transfer resources from production of one good to another, it is generally true that diminishing returns set in, implying that the extra output that is obtained will decline as resources are transferred. Moreover, the resources transferred from the production of one good may be less suitable to the production of another good (for example, not all labor is alike).

Now look at Figure 9.16. Beginning at point A, resources moved from the production of C_0 to C_1 results in a smaller loss of present consumption than if we were to begin moving resources at point B. This illustrates the principle of increasing opportunity cost. The slope of the intertemporal production possibility frontier is known as the economy's **Marginal Rate of**

Transformation (MRT) in production. The MRT is the measure of the opportunity cost of goods in production.

Finally, here is the definition in intertemporal productive efficiency.

Definition of Intertemporal Efficiency

■ An economy is intertemporally efficient if it is producing on the frontier of the intertemporal production possibility surface.

By producing along the frontier of the PPF, the economy is using all of its resources efficiently in the sense that it is not possible to produce more present consumption without giving up some future consumption. There are reasons why an economy may not produce on the frontier of the intertemporal PPF. For example, there may be institutional restrictions preventing markets from operating in the ways we have assumed. But we will not be concerned with those issues here (a course in microeconomics will say more about these matters). The next section allows us to determine which point on this surface is the welfare-maximizing one for consumers in society.

9.5 INTERTEMPORAL EFFICIENCY AND WELFARE

An economy that functions efficiently can provide an allocation of goods over time that is consistent with optimal welfare for the members of society. In order to determine if an economy is doing so, we will need a definition of maximal household welfare to use in our analysis. For this purpose, the concept of **Pareto Optimality** will be essential. Its definition follows.

Definition of Pareto Optimality

■ An allocation of goods is Pareto Optimal if it is not possible to reallocate goods, making one person better off, without making another person in the economy worse off.

This definition of welfare maximization reflects the fact that we cannot make interpersonal utility or welfare comparisons. That is, if one person's welfare improves by a reshuffling of the goods produced in an economy but another person's welfare declines, we are unable to make definitive statements about the efficacy of such a reallocation. To do so would require that we decide if one person's gain is, in some sense, enough to offset another's loss. There is no objective way to make such comparisons. But if by a reallocation of goods one person gains welfare, and no other person has a welfare loss, that reallocation unambiguously raises overall welfare in the economy; such a reallocation is said to be **Pareto-Efficient**. Thus our definition of a welfare maximum amounts to the statement that there are no Pareto-efficient reallocations possible in the economy. If there were, we would not have achieved a welfare maximum in the first place.

With this definition, we can now investigate the welfare properties of an economy. We will do so in an economy with homogeneous (identical) consumers and then with heterogeneous consumers. The goal will be to determine what resource allocations will be Pareto-optimal in each environment.

A Robinson Crusoe Economy

The economy we study first is one where there is only one consumer, sometimes referred to as a Robinson Crusoe economy. Robinson is a representative consumer, a device for representing all households in society. Households are thus assumed to be homogeneous (we allow for heterogeneity later). In this economy, the representative consumer only has production opportunities available; that is, resources can be allocated to the production of consumption goods in each of two periods so as to achieve a welfare maximum for the individual. What we seek is to learn how that allocation of production will be done in a manner that is consistent with maximizing intertemporal welfare. Figure 9.17 demonstrates the solution to this problem.

Our representative consumer wants to be on the highest indifference curve that can be reached, given the principle that individuals want to maximize their welfare. But this maximization is constrained by the intertemporal transformation surface; the PPF provides the relevant constraint because, given the economy's technology, it determines the production possibilities that are available in the economy. Robinson Crusoe achieves the highest level of welfare when the slope of the PPF is just equal to the slope of the indifference curve given by the **marginal rate of substitution (MRS)**. At this point any reallocation of production or consumption would lead to a lower level of welfare. These welfare properties are summarized below.

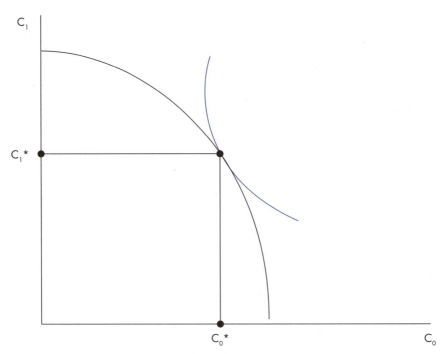

FIGURE 9.17 Intertemporal Pareto Optimality

In an economy with only production opportunities, a Pareto optimal allocation of goods occurs where the Marginal Rate of Transformation (MRT) in production is equal to the Marginal Rate of Substitution (MRS) in consumption.

Proposition About Intertemporal Optimality in a Production-Only Economy

■   In an economy where there are only productive opportunities, an allocation of goods is Pareto optimal when the Marginal Rate of Transformation (MRT) in production is just equal to the Marginal Rate of Substitution (MRS) in consumption.

This discussion illustrates how an economy will achieve a welfare maximum with homogeneous consumers in society. But this is not a very realistic case because in actual economies, there is both production and exchange occurring. Firms are producing goods for consumption by households who are, in turn, borrowing or lending to achieve their own welfare maxima. We now turn to the situation where we have two classes of households so that we can examine the welfare properties of an economy with heterogeneous consumers.

Heterogeneous Consumers

In our discussion of the household in Chapter 4, we examined the behavior of households who were borrowers and those who were lending. So it seems natural to use these two classes of consumers in this section regarding welfare maximization with heterogeneous consumers. The analysis in this section differs from the Robinson Crusoe economy because now households exist in an economy with both production and exchange opportunities. Households have access to a capital market where they can borrow or lend in line with their preferences with the aim of maximizing their intertemporal welfare. Figure 9.18 illustrates the welfare characteristics of this economy.

Consumers solve their optimization problems with the same outcomes we discussed in Chapter 4: the marginal rate of substitution (MRS) in consumption will be just equal to $1 + r$ where r denotes the real interest rate. The slope of the line labeled (M, M′) has slope $-(1 + r)$. The term $1 + r$ measures the terms of trade between present and future consumption made available to households through the capital market. Alternatively, the real interest rate measures the rate at which present and future consumption can be traded in the capital market. The economy efficiently uses its resources because it is producing along the frontier of the PPF. Production is occurring at point A in the diagram but no household is consuming these amounts of present and future consumption. Rather the existence of the capital market permits borrowers to consume more than the amount of present consumption produced by firms and lenders can consume less than this amount. Similarly, lenders get to consume more future consumption than the amount produced at point A and borrowers consume less. Therefore this diagram illustrates a critical property of equilibrium: households are actually consuming outside of the economy's intertemporal PPF.[8]

---

8 The property that we are discussing here is very similar to the argument about the gains from international trade where it is the case that trading countries will be able to consume outside their PPFs when each country trades according to its comparative advantages.

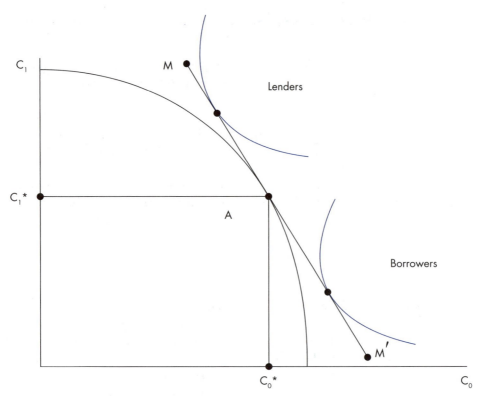

FIGURE 9.18 Intertemporal Pareto Optimality

In this economy, production occurs at point A but consumers can borrow or lend in the capital market to maximize their welfare. A Pareto optimal allocation of goods occurs where the Marginal Rate of Transformation (MRT) in production is equal to the Marginal Rate of Substitution (MRS) in consumption. The latter is equal to $1 + r$ where r is the real interest rate.

This equilibrium shows that the existence of both production and exchange opportunities through the capital market permits households to consume outside of the technological constraints facing the economy. That is, compare Figures 9.18 and 9.17 and notice that in the production-only economy, Robinson Crusoe maximized welfare at a point of tangency with the PPF. In that economy, equilibrium occurred where MRS = MRT. But the consumers in this economy have another option; they can trade with other consumers to rearrange consumption consistent with maximizing their welfare. Because of this additional feature of the economy, namely that there is both exchange and production occurring, households are consuming outside the economy's intertemporal PPF. Consumers experience a welfare gain due to the existence of a capital market. These properties of this economy are summarized below.

Proposition About Intertemporal Optimality

■ In an economy with both production and exchange activity, the economy achieves both productive efficiency and Pareto optimality when the MRT in production is equal to

$1 + r$, the terms of trade between present and future consumption determined in the capital market and where the MRS in consumption for consumers also equals $1 + r$. Overall optimality is given by the result that MRT $= 1 + r =$ MRS.

The real interest rate, prevailing in the capital market, is at its equilibrium level; that is, the real interest rate is such that what lenders wish to lend is just equal to the amount that borrowers wish to borrow. If this were not the case, there would be an excess supply or demand for loans, causing the real interest rate to change to eliminate these excess demands and supplies. Therefore there is no excess supply or demand for loans when the economy has achieved this welfare optimum. There are no Pareto-Efficient reallocations of goods that may be done because doing so would reduce the welfare of one group while raising the welfare of another group. The economy is using its resources efficiently by producing along the frontier of the PPF.

The real interest rate, given by the slope of the line along which households can trade present and future consumption, is related to both the preferences of households and the technology of firms. In the equilibrium displayed above, the real interest rate is equal to the MRS of households, thereby being equal to the ratios of the marginal utilities in consumption for households, and it is also equal to the MRT in production. The latter reflects the return to investment in the economy. This return is the extra future output that can be consumed by foregoing present consumption and moving resource to the production of future consumption. Thus the real interest rate reveals information about the rate at which households are willing to trade present and future consumption as well as the rate at which they can substitute present and future consumption through production.

Time Preference

An important concept in intertemporal macroeconomics is that of time preference, an idea related to the two-period utility function that we have used in this chapter and earlier in the book. At this point we can introduce time preference and show how it is related to the equilibrium that we just established for an economy that has a Pareto optimal allocation of goods.

You may recall from our discussion in Chapter 4 that the Marginal Rate of Substitution (MRS) in consumption was defined as the ratio of the marginal utilities of the goods consumed by the household. That definition is

$$\text{MRS} = \frac{\text{MU}_{C_0}}{\text{MU}_{C_1}}.$$

Here we have $\text{MUC}_0 = \Delta U / \Delta C_0$ and, $\text{MUC}_1 = \Delta U / \Delta C_1$, expressions measuring the marginal utility of consumption within each period. This ratio has a particularly simple form if we use the utility function

$$U(C_0, C_1) = U(C_0) + \frac{U(C_1)}{1 + \rho}.$$

The parameter ρ (the Greek character rho) is assumed to satisfy $0 < \rho < 1$ so that this parameter is like a discount rate. If the household were consuming the quantities $C_0 = C_1$, the utility from future goods would be less than the utility from present goods simply because the household must wait for future goods and it would prefer to consume now rather than later. Put differently, the household's welfare is unchanged if it foregoes one unit of consumption today in return for $1 + \rho$ units next period. For this reason, time preference is sometimes called the "rate of impatience," a parameter measuring the extent to which the household must be compensated to wait for consumption. Now note that the equilibrium in Figure 9.18 can be written as

$$MRS = (1+\rho)\frac{MU_{C_0}}{MU_{C_1}} = 1+r = MRT$$

Economists take preferences as given so that the time preference parameter, ρ, is usually assumed exogenous but note how important it is to the economy's characteristics. The larger this parameter, all else equal, the higher the real interest rate must be in the economy to induce consumers to postpone consumption. Thus high time preference economies will tend to have lower capital stocks. The reason is that if there are diminishing returns in production for productive inputs, a lower capital stock is associated with a higher MP of capital and thus a higher real interest rate. Economies with "impatient" consumers prefer more current consumption compared to low time preference economies where consumers are more willing to wait for consumption. An interesting question is what determines a consumer's time preference. This parameter may be related to demographic characteristics such as the age of consumers.[9] If this is true, then the aggregate time preference parameter will vary with the age distribution of the population.

The Time Profile of Consumption

The time preference parameter, introduced above, can be used to establish the behavior of consumption over time. This is also a way of establishing a precise set of conditions under which there will be consumption smoothing by households, an idea introduced in Chapter 4 when we discussed the two-period model of consumer behavior. As you will now see, the size of the time preference parameter, relative to the real interest rate, determines whether consumption rises or falls over time, or is constant.

Toward this end, return to the expression above where the time preference parameter was introduced. To begin, suppose that time preference and the real interest rate are the same, $r = \rho$. Observe that the condition above implies that $C_0 = C_1$ as shown below.

$$(1+\rho)\frac{MU_{C_0}}{MU_{C_1}} = 1+r \Rightarrow \left.\frac{MU_{C_0}}{MU_{C_1}}\right|_{\rho=r} = 1 \Rightarrow C_0 = C_1$$

---

9 Parents have been known to describe their children as acting as though "there is no tomorrow." This may be interpreted as a consumer with a very high value of time preference so that the utility of future consumption is of little importance to such a consumer.

This shows that the exact condition, causing complete consumption smoothing over time, is just the fact that the real interest rate and time preference are equal. This makes good intuitive sense; the real interest rate is the return to saving and time preference is the amount of compensation that consumers require to compensate them for waiting to consume. If $r < \rho$, the condition above implies that $C_0 > C_1$; consumers would want relatively more consumption in the first period because the capital market provides less compensation for waiting to consume than they require to be indifferent between present and future consumption. If $r > \rho$, the capital market provides more compensation for waiting than households require for indifference and so $C_0 < C_1$. Thus the time path of consumption is determined independently of the time path of incomes and is set only by the real interest rate and time preference.

Capital Market Imperfections

In Chapter 4, we examined the role of borrowing restrictions in the theory of consumer choice, showing that borrowing restrictions reduce household welfare for households wishing to borrow; that is, their economic welfare is reduced from the welfare level that would occur if there were capital markets available allowing them to borrow or lend to maximize intertemporal welfare. In the aggregate economy, we might ask how capital market imperfections, eliminating the ability of households to borrow or lend, affect aggregate economic welfare and here we can show that the absence of a capital market will also reduce aggregate welfare. To show this merely requires that we combine the results from our Robinson Crusoe economy with those we obtained for the economy with production and exchange opportunities.

For simplicity, we need only look at one class of household, borrowers, to see how they are affected by the absence of a capital market. Figure 9.19 illustrates how this capital market imperfection will affect the welfare of borrowers. The absence of a capital market changes the opportunity set confronting households. If they could borrow or lend, the real interest rate would be given by the slope of the line with end-points M and M'. With this opportunity set they would like to consume at point B, presumably trading with lenders to achieve this outcome. But they are unable to achieve this consumption bundle because of the imperfection in the capital market; the opportunity set now is given by the PPF and thus they can only obtain the welfare maximum associated with the production-only economy and this consumption point occurs at point D. Borrowers are now unable to consume outside of the economy's transformation surface which they were able to do when there were no capital market imperfections. In equilibrium however, it will still be true for these borrowers that MRT = MRS. The capital market imperfection does not change this equilibrium condition but it does unambiguously reduce economic welfare.

This completes our discussion of intertemporal optimality. Our results clarify what economists mean by intertemporal efficiency and optimality and demonstrate how consumer welfare is maximized by giving consumers access to a capital market where they can rearrange consumption by borrowing or lending. This framework may be used to illustrate the process of economic growth and the connection between economic growth and economic welfare. We now take up this question as a prelude to a more complete treatment of this topic in the next chapter.

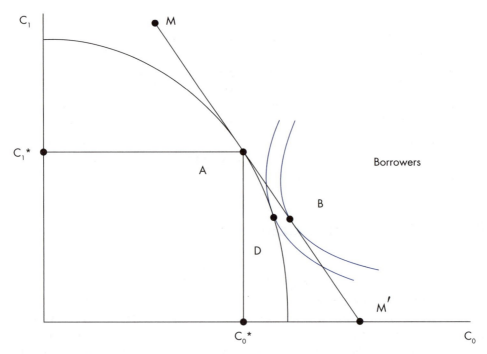

FIGURE 9.19 Capital Market Imperfections and Economic Welfare

In this economy, there are capital market imperfections that prevent households from borrowing to maximize welfare. Without this restriction, borrowers would consume at point B but they are unable to achieve this outcome and so they consume at point D.

9.6 ECONOMIC GROWTH: AN INTRODUCTION

The crucial insight of the theory of economic growth is that increases in resources (labor, capital, and other factor inputs) are the driving force behind the steady growth in living standards over time. Increased factor supplies arise in a number of ways. Households save and the capital market channels these funds to firms who invest in new capital goods, thereby increasing the economy's capital stock. Labor supply can increase from immigration or by increased labor force participation by households. To say that living standards rise due to economic growth, it is implicitly meant that economic growth is associated with higher levels of economic welfare enjoyed by the citizens of a growing economy. The framework that we just developed, addressing the questions of intertemporal welfare and productive efficiency, can be adapted to illustrate the economic welfare effects attached to economic growth.

How will increasing levels of factor inputs, available to consumers, affect their welfare? We will illustrate the answer to this question by using the Robinson Crusoe economy described earlier in this chapter. You should have no trouble answering this question for the exchange and production economy by adapting the argument below. The welfare effects are easy to see and are shown in Figure 9.20. In the classical world, markets are clearing because of flexible

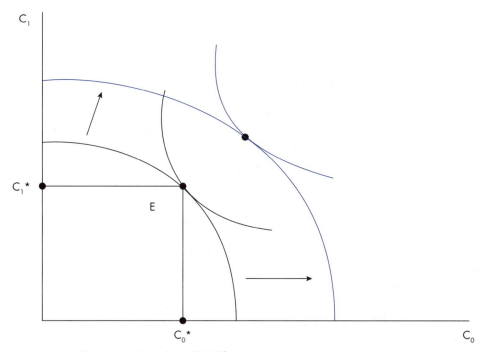

FIGURE 9.20 Economic Growth and Welfare

In this representative consumer economy, economic growth results in an expanded resource base. With more factor inputs available, the economy can produce more of both present and future consumption. The household has higher economic welfare over time as the economy grows.

wages and prices; thus increased factor supplies translate into more output produced because these additional inputs will be employed in production (there is no possibility of involuntary unemployment in the classical world). Thus this extra output is being consumed by households and the extra consumption generates higher economic welfare. This is illustrated by a shifting out of the economy's PPF and, as a result, the representative household can reach higher levels of economic welfare given by the tangency points between the PPF and the indifference curves. It is also possible that technical progress will shift out the PPF, increasing economic welfare.

This analysis just touches the surface of the literature on growing economies which has grown very rapidly in recent years. There are many interesting implications of growth models capable of empirical testing. The implications of this area of macroeconomics offer important insights into the future welfare of the citizens in developed and underdeveloped countries and have many implications for economic policy. This is the subject matter of the next chapter.

9.7 CONCLUDING REMARKS

This chapter has provided an analysis of intertemporal economics in a classical setting. That is, the behavior of the aggregate economy was examined when there is market clearing in all markets, the critical characteristic of classical economic models. The concept of Potential GDP was established and it was shown that this level of output is that occurring when the labor market is in equilibrium or, equivalently, when the unemployment rate is at its natural rate. Further, Potential GDP was shown to vary with the level of technology, the capital stock, and labor supply. The analysis leads to the conclusion that Potential GDP is independent of the price level and the real interest rate, leading us to say that Potential GDP is determined on the "supply-side" of the economy. The classical model was used to study a number of exercises in comparative statics. Shocks to the supply-side of the economy and changes in transitory or permanent government expenditures were investigated, providing insights into changes in the real equilibrium of the economy that would result from these events.

Using these ideas, we established the welfare properties of the two-period economy, first establishing the existence of the intertemporal transformation surface, showing that an economy achieves intertemporal production efficiency when it produces along the frontier of this surface. We combined this analysis with household preferences, determining the important concept of Pareto Optimality. That analysis determined the conditions that must hold if no consumer may be made better off without making another consumer worse off, the condition that must hold for Pareto Optimality to exist in the economy. We showed that if the economy has both production and exchange opportunities available to consumers, households are able to consume outside the economy's transformation surface.

The classical world provides crucial insights into the optimality properties of aggregate economies. But you should regard this as only a part of the picture of the world around you. Economies grow over time and our classical analysis said little about this although we used it to introduce the idea of economic growth. We will need to substantially expand the classical analysis if we wish to do a more complete job of understanding growing economies. This is why we devote a separate chapter to the study of economic growth. But there is also reason to believe that economies depart from the classical ideal. Business cycles are a recurrent feature of industrialized economies and economists view these cycles using economic models where mechanisms exist allowing the economy to depart from the classical equilibrium studied in this chapter. Much more will be said about these departures from the classical equilibrium when we take up cyclical fluctuations in a later chapter.

Key Ideas

- Potential GDP is the level of real output produced in the economy when the labor market is in equilibrium.
- Potential GDP is independent of the price level and the real interest rate.
- Potential GDP will change with the levels of the capital stock, technology, and labor supply.
- The classical model shows that variations in the capital stock, technology, and labor supply change the real equilibrium of the economy.
- The classical model shows that variations in goods demand only affect the real interest rate in the economy.

- The intertemporal production possibility frontier (PPF), also referred to as the intertemporal transformation surface, gives the combinations of present and future consumption that can be produced, given the economy's technology and resource base.
- Intertemporal productive efficiency is defined to be the situation where the economy is producing on the frontier of the intertemporal PPF.
- Pareto-Efficient reallocations are ones where goods may be reallocated so that at least one household is made better off without another household being made worse off.
- Pareto Optimality is the situation where it is not possible to make one household better off without making another household worse off and no Pareto-efficient reallocations of goods exist.
- Pareto Optimality has been achieved in the economy when the marginal rate of transformation (MRT) in production is equal to the marginal rate of substitution (MRS) in consumption which is in turn equal to one plus the real interest rate.
- The existence of both exchange and production opportunities in the economy means that consumers may consume at positions outside the economy's PPF.
- The lack of a capital market reduces economic welfare from what it would be when consumers may borrow or lend in maximizing their welfare.
- Time preference is the amount of compensation that households require to make them indifferent between present and future consumption.
- Consumption rises (falls) over time if the real interest rate is below (above) the rate of time preference.
- Economic growth expands the resource base of the economy, allowing the production of more present and future consumption, and thus raising economic welfare.

Key Terms

Stationary Economy

Comparative Statics

Autonomous

Permanent Change in
Government Expenditures

Production Possibility
Frontier (PPF)

Increasing Opportunity Cost

Intertemporal Transformation
Surface

Marginal Rate of
Transformation (MRT)

Time Profile of
Consumption

Production Function

Labor Market Equilibrium

Goods Demand
Schedule

Exogenous Variables

Demand Shock

Monetized Economy

Neutrality of Money

Opportunity Cost

Pareto Efficiency

Marginal Rate of
Substitution (MRS)

Real Interest Rate

Capital Market
Imperfection

Potential GDP

Endogenous Variables

Barter Economy

Pareto Optimality

Intertemporal Productive
Efficiency

Time Preference

Questions for Study and Review

Review Questions

1. Explain how Potential GDP is determined in the classical economy.
2. What happens to Potential GDP when there is a transitory negative supply shock?
3. Explain how Potential GDP is affected by: an increase in labor supply, or a decline in the capital stock.
4. Explain what happens to the real interest rate when there is a transitory increase in government expenditures.
5. What conditions arise in the aggregate economy if intertemporal optimality holds?
6. Explain what it means to have a Pareto-efficient reallocation of goods in the economy.

Thought Questions

1. What will happen to the level of Potential GDP if there is a reduction in the marginal tax rate faced by households?
2. What determines the real interest rate in the classical economy?

Numerical Questions

1. Consider the following economy with a classical labor market. Production function: $Y = 100 \cdot K^{0.2} \cdot L^{0.7}$, $MP_L = 70 \cdot K^{0.2} \cdot L^{-0.3}$, Labor Supply: $L^S = 10 \cdot [(1 - t) \cdot w]^2$. *Definitions*: Y = Output, L = Labor, K = Capital Stock, t = Marginal Tax Rate, w = Real Wage Rate.

    a) Find the labor demand schedule.
    b) Calculate the equilibrium levels of w and L, and the total after-tax income of workers. Assume that $t = 0$ and $K = 100$.
    c) Find the level of Potential GDP.
    d) Find the equilibrium levels of w, L, and Potential GDP when $t = .25$ and $K = 100$.
    e) Find the equilibrium levels of w, L, and Potential GDP when $t = .25$ and $K = 125$.

2. The economy has the following components of goods demand: $C = 1000 - .7 \cdot r$, $I = 760 - .3 \cdot r$, $G = 2250$, $Y^P = 4000$. *Definitions*: C = Consumption, I = Investment, G = Government Spending, Y^P = Potential GDP, r = Real Interest Rate.

    a) Find the level of the real interest rate using the information above.
    b) Find the levels of C and I using the information above.
    c) If G rises by one unit, find the levels of r, C, and I.
    d) Suppose that the investment schedule changes to $I = 765 - .3 \cdot r$. If all other relationships are as given above initially, compute r, C, and I.

Data Questions

1. Go to the St. Louis Federal Reserve database and find data on Potential GDP. Use that data and data on actual real GDP to graph the deviations of real GDP from its trend level.

For further questions, multiple choice quizzes, and weblinks related to this chapter, visit www.routledge.com/textbooks/rossana

References and Suggestions for Further Reading

Feldstein, M. (1986) "Supply-Side Economics: Old Truths and New Claims," *American Economic Association Papers and Proceedings*, 76 (2) (May): 26–30.

Fisher, M.E. and Seater, J.J. (1993) "Long-Run Neutrality and Superneutrality in an ARIMA Framework," *American Economic Review* 83 (3) (June): 402–15.

Hirshleifer, J. (1970) *Investment, Interest, and Capital*, Englewood Cliffs, NJ: Prentice-Hall.

Nelson, C.R. and Plosser, C.I. "Trends and Random Walks in Macroeconomic Time Series," *Journal of Monetary Economics* 10 (2), 139–62.

Chapter 10

Economic Growth

LEARNING OBJECTIVES

The subject of this chapter is economic growth, the study of those forces that cause economies to grow in size over substantial periods of time. We do not permit business cycles in the economic models of this chapter, focusing instead on the economy in general equilibrium. We try to identify why countries grow and what determines their equilibrium growth rate. We also focus on the role of technical progress, and how to measure it, since improvements in technology must surely be a big part of the economic growth story. Here are a few of the questions that we address in this chapter.

■ How can we measure technical progress?

■ What determines the rate at which the economy grows in a growth equilibrium?

■ How does technical progress affect the economy's equilibrium growth rate?

■ Is there an optimal savings rate in the economy?

■ What are the empirical implications of economic growth theory?

Living standards have been rising for centuries in the U.S. and around the world because there are forces at work in economic systems that cause per capita output and incomes to rise consistently over time. The task of this chapter is to provide an analysis of some of the reasons for this sustained economic progress.

To gain some perspective about how economies have grown over the years, consider Table 10.1. The data are estimated levels of per capita output for selected countries spanning the period 1820 to 1989. The data are measured in dollars using 1985 U.S. prices for each country. As an example, consider the United States where there has been a seventeen-fold increase in real per capita output over the sample period. In the other countries, these increases range from 9.5 times the 1820 level to 15 times that initial level. These numbers give you a perspective on the substantial increases in the sizes of these economies over a 170-year time span.

The table also can be used to compute compound growth rates for each country spanning 1820 to 1989 and these rates are displayed in the last line of the table. These long-run growth rates may seem similar at first glance (they range from 1.3 percent to 1.7 percent) but even small differences in these growth rates will have large consequences over time in the level of per capita GDP. Consider the United Kingdom which grew at a 1.3 percent rate in the sample period. If this growth rate were just 1.4 percent, the 1989 level of per capita real GDP would be 10.5 times larger than it was in 1820, rather than 9.5 times as large using the lower growth rate. The implication of this simple exercise is just this; the long-run growth rate of an economy is a crucial determinant of long-run economic welfare.

TABLE 10.1 GDP per Capita in Selected Countries, 1820–1989

Year	United States	United Kingdom	France	Germany	Australia
1820	1048	1405	1052	937	1242
1870	2247	2610	1571	1300	3123
1913	4854	4024	2734	2606	4523
1950	8611	5651	4149	3339	5931
1973	14103	10063	10323	10110	10331
1989	18317	13468	13837	13989	13584
1820–1989					
Growth Rate (%)	1.7	1.3	1.5	1.6	1.4

Source: Dynamic Forces in Capitalist Development, by Angus Maddison, Oxford University Press (1991), p. 8. Data are measured in dollars at 1985 U.S. prices.

The growth rates displayed in the table actually understate the dispersion in growth rates that has been observed in various economies. Table 10.2 gives growth rates of real GDP per capita for selected countries covering the time interval 1960–2000. Fifteen countries are contained in the table, covering various parts of the world. The average rate of growth across all countries is 3.1 percent. The table illustrates a remarkable degree of dispersion in the growth rates of these countries. Argentina displays the lowest growth rate at 1.0 percent; Taiwan has the highest growth rate of 6.6 percent. Economies with such high growth rates have been described as "growth miracles" because growth rates like the one in Taiwan generate substantial increases in per capita output in a relatively short time. For example, in South Korea, with a growth rate of 5.9 percent, real output per capita doubles in about 12 years. In the Philippines, with a growth rate of 1.3 percent, it doubles in 55 years! Economic welfare certainly depends upon factors other than real output per capita but it seems reasonable to conclude that living standards in South Korea are rising faster than they are in many other countries.

The table also reveals a tendency for underdeveloped economies to grow faster than developed economies, an empirical fact known in the economic growth literature as **absolute convergence**. In Table 10.2, Hong Kong, South Korea, and Taiwan, underdeveloped countries in 1960, are shown to grow faster than the United States but the relationship is not exact; Mexico was also an underdeveloped country in 1960 but it has grown more slowly than the United States. The theory of economic growth offers an explanation for convergence and we will use this evidence as a way of assessing the ability of economic growth models to explain the growth rates of actual economies. Here are the topics that will be addressed in this chapter.

The first topic that will be examined is **growth accounting**. The theory of economic growth demonstrates that the growth of factor inputs and technology are the sources of economic growth. Growth accounting is an empirical method, designed to quantitatively assess how much of the growth rate in output is contributed by each source of growth. An interesting by-product of this analysis is that it will be shown that it is possible to measure the extent of technological progress in the economy as the residual from a growth accounting exercise.

The next topic covered will be a one-sector model of economic growth, a model which will illustrate the forces that determine the long-run growth rate of an economy. This analysis will show that the growth of the labor force is the crucial parameter driving the growth rate of the economy. We will also test the empirical predictions of this model. The basic one-sector model

TABLE 10.2 Growth Rates in Real per Capita GDP for Selected Countries (%), 1960–2000

Argentina	1.0	Hong Kong	5.2	Spain	3.4
Australia	2.9	Japan	4.2	Sweden	2.1
Brazil	2.7	South Korea	5.9	Taiwan	6.6
Canada	2.3	Mexico	1.9	United Kingdom	2.0
France	2.6	Philippines	1.3	United States	2.5

Source: Alan Heston, Robert Summers and Bettina Aten, *Penn World Table Version 6.1*, Center for International Comparisons at the University of Pennsylvania (CICUP), October 2002. The growth rate for Taiwan uses an end year of 1998.

predicts that the growth rates of economies will converge over time and we can use actual growth rate data as a test of the model. We will also study the welfare implications of this model because it turns out that it is possible to establish how to choose an economy's savings rate in order to maximize the consumption per person in the economy.

Finally, we will study reasons why economies need not converge to the same equilibrium growth rates. This discussion will require that we look at the properties of the **production function** and the role of technical progress in generating economic growth. The basic one-sector model, described above, omits technical progress for the sake of simplicity. A moment's reflection should convince you that this is a crucial omission; for example, the Industrial Revolution and the development of personal computers are examples of new inventions that have had an enormous impact upon economic welfare and productivity. We will incorporate a simple form of technical progress into the basic one-sector model to observe the implications of technical progress for economic growth and we will study the role of knowledge in economic growth.

This chapter is designed to introduce you to an area of increasing interest for economists. Economic growth was a neglected area of study for a time but now has been revived as an active area of research. The chapter is an introduction to the reasons why living standards have improved over long stretches of economic time.

10.1 GROWTH ACCOUNTING

The basic insight from the economic growth literature is that economic growth is caused by the growth of factor inputs used in production and by technical progress. Growth accounting is an empirical method that is used to quantitatively assess the contribution of each source of growth to the actual growth of output. As you will see, this method provides an indirect estimate of the extent of technical progress, an economic concept that is not directly observable but is crucial for explaining the rise in living standards that we have enjoyed.

Accounting for Economic Growth

To see how we can account for economic growth empirically, we begin by imagining how we should measure the services of capital and labor in production. These magnitudes are flows (i.e., they have a time dimension) and so, however they are measured, they should capture the flow of capital and labor services in production per unit of time. For capital, the product of the number of machines and their hours of usage is a reasonable measure of the services of capital. Labor services in production could similarly be measured by the man-hours used to produce output, given by the product of the number of workers and the hours worked by each worker. The production function is

$$Y = T \cdot F(K, L)$$

where K and L measure, respectively, the services of capital and labor. The parameter T is defined below.

Definition of The Production Function Parameter T

■ In the production function Y = T·F(K, L) where K and L measure, respectively, the services of capital and labor, the parameter T is known as the **Solow residual** or **Total Factor Productivity**.

This parameter measures technical progress; as T rises, the economy is technically able to produce more output from a given resource base. Our exercise in growth accounting will provide a means of measuring this important parameter, an interesting and perhaps surprising implication of growth accounting.

Applying the change operator to the production function yields (see the appendix for the derivation)

$$\frac{\Delta Y}{Y} = \frac{\Delta T}{T} + \left[\frac{MP_K \cdot K}{Y}\right] \cdot \frac{\Delta K}{K} + \left[\frac{MP_L \cdot L}{Y}\right] \cdot \frac{\Delta L}{L}.$$

This is an important expression in growth accounting, enabling us to measure the magnitude $\Delta T/T$. To see how T can be measured, examine

$$\frac{MP_L \cdot L}{Y}$$

and note that this ratio is actually a measure of the share of the economy's output paid to labor. This is true because the numerator is the product of the Marginal Product (MP) of labor and the quantity of labor services, L. If factor input markets are competitive, workers are paid real factor prices equal to their marginal products (you should recall our profit maximization conditions described elsewhere in the book) and so, for labor, this numerator is the product of the real wage and the quantity of labor used in production. This share has been measured to be approximately .67 and, under certain restrictions on the technology, this implies that the output share for capital is about .33.[1] You can now see how it is that we can determine the growth of technology, $\Delta T/T$. If we can measure the growth of output, and if we measure inputs as described above and their growth over time, then we can compute a measure of technical progress as a residual using the estimated factor shares for capital and labor.

Economists have computed measures of the Solow residual and Table 10.3 provides estimates of the growth in technology for a number of sectors in the U.S. economy. These estimates are adjusted for, among other things, the costs of adjustment or installation costs associated with investment in capital goods.[2] The results show that, in all sectors but nondurable manufacturing, there was a substantial increase in the growth of technology in the latter part of the 1990s. You may recall that this was a period of substantial increases in real output in the economy and the government's budget turned from a deficit to a surplus. In

---

1 If the technology displays constant returns to scale (defined below) and if input markets are competitive, then it can be shown that all of the economy's output is exhausted by payments to the factors of production, capital and labor. That is, factor payment shares sum to unity.

2 See Chapter 5 for a discussion of these costs and their effect upon the investment decisions of firms.

TABLE 10.3 Estimated Annual Growth in Technology (%)

	1987–1999	1990–1995	1995–1999
Private Sector	2.0	1.2	3.1
Durable Manufacturing	4.6	3.4	6.7
Nondurable Manufacturing	1.2	1.4	0.9
Non-manufacturing	1.7	0.9	2.7

Source: "Productivity Growth in the 1990s: Technology, Utilization, or Adjustment?" by Susanto Basu, John G. Fernald, and Matthew D. Shapiro, *Carnegie-Rochester Conference Series on Public Policy 55* (2001), pp. 117–65.

addition, the stock market generated historically high returns to stockholders. These estimated Solow residuals suggest that the booming 1990s were caused by this rapid growth in technology.[3]

However there were past estimates of Total Factor Productivity low enough to cause widespread concerns that real wages and thus living standards would fall because U.S. residents were not saving enough. After 1973, for example, there were measures of the growth in the Solow residual that were low by historical standards. This period was referred to as the **Productivity Slowdown** and these measures are documented elsewhere.[4]

Having seen how to measure the various sources of economic growth, we are now in a position to study the implications of economic growth models. We now turn to developing economic models of a growing economy that provide much of the foundation for our understanding of the forces that govern economic growth.

10.2 THE SOLOW GROWTH MODEL

This section describes the first systematic attempt to use an economic model establishing why economies grow over time. The model was developed by Nobel laureate Robert Solow whose work started the modern research literature on economic growth. The model assumes that the economy does not experience business cycles and so it is in the classical tradition of economic analysis. In the analysis, a lower case character refers to a magnitude measured in per capita terms.

---

3 There has been a considerable amount of analysis regarding the causes of this period of historically high growth. For further discussion, see "The Resurgence of Growth in the Late 1990s: Is Information Technology the Story," by Stephen Oliner and Daniel E. Sichel, *Journal of Economic Perspectives* 14, No. 4 (Fall 2000), pp. 3–22.

4 See *Trends in American Economic Growth, 1929–1982* by Edward F. Denison, Brookings Institution (1985).

The Production Function

For simplicity, we initially abstract from technical progress in the basic model of economic growth that is discussed here but we will add in technical progress at later point in the chapter. A form of the technology is needed that will be convenient for our purposes. The technology will be assumed to display **constant returns to scale**. A definition of this property follows.

Definition of Constant Returns to Scale

■ A technology displays constant returns to scale if it has the property that changing all inputs in production by the same proportion causes output to rise by the same proportion. That is, $z \cdot Y = F(z \cdot K, z \cdot L)$.

Constant returns to scale should *not* be confused with the concept of diminishing returns, a similar concept that we have repeatedly used in the book.[5] To see why the constant returns assumption is useful in this context, suppose that we choose $z = 1/L$, giving

$$\frac{Y}{L} = y = F\left(\frac{K}{L}, 1\right) = f(k), k = \frac{K}{L}.$$

The production function now reduces to one that is very simple, relating output per capita ($y = Y/L$) to the quantity of capital per capita ($k = K/L$). This production function is displayed in Figure 10.1 and it will have a familiar shape because we will assume that there are diminishing returns to the capital–labor ratio, k. That is, we assume that the MP of capital per unit of labor is positive and diminishing.

The Evolution of the Capital–Labor Ratio

The model that we will use ignores government and applies to a closed economy (there is no international trade in the economy). Starting from the basic NIPA identity, an equation showing how the capital–labor ratio evolves may be derived (see the Appendix) and that equation is

$$\Delta k = s \cdot f(k) - (n + \delta) \cdot k$$

where $\Delta k = k - k_{-1}$ is the change in the capital–labor ratio, k. This expression neatly summarizes all of the determinants of the capital–labor ratio in the Solow growth model.

The first term on the right side of this equation captures the activity that raises the capital–labor ratio. Saving by households is added to the capital stock because firms invest these funds and purchase additional new capital goods, adding them to their existing stock of

---

5 Diminishing returns is a concept referring to the change in the MP of an input as the input's usage rises, all other inputs held constant.

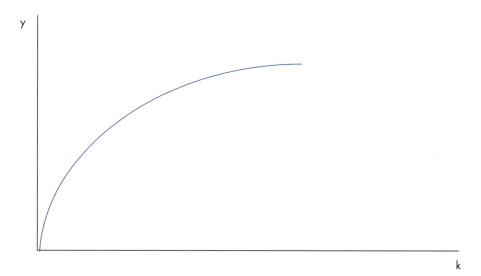

FIGURE 10.1 The Per Capita Production Function

The per capita production function relates output per capita, y, to capital per head, k, and it displays diminishing returns to k.

capital. The parameter s is the **Marginal Propensity to Save** and it obeys the restriction $0 < s < 1$. This parameter measures the increase in saving per capita that occurs if a one unit increase in output per capita is produced. For now, this parameter is fixed, one limitation of our analysis. Later we will discuss how this parameter can be chosen in an optimal fashion.

The last term of the right side of the expression shows the two forces that can reduce the capital–labor ratio. We assume that the population is growing over time and population growth can lower the ratio ($\Delta L/L = n > 0$) and this is captured by the term $n \cdot k$. Finally, the capital stock depreciates at the rate δ ($0 < \delta < 1$) and this is picked up by the term $\delta \cdot k$.[6] The equation can be illustrated graphically and this is to be found in Figure 10.2.

An equilibrium in this model is, by definition, a position where per capita economic variables remain fixed over time. A formal definition of equilibrium follows.

Definition of Steady-State Equilibrium

■ A steady-state equilibrium in a growing economy is a situation where per capita economic magnitudes remain constant over time.

The diagram is drawn under the assumption that there exists a well-defined equilibrium in the model which need not be the case.[7] But if there is such an equilibrium, it occurs at the level

6 Remember that the basic accounting identity for capital goods obeys $\Delta K = I - \delta \cdot K$ where I is gross investment and $\delta \cdot K$ is replacement investment, with the parameter δ giving the rate at which capital goods depreciate.

7 The existence of an equilibrium capital–labor ratio requires that $sf(k) < (n + \delta) \cdot k$ and later we will discuss other reasons why there may not be such an equilibrium in the economy.

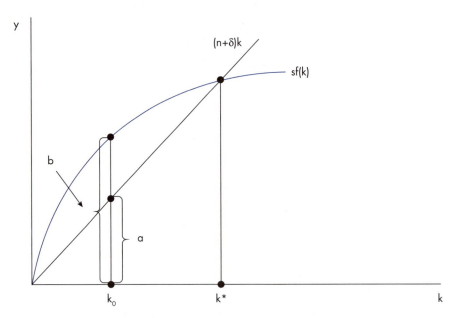

FIGURE 10.2 The Solow Growth Model

At the initial capital–labor ratio k(0), the level of output produced, measured by the distance b, exceeds the output needed to keep k(0) constant, given by the distance a, so the capital–labor ratio rises. Equilibrium occurs where saving is just enough to offset population growth and depreciation, keeping the capital–labor ratio constant. This occurs at k*.

denoted by k* (the asterisk indicates an equilibrium value of a magnitude). At this point, the amount of saving that is done, s·f(k*), is just enough to offset the effects of population growth and depreciation of the capital stock, (n + δ)·k*. Therefore this is an equilibrium (or steady-state) position in the economy because, without any changes in the exogenous parameters in the economy (s, n, and δ), this position will be maintained indefinitely.

The Warranted Rate of Growth

There is a key parameter in the Solow model that is often referred to as the **warranted rate of growth**. To understand why this parameter is so important, observe what it means for the economy to be in equilibrium.

If the economy finds itself at the position k* in Figure 10.2, it is true that the capital–labor ratio, k, is constant but that does not mean that the capital stock, K, is constant. What is true is that, in equilibrium,

$$\Delta k = 0 \Rightarrow \frac{\Delta K}{K} = \frac{\Delta L}{L} = n$$

and this shows that, in equilibrium, the capital stock must be growing at the same rate as the labor force. Similarly, the fact that output per capita is constant (this follows from the fact that k is constant) merely means that output is growing at the same rate as the labor force. This shows that the population growth rate is the key parameter in the Solow growth model because it pins down the equilibrium growth rates of important magnitudes in the economy. For this reason, the **population growth rate is the warranted rate of growth**. Thus in equilibrium we have

$$\Delta k = 0 \Rightarrow \frac{\Delta K}{K} = \frac{\Delta L}{L} = \frac{\Delta Y}{Y} = n$$

The growth rate of the population thus determines how rapidly the economy will grow once it settles down into an equilibrium. We summarize this idea in the following propositions.

Propositions About a Steady-State Growth Equilibrium

■   The warranted rate of growth of the economy is equal to the population growth rate.
■   In equilibrium, output and the capital stock grow at the warranted rate of growth.

An explicit numerical analysis is also useful for understanding the equilibrium properties of the Solow model (see the Appendix). Having established the equilibrium of the model, it is now important to understand how the economy achieves this equilibrium position when the economy has a capital–labor ratio that differs from its equilibrium level. This path to equilibrium is known as the **dynamic adjustment path** and we analyze its properties now.

Transitional Dynamics

If the economy is not in steady-state equilibrium, there are forces in the economy that will cause it to move towards this equilibrium. For this reason, the equilibrium in the Solow model is said to be **stable**; if the equilibrium were **unstable**, the economy would not again reach an equilibrium if an event occurred that caused the economy to move away from its equilibrium.

To understand the forces that drive the economy to its equilibrium, return to Figure 10.2 and assume that the economy begins at the point k(0), its initial capital–labor ratio. The capital–labor ratio will be rising at this point; the amount of saving needed to maintain k(0) is given by the distance (a) in the diagram. But the economy is saving more than this amount; it is saving the amount given by the distance (b) in the diagram. Since k is rising, so also is y (output per capita). The economy is growing faster than the warranted growth rate. The process will continue until the economy settles down at its equilibrium. If the initial capital–labor ratio were above k*, output per capita would be falling and so output would be growing at a rate less than the warranted rate of growth.

With this analysis in place, it is now possible to carry out some exercises where we determine the response of the economy to changes in the parameters in the model. We begin by studying the effects of alternative savings rates.

Changing the Savings Rate

The economy's saving rate is a crucial determinant of the economy's capital–labor ratio. Now we ask how an increase in this key parameter will affect the equilibrium of the economy. Figure 10.3 illustrates the effects of a higher value of the savings rate parameter, s.

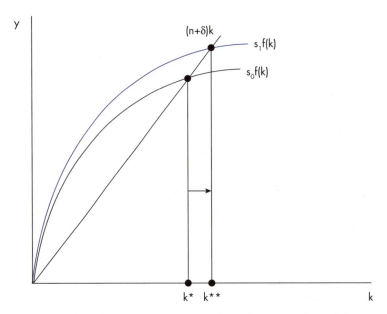

FIGURE 10.3 A Higher Savings Rate in the Solow Growth Model

A higher savings rate ($s_1 > s_0$) will shift up the economy's savings function sf(k), leading to a higher capital–labor ratio in equilibrium.

The higher savings rate means that, at any level of output, the economy will now add more to its existing capital stock. This parameter increase thereby shifts up the savings function $s \cdot f(k)$ and means that, at the original steady-state equilibrium position, the capital–labor ratio will begin to rise. The capital–labor ratio rises subject to diminishing returns, implying that increases to the flow of per capita output produced will diminish as k rises. Eventually the economy settles down to a new equilibrium, denoted by k**, a level of the capital–labor ratio that is higher than it was previously (k** > k*). What can we say about the responses of the key economic magnitudes in this economy?

A higher savings rate increases capital per head, output per capita (there is a positive relationship between y and k through the production function), consumption, and savings per capita. But the warranted rate of growth has not changed so, in the steady-state output, the capital stock and other variables continue to grow at the same rate as in the previous equilibrium.

It may seem at first glance that this scenario unambiguously raises economic welfare in the economy because of the higher steady-state level of output and consumption that results from a higher savings rate. But this cannot be claimed in this case because, as long as utility is increasing in real consumption, households initially made themselves worse off (they consumed less) in the initial equilibrium when they chose a higher savings rate. Thus there is an initial welfare loss and a welfare gain in the future associated with this higher savings rate but we have no criterion available telling us how to decide if this amounts to an overall welfare gain to households. Later we will come back to the issue of household welfare in the Solow model where it will be seen that we can make some economic welfare judgments in the context of the Solow model if we restrict our attention to cases where a policy change causes consumption to rise or fall at all instants of time.

Changing the Population Growth Rate

As a final exercise, we now ask how an increase in the population growth rate will affect the economy. You can actually think of this exercise as a policy change. For example, imagine that the population growth rate changes due to a new immigration policy rather than a change in birth rates. Figure 10.4 illustrates this case and here we will find that the equilibrium growth rate of the economy will be changed.

A higher population growth rate shifts up the ray through the origin. This ray gives the amount of saving that must be done to maintain a given capital–labor ratio and now, due to a higher population growth rate $(n_1 > n_0)$, the economy does not save enough to maintain its initial capital–labor ratio and so the capital–labor ratio falls. Output per capita falls as well and eventually the economy converges to a new equilibrium where per capita values of capital, output, consumption, and saving are now lower. But the economy grows faster in the new equilibrium. The warranted rate of growth, the population growth rate, has increased and so, in the new equilibrium, output, capital, and other economic magnitudes must grow faster than before because of the higher rate at which the population is growing. Table 10.4 summarizes

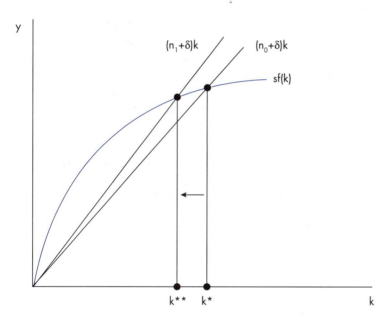

FIGURE 10.4 A Higher Population Rate in the Solow Growth Model

A higher population growth rate $(n_1 > n_0)$ will reduce the capital–labor ratio in equilibrium.

TABLE 10.4 Comparative Static Exercises in the Solow Model		
Variable Changing	Equilibrium Level	Equilibrium Growth Rate
$s \uparrow$	$k^* \uparrow, y^* \uparrow, c^* \uparrow, s^* \uparrow$	Unchanged
$n \uparrow$	$k^* \downarrow, y^* \downarrow, c^* \downarrow, s^* \downarrow$	Higher

the results from these two exercises regarding changes in the savings rate and population growth rate. Further, you should be able to carry out a similar analysis regarding a change in the **depreciation rate**.

Welfare Implications: The Golden Rule

The Solow growth model has limited normative implications about the optimal growth of an economy. The reason is that the model does not have a utility (welfare) criterion to use in assessing the effects upon economic welfare of alternative policies that might be pursued by the public or policymakers. For example, suppose that economic welfare depends solely upon the level of per capita consumption in the economy and consider the exercise carried out above concerning the effects of a higher saving rate. A higher saving rate involves less consumption now in return for more consumption in the future. We have no way of knowing if such a policy is welfare-enhancing for the inhabitants of an economy because to establish optimality requires a utility function that can determine the net effect upon economic welfare of a decline and subsequent increase in consumption per capita. But there is a limited sense in which the Solow model can answer welfare questions if we are content to restrict ourselves to situations in which we compare cases where the level of per capita consumption, resulting from one policy choice, is always higher or lower than the level of consumption resulting from an alternative policy choice. We can make such comparisons in the steady-state equilibrium of a growing economy. It is then possible to establish a condition that must hold if steady-state consumption, and thus economic welfare, is to be at a maximum. This condition is known as the **Golden Rule of Economic Growth**. The question that we will ask is this; what condition must hold if an economy is to enjoy the highest level of per capita consumption (and thus welfare) in the steady-state equilibrium of a growing economy? Equivalently, how should the savings rate in an economy be chosen in order to maximize steady-state consumption per capita?

To answer these questions, observe that, in the steady state, we have

$$s{\cdot}f(k^*) = (n + \delta){\cdot}k^*$$

$$c^* = y^* - s{\cdot}f(k^*) = (1 - s){\cdot}f(k^*)$$

$$c^* = f(k^*) - (n + \delta){\cdot}k^*$$

The first equation above holds because the capital–labor ratio is constant in equilibrium. The second equation merely provides the definition of consumption per capita. The third equation provides an equivalent definition of consumption per capita that is valid only in the steady state. The components of this latter equation can be graphed and this is provided in Figure 10.5.

The figure shows that the maximal distance between consumption and savings is at the point k^{**}. This maximal consumption occurs when the slopes of the two lines are equal, a condition given below.[8]

---

8 A necessary condition for a function to be at a maximum with respect to the choice of a variable is that the slope of the function with respect to that variable be set equal to zero. The slope in this case is the MP of k minus $n + \delta$.

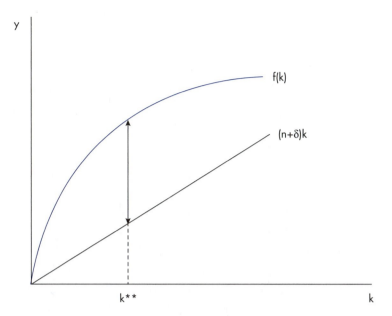

FIGURE 10.5 The Golden Rule of Economic Growth

The graph determines the optimal capital/labor ratio, k**, where steady-state consumption is at a maximum. This occurs when the slope of each line is identical, or where the MP_k equals n+δ. This determines the optimal savings rate for the economy.

$$f'(k^{**}) = n + \delta$$

So, at this point, a condition holds that is known as the Golden Rule of Economic Growth. This condition states that, in order to maximize steady-state consumption, the savings rate should be set so that the marginal product (MP) of capital per head must be equal to the sum of the population growth rate and the rate of depreciation. This analysis illustrates that there are important welfare consequences associated with the economy's savings rate and its resulting capital–labor ratio, explaining why policymakers have often expressed concern about the level of the U.S. savings rate as compared to other economies (see Table 10.5 below). You may recall from Chapter 3 that we discussed the notion of **time preference**, the idea that households prefer to consume now, rather than later when making their consumption decisions. The rate of **time preference** is that amount that must compensate people for waiting to consume goods and services. Call this rate ρ (the Greek symbol rho) and $0 < \rho < 1$. Then in an economy that has optimizing households whose preferences display time preference, the optimal savings rate should obey the **Modified Golden Rule**. That rule is given below.

$$f'(k^{**}) = \rho + n + \delta$$

This expression differs from the Golden Rule given earlier only because we have included the time preference rate, ρ. The rule states that the capital–labor ratio should be lower than it

TABLE 10.5   Household Savings Rates in Selected Countries

	1996	1997	1998	1999	2000
Australia	5.5	3.7	2.3	2.1	4.0
Austria	9.6	7.1	8.0	7.7	6.7
Belgium	17.0	15.7	14.5	14.1	13.4
Canada	7.0	4.9	4.9	4.1	4.8
Czech Republic	16.6	15.5	14.7	14.5	9.2
Denmark	5.6	3.6	5.0	1.7	4.0
Finland	2.0	4.4	3.1	3.8	0.3
France	10.0	11.3	10.8	10.4	10.8
Germany	10.8	10.4	10.3	9.8	9.8
Italy	21.2	18.1	15.0	13.9	12.3
Japan	10.9	10.2	11.6	10.6	10.3
South Korea	16.9	16.5	23.1	17.5	11.8
Netherlands	13.6	13.4	12.9	9.6	6.7
New Zealand	0.6	–0.7	–1.5	–0.3	–0.8
Norway	2.2	2.8	5.8	5.5	4.7
Portugal	11.2	9.8	8.9	8.5	10.1
Spain	14.2	13.4	12.2	10.8	10
Sweden	7.1	4.5	3.2	3.4	2.3
Switzerland	8.7	10.1	8.6	8.9	8.3
United Kingdom	9.1	9.5	6.0	5.1	4.2
United States	4.8	4.2	4.7	2.6	2.8

Source: 2002 OECD Economic Outlook

would be in an economy without time preference since households want more current consumption, and thus less saving and investment, when they prefer current, rather than later, consumption. So in order to satisfy these preferences for current consumption, a lower savings rate, and thus a lower value of k, should be chosen.

Dynamic Inefficiency

There is an additional issue related to economic welfare in a growing economy that is known as **dynamic inefficiency**. A definition of this concept follows.

Definition of Dynamic Inefficiency

■   A growing economy is dynamically inefficient if it has a capital–labor ratio that is above the level of the capital-labor ratio consistent with the Golden Rule.

If this is the case, then economic welfare, both in and out of the steady state, can be increased by setting a lower savings rate, thereby raising consumption per capita and thus reducing the capital–labor ratio to its Golden Rule level. Figure 10.6 illustrates dynamic inefficiency.

If the economy has the savings rate s_1, it achieves the level of the capital–labor ratio denoted by k*. This magnitude is above the Golden Rule level denoted by k**. If the economy achieves the level k*, the savings rate should be reduced in the economy because there will be an increase in economic welfare attached to a lower savings rate. The reason is that consumption per capita will rise at each instant of time and, eventually, consumption per capita will achieve its Golden Rule level. Thus we can say that economic welfare unambiguously rises in an economy that is dynamically inefficient when a lower saving rate is chosen by households.

This analysis illustrates the close connection between savings rates and the level of economic welfare. This analysis also explains why policy discussions in the U.S. and elsewhere frequently will focus on the level of household savings rates. Particularly in the U.S., policies are often discussed that might raise household savings rates since these rates are low enough in the U.S. to cause concerns that capital formation is below the level necessary to accommodate a higher growth rate for the economy and, presumably, higher economic welfare. Table 10.5 provides data from the OECD for five years ending in 2000. The data measure the fraction of household disposable income that is saved by households and inspection of the table reveals that the U.S. is consistently among the countries with the lowest savings rate. For these reasons, there are often debates in the U.S. about policy interventions, for example cutting marginal tax rates, designed to stimulate household savings because a lower marginal tax rate would raise the after-tax return to saving and thus, it is hoped, raise household saving.

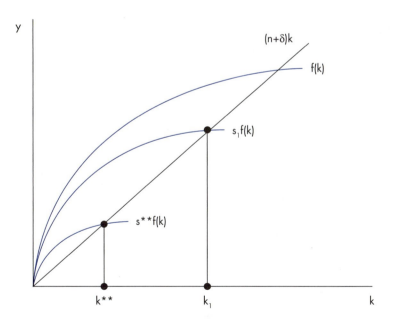

FIGURE 10.6 Dynamic Inefficiency in the Solow Growth Model

In the diagram, k** denotes the Golden Rule level of capital per head and s** denotes the savings rate leading to this level of k. A savings rate higher than the Golden Rule level ($s_1 > s**$) leads to a capital–labor ratio above its Golden Rule level. If the savings rate is reduced from s_1 to s**, consumption per capita rises at all points in time. An economy maintaining the level of k_1 is said to be dynamically inefficient.

10.3 THE EMPIRICAL IMPLICATIONS OF THE SOLOW MODEL

The Solow growth model has the virtue of simplicity and there has been considerable interest by economists in testing its empirical implications. Here we examine some of the empirical implications of the Solow model and confront the model with economic data to see how well it explains the actual growth rates of various economies.

Convergence

An important implication of the Solow growth model is known as **absolute convergence**. To understand this concept, take the equation describing the evolution of the capital–labor ratio in the Solow model and divide through by k to get

$$\frac{\Delta k}{k} = \frac{s \cdot f(k)}{k} - (n + \delta).$$

Figure 10.7 has a graph of the two components of this expression that determine the growth rate of k.

The equation above shows that the growth rate of the capital–labor ratio is determined by the difference between two terms, each of which is graphed in Figure 10.7. In the figure, k(0) is the initial capital–labor ratio in the economy. The length of the arrows in the diagram indicates the size of the economy's growth rate. At the initial value of k, the growth rate of the economy is at its highest level. As the level of k grows over time, the growth rate of the economy declines towards zero because per capita magnitudes are constant in the equilibrium of this economy. Since the labor force grows at a constant rate, this property means that output grows faster than

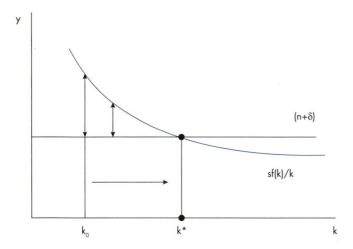

FIGURE 10.7 Convergence in the Solow Growth Model

The growth rate of the economy is given by the distance between the two curves in the figure. This distance declines as the level of k grows towards equilibrium.

the labor force until it reaches equilibrium, at which point it grows at the same rate as the labor force. The behavior of the economy's growth rate is a consequence of the assumption made about the technology of the economy, namely that it displays diminishing returns to capital per unit of labor. Thus if two economies are the same in every way, differing only with regard to their initial levels of capital and output per head, they will converge to the same long-run growth rate. Equivalently, the two economies will eventually have identical growth rates.

This implication has been interpreted to mean that underdeveloped countries should grow faster than developed ones because less-developed countries have smaller capital–labor ratios compared to developed economies. Thus, to test this model, one might look for a negative relationship between the growth rate of the economy and its initial level of output per capita. Figure 10.8 provides such empirical evidence.[9] What we are looking for is a negative relationship in Figure 10.8 and the data provides some evidence confirming this prediction. The figure contains what appears to be a negative relationship between the initial level of y and the country's growth rate but this relationship is far from exact. If the theory was strongly evident in the data, all of the points in the figure would cluster tightly about a negatively sloped line but, as inspection of the data shows, there are a number of data points that lie a considerable distance away from the line. Thus it is reasonable to interpret this data as providing, at best, weak evidence confirming that economies converge over time as predicted by the Solow model. But there is somewhat stronger evidence supporting convergence in other data sets.[10]

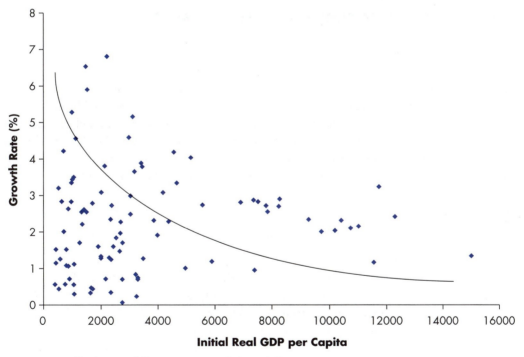

FIGURE 10.8 Evidence of Convergence in Selected Countries

9 See fn. 2 for the source of the data in this figure.

10 For example, in *Economic Growth*, Second Ed., by Robert J. Barro and Xavier Sala-i-Martin (MIT Press 2004), p. 40, there is data for OECD countries that provides stronger evidence supporting convergence.

There is an additional empirical prediction from the Solow model that merits mention. Recall that underdeveloped economies have smaller capital–labor ratios compared to developed economies. Given our assumptions about the curvature of the production function, namely that it displays diminishing returns to the capital–labor ratio, we should expect loanable funds to flow from developed to underdeveloped countries. The reason is that the returns to capital, measured by the marginal product of capital per head, would be higher in underdeveloped countries since they have low capital–labor ratios. Thus investors will achieve higher profits by investing in these emerging economies. But in fact, it has been observed that these capital flows do not occur, providing additional evidence against the Solow model.[11]

To summarize the empirical evidence, there is weak evidence in support of the Solow one-sector model of economic growth. That is, there is some evidence that economies converge in their growth rates as predicted by the Solow model but there is also ample evidence suggesting that this convergence does not occur for many economies. For these reasons, economists have searched for reasons why the growth rates of economies can diverge permanently over time since this seems to be an empirical fact for many countries. This search for an empirical explanation has led to models that explicitly incorporate technical progress, an important element of an economy ignored in the one-sector model studied above. The role of technical progress will be the subject of a later section.

10.4 GROWTH WITHOUT CONVERGENCE

Since Figure 10.8 shows that there are many countries that have low initial levels of real output per capita and are not growing at rates that seem consistent with the empirical implications of the Solow model, this section will catalog several reasons why the growth rates of economies may diverge permanently, rather than converge to a common rate as predicted by the Solow model. This class of economic model is known as the **endogenous growth model** because the growth rate of the economy is determined endogenously (within the model) rather than being given by exogenous forces as in the standard Solow model. One issue arising in this literature concerns reasons why the production function may not have diminishing returns.

The AK Model

If you look back at Figure 10.5, it is evident that convergence arises in the Solow model because the model assumes there are diminishing returns to the capital–labor ratio, k, in the aggregate production function. If this property were not present, convergence would no longer be implied by the growth model. We illustrate this fact using the so-called AK model.

Suppose the economy is characterized by the production function

$$Y = A \cdot K$$

---

11 This observation is made by Robert E. Lucas Jr. in "On the Mechanics of Economic Development," *Journal of Monetary Economics* 22, No. 1 (July 1988), p. 17.

so that the per-capita production function is

$$y = A \cdot k.$$

Thus the technology no longer displays diminishing returns to inputs in production. In our discussion of convergence, we used the expression

$$\frac{\Delta k}{k} = \frac{s \cdot f(k)}{k} - (n + \delta)$$

and, with the new technology we employ, this now becomes

$$\frac{\Delta k}{k} = s \cdot A - (n + \delta).$$

Figure 10.9 displays the implications of this model. As long as $s \cdot A > n + \delta$ which we assume to be the case, per capita magnitudes in the economy will not be constant at any time. The capital–labor ratio k (and output y) will grow at a constant rate that is independent of k. Also the economy's growth rate is a function of the savings rate so that, if a rich country has a higher savings rate than a poor country, the rich country will always grow faster than the poor country. But even if economies are the same in every way (that is, identical values of s, δ, and n), differing only with regard to their initial capital–labor ratios, the AK model implies that these economies will always grow at the same per capita rate. An obvious question to ask is what reason we might have to think that aggregate production functions do not display diminishing returns to inputs in production. One possible answer arises if we think of capital

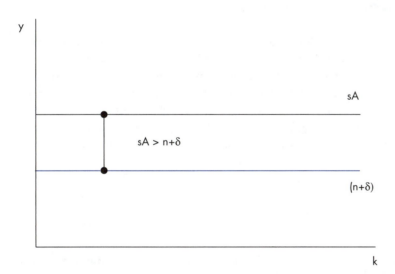

FIGURE 10.9 The AK Growth Model

The growth rate of the economy is given by the distance between the two curves in the figure. This distance is independent of k so the economy will not converge to constant per capita magnitudes. The growth rate of k and y depends upon the parameters s (the savings rate), δ (the depreciation rate), and n (the population growth rate).

as being more than just physical goods used in production. Suppose that capital also contains the stock of knowledge available to the public. There seems to be no good reason to apply diminishing returns to the use of knowledge and, related to this is the idea of **knowledge spillovers** in production.[12]

This argument is based upon the idea that research and development (R&D) carried out by one firm will increase the aggregate stock of knowledge in the economy and the new knowledge, created by one firm, will spill over to other firms who will be able to use this new knowledge within their own production processes. For this to occur, it must be the case that the research results obtained by one firm cannot be hidden (or be perfectly patented) from other firms in the economy. Thus R&D creates a **knowledge externality**; the knowledge created by one firm has a positive productivity effect upon all other firms.[13] It has been argued this externality eliminates diminishing returns and may even cause **increasing returns** in production.[14] An economy where firms are producing new knowledge through R&D can thereby grow at faster rates than other countries where less new knowledge is produced.

10.5 AN EXTENDED SOLOW MODEL

In this section we take up extensions to the Solow model that may account for its inability to explain the empirical evidence about the growth rates of economies. The first issue is the obvious one of technical progress where we discuss how the Solow model can be augmented by a simple form of technical progress. We then move on to consider the role of knowledge in the Solow model by extending the basic model to include the stock of knowledge.

Growth with Technical Progress

A moment's reflection reveals that technical progress must be a crucial source of economic growth. The living standards that we enjoy are generated to an important extent by the productivity improvements associated with new technologies as were implemented during the Industrial Revolution, when new types of capital goods were invented, and more recently by the invention of the personal computer which has generated important management efficiencies within firms. These ideas suggest that the production function that we have used must be augmented by factors associated with technological progress. We first consider how to augment the production function to account for technical progress.

Consider the aggregate production function written below.

$$Y = T \cdot F(\alpha \cdot K, \beta \cdot L)$$

---

12 This is suggested by Paul M. Romer in "Increasing Returns and Long-Run Growth," *Journal of Political Economy* 94, No. 5 (October 1986), pp. 1002–37.

13 An externality generally refers to a situation where the activities of an individual household or firm have an impact upon the behavior of other households and firms. A classic example is smoking where smoking by an individual creates second-hand smoke which may adversely affect the health of non-smokers.

14 An economy would have increasing returns if the marginal physical product of capital per head rises with the level of capital per head, k.

In this expression, Y again refers to output and T is a parameter representing one form of technical progress. In addition, there are two inputs in production, each of which is measured to account for the technical progress associated with it.

The parameter T is a measure of **Hicks-neutral technical progress**, named after the economist Sir John Hicks. This captures the idea that more output can be produced from the same resource base and technology. This may capture the effects of **learning-by-doing**, the idea that as time passes the managers of firms learn their production techniques more thoroughly, thus learning how to produce more efficiently. But learning-by-doing could also be associated with inputs in production as you will see below.

The parameter α (the Greek symbol alpha) is known as **Solow-neutral technical progress**, named after the economist Robert Solow. This can be thought of as a measure of the quality of the capital goods used in production and thus, as the quality of capital goods rises, so does output produced even though the stock of physical capital goods and their utilization (given by K) are fixed. A good example of this form of technical progress would be computers. Computers are one type of capital good used by firms and certainly today's computers are much higher in quality than those from a decade ago.

The parameter β (the Greek symbol beta) is known as **Harrod-neutral technical progress**, named after the economist Sir Roy Harrod. This parameter can be associated with changes in the quality of the labor force. It is frequently thought that this parameter is associated with the education of the labor force, the idea being that the labor force becomes more productive as it increases its **human capital**, that is, its stock of knowledge. Thus a higher quality labor force could increase output produced, for the same stock of workers and hours worked per worker. Certainly **learning-by-doing** could also be associated with the labor force as learning on the job could be viewed as an increase in the human capital stock of workers, enhancing their productivity. There is evidence supporting the existence of learning-by-doing that, interestingly, has been obtained from the construction of Liberty ships during World War II (see **Doing Economics**: Learning-by-Doing in World War II).

Hicks-neutral technical progress does not distort input decisions by firms whereas the other two types of technical progress, the Harrod and Solow types, will change the input mix used by firms in production. To see why, recall that profit-maximizing firms obey the optimality conditions

$$MP_K = \frac{\Delta Y}{\Delta K} = \frac{U_K}{P}, MP_L = \frac{\Delta Y}{\Delta L} = \frac{W}{P}$$

which are the profit-maximizing conditions obeyed by firms that were derived earlier in the book. Recall that U_K is the nominal user cost of capital, W is the money wage rate, and P is the price level. Combining these conditions yields

$$\frac{MP_L}{MP_K} = \frac{W}{U_K}.$$

This last expression shows that profit-maximizing firms equate the ratio of the marginal products of the two inputs to their factor price ratio, sometimes referred to as the **wage-rental ratio**. Using this last expression, it is easy to see how each form of technical progress will affect the ratio above. For the sake of discussion, assume that firms operate in competitive input markets so that factor input prices are given to firms and are independent of the firm's actions.

For the Hicks-neutral variety of technical progress, T appears in the numerator and the denominator of the ratio of marginal products; thus changes in T have no effect on the relative marginal products of inputs. For the other two types of technical change, the ratio of marginal products will generally vary as technical change occurs and so firms will change their usage of inputs in production as these types of technical progress occur.

With these definitions of technical progress, we can now examine how the growth of output can be affected by the existence of technical progress. However, it turns out that we can only consider the Harrod-neutral variety because it can be shown that a balanced-growth equilibrium can only arise when there is only technical progress of the Harrod type.[15] The production function that we will use can be written as

$$Y = F(K, \beta \cdot L)$$

where the product βL is known as **efficiency units** of labor. Now define

$$\hat{k} = K / \beta \cdot L$$

which is the definition of capital per efficiency unit of labor. It turns out (see the Appendix) that the expression that governs the evolution of this magnitude is very similar to the equation used above in the standard Solow model. This new expression is

$$\Delta \hat{k} = s \cdot f(\hat{k}) - (n + \delta + x) \cdot \hat{k}$$

All magnitudes are defined as they were previously but there is one new parameter in the above expression. The growth rate of Harrod-neutral technology is $\Delta \beta / \beta = x > 0$. This parameter may vary across countries and its presence means that output per capita will no longer be constant in equilibrium.

To see this last point, simply note that, in equilibrium, capital and output per efficiency unit of labor will be constant and these facts imply that

---

Doing Economics: Learning-by-Doing in World War II

During World War II, shipyards in the United States built Liberty ships, vessels that carried supplies to armies engaged in battle. These ships were all identical; that is, their construction was carried out using standardized blueprints. Data is available on the man-hours used per ship built as the number of completed ships increased. Over the period December 1941 to December 1944, over two thousand ships were built and, in the figure below, data for two shipyards is plotted illustrating the relationship between man-hours used to build each ship and the number of ships completed. A clear negative relationship is evident, showing that the more ships were built, the fewer man-hours were needed to produce each ship. This is compelling evidence of the existence of learning-by-doing in production.

---

15 See Barro and Sala-i-Martin (2004, pp. 78–80) for a proof of this proposition.

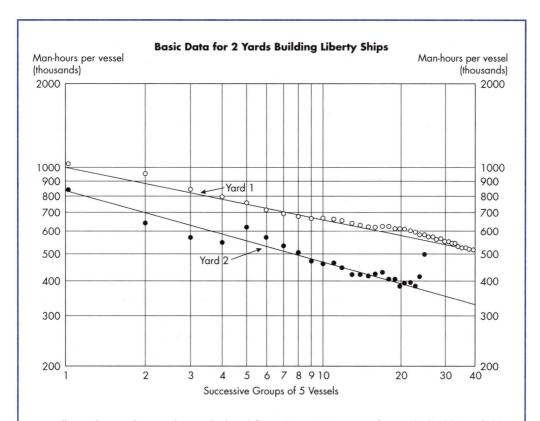

Basic Data for 2 Yards Building Liberty Ships

Man-hours per vessel (thousands)

Man-hours per vessel (thousands)

Successive Groups of 5 Vessels

For all ten shipyards, man-hours declined from 12 to 24 percent for each doubling of ship production.

What the figure does not show, however, is the source of the apparent learning-by-doing. It could be that managers became more efficient or workers on the job could have improved their skill at completing their tasks. These are unresolved issues in economic growth theory.

Source: "Making a Miracle," by Robert E. Lucas Jr., *Econometrica* 61, No. 2 (March 1993), pp. 251–72.

$$\Delta Y / Y = n + x.$$

Now, in equilibrium, output will grow faster than it did in our earlier model because it now grows at a rate equal to the sum of the population and technical progress growth rates. Alternatively, output per capita will no longer be constant in equilibrium since it now grows at the rate of technical progress. We conclude that the existence of technical progress can explain why countries will not converge to the same growth rate in equilibrium.

Human Capital in the Solow Model

The Solow model has the implication that capital should flow from developed to underdeveloped countries because of diminishing returns in production. As the capital–labor ratio rises, the marginal product of capital declines so that underdeveloped countries, with low capital per head, should produce higher investment returns than developed economies where capital per head is higher. Because this investment pattern has not been observed empirically, economists have searched for possible explanations of this empirical evidence. One possible explanation is related to the stock of human capital in underdeveloped countries.

Individuals acquire knowledge through on-the-job training and, most importantly, their education. Human capital refers to the stock of knowledge acquired by individuals that they use in their work. If the residents of a society have low levels of human capital, intuition suggests that higher levels of capital goods will not enhance the productivity of workers if they do not possess the human capital necessary to use that physical capital productively. A simple extended version of the Solow model, augmented to include human capital, verifies this intuitive explanation.[16]

Consider the aggregate production function

$$Y = K^a \cdot H^b \cdot (\beta \cdot L)^{1-a-b}$$

where Y is output, K is the stock of physical capital, H is the stock of human capital, and βL is the labor force measured in efficiency units. We have used, for simplicity, a particular functional form to specify the technology; the production function is in **Cobb-Douglas** multiplicative form. We can divide both sides of this expression by effective units of labor, $\beta \cdot L$, to get

$$\hat{y} = \hat{k}^a \hat{h}^{\cdot b}.$$

where $\hat{y} = Y/\beta L$, $\hat{k} = K/\beta L$, and $\hat{h} = H/\beta L$. It is assumed that $a + b < 1$.[17] Lower case magnitudes are thus measured per efficiency unit of labor. Using these definitions, we can derive the accumulation relationships for physical and human capital (see the Appendix), given below.

$$\hat{k} - \hat{k}_{-1} = s_k \hat{k}^a \hat{h}^b - (n + \delta + x)\hat{k}$$
$$\hat{h} - \hat{h}_{-1} = s_h \hat{k}^a \hat{h}^b - (n + \delta + x)\hat{h}$$

Recall that n is the growth rate of the labor force, x is the growth rate of the technical progress parameter β, and δ is the depreciation rate of the capital stock. The exogenous savings parameters are given by s_k, the fraction of output saved that is used to augment the stock of physical capital, and s_h, the fraction of output saved that is used to augment the stock of human capital. If we are in the steady-state equilibrium of the economy so that $k - k_{-1} = h - h_{-1} = 0$, we have

$$0 = s_k \hat{k}^{*a} \hat{h}^{*b} - (n + \delta + x)\hat{k}^*$$
$$0 = s_h \hat{k}^{*a} \hat{h}^{*b} - (n + \delta + x)\hat{h}^*$$

---

16 The version of the Solow model described here is studied in "A Contribution to the Empirics of Economic Growth," *Quarterly Journal of Economics* 107, No. 2 (May 1992), by N. Gregory Mankiw, David Romer, and David N. Weil.

17 This assumption guarantees that there is a well-defined equilibrium in the model.

Equilibrium values are denoted by an asterisk (*). We now have two equations that determine the steady-state levels of each capital stock. We can solve these two equations to get solutions for each type of capital. For physical capital we get

$$\hat{k} = \left\{ \frac{s_k^{1-b} \cdot s_h^b}{n + x + \delta} \right\} \cdot \frac{1}{1-a-b}$$

This expression illustrates the important point that the physical capital stock depends upon the savings rates for each type of capital. As s_h rises, so too will the level of physical capital, and by implication, output per unit of labor. Underdeveloped countries will therefore have lower levels of physical capital per efficiency unit of labor if they invest, compared to developed economies, relatively small fractions of their output in human capital. Thus we have established that how much a society saves (that is, how large is the savings rate s_h) to raise human capital, will determine the level of living standards in the long run.

10.6 THE ROLE OF GOVERNMENT

In the foregoing discussion, technical progress was treated as though it was an exogenous process but this is clearly inaccurate. Firms devote resources (labor and capital) to research and development and their resource allocation decisions are conditioned by the incentives they face. These incentives may result in less R&D expenditures by firms than would be desirable, from society's point of view, which leads to a role for government to use its policies to induce firms to undertake more R&D than they might otherwise do. This need arises from several special characteristics of knowledge.

The first unusual characteristic is **nonrivalry**; unlike ordinary goods such as food, the consumption of knowledge by one entity does not affect the quantity of knowledge that may be consumed by others. The second feature of knowledge that is unusual is **nonexcludability**; the firm that invents a new production process cannot exclude others from using it unless some action is taken by government to prevent this use by others. This latter aspect of knowledge is what causes concerns by policymakers that firms will not undertake enough R&D from society's point of view; if others can use the fruits of its research, a firm will not earn the return from its research that it otherwise would get and so may do less R&D than it would if it could exclude others from using its ideas. For this reason, governments give **patent protection** to new ideas. The patent is an attempt to exclude others for a period of time from using the new ideas generated by a firm.

More generally, government intervention is often needed due to the existence of **externalities**. An externality means that the actions of one economic agent have an impact upon the welfare of other agents in the economy. A standard example of a negative externality is pollution by firms. If firms pollute the air we breathe, this can cause health problems in the population, reducing their welfare. Governments take a variety of steps to reduce the second-party effects of pollution. But knowledge is an example of a positive externality. New knowledge gained by one firm can enhance the productivity of other firms as well and, because an individual firm takes no account in its own actions of how the externality benefits a society as a whole, firms are likely to invest less in R&D than would be desirable from a social point of view. And so governments can institute policies designed to induce firms to engage in more R&D than they might otherwise do. Aside from the patent protection provided by government, governments may also offer tax incentives to firms engaging in R&D to induce them to increase their R&D activities.

More generally, economic growth requires an institutional framework in an economy that is hospitable to it. A government must enforce the provisions of a legal system for the protection of property rights. The enforcement of property rights by the government is essential for individuals and firms making investment decisions, permitting the returns from investment to be captured by those making the investments. Additionally, if human capital accumulation is to occur, an educational system is required in a society. In short, institutions matter if an economy is to create wealth and grow over time.[18]

10.7 CONCLUDING REMARKS

Economic growth is the fundamental determinant of economic welfare when viewed from a long-run perspective. This chapter presents some of the basic ideas that economists have developed providing some of the reasons for these sustained increases in economic welfare occurring over long periods of time.

The basic insight of the economic growth literature is that output grows over time due to the growth of inputs such as capital and labor and because of the growth in technology. Growth accounting is an empirical method which can be used to assess the contribution of each source to the growth of output and the method also provides a means of measuring technical progress. The basic one-sector model of economic growth was discussed where it was observed that, in the long-run equilibrium of the model, all per capita economic magnitudes were constant. This was shown to imply that the key parameter in the model was the population growth rate because all economic magnitudes grow at this rate in equilibrium. This model's empirical predictions were studied. This model implies that all countries should converge to the same equilibrium growth rate and it was observed that there was evidence, albeit weak, in support of the model. Since some countries' growth rates do not converge as predicted by the model, we next examined reasons why this convergence may not occur. It was shown that technological progress, in the form of human capital accumulation, could provide such an explanation if countries differ in the rate at which their populations improve their skills over time. Finally, we observed that there may be a role for government in using its policies to promote R&D within firms. The reason is that there are external effects associated with new knowledge and it is likely that competitive economic systems will not devote appropriate amounts of resources to R&D from society's perspective since firms do not take account of these external effects when they make their R&D decisions.

The economic growth literature has grown enormously in the past twenty years. This chapter provides only an introduction to the many ideas developed in this area of economic analysis. If your interests lead you to pursue more course work in this area, this chapter should provide an adequate foundation as a basis for further study.

---

18 For a discussion of the relationship between institutions and growth, see "The Colonial Origins of Comparative Development: An Empirical Investigation," by Daron Acemoglu, Simon Johnson, and James A. Robinson, *American Economic Review* 91, No. 5 (December 1991), pp. 1369–401.

Key Ideas

- The basic insight of the theory of economic growth is that growth is determined by the growth of inputs used in production and by the growth of technology.
- Growth accounting is an empirical method designed to assess the contribution of each source of growth to the actual growth of output.
- A by-product of a growth accounting exercise is that it can provide a measure of the growth of technology, known as the Solow residual.
- The basic one-sector model of economic growth has an equilibrium determined by three parameters: the population growth rate, the savings rate, and the depreciation rate of the capital stock.
- All per capita magnitudes are constant in the equilibrium of the one-sector growth model, a fact implying that all economic magnitudes grow at the population growth rate.
- A higher savings rate raises the equilibrium capital–labor ratio and output per capita in the one-sector model while a higher population growth rate reduces both magnitudes in equilibrium.
- In the Solow model extended to include human capital (the stock of knowledge), the savings rate for human capital affects the long-run level of the capital–labor ratio.
- The Golden Rule of Economic Growth is a rule stating how to choose the savings rate in an economy in order to maximize steady-state consumption. The rule states that the savings rate should be chosen in order to get a capital–labor ratio where the marginal product of capital per head is equal to the sum of the population and depreciation rates.
- In an economy with time preference, the Modified Golden Rule states that steady-state consumption per capita will be maximized by setting the savings rate to yield a capital–labor ratio where the marginal product of the capital–labor ratio is equal to the sum of the time preference rate, the population growth rate, and the depreciation rate.
- The AK model of economic growth shows that economies need not converge to the same equilibrium growth rate if the production function does not display diminishing returns to the capital–labor ratio.
- Growth with technical progress can prevent economies from converging to the same equilibrium growth rate.
- An externality is a situation where the actions of a private individual or firm can affect the welfare of other individuals or the activities of other firms.
- There are externalities associated with the production of knowledge by firms since new ideas, developed by one firm, can spill over into other firms, raising the productivity of these other firms.
- Governments may use tax policies to stimulate R&D spending because there are knowledge externalities associated with R&D undertaken by individual firms.

Key Terms

Absolute Convergence	Harrod-Neutral	Increasing Returns	Warranted Rate
Total Factor Productivity	Technical Progress	Solow-Neutral	of Growth
Marginal Propensity	Wage-Rental Ratio	Technical Progress	Golden Rule of
to Save	Externality	Human Capital	Economic Growth
Population Growth	Growth Accounting	Efficiency Units	Dynamic Inefficiency
Rate	Production Function	Patent Protection	Knowledge
Stable Equilibrium	Steady-State	Solow Residual	Externality
Modified Golden Rule	Equilibrium	Constant Returns	Learning-by-Doing
Knowledge Spillovers	Depreciation Rate	to Scale	Nonrivalry
Hicks-Neutral Technical	Unstable Equilibrium	Dynamic Adjustment	AK Model
Progress	Time Preference	Path	Nonexcludability

Questions for Study and Review

Review Questions

1. Explain how the long-run growth rate of the economy will be affected by changes in each of the following parameters: the saving rate, the population growth rate, and the depreciation rate.
2. What is meant by the phrase "endogenous growth"?
3. What determines the economy's long-run growth rate in the Solow growth model?
4. Define constant returns to scale.
5. What is the Golden Rule of economic growth?
6. How does technical progress affect the long-run growth rate of the economy?

Thought Questions

1. According to the Bureau of Economic Analysis (BEA), the savings rate of Americans increased to over 4 percent in the first quarter of 2009. One year ago, the savings rate was less than 1 percent (http://www.bea.gov/briefrm/saving.htm).

   a) Discuss the implications of this changed behavior on the steady-state capital – labor ratio in the U.S.
   b) Businesses are worried about this development because consumer spending falls when households save more. Are their expectations in line with the predictions of the steady state consumption of the Solow model?

2. Comment on the following statement: "The Solow model predicts that all countries converge to the same steady state capital stock and the AK-model predicts that countries grow without convergence."
3. Suppose that the economy has a government sector where per capita government spending is given by $g = \gamma \cdot f(k)$ where $0 < \gamma < 1$. Derive an expression describing the evolution of the capital–labor ratio in the economy. If γ rises, what will happen to the equilibrium capital–labor ratio, k^*, in the economy?

Numerical Questions

1. Country A and Country B both have the production function: $Y = F(K,L) = K^{1/2} \cdot L^{1/2}$. Assume that, in both countries, capital depreciates at a rate of 10 percent each year (for simplicity assume no population growth). Assume further that country A saves a constant 20 percent of its income each year and that country B saves 30 percent.

   a) Find the "per-worker" form of the production function.
   b) Using the equation from a) and the steady-state condition of the Solow model, compute the steady-state level of capital per worker for each country.
   c) Compute the steady-state level of consumption per worker in each country.
   d) The Golden Rule is defined as the level of capital that allows the greatest level of consumption in steady state. Calculate the consumption-optimizing stock of capital per worker. Which of these two countries has a steady state closer to the golden rule steady state?
   e) Calculate the saving rate necessary to achieve the golden rule level of capital stock.

2. Let the production function be given by $Y = T \cdot K^{.3} \cdot L^{.7}$ where K is the capital stock, L measures labor services, and Y is real output. Compute the growth rate of the Solow residual if the capital–labor ratio grew by 2 percent and output grew at 4 percent.

Data Question

Go to the Bureau of Labor Statistics web site (www.bls.gov) and find estimates of productivity growth for U.S. manufacturing industries

For further questions, multiple choice quizzes, and weblinks related to this chapter, visit www.routledge.com/textbooks/rossana

References and Suggestions for Further Reading

Acemoglu, D., Johnson, S. and Robinson, J.A. (1991) "The Colonial Origins of Comparative Development: An Empirical Investigation," *American Economic Review* 91 (5) (December): 1369–401.

Barro, R.J. and Sala-i-Martin, X. (2004) *Economic Growth*, Second Ed., Boston: MIT Press.

Basu, S., Fernald, J.G. and Shapiro, M.D. (2001) "Productivity Growth in the 1990s: Technology, Utilization, or Adjustment?" *Carnegie-Rochester Conference Series on Public Policy* 55: 117–65.

Denison, E.F. (1985)*Trends in American Economic Growth, 1929–1982*, Baltimore, MD: Brookings Institution.

Heston, A., Summers, R. and Aten, B. (2002) *Penn World Table Version 6.1*, Center for International Comparisons at the University of Pennsylvania (CICUP), (October).

Lucas, R.E. Jr. (1988) "On the Mechanics of Economic Development," *Journal of Monetary Economics* 22 (1) (July): 3–42.

— (1993) "Making a Miracle," *Econometrica* 6 (2) (March): 251–72.

Maddison, A. (1991) *Dynamic Forces in Capitalist Development*, Oxford: Oxford University Press, p. 8.

Mankiw, N.G., Romer, D. and Weil, D.N. (1992) "A Contribution to the Empirics of Economic Growth," *Quarterly Journal of Economics* 107 (2) (May): 407–37.

Oliner, S. and Sichel, D.E. (2000) "The Resurgence of Growth in the Late 1990s: Is Information Technology the Story?," *Journal of Economic Perspectives* 14 (4) (Fall): 3–22.

Romer, P.M. (1986) "Increasing Returns and Long-Run Growth," *Journal of Political Economy* 94 (5) (October): 1002–37.

Solow, R.M. (1956) "A Contribution to the Theory of Economic Growth," *Quarterly Journal of Economics* 70 (1) (February): 65–94.

APPENDIX: DERIVING THE GROWTH ACCOUNTING FORMULA

To derive the growth accounting relationship used earlier in the chapter, begin with the production function

$$Y = T{\cdot}F(K,\ L)$$

where T denotes the level of technology (the Solow residual), K refers to the flow of capital services, and L is the flow of labor services used in production. Apply the change operator to this expression to get

$$\Delta Y = \Delta T{\cdot}F(K,L) + T{\cdot}F_K(K,L){\cdot}\Delta K + T{\cdot}F_L(K,L){\cdot}\Delta L$$

$$\Delta Y = \Delta T{\cdot}F(K,L) + MP_K{\cdot}\Delta K + MP_L{\cdot}\Delta L.$$

Each of the terms on the right side of the above expressions decomposes the change in output into each of the sources of the change in output. The first term to the right of the equal sign captures the effect of a change in technology on the change in output, the second term captures the effect of the change in the services of capital, and the last term captures the effect of the change in the services of labor. Now multiply each term in the expression by unity to get the following.

$$\frac{\Delta Y}{Y}{\cdot}Y = \frac{\Delta T}{T}{\cdot}T{\cdot}F(K,L) + MP_K{\cdot}\frac{\Delta K}{K}{\cdot}K + MP_L{\cdot}\frac{\Delta L}{L}{\cdot}L$$

Divide through this expression by output to get

$$\frac{\Delta Y}{Y} = \frac{\Delta T}{T} + \frac{MP_K{\cdot}K}{Y}{\cdot}\frac{\Delta K}{K} + \frac{MP_L{\cdot}L}{Y}{\cdot}\frac{\Delta L}{L}.$$

This last expression is the one used earlier in the chapter to explain how to measure the growth in the Solow residual.

Deriving the Solow Growth Model

In this appendix, we derive the key equation that determines how the economy's economic magnitudes change over time in the Solow model of economic growth. To do so, begin with the NIPA relationship

$$Y = C + 1 \Rightarrow \frac{Y}{L} = \frac{C}{L} + \frac{I}{L}$$

where C refers to household consumption, and I is gross investment. We abstract from government and have taken the standard closed-economy NIPA relationship and expressed it in per capita form by dividing through by the quantity of labor, L. Now substitute the production function (y = f(k)) into the NIPA expression above, giving

$$f(k) - c = \frac{I}{L}. \tag{A.1}$$

where c = C/L. We assume that the economy's households save a fixed fraction of income so that per capita savings are given by s·f(k) = f(k) − c with 0 < s < 1. In addition, the capital stock obeys the accounting identity

$$\Delta K = I - \delta \cdot K, \, 0 < \delta < 1$$

where δ is the depreciation rate, the fraction of the capital stock that wears out at each instant of time. Now express the accounting relationship for the capital stock in per capita terms by dividing through by L to yield

$$\frac{\Delta K}{L} = \frac{I}{L} - \delta \cdot \frac{K}{L} \Rightarrow \frac{I}{L} = \frac{\Delta K}{L} + \delta \cdot k$$

and use this expression to eliminate ΔK/L from (A.1) above. This gives

$$sf(k) = \frac{\Delta K}{L} + \delta \cdot k. \tag{A.2}$$

Note that we have used our assumption about savings behavior in this last equation. One last substitution is required to derive the equation that we seek. And that substitution uses

$$\frac{\Delta k}{k} = \frac{\Delta K}{L} - n \cdot k$$

where n is the growth rate of the population (ΔL/L = n > 0). Use this last expression to eliminate (ΔK/L) from (A.2), giving us

$$\Delta k = s \cdot f(k) - (n + \delta) \cdot k.$$

This equation determines how the capital–labor ratio, k, evolves over time in the Solow growth model.

Computing the Equilibrium of the Solow Model

To carry out a numerical analysis of the Solow model requires that we assume values for the parameters in the model and that we adopt an explicit functional form for the production function in the model. We will assume the following values (%) for the various parameters in the model.

Population Growth: n = .03   Savings Rate: s = .25   Depreciation Rate: δ = .01

As for the production function, we will use one known as a Cobb-Douglas production function that is given below.

$$Y = K^{.33} \cdot L^{.67}$$

Recall that we assume that the economy's technology displays constant returns to scale. To see that this is true in the above production function, divide both sides of the equation by L to yield

$$Y/L = y = K^{.33} \cdot L^{.67}/L = K^{.33} \cdot L^{.67}L^{-1} = K^{.33} \cdot L^{-.33} = k^{.33}$$

Using this functional form and the parameter values above, the Solow model now becomes

$$\Delta k = .25 \cdot k^{.33} - (.03 + .01) \cdot k.$$

Equilibrium occurs when $\Delta k = 0$ which gives

$$.25 \cdot k^{*.33} = (.03 + .01) \cdot k^*.$$

Solving this expression for k* (the asterisk denotes the equilibrium value of k) gives

$$k^* = 15.4.$$

We can compute the other per capita economic magnitudes for the model using this value for k as well and these are given below.

$c^* = (1 - .25) \cdot k^{*.33} = 1.85$ $s^* = .25 \cdot k^{*.33} = .62$ $y^* = k^{*.33} = 2.47$

The Solow Model with Technical Progress

Using the NIPA identity, we have

$$Y = C + I \Rightarrow \frac{Y}{\beta \cdot L} = \frac{C}{\beta \cdot L} + \frac{I}{\beta \cdot L}.$$

where the symbol β (the Greek symbol beta) is a technical progress parameter associated with the labor force. If output obeys the production function

$$\hat{y} = f(\hat{k}), \hat{y} = \frac{Y}{\beta \cdot L}, \hat{k} = \frac{K}{\beta \cdot L}$$

then if a constant fraction of the economy's output is saved we can rewrite the NIPA equation to yield

$$sf(\hat{k}) = \frac{I}{\beta \cdot L} = \frac{\Delta K + \delta \cdot K}{\beta \cdot L} = \frac{\Delta K}{\beta \cdot L} + \delta \cdot \hat{k}$$

Finally, a bit of algebra gives the following expression.

$$\frac{\Delta K}{\beta L} = \Delta \hat{k} + (n+x) \cdot \hat{k}, \frac{\Delta \beta}{\beta} = x > 0.$$

Inserting this last expression into the previous one yields the equation in the text.

The Solow Model with Physical and Human Capital

Human capital evolves according to

$$\Delta H = I_H - \delta \cdot H$$

where Δ is the change operator, H is the stock of human capital, and I_H is gross investment in human capital. Divide both sides of this equation by $\beta \cdot L$ to get

$$\frac{\Delta H}{\beta \cdot L} = \frac{I_H}{\beta \cdot L} - \delta \cdot h$$

where we have used the definition $h = H/\beta \cdot L$. Apply the change operator to this last expression to get

$$\Delta h - (n+x) \cdot h = \frac{\Delta H}{\beta \cdot L}.$$

Use this last expression with one derived above it to get

$$\Delta h - (n+x) \cdot h = \frac{I_H}{\beta \cdot L} - \delta \cdot h.$$

We assume that

$$\frac{I_H}{\beta \cdot L} = s_h \cdot y = s_h \cdot k^a \cdot h^b$$

so substituting this expression into the one preceding it gives

$$\Delta h = s_h \cdot k^a \cdot h^b - (n + x + \delta) \cdot h.$$

The capital per head equation is derived using steps used in the section of this appendix deriving the capital equation in the Solow model with technical progress attached to labor.

Chapter 11

Aggregate Demand

LEARNING OBJECTIVES

In this chapter, the **aggregate demand** schedule is derived. This will be one component of our business cycle models used in subsequent chapters. The aggregate demand relationship incorporates goods and financial market equilibrium into one locus of points. You will see that this schedule is affected by changes in fiscal and monetary policy and it may also be affected by the actions of the private sector. Shifts in this schedule are one reason why recessions may arise in the economy. Here are a few of the questions that we seek to answer in this chapter.

- What is the relationship between the real interest rate and output such that the goods market is in equilibrium?

- What is the relationship between the real interest rate and output such that the money and bond markets are in equilibrium?

- How can the aggregate demand schedule be derived from the goods and **money market equilibrium** relationships?

- How do monetary and fiscal policies affect the position of the aggregate demand schedule?

Economic models of the **business cycle** use a device called the aggregate demand schedule as one of their components. This schedule represents equilibrium in the goods and financial markets and it incorporates the behavior of the private sector and the government into one part of business cycle models, showing how changes in the behavior of these economic agents can affect equilibrium in the goods and financial markets. The task of this chapter is to show how this component of business cycle models can be derived.

It is important to stress that this version of aggregate demand will differ from the one that was developed in Chapter 9. The one that you saw previously was designed for the classical model and did not contain the level of output in sectoral demands for goods. Output was determined on the supply side of the economy in the classical model and so it was independent of aggregate demand. Here we develop a version of the aggregate demand schedule that is intended for the analysis of business cycles. In this style of economic model, aggregate demand does have a role to play in the determination of the level of output (indeed we will see that the aggregate demand schedule can shift and change the level of output) and so the aggregate demand schedule in this chapter will be an economic relationship that involves the level of output.

The first part of the derivation of this aggregate demand schedule concerns the goods market. Equilibrium in the goods market will occur when there are no unintended changes in inventories held by firms. Using our analysis of household behavior and the behavior of the firm developed in earlier chapters, we will show how the real interest rate is determined by the interaction of **national saving** and the investment demand for goods by firms. That analysis will allow us to determine a **goods market equilibrium** locus involving the real interest rate and the level of output. This last relationship, known as the **IS schedule**, will be the goods market component that we need for later purposes. We will establish its properties (its slope and what causes it to shift) because we will need to know these characteristics for later analysis.

The next part of the derivation of aggregate demand involves the money and bond markets. This analysis depends upon our discussion of those markets in Chapter 7 where it was shown how the interest rate was determined in the money and bond markets. Using this theory of the financial markets, we will show that it is possible to obtain a relationship between the real interest rate and output that is consistent with equilibrium in both the money and bond markets. This schedule is known as the **LM schedule**, the second building-block for the aggregate demand schedule. We will also establish its properties for later use.

The next step in the analysis is to take the preceding two models of the financial and goods markets and combine them into what we will call the aggregate demand schedule. This schedule is a relationship between the price level and the level of output and each point on this line represents equilibrium in the goods and financial markets. This is a critical component of business cycle analysis because it is one (but not the only) part of business cycle models where private sector and policymaker behavior are located. Any changes in the behavior of the private sector, or policy changes by the government or the Fed, affect the aggregate demand for goods and may ultimately have an impact upon the level of output and other magnitudes over the business cycle. Thus understanding cyclical fluctuations will require a careful analysis of the determinants of aggregate demand. You will need to know why it slopes the way it does and what may cause it to shift.

The final part of this chapter is a brief introduction into business cycle analysis. Business cycles are analyzed by using the aggregate demand schedule derived in this chapter along with a model of the supply-side of the economy. In Chapter 8, we developed several variants of economic models of the labor market that are a part of the foundation for this supply discussion. Chapter 12 will show in detail how each of these labor market models translates into a theory of the supply of output in the aggregate economy. Most of those theories of the supply-side have the feature that there are two versions of the supply-side: an equilibrium one and another representing disequilibrium. In this section, we will introduce you to the methodology of using those models of the supply-side, in conjunction with the aggregate demand schedule, to carry out the analysis of cyclical fluctuations, leaving a more thorough analysis of these ideas until the next chapter.

Once you learn the material in this chapter, you should understand how the aggregate demand schedule arises from goods and financial markets and how monetary and fiscal policy tools can affect the position of the aggregate demand schedule.

11.1 THE GOODS MARKET

Goods market equilibrium is represented by the IS schedule and its definition is given below.

Definition of the IS Curve

■   The IS curve is an equilibrium schedule for the real interest rate and output such that the goods market is in equilibrium. Goods market equilibrium occurs when there is no unintended inventory accumulation.

Before we derive this schedule, it is useful to recall several features of our analysis of the household in Chapter 4.

That analysis established that real household saving was determined by current and future real after-tax income and the real interest rate. Saving was found to be increasing in the level of current after-tax income and, if the substitution effect dominated the income effect, saving would rise with the real interest rate. With these observations in mind, consider the closed-economy NIPA relationship

$$Y = C + I + G$$

where Y denotes real output, C is real household consumption spending, I is real investment spending by firms, and G refers to real government expenditures. This is an **identity**, that is, it holds by definition. We now want to inject some economic content into this identity by thinking of it as a representation of equilibrium behavior. Towards this end, imagine that the right side of this expression is the planned demand for goods by the private sector and government. The left side is now the supply of goods in the economy so that supply and planned demand are equal. Equilibrium in the goods market occurs when the planned demand for goods is equal to supply so that there are no unintended changes to the level of inventories held by firms. Rewrite the above relationship as

$$Y - C - G = I$$

$$S^P - G = I.$$

In the expression above, S^P stands for **private saving** ($S^P = Y - C$) and national saving is defined as $S^P - G$. The last expression now states that goods market equilibrium occurs when national saving is equal to investment. Our analysis of the household established some of the economic magnitudes that determine S^P (namely current after-tax real income and the real interest rate) and our analysis of investment by firms showed that investment was inversely related to the real interest rate. These observations lead us to write

$$S^P(Y_0, r) - G_0 = I(r).$$

We can display these expressions in a graph and this is done in Figure 11.1. The real interest rate, r_0, is the real interest rate where the goods market is in equilibrium. The savings relationship is drawn under the assumption that there are particular values of output and government spending that prevail in the economy, Y_0 and G_0. Firms are demanding goods for

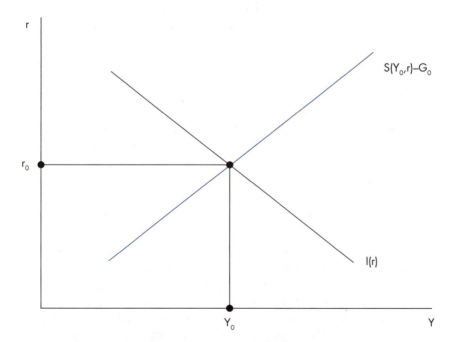

FIGURE 11.1 Goods Market Equilibrium

Equilibrium in the goods market occurs at the point (r_0, Y_0). This is the place where the demand for savings is just equal to the supply of savings.

investment in new plant and equipment and funds for these projects are provided through national saving. If the real interest rate differs from r_0, then economic forces come into play that would cause the real interest rate to change. For example, at an interest rate below r_0, firms would demand funds in excess of what is being provided through national saving. As a result, the real interest rate would rise, reducing the level of investment until it is equal to the level of national saving.

We can derive the IS curve by varying the level of real output and observing the response of the real interest rate when the goods market is in equilibrium but, before we do so, it is useful to point out that there are other determinants of these schedules that can shift their positions. You will recognize these factors once the intertemporal nature of the decisions made by households and firms is considered. First consider the behavior of the household.

Our two-period analysis of the household in Chapter 4 showed that saving and consumption were determined by three factors: current and future after-tax real income along with the real interest rate. Two of these magnitudes are built into the savings schedule contained in Figure 11.1 but future after-tax real income is not. The implication of this is that any changes in the perceptions of households regarding future after-tax real income will cause a shift in the saving schedule displayed in Figure 11.1. This is completely consistent with our analysis in Chapter 4 where we showed that current consumption would rise with an increase in future after-tax real income. Thus one factor that can shift the current saving schedule is the household's expectations about its future disposable real income.

As for firms, recall from our discussion in Chapter 5 that firms make their investment decisions in a forward-looking manner just as households do. So in deciding upon the appropriate amount of current investment to undertake, firms must look ahead at estimated future values of the economic determinants of investment. We argued in Chapter 5 that it was important for firms to do this because there are planning and installation costs attached to new investment projects. If firms make mistakes in forecasting the future, they discover that their profits have declined because they undertook certain investment projects that they would not have carried out with better forecasts of the future. So, for example, if firms foresee a future cut in the corporate tax rate and they are certain that this cut in the tax rate will take place, they will increase investment now in anticipation of this cut in the user cost of capital.

The bottom line from this discussion about the forward-looking behavior of households and firms is that expectations about future economic magnitudes relevant to households and firms can change and, if they do, current saving and investment will change as well. We will refer to these forces as "**exogenous** shift factors" because they are determined outside the scope of our analysis which is focused upon the behavior of economic agents in the current period. But in our analysis below, we will indicate how these exogenous forces affect the economic relationships that interest us.

Figure 11.2 provides the graphical derivation of the IS schedule. At the original level of output, Y_0, the real interest rate that achieves goods market equilibrium is r_0. The level of national saving is denoted in the figure as $S^P(Y_0, r) - G_0$. If current output (income) rises to Y_1, household saving increases at any level of the real interest rate. The new level of national saving is now $S^P(Y_1, r) - G_0$. As a result of the additional funds made available by households, the real interest rate must fall until national saving and investment are again equal. The implication of the analysis is that there is an inverse relationship between the real interest rate and the level of output consistent with goods market equilibrium. The IS curve, derived in the right panel

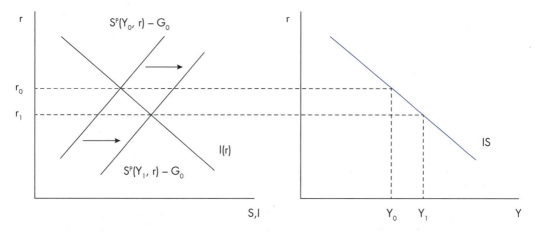

FIGURE 11.2 Deriving the IS Curve

The goods market is in equilibrium at the interest rate r_0 when output is at the level Y_0. If output rises ($Y_1 > Y_0$), private saving increases at any real interest rate, reducing the level of the real interest rate at which goods market equilibrium occurs.

of Figure 11.2 that we sought to obtain, displays this inverse relationship between the real interest rate and the level of output.

The IS curve can change its position for a variety of reasons. We now investigate how those economic events can cause shifts in the goods market equilibrium locus that we just derived.

To see how inventories figure into our discussion, imagine that the economy was in a situation where it produced a level of output inconsistent with goods market equilibrium. Figure 11.3 illustrates the connection between the IS curve and inventory changes. At an interest rate of r_0, the economy should be producing the level of output Y_0 but suppose that firms were producing the higher level, Y_2. At this higher output level, inventories rise unexpectedly. Since holding inventories is costly (recall our discussion of inventory holding costs from Chapter 4), firms will reduce production, causing output to fall from Y_2 to Y_0. If firms were producing at Y_1, inventories would fall unexpectedly, causing firms to hold inventories at levels where they may stock out, causing a loss of customer good will. So firms would increase production to Y_0. Whenever the economy is producing at levels off the IS curve, there are unexpected changes in inventories that will lead to production adjustments by firms. When we describe how an economy responds to various shocks, we will therefore use inventory behavior to motivate why production will change in the economy.

Shifts in the IS Curve

The position of the IS curve is determined by any of the factors that can cause the national saving or investment schedules to shift. These factors are exogenous, that is, determined outside of the economic model that we are studying. These factors include tools associated with fiscal policy (government expenditures and taxes) but they might also include factors that are not explicitly incorporated into our analysis, such as expectations about future economic magnitudes. As a first example, consider a decline in the investment demand schedule,

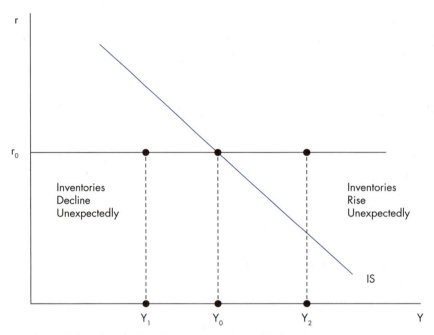

FIGURE 11.3 Unintended Inventory Changes and the IS Curve

At interest rate r_0, goods market equilibrium occurs at output level Y_0. If Y_1 is produced by firms, inventories fall unexpectedly. If output level Y_2 is produced, inventories rise unexpectedly.

implying that there will be a lower level of investment demand by firms at any value of the real interest rate. This may occur because firms perceive lower returns to investment in the future possibly because they foresee an increase in the corporate tax rate, causing them to reduce new plant and equipment spending now in anticipation of these future lower returns.[1] Alternatively, the relative price of investment goods may be expected to rise in the future. Both of these possibilities increase the future user cost of capital. Figure 11.4 provides the graphical details of this change in the behavior of firms.

The national saving schedule is $S^P(Y_0, r) - G_0$ and Y_0 is the fixed level of real output. The original investment demand schedule is $I_0(r)$ and the new investment demand schedule is given by $I_1(r)$. Because there has been a decrease in investment at any level of the real interest rate, saving now exceeds investment at the original level of the real interest rate and output. As a result, the real interest rate must fall to increase the level of investment and to reduce national saving. As this occurs at the fixed (by assumption) level of real output, this means that the IS curve has shifted to the left as a result of the decreased investment demand by firms.

As a second example, consider a transitory increase in government spending. If the increase is transitory, this means that total government expenditures rise but will ultimately return in the future to their permanent level (the present value of transitory government spending is zero). We have argued that governments finance transitory spending with bond issue.

---

1 Recall our discussion of investment in Chapter 4 showing that, due to costs of adjustment, firms will change their investment behavior in anticipation of changes in economic incentives.

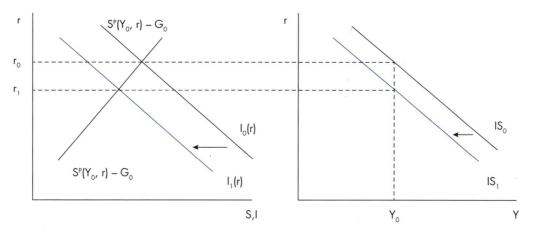

FIGURE 11.4 Shifting the IS Curve Due to a Shift in Investment

The goods market is initially in equilibrium at the interest rate r_0 when output is at the level Y_0. If there is an exogenous decrease in investment, the interest rate that clears the goods market must fall at the initial level of real output. This implies a leftward shift in the IS curve.

Household taxes will not increase. These additional bonds absorb some of the savings generated by households. Equivalently, more of the economy's current output is used by the government, leaving less output and income available as aggregate saving. The end result is that there will be a net decline in national saving at any level of the real interest rate.

Alternatively, the additional government spending could be permanent in which case there will be a permanent increase in taxes paid by households (the present value of household taxes will increase). How will households respond to the increase in government spending and taxes? We showed in Chapter 4 that, for every dollar that household disposable income declines, household consumption falls by less than a dollar.[2] When the government raises current lump-sum taxes to pay for additional permanent spending, current household spending will fall but by less than the increase in government spending. Thus there is a net decline in saving in the economy, just as in the transitory government spending case. Figure 11.5 illustrates both of these cases.

The investment demand curve is unaffected by changes in government expenditures. The original level of national saving is given by $S^P(Y_0, r) - G_0$ and government expenditures rise to G_1 $(G_1 > G_0)$ so the new national saving schedule is $S^P(Y_0, r) - G_1$. Since the increase in government expenditures more than offsets the decline in household consumption that may occur, there will be a net decline in national saving at any level of the real interest rate. At the original real interest rate, this implies that there will be an excess demand for goods for investment purposes, requiring that the real interest rate must rise, reducing investment and increasing national saving. This means that at the original level of real output, Y_0, a higher real interest rate is consistent with goods market equilibrium. This fact implies that the IS curve has shifted to the right.

2 The **marginal propensity to consume**, a parameter found to be between zero and unity, measures the size of the decline in household consumption.

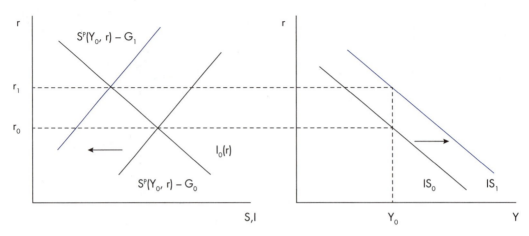

FIGURE 11.5 Government Expenditures and the IS Curve

The goods market is initially in equilibrium at the interest rate r_0 when output is at the level Y_0. If there is an exogenous transitory increase in government expenditures, the interest rate that clears the goods market must rise at the initial level of real output. This implies a rightward shift in the IS curve.

The final example that we consider concerns a cut in lump-sum taxes that are paid by households. To understand this case requires that we address an issue taken up in Chapter 4 known as **Ricardian Equivalence**. As you may recall, the response by households to a tax cut turns on how they perceive the future tax liabilities that are attached to a tax cut. If consumers are Ricardian, they know that the government must satisfy an intertemporal budget constraint, and that a tax cut now, with constant government expenditures, implies a tax increase in the future. They will save the tax cut that they receive because they are forward-looking and perceive the future taxes that are implied by the tax cut. Put differently, their consumption choices will be unaffected by a tax cut. If consumers are not Ricardian, they will not foresee these future taxes and will believe that their wealth has increased due to the tax cut. And in this case, they will spend part of the tax cut. Thus if we are to know how the IS curve will be affected by a tax cut, we need to base our answer upon the reaction of households to the tax cut. If they are Ricardian, the tax cut will not affect consumption demands by households and so the IS curve will be unaffected by the tax cut. If the public is not Ricardian, that is, they do not see the future taxes implied by the tax cut, a tax cut increases the demand for goods by households at any level of the real interest rate. This means that, at any level of real output, savings by households will decline and the real interest rate clearing the market will rise. Thus the IS curve will shift to the right. Graphically, the story looks much like Figure 11.4 except the shift in the curve $S^P(Y, r)$ – G is caused by a shift in the savings schedule, rather than by government expenditures, G.

Table 11.1 summarizes the possible cases where changes in economic magnitudes can shift the IS curve. In addition to the cases already discussed, the table also contains two other possible scenarios. There are exogenous forces that can shift saving or, equivalently, household consumption. Consumption could shift due to changes in the expectations of households regarding their future real after-tax incomes. The important point to keep in mind is that the shift in the curve is exogenous, that is, determined outside of the IS framework. These shifts in the IS curve are related to the Keynesian multipliers taught to students in introductory economics courses (see **Doing Economics**: Keynesian Multipliers and Fiscal Policy).

TABLE 11.1 Causes of Shifts in the IS Curve

Exogenous Factor	Response of the IS Schedule
Investment ↑	IS shifts →
Government Expenditures ↑	IS shifts →
Lump-Sum Taxes ↓	
Ricardian Consumers	IS Unchanged
Non-Ricardian Consumers	IS shifts →
Private Saving ↑	IS shifts ←
Household Consumption ↑	IS shifts →

This completes our derivation of the IS curve, the goods market component of the aggregate demand schedule. We now need to develop the financial component of aggregate demand, the subject of the next section.

11.2 THE FINANCIAL MARKET

The analysis of the money market from Chapter 7 is what we will use to obtain a relationship between the interest rate and real income that represents financial market equilibrium. This is called the LM schedule and its definition is given below.

Doing Economics: Keynesian Multipliers and Fiscal Policy

In introductory macroeconomics courses, students learn how to compute Keynesian multipliers, named after the economist John Maynard Keynes who developed the economic models upon which multiplier analysis is based. These multipliers actually measure the change in output given a change in an exogenous variable such as government spending at a fixed interest rate or, equivalently, they measure shifts in the IS curve. These multipliers may be derived using the IS schedule in the model spelled out in the Appendix to this chapter.

Keynesian multipliers have been used in economic policy analysis recently. The economy entered a recession in December 2007. The Obama Administration supported a stimulus bill, ultimately signed into law in February 2009 and known as the American Recovery and Reinvestment Act, partly on the grounds that the additional government spending in the bill would increase economic activity. There were reports in the media that the Administration expected that, for every dollar in additional government spending in the bill, income would rise by 1.5 dollars. That is, the Administration operated under the assumption that the government spending multiplier was 1.5. So multiplier analysis was used to justify an economic policy thought to raise real GDP.

Definition of the LM Curve

■   The LM curve is an equilibrium schedule for the interest rate and output such that the money and bond markets are in equilibrium.

As the definition states, at each point on the LM curve, the money and bond markets are in equilibrium. That is, the interest rate has adjusted so that there is no excess supply or demand for money and bonds. Before we begin our derivation of the LM curve, it is useful to review our findings about the demand for money that were presented in Chapter 7.

The motive for holding money is that money is used as the **medium of exchange** so that money is held by households because they will use it to buy goods and services. Money has an opportunity cost, measured by the interest rate, and money demand is inversely related to this interest rate. At a higher interest rate, households demand more bonds because the return on bonds has risen and therefore they demand less money and more bonds. We will assume that there is no **expected inflation** in the economy for simplicity. Thus there is no difference between the real and nominal interest rates.[3] Money demand is increasing in the level of consumption; consumption is replaced here by real income for simplicity. Thus money demand rises with an increase in real income because as real income rises, planned consumption rises and so households will plan to hold more money to pay for the additional goods and services that they plan to consume. With these preliminary ideas established, we can now explain how to derive the LM schedule. Figure 11.6 illustrates how to find this money and **bond market equilibrium** locus.

The figure shows the money market with two levels of real income, Y_0 and Y_1, and the corresponding demand schedules for money. The LM curve is found by observing how the

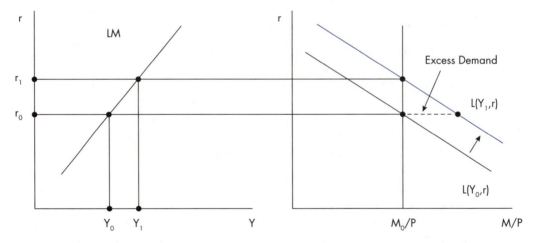

FIGURE 11.6 The LM Curve

The LM curve is derived by observing how the interest rate, clearing the money and bond markets, changes with income. Money demand, L(Y, r), rises with income ($Y_0 < Y_1$) so the interest rate clearing the money market must rise with real income.

---

3 See the Appendix for a discussion of including inflation into the analysis of the aggregate demand schedule.

equilibrium interest rate, set in the money and bond markets, changes with real income. Because the demand for money rises with an increase in real income, the LM schedule has a positive slope. The reason is that when real income rises from Y_0 to Y_1, there is an initial excess demand for money at the original interest rate, r_0. From our earlier analysis of the financial markets, we know that there will be a corresponding excess supply of bonds. No additional money will be provided by the Fed because we assume that the overall supply of real money balances is fixed.

Therefore, to acquire additional cash for transaction purposes, the public begins to sell bonds, bond prices fall, and the bond yield (interest rate) rises. The interest rate will continue to rise until the excess demand for money has been eliminated. Thus, the LM schedule displays a positive relationship between the interest rate and real income. Having established the slope of the LM schedule, we now investigate factors causing it to shift.

Shifts in the LM Schedule

Two magnitudes are contained in our economic framework that will shift the LM schedule. Here we show how these magnitudes, the price level and the nominal money supply, will cause such a shift. Figure 11.7 illustrates these cases. In both cases, we fix the level of real income and ask how the interest rate, clearing the money and bond markets, will change with the level of real money balances supplied to the economy. This change in supply can occur either because of an increase in the nominal money supply ($M_0 < M_1$) by the Fed or by a fall in the price level ($P_0 > P_1$).[4] Either of these events will cause an increase in the supply of real balances shown in Figure 11.7. The figure demonstrates that the interest rate, clearing the financial markets, will fall at any level of real income. The reason is that with an increase in the supply of real balances, there is initially an excess supply of money (and an excess demand for bonds) at the interest rate r_0. Thus there must be a lower level of the interest rate clearing the money and bond markets at the original interest rate and output level Y_0. Now carry this observation over to the left panel in the figure, and it is evident that the LM curve must have shifted to the right if either the nominal supply of money rises or the price level falls.

The final case concerns a shift in the LM schedule caused by an exogenous force, not explicitly built into our economic analysis of the financial market, affecting the demand for money. Just as for household and firm behavior embedded in the IS curve discussed above, there can be exogenous changes in household behavior in this money market. Here we imagine that there is a transitory increase in money demand in the economy. If such a transitory shift occurs, the LM curve will also temporarily shift. Figure 11.8 provides the graphical details.

In the figure, the initial level of money demand is denoted by L_0. There is an exogenous shift in money demand denoted by L_1. The interest rate clearing the financial markets is no longer r_0 because, once the shift in money demand has occurred, there is an excess demand for money at this interest rate. By assumption, there will be no increase in the supply of

---

4 Note that the price level is just an exogenous parameter at this stage of our analysis so it is appropriate to treat it as an exogenous shift parameter of the LM schedule. Later, we will develop models where the price level is determined within the economic framework so that, in those models, the price level cannot be treated as an exogenous parameter.

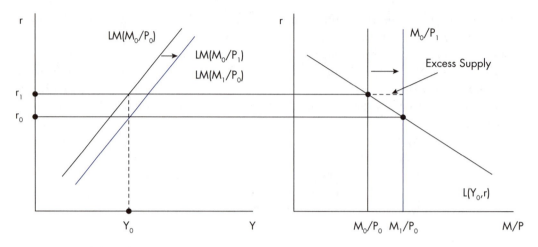

FIGURE 11.7 Shifting the LM Curve

The LM curve shifts by observing how the interest rate, clearing the money and bond markets, changes with the level of real money balances supplied at a fixed level of income. The level of real money balances supplied can rise by an increase in the nominal money supply ($M_0 < M_1$) or by a fall in the price level ($P_0 > P_1$). In either case, the initial increase in the supply of real money balances creates an excess supply of real money balances, reducing the real interest rate that clears the financial markets at any level of real output.

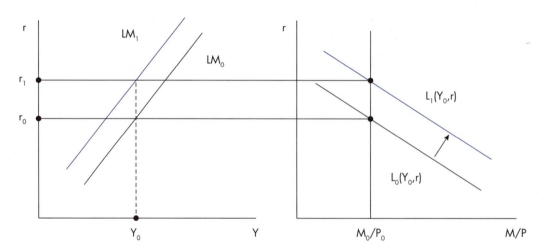

FIGURE 11.8 Money Demand Shifting the LM Curve

The LM curve shifts by observing how the interest rate, clearing the money and bond markets, changes with an exogenous shift in the demand for money. The interest rate clearing the financial markets must rise when money demand changes from L_0 to L_1. This causes a shift in the LM schedule from LM_0 to LM_1.

real balances by the Fed. As a result, the interest rate must rise to eliminate the excess demand for money. This implies that there is a higher interest rate at the level of output, Y_0, which is consistent with financial market equilibrium. The LM schedule has shifted to the left. Table 11.2 provides a summary of our results regarding factors that shift the LM schedule.

TABLE 11.2 Factors Shifting the LM Schedule

Shift Variable	Response of LM
Nominal Money Supply ↑	LM shifts →
Price Level ↓	LM shifts →
Money Demand Shift ↑	LM shifts ←

We are now in a position to derive the economy's aggregate demand schedule. This schedule combines our IS and LM analysis into one equilibrium relationship consistent with financial market and goods market equilibrium.

11.3 AGGREGATE DEMAND

The aggregate demand schedule is defined as follows.

Definition of the Aggregate Demand Curve

■ The aggregate demand schedule is an equilibrium relationship for price and output such that there is equilibrium in the goods market, the money market, and the bond market.

This relationship arises by combining the analysis of the goods and financial markets, then observing how a change in the price level will affect equilibrium in those markets. Figure 11.9 provides the graphical derivation of this relationship.

Start by assuming that the price level declines. Our analysis of the LM curve showed that this decline in the price level results in an increase in the supply of real money balances in the economy, reducing the real interest rate that clears the financial markets. The real supply of money therefore rises from M_0/P_0 to M_0/P_1. This implies a shift in the LM schedule to the right, the real interest rate declines, and the level of output increases because the investment demand for goods by firms increases. This increase in output increases the transactions demand for money, shifting money demand to the right. The end result is that a lower price level results in a decline in the real interest rate, thereby increasing the demand for output. This establishes that a fall in the price level is associated with an increase in the demand for goods that is consistent with equilibrium in the goods, money, and bond markets. There is a negative slope to the aggregate demand schedule as shown in Figure 11.9.

The Appendix provides an algebraic derivation of the aggregate demand schedule. That analysis reveals that there are several factors that will cause the aggregate demand curve to shift, and we now discuss how each of these magnitudes positions the aggregate demand schedule.

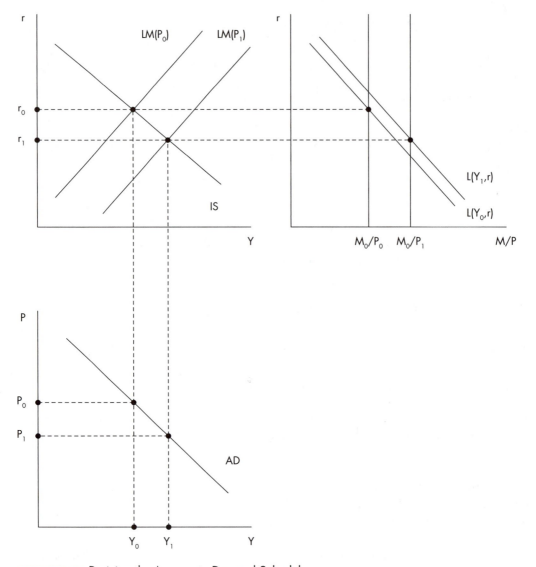

FIGURE 11.9 Deriving the Aggregate Demand Schedule

The aggregate demand curve is obtained by observing how a change in the price level affects equilibrium in the goods, money, and bond markets. The level of real money balances supplied rises with a fall in the price level ($P_0 > P_1$). This causes a decline in the interest rate clearing the money market, causing the LM curve to shift right. A lower real interest rate raises the investment demand for goods. A lower price level results in a higher demand for goods.

Shifts in Aggregate Demand

Any economic magnitude that can shift either the IS or LM curves (aside from the price level) will shift the position of the aggregate demand schedule. We begin with an increase in the nominal money supply by the Fed and show how this translates into an increase in the demand for goods at any level of prices. Figure 11.10 gives the derivation.

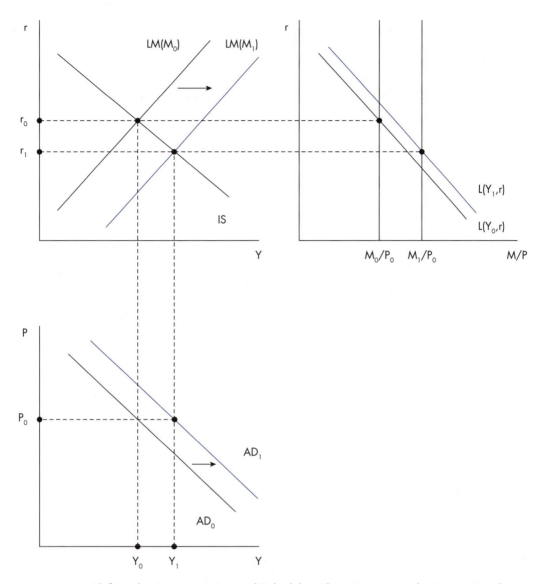

FIGURE 11.10 Shifting the Aggregate Demand Schedule with an Increase in the Money Supply

The aggregate demand curve shifts with an increase in the nominal supply of money. When the Fed increases the money supply ($M_0 < M_1$), there will be a decline in the interest rate clearing the money market, causing the LM curve to shift right. A lower real interest rate raises the investment demand for goods for a given level of prices. Therefore an increase in the money supply shifts the aggregate demand schedule to the right.

The initial supply of real balances is M_0/P_0 and now the nominal money supply rises to M_1 ($M_1 > M_0$). The price level is assumed fixed so that we can ascertain how the level of output demanded will change at this fixed price level. The increased supply of real money balances generates an excess supply (demand) for money (bonds). This causes the real interest rate to decline to eliminate the excess supply of money. The reduced real interest rate increases the investment demand for goods at any value of the price level. This increased level of output demand implies that the aggregate demand schedule has shifted rightward with the increase in the nominal supply of money.

Next we look at a case where there is an event causing the IS curve to shift. Figure 11.11 illustrates the case of a transitory increase in government expenditures. Previously we pointed out that the government finances this increase with bond issue. When bonds are issued, these new securities will absorb some of the saving that is done by households, shifting the IS

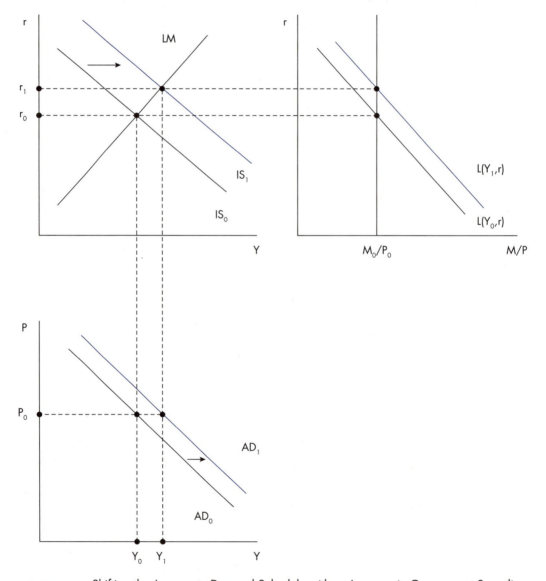

FIGURE 11.11 Shifting the Aggregate Demand Schedule with an Increase in Government Spending

The aggregate demand curve shifts with a transitory increase in government expenditures. When government expenditures rise $(G_0 < G_1)$, there will be an increase in the demand for goods at any level of the real interest rate and the price level.

TABLE 11.3 Factors That Shift the Aggregate Demand Schedule

Shift Variable	Response of Aggregate Demand
Government Expenditures ↑	AD shifts →
Lump-Sum Taxes ↓	
Ricardian Consumers	AD Unaffected
Non-Ricardian Consumers	AD shifts →
Nominal Money Supply ↑	AD shifts →
Investment ↑	AD shifts →
Private Saving ↑	AD shifts ←
Household Consumption ↑	AD shifts →

curve to the right and thus increasing the level of output. Thus at a given price level, there is a higher level of output consistent with goods market and financial market equilibrium. We conclude that the aggregate demand schedule shifts rightward with an increase in government expenditures.

Finally, there can be exogenous shifts in economic relationships that cause the aggregate demand schedule to change its position. An increase in the demand for goods by households (or, correspondingly, a reduction in household saving), and an increase in the investment demand for goods by firms will cause a rightward shift in the aggregate demand schedule. An increase in the demand for money will cause a leftward shift in the LM schedule and a consequent leftward shift in the aggregate demand schedule. Table 11.3 summarizes all of the factors that can cause a change in the position of the aggregate demand schedule.

This completes our analysis of the aggregate demand schedule. We now use it to introduce the analysis of the business cycle, a subject that will occupy us in later chapters. To understand the source of economic fluctuations, the analysis of the labor market and the supply-side of the economy must be combined with the aggregate demand schedule, giving us a complete model of the aggregate economy to be used to study the business cycle.

11.4 THE BUSINESS CYCLE: AN INTRODUCTION

The model frameworks that we will use to analyze the business cycle all contain an aggregate demand schedule. But the analysis of cyclical fluctuations requires more than this. Studying business cycles requires that we introduce the concept of an **aggregate supply** schedule to use in studying the business cycle. Figure 11.12 displays this economic framework. In Chapter 9, you saw the derivation of the classical supply schedule. In Figure 11.12, that classical supply curve is the vertical line, labeled LRAS (Long-Run Aggregate Supply), and it arises when there is a general equilibrium in the labor market. That is, the labor market is clearing, meaning that there is no excess supply or demand for labor and unemployment is at its natural rate. Further, there are correct price expectations on the part of all agents in the economy. In Chapter 12, you will see derivations of aggregate supply schedules that arise when the economy is not in a general equilibrium, either because there are incorrect price expectations or because there is

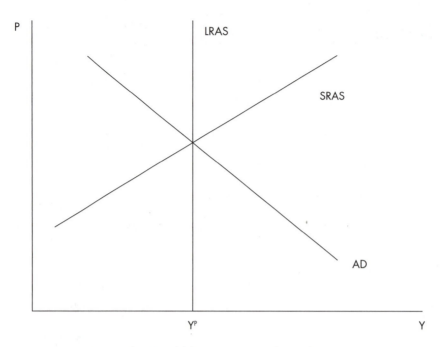

FIGURE 11.12 A Complete Model for Business Cycle Analysis

A complete model of the business cycle requires the aggregate demand schedule along with a model of the supply-side of the aggregate economy. The latter will have equilibrium (LRAS) and disequilibrium (SRAS) components allowing us to explain economic behavior when the economy is in and out of equilibrium.

an excess supply or demand for labor in the labor market. In that setting, a rise in the price level will induce firms to increase their supply of output although this will not be a permanent increase in production.

One class of business cycle model is illustrated in Figure 11.13. The aggregate demand curve has departed for unspecified reasons from the level AD_0 (denoted by the dotted lines). As a result, output can deviate from its potential level, Y^P. Potential GDP is taken to be **stationary**, that is, it is fixed over time.[5] The economy moves into a boom or a recession depending upon the shift in aggregate demand that occurs. But these deviations are transitory. That is, forces will be set in motion that will cause the economy to move back towards its potential level. It may take a substantial amount of time to return to Y^P (and we will have reasons to expect this to be the case) but output is stationary about its potential level.

An alternative style of model is illustrated in Figure 11.14. Here it is assumed that the economy is always in general equilibrium. That is, markets are always clearing and expectations are correct. This class of model, called the real business cycle model, imagines that output fluctuations are the result of shocks to the supply-side of the economy. But the implications of this model are quite different from the previous model we discussed above.

---

5 This is actually true only for the purposes of analyzing this model of the business cycle. It is possible to think of Y^P as obeying a trend over time in which case the business cycle model attempts to explain why output can deviate from its trend over time.

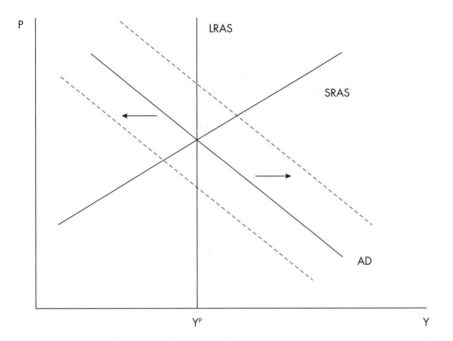

FIGURE 11.13 Cyclical Fluctuations Caused by Aggregate Demand

One style of business cycle model explains business cycles as transitory deviations in output from its potential level caused by shifts in aggregate demand. Output is stationary about its potential level.

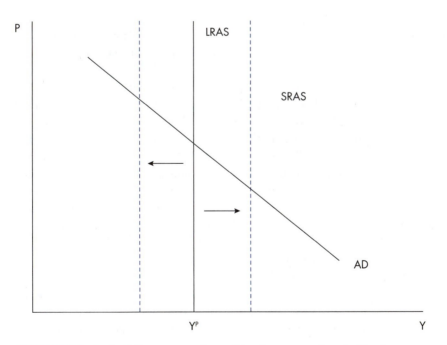

FIGURE 11.14 Cyclical Fluctuations Caused by Aggregate Supply Shocks

The real business cycle model explains output fluctuations as caused by permanent shocks to the supply-side of the economy. All economic magnitudes change permanently in response to these shocks.

One difference concerns the time series properties of economic magnitudes. In the model where cycles arise from shocks to aggregate demand, deviations of output from its potential level are transitory; output returns to Y^P eventually. But in the real business cycle model, permanent shocks cause output to permanently move away from Y^P. Output and other economic magnitudes are not stationary through time.

A second difference concerns the welfare implications of economic fluctuations. In the real business cycle model, economic agents are always optimizing and achieving the best outcomes that they can, given their constraint sets. In the case of cycles induced by aggregate demand shocks, there are some welfare losses occurring to economic agents because markets are not in full equilibrium. Therefore, some individuals in the economy may be made better off by policy interventions by the government or the Fed.

This discussion suggests that there is a need to use empirical evidence as a way of discriminating between competing theories of the business cycle and this is indeed the case. It will therefore be important to draw out the time series implications of each model of the business cycle and confront these predictions with empirical evidence in order to see how well the predictions of each economic model match up with actual economic data. As you will see, no aggregate economic model can explain all of the stylized facts that economists have uncovered regarding cyclical fluctuations. But each model does have the capability to explain at least some of the features of business cycles that are common to a variety of industrialized economies.

11.5 CONCLUDING REMARKS

This chapter shows how to obtain the aggregate demand schedule, an important component of the aggregate economic models used to study business cycles. This relationship is one involving the price level and output, and it represents equilibrium in the goods, money, and bond markets.

We derived this relationship by first looking at the goods market. Using the NIPA identity, we argued that goods market equilibrium should mean that there are no unintended inventories being accumulated in the economy. Then we built a model of the goods market using results from previous chapters regarding the savings decisions by households and the determinants of investment by firms. This analysis led to a relationship between the real interest rate and output, called the IS schedule, where the planned demand for goods equaled the supply of goods. We found that the IS curve had a negative slope because the demand for investment rises as the real interest rate falls. The curve could shift due to changes in fiscal policy variables (taxes and government expenditures), and any exogenous shifts in the economic relationships arising in the goods market.

There is a corresponding relationship between the real interest rate and output, called the LM schedule, which represents equilibrium in the financial markets (money and bonds). We found that, in these markets, the real interest rate would rise as real output increases as a result of the increase in the demand for money that occurs with rising real income. A change in the real money supply shifts the LM curve and any exogenous shift in money demand will do so as well.

Finally we derived the aggregate demand schedule from the analysis of goods and financial market equilibrium. We found that the aggregate demand schedule displayed an inverse relationship between the price level and the level of output because an increase in the real supply of money lowers the real interest rate, raising the investment demand for goods, and thus the aggregate demand for goods. Any magnitude that would shift the IS and LM schedules was found to shift the aggregate demand schedule.

The last topic that was discussed in this chapter was an introduction to business cycle analysis. The aggregate demand schedule is one building-block of a complete economic framework for the study of business cycles. By combining this demand schedule with a model of the supply-side of the economy, it was shown how business cycles can be analyzed. The next chapter contains a much more detailed analysis of the supply-side of economic models, thus preparing you for a much more thorough discussion of cyclical fluctuations.

Key Ideas

- The IS curve is an equilibrium schedule for the interest rate and output such that the goods market is in equilibrium.
- Goods market equilibrium occurs when the planned demand for goods by households, firms, and the government equals the available supply of goods.
- Goods market equilibrium occurs when there is no **unintended inventory accumulation**.
- An identity is a relationship between economic magnitudes that holds as a matter of definition.
- Private saving rises with the real interest rate as long as the substitution effect dominates the wealth effect.
- The IS curve displays an inverse relationship between the real interest rate and real output because, as the real interest rate falls, the planned demand for investment goods by firms rises.
- The IS curve displays an inverse relationship between the real interest rate and real output because, as real output rises, national savings increases, causing an excess supply of savings, thereby reducing the real interest rate.
- The IS curve will shift rightward with an increase in government expenditures or with a decline in lump-sum taxes as long as households do not foresee the future tax implications of the tax cut. Either event increases the planned demand for goods at any level of the real interest rate.
- Exogenous shifts in investment or household savings will shift the IS curve. If either event occurs, there will be a change in the planned demand for goods at any level of the real interest rate.
- The theory of Ricardian Equivalence states that consumers will not spend a tax cut as they will foresee the future tax increases implied by a tax cut.
- The LM curve is an equilibrium schedule for the interest rate and output such that the money and bond markets are in equilibrium.
- The LM schedule displays a positive relationship between the real interest rate and output because, as real output rises, the transaction demand for money increases, and the real interest rate must rise to eliminate the excess demand for money.
- An increase in the nominal money supply will shift the LM schedule to the right. An increase in the money supply creates an excess supply of money, causing the real interest rate that clears the money market to decline at any level of output.

■ A decline in the price level will shift the LM curve to the right because a price decline increases the supply of real money balances. An increase in the real money supply creates an excess supply of money, causing the real interest rate that clears the money market to decline at any level of output.

■ An exogenous increase in the demand for money will shift the LM curve leftward. An increase in money demand creates an excess demand for money, increasing the real interest rate that clears the money market at any level of output.

■ The aggregate demand schedule is an equilibrium relationship for price and output representing equilibrium in the goods market, the money market, and the bond market.

■ Aggregate demand displays an inverse relationship between price and output. As the price level rises, the supply of real money balances rises, reducing the real interest rate at any level of output. The decline in the real interest rate increases the planned demand for investment by firms and thus aggregate demand.

■ Aggregate demand shifts rightward with an increase in government expenditures or a decline in lump-sum taxes as long as households do not foresee the future tax implications of a tax cut. Either event increases the planned demand for goods at any level of prices in the economy.

■ Aggregate demand will shift if there are exogenous shifts in investment, saving by households, or the demand for money.

Key Terms

IS Schedule

Goods Market Equilibrium

Marginal Propensity
  to Consume

Money Market
  Equilibrium

Expected Inflation

Business Cycle

Identity

Private Saving

Ricardian
  Equivalence

Bond Market
  Equilibrium

Aggregate Demand

Stationary

Unintended Inventory
  Accumulation

National Saving

LM Schedule

Medium of
  Exchange

Aggregate Supply

Exogenous

Questions for Study and Review

Review Exercises

1. Define the IS curve, the LM curve, and the AD curve.
2. Explain how the IS and LM schedules are affected by shifts in each of the following factors: government spending, lump-sum taxes, the money stock, the price level.
3. Explain how the aggregate demand schedule is affected by shifts in each of the following factors: government spending, lump-sum taxes, the money stock, the price level.

Thought Exercises

1. Suppose that taxes are of the lump-sum variety. What happens to the AD schedule when there is a balanced-budget increase in government expenditures?
2. What happens to the slope of the aggregate demand schedule when investment becomes increasingly interest-elastic?
3. What happens to the slope of the aggregate demand schedule when the marginal tax rate increases?
4. Suppose that the money supply is a multiple of the Monetary Base. How would an increase in the Monetary Base affect the aggregate demand schedule?

Numerical Exercises

1. Suppose you have the following information for an economy: $C = 1000 + .65 \cdot (Y - T) - 1000 \cdot r$, $I = 600 - 1000 \cdot r$, $T = -150 + .3 \cdot Y$, $G = 500 - .07 \cdot Y$, $M^D/P = 60 + .7 \cdot Y - 500 \cdot i$, $M^S = M_0$. *Definitions*: Y = Output, P = Price Level, C = Consumption, I = Investment, G = Government Expenditures, T = Tax Receipts, M^D = Money Demand, M^S = Money Supply, r = Real Interest Rate, i = Nominal Interest Rate.

   a) Derive the IS schedule.
   b) Derive the LM schedule.
   c) Derive the AD schedule.

2. Congress wishes to stimulate the economy. Suppose you are a policy analyst. It is your job to analyze the macroeconomic effects of a permanent tax cut. You have worked out the following very simplified model to characterize the basic features of the U.S. economy. $Y = 4 \cdot K + 5 \cdot L$ where $K = 1,000$ and $L = 800$, $G = 3,000$, $T = 3,000$, $I = 2,000 - 6,000 \cdot r$, $C = 600 + .6 (Y - T) - 3,000 \cdot r$. *Definitions*: Y = Full-Employment Output, K = Capital Stock, L = Labor Services, C = Consumption, I = Investment, r = Real Interest Rate, T = Taxes, G = Government Spending.

   a) Compute the equilibrium values of investment and consumption, as well as the consumption and investment shares, before the tax cut if consumers are not Ricardian.
   b) Suppose that taxes fall to $T = 2,700$. Compute the equilibrium values of investment and consumption, as well as the consumption and investment shares, after the tax cut if consumers are not Ricardian.

3. Suppose the economy has the following consumption and investment schedules. $C = 1,000 + .65 \cdot Y - 1,000 \cdot r$, $I = 600 - 1,000 \cdot r$. *Definitions*: Y = Income, C = Consumption, I = Investment, r = Real Interest Rate.

   a) Derive the national saving schedule for the economy.
   b) If government spending is $G = 500$, and if output $Y = 5,500$, find the real interest rate that clears the loanable funds market.
   c) Suppose that government spending rises to $G = 550$. Find the real interest rate that clears the loanable funds market.

4. Suppose the economy has the following consumption and investment schedules. $C = 1,000 + .65 \cdot Y - 1,000 \cdot r$, $I = 600 - 1,000 \cdot r$. *Definitions*: Y = Income, C = Consumption, I = Investment, r = Real Interest Rate.

a) Derive the national saving schedule for the economy.

b) If government spending is G = 500, and if output Y = 5,500, find the real interest rate that clears the loanable funds market.

c) Suppose that government spending rises to G = 550. Find the real interest rate that clears the loanable funds market.

For further questions, multiple choice quizzes, and weblinks related to this chapter, visit www.routledge.com/textbooks/rossana

APPENDIX: DERIVING THE AD SCHEDULE

In this appendix, an algebraic derivation of the aggregate demand schedule is presented. The behavioral relationships will be assumed linear for simplicity. We begin with lump-sum taxes but we will extend our results later to incorporate a flat tax schedule and there is initially no inflation (inflation is added later). Thus there is initially no difference between the real and nominal interest rate. Here are the components of the IS schedule.

Consumption: $C = c_0 + c_1 \cdot Y^D$, $c_0 > 0$, $0 < c_1 < 1$ Disposable Income: $Y^D = Y - T$

Investment: $I = i_0 - i_1 \cdot r$, $i_0 > 0$, $i_1 > 0$,   Government Expenditures: $G = G_0$,

Tax Receipts: $T = T_0$,   Government Surplus (Deficit): $T - G$

The LM schedule requires the following information.

Money Demand: $\dfrac{M^D}{P} = k_0 + k_1 \cdot Y - k_2 \cdot r$, $k_0 > 0$, $k_1 > 0$, $k_2 > 0$

Money Supply: $\dfrac{M^S}{P} = \dfrac{M_0}{P}$

To derive the IS schedule, form the NIPA relationship $Y = C + I + G$ and, into this expression, substitute the assumptions we are making about each of its components. The result of these substitutions is given below.

$$Y = c_0 + c_1 \cdot (Y - T_0) + i_0 - i_1 \cdot r + G_0$$

Now solve this for the interest rate to obtain the IS schedule.

$$IS : r = \frac{c_0 - c_1 \cdot T_0 + i_0 + G_0}{i_1} - \left[\frac{1 - c_1}{i_1}\right] \cdot Y$$

The slope of this curve is given by $-(1 - c_1)/i_1 < 0$ and the curve will shift if taxes or government expenditures change. To obtain the LM schedule, set the supply of money equal to money demand to obtain

$$\frac{M_0}{P} = k_0 + k_1 \cdot Y - k_2 \cdot r.$$

Solve this for the interest rate to get

$$r = \frac{k_0}{k_2} - \frac{1}{k_2} \cdot \frac{M_0}{P} + \frac{k_1}{k_2} \cdot Y.$$

The slope of this schedule is $k_1/k_2 > 0$ and it shifts with a change in the money supply.

To derive the AD schedule, eliminate the interest rate from the IS and LM schedules in the following way.

$$\frac{k_0}{k_2} - \frac{1}{k_2} \cdot \frac{M_0}{P} + \frac{k_1}{k_2} \cdot Y = \frac{c_0 - c_1 \cdot T_0 + i_0 + G_0}{i_1} - \left[\frac{1 - c_1}{i_1}\right] \cdot Y$$

Now solve this last expression for the level of real output Y. Some algebra gives

$$AD: Y = \frac{k_2 \cdot (c_0 - c_1 \cdot T_0 + i_0 + G_0) - k_0 \cdot i_1}{(1 - c_1) \cdot k_2 + k_1 \cdot i_1} + \left[\frac{i_1}{(1 - c_1) \cdot k_2 + k_1 \cdot i_1}\right] \cdot \frac{M_0}{P}$$

The first term to the right of the equal sign captures the effects of magnitudes associated with fiscal policy (government expenditures and taxes), among other things, that can shift the AD schedule. The last term captures the effect of the money supply on the AD schedule (it shifts the curve) and it enables us to compute the slope of the AD schedule. The coefficient preceding the level of real money balances is positive. This implies two things; it shows that an increase in the nominal money supply shifts aggregated demand rightward. It also shows that the slope of the aggregate demand schedule is negative.

The Flat Tax

Now suppose that we have the flat tax schedule

$$\text{Tax Receipts: } T = T_0 + t \cdot Y, \, 0 < t < 1$$

where t is the marginal tax rate ($0 < t < 1$). The corresponding definition of the government surplus (deficit) is given below.

$$\text{Government Surplus (Deficit): } T_0 + t \cdot Y - G_0$$

The LM curve is unaffected by this change but the new IS schedule is found by forming

$$Y = c_0 + c_1 \cdot (Y - T_0 - t \cdot Y) + i_0 - i_1 \cdot r + G_0$$

and, solving this for Y, gives the IS schedule

$$IS : r = \frac{c_0 - c_1 \cdot T_0 + i_0 + G_0}{i_1} - \left[\frac{1 - c_1 \cdot (1-t)}{i_1} \right] \cdot Y.$$

Solving for the AD schedule using the same method as above gives the new AD schedule.

$$AD : Y = \frac{k_2 \cdot (c_0 - c_1 \cdot T_0 + i_0 + G_0) - k_0 \cdot i_1}{[1 - c_1 \cdot (1-t)] \cdot k_2 + k_1 \cdot i_1} + \left[\frac{i_1}{[1 - c_1 \cdot (1-t)] \cdot k_2 + k_1 \cdot i_1} \right] \cdot \frac{M_0}{P}$$

Simply set t = 0 and you will see that this AD schedule reduces to the one derived previously in this appendix which is as it should be.

Inflation

The final aspect of the AD schedule to be demonstrated is how to find the AD schedule when there is inflation in the model. In this version of the model, nominal and real interest rates differ by the rate of expected inflation. If the nominal interest rate is denoted by i and if the real interest rate is denoted by r, then $r = i - \Delta P^e / P$ where P stands for the price level and e denotes an expectation, and the money demand schedule must now include the nominal interest rate as given below.[6]

$$\frac{M^D}{P} = k_0 + k_1 \cdot Y - k_2 \cdot i$$

We can form the LM schedule as before by solving this expression for the nominal interest rate. But the IS curve will contain the real interest rate because investment depends upon the real interest rate. Eliminating the nominal interest rate from the IS and LM schedules gives the resulting AD schedule given below.

$$Y = \frac{k_2 \cdot (c_0 - c_1 \cdot T_0 + i_0 + G_0) - k_0 \cdot i_1}{[1 - c_1 \cdot (1-t)] \cdot k_2 + k_1 \cdot i_1} + \left[\frac{i_1}{[1 - c_1 \cdot (1-t)] \cdot k_2 + k_1 \cdot i_1} \right] \cdot \frac{M_0}{P}$$

$$+ \left[\frac{k_2 \cdot i_1}{[1 - c_1 \cdot (1-t)] \cdot k_2 + k_1 \cdot i_1} \right] \cdot \frac{\Delta P^e}{P}$$

The coefficient preceding expected inflation is positive. At a given nominal interest rate, a higher rate of expected inflation implies a lower real rate of interest, higher investment demand for goods, and thus a higher level of aggregate demand.

---

6 In Chapter 7, there is a discussion showing that money demand is determined by a real interest differential which reduces to the nominal bond rate when money does not pay interest.

Chapter 12

The Business Cycle

LEARNING OBJECTIVES

This chapter is the culmination of all of the economic models developed earlier in this book. Here we describe a variety of economic models of the business cycle using the microfoundations described in previous chapters and using ideas from the classical model of the economy. These models use several theories of the supply-side of the economy and attempt to explain business cycles originating from the demand side and the supply-side of the aggregate economy. It will be seen that business cycles can arise from the actions of the public as well as the actions of policymakers. We also try to use each model to explain the time series properties of macroeconomic data. Here are a few of the questions that we address in this chapter.

- How do shifts in the aggregate demand schedule cause recessions?
- How do supply-side shocks cause economic fluctuations?
- Can policymakers cause recessions?
- Which model of the business cycle does the best job of explaining the time series properties of macroeconomic data?

Macroeconomics emerged as an area of economic analysis and research in response to the Great Depression. During this event, there was an enormous increase in the unemployment rate (at one point, almost 25 percent of the workforce was unemployed and searching for work) and there was an extraordinary reduction of about 30 percent in the level of real output produced. These facts caused economists to devote a great deal of thought to the features of an aggregate economic system that might cause output in an economy to decline, sometimes dramatically. The task of this chapter is to describe economic models of an economy that may explain the causes of these fluctuations in economic activity.

The models that will be described in this chapter fall into two broad categories: market-clearing models and models where markets do not clear. Market-clearing models are attractive to many economists because such models have the property that all trades, mutually advantageous to the participants in markets, are being carried out. Further, market-clearing models are consistent with optimizing behavior by economic agents; that is, they are precisely consistent with utility-maximizing and profit-maximizing behavior by households and firms. But empirical observation has caused some economists to question the market-clearing paradigm. These economists believe that markets do not clear, at least for a time, leading them to advocate economic models that incorporate wage and sometimes price rigidities. There are elements of truth to each style of economic model and one of our tasks in this chapter will be to draw out the strengths and weaknesses of each approach.

We begin the analysis by describing alternative theories of the supply-side of the economy. The first model framework that we examine will be the New Classical model that is based upon the assumptions that the labor market clears and that there is incomplete information in the labor market. Unlike firms, labor suppliers will operate under incomplete information about the price level. In this labor market, unexpected movements in the price level will cause changes in real wages and thus labor services used in production by firms. This labor market will give rise to output supply curves associated with both correct and incorrect price expectations. Incorrect price expectations are one of the reasons why output may deviate from its potential level.

We next discuss a variant of the classical model that incorporates shocks to the technology used by firms. These **technology shocks** permanently shift labor demand and output produced in the economy. All markets clear in this model and expectations are correct for all participants in the labor market. The level of output supplied is thus determined by the realizations of these supply-side disturbances.

The final supply-side model that we discuss is based upon the Keynesian notion that money wages and possibly prices are fixed for substantial periods of time. In this model it will be assumed that wages are fixed, say by bargaining agreements, and that employment is determined by the labor demand of firms. Output can deviate from potential GDP if inventories change unexpectedly, causing firms to vary output supply to replenish depleted stocks of inventories. There will be no short-run change in wages (and possibly prices) in this model while inventories are rebuilt but, in the future, wages and prices will change over time as wage and price agreements are renegotiated.

Business cycles will then be studied using each of these supply-side models and we will assess the empirical predictions of each model regarding the time series properties of macroeconomic data, comparing the predictions of each model with the actual time series properties of the data. In the New Classical model, business cycles will arise because unexpected shifts in aggregate demand will fool labor suppliers into working more than they should and, as their incorrect expectations adjust over time, these adjustments to price expectations will result in fluctuations in labor supply and therefore output produced in the economy. We will also observe how differently the economy can behave under alternative assumptions about these expectations. It will be apparent that only unexpected movements in aggregate demand will have real effects upon the economy. The model will serve to illustrate how important expectation formation is to the behavior of the macroeconomic system.

We will next examine another classical style of model, known as the Real Business Cycle (RBC) model of the economy. The hallmark of this model is that shocks to the supply-side of the economy, so-called technology shocks, are the sources of economic fluctuations in the economy. It is assumed in this model that all markets clear so that fluctuations in real GDP are just a manifestation of shifts in potential GDP in the economy. This style of model has very different implications for the economy because it views changes in real GDP as always being consistent with profit and utility maximization by households and firms.

In contrast, the Keynesian business cycle model that we will next discuss is built on the assumption that markets do not clear at all instants of time. The model assumes that money wages, prices, or both do not adjust to clear markets because there are multi-period agreements in force that prevent adjustments in these magnitudes. In this model, an increase in aggregate demand will be met by expanding production and output so that business cycles are caused by unanticipated shifts in aggregate demand. Over time, the economy will return to equilibrium as wage and price agreements are renegotiated.

Our last cyclical analysis concerns transitory shifts in aggregate supply. In that analysis, it will be seen that an economy can experience a rising price level along with declining output. This will be seen to generate price and output behavior that is different from what will be observed when shocks originate in the aggregate demand schedule where price and output move in the same direction.

Finally, in all of the models in this chapter, Potential GDP is assumed fixed. This means that we are assuming that we have a **stationary economy**, one where potential GDP is unchanging over time. Our analyses in Chapters 3 and 10 showed that this is incorrect but this difference will not be a source of error in our analysis. The reason is that the economic models discussed in this chapter are designed to explain departures from potential GDP, whether or not this equilibrium is constant. However it is important to explain how **nonstationarity**, the property that output seems to consistently rise or trend upward over time, arises in the each of the economic models in this chapter. As we will see, the origins of that time series property will differ in some of the models discussed below.

12.1 THE NEW CLASSICAL MODEL OF AGGREGATE SUPPLY

In Chapter 8, we described a labor market where firms knew the current price level when making their labor input decision but households operated under incomplete information about prices, requiring that they forecast the real wage in making their labor supply decision. Here we want to use that labor market model to derive supply curves for output. These supply curves (the supply-side of the model) will be two elements of the New Classical model of cyclical fluctuations. Figures 12.1 and 12.2 illustrate how to obtain these supply curves. The Appendix to this chapter contains an algebraic derivation of the supply schedules derived in these first two figures.

The demand for labor is downward-sloping because a consequence of profit-seeking behavior by firms is that own-factor price effects are negative if inputs in production are subject to diminishing returns in production. Labor supply is increasing in the expected real wage because it is assumed, as we have discussed previously, that substitution effects dominate income effects in describing the effect on labor supply of a shift in the expected real wage. Money wages are taken to be flexible. This means, by definition, that if there is an excess supply or demand for labor in the labor market, money wages will adjust to eliminate an excess demand or supply.

Figure 12.1 illustrates an initial equilibrium in the labor market. Equilibrium now means something more than just quantity demanded equals quantity supplied; we must also address the issue of whether expectations are correct. In the figure, it is initially assumed that expected and actual prices are the same so that price expectations are correct. This leads us to define a market equilibrium in the following way.

Definition of a Market Equilibrium

■ In a model where expectations must be formed by economic agents (households and firms), equilibrium in a market is defined to be a situation where there is no excess supply or demand in the market and price expectations are correct.

As you will see below, an interesting situation can arise in this type of market; the market can have incorrect price expectations and yet there may not be any excess supply or demand in the market. In such a situation, forces will be set in motion that will disturb the price and quantity set in the market. These forces help explain why prices and quantities change in the economy.

At the initial money wage, denoted by W_0, the labor market is in equilibrium with correct price expectations. To derive the supply curves, we do two experiments; the actual price level rises to P_1 ($P_0 > P_1$), and then we observe the response of output supply when the price change is either unanticipated or anticipated. Definitions of these terms follow.

Definitions of Price Changes

■ An **unanticipated price change** is one where actual prices change but the price expectations of labor suppliers are constant.

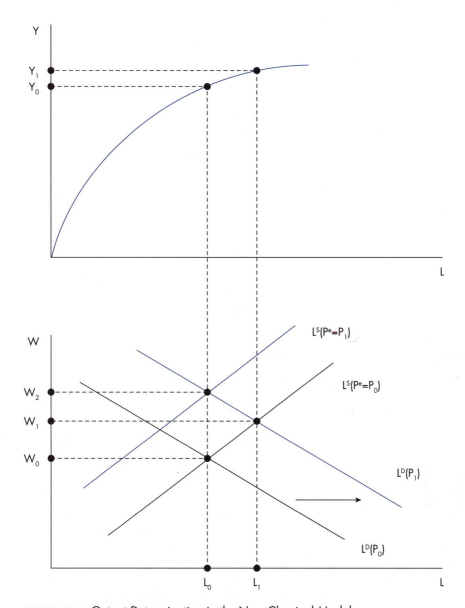

FIGURE 12.1 Output Determination in the New Classical Model

The actual price level rises to P_1 ($P_1 > P_0$), causing labor demand to shift to the right. If price expectations rise at the same instant as the actual price level, labor supply shifts left, keeping labor input and output constant at their initial levels. If price expectations do not change when actual prices do, labor input in production rises because real wages decline and thus output supplied rises.

■ An **anticipated price change** is one where the change in actual prices is correctly perceived by labor suppliers who change their price expectations such that their price expectations remain correct.

Two supply curves thus arise; one is called the short-run aggregate supply curve (SRAS) where price expectations are incorrect at all but one point. The second is the long-run aggregate

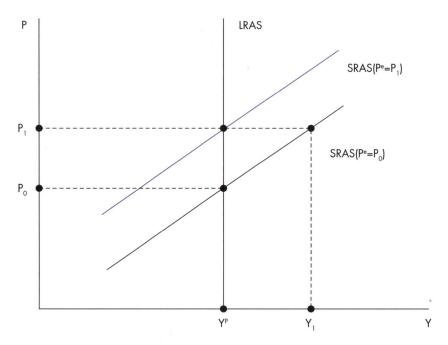

FIGURE 12.2 Output Supply in the New Classical Model

If the price level rises from P_0 to P_1, and if this price increase is anticipated by labor suppliers, then output remains fixed at the level of potential GDP, Y^P. If the price increase is unanticipated, output supply will rise above potential GDP to the level Y_1. If the expected price level rises, the short-run supply curve shifts to the left.

supply curve (LRAS) where price expectations are correct at all points. To understand the implications of these supply schedules, begin with the case where a price increase is anticipated.

In this case, the increase in the price level is recognized by all participants in the labor market. Firms demand more labor at any level of money wages because, at a given money wage rate, a higher price level implies lower real wages and firms will therefore want to hire more labor. Labor suppliers, however, observe that the real wage has fallen at any level of money wages and so they supply less labor. These events cause an excess demand for labor in the labor market, causing money wages to rise as firms compete to hire more labor. But the interaction of these forces causes real wages to remain constant ($\Delta W/W = \Delta P/P$). Ultimately, labor used in production and output produced remain fixed.

Now consider an increase in the price level that is unanticipated by labor suppliers but recognized by firms. Labor demand shifts in the same way, and for the same reasons, as it did when the increase in the price level was fully anticipated. But now there will be no shift in labor supply because households supplying their labor services do not recognize the increase in the price level and its resulting decline in real wages. As a result, there will be an excess demand for labor and money wages rise but, in this case, they rise by less than the price level ($\Delta W/W < \Delta P/P$). The end result is that real wages fall, labor services used in production and output supplied, will increase.

There is a simple equation that can be used to describe the supply curve that was just graphically derived and it is given below.

$$Y^s = Y^P + \gamma \cdot (P - P^e), \gamma > 0$$

In this expression, γ (the Greek symbol gamma) is positive. As this supply function shows, departures from full employment occur because of forecast errors made by the public. If prices are higher than expected, output will be above potential GDP. If prices are lower than expected, output will lie below potential GDP. This equation is known as the Lucas supply function.[1]

Note also that this equation establishes that the supply curve shifts with changes in the level of price expectations because the equation implies that

$$\left. \frac{\Delta Y^s}{\Delta P^e} \right|_{\Delta P = 0} = -\gamma < 0$$

This result shows that at a given level of actual prices, a higher level of expected prices will reduce the amount of output supplied in the economy. The short-run supply curve (SRAS) shifts to the left in this case. When labor suppliers think that the price level has risen, they will also think that real wages have declined and so will reduce their labor supply. As a result, the actual real wage rises, reducing employment and output at any level of actual prices in the economy (see Figure 12.2 above).

Finally, it should be kept in mind that Potential GDP can change because of shifts in the capital stock, marginal tax rates, and possibly other magnitudes. If any of these events occur, the position of the supply curve will change to reflect these events.

This aggregate supply equation and our graphical derivation of it illustrate how crucial expectations are to the behavior of the economy. Departures from full employment (Potential GDP) require that labor suppliers be unaware (or fooled) by a change in the price level; equivalently, there must be a forecast error by the public for output to deviate from full employment. Later you will see that this same characteristic is present in the complete version of the New Classical model of the aggregate economy that will be discussed below. These incorrect expectations will be used to explain cyclical fluctuations in the New Classical model of the economy. Later in the book, we will also use this supply schedule to study the implications of optimal forecasting mechanisms that might be used by the public.

12.2 SHOCKS TO AGGREGATE SUPPLY

A recent line of economic research, known as the real business cycle literature, stresses that shocks to the economy's technology are an important source of economic fluctuations.[2]

---

1 This supply function was suggested as a description of the supply side of aggregate economies by Robert E. Lucas in "Some International Evidence on Output-Inflation Tradeoffs," *American Economic Review* 63, No. 2 (June 1973), pp. 326–34. The Appendix to this chapter contains an algebraic derivation of this supply function.

2 This literature was initiated by Charles I. Plosser and John B. Long in "Real Business Cycles," *Journal of Political Economy* 91, No. 1 (February 1983), pp. 39–69.

In order to study this type of business cycle model, it is necessary to show how these so-called technology shocks can affect the supply-side of an economy. We do so in Figure 12.3.

The technology is now written as

$$Y = T \cdot F(K, L)$$

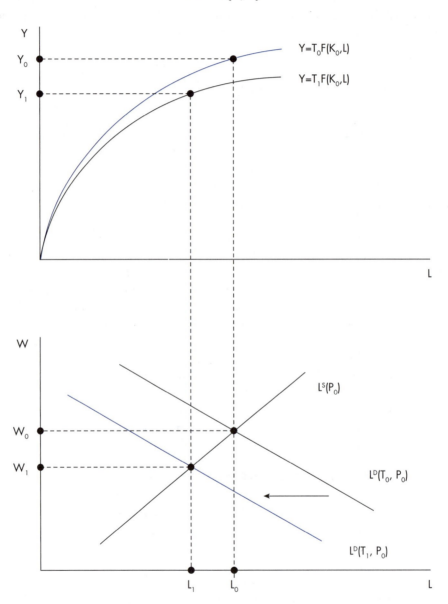

FIGURE 12.3 Output Determination in the Real Business Cycle Model

A negative shock to the technology is given by a reduction in T ($T_1 < T_0$). Labor demand shifts to the left. In equilibrium (note that price expectations are assumed to be correct for all labor market participants), labor input set in the market falls and so will the level of output produced. Potential GDP declines temporarily if the technology shock is transitory, permanently if the negative shock is permanent.

where T stands for a shock to the aggregate production function. In Chapter 10, we referred to T as **Total Factor Productivity** or the **Solow residual**. Shocks to the production function can be either transitory or permanent. As these names suggest, a **transitory shock** is one that occurs for a time and then disappears. A **permanent shock** is one persisting forever. Changes in this magnitude affect the marginal products of factor inputs in production and they will also change the level of Potential GDP. To see how, imagine that there has been a transitory negative shock to the production function, thereby reducing the level of the technical progress parameter, T. An example of this phenomenon might be a drought that temporarily reduces the production of farmers. The productivity of labor and capital will decline as, with less water available for production, these inputs will generate less output at the margin. Thus the demand for labor will decline at any level of money (and real) wages.[3] Labor used in equilibrium will decline and thus so will the output produced in the aggregate economy. The implication of these ideas is that Potential GDP has declined.

This style of analysis assumes that there is market clearing at all times and that the economy is in equilibrium. Thus there is no reason to distinguish between actual and expected magnitudes because expectations are correct. This assumption is reflected in Figure 12.3 where only actual prices are contained in the figure. So it is appropriate to think of this model as of the classical variety where the economy is observed only in equilibrium states.

Because of these technology shocks, real magnitudes such as Potential GDP will change as these shocks are realized. We will see later that this class of model raises provocative questions regarding the origins of business cycles; its advocates have argued that certain characeristics of actual economies (to be discussed below) indicate that the sources of business cycles must come from the supply-side of the economy rather than the demand side. This reasoning challenges conventional views of what is meant by the business cycle.

12.3 KEYNESIAN MODELS OF AGGREGATE SUPPLY

One criticism of the New Classical model of the labor market is that empirical evidence seems to contradict the assumption of flexible money wages that is a crucial part of that model of the labor market. In many if not most occupations, nominal wages are fixed for substantial periods of time (you have no doubt observed this fact in your own work experience). As a result, Keynesian economics is based upon the assumption that wages (and possibly prices) do not adjust to clear markets at least for some period of time. The labor market that we examine in this section will be based upon the assumption that money wages are unable to adjust to market forces because they are set for multiple time periods and sectors of the economy renegotiate wages at differing points in time.[4] The aggregate wage rate for the economy has,

---

3 The relevant marginal productivity condition for a profit-maximizing firm would be $MP_L(T) = W/P$ (the marginal product of labor depends upon T) so, at any level of real wages, a decline in T reduces the MP_L (the marginal product of labor).

4 This model of the labor market was studied by Stanley Fischer in "Long-Term Contracts, Rational Expectations, and the Optimal Money Supply Rule," *Journal of Political Economy* 85, No. 1 (February 1977), pp. 191–205 and by John B. Taylor in "Aggregate Dynamics and Staggered Contracts," *Journal of Political Economy* 88, No. 1 (February 1980), pp. 1–23.

as its components, the wages set in the various sectors of the economy; thus at any point in time, the aggregate wage rate is fixed because its components cannot adjust for a time to changes in economic forces. Figure 12.4 illustrates the workings of the labor market and output determination in this model.

To understand how this model works, it helps to imagine a bargaining situation where workers and firms set money wages for several periods of time, choosing what they believe will

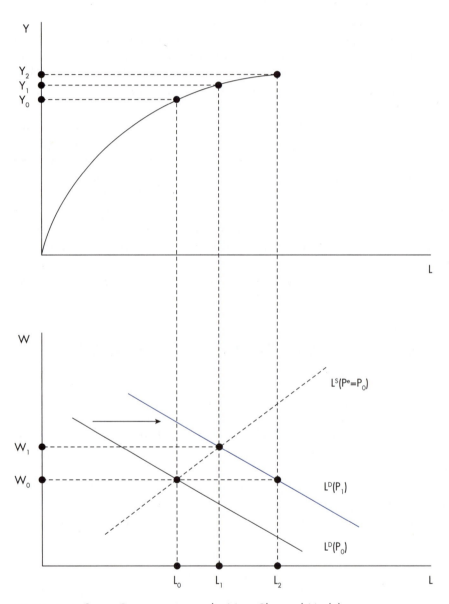

FIGURE 12.4 Output Determination in the New Classical Model

The actual price level rises to P_1 $(P_1 > P_0)$. Labor demand therefore shifts to the right. Labor input rises to L_2, causing output to rise to Y_2 because money wages are fixed at W_0. If money wages were flexible, labor input would only rise to L_1 $(L_1 < L_2)$.

be the equilibrium money wage rate for this period. In Figure 12.4, W_0 denotes the initial market clearing wage rate when all market participants believe that prices will be at the level P_0. If prices turn out to be higher than P_0, this will generate an increase in labor demand but, with fixed money wages, there will be an excess demand for labor. Then the question arises as to how we can determine the level of employment set in the labor market because money wages are fixed by prior agreement and so cannot adjust to eliminate the excess demand for labor. The crucial assumption in the New Keynesian model that answers this question is given in the following proposition.

Proposition About Employment Determination in the New Keynesian Model

■ In the New Keynesian model of the labor market, employment is determined by the demand for labor by firms.

Now if there is a situation where there is an excess demand for labor, money wages will not adjust as they would in the New Classical model and we read employment from the labor demand schedule. Thus if the price level rises unexpectedly to P_1, Figure 12.4 shows that employment rises to L_2. The figure also shows that there will be a larger employment increase in the New Keynesian model as compared to the New Classical labor market model. If money wages were allowed to adjust as in the New Classical model, employment would only rise to L_1 ($L_1 < L_2$). Thus for a given increase in the price level, employment and output rise by more when money wages are fixed than they would in a world with flexible money wages. Figure 12.5 illustrates the short-run (SRAS) supply schedule for the New Keynesian version of the labor market. It has a flatter slope than the one arising from the New Classical model of the labor market which reflects the effects of our assumptions about the workings of the labor market (specifically, that money wages are fixed).

Finally, the short-run supply curve is positioned by the initial money wage rate that was negotiated in the market. A higher money wage translates into a higher real wage rate at a given actual price level. Because the real wage has risen, labor demand declines so actual employment falls and so does output produced. The aggregate money wage is thus a shift parameter in the aggregate supply curve. As wage contracts come up for renegotiation, the aggregate wage will change, reflecting these new wage agreements; the aggregate supply curve will shift accordingly.

Menu Costs

The New Keynesian labor market is built upon the assumption that money wages are rigid for a time due to multi-period contracting. There is a related idea that is relevant to product markets. And that idea is that there are costs attached to changing the prices of goods and services, called **menu costs**, causing firms to keep the prices at which they sell goods to be fixed for some time.[5]

---

5 This idea was suggested by N. Gregory Mankiw in "Small Menu Costs and Large Business Cycles: A Macroeconomic Model of Monopoly," *Quarterly Journal of Economics* 100, No. 2 (May 1985), pp. 529–37.

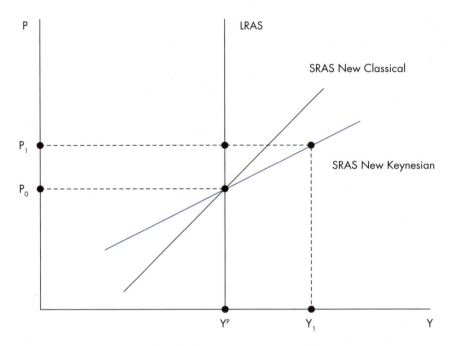

FIGURE 12.5 Output Supply in the New Keynesian Model

If the price level rises from P_0 to P_1, and if this price increase is anticipated by labor suppliers, then output remains fixed at the level of potential GDP, Y^P as the SRAS curve will shift up. If the price increase is unanticipated, output supply will rise above potential GDP to the level Y_1. The New Classical SRAS curve has a steeper slope than the New Keynesian SRAS curve because money wages are flexible in the New Classical labor market.

This idea is close in spirit to the idea of capital stock adjustment costs that was discussed in Chapter 5 regarding the investment decisions of firms. Firms must bear costs attached to changing the prices of the goods that they sell. Labor must be devoted to the act of changing posted prices (thus these are called menu costs using the imagery of new menus being printed by restaurants) and, because it is costly to do this, firms will be unwilling to change prices very frequently to avoid these menu costs (see **Doing Economics**: How Large Are Menu Costs?). There is also the additional and related idea that firms may contract with the buyers of their products using multi-period contracts, just as there are for wage contracts.[6] If so, then firms cannot change the prices at which they sell goods until contracts are renegotiated. These ideas suggest that firms cannot (or will not) change the prices at which they sell goods for a time and, if we combine these notions with our Keynesian assumption of rigid money wages, we get a variant of the New Keynesian supply curve displayed in Figure 12.6. If there is an increase in the demand for goods that firms experience, they cannot change prices but they will experience unanticipated declines in inventories which would presumably cause them to increase production. The reason is that an unanticipated increase in the demand for goods may

6 This issue was studied by Dennis Carlton in "Contracts, Price Rigidity, and Market Equilibrium," *Journal of Political Economy* 87, No. 5 Part 1 (October 1979), pp. 1034–62.

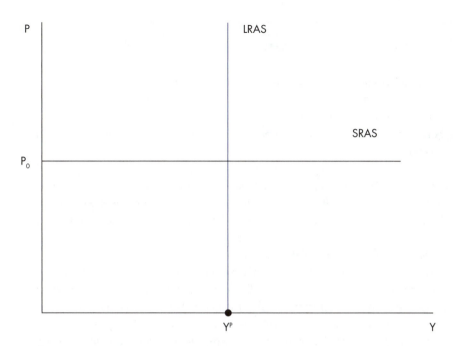

FIGURE 12.6 Output Supply with Menu Costs

If firms will not change prices because it is costly to do so or because they have multi-period contracts with their buyers, then, firms can only vary output in the short run but not the price at which they are willing to sell goods. As a result, the SRAS schedule is horizontal. The long-run supply curve, LRAS, remains as it was in earlier models.

cause inventories to be depleted (or firms may actually have stock-outs), raising the risk of lost customer sales and goodwill.

As we will see, this version of the short-run supply curve has some appealing empirical predictions. Specifically, aggregate demand changes will not have any price or inflation effects over short time horizons in the presence of this supply schedule. This property seems to match up well with the available empirical evidence in industrialized economies, making this approach to the supply-side an attractive one for many economists.

This completes our discussion of the supply-side of aggregate macroeconomic models. Notice that none of our supply-side discussions differs about the long-run properties of the economy; the classical world is always the model of the long-run for the aggregate economy. The alternative supply-side models do, however, disagree in their descriptions of the short-run supply behavior of the economy. These differences can be justified in part by the time horizon held in mind when choosing a model framework for analysis. The longer the time horizon that one wishes to use, the more reasonable it is to assume that prices are flexible. Thus a Keynesian model can be viewed as one that applies to time periods short enough that it is reasonable to assume that wages (and possibly prices) are fixed. The New Classical model can be viewed as one applying to a longer time period where the prices of goods and labor can respond to market forces. Whatever story about the supply-side we choose to use, we must combine that supply-side framework with an aggregate demand schedule, thereby enabling us to discuss the origins of cyclical fluctuations.

Doing Economics: How Large Are Menu Costs?

If menu costs are to be taken seriously as an explanation for the short-run supply schedule in the aggregate economy, it is necessary to find empirical evidence showing that menu costs are of a sufficient magnitude that they cause firms to avoid changing prices as frequently as they might if these menu costs did not exist. Economists have found some evidence using data for supermarket chains.

The data was obtained for five supermarket chains making up a large share of the retail grocery trade in the U.S. There was an important difference between these chains; one chain was subject to an item-pricing law (there must be a separate price tag on each item rather than just on the shelf) and the other four chains were not. The menu costs measured in the study consisted of labor costs for price and sign changes, the costs of printing and delivering price tags, the costs of mistakes, and the cost of in-store supervision of the price change process. There were other types of menu costs that the authors were unable to measure.

It was found that menu cost averaged about .70 percent of revenues and averaged over $105,000 per store. As might be expected, the chain subject to the item-pricing law changed prices much less frequently than the other four chains. The four chains not subject to an item-pricing law changed, on average, 3916 prices per week. The firm subject to item pricing changed 1578 prices per week. Further, management reported that at least 20 percent of the items whose cost to the firm had risen in a week would not have their prices changed because it was unprofitable to do so.

Finally, the chain subject to item pricing had over 400 products exempt from item pricing. The chain changed prices over three times as frequently for products exempt from this law than for products subject to the law.

Source: "The Magnitude of Menu Costs: Direct Evidence From Large U. S. Supermarket Chains," by Daniel Levy, Mark Bergen, Shantanu Dutta, and Robert Venable, *The Quarterly Journal of Economics* 112, No. 3 (August 1997), pp. 791–825

12.4 CYCLICAL FLUCTUATIONS

A complete economic model of cyclical fluctuations uses the aggregate demand schedule from Chapter 11 and one of the supply-side discussions above. In this section, we will draw out the determinants of cyclical fluctuations using each model of the supply side of the economy. We will not, however, be specific as to the causes of the shifts in the aggregate demand curve that set off these cyclical fluctuations because we don't need to be. Many, but not all, of the characteristics of business cycles do not depend upon the precise reason for the shifts in aggregate demand that occur and so we need not consider these reasons at this stage of our analysis. However, for convenience, Table 12.1 contains all of the factors that can shift the aggregate demand (AD) schedule described in Chapter 11. It has become customary to refer to shifts in the AD schedule as "shocks" to AD and we will do so here. Later in the book, we

TABLE 12.1 Factors That Shift the Aggregate Demand Schedule

Shift Variable	Response of Aggregate Demand
Government Expenditures ↑	AD shifts →
Lump-Sum Taxes ↓	
Ricardian Consumers	AD Unaffected
Non-Ricardian Consumers	AD shifts →
Nominal Money Supply ↑	AD shifts →
Investment ↑	AD shifts →
Private Saving ↑	AD shifts ←
Household Consumption ↑	AD shifts →

will look more closely at the sources of movements in the aggregate demand schedule because there are, in fact, some issues that arise (notably with respect to economic policy) when an economic policy variable shifts the aggregate demand schedule.[7] We begin our analysis of the business cycle with the New Classical case.

Finally, note that shocks to aggregate demand could be permanent or transitory. We carry out our discussion using permanent shifts in AD but will indicate later how our analysis differs if the shifts in AD are of the transitory variety.

Business Cycles in the New Classical Model

Figure 12.7 sets up this model of the economy. Initially the economy is in **full equilibrium** where price expectations are correct. There are no excess supplies or demands for goods or financial assets in any of the markets in this economy. There is no ongoing inflation in the economy as the price level is constant over time. Begin by assuming that there is a shock (or a permanent shift) to the aggregate demand schedule, shifting the aggregate demand schedule rightward. You may think of this as a change in, say, investment spending by firms due to their expectations about improved profitability of investment returns in the future. We will initially assume that this shock is unanticipated by labor suppliers. Hence there is no change in the aggregate labor and supply schedules.

The initial shift in aggregate demand causes an excess demand for goods in the economy. Firms experience unanticipated reductions in inventory stocks and, as a result of this excess demand for goods, the price level rises to the level P_1. This rising price level generates an excess demand for labor, causing firms to bid up nominal wages as they try to hire more labor. Since labor suppliers do not correctly perceive the increase in the price level but see nominal wages

---

7 To give one example, the economy's long-run equilibrium can be affected by fiscal policy because the capital stock, and thus potential GDP, can be affected by fiscal instruments such as tax rates.

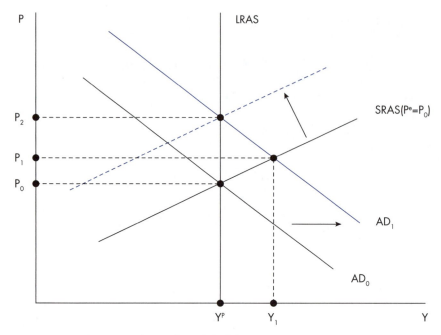

FIGURE 12.7 The New Classical Model of the Economy

The economy is initially in full equilibrium at Potential GDP, Y^P, and with the price level at P_0. An unanticipated permanent increase in aggregate demand causes output to rise to the level Y_1 and the price level rises to P_1. Labor input in production rises, the unemployment rate falls, real wages and the real interest rate decline. Long-run equilibrium will occur at Potential GDP and a price level above P_1.

rise, they believe that real wages have increased and are fooled into working more. In fact, real wages have declined ($\Delta W/W < \Delta P/P$) and, because firms are aware of this fact, they use more labor in production because labor is now a cheaper input in production (its real factor price has declined). Output produced therefore rises and the economy enters a boom, achieving the point (P_1, Y_1). The unemployment rate falls below the natural rate of unemployment as some of the economy's unemployed job searchers find jobs.

At this point in the analysis, it is important to define two notions of equilibrium that we must use to interpret economic behavior in aggregate economic models. These definitions are given below.

Alternative Definitions of Equilibrium

- A general equilibrium is one where all goods and financial asset markets do not display excess demands or supplies and the expectations of economic agents are correct.
- A **temporary equilibrium** is one where all goods and financial asset markets do not display excess demands or supplies but the expectations of economic agents are incorrect.

These definitions are useful in understanding the events occurring in the economy as a result of a shift in aggregate demand; when the economy is in a temporary equilibrium, we can use this fact to explain further changes that will occur in the economic system.

In the New Classical model, the position given by the pair (P_1, Y_1) is only a temporary equilibrium simply because price expectations will not be fixed forever. Eventually, labor suppliers will become aware that the price level has risen (equivalently, they get the "news" that the price level has gone up) and so they will adjust their price expectations accordingly. As they do so, the aggregate supply curve will shift leftward. As this occurs, output and employment will decline because the real wage will rise. The unemployment rate will rise towards the natural rate and the price level will continue to increase. The final resting point for the economy is again at Potential GDP but the price level will reach a new higher level (given by the intersection of the aggregate demand curve and the dotted aggregate supply schedule). Once this new higher price level is reached, no further increases in the price level will occur. That is, there will be no continuing inflation in this economy (more will be said about inflation in the next chapter). This final position is a general equilibrium; no excess supplies or demands exist in product, input, or asset markets and there are correct price expectations. The bottom line in the New Classical model is this: business cycles are due to unanticipated shocks to the aggregate demand schedule. Our findings are summarized in the following proposition.

Propositions About the Origin of Business Cycles in the New Classical Model

- ■ In the New Classical model, business cycles are caused by unanticipated shocks to the aggregate demand schedule.
- ■ A permanent unanticipated shock to the aggregate demand schedule will change real economic magnitudes in the economy in the short run while the price expectations of labor suppliers are incorrect.
- ■ The long-run effect of a permanent shift in the aggregate demand schedule will be to raise nominal magnitudes (e.g., money wages and the price level) but there will be no change in any real economic magnitudes in the economy once price expectations have fully adjusted.

There will be some qualifications to these results discussed in subsequent chapters.[8]

A Recession in the New Classical Model

If the aggregate demand schedule unexpectedly shifts to the left, the economy will enter a recession. To work through this example, return to Figure 12.7 and imagine that the economy is initially in a general equilibrium with aggregate demand schedule given by AD_1. Then a reduction in aggregate demand, shifting the AD schedule to AD_0, causes the economy to enter a temporary equilibrium with reduced output and a lower price level. You should be able to work out the sequence of events leading the economy to ultimately achieve a new general equilibrium at Potential GDP and price level P_0 (see **Doing Economics**: The Volcker Disinflation).

---

8 Potential GDP can change in response to shifts in aggregate demand depending upon the precise reasons behind the movement in aggregate demand. For one example of this possibility, see fn. 7 above.

Transitory vs. Permanent Shocks to Aggregate Demand

Suppose that the shock to the AD schedule is transitory rather than permanent. As an example, imagine that there is a transitory decline in consumer spending because of increased consumer pessimism about future real incomes. In this case, we would have an unanticipated leftward shift in aggregate demand and the economy would enter a recession. Real wages would increase and firms would hire fewer workers, causing the unemployment rate to rise above the natural rate. The economy would be in a temporary equilibrium with a lower price level and output below Potential GDP. How then does this case differ to the one where the shock to AD is permanent?

The answer lies simply with the realization that the AD schedule will return to its original position once consumers realize that their views about the future are wrong, causing them to increase their spending. The ultimate resting place for the economy will be at the position where it began before consumers reduced their spending. Thus the difference between the two cases is that with a transitory change in spending, the economy returns to its original general equilibrium position whereas, in the permanent case, there will be a new general equilibrium with changed nominal magnitudes (and unchanged real magnitudes), in the new general equilibrium.

The Time Series Implications of the New Classical Model

The New Classical model has implications for the time series characteristics of macroeconomic data and the business cycle. Transitory changes in real output (and other real magnitudes) are caused by unanticipated shocks to aggregate demand, whatever the cause of the shift in the aggregate demand schedule. Thus we associate deviations in output from full employment with fluctuations in the aggregate demand schedule. We conclude that, in the context of the New Classical model of the economy, the transitory component of economic time series is generated by these unanticipated shocks to aggregate demand.

But macroeconomic time series have a permanent component as well; we have shown previously that nearly all macroeconomic data are nonstationary (that is, their average value is changing over time). The New Classical model implies that if we are to rationalize the nonstationary nature of potential GDP, it cannot be done by appealing to any movements in the aggregate demand schedule since shifts in aggregate demand can only cause temporary movements in the economy away from its long-run equilibrium. So to explain why real GDP and other economic time series are nonstationary, we must look for another explanation of this time series fact. One obvious possibility is that there is growth in Potential GDP, say by a trend over time in this magnitude. If the model is to explain the nonstationary nature of real GDP, this trend will account for it. In fact, the presence of such a trend has been the customary rationale for the time series characteristic of nonstationarity in real output.[9]

An important additional property of economic time series is **serial persistence**, the feature of time series where they stay above or below their trend for several periods of time. In the New

---

9 Charles R. Nelson and Charles I. Plossser make this claim in their provocative paper "Trends, Random Walks, and Macroeconomic Time Series: Some Evidence and Implications," *Journal of Monetary Economics* 10, No. 2 (September 1982) pp. 139–62.

Classical model, this persistence can be explained in several ways. One possibility would be by the sluggish adjustment of price expectations through time. If it takes several periods for these price expectations to adjust, moving the economy towards the new full equilibrium, then these sluggish expectation adjustments will generate serial persistence in all economic time series.

Second, the aggregate demand schedule could continually shift in such a way as to keep output above or below trend, say by the choices made by economic policymakers.[10] Finally, costs of adjustment can also generate serial persistence. The aggregate demand and supply schedules may both display sluggish movements over time due to these forces. On the supply side, if it is costly to hire and train new workers, firms will only gradually add to the workforce so that output supply will reflect this gradual change in labor input and thus output supply. On the demand side, investment displays partial adjustment due to the costs of adding new capacity. Thus the aggregate demand schedule will also mirror these slow adjustments over time.

Doing Economics: The Volcker Disinflation

In 1979, Paul Volcker became chairman of the Board in the U.S. Federal Reserve System. At the time that he took this position, the U.S. was experiencing high inflation which Volcker acted to reduce by pursuing a restrictive monetary policy, thus reducing the growth rate of the money supply. The result is described in the figure below.

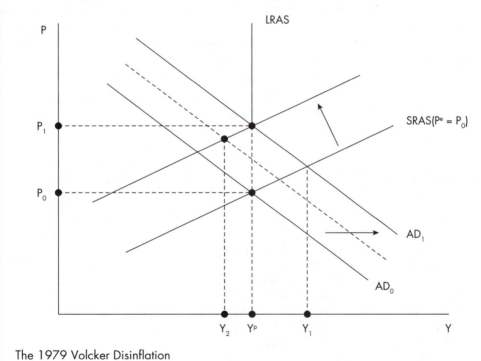

The 1979 Volcker Disinflation

(continued)

10 When we discuss the Phillips Curve in Chapter 13, a relationship that relates inflation and unemployment, we will discuss attempts by policymakers to keep the unemployment rate persistently below its natural rate.

The economy was initially experiencing inflation measured by the movement from P_0 to P_1. The Fed reduced the growth rate of the money supply, causing the AD schedule to shift leftward, given by the dotted line in the diagram. The economy entered a recession with a temporary equilibrium price level reduced from what it would otherwise have been and output was below its potential level.

The reduction in the money stock caused the AD schedule to be that given by the dotted line but, due to the fact that there was no change in expectations by the public, the SRAS schedule set by the public was the one given by the expected price level, P_1. As a consequence, the economy entered a recession. Rather than achieving the price-output combination (P_1, Y^p), the economy entered a temporary equilibrium with reduced output and price level.

Inflation is **procyclical** in the New Classical economy because when the economy enters a boom, the price level begins to rise; the price level would fall in a recession. Real wages are **countercyclical**; output rises in the short run because real wages fall. This implies that employment is procyclical. The unemployment rate is countercyclical, falling below the natural rate when output rises above its potential level. The real interest rate is also countercyclical. The IS curve implies an inverse relationship between the real interest rate and output so when output is above potential GDP, the real interest rate would be lower than its full equilibrium level. These time series properties are summarized in Table 12.2. Most of these implications are empirically verifiable with the notable exception of the real wage rate which we know to be procyclical. Thus this model seems to do a reasonable job of providing an economic explanation of the time series properties of most major macroeconomic time series. However there are economists who take issue with the assumption that output is

TABLE 12.2 Time Series Properties of Macro Data in the New Classical Model

Time Series	Business Cycle Property
Employment	Procyclical
Unemployment	Countercyclical
Real Wages	Countercyclical
Price Level	Procyclical
Real Interest Rate	Countercyclical
Output	Nonstationarity Due to Trend in Potential GDP
	Serial Persistence Due to:
	Sluggish Adjustments in Expectations
	Adjustment Costs
	Persistent Shifts in Aggregate Demand

nonstationary because Potential GDP contains a trend. We will discuss another model of business cycles below (the Real Business Cycle model) that provides an alternative explanation for his apparent nonstationarity.

An Alternative Expectation Formation Scheme

In the analysis above, a departure from Potential GDP was caused by the fact that aggregate demand shifted in a way that was unanticipated by labor suppliers. Put differently, the price expectations of households supplying labor turned out to be wrong as a result of an unanticipated shift in aggregate demand. Here we suggest how differently the economy will behave if these households are not fooled by the shock to aggregate demand.

If the shift in aggregate demand has an impact upon the price level that is correctly foreseen by the public, then there will be a shift in the aggregate supply curve SRAS that is coincident with the shift in aggregate demand. This fact prevents any real magnitudes from departing from their general equilibrium levels. The end result is that there will be no departure of the economy from Potential GDP. In Figure 12.7, the price level will move up from P_0 directly to P_2. The shift in aggregate demand will have no real, only nominal, economic effects in the economy. This illustrates how crucial expectation formation is to the functioning of the economy. In Chapter 13, we will investigate the properties of aggregate economic models when there are no systematic forecasting errors by the public. When the public makes no such errors, this fact will have important consequences for the economic effects of economic policy.

Self-Fulfilling Expectations

Business cycles can be entirely caused by the expectations of economic agents. Expectations can affect the current consumption choices by households and investment decisions of firms.[11] Here it is easy to show that the expectations of labor suppliers can change, causing the economy to move into a recession. The exercise will also show that, to some extent, expectations can be self-fulfilling. That is, if the public chooses to expect a higher price level, that fact can cause an increase in the actual price level.

To see how this can occur, return to Figure 12.7 and imagine that the economy starts at the general equilibrium given by the pair (P_0, Y^P). Now assume that the supply curve given by the dotted line in the figure is caused by higher price expectations on the part of labor suppliers. This causes a leftward shift in the original SRAS schedule. The labor supply curve has shifted leftwards as well, setting off an excess demand for labor. Money wages and real wages will rise

---

11 In Chapter 5, it was shown that consumers make their consumption choices by looking in part at expected future incomes. If those expectations change, so too will their current consumption choices. For firms, the analysis of Chapter 6 revealed that current investment depends upon all future levels of the discount rate, factor prices, tax rates, and possibly other magnitudes. Shifts in the expectations of firms about any of these magnitudes will change current investment spending by firms. Thus the expectations of firms and households help to position the aggregate demand schedule and when these expectations change, so will the aggregate demand schedule. Therefore a shift in these expectations could cause a recession or boom in the economy.

as a result (the actual price level is unchanged as this unfolds). The result is less labor used in production and less output produced. The reduction in supply sets off an excess demand for goods, raising the price level. Thus an increase in price expectations causes the actual price level to rise. The resulting temporary equilibrium is given by the intersection of the dotted SRAS curve and the original aggregate demand schedule, AD_0. The economy is now in a recession. As is true of all temporary equilibria, the economy will not remain in recession forever as labor suppliers will learn that their expectations are incorrect and adjust their expectations accordingly.

This completes our analysis of the New Classical model. The basic viewpoint of the model is that cyclical fluctuations occur as a result of unexpected shocks to aggregate demand with a given level of potential GDP, causing transitory deviations in output from its general equilibrium level. But Potential GDP may not be fixed. Technology shocks to the supply-side of the economy can change the level of Potential GDP. We now pursue this possibility in the context of the Real Business Cycle model.

Real Business Cycles

Figure 12.8 illustrates a cyclical fluctuation in the Real Business Cycle (RBC) approach to the business cycle. To see how a recession can arise, we assume that there is a negative permanent shock to aggregate supply, reducing the level of production at any level of input usage.

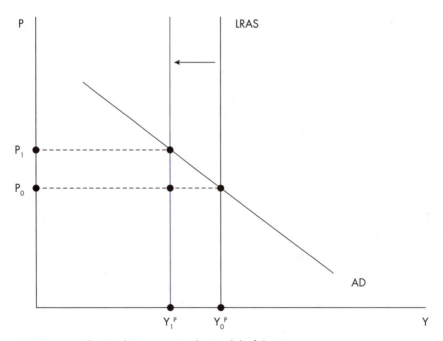

FIGURE 12.8 The Real Business Cycle Model of the Economy

The economy is initially in full equilibrium at Potential GDP, with the price level at the level P_0. A negative shock to the economy's technology will reduce Potential GDP at any level of prices, reducing output and raising the price level.

This negative technology shock will reduce the marginal productivity of labor, reducing the demand for labor at any level of real wages. To see this, if the production function is Y = T·F(K, L), the profit-maximizing choice of labor by the firm is now given by

$$MP_L(T) = \frac{\Delta Y}{\Delta L} = W/P.$$

Not surprisingly, the productivity of labor is now directly affected by the technology parameter, T. A decline in this parameter reduces the productivity of labor, reducing labor demand at any level of real wages. If there is no change in labor supply by households, real wages fall; employment and output decline. With reduced employment, there will be a higher unemployment rate. The price level will rise as the decline in full-employment GDP sets off an excess demand for goods, thus raising the price level. The real interest rate has increased and investment is correspondingly reduced. Table 12.3 summarizes the implications of the real business cycle approach for various economic time series. As is evident in the table, the results for the price level are inconsistent with the available evidence but, beyond that, the model fits the facts reasonably well.

Regarding the nonstationarity and persistence implications of this model, the ability of the RBC model to rationalize these time series properties depends simply upon the characteristics of the shock to the supply-side of the economy. If these shocks are permanent, then all economic magnitudes will be nonstationary (all economic magnitudes change permanently) and they will also appear to be serially persistent. The reason is that if a shock is permanent, it will change the levels of economic magnitudes to new levels and those new levels are permanent, lasting over time. Transitory shocks on the supply-side are inconsistent with these time series properties of macroeconomic data because they could not explain the evident trends that are observed in macroeconomic data. Therefore the ability of the RBC model to rationalize nonstationarity comes down to the existence of permanent shocks to the economy's supply-side. Absent these shocks, the model cannot account for the apparent trends in macroeconomic time series without resorting to additional assumptions about potential GDP.

It is important to stress that the RBC model also has a rather different view of the economy and its business cycles compared to the other models that we discuss in this chapter. In the

TABLE 12.3 Time Series Properties of the Real Business Cycle Model

Time Series	Business Cycle Property
Employment	Procyclical
Unemployment	Countercyclical
Real Wages	Procyclical
Price Level	Countercyclical
Real Interest Rate	Countercyclical
Output	Nonstationarity Due to Permanent Supply-Side Shocks
	Serial Persistence Due to Permanent Supply-Side Shocks

real business cycle approach, the economy is always in an equilibrium state where all markets clear and economic agents are optimizing their objectives subject to their constraint sets. Households are thus maximizing welfare and firms maximize profits. There is no scope for thinking of this economy as if it is performing in some suboptimal way, whatever we might mean by the word suboptimal. In contrast, the other models in this chapter view the economy as fluctuating about Potential GDP; the level of Potential GDP is associated with optimizing behavior by economic agents. Thus if the economy is not at Potential GDP, there are welfare losses of some sort that are present, suggesting that it is desirable to use economic policy to manage the economy with the aim of keeping it near Potential GDP. In the RBC model, policy interventions are not implied by any change in the level of real output.

Regarding business cycles, the real business cycle approach assumes that Potential GDP is itself changing in response to technology shocks so that the evident trend in real GDP is simply the result of the realizations of these technology shocks. The economy is not fluctuating about a trend; there is no deterministic trend in Potential GDP. The trend appears to exist merely as a consequence of permanent movements in Potential GDP (that is, it is illusory). In the other models in this chapter, Potential GDP is a magnitude growing over time due to forces like population growth. Business cycles in those models are fluctuations in real output about trend.

There is little doubt that there are shocks to the supply side of the aggregate economy since these shocks can be observed after they occur even if economic agents do not know the values of these shocks when they make their decisions. Thus it is reasonable to think that the cyclical fluctuations that occur are in part due to these supply-side disturbances. But one reason that many economists are skeptical of the RBC model is that, while it is easy to think of examples of transitory shocks to output supply such as droughts, it is hard to think of any permanent negative shocks to the supply-side of the economy that might be used to explain recessions and, at the same time, the nonstationary and persistent of those recessions. Without such empirical validation after the fact, many economists doubt that technology shocks are the primary source of recessions, preferring instead to use other models, such as the other aggregate economic models described in this chapter, to explain the origins and time series characteristics of the business cycle.

Business Cycles in the New Keynesian Model

In the New Keynesian models, we derived supply curves using the notion that money wages (and possibly prices) are fixed for some periods of time. Now we use that concept to investigate departures from Potential GDP. The menu cost model will serve to illustrate the main issues in this economic framework. Figure 12.9 provides the graphical details of the analysis.

An increase in aggregate demand cannot have any initial impact upon nominal wages or prices in the economy because these magnitudes have been set by pre-existing multi-period agreements. However the increase in the demand for goods will cause inventories of finished goods to decline unexpectedly. Firms, wishing to avoid stock-outs, will raise production and so will use more labor in production. Some of these workers will be hired from the pool of unemployed job searchers so that the unemployment rate will decline. The short-run impact of the increase in aggregate demand is to raise output without any change in the price level. This

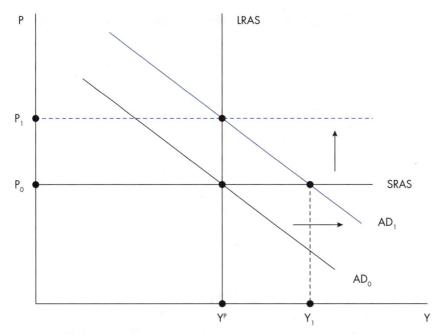

FIGURE 12.9 The Menu Cost Keynesian Model and the Business Cycle

In the Keynesian model with menu costs, an increase in aggregate demand has no short-run impact upon prices and wages because these magnitudes are set in pre-existing multi-period agreements. Inventories will decline unexpectedly, thereby inducing firms to expand production by hiring more workers.

is an empirically attractive feature of the Keynesian model because this prediction about short-run effects matches up quite well with the actual performance of industrialized economies.[12]

But this departure from Potential GDP is only a temporary equilibrium. The increase in the demand for goods will eventually induce firms to raise prices on the goods they sell once agreements with their buyers expire and can be renegotiated. When this begins to happen, there will be an incentive for money wages to rise in response to the higher prices set by firms. When wage agreements expire and are renegotiated, higher money wages will be set. As a result, the SRAS curve will start to shift up over time and this process will continue until a new long-run equilibrium is reached at the price P_1. With no further changes in aggregate demand, this is a new general equilibrium for this economy.

Note the long-run equilibrium in the Keynesian model as compared to the New Classical model; they are identical. As pointed out earlier in this chapter, the classical long run is not a matter of dispute among economists as economists of every stripe agree that, if one waits long enough, the economy will settle down to a classical equilibrium. The differences among economists center around their beliefs about the style of model that best represents the short-run behavior of the economy.

---

12 However it should also be remembered that how plausible it is to have fixed prices and wages is dependent upon the time horizon that one has in mind. The shorter that time horizon, the more plausible it is to assume fixed wages and prices in an economic model.

The Business Cycle Properties of the Menu Cost Model

Regarding the nonstationarity of real GDP, the New Keynesian model must rely on a trend being present in real GDP. Otherwise, this model cannot explain this time series property of macroeconomic data. Serial persistence can be explained in the New Keynesian model by the sluggish adjustment of wages and prices. Potential GDP differs from its potential level while wages and prices are adjusted over time. The more rapidly these prices and wages adjust, the more quickly real GDP will return to Potential GDP. In addition, this model can account for serial persistence due to costs of adjustment or persistent shifts in aggregate demand.

Real wages must fall if output is to rise above Potential GDP since the only way that employment and output can rise is if real wages fall, consistent with the labor demand schedules of firms. Thus real wages are countercyclical and employment is procyclical while unemployment is countercyclical. The price level is procyclical, rising while output is above trend. The real interest rate is countercyclical. Table 12.4 summarizes these cyclical implications.

Which Model Best Explains the Data?

No consensus has emerged with economists settling on one single model of cyclical fluctuations. Each model framework cannot explain all of the time series macroeconomic facts. There is at least one stylized fact that differs from the predictions of each model. But the most compelling difference between models is the justification for the nonstationarity evident in macroeconomic data. The statistical methods available to economists do not distinguish well between nonstationarity due to trends as opposed to nonstationarity caused by permanent shocks to the macroeconomic system.[13] Until it is possible to discriminate between these two alternatives, there will continue to be disagreement about the model which best describes the

TABLE 12.4 Time Series Properties of the New Keynesian Model

Time Series	Business Cycle Property
Employment	Procyclical
Unemployment	Countercyclical
Real Wages	Procyclical
Price Level	Procyclical
Real Interest Rate	Countercyclical
Output	Nonstationarity Due to Permanent Supply-Side Shocks
	Serial Persistence Due to Permanent Supply-Side Shocks

---

13 The paper by Nelson and Plosser, cited earlier in this chapter, attempts to statistically discriminate between these two possible nonstationarity alternatives. Their evidence is that macroeconomic data have nondeterministic nonstationarity with the possible exception of the unemployment rate.

macroeconomic system. But we can summarize these models as far as their implications for the origins of business cycles.

The New Classical, New Keynesian, and Menu Cost models all treat the business cycle as originating from unanticipated shocks to aggregate demand. The Real Business Cycle model describes business cycles as originating from shocks to aggregate supply. It is of course true that aggregate economies experience shocks to both aggregate demand and supply and, for the purposes of analyzing a particular episode in economic history, one particular model among those available may be most the most suitable one for understanding and interpreting economic events. For example, the U.S. recession beginning in December 2007 appears to be one originating on the aggregate demand side of the economy. The reason is that there is evidence suggesting that the housing sector initiated the decline in economic activity due to mortgage defaults by homeowners, with the result that banks experienced loan losses, impairing their ability to originate loans to the private sector (see **Doing Economics**: The Recession of 2007). For other cyclical episodes, another model may be most appropriate. The non-cyclical aspects of shocks to energy prices would seem to be analyzed best in a real business cycle model since the disturbance to the economy originated on the supply-side of the economy, specifically, the energy sector. Thus each style of model can capture certain aspects of the business cycle experienced in industrialized economies.

12.5 TRANSITORY SHOCKS TO AGGREGATE SUPPLY

Our discussion of the business cycle has not addressed one type of cyclical episode experienced by industrialized economies. In Chapter 9, we discussed shocks to aggregate supply from the viewpoint of an equilibrium classical model of the economy. But there can be changes in the supply of inputs to an economy that can cause a recession. Here we examine the economic effects of transitory shocks to aggregate supply using our AD-AS framework.

Recall that we used the production function

$$Y = T \cdot F(K, L)$$

where T stands for technology, K is capital, and L is labor. Firms use intermediate inputs like raw materials and energy in producing output and these were omitted in most of our previous analysis. But suppose that there is a transitory reduction in the supply of these intermediate inputs as the relative prices of intermediates inputs rise. A good example of this would be relative gasoline prices rising to historically high levels in 2008 and declining thereafter. The result is displayed in Figure 12.10 using a menu cost model of the economy.

The decline in raw materials supplies and implied increase in relative raw materials prices will reduce the amount of output produced at any level of prices. Equivalently, a given supply of output will only be supplied at a higher price level, implying an upward shift in the SRAS schedule. The result is that the economy enters a recession, with declining output and higher price level. There will be a decline in the demand for labor consistent with the decline in output produced. Firms will see rising inventories, causing them to reduce output. But notice how price and output behave in this scenario compared to what we observed with aggregate demand shocks.

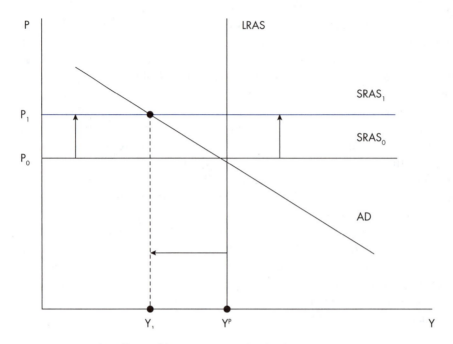

FIGURE 12.10 The Effects of Transitory Supply Shocks

The economy experiences a transitory increase in the relative price of intermediate inputs, raising the supply-price of output. The SRAS schedule shifts up, causing the economy to experience a reduction in output and a higher price level.

In a recession caused by a negative aggregate demand shock, price and output move the same way; they both decline. In the case of a transitory supply shock, the price level rises while output falls. This price-output pattern has been called "**stagflation**" in the media but this is not inflation as we mean it. The reason is that the price level will stop increasing at some point in our model but it rises continually when there is ongoing inflation. Nonetheless prices rising at the same time as declining output (or rising unemployment) have often been confused with inflationary behavior but there should be no confusion about this in your mind as we have been careful to define the origins of inflation (as in Chapter 7).

This completes our survey of the economic models that are the workhorses of modern business cycle studies. We have not mentioned the Great Depression, the motivating event for the study of business cycles. This depression is the largest cyclical decline in economic activity that has been observed in the U.S. economy and this is treated separately (see **Doing Economics**: The Great Depression).

12.6 CONCLUDING REMARKS

Macroeconomics became an important subspecialty of economics because of the existence of business cycles. Providing an explanation of these important economic phenomena has preoccupied the research efforts of many economists and this chapter sets out several of the models that have been devised to explain the sources of the fluctuations in economic activity.

These models fall into two broad categories: those that assume market-clearing and those that do not. Two models using the market-clearing paradigm are the New Classical model and the Real Business Cycle (RBC) Model. The New Classical model uses expectational errors about the price level to rationalize departures from Potential GDP. When these errors occur, real wages will change and this causes labor input in production and output to change. Thus unanticipated changes in aggregate demand cause cyclical fluctuations. In the RBC approach, technology shocks are the sources of economic fluctuations. When these shocks occur, Potential GDP changes and so cyclical fluctuations are just the manifestation of these technology shocks.

Doing Economics: The Recession of 2007

The most recent recession experienced in the U.S. and other countries began in December 2007, according to the Business Cycle Dating Committee of the National Bureau of Economic Research. A peak in economic activity, and thus the beginning of a recession, occurred during this month. The committee looks at a variety of economic data in reaching their decision but a look at the data on real GDP indicates why this decision was made.

Quarter	Real GDP	Annual Growth Rate
2007:1	11,357.8	.05
2007:2	11,491.4	4.71
2007:3	11,625.7	4.68
2007:4	11,620.7	.17
2008:1	11,646.0	.87
2008:2	11,727.4	2.80
2008:3	11,712.4	−.51
2008:4	11,522.1	−6.50
2009:1	11,360.5	−5.61

The data reveals a small decline in real GDP in the fourth quarter of 2007, the quarter in which the recession began. The end of the recession was June 2009 but the data reveal two subsequent quarters of positive growth followed by three quarters of negative growth. The data show that recessions are not always characterized by consistency in the data (there is a mixture of positive and negative growth) so that the recession can appear to be over when, in fact, it is not.

Doing Economics: The Great Depression

The National Bureau of Economic Research (NBER) dates the contraction in economic activity, known as the Great Depression, as an economic contraction beginning in August 1929 (peak) and ending in March 1933 (trough). To get an idea of how extreme this event was in recorded

(continued)

business cycle history, consider the following measures of its severity. The duration of this contraction was far longer than the typical contraction measured by the NBER. The Great Depression lasted 43 months (from the peak in economic activity to its trough) whereas the average duration reported by the NBER, for all recorded episodes covering the period 1854–2001, is 17 months. In 1929, the unemployment rate was 3.2 percent, rising to 23.6 percent in 1933. Real GNP was 203.6 in billions of 1958 dollars, falling to 141.5 in 1933 measured in the same units, a decline of just over 30 percent.* These are remarkable facts about the changes in economic activity that occurred between 1929 and 1933, unlike anything seen since the beginning of the twentieth century. What caused this terrible event now known as The Great Depression?

The classic answer to this question was provided by Milton Friedman and Anna J. Schwartz in their seminal study of the U.S. financial system.** They compiled historical monetary statistics, also studying the behavior of the Federal Reserve policy during this period. Their conclusion from these efforts was that there was a monumental failure of monetary policy by the Federal Reserve that allowed a recession to deteriorate into an historic collapse in economic activity. Here are a few statistics that support their analysis.

In the table below, you will see statistics on the money stock and its components at the beginning and end of the Great Depression. As you can see from the table, there was an enormous decline in the stock of money during this contraction; it fell by just over one-third. Moreover, you will recall from our discussion in Chapter 7 that households choose a currency–deposit ratio that reflects in part their needs for currency in purchasing goods and services. But there is another reason for choosing to use currency rather than bank deposits; currency is safer than commercial bank deposits because banks can fail (and they did during the Great Depression) so the currency–deposit ratio can also reflect the perceived risk of banks. This ratio more than doubled during this time period. Bank failures led to bank panics and the closing of banks during a bank holiday. The wealth of many households was severely reduced if not completely wiped out due to these bank failures. Friedman and Schwartz documented the behavior of the Federal Reserve during this period and argue that the Fed caused the Great Contraction and the partial collapse of the banking system.

	Currency	Commercial Bank Deposits	Money Supply	Currency-Deposit Ratio
August 1929	3919	42359	46278	.09
March 1933	5509	24461	29970	.23

* See the Department of Commerce publication *Historical Statistics of the United States, Colonial Times to 1970*, Part 1.
** See *A Monetary History of the United States, 1867–1960*, Princeton University Press for the National Bureau of Economic Research (1963).

Alternatively, New Keynesian models operate under the assumption that wages and possibly prices are fixed for substantial periods of time which seems plausible based upon empirical observation. As a result, an unanticipated shift in aggregate demand will cause inventories to fall unexpectedly, inducing firms to raise production in order to replenish depleted stocks of finished goods. Just as in the New Classical model, cyclical fluctuations are caused by shocks to the aggregate demand schedule.

Neither the New Classical nor the New Keynesian models disagree about the long run in the aggregate economy. In the long run, the economy is classical in its behavior in all models. The RBC model presumes that the classical model holds at all instants of time.

Models differ in important ways regarding the time series properties of macroeconomic data. The New Classical and Keynesian models must rely on a trend in Potential GDP to be able to explain the nonstationarity of macroeconomic data. The RBC model regards nonstationarity as arising because technology shocks to the supply-side of the economy are permanent so nonstationarity appears as a result of the realizations of these technology shocks. Serial persistence occurs in the RBC model because technology shocks permanently affect real economic magnitudes so that this model does not require other mechanisms to generate this time series characteristic. The New Classical and Keynesian models require sluggish adjustments in wages, prices (or expected prices), and possibly costs of adjustment to explain serial persistence.

Every model does a reasonable job of explaining the time series behavior of economic variables. No model can explain all of the key characteristics of every economic time series.

Key Ideas

- The New Classical model of the labor market assumes that money wages are flexible. Firms have correct information about the price level but labor suppliers do not. Labor suppliers form an expectation of the price level in making their labor supply decisions.
- In the New Classical model, an unexpected increase in the price level fools labor suppliers, making them think that real wages have increased although they have in fact declined. Labor services and output produced will rise.
- In the New Classical labor market model, an anticipated increase in the price level causes coincident shifts in labor demand and supply. As a result, real variables are unchanged but money wages rise at the same rate as prices.
- In the New Keynesian model, wages and possibly prices are fixed so that the short-run supply curve is horizontal or nearly so. Firms are willing to supply more output at these fixed prices and wages because they wish to replenish depleted inventory stocks.
- The long-run equilibrium of the New Classical and New Keynesian models is the classical model of the economy where all prices and wages are flexible and there are correct expectations.
- The Real Business Cycle (RBC) model of the supply side assumes that prices and wages are flexible but permanent technology shocks shift the level of potential GDP.
- The New Classical model implies that unanticipated shocks to aggregate demand cause cyclical fluctuations. These shocks cause price forecast errors by labor suppliers who are fooled into working more than they would if they knew that real wages had fallen.
- The New Keynesian model uses unanticipated shocks to aggregate demand to explain business cycles. These shocks cause an excess demand for goods resulting in depleted inventory stocks.
- The RBC model asserts that technology shocks permanently shift Potential GDP. Thus these technology shocks are the cause of the apparent cycles in economic activity.

Key Terms

Stationary Economy

Anticipated Price
   Change

Temporary Equilibrium

Technology Shocks

Countercyclical

Nonstationarity

Transitory and
   Permanent
   Shocks

Total Factor Productivity

Menu Costs

Stagflation

Unanticipated Price
   Change

Full Equilibrium

Solow Residual

Serial
   Persistence

Procyclical

Question for Study and Review

Review Exercises

1. Why does the short-run aggregate supply schedule have a positive slope in the New Classical model of the economy's supply-side?
2. Why does the short-run aggregate supply schedule have a positive slope in the New Keynesian model of the economy's supply-side?
3. Why does the short-run aggregate supply schedule have a zero slope in the menu cost model of the economy's supply-side?
4. How does an unanticipated shift in aggregate demand caused by a rise in the money supply affect real and nominal variables in the New Classical economy?
5. How does an unanticipated shift in aggregate demand caused by a rise in the money supply affect real and nominal variables in a menu cost economy?
6. How does a negative supply shock affect the aggregate levels of price and output in a real business cycle model of the economy?
7. Why will a shift in the aggregate demand schedule have no effect upon real magnitudes in the long run?
8. Why is inflation procyclical?

Thought Exercises

1. How does a negative supply shock affect the aggregate levels of price and output in a New Classical model of the economy?
2. How does a negative supply shock affect the aggregate levels of price and output in a New Keynesian model of the economy?
3. Suppose there is an anticipated increase in aggregate demand. What will happen to the price level and output in the short run and the long run?

Numerical Exercises

1. Assume that output is produced with the production technology $Y = 10 + .3 \cdot K + .6 \cdot L$. Further consider the following relationships in the labor market: $L^S = 10 + 5 \cdot (W - P^e)$ and $L^D = 25 + .75 \cdot K - 2.5 \cdot (W - P)$. *Definitions*: Y = Output, L = Labor, W = Money Wage, P = Price Level, W – P = Real Wage, P^e = Expected Price Level, L^D = Labor Demand, L^S = Labor Supply, K = Capital Stock.

a) Derive an equation for the AS curve.
b) What is the level of LRAS (Potential GDP) when the capital stock in long-run equilibrium equals 100 units?

2. Consider the following information about an aggregate economy. Consumption $C = 500 + .7 \cdot (Y - T)$, Taxes: $T = -25 + .2 \cdot Y$, Investment: $I = 500 - 5000 \cdot r$, Government: $G = 100$, Money Demand: $m^D - P = 100 + .3 \cdot Y - 2000 \cdot i$, Money Supply: $m^s = m_0$. *Definitions*: Y = Output, P = Price Level, C = Consumption, T = Tax Receipts, I = Investment, r = Real Interest Rate, G = Government Expenditures, m = Money Stock, i = Nominal Interest Rate, p^e = Expected Inflation Rate. The money market is always in equilibrium.

a) Derive an aggregate demand schedule of the form $Y = y_0 + y_1 \cdot (m_0 - p) + y_2 \cdot \pi$, finding numerical values for the parameters y_0, y_1, and y_2. (Hint: Form the IS and LM equations and solve the two by eliminating the nominal interest rate from the two expressions.)
b) Suppose that expected inflation is zero, Potential GDP is 1500, and the money supply is 400. If the economy is in a general equilibrium, find the values of the price level and the real interest rate.

3. Consider the following information for an aggregate economy. Aggregate Demand: $y^D = 100 + 25 \cdot (m^s - P)$, Aggregate Supply: $y^s = 1500 + .4 \cdot (P - P^e)$. The expected rate of inflation is zero. *Definitions*: y = Output, P = Price Level, P^e = Expected Price Level, m = Money Stock.

a) If the economy is in a general equilibrium at full employment with $m^s = 150$, find the equilibrium levels of output, the price level and the expected price level.
b) Now suppose that there is an unexpected increase in the money stock to $m^s = 160$. Find the temporary equilibrium levels of the price level and output.

For further questions, multiple choice quizzes, and weblinks related to this chapter, visit www.routledge.com/textbooks/rossana

References and Suggestions for Further Reading

Carlton, D. (1979) "Contracts, Price Rigidity, and Market Equilibrium," *Journal of Political Economy* 87 (5) Part 1 (October): 1034–62.

Friedman, M. and Schwartz, A.J. (1963) *A Monetary History of the United States, 1867–1960*, Princeton University Press for the National Bureau of Economic Research.

Historical Statistics of the United States, Colonial Times to 1970, Part 1, US Department of Commerce.

Levy, D., Bergen, M., Dutta, S. and Venable, R. (1997) "The Magnitude of Menu Costs: Direct Evidence From Large U. S. Supermarket Chains," *The Quarterly Journal of Economics* 112 (3) (August): 791–825.

Lucas, R.E. Jr. (1973) "Some International Evidence on Output-Inflation Tradeoffs," *American Economic Review* 63 (2) (June): 326–34.

Mankiw, N.G. (1985) "Small Menu Costs and Large Business Cycles: A Macroeconomic Model of Monopoly," *Quarterly Journal of Economics* 100 (2) (May): 529–37.

McCallum, B.T. (1980) "Rational Expectations and Macroeconomic Stabilization Policy: An Overview," *Journal of Money, Credit, and Banking* 12 (4) Part 2 (November): 716–46.

Nelson, Charles R. and Plosser, Charles I. "Trends and Random Walks in Macroeconomic Time Series," *Journal of Monetary Economics* 10, No. 2, 139–162. (Ch. 12)

Plosser, C.I. and Long, J.B. (1983) "Real Business Cycles," *Journal of Political Economy* 91 (1) (February): 39–69.

Taylor, John B. "Aggregate Dynamics and Staggered Contracts," *Journal of Political Economy* 88, No. 1, February 1980, pp. 1–23. (Ch. 12)

APPENDIX: THE NEW CLASSICAL AND KEYNESIAN MODELS OF AGGREGATE SUPPLY

In this appendix, we will set out the analytical framework for the New Classical and New Keynesian models of aggregate supply. The objective will be to derive aggregate supply equations for each supply-side model to support the graphical discussions given earlier in the chapter.[14] All equations are linear for simplicity while retaining the economic content consistent with utility and profit maximization.

The New Classical Model

The labor market consists of the following three equations.

$$\text{Labor Demand: } L^d = n_0 - n_1 \cdot (W - P), \; n_0 > 0, \; n_1 > 0$$

$$\text{Labor Supply: } L^s = n_2 + n_3 \cdot (W - P^e), \; n_2 > 0, \; n_3 > 0$$

$$\text{Market Equilibrium: } L^d = L^s = L$$

Definitions: L = Labor, W = Money Wage, P = Actual Price Level, P^e = Expected Price Level. The equations are consistent with our labor market discussion in Chapter 7. The labor demand schedule has a negative own-factor price effect and labor supply is increasing in the expected real wage which assumes that substitution effects dominate income effects.

To obtain the aggregate supply equation, we will need to solve the labor market equations for the level of labor services, L, by eliminating the money wage rate. Solve each equation for W and equate the resulting two expressions as follows. Using the fact that $L^d = L^s = L$ gives

$$\frac{n_0 - L}{n_1} + P = W = \frac{L - n_2}{n_3} + P^e$$

A bit of algebraic manipulation allows us to solve for L as follows.

---

14 A much more thorough derivation of the material in this appendix may be found in "Rational Expectations and Macroeconomic Stabilization Policy: An Overview," by Bennett T. McCallum, *Journal of Money, Credit, and Banking* 12, No. 4 (Part 2, November 1980), pp. 716–46.

$$L = \frac{n_0 \cdot n_3 + n_1 \cdot n_2}{n_1 + n_3} + \left[\frac{n_1 \cdot n_3}{n_1 + n_3}\right] \cdot (P - P^e),$$

$$\frac{n_0 \cdot n_3 + n_1 \cdot n_2}{n_1 + n_3} > 0, \quad \frac{n_1 \cdot n_3}{n_1 + n_3} > 0$$

The expression above has two positive coefficients. The intercept is positive and this can be interpreted as the "natural" employment level. The reason is that if the forecast error is zero (that is, when $P = P^e$), employment is the positive amount given by the first term on the right side of the labor equation above. If there is an actual price level that is above the expected price level, employment is above the natural level, a level consistent with our discussion of the New Classical labor market.

Using the analysis of the labor market, we can then derive the aggregate supply curve. First we must use the production function

$$Y^s = y_0 + y_1 \cdot L, \quad y_0 > 0, \quad y_1 > 0,$$

assumed linear for simplicity. Output is increasing in the level of labor input and has a positive intercept. Substitute the expression for labor, derived above, into the production function to get

$$Y^s = y_0 + y_1 \left[\frac{n_0 \cdot n_3 + n_1 \cdot n_2}{n_1 + n_3} + \left[\frac{n_1 \cdot n_3}{n_1 + n_3}\right] \cdot (P - P^e)\right]$$

and then rewrite this as

$$Y^s = \left[y_0 + \frac{y_1(n_0 \cdot n_3 + n_1 \cdot n_2)}{n_1 + n_3}\right] + \left[\frac{y_1 \cdot n_1 \cdot n_3}{n_1 + n_3}\right] \cdot (P - P^e)$$

Observe the term within the brackets of this last expression. It is the level of output produced when labor is at its natural level. Thus we call this the natural level of output, denoted in the text by Y^p. The term preceding the forecast error is positive which is plausible; if there is a positive forecast error, labor input used in production will rise above the natural level and so, with more labor used in production, there will be more output produced. Incorporating these results, we write the New Classical supply curve as

$$Y^s = Y^p + \gamma \cdot (P - P^e), \quad Y^p > 0, \quad \gamma > 0.$$

This last expression is the supply curve that we used in the graphical discussion of the New Classical model earlier in the chapter.

The New Keynesian Model

The New Keynesian supply curve can be derived by using some of the elements of the New Classical model above. Specifically, substitute the labor demand schedule into the production function to get

$$Y^s = y_0 + y_1 \cdot [n_0 - n_1 \cdot (W - P)]$$

$$Y^s = [y_0 + y_1 \cdot n_0] + y_1 \cdot n_1 \cdot P - y_1 \cdot n_1 \cdot W$$

As stated in the text, the New Keynesian supply curve has an intercept that can be interpreted to be Potential GDP. It has a positive intercept ($y_0 + y_1 \cdot n_0 > 0$) and the slope of this curve is also positive ($y_1 \cdot n_1 > 0$). And now we interpret W to be the wage set by contract and so the contract wage, W, appears as a shift parameter in this supply schedule as was stated in the text. A higher value of the contract wage shifts the aggregate supply curve to the left. That is,

$$\left. \frac{\Delta Y^s}{\Delta W} \right|_{\Delta P = 0} = -y_1 \cdot n_1 < 0$$

Interestingly, if the contract wage is set in relation to the expected price level, P^e, then the New Keynesian supply curve reduces to one much like that we derived above for the New Classical case. Suppose the wage is set using

$$W = w_0 + P^e$$

which can be interpreted to mean that the money wage is set to achieve a desired real wage. Substitute this contract equation into the supply schedule above to get

$$Y^s = [y_0 + y_1 \cdot n_0] + y_1 \cdot n_1 \cdot (P - W)$$

$$Y^s = [y_0 + y_1 \cdot n_0] + y_1 \cdot n_1 (P - w_0 - P^e)$$

$$Y^s = [y_0 + y_1 \cdot (n_0 - n_1 \cdot (w_0)] + y_1 \cdot n_1 \cdot (P - P^e).$$

This last expression is very similar to the supply curve we derived for the New Classical case. Its parameters are different but the same economic variables appear in it (the level of output and the forecast error for the price level) as we found in the New Classical supply curve. To achieve this similarity, it only required that we assume that money wages are set in relation to the expected price level.

Chapter 13

Inflation, the Phillips Curve and Expectations

LEARNING OBJECTIVES

This chapter describes the origin of inflation and it considers the relationship between inflation and unemployment, a relationship evident in macro-economic data. The AD-AS framework developed earlier in the book can explain the cause of inflation and how an unemployment–inflation tradeoff can exist. That discussion will lead us to consider how expectations are formed by the public and to develop explicit descriptions of economic policy known as policy rules. Here are some specific topics discussed in this chapter.

■ The AD-AS framework is used to explain how inflation can occur.

■ The chapter discusses the relationship between inflation and unemployment known as the Phillips Curve in both its original and modern forms.

■ The chapter provides a discussion showing how the Phillips Curve relationship emerges from the AD-AS framework.

■ The Phillips Curve discussion shows that expectations are crucial to an economy's behavior so there will a discussion of how the economy behaves under alternative expectation formation methods.

■ One way of forming expectations is found to require that the public be very knowledgeable about the economy including knowledge of how economic policy will be conducted.

Inflation has been a recurring feature of industrialized economies. One of the main achievements of macroeconomists is their ability to explain the cause of inflation. The first part of this chapter provides the explanation for what it is that causes the price level to rise systematically and you will see that this explanation involves the central bank and its control of the money supply.

Further, it was widely believed during the early 1960s that there was a tradeoff between inflation and unemployment that could be exploited by policymakers and this tradeoff was a prominent part of policy discussions during this time period. Subsequent to this time period, however, this tradeoff seemed to disappear, creating a puzzle that economists attempted to solve. One purpose of this chapter is to describe the solution that was found to this puzzle.

Our chapter begins with a discussion of inflation, showing how it can arise in the familiar AD-AS framework developed in Chapter 12. It will be seen that inflation is of monetary origin so the behavior of the central bank is crucial to the explanation of inflation in the economy.

The original Phillips Curve was an empirical relationship observed over a substantial period of time. Our next discussion in this chapter looks at the original Phillips Curve, then looks at some more recent data, showing how different the tradeoff seems to be depending upon the sample period that is chosen for display.

The modern version of the Phillips Curve is then presented. This newer version stresses the importance of the expected rate of inflation as a component of the inflation–unemployment tradeoff. A change in these inflation expectations can thus be used to explain why the inflation–unemployment tradeoff could shift over time. This discussion will lead us to consider the possibility that a policymaker could try to continually keep the unemployment rate below its equilibrium level. This part of the discussion will show how crucial is the way expectations are formed by the public because the public would need to form their inflation expectations in such a way that this policy option is possible.

Then we will establish how the Phillips Curve can arise from the familiar AD-AS framework. This analysis will show that the modern-day Phillips Curve arises quite naturally from this familiar model of the economy. The exercises done here will further emphasize the importance of inflation expectations in explaining the origin of an inflation–unemployment tradeoff.

Expectation formation is therefore our next topic for discussion and here we will contrast the implications of two ways of forming expectations. The first is very simple, where the public only looks into the past to form its expectations. The second assumes that the public is very sophisticated in its behavior, using an enormous amount of information in forming expectations. This analysis will have the remarkable implication that only the unpredictable part of monetary policy can affect real economic magnitudes.

The final topic for discussion might best be described as "Beware of Economists Bearing Economic Forecasts!" We will discover that if it were really true that the public uses a large body of economic data in forming inflation expectations, that fact would mean that they knew the policy rules used by the central bank. Then if this **policy rule** were to change, it would be virtually impossible to predict the effects of this policy change on the economy. Thus policy analysis, predicting the effects of a policy change, is unlikely to be of much use to the public.

13.1 THE ORIGIN OF INFLATION

In the models described in the previous chapter, the price level only varied while the economy was not in a general equilibrium. Once the economy reached a long-run equilibrium, the price level became constant over time. Here we want to study how inflation can arise in the aggregate economy. For this purpose, we will use the New Classical model of the economy although much the same story would arise in the New Keynesian model discussed in this chapter.[1]

We begin with two definitions of inflation.

Definitions of Inflation

- **Unanticipated inflation** is an inflation rate that the public does not correctly forecast.
- **Anticipated inflation** is an inflation rate that the public correctly forecasts.

Obviously, these definitions are analogous to our earlier definitions of anticipated and unanticipated price changes. We begin our analysis by showing how inflation can arise when it is fully anticipated. Figure 13.1 illustrates this case.

Recall that inflation is defined as a continual or ongoing increase in the prices of all goods and services in the economy. Therefore the price level can only rise due to a continual shift in aggregate demand; the short-run supply schedule, SRAS, shifts only due to changes in expectations by labor suppliers. What causes this shift in aggregate demand? Recall that in Chapter 7, we showed that if the velocity of money is constant, money growth translates directly into inflation.[2] And as we show when we discuss economic policy, there must be a monetary explanation underlying the shift in aggregate demand. All that matters here is that there must be a continual increase in aggregate demand to generate continual increases in the price level.[3]

---

1 The RBC model was designed to show that cyclical fluctuations could arise in barter systems so there is no role for monetary forces. Inflation has its origin in monetary policy as will be discussed in this chapter.
2 Remember that the velocity of money is defined as the ratio of nominal GDP to the money stock.
3 Remember that there are no shocks to the supply-side of the economy by assumption. Supply-side shocks generate one-time changes in the price level, not the ongoing increase in the prices of all goods and services in the economy which is what is meant by inflation. As a result, the origin of inflation must be found in the behavior of the aggregate demand schedule. As a matter of empirical observation, it may be difficult to disentangle these two sources of price level changes but there is no problem in doing so conceptually.

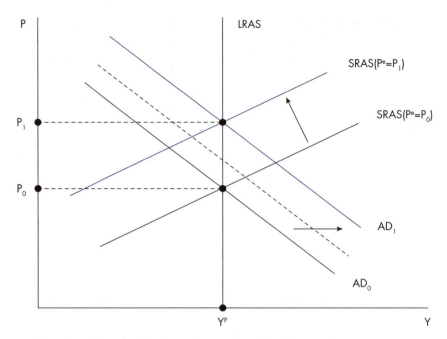

FIGURE 13.1 Inflation in the New Classical Model of the Economy

The economy is initially in full equilibrium at Potential GDP, Y^P, and with the price level at the level P_0. An anticipated increase in aggregate demand causes a shift in aggregate supply that is coincident with the shift in aggregate demand. As a result, output remains at Potential GDP and all real economic magnitudes stay at their full equilibrium levels. Nominal magnitudes, such as wages and prices, rise at the same rate.

Anticipated Inflation

Anticipated inflation arises when labor suppliers recognize the continuing shifts in aggregate demand that will generate inflation. As a result, they expect a higher price level to occur and adjust their expectations accordingly and, most importantly, their price (inflation) expectations are correct. Thus the actual (and expected) price level rises from P_0 to P_1 displayed in Figure 13.1 and the economy remains at Potential GDP. All other real economic magnitudes remain at their full equilibrium levels but nominal magnitudes are not constant. They rise as prices do. For example, money wages rise at the rate of inflation so as to keep real wages constant ($\Delta W/W = \Delta P/P$). Thus if real wages remain fixed, so labor used in production must be constant.

In addition, real and nominal interest rates no longer coincide. Recall that our definition of the real interest rate is

$$r = i - \Delta P^e/P.$$

where r denotes the real interest rate and i is the nominal rate of interest. Since we are in full equilibrium, actual and expected inflation rates are the same ($\Delta P^e/P = \Delta P/P$) so the real interest rate differs from the nominal interest rate by the rate of the fully anticipated price inflation that is occurring in the economy. This fact also makes it easy to see the connection between the rate of inflation and nominal interest rates, a relationship referred to as the **Fisher Effect**, named after the American economist Irving Fisher who first postulated this relationship. Suppose that the real interest rate in equilibrium is fixed, say because the capital stock and its marginal productivity are fixed in equilibrium. Then there is a one-to-one relationship between the nominal interest rate and inflation. A higher rate of inflation will be associated with a higher nominal interest rate so as to keep the real interest rate constant.[4] Thus economies experiencing rising inflation should be observed to have rising nominal interest rates as well.

This empirical relationship between nominal interest rates and inflation is shown in Figure 13.2. The figure plots annual data for the one-year government bond yield and the annual rate of inflation in the Consumer Price Index (CPI). The use of annual data serves two purposes. It simplifies the graph making it somewhat easier to discern the relationships of interest but, further, the use of annual data essentially removes the business cycle, a phenomenon that we

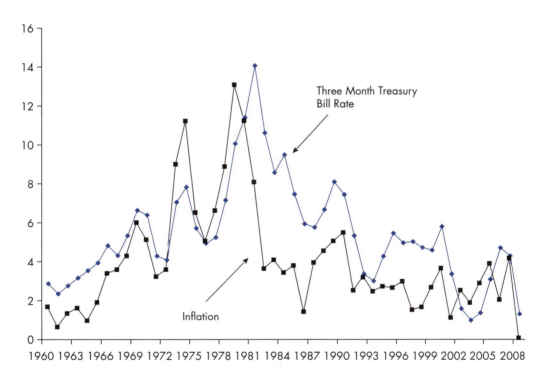

FIGURE 13.2 Inflation and the Three Month Treasury Bill Rate

Source: St. Louis Federal Reserve Bank FRED Database

---

4 Inflation can have real effects on the general equilibrium of an economy. This is discussed more fully later in the book but here we give just one reason why this might be the case. Inflation can increase marginal tax rates in the economy. If the tax code taxes nominal, rather than real, income as has been the case historically, then as incomes rise to keep pace with prices, households find themselves pushed into higher tax brackets with correspondingly higher marginal tax rates. These higher tax rates can distort the saving and labor supply decisions of households.

usually observe at monthly or quarterly data frequencies. The Fisher effect is not a cyclical relationship and so the use of annual data eliminates cyclical movements in the data, allowing us to focus on a long-run phenomenon. The figure shows a distinct positive correlation between the two series in the figure; a higher inflation rate is clearly associated with a higher nominal bond yield and so the data do provide some confirmation of the Fisher effect. But something else is evident in the figure.

Our discussion about the Fisher effect used a constant real interest rate as a device for providing the motivation for the Fisher relationship. But the real interest rate implied by Figure 13.2 is not constant as is evident from Figure 13.3. This figure shows that the real interest rate, derived by simply subtracting the inflation rate from the nominal bond yield, is not constant over time. It is positive and quite variable over most of the 1960–2001 time period in the figure and it is actually negative over a small number of years. You should be careful *not* to draw the conclusion from this figure that households and firms were actually expecting negative real interest rates. The real interest rate used by households and firms in their economic decision-making involves expectations of inflation and these expectations are not given in the figure. What the figure shows are real interest rates "after the fact" (sometimes called the ex post real interest rate) because inflation has been realized. But the actual rate of inflation need not be the same as the inflation rate expected by the public when their economic decisions are made.

You should also realize that the use of the New Classical model is not central to the analysis just completed. If we were to use any Keynesian style of model, we would still observe the same effects of anticipated inflation as we did in the New Classical model. For example, if wage agreements are being negotiated, all participants would recognize the inflation that is certain to occur and these wage bargains would incorporate this inflation rate into negotiated wage

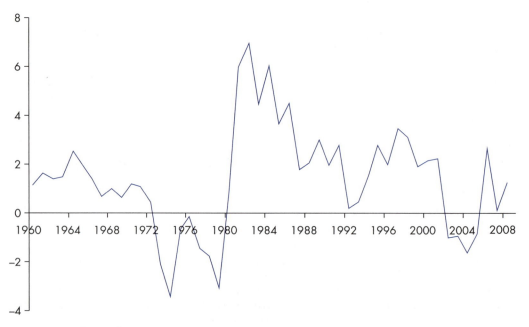

FIGURE 13.3 The Real Interest Rate

packages. Similarly pricing agreements between buyers and sellers would include this correctly anticipated inflation. Thus the economy would remain at a full equilibrium just as we showed in the New Classical model of the economy.

In future periods, aggregate demand and supply would continue to slide up along the LRAS line, increasing prices by the exact same percentage in each period. As long as these continuing shifts in aggregate demand are correctly anticipated, the economy remains at its full equilibrium level.

This analysis shows that the economy's real equilibrium is independent of the rate of inflation caused by continuing shifts in aggregate demand when that inflation is fully anticipated. The cyclical behavior of inflation requires that we examine the causes of unanticipated inflation, an issue that we now discuss.

Unanticipated Inflation

Unanticipated inflation occurs when there is an unexpected change in the aggregate demand curve, leading to a realized rate of inflation that differs from the inflation rate expected by the public. This is also illustrated in Figure 13.1 by the dotted line lying between the aggregate demand curves AD_0 and AD_1. This intermediate aggregate demand curve is one that was not anticipated by labor suppliers (as an example, there may have been some unexpected negative shock to aggregate demand in the economy) who were expecting that aggregate demand would be the one given by AD_1. As a result, their price expectations are now incorrect. The price level will be lower than the one they were anticipating (equivalently, the inflation rate is below the level they expected); real wages will therefore rise above their equilibrium level, reducing employment and output. The unemployment rate will be above its natural level (the unemployment not due to the business cycle). The economy has entered a recession because the inflation rate is below the level anticipated by the firms and households in the economy. Unanticipated inflation is therefore a phenomenon associated with an economy that is in disequilibrium. Inflation is **procyclical**, declining when output is below Potential GDP. You should be able to work out the case where the aggregate demand curve is above the level anticipated by the public, thus causing inflation above the level anticipated by the public. The economy will enter a boom with the unemployment rate below its natural level.

This completes our discussion of inflation in a model of the business cycle. We now discuss an empirical relationship involving inflation and its relation to unemployment.

13.2 THE PHILLIPS CURVE

Economist A. W. Phillips published empirical research in 1958 showing what appeared to be a stable relationship between money wage rates and unemployment for the U.K. economy.[5] Figure 13.4 is the original diagram, taken from Phillips' original article, showing the tradeoff

---

5 See "The Relation Between Unemployment and the Rate of Change of Money Wage Rates in the United Kingdom, 1861–1957," *Economica* 25, No. 100 (November 1958), pp. 283–99.

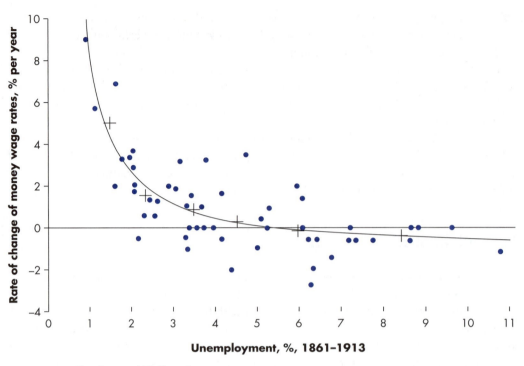

FIGURE 13.4 The Original Phillips Curve

between the growth rate of money wage rates and the unemployment rate in the U.K. There is a negative tradeoff evident in the data and the relationship arises over a substantial time period. Thus an economy with high (low) wage growth will have a low (high) unemployment rate.

Since economists tend to view wage rates as positively related to output prices, this evidence can be interpreted to mean that there is a negative tradeoff between inflation and the unemployment rate, with a higher inflation rate appearing to be associated with a lower unemployment rate. This appears to be the case in Figure 13.5. This figure provides a graph of annual U.S. data for the unemployment rate and the GDP deflator as the measure of the price level. A quick look at this figure shows how one might form the opinion that there is such a tradeoff that can be exploited. This empirical research showing the connection between the inflation rate and the unemployment rate was extremely influential in creating the professional opinion that policymakers, using their monetary and fiscal policy tools, could exploit a tradeoff between inflation and unemployment in line with their own preferences.

Figure 13.5 contains Phillips Curve data covering the period 1950–1965. With the exception of a few data points, the data seem to be clustered about a line with a negative slope (this tradeoff line has been drawn in the chart for convenience). Thus the data seem to confirm Phillips' analysis that there is a negative tradeoff between inflation and unemployment. It is fair to say that economic policy was dominated during the 1960s by the view that politicians, and the economists who advised them, could manipulate economic policy so as to pick whatever point along the curve was desired by elected leaders. But Figure 13.6, covering the period 1965 to 1980, reveals that this tradeoff, if there really was such a tradeoff, was not a very stable one.

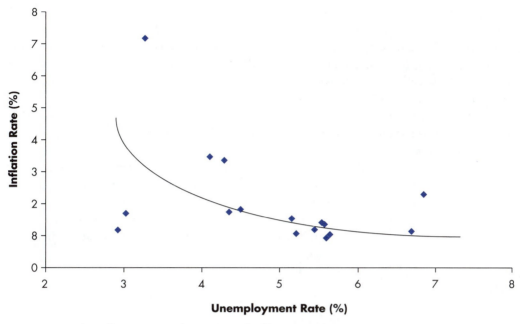

FIGURE 13.5 The Inflation–Unemployment Tradeoff, 1950–1965

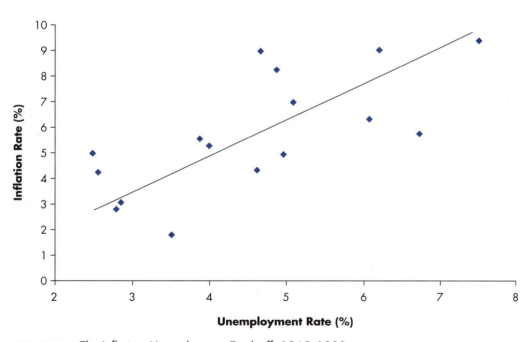

FIGURE 13.6 The Inflation–Unemployment Tradeoff, 1965–1980

This chart contains the same two data series but measured over a later time period, 1965 to 1980. The impression conveyed by this figure is remarkably different from that suggested by Figure 13.5. Now it appears that there is a positive tradeoff between inflation and unemployment (again a tradeoff line is drawn in the graph for convenience), with a higher rate of inflation apparently associated with a higher unemployment rate. How can this change in the Phillips Curve tradeoff be explained?

Economists Milton Friedman and Edmund Phelps provided an explanation, introducing what is now known as the **expectations-augmented Phillips Curve**.[6] Figure 13.7 displays this version of the Phillips Curve.

In the figure, U^N is the natural unemployment rate. You will recall from our discussion of labor markets in Chapter 8 that this magnitude is the sum of all types of unemployment that are not cyclical. That is, all of the job-searchers who make up this fraction of the labor force have not lost their jobs due to cyclical layoffs. The vertical line rising up from the natural unemployment rate is the long-run Phillips Curve. It implies that there is no tradeoff between

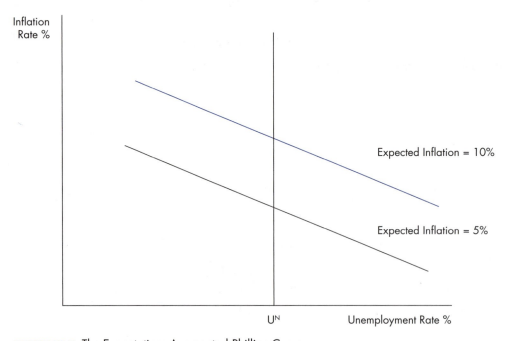

FIGURE 13.7 The Expectations-Augmented Phillips Curve

The natural unemployment rate is U^N and the vertical line above it is the long-run Phillips Curve. This line implies that there is no long-run tradeoff between inflation and unemployment when inflation is fully anticipated. There is a short-run Phillips Curve for each level of expected inflation and there is an inflation-unemployment tradeoff when inflation is unanticipated. The actual and expected rates of inflation are the same at the point where the long-run and short-run Phillips curves intersect.

---

6 See Milton Friedman, "The Role of Monetary Policy," *American Economic Review* 58, No. 2 (March 1968), pp. 1–17 and Edmund Phelps ed., *Microeconomic Foundations of Employment and Inflation Theory*, W. W. Norton and Company, New York (1970).

inflation and unemployment in the long run. But there are a series of short-run Phillips Curves, each one associated with a particular level of the expected rate of inflation. These short-run curves show that there is a tradeoff between inflation and unemployment, given the level of expected inflation. Thus the Friedman-Phelps explanation for the data in Figures 13.5 and 13.6 is that there is no stable tradeoff between inflation and unemployment because the tradeoff will shift over time as the public changes their expectations of inflation. To understand this modern form of the Phillips Curve, the crucial distinction that needs to be made is whether inflation is anticipated or unanticipated.

As we have stressed earlier in Chapter 12, one property of an economic equilibrium in an economy is that expectations are correct. Not surprisingly then, the long-run Phillips Curve corresponds to a situation where expectations of inflation are correct, meaning that inflation is fully anticipated by the public. An economy that is in disequilibrium is one where, among other things, expectations are incorrect. Here this means that inflation is unanticipated by the public. Thus the expectations-augmented Phillips Curve implies that an economy can be in equilibrium at the natural unemployment rate at any level of inflation as long as that inflation is fully anticipated by the public. If the rate of inflation differs from what is expected by the public, there is unanticipated inflation in the economy and the unemployment rate can differ from its natural rate. This disequilibrium is temporary as we have argued previously in Chapter 12 on the business cycle. But this Phillips Curve also has implications about the ability of policymakers to keep the unemployment rate below it natural rate.

Figure 13.8 illustrates what must happen to the inflation rate if policymakers attempt to keep the unemployment rate below the natural rate of unemployment. In the figure, the natural rate of unemployment is 6 percent and it is assumed in the figure that policymakers want to keep the actual unemployment rate at 4 percent. The expectations-augmented Phillips Curve implies that if policymakers try to carry out this policy, it will require increasing the rate of inflation to accomplish this objective. As the public comes to expect a higher level of inflation, shifting up the short-run Phillips Curve, it will take increasing inflation to keep the unemployment rate below 6 percent. Needless to say, this process will continue, with continually rising inflation required to keep the unemployment rate below its equilibrium level. Milton Friedman referred to this phenomenon as the **Accelerationist Hypothesis**; its definition is given below.

The Accelerationist Hypothesis

■ The expectations-augmented Phillips Curve implies that an attempt to keep the unemployment rate below its natural rate requires continual accelerating inflation.

It is important to realize that the Accelerationist Hypothesis implies that a policymaker must continually create unexpected inflation in order to achieve her policy objective of reducing the unemployment rate. If inflation is costly to society (we will discuss the costs of inflation when we discuss economic policy later in the next chapter of the book), then a policy of constantly creating unexpected inflation imposes costs on society and this fact raises questions about why it would be proper for a policymaker to behave in this way. We postpone additional discussion about this issue until we discuss economic policy but there is another aspect of the Accelerationist Hypothesis that deserves comment.

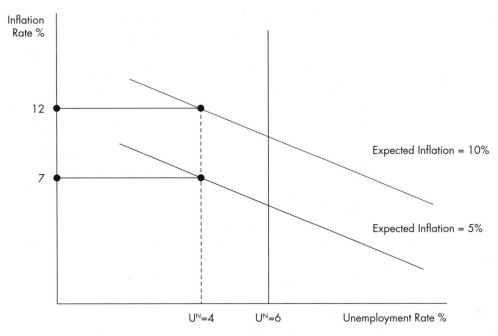

FIGURE 13.8 Keeping Unemployment Below the Natural Rate

The expectations-augmented Phillips Curve has the implication that attempts by policymakers to keep actual unemployment below the natural rate of unemployment will require accelerating the rate of inflation. In the figure, trying to keep unemployment at the rate of 4 percent, less than the natural rate of 6 percent, will require a rising inflation rate as the inflation expectations of the public rise.

The essence of the Accelerationist Hypothesis appears to be that the public can be systematically fooled by policymakers. This must be true in order for unemployment to be continually kept below the natural rate of unemployment; there must always be unanticipated inflation in the economy. But it seems reasonable to suppose that the public would eventually catch on to the policymaker's behavior because, as we have frequently argued, it is in the public's interest to forecast inflation accurately. In fact, it would seem very odd to economists if the public never learned of the policymakers' actions. If the public does indeed come to recognize the behavior of policymakers, there would be a change in the way that expectations are formed by the public, enabling them to adjust their inflation expectations to these systematic attempts at creating unanticipated inflation. This suggests that the Accelerationist Hypothesis can occur only because expectations are formed so as to permit the creation of continual unanticipated inflation.

These ideas indicate why economists have developed economic models where economic agents cannot be continually fooled. Later in this chapter we will discuss the idea of **rational expectations**, a way of forming expectations where the public cannot be systematically fooled about inflation or other economic magnitudes. Now we show how the expectations-augmented Phillips Curve arises using our familiar aggregate demand-aggregate supply framework.

13.3 THE PHILLIPS CURVE AND THE AD-AS MODEL

In this section you will learn how the Phillips Curve is related to the AD-AS model that we have used. You will see that the Phillips Curve is really implied by that model and it is completely consistent with it. This will be demonstrated using the New Classical model of the economy but the model of the economy that we use is not essential to our purposes. Before we carry out this graphical derivation, it is very useful to examine an equation for the expectations-augmented Phillips Curve, then comparing it to the Lucas supply curve that we have already used.

The modern version of the Phillips Curve can be written as

$$U = U^N - \lambda \cdot (\pi - \pi^e), \lambda > 0$$

where π (the Greek symbol pi) is the rate of price inflation, π^e is the expected rate of inflation, U is the unemployment rate, and U^N is the natural unemployment rate. The parameter λ (the Greek symbol lambda) is a parameter controlling how the gap between the actual and expected rate of inflation affects the unemployment rate. This parameter is positive implying that if inflation is below the level expected by the public, the unemployment rate will be above the natural rate (the economy is in a recession). If inflation is higher than expected, the economy is in a boom with the unemployment rate below the natural rate.

Now compare this equation to the Lucas supply function given below.

$$Y^s = Y^P + \gamma \cdot (P - P^e), \gamma > 0$$

As before, Y^s is output supply, Y^P is the level of Potential GDP, P is the price level, while P^e is the expected price level. The symbol γ (the Greek symbol gamma) controls how the price forecast error, $P - P^e$, affects the level of output supplied. Note that the supply schedule implies that if the price level is above (below) the level expected by the public, then output is above (below) its potential level. If the price level is higher (lower) than expected, the inflation rate is also above (below) the expected rate of inflation. If output is above its equilibrium level, the opposite is true of the unemployment rate; it will be below its equilibrium rate. If output is below its potential level, the unemployment rate is above its natural rate. This comparison should make clear that the expectations-augmented Phillips Curve is simply an alternative way to represent the implications of the Lucas supply function. With this comparison made, we can turn to a graphical derivation using the AD-AS framework. Figure 13.9 illustrates the salient details. We begin by showing how the long-run Phillips Curve corresponds to certain actions occurring in the AD-AS framework.

You may recall that we represented steady anticipated inflation as a situation where the AD and AS schedules simply slide up the vertical Potential GDP line, always intersecting at the level of Potential GDP. As you also know, associated with Potential GDP there is the natural unemployment rate in the top panel of Figure 13.9, denoted U^N. Now look at the bottom panel of Figure 13.9 and note that point A corresponds to point A in the top panel of the same figure. That corresponds to a rate of inflation given by the movement in prices between P_0 and P_1. If the inflation rate were higher than this level, we would have the AD and AS schedules intersect

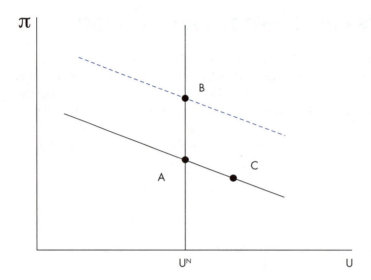

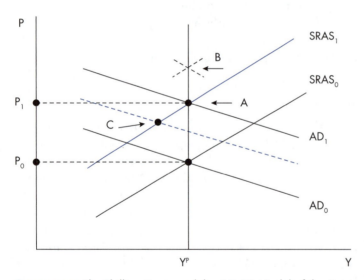

FIGURE 13.9 The Phillips Curve and the AD-AS Model of the Economy

The long-run Phillips Curve corresponds to a steadily shifting pair of AD and AS schedules that always intersect at Potential GDP. If there is an unexpected shift in AD, say it only shifts to the dotted line in the bottom panel rather than to AD_1, this unexpected shift corresponds to a move along a short-run Phillips Curve.

at a price level higher than P_1 and this would be the situation, in the bottom panel, where the two dotted lines intersect the LRAS schedule, denoted by point B. In the upper panel, this higher anticipated inflation scenario would correspond to point B where the dotted short-run Phillips Curve intersects the vertical long-run Phillips Curve. Thus the vertical long-run

Phillips Curve corresponds to a situation where the AD-AS schedules are continually shifting up and intersecting along the LRAS line.

As for the short-run disequilibrium situation, imagine that households and firms were expecting the shift in aggregate demand represented by the curves AD_0 and AD_1. However for unspecified reasons, the AD_1 curve does not arise (possibly the Fed decided to try to reduce the economy's rate of inflation) but rather the one represented by the dotted AD line occurs between AD_0 and AD_1. This means that the price level will not rise to P_1; rather the price level will rise by a smaller amount and the economy enters a recession. The temporary equilibrium for the economy is given by point C and this point corresponds to point C in the upper panel of the figure. Finally the economy could be in a recession if inflation declines from any amount, meaning that we could move along any short-run Phillips curve temporarily.

This discussion makes it clear that there is a very close correspondence between the expectations-augmented Phillips Curve and our workhorse AD-AS framework. As the discussion above made clear at several points, much of what we say about the short-run Phillips Curve depends importantly upon the manner in which expectations are formed. What we take up now is the study of how an economy behaves under alternative expectation formation schemes that may be used by the public.

13.4 EXPECTATION FORMATION

The characteristics of any economic model of the business cycle depend in a crucial way upon the manner in which economic agents form their expectations about the magnitudes that affect their welfare. In this section, we illustrate this fact by discussing two forms of expectation formation, showing that they have radically different implications about the affects of shifts in aggregate demand upon the level of output. These forecasting schemes are polar opposites; one is simple and easy to carry out and the other is a far more complex way of forming expectations. Economists do not know for certain how expectations are formed by the public but these two cases provide the boundaries of how the public can behave and thus these are useful benchmark cases for study. We begin with the simpler case: backward-looking expectations.

Backward-Looking Expectations

Economic systems are complex and in such an environment, it is reasonable to suspect that households and firms would use rules-of-thumb to form expectations about economic magnitudes affecting their welfare. We might argue that, because it is not possible for economic agents to really know the process determining the economic variables that they need to forecast, experience is likely to lead them to use an expectation formation scheme that is simple yet accurate at least some of the time. Here is a very simple rule-of-thumb for forecasting the price level that is consistent with these notions.

$$P^e = P_{-1}$$

Here P^e denotes the expected price level and P_{-1} is the price level last period. This expectation formation scheme is backward-looking; the individual forming an expectation of the price level always assumes that the expected price level will be what it was last period.[7] This mechanism has the virtue of simplicity but it also has several troubling implications; economic agents forming expectations in this way will always be fooled by aggregate demand shocks (this will be shown below) and the public is ignoring many informative types of economic data that might be useful in forecasting the price level. For example, the public could use data on the money stock to help them in their forecasting since data on the money stock are readily available from the Fed and yet they are not using this data. Why they would ignore so much relevant data? Figure 13.10 illustrates the role of backward-looking expectations in a New Classical model of the economy.

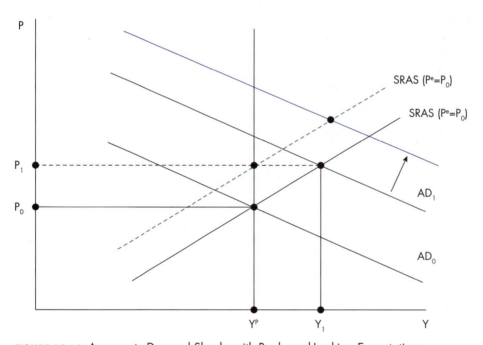

FIGURE 13.10 Aggregate Demand Shocks with Backward-Looking Expectations

An aggregate demand shock shifts the AD schedule from AD_0 to AD_1. Labor suppliers expect the price level to be P_0 and so output departs from Y^P because labor suppliers are fooled by the aggregate demand shock. Next period, having learned that the price level rose to P_1, labor suppliers now expect P_1 to be the price level, shifting SRAS to the dotted SRAS line but, if there any further shocks to AD such as one shifting AD to the dotted AD line in the figure, labor suppliers will be fooled again about the price level.

---

7 This is actually a special case of a forecasting mechanism known as adaptive expectations. In that mechanism, economic agents form expectations by using sums of lagged values of variables with declining weights. So to forecast the price level, one would use an infinite sum of lagged values of the price level. If the weights in this sum decline, more recent lagged values of the price level have a bigger impact upon expectations than lagged prices from the distant past. For simplicity, we only use one lagged value of the price level in our discussion here.

The figure shows an economy that is initially in equilibrium at Potential GDP. A shock to aggregate demand occurs, shifting out the AD schedule. Labor suppliers continue to expect the price level to be at its initial level, P_0. As a result, the shock to aggregate demand sets off an excess demand for goods, the price level rises, and output rises above its potential level (the economy enters a boom period). Labor suppliers have been fooled about the price level and, as a result, they work more than they should because they incorrectly believe that the real wage has risen. They see money wages rise but do not realize that prices have risen. But this situation will not persist indefinitely.

Sooner or later, the public will come to realize that the price level has risen and they will adjust their expectations using the backward-looking process we discussed above. They will now expect the price level to be P_1, shifting the SRAS schedule accordingly. But a consequence of backward-looking expectations is that labor suppliers will always be one step behind a shock to aggregate demand. If there is a further shift in aggregate demand, as illustrated by the dotted AD line in Figure 13.10, labor suppliers will be wrong again about the price level; the actual price level will not be P_1 but it will be at some higher level. The implication of this exercise is that labor suppliers will always be fooled by shocks to aggregate demand because these shocks will always be unanticipated by the public.

This analysis makes clear that the Accelerationist Hypothesis that we discussed above requires an expectation scheme of this sort to permit a policymaker to try to systematically fool the public. This implication is a troubling one to economists for the following reason. Since households and firms have incentives to have correct expectations because their welfare is at stake, it is hard to believe that they would permit themselves to continually be fooled by shocks to aggregate demand. We would expect the public to exhibit some sort of learning that might improve their forecasting accuracy about shocks to aggregate demand.

We now discuss a form of expectation formation that results when such learning has occurred. As you will see, this type of expectation requires that the public process a very large amount of information in order to carry out their forecasting.

Rational Expectations

Households and firms have strong incentives to form correct expectations about the economic magnitudes that affect their welfare. Our discussion in Chapter 5 about the investment decisions of firms showed that the decision to add capital goods involves forecasts of the price level, among other variables, into the future. If firms incorrectly forecast the price level, they may find that the acquisition of new capital actually lowers, rather than raises, profits. Similarly our discussion in Chapter 8 showed that labor suppliers would make incorrect labor supply decisions if they make forecast errors regarding the real wage rate, supplying more or less labor supply than is utility-maximizing. Since economists tend to think of all economic actors as pursuing optimal behavior, it is natural to think that firms and households will adopt forecasting mechanisms that have some optimality properties since, to do otherwise, will lead to reduced profits and/or welfare. Rational expectations are a way of optimally forecasting economic magnitudes that make economic sense when households and firms are pursuing utility and profit maximization. The definition of a rational expectation is given below.

Definition of Rational Expectations

■ A **rational expectation** of an economic magnitude is an expectation with the property that there are no systematic errors made in forecasting the economic variable of interest.

It is important to stress that we are *not* saying that the public is always right in making an economic forecast. We *are* saying that their errors are not systematic. An example may serve to clarify this definition.

Suppose that a firm is interested in forming an expectation of the level of the money supply because the managers of the firm believe that the money supply will have an impact upon the demand for the goods produced by the firm (the managers of this firm have taken the intermediate macroeconomics course in which you are now enrolled!). The firm has economists on staff who have used statistical methods showing that the policy rule used by the Federal Reserve is well-represented by the following expression.

$$\text{Monetary Policy Rule: } m^s = m_0 - m_1 \cdot [\pi_{-1} - \pi^T] + \varepsilon$$

In this expression, m^s refers to the money supply, π is the rate of inflation, π^T is the target inflation rate chosen by the Fed, and the parameters m_0 and m_1 tell us how the Fed sets the money stock in relation to the gap between the actual rate of inflation and its target. Suppose that both of these parameters are positive ($m_0 >$ and $m_1 > 0$). Apart from the last term in the equation (to be described shortly), this policy rule states that the Fed will set the money stock at a constant level m_0 if last period's inflation rate, π_{-1}, was equal to its target level, π^T. If the inflation rate last period exceeded the target, the money stock will be reduced below m_0. If the inflation rate last period was less than the target, the money stock will be increased above m_0. The target inflation rate chosen by the central bank may even be publicly announced by the Fed. This is not an unreasonable way to imagine that monetary policy is set (although it is quite simple) and it has been argued by some economists that the Fed should adopt a rule similar to this one, announced openly to the public. Rules of this type have received a great deal of attention in discussions of how actual monetary policy should be conducted (see Chapter 14 for further discussion about policy rules).

Now consider the last term in the expression, ε (the Greek symbol epsilon). This is meant to capture the control errors that the Fed will have in hitting money stock targets. There are random shocks that hit financial markets often enough that it is reasonable to expect that the Fed would not be able to hit any money stock target exactly. Assume that this magnitude is completely unpredictable; this means that it cannot be predicted by anyone in advance of its realization (the actual value that it takes). Further, assume that, on average, it takes the value zero but its realized value in any period may not be zero, being either positive or negative.[8] If the firm wants to form a rational expectation of the money stock, how should it do so? The firm cannot forecast the control error, ε, and so can only ignore it (equivalently, it will assume that it takes its average value of zero). But the remaining elements of the policy rule are the systematic parts of monetary policy and the firm must use these parts to avoid systematic errors

---

8 For those familiar with statistical concepts, we are assuming that the control error is a random variable with a mean (average) or expected value of zero.

in predicting the money supply. This leads us to the following conclusion. Since a rational expectation of the money supply is one where there are no systematic errors, the firm must use

$$m_0 - m_1 \cdot [\pi_{-1} - \pi^T]$$

as its rational expectation of the supply of money. This systematic part of the money stock has been termed **expected money** in economic research on rational expectations. The remaining part of the policy rule, ε, is known as **unexpected money**. The expected money supply is that portion of the policy rule that is predictable and therefore known to the public if they are to avoid systematic errors in forecasting the level of the money supply. It is important to recognize how strong a statement we are making about what the public knows about the Fed's policy actions.

We are assuming that the public knows that the Fed has an inflation target and that the public knows its value. The public also knows how the money supply will deviate from its equilibrium value if inflation is not at the target level set by the Fed. This means that the public knows the parameter m_1. Finally, the public knows the value of the money stock that the Fed will set if the inflation target is hit exactly, m_0. The public thus has an extraordinary level of knowledge about the Fed's policy behavior. It certainly seems unlikely that the public actually knows the policy rule in use at the Fed even if there is one in use; at least in the U.S., the central bank has never announced any explicit policy rule of the sort we are discussing, preferring instead to look at many things, including inflation, in choosing how to set the money supply.[9]

The **unexpected money supply,** ε, is the component of the monetary policy rule that cannot be predicted by the public or even controlled by the Fed. The best that the public can do is to assume that this component of the money stock will be at its average value that we assume to be zero. An implication of rational expectations, and one that has been very controversial among economists, is that only unexpected money can affect real magnitudes in the economy. This characteristic is known as the **Policy Ineffectiveness Proposition** and a statement of this proposition is given below.

The Policy Ineffectiveness Proposition

■ In a New Classical model of the aggregate economy, only the unanticipated portion of the money supply will have an impact upon the real economic magnitudes in an economy where the public has rational expectations.

This proposition has been demonstrated in the context of the New Classical model although, in principle, it could arise in other models of the economy. We now discuss this proposition in the AD-AS framework.

Figure 13.11 illustrates the implications of rational expectations and the theory of economic policy. Suppose for simplicity that the supply-side is known to all members of the public and

---

9 One debate in the area of economic policy concerns the choice of rules rather than discretion in economic policy. Advocates of rules believe that a central bank should be required to announce a policy rule like the one we are discussing here. Others believe that these rules would be too confining and that a central bank should look at more economic data than just an inflation target. We will take this up later in the book in Chapter 14 on economic policy.

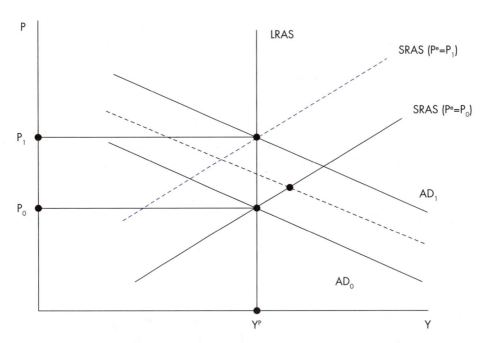

FIGURE 13.11 Predictable Aggregate Demand Shocks with Rational Expectations

A predictable aggregate demand shock shifts the AD schedule from AD_0 to AD_1. The public recognizes this shift in aggregate demand and raises its price expectations at the same instant that the AD shock occurs. The result is that the economy remains at Potential GDP. An unanticipated shock to AD causes the AD schedule to shift to the dotted line, causing an economic boom. Output will rise above Potential GDP.

that it is not subject to shocks of any kind (although we know this is not true). The figure illustrates what will happen if there is any systematic (predictable) shock to aggregate demand from any source, given by the shift of the aggregate demand schedule from AD_0 to AD_1. The public's expectations about the price level will shift coincidently with the shock to the AD schedule such that there will be no departure of the economy from Potential GDP. Only the price level and other nominal magnitudes respond to a predictable shock to aggregate demand. All real variables remain unchanged.

In contrast, suppose there is an unanticipated shock to the AD schedule, such as the one represented in Figure 13.11 by the dotted AD line between the AD_0 and AD_1 curves. This change to the AD schedule cannot be anticipated by the public and so the economy will enter a temporary boom with output rising above its potential level. Only unanticipated shocks to aggregate demand have real effects. So if the unpredictable shock to aggregate demand is unanticipated money, then the shift in the AD curve will not be anticipated by the public and the shock will affect output and other real magnitudes in the economy.

In fact, if the public is to form a rational expectation of the price level, they must know much more than just the systematic part of the central bank's policy rule. They must know all of the systematic determinants of the price level (that is the only economic variable that they must forecast in our New Classical model) which means knowing far more than the systematic shocks to aggregate demand. The public must know all of the systematic components of aggregate supply and demand in so far as they have any predictive ability for the price level. The Appendix shows just how much knowledge the public must have to avoid systematic forecast errors about the price level. This is why some economists are skeptical about rational expectations since it implies such extreme informational requirements.[10] It is hard to believe that the public has as much knowledge about the structure of the economy as they would need to have in order to avoid systematic errors in forecasting various economic magnitudes. Empirical evidence on rational expectations is mixed so the empirical record is unclear as to whether or not the public has rational expectations (see **Doing Economics**: The Livingston Price Expectations Survey).[11] Nonetheless, this expectation mechanism has its appeal to economists if only because utility-maximizing individuals should wish to form expectations in this manner.

Before leaving this topic, it is important to stress that rational expectations does not necessarily prevent the money stock from having a role in stabilizing output in certain types of economic models. For example, in Keynesian models where nominal wage contracts are set for more than one period, money can have real output effects.[12] And even in a New Classical style model, money can have output effects if the central bank has more information than the public about the economic shocks hitting the economy.[13] We discuss these issues further when we discuss monetary policy later in the book.

The Lucas Critique

Another important insight to emerge from the rational expectations literature is the **Lucas Critique**. Robert E. Lucas is a Nobel laureate at the University of Chicago who stated this proposition.[14] This idea has been extremely influential because it suggests that there are very few parameters in an economy that are truly fixed. This can be illustrated in the following way.

Suppose that the Fed is using the policy rule that we discussed above, reproduced here for convenience.

$$\text{Monetary Policy Rule: } m^s = m_0 - m_1 \cdot [\pi_{-1} - \pi^T] + \varepsilon$$

---

10 See, for example, Benjamin M. Friedman, "Optimal Expectations and the Extreme Information Assumptions of 'Rational Expectations' Macromodels," *Journal of Monetary Economics* 5, No. 1 (January 1979), pp. 23–41.

11 See Frederic Mishkin, *A Rational Expectations Approach to Macroeconometrics*, University of Chicago Press (for the NBER), Chicago (1983).

12 See Stanley Fischer, "Long-Term Contracts, Rational Expectations, and the Optimal Money Supply Rule," *Journal of Political Economy* 85, No. 1 (February 1977), pp. 191–205.

13 See Robert J. Barro, "Rational Expectations and the Role of Monetary Policy," *Journal of Monetary Economics* 2, No. 1 (January 1976), pp. 1–32.

14 See "Econometric Policy Evaluation: A Critique," in *Studies in Business Cycle Theory*, MIT Press, Cambridge (1982), pp. 104–30.

Doing Economics: The Livingston Price Expectations Survey

The research on rational expectations made it very clear to economists that knowledge of how expectations are formed by the public was important in determining whether rational expectations models were good descriptions of actual economies. This caused economists to search for some evidence on how expectations were actually formed by the public.

One such source of public forecasts was a survey done by Joseph Livingston, a newspaper columnist who regularly queried professional economists regarding their expectations about inflation and other economic magnitudes. This survey provided a rich source of data on an actual measure of inflation expectations and so this data was studied extensively by economists to see if it implied that inflation forecasts were rational.

This research found that inflation expectations were not fully rational because relevant information was not used efficiently by inflation forecasters. Specifically, inflation forecast errors were statistically related to money growth, information that was available to the forecasters in formulating inflation forecasts. Money growth should have been built into inflation forecasts but appeared to be ignored by inflation forecasters.

References: "What do Economists Know? An Empirical Study of Experts' Expectations," by Bryan W. Brown and Shlomo Maital, *Econometrica* 49, No. 2 (March 1981), pp. 491–504 and "The Livingston Survey: Still Useful After All These Years," by Dean Croushore, *Business Review*, Federal Reserve Bank of Philadelphia (March/April 1997), pp. 1–12.

This rule states that the Fed targets inflation only and pays no attention to other potential targets such as real output. Now suppose that the Fed decides to begin targeting output as well as inflation, changing its policy rule to the expression below.

$$\text{New Monetary Policy Rule: } m^s = m_0 - m_1 \cdot [\pi_{-1} - \pi^T] - m_2 \cdot [Y_{-1} - Y^P] + \varepsilon$$

Now if output was above Potential GDP last period, the money supply will decline (we assume that $m_2 > 0$) all else the same. Now we wish to ask the following question. When the Fed changes its policy rule from one only targeting inflation (where $m_2 = 0$) to one targeting both inflation and output ($m_2 \neq 0$), can we predict how this change in the policy rule will affect the economy? Lucas suggested that the answer to this question is almost certainly no; we cannot predict the effects of this change in the policy rule. His reasoning was as follows.

Economic agents make their decisions in response to the incentives that they face and in response to the economic policies of the Fed and the government. The decision rules that they use, say for the demands for goods or factor inputs in production, are derived by the public for given policy rules used by the central bank and the government. When those policy rules change, it is reasonable to expect that the public will form new decision rules needed to pursue their objectives (welfare and profit maximization) appropriate to the new policy rules now in force (see **Doing Economics**: The 1979 Policy Change by the Fed). In order to predict the economic effects of the new Fed policy rule, it would be necessary to know how the decision rules of the public will change and this is almost impossible to know. This implication of the actions of optimizing economic agents is sometimes called the **Policy Invariance Principle**. We can summarize this idea in the following way.

Proposition: The Policy Invariance Principle or Lucas Critique

- The decisions rules obeyed by households and firms will contain parameters that are functions of (or depend upon) the parameters of the policy rules used by policymakers.
- To predict the effects of a change in a policy rule requires that we know the relationship between the parameters in the decision rules used by the public and the parameters of policy rules used by policymakers.

Lucas was led to develop this critique of economic policy evaluation after thinking about the "spectacular" failures of economic forecasters to predict the inflation that emerged in the 1970s. No professional forecaster foresaw the U.S. inflation in the 1970s and this is the explanation devised by Lucas to rationalize this inability to foresee this extraordinary inflation.

The news media regularly contain forecasts by professional economists. Inflation and the effects of Federal Reserve monetary policies, among other things, are items that are regularly forecasted. The point of the Lucas Critique is that it is prudent to pay little attention to these predictions because economists have little knowledge of the relationships between the parameters of policy rules and the parameters of the decision rules used by the public.

You might be wondering if there any parameters in an economy that are really invariant to changes in the parameters of policy rules. Economists have identified two groups of parameters that are immune to the effects of changes in policy rules. Those would be parameters associated with the tastes (utility functions) of households and the parameters of the technologies used by firms to produce output.[15]

Doing Economics: The 1979 Policy Change by the Fed

In October 1979, Paul Volcker was the Chairman of the Federal Reserve Board. He and his colleagues changed the way in which monetary policy was conducted, a well-known example of a change in the policy rule (sometimes called a regime change) used by the Fed. The reason, as you will see, was to get the money stock under control.

The Fed had been using a policy rule of pegging the Federal Funds interest rate in a very narrow band and then decided to increase the range over which the Federal Funds rate could vary. The money market diagram below illustrates this change in policy rule when there are unpredictable disturbances to money demand given by the dotted lines in the diagram.

(continued)

---

15 It may be that even the second parameter group, those associated with technology, are not immune to government policies. The government gives tax incentives to firms to carry out research and development and to the extent that these tax incentives lead to improvements in technology, even the technologies of firms are affected by the policy rules of the government.

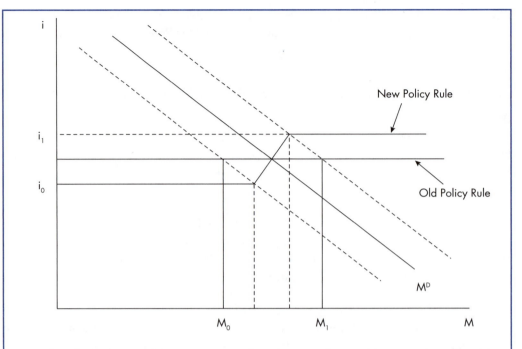

When the Fed pegged the interest rate, the money stock varied between the values M_0 and M_1. By allowing the interest rate to vary over the wider range, i_0 to i_1, the money stock would vary over a smaller range, given by the dotted vertical lines between M_0 and M_1. Thus the effect of widening the range over which the Federal Funds rate could vary was to prevent the money stock from fluctuating as much as it would when the interest rate was held fixed by the Fed.

There was an additional reason for the policy change. The Chairman of the Fed regularly would testify before a congressional committee and the chairman would report money stock targets during this testimony. The Fed frequently would not hit its money stock targets and so part of the reason for the policy change was to enable the Fed to hit the money stock targets that it would report to Congress.

13.4 CONCLUDING REMARKS

Inflation has been a persistent feature of aggregate economies and one objective of this chapter has been to draw out the origins of inflation. Our analysis revealed that inflation is a monetary phenomenon, illustrated by a continuing increase in the money stock, causing persistent shifts in aggregate demand.

Policymakers thought at one time that they could choose a particular combination of unemployment and inflation in a manner consistent with their own preferences. This tradeoff was known as the Phillips Curve, named after the economist who first established this empirical relationship. This apparent tradeoff disappeared in the 1970s and beyond, prompting a search for an explanation of why the Phillips Curve had changed.

The solution that was found added inflation expectations to the Phillips Curve and this new version showed that there was an inflation–unemployment tradeoff for a given level of inflation expectations. Once those expectations change, so too will the curve reflecting the tradeoff between inflation and unemployment. This new version, called the expectations-augmented Phillips Curve, can be derived from the AD-AS framework that we have developed for the analysis of the business cycle.

That framework showed how crucial expectation formation is to the appearance of a Phillips Curve tradeoff. If the public uses a simple rule-of-thumb in forming expectations, one where they only use a past price level as their expectation, then it is possible for a policymaker to systematically fool the public about inflation and, as a result, keep the unemployment rate below the natural rate. If the public does not make systematic errors in forming expectations, an idea called rational expectations, systematic elements of monetary policy no longer have any real effects on the economy. If the public does form expectations in this way, any time there is a change in the policy rule used by the central bank, households and firms will reformulate their optimal decision rules, making it virtually impossible to predict the economic effects of a policy rule change.

This chapter has introduced you to some of the issues that arise in connection with economic policy. The next chapter continues the analysis of economic policy in more detail.

Key Ideas

- Inflation is the continuing increase in the level of all prices in the economy.
- Inflation is caused by continual rightward shifts in aggregate demand, causing continual increases in the expected price level.
- Data prior to 1965 gave the appearance that there was a negative tradeoff between inflation and unemployment.
- Data subsequent to 1965 showed a very different tradeoff between inflation and unemployment, leading to the development of the expectations-augmented Phillips Curve.
- The modern Phillips Curve shows that there is an inflation–unemployment tradeoff for a given rate of expected inflation. At a higher level of expected inflation, a given unemployment rate will be associated with a higher rate of inflation.
- Depending upon how the public forms expectations, it may be possible for a policymaker to try to continually keep the unemployment rate below the natural rate of unemployment, an idea known as the Accelerationist Hypothesis.
- If the public has rational expectations, they do not make systematic errors in forecasting economic variables affecting their welfare.
- When the public uses rational expectations, the central bank cannot systematically affect any real variables in the economy. Only the unpredictable component of policy has real effects.
- If the public does use rational expectations, any change in a policy rule will cause households and firms to reformulate their optimal decision rules, making it difficult to predict the economic effects of a change in policy. This is known as the Lucas Critique of policy evaluation.

Key Terms

Phillips Curve

Expectations-Augmented
  Phillips Curve

Unexpected Money

Rational Expectations

Policy Ineffectiveness
  Proposition

Fisher Effect

Inflation-Unemployment
  Tradeoff

Unanticipated Inflation

Accelerationist
  Hypothesis

Policy Rule

Anticipated Inflation

Expected Money

Backward-Looking
  Expectations

Lucas Critique

Policy Invariance
  Proposition

Questions for Study and Review

Review Exercises

1. How does the original Phillips Curve differ from the modern version of the Phillips Curve?
2. How do economic agents form a rational expectation of an economic magnitude?
3. What must be true about the expectations of the public that would allow the Fed to keep the unemployment rate consistently below the natural rate of unemployment?
4. What is the Lucas Critique of policy evaluation?
5. What kind of monetary policy can affect real output in a New Classical model of the economy with rational expectations?
6. Use the AD-AS framework to explain how rising inflation can be associated with rising unemployment.
7. Use the AD-AS framework to explain how declining inflation can be associated with rising unemployment.

Thought Exercises

1. If there is a decline in the natural rate of unemployment due to, say, the changing demographics of the labor force, how does this affect the expectations-augmented Phillips Curve? How would this affect the Lucas Supply Curve?
2. If economic agents have rational expectations, what kind of monetary policy would exploit the short-run Phillips Curve tradeoff?
3. Explain how the natural rate of unemployment will be affected in each of the following scenarios.

   a) The government institutes a free employment service, posting job vacancies and registering and screening unemployed workers for their suitability to vacant jobs.

b) A technological breakthrough occurs where a new non-oil based fuel for automobiles is developed that is not only cheaper than gasoline but is friendlier to the environment.

c) The government launches job training programs to train unemployed workers.

Numerical Exercises

1. An economy has the following relationships. IS: $y = 100 - 1{,}000 \cdot i + g$, LM: $m - p = 200 + .5 \cdot y - 500 \cdot i$, AS: $y^s = 800 + .6 \cdot (P - P^e)$. *Definitions*: y = Output, i = Interest Rate (expected inflation is zero), P = Price Level, P^e = Expected Price Level, g = Government Spending, m = Money Supply.

   a) Derive the aggregate demand schedule for this economy.
   b) Derive the solution for the price level that agents must use to form a rational expectation of the price level.
   c) If $g = 150$ and $m = 1{,}000$, derive the value of the price level expected by rational economic agents. (Hint: When you use the price solution to form P^e, remember that the P^e appears on both sides of your price solution.)

2. The economy has the following Phillips Curve relationship: $\pi = \pi^e - 3 \cdot (U - U^N)$ where π is the inflation rate, π^e is the expected rate of inflation, U is the unemployment rate and U^N is the natural rate of unemployment, fixed at $U^N = .045$.

   a) Suppose that the central bank tries to keep the actual unemployment rate at .035. If inflation expectations rise from 5 to 10 percent, by how much must the actual inflation rate rise to keep the unemployment rate below the natural rate of unemployment?
   b) If inflation expectations are 5 percent, what will be the actual rate of inflation if the central bank causes the unemployment rate to rise to .055?
   c) Suppose that the economy has a 3-year rising inflation experience given by the following data: Year 1: $\pi = .08$ $\pi^e = .05$, Year 2: $\pi = .09$ $\pi^e = .07$, Year 3: $\pi = .10 = \pi^e$. Compute the actual unemployment rate in each period.

Data Exercises

Economagic (www.economagic.com) is an excellent source for macroeconomic data. Use this data source to answer each of the following questions.

1. The economist Arthur Okun served on the Council of Economic Advisors and suggested that there was a relationship between the percentage gap of real output from real Potential GDP and the gap between the unemployment rate and the natural unemployment rate. Find data on real GDP, Real Potential GDP, and the

actual and natural unemployment rates. Do a scatter plot using annual data for two decades of your choosing and observe the relationship between these two gaps during the 20-year period that you chose.

2. Do a scatter plot of annual inflation and the annual unemployment rate for the decade of the 1960s and the 1970s. Observe any differences in the relationship between these two decades. Then do a scatter plot, for the same two decades, of the inflation rate and the cyclical unemployment rate, observing any differences between the two decades.

For further questions, multiple choice quizzes, and weblinks related to this chapter, visit www.routledge.com/textbooks/rossana

References and Suggestions for Further Reading

Barro, R.J. (1976) "Rational Expectations and the Role of Monetary Policy," *Journal of Monetary Economics* 2 (1) (January): 1–32.

Brown, B.W. and Maital, S. (1981) "What do Economists Know? An Empirical Study of Experts' Expectations," *Econometrica*, 49 (2) (March): 491–504.

Croushore, D. (1997) "The Livingston Survey: Still Useful After All These Years," *Business Review*, Federal Reserve Bank of Philadelphia (March/April) 1–12.

Fischer, S. (1977) "Long-term Contracts, Rational Expectations, and the Optimal Money Supply Rule," *Journal of Political Economy* 85 (1) (February): 191–205.

Friedman, B.M. (1979) "Optimal Expectations and the Extreme Information Assumptions of 'Rational Expectations' Macromodels," *Journal of Monetary Economics* 5 (1) (January): 23–41.

Friedman, M. (1968) "The Role of Monetary Policy," *American Economic Review*, 58 (1) (March): 1–17.

Lucas, R.E. Jr. (1982) "Econometric Policy Evaluation: A Critique," in *Studies in Business Cycle Theory*, Cambridge, MA: MIT Press, pp. 104–30.

McCallum, B.T. (1980) "Rational Expectations and Macroeconomic Stabilization Policy: An Overview," *Journal of Money, Credit, and Banking* 12 (4) Part 2 (November): 716–46.

Microeconomic Foundations of Employment and Inflation Theory (1970) edited by Edmund S. Phelps, New York: W. W. Norton and Company.

Mishkin, Frederic F. (1983) *A Rational Expectations Approach to Macroeconometrics*, University of Chicago Press (for the NBER).

Phillips, A.W. (1958) "The Relation Between Unemployment and the Rate of Change of Money Wage Rates in the United Kingdom, 1861–1957," *Economica* 25 (100) (November): 283–99.

APPENDIX: FORMING A RATIONAL EXPECTATION

In this appendix, a linear macroeconomic model will be specified and it will be used to show how an economic agent would need to use the structure of the model to form a rational expectation of the price level.[16] This exercise should make clear just how much information the public would need to have if it were to form a rational expectation of the price level. We will also show that only unanticipated money has real effects. Begin by specifying the elements of a New Classical model of the economy in linear form.

$$\text{IS Curve: } y = a_0 - a_1 \cdot i + u$$

$$\text{Money Demand Schedule: } m^d - p = a_2 + a_3 \cdot y - a_4 \cdot i + v$$

$$\text{AS Curve: } y = a_5 + a_6 \cdot (p - p^e) + w$$

$$\text{Monetary Policy Rule: } m^s = m_0 + e$$

Definitions: y = Output, i = Nominal Interest Rate, p = Price Level, m = Money Stock, u, v,w,e = Unpredictable Shocks.

The IS schedule has been simplified by assuming that there is no ongoing inflation in the economy. All of the parameters, a_i $i = 1,\ldots,6$ in the equations above, are positive. Each equation should be familiar to you based upon your reading of earlier chapters where each part of this model was discussed at length. Each equation, including the monetary policy rule, has an unpredictable shock term included in it. To form a rational expectation of the price level requires the following steps.

First find the aggregate demand schedule by eliminating the nominal interest rate, i, from the IS and LM schedules while using the monetary policy rule. This operation gives

$$\frac{a_2 + a_3 \cdot y + v - (m_0 + e - p)}{a_4} = i = \frac{a_0 - y + u}{a_1}$$

Now do some algebra to derive the Aggregate Demand schedule given below.

$$y = b_0 + b_1 \cdot (m_0 - p) + x$$

$$b_0 = \frac{a_4 \cdot a_0 - a_1 \cdot a_2}{a_4 + a_1 \cdot a_3}, b_1 = \frac{a_1}{a_4 + a_1 \cdot a_3} > 0, x = \frac{a_4 \cdot u + a_1 \cdot (e - v)}{a_4 + a_1 \cdot a_3}$$

In the above AD schedule, x is a composite disturbance containing all of the shocks found on the aggregate demand side of the economy.

---

16 This derivation borrows from Bennett T. McCallum, "Rational Expectations and Macroeconomic Stabilization Policy: An Overview," *Journal of Money, Credit, and Banking* 12, No. 4 Part 2 (November 1980), pp. 716–46.

We now must obtain an expression listing all of the variables that determine the price level to be used by the public in forming a rational expectation. To do this, we assume that the price level is flexible, equating aggregate demand to aggregate supply. Set AD = AS and solve the resulting expression for the price level. These steps give

$$b_0 + b_1 \cdot (m_0 - p) + x = y = a_5 + a_6 \cdot (p - p^e) + w$$

$$p = \frac{b_0 + b_1 \cdot m_0 + x - a_5 + a_6 \cdot p^e - w}{a_6 + b_1}$$

where this last expression lists all of the economic magnitudes that determine the price level. These are: expected money (m_0), the expected price level (p^e), Potential GDP (a_5), and all of the shocks that affect AD and AS. This price solution is what the public must use to form a rational expectation of the price level.

Using this equation, we can compute the forecast error, $p - p^e$, which is a part of the aggregate supply schedule. This forecast error is given below.

$$p - p^e = \frac{x - w}{a_6 + b_1}, x = \frac{a_1 \cdot (e - v) + a_4 \cdot u}{a_1 \cdot a_3 + a_4}$$

Substitute this last expression into the aggregate supply schedule to get

$$y = a_5 + a_6 \cdot (p - p^e) + w$$

$$= a_5 + a_6 \cdot \left[\frac{x - w}{a_6 + b_1} \right] + w$$

which states that output is determined entirely by unpredictable random shocks. This illustrates the Policy Ineffectiveness Proposition stated earlier in the chapter because expected money, m_0, has no impact upon output.

Chapter 14

Macroeconomic Policy

LEARNING OBJECTIVES

This chapter examines the role of economic policy in the aggregate economy, beginning with a discussion of the policy goals that might be used by policymakers. We then take up issues about the implementation of policy and the effects of policies upon the economy, issues common to monetary and fiscal policy. We turn next to issues specific to either monetary or fiscal policy. Here are some of the questions we try to answer in this chapter.

- What goals should the government and central bank try to achieve?

- How long does it take for economic policies to affect the economy?

- Should policymakers follow explicit rules or should they use their discretion in setting economic policy?

- How does the policymaker's **credibility** affect the reaction of the economy to shifts in economic policy?

- Should the Fed peg the interest rate or the money stock in carrying out its policies?

- How does an income tax act as a stabilizing force in the economy?

- What kinds of tax cuts will change the spending decisions of economic agents?

The performance of a modern industrialized economy is importantly influenced by the macroeconomic policies pursued by the government and the central bank. In this chapter, we discuss issues related to the conduct of those policies.

Our first task will be to list the possible goals that policymakers might have. Some of these goals are related to the business cycle, when an economy may be in disequilibrium, but they may also apply to economic magnitudes when the economy is at Potential GDP. Having specified the possible goals of economic policy, the next objective is to discuss a series of issues related to how policies should be carried out to achieve these policy goals. This discussion will address the important issue of whether policymakers should commit themselves to explicit rules describing their goals and how they will achieve them. You will also see that policymakers will not be able to achieve their objectives if they ignore the fact that the public's behavior is forward-looking, depending upon the present and future economic policies that are implemented. We will also show how the effects of economic policy depend upon the credibility of policymakers, how **supply shocks** pose a difficult dilemma for policymakers, and how politics can influence economic policy.

Regarding monetary policy, we will examine the question of whether the Fed should peg the interest rate or the money stock if its goals are to keep the price level and output at their full-employment levels. It turns out that how the Fed should conduct policy depends on the sources of the shocks in the economy. We will also study examples of explicit rules for monetary policy, such as the **Taylor Rule**, which has been widely discussed as a method of carrying out monetary policy. We also discuss the long-run implications of monetary policy.

Regarding fiscal policy, we will show why it is that the tax code can act to stabilize the economy over the business cycle. We will discuss the issue of tax cuts and how their effects depend upon whether they are permanent or transitory in nature. Finally, coordinated monetary and fiscal policies will be examined, showing how a government deficit can be financed in part by printing money, and how money finance makes fiscal policy have a larger impact upon aggregate demand as compared to other financing methods. We will also discuss the long-run relationship between Potential GDP and the elements of fiscal policy.

When you have completed your study of this chapter, you should have a good understanding of the tools available to policymakers and how they may wish to use those tools. You should also have some appreciation of the power (and limitations) of economic policy to affect our economic affairs.

14.1 POLICY GOALS

In this section, we will be concerned with the possible policy goals that might be chosen by the government and the central bank. Policy goals are usually tied to unemployment and inflation but it is sometimes true that the exchange rate is a variable of concern to the central bank.

Unemployment

Policy prescriptions about reducing unemployment depend upon the kind of unemployment that is the topic of discussion. What we prescribe depends upon whether the natural rate of unemployment or **cyclical unemployment** is the magnitude that we wish to change. We discuss policies designed to reduce unemployment for each type of unemployment.

Reducing the Natural Rate of Unemployment

Our discussion of unemployment in Chapter 8 showed that the **natural unemployment rate** refers to the unemployment that occurs in the economy that is independent of the business cycle. This is related to the demographic characteristics of the individuals in the labor force (gender, race, age, education, and possibly other factors) and to the characteristics of labor markets. As such, this type of unemployment is not really within the domain of macroeconomics (it is more properly the concern of labor economics).

It is also important to remember that labor markets are designed to match workers with jobs in a world with incomplete information about job vacancies, as well as job and worker characteristics. It is in the interests of society to have good matches made in the labor market. Good matches take time to occur so some of the unemployment that occurs is beneficial in the sense that unemployment is something that goes on while the matching process is carried out. However we can mention some ideas that might reduce the natural rate of unemployment.

1. The acquisition of **human capital** (education) is subsidized in the economy through the spending and tax policies of government. One reason for this subsidy is that there is an externality associated with education; all of society is thought to benefit when individuals are educated and thus better able to make informed decisions as voters. A second reason is that a college education leads to substantially higher lifetime earnings for college graduates as compared to those who do not have a college education. Thus education is a way of enhancing the welfare of the citizens in society. But it is also true that college graduates have lower unemployment rates compared to those who have not completed college. Thus an increase in the fraction of the population with a college degree may lower the natural rate of unemployment.

2. **Unemployment compensation** programs can have the effect of raising the natural rate of unemployment if these programs replace too much of the income lost by laid-off workers. To take an extreme example, suppose that the replacement rate was one for one; that is, for every dollar of lost after-tax income, an unemployment compensation program paid out a dollar of after-tax income. A layoff thus involves no lost disposable income for the individual experiencing it and we would expect that this replacement rate would reduce the job search activities of a worker on layoff. Put differently, unemployment may be too attractive a state to make an individual look very hard to find a new job. Note that the crucial issue is not the existence of the program but how much lost income is replaced (the replacement rate). Replacement rates are not typically one for one but, the more generous the replacement rate, the higher is the unemployment rate in equilibrium.[1]

---

1 For some empirical evidence on this issue, see Martin S. Feldstein, "The Effect of Unemployment Insurance on Temporary Layoff Unemployment," *American Economic Review* 68, No. 5 (December 1978), pp. 834–46.

3. **Minimum wages** can cause an increase in the natural rate of unemployment. As we showed in Chapter 8, if the real wage is driven above its equilibrium value, there will be unemployment in excess of what would occur in labor market equilibrium. There is also considerable empirical evidence showing that the minimum wage causes unemployment. Thus one way to reduce the natural rate of unemployment would be to eliminate or reduce the minimum wage.

4. Equilibrium unemployment is partly a result of structural change in the economy. Technical progress can cause new firms to spring up and old ones to die off. Those unemployed as a result of the death of firms may have skills specific to the industry that is in decline and so may not have an easy time finding employment in alternative occupations. Thus worker retraining is often suggested as a government program to help unemployed workers find new careers using newly acquired skills. And so the government can subsidize training for workers who experience structural unemployment.

Reducing Cyclical Unemployment

Workers who are laid off during a recession suffer a loss of income that may or may not be reduced by unemployment compensation. Even if they do have access to a government program replacing lost income, these programs last for only a fixed period and so the longer they are unemployed, the closer they get to the time when they exhaust their benefits. Most economists agree that cyclical unemployment is largely involuntary, involving substantial welfare losses to those experiencing it. Income loss clearly reduces household welfare and, for this reason, many economists advocate policy interventions by the government and/or the central bank to reduce the length and severity of recessions.

While there is broad agreement among economists about the need for policies to combat a recession, there are disagreements among economists about how this policy should be carried out. This disagreement involves the choice between discretion in setting economic policy or the use of rules to combat recessions. We discuss this difference later in the chapter.

Inflation

Price stability is often given as a policy goal of central banks because inflation imposes costs on a society. However, the costs of inflation depend upon whether or not it is anticipated by the public. We discuss the costs of inflation appropriate for each type of inflation.

The Costs of Anticipated Inflation

An inflation that is anticipated is one that is recognized by the public and is correctly predicted by them in their economic affairs. An economy that does experience inflation in equilibrium will have costs imposed on its members of the following sort.

1. Anticipated inflation involves what are sometimes called **shoe-leather costs**. This refers to the increased transaction costs born by the members of an economy because inflation will cause them to hold less money. Holding a cash balance involves a loss of purchasing power

when all prices are consistently rising. If the inflation rate rises, people will hold less money. In the framework of the Baumol-Tobin model of money demand discussed in Chapter 7, people will make more "trips to the bank" to finance a given volume of goods that they plan to purchase. This increase in transactions costs imposes a welfare loss on the households in an economy.

2. When there is ongoing anticipated inflation, firms bear the resource costs of changing prices which we have called **menu costs**. This refers to the use of labor and capital that must be devoted to changing posted prices or, more generally, to building price increases into the sales and production process.

3. If tax payments are not indexed to the price level, tax rates can rise with inflation. We explained in Chapter 6 that when the tax code is progressive (meaning that tax rates rise with income) and when taxes are computed on nominal, as opposed to real, income, taxpayers can be pushed into higher tax brackets when their nominal incomes rise with prices. So even though a household cannot buy any more goods when its income rises by exactly the same percentage as prices, taxpayers can find themselves facing a higher marginal tax rate (MTR). As a result of a higher MTR, labor supply decisions can change; empirical evidence shows that a higher MTR will reduce labor supply and thus Potential GDP. In addition, households have a greater incentive to search for investments whose returns have favorable tax treatment. So the investment decisions of the public will change with a higher tax rate.[2] These investment choices may not be optimal for society as a whole because they are driven by tax considerations, not by the underlying profitability of the investment.

4. An extremely high inflation is called a **hyperinflation**. This type of inflation has not been observed in the U.S. and other industrialized economies but there have been countries in Latin America and in the German Weimar Republic during the 1920s where inflation rates at times were as high as 1,000 percent or more *per month*! Extreme inflation rates of this magnitude can cause enormous changes in an economy. For example, **payments periods** can change. People might be paid once every two weeks when inflation rates are at a moderate level. But when inflation is extremely high, workers may wish to be paid more frequently, even every day, so that they can buy goods before they rise in price. In the limit, an economy will no longer be **monetized** (use money in trade for goods) when there is extremely high inflation, reverting instead to **barter** which we know to be a very inefficient way of carrying out transactions. In such a situation, the costs of inflation are enormous.

The Costs of Unanticipated Inflation

1. The **rational expectations** literature emphasizes the idea that economic agents must decide if there are relative or absolute price changes occurring in the economy when they do not have complete information about the state of the economy. Thus imagine that a

---

2 For example, there are tax benefits associated with real estate so higher marginal tax rates could induce households to hold physical assets such as real property as opposed to bonds or other financial assets.

competitive firm observes an increasing price for its output. This could mean that all prices in the economy are rising or it could mean that its price is rising relative to all other prices in the economy. If its relative price is rising, the firm should produce more. If all prices are rising, the firm should not change its production level. Because there is **incomplete information** in an economy, the price increase observed by the firm is a **noisy signal**, meaning that the firm does not know whether relative or absolute price changes are occurring simply by observing the behavior of its own price. The firm is forced to make resource allocation decisions that could turn out to be wrong, implying that its profits could decline from what they would be if alternative decisions were made. Or the firm must devote resources to finding out whether absolute prices or relative prices are changing which also affects the firm's profits. Prices serve as signals about how firms and households should allocate resources and this function of prices is impaired when there is unanticipated inflation.

2. There can be institutional features of an economy that cause unanticipated inflation to impose real costs on a society. Suppose loan contracts cannot be written with adjustable nominal interest rates. This was the case in the U.S. for a considerable period of time for certain types of loan transactions. Then unanticipated inflation can cause serious problems for banks making fixed-rate loans while offering deposits that also have fixed rates. Suppose that a bank has made mortgages at a fixed nominal interest rate of 6 percent while paying its depositors a nominal interest rate of, say, 3 percent at a time when there was no ongoing inflation. Now imagine that the inflation rate rises unexpectedly to 4 percent per year. The bank's depositors will find themselves earning a negative real return on their deposits (they earn 3 percent on their deposits but the inflation rate is now 4 percent) and so they will search for assets yielding higher nominal returns. Our discussion of the Fisher Effect in the last chapter leads us to predict that nominal interest rates will rise in the economy. When depositors find assets with higher nominal interest rates, they will withdraw funds from their bank deposits, a phenomenon known as **disintermediation** in the banking sector. This loss of funds could ultimately result in the bankruptcy of individual banks; banks need deposits to acquire income-earning assets in order to earn profits. A bank would like to offer higher rates to its depositors to stem the deposit outflow that it is experiencing. But suppose that it cannot due to regulatory restrictions. It can't raise the rate on its mortgage loans because these are fixed. Thus there is a real possibility of bankruptcy facing a bank in this situation and bankruptcy damages the welfare of the households owning the bank in their role as stockholders. Therefore institutional features of the financial system, such as deposit rate restrictions, can cause financial instability and possible bank bankruptcy. In these circumstances, unanticipated inflation can have real effects in the banking sector by causing bank bankruptcies, reducing the ability of banks to serve as financial intermediaries. If the bank can raise the rate it pays on deposits, it will raise the rate that it pays depositors to stem the loss of funds that it will experience if interest rates rise elsewhere. But then the bank can find itself losing money if it pays more for deposits than it earns on its income-earning assets. Bankruptcy may result.

3. Related to the previous issue is the idea that there can be a redistribution of wealth between debtors and lenders when there is unanticipated inflation. If a bank is losing deposits and eventually is bankrupt, its stockholders lose their wealth held in the form of bank stock. Even if bankruptcy does not occur, a bank earning a negative real interest rate

causes its stockholders to lose welfare while debtors, borrowing at the negative real rate of interest, gain in welfare. Labor suppliers may discover that their real wage is lower than they expected it to be, resulting in reduced welfare. In all of these cases, there is an incentive for individuals and firms to forecast inflation to avoid welfare losses, thus requiring that resources (labor and capital) be devoted to forecasting inflation.

The Exchange Rate

You should recall from our discussion in Chapter 7 that central banks usually carry out their monetary policies by purchasing or selling government bonds. But they can trade in assets other than bonds. Central banks have periodically bought and sold foreign exchange, attempting to change the equilibrium exchange rate for their own and other currencies.

1. One reason for this policy is that, in a **flexible exchange rate** system, exchange rates can be volatile and this volatility has induced central banks to intervene in foreign exchange markets to try to reduce this apparent volatility. The concern about **exchange rate volatility** is based upon the idea that it can be damaging to international trade between countries. For example, exchange volatility could make firms reluctant to ship goods abroad because the revenue that they would earn could be reduced by exchange rate depreciation. This risk might reduce goods flows between countries. Or firms may build plants abroad, rather than ship finished goods abroad, because of exchange rate volatility. This reduces the international division of labor, reducing the gains from trade.[3] But the purchase or sale of foreign exchange by a central bank could affect a country's money supply and thus possibly inflation. And so a central bank that is intervening in the foreign exchange market must also ensure that these actions do not prevent it from achieving its inflation target.
2. Another reason that a central bank may buy or sell foreign exchange is that the central bank may be responsible for maintaining a **fixed exchange rate**. An exchange rate is a ratio expressing how much foreign currency can be obtained in a trade for domestic currency. The market can lead to volatile exchange rates when these rates are set in unfettered markets; it may be desirable for a country to adopt a fixed exchange rate, requiring the central bank to maintain a fixed rate of exchange. We will see below that this will require the central bank to pursue monetary policies consistent with the maintenance of a fixed exchange rate regime.

Now we address questions applying to both monetary and fiscal policy. These issues include how policies should be conducted and why policies might not achieve their objectives.

---

3 Trading between countries is beneficial to society for the same reason that it is beneficial for most of us to trade with farmers for food rather than growing our own food. We could grow our own food but find it in our interest to spend our time doing things other than growing food, buying food from farmers instead. Countries specialize in production just as individuals do. That specialization is welfare-improving for all parties; if this were not the case, voluntary trading would not occur.

14.2 ISSUES COMMON TO MONETARY AND FISCAL POLICY

There are a number of economic policy topics that are common to both monetary and fiscal policy. We first take up these issues and then move on to aspects of economic policy that are specific to monetary or fiscal policy.

Countercyclical Policy

One goal of either monetary or fiscal policies is to reduce the severity of, or eliminate, recessions that may occur. Note that the real business cycle literature treats changes in the level of output as consistent with optimizing behavior by households and firms. In such a framework, we could not claim that policies to raise output can be justified on welfare grounds simply because utility maximization occurs at all times in the RBC framework. If one subscribes to other forms of aggregate economic model, and there are many economists that do, then reductions in output can be associated with welfare losses; such welfare losses can then be used to justify countercyclical macroeconomic policies designed to combat recessions. Figure 14.1 illustrates the intent of these policies.

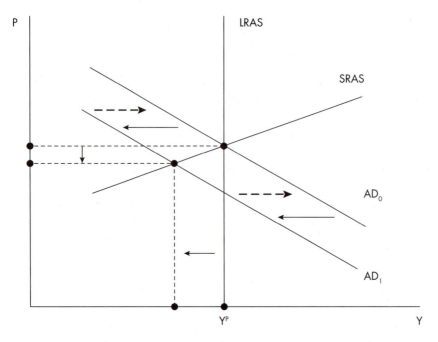

FIGURE 14.1 Combating a Recession with Discretionary Economic Policy

Initially let the economy be at the level of potential output, Y^P, with price level P_0. Suppose that the economy experiences a recession caused by an unexpected negative shock to the aggregate demand schedule. Proponents of discretionary economic policy would advocate the use of fiscal and monetary policy to move the AD schedule, shown by the dashed arrows, back towards its initial position, AD_0, so as to reduce or eliminate the recession.

We imagine that the economy has entered a recession for reasons unrelated to economic policy in a New Classical model of the economy. For example, there could have been an unexpected negative shock to consumer spending, causing a transitory leftward shift in the aggregate demand schedule. The economy enters a recession with price and output falling below their equilibrium levels. The unemployment rate has risen above the natural rate, employment has declined, and real wages have increased (price expectations are assumed fixed and so money wages rise after a leftward shift in the demand for labor). In the figure, the aggregate demand schedule has shifted from AD_0, its initial position, to AD_1, the AD schedule that arises after the unexpected shift in consumer spending.

The goal of policy is simple to describe. Monetary and/or fiscal policies will be set so as to shift the aggregate demand schedule from its recession level of AD_1 rightward towards the pre-recession level given by AD_0. If this can be accomplished, the effects of the negative shock to aggregate demand will be attenuated; the unemployment rate will decline and output will increase. Presumably, the policy variables that are changed, say government spending, tax rates, the money supply and so on, will return to their pre-recession values once the negative shock to consumer spending dissipates. The most recent recession provides some evidence consistent with this view because the U.S. and countries in the European Union carried out fiscal policies designed to moderate the most recent recession in world economies (see **Doing Economics**: 2009 Stimulus Packages).

Lags in Policy Effects

Implicit in the discussion above about countercyclical policy was the assumption that policy changes could be timed properly regarding their effects upon the economy. But it takes time for monetary and fiscal policies to take effect on the economic system. Economists have identified two types of lags in economic policy.

Inside lags refer to the time it takes, within a policymaking body, for policymakers to recognize the need for action and the time it takes to reach agreement about a policy change to carry out. **Outside** lags refer to the time it takes for an economic policy to affect the economy. For fiscal policy, it takes about six months for a change in tax rates and/or government spending to affect economic activity. For monetary policy, Milton Friedman established a six-month outside lag for monetary policy to affect real output and about two and a half years for monetary policy to affect inflation; he also argued that these lags were variable, making it difficult for policy to affect economic activity with the appropriate timing.

Doing Economics: 2009 Stimulus Packages

The U.S. and other industrialized countries passed economic stimulus packages designed to combat recessions ongoing in many countries during 2009. In the U.S., the recession began in December 2007 as determined by the NBER (National Bureau of Economic Research) in December 2008. The NBER chooses starting dates "after the fact" so the recession was well under way before it was officially determined that a peak in economic activity had occurred.

(continued)

President Obama signed the stimulus bill (the American Recovery and Reinvestment Act) in February 2009. Note the difference between the starting date of the recession (December 2007) and the date the bill was signed (February 2009). The difference between these dates (over one year) suggests the difficulty of timing fiscal policy to ameliorate a recession. Equivalently, the length of the inside lag is long enough to make it difficult to time fiscal policy appropriately.

Proponents of this package pointed to the spending contained in the bill, widely reported to be $787 billion, using standard Keynesian arguments to suggest that this spending would raise GDP although, as noted by the CBO (Congressional Budget Office), most of the spending would occur in 2010 and 2011. The size of the multiplier has an important impact on the ultimate increase in GDP arising from the stimulus package. Some economists suggested a multiplier value of 1.5, suggesting that the ultimate spending increase would be about $1.2 trillion.

Other economists expressed skepticism about simple Keynesian prescriptions for the effects of additional government spending. They argued that simple Keynesian analyses ignore the implied tax liabilities of the additional government spending. The government budget constraint states that the present value of spending and taxes must be equal so more spending today implies more taxes in the future. These economists argue that consumer spending will be reduced from what is assumed in Keynesian models due to these implied future tax liabilities, arguing that the multiplier for government spending is much less than unity.

Finally, transitory tax cuts were contained in the stimulus package. Our analysis in Chapter 4 showed that consumers would spend in relation to their **permanent income** and permanent income is not much affected by transitory tax cuts. Thus our theory of the consumer indicates that these transitory tax cuts will not have much impact upon consumer spending.

One undeniable aspect of the stimulus package is that it will increase the government deficit. The recession reduces tax receipts so the deficit will rise but, along with the stimulus package, the government deficit is expected by the CBO to reach 12 to 15 percent of GDP in 2009, a level never seen in the U.S. since World War II.

Rules Versus Discretion

Policy can be conducted using explicit **rules** to describe how policymakers will behave (see the discussion later in this chapter on the Taylor Rule). These rules can specify the goals of policy (price stability, reducing the severity of recessions, and so on) and how the policymakers will attempt to achieve their goals. Alternatively, policy can be carried out without any explicit rules describing the behavior of policymakers, behavior known as **discretion**. There has been a lengthy debate among economists about which of these two alternatives will lead to the best outcomes for the macroeconomic system.

Early proponents of rules were economists known as **monetarists** and the most prominent of these individuals was Milton Friedman. There were a number of policy positions associated with these economists and one of them was the belief that the Fed should follow a **k-percent**

rule regarding the growth rate of the money stock. This position implies that the Fed should allow the money stock to grow at a fixed percentage, irrespective of the state of the economy, and this growth rate should be designed to achieve approximate price stability. Thus these economists explicitly rejected the view that money should be used as a tool for stabilizing the economy. The reasons why these economists adopted this position have partly to do with the lags associated with economic policy.

Friedman believed that the **lags** between money, output, and prices were long and variable based upon his research on monetary economics and the central bank.[4] He documented the time it took for a change in the money supply to affect output and prices and found that these lags were not fixed in length and so, as a result, it was possible that monetary policy could actually be destabilizing. Thus a recession could be made more severe if the Fed could not implement its policies to take effect at just the right time. Generally it was Friedman's belief that economists simply did not know enough to use the money supply in just the right way to reduce economic fluctuations.

Further, economists were aware that a central bank may be subject to political pressure to accommodate political objectives. Thus a politician running for reelection may wish to see the central bank expand the money supply to create an economic boom as an aid to his/her reelection campaign (see the section below on the **Political Business Cycle**). The central bank might be pressured into expanding the money supply in the period preceding election campaigns.

Friedman was also acutely aware that the Fed had been a destabilizing force in the economy. His research with Anna J. Schwartz on the history of the U.S. central bank led him to conclude that Fed policy mistakes were the most important cause of the Great Depression. Thus if the Fed were prevented from engaging in business cycle stabilization, this would eliminate one major source of risk for the economy. If the Fed let the money stock grow at a constant rate, there would be little chance that the Fed would cause a severe recession or high inflation.

Finally, the rational expectations literature stresses the idea that the public will acquire information about the behavior of policymakers and use it to maximize their own economic welfare. It follows that when rules are used and publicly announced by policymakers, economic agents will be better able to maximize their own welfare. Thus many economists are generally in favor of rules that are simple and easily understood by the public.

But there are other economists who believe that monetary and fiscal policies can and should be used as stabilization tools. Keynesian economists favor economic models where nominal rigidities exist permitting the Fed and the government to pursue aggregate demand management. Since a rising unemployment rate clearly involves welfare losses to those losing their jobs in recessions, these economists regard it as the responsibility of the government to minimize the severity of recessions. These economists advocate active stabilization actions by policymakers to reduce the welfare losses to society of cyclical unemployment.

---

4 See *A Monetary History of the United States, 1867–1960*, Princeton University Press for the National Bureau of Economic Research (1963) by Milton Friedman and Anna J. Schwartz.

Time Inconsistency

Economists Finn E. Kydland and Edward C. Prescott[5] have suggested that economic policy will be inconsistent over time with the goals of policy. The reason for their position depends upon the manner in which, they believe, economic policy is carried out.

Kydland and Prescott argue that policymakers often conduct policy without taking account of the reactions of households and firms to the future policies that they will face. In their view, policy is set in the following way; policymakers consider their own preferences, the current state of the economy, and how that state is affected by current and past economic policies. They then carry out policies designed to achieve outcomes believed to be consistent with their policy preferences. But because no account is taken of how the public will react to future policies, the actual outcomes that occur will not be the ones that policymakers wish to achieve. They use a Phillips Curve example to illustrate their point.

Figure 14.2 is a diagram of the expectations-augmented Phillips Curve that we discussed in Chapter 13. Imagine that the economy is in full equilibrium with an inflation rate of 3 percent

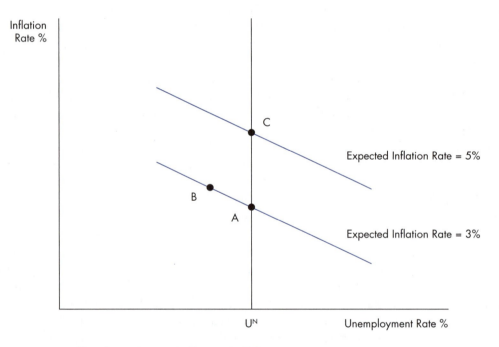

FIGURE 14.2 Time Inconsistency in Economic Policy

Let the economy be initially at the natural unemployment rate U^N with a fully anticipated inflation rate of 3 percent. When economic policy attempts to reduce unemployment and raise inflation, policymakers will expect the economy to move from point A to point B because they take no account of the reaction of the public to future policies. The economy will in fact move from A to point C. The policymaker achieves higher inflation without any offset in lower unemployment.

---

5 See Kydland, F.E. and Prescott, E.C. (1977) "Rules Rather Than Discretion: The Inconsistency of Optimal Plans," *Journal of Political Economy* 85 (3) (June): 473–92.

and an unemployment rate that is at the natural rate, U^N. Now suppose that there is a decision made to try to reduce the unemployment below the natural rate. The policymaker will expect the economy to move from point A to point B in the diagram because no account will be taken of how expectations will change as a response to future economic policy. What will in fact occur is a move from point A to point C. If the public has rational expectations, they will foresee the plans of the policymaker and adjust their expectations accordingly. Thus the policymaker only achieves higher inflation, which is undesirable, and does not accomplish the reduced unemployment that is presumably regarded as desirable. Over time, the policy outcome will be inconsistent with the preferences of the policymaker.

The argument above assumes that the public has rational expectations but Kydland and Prescott stress that this is inessential to their argument. All that matters is that the public take account, in some way, of the future actions planned by the policymaker.

For fiscal policy there is a similar situation that arises when the government tries to evaluate the effect of tax cuts upon the tax revenue it will get. Our discussion in Chapter 8 showed that changes in tax rates affect labor supply. If labor supply changes now and in the future, these changes will have an impact upon the tax revenues received by the government. Governments often do not take account of these dynamic labor supply effects when they try to evaluate the effects of future tax cuts on tax revenues and economic activity.

Credibility

The fact that economic agents form expectations about the future raises the issue of credibility in economic policy. There are a number of contexts where we have seen how future economic conditions affect current behavior.

Our discussion about the household in Chapter 4 showed that future income affects the current consumption choices of the public. Future income is affected by taxes and so the household will make its current consumption choices in part due to expectations about future taxes. The theory of investment in Chapter 5 revealed that the entire future path of wages and prices affects current investment decisions of the firm. Firms will make decisions in part on the user cost of capital and how it will be affected by corporate taxes now and in the future. Thus if the government were to implement a tax increase in the future, how the public reacts now depends upon the credibility of the government's tax policies.

When a government or the central bank announces policy objectives, the question then arises as to whether the public will treat these announcements as credible. There are examples of statements about policy goals by the government and central banks that were not ultimately pursued for various reasons. If the public observes policy statements that are not ultimately carried out, how will they react to future policy announcements? Will they believe them in the future or take a "wait and see attitude" regarding the policy? The answer has important implications for economic policy, as we now demonstrate.

Inflation need not be costly to eliminate if economic policy is credible. Thus an economy could have a **painless disinflation** if the Fed is credible when it announces a lower inflation target. Figure 14.3 illustrates how this occurs. We have a situation in the diagram where there is an ongoing anticipated inflation and the Fed has decided to reduce inflation and thus lowers its price level target, implying that an aggregate demand schedule will materialize that is not

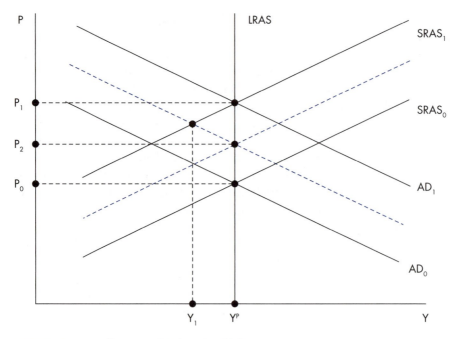

FIGURE 14.3 Disinflation and Policy Credibility

The economy is initially in full equilibrium at Potential GDP, Y^P, and with a fully anticipated inflation raising the price level from P_0 to P_1. The Fed announces that it wishes to reduce inflation, changing the AD schedule from AD_1 to the dotted AD line. If the policy is credible, the economy remains at Y^P with the price level P_2. If the policy is not credible, the economy enters a recession, with output falling to Y_1.

the one expected by the public. The announcement by the Fed informs the public about this new AD schedule. Will the public believe the announcement? Figure 14.3 shows what will happen when they do and when they do not.

If the public regards the policy announcement as credible, they will reduce their expectations of prices so that the SRAS schedule is the one that is dotted in the diagram. The result is that the economy remains at Potential GDP and disinflation is painless; there will be no recession as a result of the new Fed policy. If the public does not believe that the Fed will carry out its new policy, they will not adjust price expectations and the economy will enter a recession with output falling to the level Y_1. Now it requires a recession to convince the public that the Fed is serious about reducing inflation. Thus policy credibility has a crucial role in explaining the effects of economic policy.

As a final example, suppose that the government announces a tax cut in the future. Theory tells us that economic agents will change their behavior now in anticipation of this event but we were implicitly presuming that the government was credible. That is, there is always the possibility that the government will rescind the tax cut in the future; households and firms may not change their behavior if they believe their government is not fully committed to the tax cut.[6]

---

6 The U.S. federal estate tax is currently set to be phased out in the future. But the tax is now being debated in the Congress with members who want to eliminate it and others that wish to retain it. Thus households are unlikely to regard the phase-out as credible given ongoing debate in government.

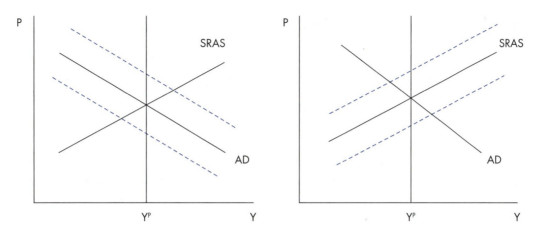

FIGURE 14.4 Price, Output, and Shocks to the AD and AS Schedules

A shock to the AD schedule moves price and output in the same direction. Thus any policy that reverses the shift in AD will achieve the goals of keeping the price level and output at their full-employment levels. A supply shock moves the price level and output in opposite directions, called stagflation. Any movement in the AD schedule as a policy response moves one variable closer to its target but that same movement will move the other variable farther away from its target, creating a dilemma for the policymaker.

The Dilemma of Supply Shocks

Supply shocks pose a dilemma for policymakers, a dilemma which does not arise when there are shocks to the aggregate demand schedule. To understand why this is so, consider Figure 14.4. The left panel illustrates the consequences for price and output of a shock to the AD schedule; the right panel does the same for a supply shock.

Notice that a shock to the AD schedule causes price and output to move in the same direction; a boom has price and output rising above their full-employment levels and a recession has them falling below their full-employment levels. If the goal of policy is to keep price and output at their full-employment levels, any monetary or fiscal policy that reverses the movement in the AD schedule allows the policymaker to hit the target levels for prices and output. There is no conflict between the goals of keeping the price level and output at full-employment levels.

A supply shock causes price and output to move in opposite directions. An adverse supply shock (a transitory shift up in the SRAS schedule) causes the price level to rise and output to fall. This situation is known as "**stagflation**." If nothing is done as a result of this supply shock, the outcomes for price and output are presumably undesirable for policymakers because the price level is rising and output is declining. But any policy designed to shift the AD schedule and reduce unemployment (or raise output) will cause a policy conflict. If there is a shift in AD to combat the recession, output may rise above its recession level but the price level will also rise. The effect on the price level is presumably inconsistent with the preferences of policymakers although the output increase may be desirable for them. A supply shock leads to policy choices whose desirability is unclear to economists and must be evaluated using the preferences of those in charge of economic policy, a preference ordering unknown to economists.

The Political Business Cycle

Economist William D. Nordhaus studied the extent to which economic policy was associated with the political objectives of politicians.[7] He suggested that there may be political motives that would induce politicians to exploit a Phillips Curve tradeoff to enhance their reelection prospects. He suggested that three conditions are necessary to permit a political business cycle to occur.

1. A government must be chosen in periodic elections.
2. The government must have sufficient knowledge and economic control to move the economy in the direction desired.
3. Voters must be myopic.

The first two conditions are obvious but the third may not be so clear. This last one amounts to saying that the voters must not have rational expectations; otherwise they would foresee the plans of the government and adjust their expectations (and votes) accordingly. If the public does not have rational expectations, and there is some reason to believe that this is the case, there will be a Phillips Curve tradeoff that the government can exploit to its electoral advantage. It would do so by first reducing the unemployment rate, just prior to an election, thereby reaping the political gains of reduced unemployment. Once an election has occurred and the inflation consequences of its past policy arise, the government can act to reduce inflation, thus generating a recession, and possibly displeasing voters. If voters' memories of the recession fade over time, the government can reduce unemployment in the latter half of the electoral period, enhancing their reelection prospects. Nordhaus provides evidence that several countries, including the U.S., seem to have followed this pattern at some points in their histories.

14.3 MONETARY POLICY

Whatever the policy goals chosen by a central bank, policymakers must choose a manner of carrying out their policies to achieve their policy objectives. This amounts to the choice of what are called **intermediate targets**. These targets are not the ultimate goals of policy. Rather they are targets chosen because of their relationship to the ultimate goals of policymakers. For a central bank, choosing an intermediate target means the choice of an interest rate or bank reserves (or, equivalently, the money stock) as the operating guide for policy. Thus we address why a central bank may wish to choose an interest rate or bank reserves as an operating target.

Pegging the Interest Rate or Reserves

The interest rate that the Fed can peg is the **Federal Funds interest rate**. As you may recall, this is the rate set in the reserves market where banks with reserves insufficient to meet their

---

7 See "The Political Business Cycle," *Review of Economic Studies* 42, No. 2 (April 1975), pp. 169–90.

reserve requirements can borrow from banks with reserves in excess of their reserve requirements. When the Fed buys or sells government bonds through open market operations, the
Federal Funds rate rises or falls as the overall supply of bank reserves changes. The Fed could
choose to set this interest rate or it could choose to peg bank reserves.

Before we proceed with this discussion, it is useful to point out that we will conduct the
analysis of interest rate pegging using the interest rate that is relevant to the demand for money,
usually thought to be a short-term interest rate such as the rate on six month Treasury Bills
(T-Bills). The Federal Funds rate does not measure the opportunity cost of money for
households since households can't borrow or lend at this interest rate but they can buy and sell
short-term debt issued by the government. However Figure 14.5 shows that the federal funds
rate and the T-Bill rate move very closely together and so little is lost by imagining that the
Fed is actually setting the interest rate that is relevant to the demand for money by the public.

To see what the Fed must do to peg the interest rate, consider Figure 14.6. Here we look
at the money market and imagine that there are shocks to money demand, causing the money
demand schedule to shift between the dotted lines in the diagram. Suppose that the Fed
chooses to set the supply of bank reserves and thus the supply of money at the level M_0. If the
central bank behaves in this way, the money stock is being used as an intermediate target and
the interest rate is being allowed to fluctuate as necessary to clear the money and bond
markets. Alternatively, if the central bank decides to fix the interest rate at the level i^T, then it
will need to adjust the supply of bank reserves, and thus the supply of money, in response to
money demand shocks. In this case, the horizontal line at the target interest rate is effectively
the money supply schedule. The nature of the alternatives is clear; when pegging the interest
rate, the money supply is endogenous (not fixed at the level chosen by the Fed) but, when the
Fed is pegging the money stock, the interest rate is endogenous. When the money supply is

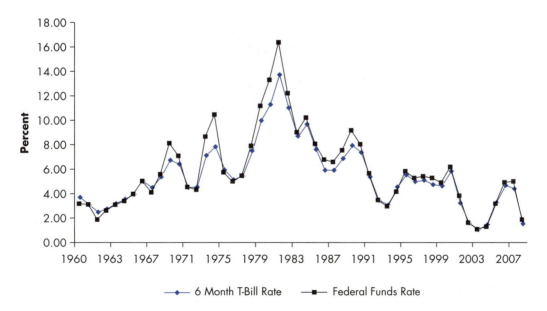

FIGURE 14.5 Federal Funds and 6 Month T-Bill Rates

Source: St. Louis Federal Reserve Bank FRED Database

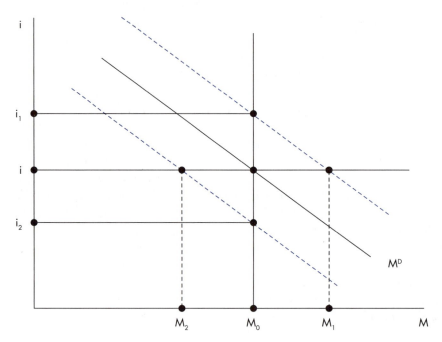

FIGURE 14.6 Pegging the Interest Rate by the Central Bank

If the Fed Pegs the money stock, it keeps the money supply at M_0 and the interest rate will fluctuate between i_1 and i_2. If the Fed wishes to peg the interest rate at the target level i^T, then the money supply is no longer exogenous. Whenever there is a shock to money demand, the Fed must move the supply of bank reserves to keep the interest rate at the level i^T.

exogenous, the interest rate will fluctuate whereas, when the interest rate is pegged, the money supply fluctuates.[8]

There is one immediate implication of this analysis. If the Fed keeps the interest rate fixed for sustained periods of time, it is likely to lose control of the money stock. And if it is attempting to hit money stock targets, it is likely to miss those targets if it keeps the interest rate fixed for too long. The Fed must be willing to change its interest rate target if it intends to hit money stock targets.[9]

But the Fed is really interested in its ultimate policy goals, such as inflation, and so its choice of intermediate targets is based upon how well these targets enable the Fed to achieve its ultimate policy objectives. Now we ask how either policy choice enables the Fed to hit price and output targets.

---

8 If the money supply is increasing in the interest rate, then the interest rate and the money stock will fluctuate with shocks to money demand. The supply of money could rise with the interest rate if banks reduce their excess reserves when the interest rate rises, thereby increasing the supply of money. Thus we have simplified the analysis by making the money supply completely inelastic with respect to the interest rate. The cost of this simplification is a certain lack of realism because both the interest rate and the money stock can be expected to fluctuate rather than just one of these two economic variables.

9 Historically the Fed has chosen a target range for the Federal Funds rate, with high, low, and mid-point values. We have omitted the bands from our discussion for simplicity. Our target value, i^T, corresponds to the mid-point of the range set by the Fed.

Hitting A Price Level and Output Target

An inflation target amounts to having a target price level that the Fed would like to achieve for the aggregate economy; we will assume that the Fed's target price level is that associated with full employment and that it knows the value of this magnitude. Further, we assume the Fed wants to keep output at its full-employment level. We will do two exercises where there are unpredictable shocks to the economy and we will want to know how the Fed should conduct its policy in the presence of these shocks. In each case, it will be clear that there is a preferred way of hitting the target price level. The crucial part of each scenario will be where the shocks in the economy originate. Figures 14.7 and 14.8 illustrate the two cases we discuss but care must be taken to be clear about the causality in each case.

In the first case, we will assume that there are unpredictable shocks to money demand and nowhere else in the economy. We need to establish how the economy will react to these shocks under each policy alternative. Begin with the case where there is a fixed supply of bank reserves and observe how shocks to the demand for money affect the AD schedule. A positive shock to money demand raises the interest rate clearing the money market at any level of real income, implying a shift to the left in the LM schedule (see Chapter 11). This in turn implies a shift to the left in the AD schedule, causing a recession and a reduction in the price level. A negative shock to money demand lowers the interest rate that clears the money and bond markets, causing a shift to the right in the LM and AD schedules. Therefore the price level rises and the economy enters a boom period. The implication is that if the central bank pegs the money supply, price and output will fluctuate in the economy.

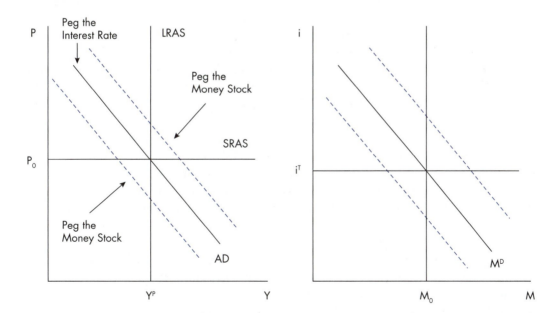

FIGURE 14.7 Monetary Policy in the Presence of Money Demand Shocks

Money demand shocks cause the aggregate demand schedule to fluctuate when the Fed pegs the money stock. When the Fed pegs the interest rate, there will be no fluctuations in the aggregate demand schedule.

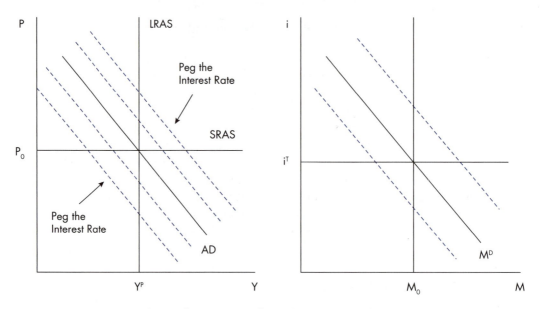

FIGURE 14.8 Monetary Policy in the Presence of Goods Market Shocks

Goods market shocks, causing the AD schedule to fluctuate, will cause shifts in money demand and the interest rate when the Fed pegs the money supply. If the Fed pegs the interest rate, the fluctuations in the AD schedule will be larger than if the Fed pegs the money stock.

Now compare this scenario with the situation that would arise if the interest rate were to be pegged at the rate prevailing without any shocks to money demand. In this case, the positive shock to money demand triggers an increase in the money supply when the Fed observes a rising interest rate. This automatically prevents a shift in the LM and AD schedules. A negative shock to money demand causes a reduction in the money supply that, once again, eliminates any shift in the LM and AD schedules. Clearly the preferred strategy is to peg the interest rate because the central bank would eliminate shocks to AD and so it would hit its target price and output levels exactly.

Now consider the situation where there are shocks to the goods market only, represented by shifts in the AD schedule (see Figure 14.8). For example, an exogenous increase in the level of consumption, at any level of the interest rate, implies a higher level of aggregate demand at any level of prices. A negative shock to consumption shifts AD to the left. If the Fed leaves the money stock at a fixed level, the price level and output will fluctuate around their full-employment values.

If the central bank pegs the money stock, then shocks to the goods market will cause price and output to move together; the price level and output rise above or fall below their full-employment levels. Pegging the interest rate, however, causes the fluctuations in the price level and output to be amplified. The reason is that a positive shock to the IS curve raises the interest rate by shifting money demand and this would induce the Fed to expand the money supply to drive the interest rate down to its target level. But this increase in the money supply causes a further shift in aggregate demand and thus a bigger increase in output. The preferred strategy in this case is to peg the money stock. Under either policy alternative, the Fed will not hit its price and output targets exactly but it will be closer to its goals if it pegs the money stock. Our findings are summarized in the following propositions.

Propositions About the Conduct of Monetary Policy

■ When the only shocks in the economy affect money demand, the Fed can hit a price and output target exactly when it pegs the interest rate.
■ When the only shocks in the economy are in the goods market, the Fed will get closer to a price and output target when it pegs the money stock.

As you have no doubt realized, there are shocks that simultaneously affect all sectors of the economy, not just one market or another. In these cases, graphical analysis is unavailable but it is possible to provide some analytical results about the appropriate way to conduct policy in these more complex cases.[10] Thus even in more difficult circumstances, it may be possible to show that it is more appropriate to choose either policy alternative discussed here.

Policy Under Rational Expectations

Our discussion about rational expectations in Chapter 13 produced the striking result that only unanticipated money can have an impact on real economic magnitudes. The reason for this finding was that rational economic agents would know the systematic parts of the monetary policy rule and so would use this information in forming their expectations. However, even if the public has rational expectations (and there is reason to be skeptical that they do), there are still ways for monetary policy to have real effects.

One possibility is if the Fed has an **informational advantage** compared to the public. The Fed has a staff of professional economists whose expertise is used in formulating monetary policy. As a result, it is possible for the Fed to have superior information, compared to the public, about the actual values of any shocks that may be affecting the economy. If the Fed knows the values of these shocks, and if the public does not know these values, then the Fed can tie the money supply to these realized shocks and thus the money stock can be used as a stabilization tool.[11] The reason is that the public will not be able to use the actual values of the shocks in forming their expectations so any part of the money supply tied to the realized value of these shocks can be used as a stabilization device.

In addition, if the economy is well described by Keynesian models with multi-period overlapping wage agreements, then there will always be sectors of the economy with workers who will be locked into contracts within a given time period. So even if the public has rational expectations, the money supply can be adjusted in relation to shocks that occur to a degree that cannot be anticipated by workers locked into wage agreements.

---

10 See William Poole, "Optimal Choice of Monetary Policy Instruments in a Simple Stochastic Macro Model," *Quarterly Journal of Economics* 84, No. 2 (May 1970), pp. 197–216.
11 This insight was provided in Robert J. Barro, "Rational Expectations and the Role of Monetary Policy," *Journal of Monetary Economics* 2, No. 1 (January 1976), pp. 1–32.

The Taylor Rule

Economist John B. Taylor has proposed a monetary policy rule that he believes to be a good description of historical Fed conduct of monetary policy (see **Doing Economics**: The Taylor Rule). Here we discuss a simplified version of this rule, showing its impact upon the aggregate demand schedule in the economy.

Figure 14.9 provides a graphical description of a Taylor rule in the simplified case where there is only inflation targeting. This is not as unrealistic as it may seem; many economists believe that inflation should be the only concern for a central bank since the money supply can only affect prices in the long run (this is what is meant by the neutrality of money). In the figure, the policy rule has a target inflation rate, π^T. The inflation rate is on the horizontal axis and the nominal interest rate is on the vertical axis. There is a line in the diagram with a slope of unity. Along this line, the real interest rate is constant (we assume that inflation expectations are correct as in equilibrium); a unit increase in the inflation rate is matched by a unit increase in the nominal interest rate. When inflation is zero, the real and nominal interest rates are the same so that the intercept of the line with unit slope gives the value of the real interest rate.

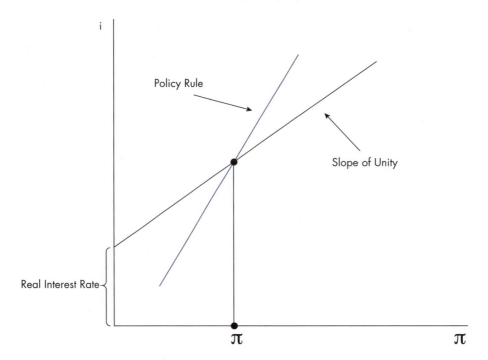

FIGURE 14.9 The Taylor Rule

In the diagram, i is the nominal interest rate and π is the inflation rate. The central bank is using only an inflation target in the diagram above. If inflation is above the target, π^T, the Fed raises the real interest rate. If inflation is below the target, the Fed reduces the real interest rate. When inflation is at its target level, the real interest rate is equal to its long-run equilibrium level.

Doing Economics: The Taylor Rule

Economist John B. Taylor proposed the following policy rule that he believed to be a close approximation to actual Fed behavior.

$$i = \pi + .5 \cdot (Y - Y^P)/Y^P + .5 \cdot (\pi - 2) + 2$$

In this expression, i refers to the nominal interest rate controlled by the Fed which is the Federal Funds interest rate, Y is real GDP, Y^P is Potential GDP (growing at 2.2 percent per year), and π is the inflation rate over the previous year. This policy rule reflects how the Fed actually carries out its monetary policies since it does so by setting the Federal Funds interest rate, the interest rate that banks pay to borrow reserves. The rule presumes that the Fed has an inflation target of 2 percent and an output target of Potential GDP. This policy rule states that if real GDP is at its potential level and if the inflation rate is 2 percent, the Fed should set the real interest rate at 2 percent, approximately the equilibrium real interest rate for the economy. The rule implies that if the rate of inflation is above target, the Fed should raise the real interest rate. Similarly, the Fed should raise the real rate of interest if the economy is in a boom (output is above its trend level). The Fed should lower the real interest rate if inflation and/or output are below their targets.

Taylor argued that this policy rule corresponds closely to Fed policy over the period 1987–1992, although the Fed never publicly claimed to be using this policy rule. There was, however, a notable departure from this rule in 1987 when the Fed significantly reduced the nominal interest rate in response to a sharp decline in the stock market. Thus the Fed was implicitly following a rules-based strategy but left open the possibility of abandoning the rule in response to extraordinary economic events.

See "Discretion Versus Policy Rules in Practice," *Carnegie-Rochester Conference Series on Public Policy,* 39 (December 1993), pp. 195–214.

The policy rule has a slope that is bigger than unity. So imagine that inflation rises above the target level, π^T. The nominal interest rate will rise by more than the increase in inflation, implying that the real interest rate increases. If the inflation rate declines below its target level, the real interest rate will fall. Thus the Fed moves the real interest rate when inflation deviates from its target level. The slope of the policy rule reflects the resolve of the Fed to hit its inflation target. The larger the slope, the greater the determination of the Fed to hit its inflation target.

If the Fed changes its target rate of inflation, the policy rule shifts to reflect the new policy preferences of the central bank. Figure 14.10 displays the case where the Fed has chosen a lower target inflation rate. At any given rate of inflation, the Fed will set a higher real rate of interest when it decides to pursue a lower inflation target. Thus the policy rule shifts up to reflect this new policy choice of lower inflation.

When a policy rule is used by the Fed or the government, this rule affects the properties of the aggregate demand schedule. For an example of how the AD schedule will change, it is

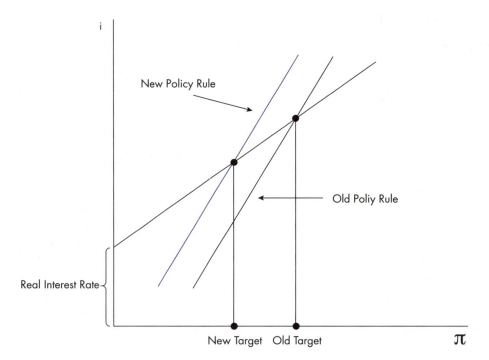

FIGURE 14.10 Changing the Inflation Target in the Taylor Rule

If a central bank chooses a lower inflation target, it sets a higher nominal interest rate at any level of inflation. The policy rule shifts up, giving a higher real interest rate at any level of inflation.

convenient to use an example of a policy rule similar to one that you have seen before. Suppose the Fed uses the policy rule

$$m^s = m_0 - m_1 \cdot (p - p^T), \ m_0 > 0, \ m_1 > 0.$$

This is a money stock rule, rather than an interest rule as discussed above. You saw a version of this rule in Chapter 13 when we discussed rational expectations. In that chapter, there was an inflation target and the money supply was based in part on the difference between actual and target inflation. That is much the same as setting the money supply based upon the difference between the actual and target price level and the version of the policy rule above is more convenient for our purposes. This policy rule can be inserted into an aggregate demand schedule (see the Appendix for the details). There are two insights that emerge from that derivation; the target price level is a shift parameter in the AD schedule and the slope of the aggregate demand schedule depends upon the parameter m_1. Figure 14.11 illustrates each of these facts. A lower target price level means that, ceteris paribus, the Fed must reduce the money supply and that causes a shift to the left in the aggregate demand (AD) schedule. But, in addition, the slope of the AD schedule depends upon how serious the Fed is in hitting its price target. If the Fed "has religion," meaning they are very committed to hitting the price target, the AD schedule is flat and the diagram shows the implication of this.

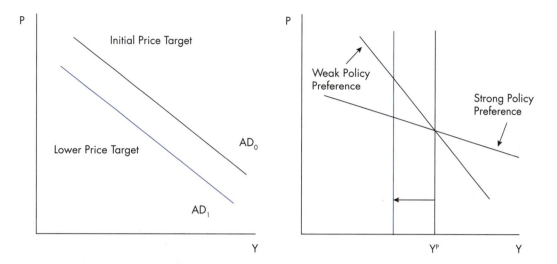

FIGURE 14.11 The Monetary Policy Rule and the Aggregate Demand Schedule

If the Fed uses a price target in its policy rule, the price target appears in the aggregate demand (AD) schedule. A lower price target causes the AD schedule to shift left as the Fed would reduce the money supply to reduce the price level. The stronger the Fed's desire to keep the price level near its target level, the flatter the AD schedule. Thus if a negative supply shock reduces Potential GDP, the price level goes up by less when the Fed has a strong preference in preventing a rise in the price level compared to the case where the Fed has a weak preference in preventing a higher price level.

Imagine a negative supply shock shifting the LRAS schedule (Potential GDP) to the left. The larger the parameter m_1, the smaller will be the effect of the supply shock on the price level and the reason is clear. The more intensely the Fed intends to hit its price target, the more it will reduce the money stock when the price level rises. The larger the decline in the money supply, the smaller will be the impact upon the price level of a negative supply shock.

Maintaining a Fixed Exchange Rate

If a country has fixed nominal **exchange rates** between its own currency and the currencies of other countries, it is the responsibility of the central bank to maintain these fixed exchange rates. This means that the central bank must pursue a monetary policy that is consistent with the maintenance of fixed exchange rates. Here we briefly discuss this policy obligation, leaving a more complete discussion for the next chapter in the book.

Let e denote the nominal exchange rate, say between the United Kingdom (UK), and the U.S. The exchange rate is an exchange ratio given by

$$e = £/\$.$$

The ratio is measured in units of foreign currency per dollar. Thus one U.S. dollar may trade for two UK pounds and the nominal exchange rate is two pounds per dollar. If e rises, the dollar fetches more pounds in the market and this is called an appreciation of the dollar. When the dollar appreciates, the pound depreciates since it trades for fewer U.S. dollars. In a flexible exchange rate system, the market sets the nominal exchange rate and so the exchange rate that prevails in the market is one where there is no excess supply or demand for currency. In a fixed exchange rate system, the nominal exchange rate need not be the one consistent with an absence of any excess supply or demand for currency. In this case the central bank is obligated to supply or demand foreign exchange to maintain the fixed exchange rate.

To see why, suppose there is a fixed exchange rate system and, for unspecified reasons, there is an excess supply of dollars at this fixed exchange rate. The central bank must buy up the excess supply of dollars, supplying pounds to carry out these transactions. This is what it must do to maintain the current value of the exchange rate. It does this by selling UK pounds out of its holdings but these reserves are finite and eventually will be exhausted. Before it uses up all of its reserves, the central bank must do something to eliminate the excess supply of dollars. As you will see in the next chapter, the central bank must pursue a monetary policy that will eliminate the excess supply of dollars.

This discussion shows that a fixed exchange rate system imposes a constraint on central banks. They must pursue monetary policies that will ensure that a fixed exchange rate system can be maintained. Thus a central bank may be required to set a monetary policy to support a fixed exchange rate that may not be the sort of policy that the central bank wishes to pursue to achieve other policy goals. There may thus be a conflict in the goals of monetary policy regarding the exchange rate and other economic magnitudes.

Monetary Neutrality

Our discussion of monetary policy as a stabilization device provided supply-side assumptions that permitted an increase in the money stock to affect real economic magnitudes. But we also pointed out that it is a classical world in the long run. Money will thus have no effect on output and other real economic variables in the long run. In the New Classical model, an unanticipated increase in the money stock would raise the price level, eventually causing inflation expectation adjustments by the public. Those adjustments, given no further increases in the money stock, would eventually cause output to return to its potential level. In the menu cost (or New Keynesian) model, a shift in aggregate demand will ultimately have no effect on real output once wage and price agreements are renegotiated and fully adjusted to the shift in the money stock. Thus the effects of monetary policy on real variables are confined to temporary equilibrium situations when the economy is not in a full general equilibrium.[12]

In the most recent recession, the Fed has responded to a negative shock to aggregate demand by increasing the money supply and the monetary base (See **Doing Economics**: Monetary Policy in 2008/2009). Once the negative shock begins to dissipate, it remains to be seen how the Fed will reduce the level of the money supply to avoid driving up the price level and thus inflation.

---

12 Note that we are excluding the case of consistently accelerating inflation due to consistently accelerating increases in the money stock. Our analysis showed that this would ultimately lead to accelerating inflation and it is reasonable to expect the public to catch on to this policy, ultimately causing this policy to have no lasting real effects.

Doing Economics: Monetary Policy in 2008/2009

With the economy in recession in 2008, the Federal Reserve was faced with the policy decision of whether and when to increase the monetary base and the money supply by reducing the Federal Funds rate. Economic activity did not decline sharply until the last quarter of 2008 (see Doing Economics: The Recession of 2007 in Chapter 12) and, as shown in the chart below, the Fed did finally increase the base but did not increase the monetary base substantially until the last quarter of 2008. The increase in the monetary base in the chart is unprecedented; never has there been such an extraordinary increase in the base in such a

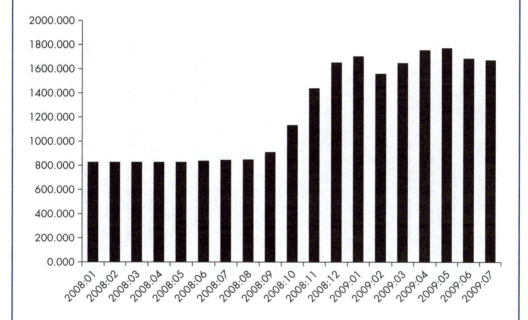

U.S. Monetary Base – Billions of SA Dollars

short time. Between January 2008 and March 2009, the monetary base more than doubled! Why was there such a large increase?

Fed officials were clearly concerned that there were many banks in danger of insolvency and that a financial panic was a real possibility. The source of the recession was primarily due to homeowner mortgage defaults. As you may recall from Chapter 8, the assets held by banks include mortgages made to individuals. If homeowners default, this reduces the value of the assets on the books of banks and, if this happens to a sufficient degree, a bank could become insolvent, resulting in bankruptcy. But there was an additional problem faced by the Fed.

Many financial institutions held assets that were tied or backed by groups of mortgages. As mortgage defaults occur, the market value of these assets became difficult to determine

(continued)

so that it was unclear how to measure a bank's net worth. These mortgage defaults, and the so-called mortgage-backed "toxic assets," impaired the ability of banks to borrow so that the private sector could not get access to lending as it needed to do business. And so the Fed not only increased bank reserves in the usual way but bought mortgage-backed assets as well as government debt. Now the Fed's balance sheet has changed, including assets that were never purchased by the Fed prior to the recession that started in December 2007.

The increase in the monetary base increases the money supply, charted below.

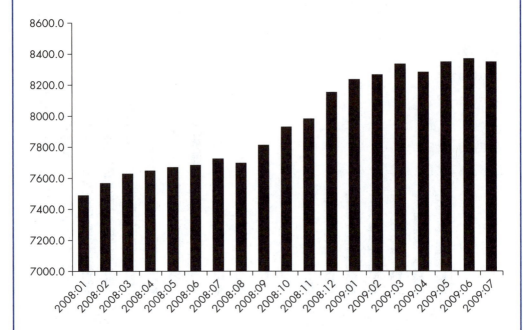

Source: St. Louis Federal Reserve FRED Database

The M2 money stock has increased by 12 percent over the period when the base doubled. And so a rising concern is that, once the recession is over, the increase in the money stock will cause the price level to rise so the Fed must devise an "exit strategy" to undo much of the increase in the money supply that has occurred. The challenge will be to reduce the money stock without causing the economy to enter another recession.

14.4 FISCAL POLICY

Economists do not study fiscal policy as a stabilization device to the degree that they study monetary policy. The reason is that monetary policy can change course with, quite literally, a conference call between central bank policymakers. For a change in fiscal policy to occur, say a change in tax rates is under consideration, there must be discussion and debate between the members of the government about the efficacy of a tax change and these discussions tend to be quite lengthy. The result is that it is difficult for fiscal policy changes to be timed appropriately relative to the business cycle. Sometimes this is described by saying that the inside lags (the time for discussion within a policymaking body) are too long for fiscal policy to be used effectively as a stabilization device. In addition, it takes time for policy changes to affect the economy (the so-called outside lags) so that, when account is taken of all of the lags involved in the policy process, fiscal policy is viewed by economists as too cumbersome for business cycle stabilization. Indeed if the policy is timed poorly, it may actually cause larger swings in economic activity than would otherwise would be the case.

But there is one aspect of fiscal policy that is not subject to these lag problems. One fiscal policy tool acts as an **automatic stabilizer**, thus requiring no action by the government to enable it to be a useful stabilizing force in the economy. And that tool is the tax code.

Automatic Stabilizers

You will recall that we have discussed from time to time the properties of a tax code that ties tax payments to income. Thus we have discussed a tax schedule written as

$$T = T_0 + t \cdot Y, \, 0 < t < 1$$

where t is the MTR (marginal tax rate). Thus tax payments rise and fall with income. This fact implies that the tax code tends to dampen fluctuations in aggregate demand compared to the case here $t = 0$. This is true for the following reasons.

Suppose that we regard business cycle fluctuations as arising from exogenous changes in the demand for goods. This could originate in the private sector because expectations affect the behavior of households and firms. If households feel better about their future prospects, they may consume more or firms might invest more if they see improved future profitability attached to investment prospects. These shifts in aggregate demand are reduced by having an MTR that is nonzero. Keynesian multipliers are lower than they would be when $t = 0$.[13] That translates into a smaller shift in aggregate demand for a given shock to consumer demand. Figure 14.12 illustrates the effects of this automatic stabilizer. The intuition behind the figure is easy.

When there is an exogenous increase in goods demand, incomes and output will rise but tax payments rise as well. This increase in tax receipts dampens the ultimate increase in the aggregate demand for goods compared to the case where tax payments do not rise. And these business cycle benefits arise without any explicit action by the government. Hence they are viewed as a potentially useful tool to dampen cyclical fluctuations in the economy.

---

13 Recall that the investment and government spending multipliers in simple Keynesian models are given by $1/[1-b(1-t)]$ where b is the marginal propensity to consume and t is the MTR. It is easy to show that $1/[1-b(1-t)] < 1/(1-b)$.

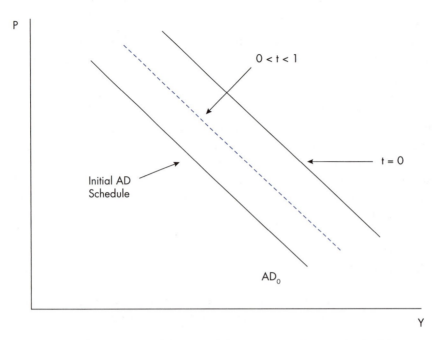

P

$0 < t < 1$

$t = 0$

Initial AD
Schedule

AD_0

Y

FIGURE 14.12 Automatic Stabilizers and the Aggregate Demand Schedule

Given a shock to the aggregate demand schedule AD_0, there will be a larger resulting shift in AD when the MTR is zero than there will be when the MTR is between zero and unity.

Transitory Versus Permanent Tax Cuts

There is another aspect of tax policy that arises when a tax change is considered by the government. And that is how households will change their behavior depending upon whether a tax cut is transitory or permanent.

Our theory of the household in Chapter 3 showed that consumption is proportional to Permanent Income as given by the expression

$$C = k \cdot Y^P, \ 0 < k < 1.$$

The factor of proportionality, k, was shown to be independent of the tax rate on income and so the impact upon consumption of a tax cut will depend upon the size of k and the effect of the tax cut on Permanent Income. Permanent Income was previously defined in the following way.

$$Y^P \cdot \left[1 + \frac{1}{1+r} + \frac{1}{(1+r)^2} + \cdots \right] = Y_0 + \frac{Y_1}{1+r} + \frac{Y_2}{(1+r)^2} + \cdots$$

Thus if we want to know the impact of a tax cut, we will first need to know how Permanent Income will change with the tax cut.

Intuition suggests that a **temporary tax cut** will have a minimal impact upon Permanent Income when compared to a permanent tax cut of the same size. As a matter of simple arithmetic, an increase in just Y_1 changes Y^P by less than the same increase applied to Y_1, Y_2, and other future incomes. For this reason, economists argue that transitory tax cuts have little impact upon household consumption because they will have a minimal impact upon Permanent Income.[14]

Coordinated Fiscal and Monetary Policy

Earlier in the book when the government budget constraint was discussed, it was pointed out that the government must issue bonds if it is running a deficit (spending exceeds tax receipts). But we also mentioned the possibility that the Fed could choose to buy up the bonds issued by the government, in which case a spending increase or tax cut would carry along with it an increase in the money supply. This is sometimes called **monetizing** the deficit (or money finance) because money, in effect, is being printed to pay for some of the government's expenditures. What we point out here is that there will be a larger increase in the demand for goods when there is money finance than there will be when bonds alone are used to finance the deficit. Figure 14.13 provides the graphical details of this case.

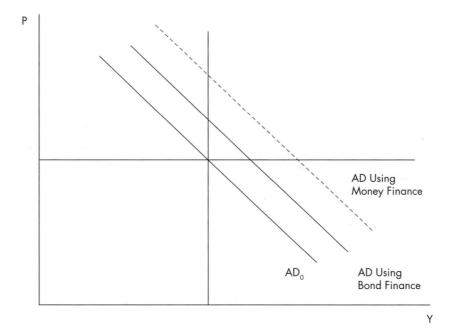

FIGURE 14.13 The Aggregate Demand Schedule and Money-Financed Fiscal Policy

The initial aggregate demand schedule is AD_0. There will be a larger shift in AD when there is money finance than there will be with bond finance.

---

14 Recall that a tax cut may not affect consumption at all if there are future tax increases that will follow the tax cut. This is the essence of the Ricardian Equivalence Proposition, discussed in Chapter 4.

Suppose that there is an increase in government expenditures financed by bond issue. We know from previous analysis that this will cause a rightward shift in the aggregate demand schedule. In Figure 14.13, think of this as generating the AD schedule labeled AD Using Bond Finance. But if the Fed buys up the bonds, the money supply expands, also causing a shift in the AD as we know from previous discussion. When money is used to finance additional government spending, both shifts are occurring and so the AD schedule given by the dotted line in the figure corresponds to a further shift in the AD schedule associated with the increase in money.

Notice that monetary and fiscal policies are more powerful when they are used in a coordinated fashion than they would be if either policy tool were used alone. That is, for given increases in government spending, there is a greater shift in the AD schedule when government spending and the money stock increase than there will be if only government expenditures, financed by bond issue, increase. This provides an explanation for the evident connection between the money supply and the government deficit noticed empirically by economists. But remember that the money supply increase is a policy choice by the central bank and may cause inflation to occur if the money stock continues to increase. A central bank may not be required to buy up any new debt issued by the government.

Fiscal Policy in the Long Run

Fiscal policy in the long run will have an impact upon Potential GDP. This can occur because of government spending and tax rate effects, each of which we now discuss.

Our analysis in Chapter 9 revealed that higher government spending will reallocate real GDP away from the private sector towards the government. This happened as a result of real interest rate effects. If the government wants a higher fraction of real GDP, it must crowd out private expenditures by increasing the real interest rate. But this implies that the economy's capital stock must be lower in equilibrium, implying a lower level of Potential GDP in the long run. To see this, consider one aspect of our discussion of investment in Chapter 5.

The accounting relationship that governs the economy's capital stock can be written as

$$K - K_{-1} = I - \delta \cdot K_{-1}$$

where K is the capital stock, I is gross investment and $\delta \cdot K_{-1}$ is replacement investment needed to replace capital goods that wear out at the positive rate δ. Net investment is given by $K - K_{-1}$, the change in the capital stock between two time periods.

Remember that in the economy's equilibrium, net investment is zero so that

$$I = \delta \cdot K$$

because there will only be replacement investment in the economy's long-run equilibrium. If the real interest rate in the long run is higher due to higher government spending, then because the theory of investment showed that there was an inverse relationship between the capital stock and the real interest rate (a component of the user cost of capital), it must be true that the capital stock is lower in the long run, implying that Potential GDP will be reduced in the long run. Thus higher government spending completely crowds out private investment; the latter leads to a smaller capital stock and Potential GDP.

Tax rates affect labor supply as you learned in Chapter 8 but it is important to distinguish between marginal and average tax rates when we discuss the effects of taxes on Potential GDP. If average taxes are raised by the government, in the long run there will be an increase in labor supply as people reduce their consumption of leisure in response to a higher average tax. As a result, Potential GDP will increase although the size of this increase is an empirical question. If marginal tax rates rise, theory is ambiguous as to the effect upon the labor/leisure choice but, if income effects are dominated by substitution effects, leisure will increase and labor supply will fall. Again the size of the tax rates/labor supply connection is open to empirical evaluation both to its sign and its size. The evidence shows that there is a negative relationship between marginal tax rates and labor supply. Thus a higher marginal tax rate will reduce labor supply and Potential GDP since the higher tax rate causes a reduction in after-tax real wages.

14.5 CONCLUDING REMARKS

This chapter has been concerned with macroeconomic policy. We began with a discussion of the goals of policy. We stated that the unemployment rate is often a goal of policymakers and it was useful to consider policies that might be used to reduce either the natural unemployment rate or cyclical unemployment. Regarding the natural rate of unemployment, structural policies might be used to reduce unemployment, such as reducing or eliminating the minimum wage, job training, and reducing the replacement rate of unemployment compensation schemes. As for cyclical unemployment, monetary and fiscal policies may be used to dampen business cycle fluctuations in these magnitudes.

Inflation is costly to society in either the anticipated or unanticipated varieties. With anticipated inflation, less money will be held by households resulting in higher transactions costs being incurred. There will be costs attached to changing posted prices, called menu costs, and in the case of extreme inflation, called hyperinflation, payments periods can shorten and a society may even revert to barter.

The exchange rate is also a possible goal variable for policymakers because exchange rate volatility may be damaging to international trade between countries. Further, central banks may be required to carry out monetary policies maintaining a fixed nominal exchange rate.

When we studied economic policy, we discussed the debate regarding using rules or discretion, suggesting that many economists support rules since it would make policy clear to households and firms, making it easier for them to use these rules in their optimizing behavior. We discussed time inconsistency leading to an inability of policymakers to hit their goals if they disregard the way economic agents react to future policies. We showed how the credibility of policymakers has an important role in explaining how actual policies affect the economy.

Regarding monetary policy, we showed how the Fed can either target the money stock or the interest rate and showed that which policy it uses depends upon the sources of shocks on the economy. The Taylor Rule was illustrated and we showed how the parameters of this policy rule affect the properties of the aggregate demand schedule. As for fiscal policy, we discussed the tax code as it acts to stabilize the economy and we showed the consequences of using money to finance some of the government's spending.

The topics in this chapter imply that there is considerable scope for the government and the central bank to change the equilibrium and business cycle characteristics of an aggregate economy. The availability of these policies suggests that cyclical fluctuations need not be as severe as they were in the past since policymakers are now better prepared to deal with the swings in economic activity known as the business cycle.

Key Ideas

- Economic policy often targets the unemployment rate, the inflation rate, and the exchange rate.
- The natural unemployment rate may be reduced by reducing the minimum wage, job training programs, and subsidizing the formation of human capital.
- The cyclical unemployment rate can be reduced by policies reducing the frequency and severity of business cycle fluctuations.
- Anticipated inflation is costly to a society because it may cause the public to reduce their money-holdings, thus causing them to bear higher menu (transaction) costs and because it imposes menu costs on society.
- A hyperinflation may cause a society to change the frequency at which its members are paid for their work and it may even cause a society to revert to barter.
- Unanticipated inflation can cause a redistribution of wealth to debtors from creditors, it may cause banks to cease to operate if there are institutional restrictions on the interest rates that banks pay, and it can reduce the ability of prices to serve as signals that guide resource allocation in a society.
- A central bank may intervene in foreign exchange markets because flexible exchange rates are volatile or because the central bank must maintain a fixed exchange rate.
- Policy can be carried out using rules that explicitly describe the goals of policy and how those goals will be achieved. Alternatively, policy can be carried out using discretion where no such rules are used.
- Policy can be inconsistent with the goals of the policymaker if policymakers do not take account of the fact that the public's actions will be determined in part by the future policies that are set.
- The economic effects of economic policy depend upon the credibility of the policymaker.
- Supply shocks pose a dilemma for policymakers because price and output move in opposite direction when a supply-side shock occurs.
- A political business cycle refers to the possibility that policymakers will manipulate the economy to improve their reelection prospects.
- The Fed can peg the interest rate or bank reserves to achieve its ultimate policy goals.
- With only money demand shocks in the economic system, the Fed should peg the interest rate to achieve its goals but, if there are only goods market shocks, it should peg the money stock.

- Only unanticipated money has real effects in an economy with rational expectations unless the Fed has an informational advantage or there are overlapping staggered contracts in labor markets.
- The Taylor Rule refers to an interest rate rule that the Fed may use to set policy.
- A central bank must pursue a monetary policy to maintain a fixed nominal exchange rate for its currency.
- In the long run money is neutral so monetary policy will not affect real magnitudes in the economy in the long run.
- A tax code tied to income reduces the size of multipliers in an economy, dampening the fluctuations in aggregate demand.
- Transitory tax cuts have little or no effect on permanent income as compared to permanent tax cuts.
- In the long run, higher government spending raises the real interest rate, reduces the economy's capital stock, and thus reduces Potential GDP.

Key Terms

Natural Unemployment Rate
Unemployment Compensation
Anticipated Inflation
Payments Period
Incomplete Information
Nominal Exchange Rate
Flexible Exchange Rate
Stagflation
Painless Disinflation
Credibility

Intermediate Targets
Monetary Neutrality
Temporary Tax Cut
Coordinated Fiscal and Monetary Policy
Cyclical Unemployment
Minimum Wages
Shoe Leather Costs
Monetize Debt
Noisy Signal
Exchange Rate Volatility

Time Inconsistency
Supply Shocks
Rational Expectations
Inside Lag
Permanent Tax Cut
Human Capital
Menu Costs 437
Barter 437
Disintermediation
Fixed Exchange Rate
Federal Funds Interest Rate

Political Business Cycle
The Taylor Rule
Outside Lag
Permanent Income
Hyperinflation
Unanticipated Inflation
Informational Advantage
Exchange rate
Automatic Stabilizer

Questions for Study and Review

Review Exercises

1. Describe policies that can change the natural and cyclical rates of unemployment.
2. Explain why inflation can be damaging to a society.
3. Explain why economists who believe in the Real Business Cycle model differ in their policy prescriptions compared to economists who subscribe to the New Keynesian model of the economy.

4.   Explain the differences between policies carried using discretion as opposed to rules.
5.   Explain what must be true for policymakers to carry out a painless disinflation.
6.   Explain how price and output respond to supply shocks as compared to how they respond to demand shocks.
7.   Describe the proper way for the Fed to hit price level and output targets when the only shocks in the economy affect the demand for money.
8.   Describe the long-run effect of higher government expenditures on the level of Potential GDP in the economy.
9.   In a rational expectations economy, under what circumstances will monetary policy affect real variables in the economy?

Thought Exercises

1.   Suppose that the Taylor Rule followed by the central bank has both an inflation gap and a real GDP gap (the difference between last period's actual real GDP and Potential GDP). Explain how changes in the GDP gap affect the Taylor Rule displayed in Figure 14.9.
2.   Can the political business cycle exist if agents in an economy have rational expectations?
3.   Suppose that an economy has a progressive income tax schedule (marginal tax rates rise with a higher ability to pay) but the tax code taxes nominal income. If the Fed chooses a higher inflation target, how will this new policy affect Potential GDP?

Numerical Exercises

1.   The market for labor is described by the following linear equations. Production Function: $Y = 4.8 + .4 \cdot L$, Labor Demand: $L^D = 6.45 - 1.67 \cdot (W - P)$, $L^S = 1 + 2 \cdot (1 - t) \cdot (W - P)$. The real wage is flexible, clearing the labor market. *Definitions*: L = Labor, W − P = Real Wage, t = Marginal Tax Rate.

   a)   If t = .25, compute the equilibrium levels of labor, output, the pre-tax and after-tax real wage.
   b)   If t = .20, compute the equilibrium levels of labor, output, the pre-tax and after-tax real wage.

2.   Consider the following market for loanable funds in the aggregate economy. Saving: $S = 50 + 300 \cdot (1 - t) \cdot r$, Investment: $I = 190 - 500 \cdot U_K$. *Definitions*: r = Real Interest Rate, t = Marginal Tax Rate (MTR), U_K = User Cost of Capital. The MTR is t = .25.

   a)   Compute the user cost of capital if there is a corporate income tax rate $t_c = .35$ and if the depreciation rate is d = .05. Note: the economy produces only one good so the purchase price of capital goods is the same as the general price level.
   b)   Using your measure of the user cost of capital, solve the saving and investment expressions for the equilibrium levels of the pre-tax and after-tax real interest rate, and the level of saving.
   c)   Let the corporate tax rate rise to $t_c = .40$, and solve the saving and investment expressions for the equilibrium levels of the pre-tax and after-tax real interest rate, and the level of saving.

3. Consider the following model of an aggregate economy. IS Schedule: $Y = 10,000 - 750 \cdot i$, Money Demand: $M^D - P = 500 + .5 \cdot Y - 500 \cdot i$, Money Supply: $M^S = 1,000 - .5 \cdot (P - P^T)$. *Definitions*: P = Price Level, Y = Output, i = Interest Rate, P^T = Target Price Level.

    a) Derive the aggregate demand schedule for this economy by finding the value of the intercept, and the coefficients attached to the target and actual price levels.

    b) Now imagine that a new policy rule is chosen, given by $M^S = 1,000 - .75 \cdot (P - P^T)$. Compute the three coefficients of the aggregate demand schedule.

Data Exercises

1. Using data on the monetary base, graph the base over the period 2006–2009. Does the data reveal the actions of the Fed in combating the recession?
2. Draw a time series graph of Federal expenditures and real GDP over the period 2006–2009. Is there evidence in the graph that the Stimulus Bill had a substantial impact upon real GDP?

For further questions, multiple choice quizzes, and weblinks related to this chapter, visit www.routledge.com/textbooks/rossana

References and Suggestions for Further Reading

Barro, R.J. (1976) "Rational Expectations and the Role of Monetary Policy," *Journal of Monetary Economics* 2 (1) (January): 1–32.

Feldstein, M.S. (1978) "The Effect of Unemployment Insurance on Temporary Layoff Unemployment," *American Economic Review* 68 (5) (December): 834–46.

Friedman, M. and Schwartz, A.J. (1963) *A Monetary History of the United States, 1867–1960*, Princeton University Press for the National Bureau of Economic Research (1963).

Nordhaus, W.D. (1975) "The Political Business Cycle," *Review of Economic Studies* 42 (2) (April): 169–90.

Poole, W. (1970) "Optimal Choice of Monetary Policy Instruments in a Simple Stochastic Macro Model," *Quarterly Journal of Economics* 84 (2) (May): 197–216.

Taylor, J.B. (1993) "Discretion Versus Policy Rules in Practice," *Carnegie-Rochester Conference Series on Public Policy*, 39 (December): 195–214.

APPENDIX: POLICY RULES AND THE AGGREGATE DEMAND SCHEDULE

The aggregate demand schedule will reflect the characteristics of the policy rules used by a central bank and the government. In this appendix, we demonstrate this fact by showing how the aggregate demand schedule will change when a central bank uses a policy rule tied explicitly to the price level.

In Chapter 13, we derived a linear aggregate demand schedule using

$$\text{IS Curve: } y = a_0 - a_1 \cdot i + u$$

$$\text{Money Demand Schedule: } m^d - p = a_2 + a_3 \cdot y - a_4 \cdot i + v$$

where y is output, i is the interest rate (inflation is ignored for simplicity), m is the supply of money, and p is the price level. There are unpredictable shocks, u and v, which we will now ignore (u = v = 0) for simplicity. We will use the policy rule

$$m^s = m_0 - m_1 \cdot (p - p^T), \; m_0 > 0, \; m_1 > 0$$

to describe the central bank policy. To derive the aggregate demand (AD) schedule, set $m^d = m^s$ to get

$$m_0 - m_1 \cdot (p - p^T) = p + a_2 + a_3 \cdot y - a_4 \cdot i.$$

Eliminate the interest rate, i, from this expression and the IS curve to get the AD schedule.

$$y^d = b_0 - b_1 \cdot p, b_0 = \frac{a_4 \cdot a_0 - a_1 \cdot a_2 + a_1 \cdot \left(m_0 + m_1 \cdot p^T\right)}{a_4 + a_1 \cdot a_3}, b_1 = \frac{a_1 \cdot \left(1 + m_1\right)}{a_4 + a_1 \cdot a_3}$$

The target price level, p^T, appears in the intercept term, establishing that this parameter will shift the AD schedule. Also note that the parameter m_1, the size of which measures the intensity of the Fed's desire to hit the price target, appears in the expression for the slope of the AD curve, b_1. Since $\Delta p / \Delta y^d = -/b_1 < 0$, as m_1 rises, the slope of the AD schedule goes to zero.

Chapter 15

The Open Economy

LEARNING OBJECTIVES

This chapter explores the linkages between economies arising from international trade in goods, services, and financial assets. Our goal in this chapter is to understand the implications of these links for business cycles and economic policy. Because domestic residents can buy goods, physical and financial assets at home and abroad, business cycles, asset returns, and inflation rates in trading countries will be linked. It will also be true that exchange rates linking the currencies of open economies can constrain the policies of central banks. Here are a few of the questions that we examine in this chapter.

- How do countries keep track of international trade in goods and financial assets?

- How are exchange rates determined?

- How do inflation rates in trading countries affect exchange rates?

- Why are asset returns in trading countries linked?

- Why are business cycles in a domestic economy transmitted abroad?

All of the economic models described in this book have so far ignored the fact that economies are open. That is, the residents of a country can buy goods produced in foreign countries and they may buy physical and financial assets in foreign countries. The purpose of this chapter is to integrate these additional aspects of economic life into an aggregate economic model.

Our first topic for discussion is the **Balance of Payments**, an accounting system that records the transactions that occur between the residents of trading countries. This accounting system has two sections; one devoted to transactions in goods and services, and the other concerned with physical and financial asset flows between countries. This discussion will list the types of economic activities linking countries, a discussion useful to understanding what economic actions generate the demand and supply for foreign exchange.

We then discuss the determination of exchange rates by studying the foreign exchange market where market forces determine the demand and supply for currencies. Foreign exchange markets have historically had differing institutional arrangements involving the central bank. For example, the central bank may need to keep an exchange rate at a fixed value. We will describe these alternative market forms and discuss the role of the central bank, if any, in each system. We conclude our discussion of **nominal exchange rates** by discussing two theories of exchange rate determination; one of these theories applies to transactions in goods markets and the other applies to activities associated with financial markets.

Our next task will be to construct an aggregate economic model suitable to an open economy. This will involve including net exports (exports minus imports) into our aggregate demand relationship and then developing the economic theory of how exchange rates and real interest rates affect the trade balance. Having described this model, we then carry out a number of exercises to illustrate the workings of our open economy model. The important lesson to be drawn from these exercises is that business cycles are linked in pairs of trading economies. Economic fluctuations originating in one country will be transmitted to other countries, an important insight omitted from our closed economy models of aggregate economies.

Our discussion in this chapter is not a substitute for a formal economics course devoted to the open economy. But this chapter will serve to introduce you to some of the macroeconomic issues arising in open economies.

15.1 THE BALANCE OF PAYMENTS

The Balance of Payments (BOP) is an accounting statement of the economic transactions by residents of a country with the rest of the world in a given time period. The accounts are a double-entry bookkeeping system and, as such, every transaction is recorded twice. Once it is recorded as a credit with a positive entry and once as a debit entry with a negative sign. Thus all items in the accounts should sum to zero but, for various reasons, they do not and so a statistical discrepancy term is added to cause the accounts to sum to zero. For a given country, any transaction generating a payment flowing into an economy is recorded as a positive entry; any transaction generating a payment flowing to the rest of the world is recorded as a negative entry. There are two sections to these accounts: the **Current Account**, and the **Capital and Financial Account**.

The Current Account

This section of the BOP contains transactions for merchandise, services, and net transfer payments between countries. **Exports** refer to goods and services produced in the domestic economy, sold to residents in a foreign country. **Imports** are goods and services produced in a foreign country, sold to domestic residents. The difference between exports and imports is called **net exports**. So if the U.S. exports goods to the residents of the U.K., payments received by U.S. residents are recorded as a positive export entry in the BOP for the U.S. and a negative import entry is recorded in these accounts for the U.K. since this imported item generates a payment from U.K. residents. When the U.S. imports goods from the U.K., payments flow to U.K. residents from U.S. residents and so these transactions are recorded as a negative entry in the BOP for the U.S. and a positive entry is made as an export from the U.K. This section of the accounts also includes service transactions such as management consulting and legal services, income receipts derived from the ownership of assets, and unilateral transfers such as foreign aid payments. If a country's exports exceed its imports, that country is said to have a **trade surplus**. If exports are less than imports, a country has a **trade deficit**.

The Capital and Financial Account

This section of the BOP has two component categories: the **Capital Account** and the **Financial Account**.

The Capital Account

This section of the BOP records transactions for capital transfers and the purchase and sale of non-produced non-financial assets. An example of a capital transfer would be the transfer of ownership of a fixed asset such as land or debt forgiveness by a government. The acquisition and disposal of patents and copyrights are examples of non-produced non-financial assets.

The Financial Account

This account includes financial transactions such as trade in stocks and bonds (portfolio investment), firms, real estate, and the transactions involving the reserve assets of a country's monetary authorities. So if a U.K. resident buys a financial asset in the U.S., this would be recorded as a positive entry in the U.S. BOP because a domestic resident receives a payment from abroad. If a U.S. resident buys an asset abroad, this is recorded as a negative entry in the U.S. because a payment is made to a foreign resident.

In principle, the BOP should sum to zero although it does not for various reasons. The intuition for this is simple. If the residents of a country import more than they export, so that the trade balance is negative, then they must sell assets or borrow to make up the difference between exports and imports. The assets drawn down could be ones sold by domestic residents; they may borrow from abroad, generating positive entries in the financial account as they do so. Alternatively, the assets declining could be the official reserves of the country's central bank as the central bank sells foreign exchange from its currency reserves.

Figure 15.1 provides a time series plot of the annual U.S. current account balance for 1947 to 2008. Persistent deficits have been the norm for most years since 1970. This suggests that U.S. residents have been selling assets or borrowing to finance these deficits in the Current Account. Table 15.1 provides annual balance of payments data for the U.S. for selected years.

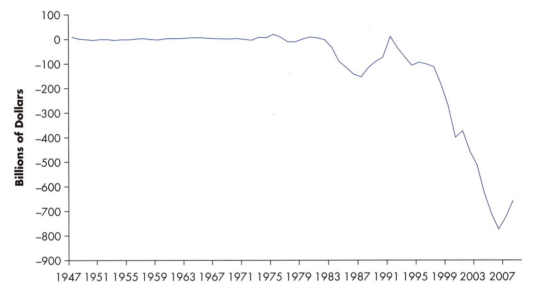

FIGURE 15.1 U.S. Current Account Balance, 1947–2008

Source: Table 4.1, Bureau of Economic Analysis

TABLE 15.1 The U.S. Balance of Payments, Millions of Dollars

	2005	2006	2007	2008
Current Account	–728993	–788116	–731214	–673265
Capital Account	–4036	–3880	–1843	–2600
Financial Account	700716	809364	767849	546590
Statistical Discrepancy	32313	–47078	–41287	129275

Source: Table 1, U.S. International Transactions, Bureau of Economic Analysis

The data confirm that the financial account has indeed been a surplus to finance the current account deficits in the U.S.

15.2 THE MARKET FOR FOREIGN EXCHANGE

The nominal exchange rate is a trading ratio between two currencies. For example, one dollar could be used to purchase two euros ($1 = €2) and the exchange rate, describing this ratio, can be expressed in one of two ways: euros per dollar (€2/$1) or dollars per euro ($1/€2). For consistency, we will always define the nominal exchange rate, e, to be measured in units of foreign currency per dollar. If e rises, the dollar fetches more euros in the market and this is called an **appreciation** of the dollar. When the dollar appreciates, the euro **depreciates** since it trades for fewer U.S. dollars.

Our discussion of the Balance of Payments described the activities of the public that generate the demands and supplies for currencies. Residents of a domestic economy will buy foreign currency, and supply domestic currency, because they wish to buy foreign goods. In addition, they may also wish to buy physical and financial assets in foreign countries. Doing so requires that domestic residents supply domestic currency in order to buy foreign currency.

Similarly, foreign residents will wish to buy goods in foreign countries as well as physical and financial assets. Thus they will supply the currency of their own country and will purchase the currencies of other countries. Figure 15.2 illustrates the market for foreign exchange that arises from all of these transactions. The market illustrated in the figure determines the nominal exchange rate for euros and the U.S. dollar.

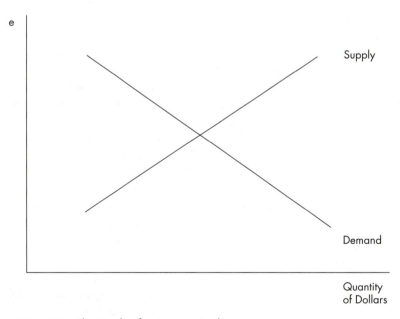

FIGURE 15.2 The Market for Foreign Exchange

The nominal exchange rate is denoted by e and is measured in units of foreign currency per dollar.

On the vertical axis, we have the nominal exchange rate, e, measured in units of foreign currency (here euros) per U.S. dollar. On the horizontal axis we measure the quantity of dollars traded in this market. The demand for dollars is downward sloping and the supply curve for dollars slopes upward. To see why, imagine that the dollar were to appreciate. When this happens, U.S. goods become more expensive abroad; if the nominal exchange rate for euros and dollars changes from €10/$1 to €20/$1, a product measured in dollar units with a price of $10 changes in price, in the foreign country, from €100 to €200. This increase in the euro price of the U.S.-made commodity causes foreign residents to buy fewer U.S. goods, and so the quantity of dollars demanded by foreign residents falls. Further, U.S. residents find foreign goods to be cheaper when measured in U.S. dollars; using the same two exchange rate values, a good produced in the Euro area, priced at €10, will fall in price from $1 to $.5. U.S. residents will buy more foreign goods, supplying more dollars in order to acquire more foreign currency.

Having established the slopes of these curves, we now need to establish how the exchange rate is determined in this market. It turns out that foreign exchange markets have operated under different institutional arrangements. We now discuss these alternatives, eventually asking which of these may be the best choice for an economy.

Exchange Rate Regimes

Exchange rate regimes differ by the degree of intervention in foreign exchange markets by central banks. In a **flexible exchange rate** system, there is no intervention by central banks and thus the market is permitted to set the exchange rate through the actions of all of the participants in the market. Therefore, in Figure 15.3, if the exchange rate is initially above the equilibrium denoted by e*, there will be an excess supply of dollars in the market. Sellers of dollars will attempt to sell dollars by reducing the rate that they will accept in trade for euros and so the dollar will depreciate until the equilibrium is reached. Below this equilibrium, there will be an excess demand for dollars and the dollar will appreciate. In an excess demand situation, those who demand dollars in trade for foreign currency will bid up the exchange rate by offering more units of foreign currency per dollar, causing the dollar to appreciate. In this type of market, therefore, excess supplies and demands for currencies will be eliminated. In a **dirty float**, private citizens buy and sell currencies, just as in the floating exchange rate case, but in addition, central banks purchase or sell currencies, often in an attempt to change the equilibrium exchange rate.

The U.S. and many other developed economies have been on a flexible exchange rate system since the early 1970s; there have been occasions where central banks have intervened in foreign exchange markets to try to change the levels of exchange rates. Figure 15.4 gives a monthly time series graph of the euro–dollar exchange rate. The data shows considerable changes in the series over time and the month-to-month, or even day-to-day, variability in the exchange rate has been an important reason for central bank market interventions.

In a **fixed exchange rate** system, the exchange rate is pegged at a fixed value and it is the responsibility of the central bank to maintain this fixed value. So first imagine that the exchange rate is pegged at the level of the equilibrium e*. There is nothing that the central bank must do to maintain this rate; quantities of currencies supplied and demanded just balance. But there may be shifts in the demand and supply curves that would warrant action by the central bank.

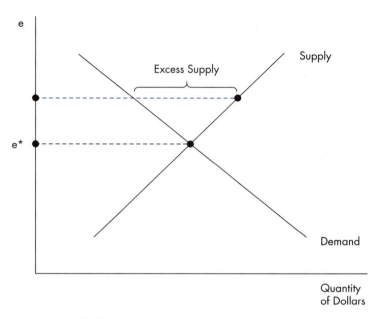

FIGURE 15.3 Exchange Rate Regimes

The nominal exchange rate is denoted by e. In a flexible exchange rate system, the market will set e* but, in a fixed exchange rate system, the central bank must maintain an exchange rate above e*.

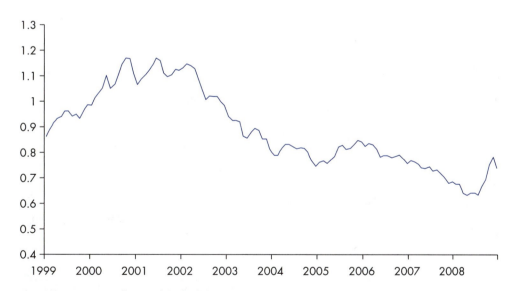

FIGURE 15.4 Euro-Dollar Exchange Rate

Source: St. Louis Federal Reserve Bank FRED Database

Suppose such shifts occur, resulting in an exchange rate pegged at a level which is above the equilibrium (see Figure 15.3 above). At this level, the dollar is **overvalued** because, if the market were allowed to set the equilibrium exchange rate, the dollar would depreciate. There is an excess supply of dollars and it is now the job of the central bank to buy these dollars by supplying foreign currency out of its stock of foreign currency reserves.[1] So in this situation, the reserves of the central bank are being depleted and eventually will be exhausted because the reserves of a central bank are not unlimited.[2] As we will now show, the central bank must pursue its monetary policy to cause the pegged exchange rate to become the equilibrium in the market. What must it do to accomplish this objective?

The answer lies in thinking about how monetary policy affects interest rates in the domestic economy. Look at Figure 15.5 and recall that if the money supply is reduced, the nominal (and real) interest rate will rise. This will cause domestic and foreign investors to change their behavior; domestic investors will find domestic assets more attractive and so will wish to buy fewer foreign assets. As a result they supply fewer dollars at any level of the nominal exchange

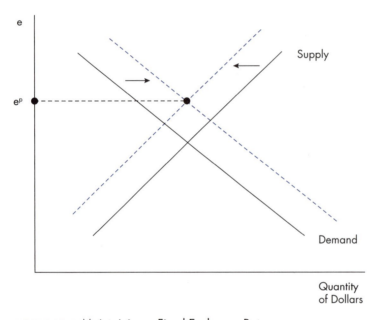

FIGURE 15.5 Maintaining a Fixed Exchange Rate

In a fixed exchange rate system, the central bank will lose foreign exchange reserves if its currency is overvalued. So it must pursue monetary policies which cause the demand and supply curves to shift so that the pegged exchange rate becomes the equilibrium exchange rate.

---

1 Recall our discussion of the Fed's balance sheet in Chapter 7. In that chapter, you saw that one entry on the asset side of the balance sheet was foreign exchange holdings by the Fed.

2 The International Monetary Fund was set up to help countries deal with situations like the one being described here. This organization could lend currencies to central banks which could then use them to maintain a fixed exchange rate. This was only a temporary situation, however, and central banks were required to take other steps, described below, to eliminate the excess demand for dollars.

rate. Foreign investors will find domestic assets more attractive and so will want to buy more of them, increasing the demand for dollars at any level of the exchange rate. These actions thus cause shifts in the demand and supply curves that act to eliminate the excess demand for dollars. In the case where the dollar is undervalued, the Fed will acquire foreign exchange reserves, and central banks elsewhere will be losing foreign exchange reserves. The Fed should pursue monetary expansion, reducing real interest rates in the U.S., and other central banks should pursue restrictive monetary policies to eliminate their foreign exchange losses.

The moral of the story is that a central bank is not free to pursue whatever monetary policy it chooses if it intends to maintain a fixed exchange rate; it must pursue a restrictive (expansive) monetary policy when its currency is overvalued (undervalued). We summarize this important insight in the following proposition.

Proposition About Monetary Policy in a Fixed Exchange Rate System

- In a fixed exchange rate system, the central bank must pursue its monetary policies consistent with the maintenance of its fixed exchange rate.

Currency Attacks

If a central bank does not pursue the monetary policy needed to maintain a fixed exchange rate, the result may be a **speculative attack** on the domestic currency by the public. Figure 15.6 illustrates what can happen in this case. Foreign exchange reserves are finite and so if a central bank continually loses foreign exchange reserves, and if these reserve losses are common knowledge, the public will come to expect a depreciation of the domestic currency. This implies that there are capital gains to be had by holding foreign currency; if the dollar is devalued (set at a new lower depreciated level), holders of foreign currency will be able to buy more dollars after the devaluation. This realization will cause domestic U.S. investors to supply more dollars as they try to hold more foreign currency. Foreign residents will demand fewer dollars because they expect the dollar currency to depreciate. The end result is that the excess supply of dollars will grow, accelerating the loss of reserves by the central bank. Ultimately, the domestic currency will need to be devalued to stem the loss of reserves by the central bank. Thus the expectations of the public about the prospects of currency devaluation will be correct.

The United States was on a fixed exchange rate system until the early 1970s when the fixed exchange rate system was abandoned. The underlying reason for this is that the U.S. was experiencing substantial inflation at that time and, as you will soon learn, a fixed exchange rate system is incompatible with inflationary monetary policies. Below we will argue that inflation is one reason why exchange rates change over time.

Capital Controls

In our discussion of exchange markets, we assumed that private individuals were free to pursue whatever actions were in their own self-interest. This is not always the case because

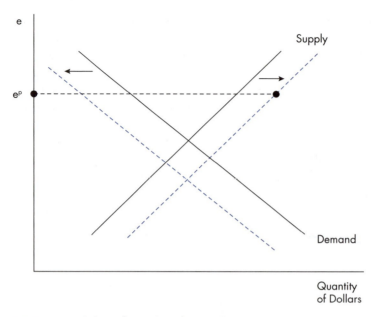

FIGURE 15.6 A Speculative Attack on a Currency

In a fixed exchange rate system, the central bank will lose foreign exchange reserves if its currency, pegged at e^p, is overvalued. If the central bank does not pursue a restrictive monetary policy, the domestic currency may be subject to a speculative attack, causing the demand and supply curves to shift as investors expect a depreciation of the overvalued currency.

governments have, from time to time, restricted the actions that private individuals could carry out in foreign exchange markets. **Capital controls** are an example of a government policy that would prevent people from buying foreign exchange for some purposes.

Suppose we return to our speculative attack example and imagine how our discussion would differ if the government could effectively prevent the private sector from engaging in the purchase or sale of foreign exchange. Then individuals would be unable to carry out the foreign exchange transactions that would lead to an increasingly **overvalued currency** and so the central bank would see smaller foreign exchange reserve losses compared to the case where there were no capital controls. This result of course depends upon the government's ability to enforce its restrictions on foreign exchange transactions and it is quite likely that individuals would seek and find ways around the government's policy restrictions. Thus the effectiveness of capital controls in foreign exchange markets depends upon the effectiveness of the government's enforcement mechanisms in preventing the private sector from engaging in certain transactions.

Which Exchange Rate System Is Best?

Fixed and flexible exchange rate systems each have their strengths and weaknesses and the system that a country adopts depends upon the circumstances in which the country finds itself.

Advocates of fixed exchange rate systems argue that flexible exchange rate systems generate extremely volatile nominal exchange rates that will damage international trade between countries.[3] If exchange rates are volatile, firms may build plants abroad rather than ship goods abroad simply because of exchange rate volatility. This would lead to a less efficient resource allocation in the world and a corresponding reduction in economic welfare. In addition, central banks are less able to pursue inflationary monetary policies if they are required to maintain a fixed exchange rate system. This imposes discipline on the institution that otherwise might be prone to causing inflation. A country and may thus experience lower inflation.

Those in favor of flexible exchange rates stress that monetary policy is free under a flexible exchange rate system to be used to combat recessions, an action that may not be possible in a fixed rate system. For this to be a virtue, the central bank must be competently managed and not prone to creating secular inflation. Advocates of these systems also must believe that it is appropriate for monetary policy to be used as a stabilizing influence in the economy, whether by using rules or discretion in carrying out such stabilization. As we indicated in Chapter 14, some economists do not believe that discretionary monetary policy should be used as a stabilization mechanism.

Currency unions, such as the EU, are an alternative to fixed exchange rate systems where a group of countries agree to use a common currency in all transactions. The advantage of such a system is that it reduces the transactions costs associated with using multiple currencies and it confers the advantages of a fixed exchange rate system at the same time. However, monetary policy must be conducted by a single institution in such an arrangement, meaning that monetary policy cannot be tailored to the needs of a single country but rather must be set for the group of countries as a whole. This implies that countries must be willing to give up the right to have their own central banks. A currency union would also involve free trade among member countries so that this arrangement confers the advantages of free trade upon member countries.

15.3 THE DETERMINANTS OF NOMINAL EXCHANGE RATES

The foreign exchange market determines the nominal exchange rate in response to economic forces prevailing in trading economies. Here, two theories of these underlying economic forces are described, one associated with goods markets and one with financial markets.

Goods Markets: Purchasing Power Parity

To understand how nominal exchange rates are determined, consider a simple example of two trading countries where there are no barriers to trade and no transactions costs associated with shipping goods abroad. Imagine further that one good can be produced and sold in either country and suppose that the following condition holds.

---

3 This exchange rate volatility is one reason why central banks have intervened in foreign exchange markets. This is an important reason why dirty floats have occurred.

$$P^{Foreign} > P \cdot e$$

In this expression, $P^{Foreign}$ stands for the foreign currency price of the good (the price at which the good sells in the foreign country), P is the domestic price of the same good, and e is the nominal exchange rate measured in units of foreign currency per dollar. If you were a U.S. goods producer, where would you want to sell your product?

Clearly the domestic producer would want to sell her product abroad because doing so generates more dollars ($P^{Foreign}/e > P$) than selling it at home. Or consider a trader in foreign exchange markets. He notices that he could buy the good in the U.S., ship it abroad and sell it, generating a sure profit.[4] These actions by the producer and currency trader would tend to eliminate the inequality in the expression above, leading to the **Purchasing Power Parity** relationship

$$P^{Foreign} = P \cdot e.$$

Economies of course produce more than one good so our discussion must recognize this obvious feature of actual economies. We can take account of this fact by imagining that, in the equation above, individual prices are replaced by price indexes. Doing so, the resulting equation yields a version of exchange rate theory called **Absolute Purchasing Power Parity**.

This theory is not thought by economists to hold exactly for a number of reasons (see **Doing Economics**: Empirical Evidence on the Law of One Price). For example, one of the assumptions in our discussion above does not hold for all goods in an economy. We assumed that all goods were tradable across economic boundaries but in fact this is not the case. There are non-traded goods, such as housing, that cannot be used for **arbitrage** opportunities and so

---

Doing Economics: Empirical Evidence on the Law of One Price

The theory of Purchasing Power Parity (PPP), discussed in the text, was motivated by an example drawn from a simple economic world that does not exist. That is, economists have devised many reasons why PPP may not hold in the world in which we actually live and so it becomes an empirical question as to the extent to which PPP holds. Economists Jonathan Haskel and Holger Wolf carried out such an empirical study of PPP using data from IKEA, a well-known retail firm that sells products in many countries. These economists studied absolute prices for more than 100 identical goods sold in 25 countries by IKEA, using actual local currency transaction prices for identical goods. This choice of data is attractive because the goods chosen are tradable and permit a direct computation of absolute and proportional violations of the law of one price.

---

4 This is called an *arbitrage* by the currency trader. Foreign currency markets are thought to have well-informed traders who would quickly exploit these profit opportunities if they were to arise.

The results from this study show typical divergences in prices from PPP of 20 to 50 percent. Further, they find no evidence that these price differences can be attributed to differences in local distribution costs. However they do find some evidence that prices converge over time to PPP levels. Thus there is considerable evidence in this study that Absolute PPP does not hold.

Reference: Jonathan Haskel and Holger Wolf, "The Law of One Price – A Case Study," *Scandinavian Journal of Economics* 103, No. 4 (2001), pp. 545–58.

there is an approximate form of the theory known as **Relative Purchasing Power Parity**. This version of the theory is written as

$$P^{Foreign} \cong P \cdot e$$

where, in the above relationship, the symbol "$\cong$" stands for "approximately." But even with this qualification, we can use this economic theory of exchange rates to derive a prediction about what determines nominal exchanges rates over time. Applying the change operator to the last expression above gives us

$$\frac{\Delta P^{Foreign}}{P^{Foreign}} \cong \frac{\Delta P}{P} + \frac{\Delta e}{e}$$

and, rearranging this expression gives

$$\frac{\Delta e}{e} \cong \frac{\Delta P^{Foreign}}{P^{Foreign}} - \frac{\Delta P}{P}.$$

This equation instructs us to look at relative inflation rates between countries as an explanation for the behavior of nominal exchange rates; this inflation differential determines the behavior of the nominal exchange rate. If the domestic economy has an inflation rate exceeding that of its trading partner, then the domestic currency will depreciate ($\Delta e/e < 0$); that is, it will fetch fewer units of foreign currency in the foreign exchange market. If the domestic economy has an inflation rate below that of its trading partner, the domestic currency will appreciate ($\Delta e/e > 0$).

Figure 15.7 provides some evidence on the relationship between inflation and nominal exchange rates in G-7 countries. On the horizontal axis we have the inflation differential between six G-7 countries versus the U.S. and on the vertical axis we have the percentage change in the nominal exchange rate. The data are annual averages and all calculations begin in 1971, ending in either 2001 or 2008 due to data availability. Since exchange rates are measured in units of foreign currency per dollar, a positive inflation differential means that foreign inflation exceeds domestic inflation and so should be associated with a positive percentage change in the exchange rate. As you can see from the diagram, there is clear evidence supporting this theory but there is not quite a one-to-one relationship between the inflation differential and the percentage change in the nominal exchange rate. There must be

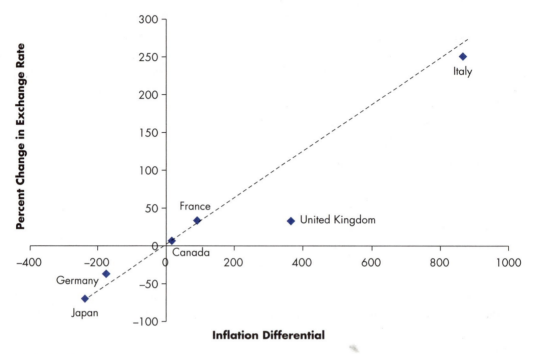

FIGURE 15.7 Inflation and Exchange Rates in G7 Countries

other forces at work, suggesting that Relative Purchasing Power Parity is not the whole story about the determinants of nominal exchange rates. For this reason, economists have come to regard Relative Purchasing Power Parity as a theory of the long-run relationships between nominal exchange rates, a relationship holding when economies are in long-run equilibrium. Such equilibria are rare if they ever occur at all outside of economic theory texts, suggesting that there must be other influences on nominal exchange rates that would explain short-run variations in exchange rates when economies are not in long-run equilibrium.

Financial Markets: Uncovered Interest Parity

The demands and supplies for currencies arise in part from transactions in financial markets. Here we discuss a determinant of nominal exchange rates associated with financial markets. **Uncovered Interest Parity** is a theory that we can use to explain the connection between interest rates across countries. The theory arises by way of the following thought experiment.

Imagine that an individual investor has the option to buy two securities. These securities are identical in every way except that each is offered in a different country. Table 15.2 provides the data on the returns obtained by holding these two securities.

If an investor invests a dollar in the home country, she will earn the return $1 + i$. Alternatively, if she invests in the foreign country, she must first convert a dollar into foreign currency using the nominal exchange rate, e. Thus one dollar buys e units of foreign currency. In units of foreign currency, she will earn $e \cdot (1 + i^{\text{Foreign}})$ where i^{Foreign} is the return on the asset in the foreign country. In the future, our investor must convert her earnings back into units of domestic

TABLE 15.2 Asset Returns in Two Countries	
Return from Home Country Assets	*Return from Foreign Country Assets*
$(1 + i)$	$(1 + i^{\text{Foreign}}) \cdot (e/e^*)$
Equilibrium Condition: $(1 + i) = (1 + i^{\text{Foreign}}) \cdot (e/e^*)$	

Note: In the table, i denotes the asset return in the home country, i^{Foreign} is the asset return in the foreign country, e is the current nominal exchange rate in units of home country currency, and e* is the future nominal exchange rate.

currency, so her total return is given by $e \cdot (1 + i^{\text{Foreign}})/e^*$ where e* is the nominal exchange rate in the future when this foreign return is to be converted back into domestic currency. At the time of her investment decision, the individual does not know the value of the future nominal exchange rate and so must form expectations in some manner about this magnitude.

In making her investment decision, suppose the investor's expectations are formed so that

$$(1 + i) > (1 + i^{\text{Foreign}}) \cdot (e/e^*).$$

In this case, the investor would prefer to hold the domestic asset since she expects it to yield a higher return. If all investors held the same expectation, then they all would be buying the domestic asset, tending to cause the domestic currency to appreciate as domestic investors reduce foreign asset purchases and foreign residents try to buy more domestic assets.

If the inequality above were reversed, our investor would prefer the foreign asset, as all investors would with the same expectation. Thus in equilibrium, we anticipate that expected returns across countries would be about the same. So our equilibrium condition in the asset markets of the two countries would therefore be

$$(1 + i) = (1 + i^{\text{Foreign}}) \cdot (e/e^*).$$

A bit of algebra (see the Appendix) takes this result and turns into one that is a bit more intuitive. That expression is given below.

$$(1+i) = (1+i^{\text{Foreign}}) - \frac{e^* - e}{e}$$

This last expression is very intuitive for it simply says that the return on domestic assets must be equal to the return on foreign assets adjusted for any expected capital gains or losses that arise due to foreign currency purchases and sales. This equilibrium condition offers several insights that are worth noting.

The first useful implication of this condition is that it clearly shows why the demands and supplies for currencies, discussed previously, are tied to portfolio decisions by the public. Any decision to buy foreign assets will require a foreign currency purchase and sale by domestic residents. The same is true for foreign residents planning to buy domestic assets.

Second, this market equilibrium condition shows that expectations about the future nominal exchange rate must be made by market participants. The exchange rate at which investment earnings, measured in units of foreign currency, will be converted back into domestic currency units is unknown to investors at the time they make their investment decisions. This is an element of uncertainty that complicates any decision to buy foreign assets because there may be unanticipated capital losses attached to investing in foreign countries that will reduce the returns on foreign assets.[5]

Finally, this condition suggests that we should see interest rates on comparable securities moving closely together. The market equilibrium condition above shows that there will be a differential between domestic and foreign returns based upon the expectations of the public about future exchange rates and the current nominal exchange rate. For example, returns in the two countries will be identical if the public expects no change in the exchange rate in the future. If the public expects capital losses on foreign currency, then the foreign return must exceed the domestic return as compensation for these capital losses on foreign exchange. Given the current and future nominal exchange rate, if an event causes nominal interest rates to change, say monetary policy in the domestic country reduces the nominal asset return i, then we can expect financial capital to flow out of the domestic economy and into the foreign economy, thus restoring the previous differential. In short, a decline in the domestic economy return should result in a decline in the foreign country return.

Figure 15.8 provides some evidence on this last point. The figure provides monthly data on three-month Treasury Bills in Canada and the U.S. It is evident that the series frequently follow a common pattern but it is also clear that there are relative level shifts in the series. These shifts in the levels of the series may reflect changes in exchange rate expectations or other factors omitted from our analysis. But the data provides some support for our interest parity discussion.

Financial market linkages exist between countries that involve other financial assets such as stock markets. Indeed recent events in Greece apparently affected U.S. stock prices (see **Doing Economics**: The U.S. Stock Market and the Greek Sovereign Debt Crisis). One aspect of globalization is the intimate connection between markets in financial assets around the world.

Doing Economics: The U.S. Stock Market and the Greek Sovereign Debt Crisis

On May 6, 2010, the U.S. stock market displayed unprecedented volatility with the Dow Jones Industrial Average (an index measuring the stock prices of a group of large U.S. corporations) falling 1,000 points in just over thirty minutes. The Dow ended the day with an approximate 300-point loss. Members of the media queried market experts who claimed that the possible insolvency of the Greek government was one factor causing this volatility. Why

---

5 There is a version of this theory, known as Covered Interest Parity, which extends this analysis by including *forward exchange rates* into the analysis. A forward exchange rate is one where individuals agree on an exchange rate between currencies to be exercised at a future time. Thus investors could use this forward exchange rate in place of the expected future exchange rate in making their investment decisions.

should the Greek government's financial problems have anything to do with the price of U.S. stocks? One possible answer to this question arises from the fact that all financial markets are linked. Domestic residents of a country can buy and sell assets at home or abroad – one aspect of globalization.

Greece is a member of the EU. The government of Greece has been running budget deficits for a number of years, with the current budget deficit at approximately 13 percent of GDP. The fear among EU policymakers, leading them to provide loans to Greece, was that the Greek government would be unable to borrow the sums necessary to cover their current deficit, leading to the insolvency of the Greek government. If the Greek government became insolvent, it would be unable to make interest payments on existing Greek government debt, making the Greek government's bonds worthless. That bond default could lead to problems for financial institutions, in Greece and elsewhere, holding Greek government bonds. Thus the insolvency of Greece could reduce the net worth of these financial institutions, possibly causing them to become bankrupt. Thus the Greek financial crisis could result in the economies of the EU entering a recession.

Our results in this chapter indicate that business cycles are transmitted internationally due to foreign trade linkages, so a recession in the EU could result in recessions in other countries, including the U.S. Thus holders of U.S. stocks may have expected the Greek debt crisis to cause a U.S. recession that would reduce U.S. corporate earnings, triggering the selling of their U.S. stocks. This scenario illustrates the extent to which financial events in any one country can have their effects transmitted globally.

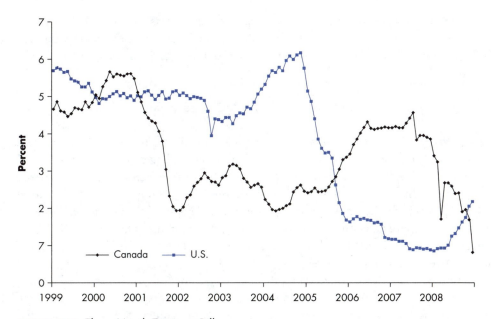

FIGURE 15.8 Three-Month Treasury Bills

Sources: Bank of Canada, St. Louis Federal Reserve Bank FRED Database

15.4 OPEN ECONOMY AGGREGATE MODELS

In this section, we develop an aggregate economic model for an open economy. Our first goal is to incorporate the trade sector into the aggregate demand schedule. We do this by first developing a relationship between net exports and the real exchange rate. We then take up a discussion of the real exchange rate and its connection to real interest rates. Piecing together the two discussions shows how net exports are related to real interest rates.

The Real Exchange Rate

Our purchasing power parity discussion can be used to introduce another measure of exchange rates that is useful to us in our open economy macroeconomic models. This new measure is called the **real exchange rate**, denoted by e_r, and it is defined below.

Definition of the Real Exchange Rate

■ The real exchange rate is defined as $e_r = e \cdot [P/P^{Foreign}]$ where P denotes the domestic price level and $P^{Foreign}$ is the price level in the foreign country. It measures the rate at which goods can be exchanged between the two countries.

In a world where absolute purchasing power parity holds, the real exchange rate would be equal to unity ($e_r = 1$) but our earlier discussion showed that this is not the case. Thus we will argue that variations in this magnitude will affect the current account in open economies.

To see what the real exchange rate measures, imagine that there is only one good produced in the world, apples. Suppose that in the U.S., apples sell for $1 per apple and that, in the EU, apples sell for €3 per apple. If the nominal exchange rate is e = €2/$, then the real exchange rate is

$$e_r = [(€2/\$)\cdot(\$1/\text{U.S. apple})]/(€3/\text{Euro apple})$$

which gives the value $e_r = .67$. One U.S. apple trades for .67 Euro apples. Thus the real exchange rate measures an exchange ratio for goods between trading pairs of countries.

If e_r increases, the real exchange rate has appreciated because a given quantity of domestic goods exchanges for more foreign goods. So in the numerical example above, if e_r rises from .67 to .8, a U.S. apple fetches more Euro apples in trade. This would occur, for example, if the dollar were to appreciate (the nominal exchange rate, e, increases), meaning that U.S. goods become more expensive abroad and foreign goods get cheaper in the U.S. If e_r declines, the real exchange rate has depreciated.

Our example was simplified by assuming that there was only one good produced in each country. As we know, economies produce many goods and services so we will need to think of the real exchange rate as including price indexes for each country in place of individual goods prices. And so if there is an appreciation of the real exchange rate, U.S. goods are becoming generally more expensive abroad and Euro area goods get cheaper in the U.S.

Net Exports and the Real Exchange Rate

Changes in the real exchange rate will have an impact upon a country's net exports. To see why, consider an increase in the real exchange rate, called a **real appreciation**. From our real exchange rate definition above, notice that the real exchange rate can rise for three reasons: the domestic price level rises, the foreign price level falls, or the domestic currency appreciates (the nominal exchange rate, e, rises). In each of these cases, net exports will fall.

Suppose that the U.S. domestic price level rises. Then residents of the U.S. economy will buy more UK goods because UK goods are now cheaper relative to U.S. goods. U.S. domestic imports rise and so net U.S. exports decline. UK residents will buy fewer U.S. goods because U.S. goods are now more expensive relative to goods produced in their own country and so U.S. exports decline, and thus net U.S. exports fall.

Now suppose that the UK price level declines, raising the real exchange rate. If UK goods get cheaper, domestic U.S. residents buy more goods imported from the UK, reducing net U.S. exports. Foreign UK residents will buy fewer goods produced in the U.S. because U.S. goods are now more expensive relative to goods produced in their own country. Thus U.S. exports decline and so net U.S. exports decline.

Finally, suppose that the domestic currency appreciates (e rises). This causes domestic goods to become more expensive abroad, causing domestic exports and thus net domestic exports to decline. Foreign goods get cheaper in the domestic economy and so domestic imports rise, reducing net domestic exports.[6] Our discussion is summarized below.

Proposition About Net Exports and the Real Exchange Rate

■ Net exports are inversely related to the real exchange rate.

Figure 15.9 provides a times series plot of the real exchange rate and real net exports for the U.S. There is an evident increase in the real exchange rate starting in the middle of the 1990s. Real net exports declined over this period and continued to decline for some time thereafter. But the real exchange rate declined beginning in about 2002 yet there was no evident increase in net exports. This suggests that there are other determinants of net exports, omitted from our discussion, which may account for this pattern in the data (see fn. 4 above).

The Determinants of the Real Exchange Rate

The real exchange rate responds to two economic determinants: real interest rates at home and abroad. This implies that net exports are dependent upon these economic magnitudes.

---

6 Net exports could initially decline if the real exchange rate depreciates, a possibility that we ignore for simplicity. The reason is that, given real net exports, a currency depreciation will initially result in higher imports when measured in units of domestic currency. Quantities of net exports will adjust over time. Thus net exports may initially fall in response to a currency depreciation and rise over time, a pattern known as the *J-Curve*.

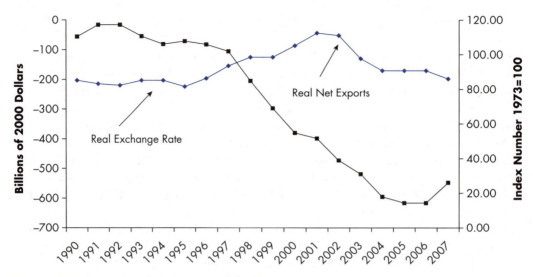

FIGURE 15.9 The Real Exchange Rate and Real Net Exports

Sources: Real Exchange Rate, Council of Economic Advisors, 2009. Real Net Exports, BEA, Table 1.1.6

To see how the domestic real interest rate affects the real exchange rate, recall that financial transactions occur between countries as their residents buy and sell financial and physical assets at home and abroad. The decision to buy these assets depends in part upon the real return provided by these assets. So if the real interest rate rises in the U.S., making U.S. assets more attractive to investors, then U.S. residents will buy fewer assets abroad, supplying fewer dollars in the foreign exchange market, and EU investors will demand more dollars in the foreign exchange market as they will wish to buy more U.S. assets. These actions will cause the dollar to appreciate, resulting in an appreciation of the real exchange rate.

Suppose now that the real interest rate rises in the EU. How will this event affect investors in the EU area and the U.S.? Clearly U.S. investors will wish to buy more EU assets, supplying more dollars to do so. Investors in the EU area will wish to buy more assets in the EU and fewer in the U.S. All of these actions lead to a depreciation of the nominal exchange rate and of the real exchange rate as well.

As we showed earlier, there is an inverse relationship between the real exchange rate and net exports so a rise in the U.S. real interest rate causes an appreciation of the real exchange rate and thus a decline in net exports. A rise in the EU real interest rate causes a depreciation of the real exchange rate and hence an increase in net exports.

Net Exports and Output

Net exports also depend upon the levels of income in the domestic and foreign economies. Imports depend upon the income of domestic residents; the higher are domestic incomes, the higher will be consumption by households, and some of this additional consumption will be imports into the U.S. We can describe this relationship as

$$IM = IM(Y), 0 < \Delta M/\Delta Y < 1$$

where IM denotes imports. The change in imports associated with a change in income is sometimes called the **marginal propensity to import** or **MPI**. We assume the MPI to be between zero and unity for the same reason that we did for the MPC (marginal propensity to consume). It is reasonable to assume that for every extra dollar of income, households will save a part of the increased income and consume part of the increased income. Part of this additional consumption will be for imports.

Domestic exports depend upon the level of foreign incomes; the higher are foreign incomes, the higher will be exports, and thus net exports, in the domestic economy.

Defining NX as net exports, Y as domestic income, $Y^{Foreign}$ as foreign income, r as the domestic real interest rate, and $r^{Foreign}$ as the foreign real interest rate, we write net exports as

$$NX = NX(Y, Y^{Foreign}, r, r^{Foreign}),$$

$$\Delta NX/\Delta Y < 0, \Delta NX/\Delta Y^{Foreign} > 0,$$

$$\Delta NX/\Delta r < 0, \Delta NX/\Delta r^{Foreign} > 0.$$

In the expressions above, we note that net exports depend upon domestic and foreign incomes, and real interest rates. We also note the response of net exports to its determinants. Table 15.3 summarizes our discussion about the determinants of net exports.

15.5 THE OPEN ECONOMY IS CURVE

The open economy IS curve can be obtained from the NIPA (National Income and Product Accounts) relationship written as

$$Y = C + I + G + NX.$$

TABLE 15.3 Net Exports, Real Incomes, and Real Interest Rates

Exogenous Factor	Response of Real Exchange Rate	Response of Net Exports
$r \uparrow$	$e_r \uparrow$	$NX \downarrow$
$r^{Foreign} \uparrow$	$e_r \downarrow$	$NX \uparrow$
Y	N.A.	$NX \downarrow$
$Y^{Foreign}$	N.A.	$NX \uparrow$

Note: In the table, Y is domestic income, $Y^{Foreign}$ is foreign real income, r is the domestic real interest rate, $r^{Foreign}$ is the foreign real interest rate, NX denotes net exports, and e_r is the real exchange rate.

Our analysis of investment demand led us to conclude that investment was inversely related to the real interest rate and we just established a relationship between net exports, domestic income, and the real interest rate.[7] We note these dependencies by rewriting the goods market NIPA equation as

$$Y = C(Y) + I(r) + G + NX(Y, r).$$

In the expression above, we suppress for now all of the shift parameters that affect this relationship. Apply the change operator to this expression to get

$$\Delta Y = C_Y \cdot \Delta Y + I_r \cdot \Delta r + NX_Y \cdot \Delta Y + NX_r \cdot \Delta r$$

$$\Delta Y = MPC \cdot \Delta Y + I_r \cdot \Delta r - MPI \cdot \Delta Y + NX_r \cdot \Delta r$$

where C_Y is the MPC (Marginal Propensity to Consume) and $NX_Y = -IM_Y = -MPI$. Remember that $NX = X - IM$ (exports minus imports) which explains the minus sign preceding the MPI. Rearranging terms in this expression gives

$$[1 - MPC + MPI] \cdot \Delta Y = (I_r + NX_r) \cdot \Delta r$$

which yields the slope of the IS curve to be

$$\frac{\Delta r}{\Delta Y} = \frac{1 - MPC + MPI}{I_r + NX_r} < 0,$$

given our assumptions about the sizes of the MPC and MPI. In this last expression, I_r is the response of investment to the real interest rate and NX_r is the response of net exports to the real interest rate; both of these responses are negative. This shows that the IS curve has a negative slope, just as it did previously in our closed-economy models. But it is now more interest-elastic than it was previously as is shown in Figure 15.10.

The reason for this increased interest elasticity is easy to understand. When there is an increase in the real interest rate, our previous analysis caused us to expect a decline in investment, thereby reducing output in the goods market. But now an increase in the real interest rate causes two types of output demand to decline: investment and net exports. As a result, output will fall by more, for a given increase in the real interest rate, than it did when net exports were not a part of our analysis.

15.6 THE OPEN ECONOMY AGGREGATE DEMAND SCHEDULE

In closed economy models, we ignored net exports and derived relationships between the price level and output consistent with equilibrium in the goods, money, and bond markets. In the

---

7 We simplify by ignoring the fact that consumption depends upon the real interest rate as established in Chapter 4.

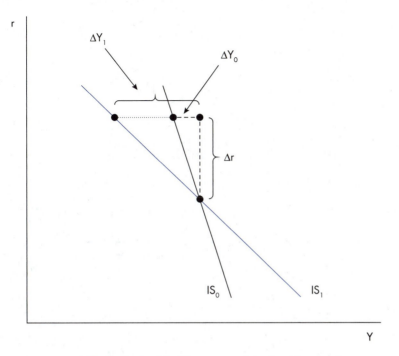

FIGURE 15.10 The IS Curve, Net Exports, and the Real Interest Rate

IS_0 is the IS curve when net exports are ignored and IS_1 is the IS curve when net exports are related to the real interest rate. In the latter case, the IS curve is more interest elastic so a rise in the real interest rate generates a larger reduction in real output since both investment and net exports decline. An increase in the interest rate in the amount Δr reduces output by ΔY_0 when net exports are not in the model and by ΔY_1 when net exports are interest elastic ($\Delta Y_1 > \Delta Y_0$).

open economy model, we derive exactly the same relationship between price and output and, in view of our discussion above about the open economy IS curve, your intuition should be that the open economy aggregate demand schedule should look very similar to its closed-economy counterpart. This is true as we now demonstrate.

Consider Figure 15.11, identical to Figure 11.8 in Chapter 11. The aggregate demand schedule is derived using the following thought experiment. Starting from the initial price level, P_0, ask what will happen in the goods, money, and bond markets when there is a decline in the price level. The decline in the price level causes an increase in the real money supply, M/P, causing an excess supply of money that reduces the interest rate consistent with equilibrium in the financial markets (money and bonds). This causes a rightward shift in the LM schedule because there is now a lower interest rate consistent with financial market equilibrium at any level of output. This increases the level of output consistent with goods market equilibrium because investment and net exports increase when the interest rate declines. This means that at a lower price level, there is a higher level of output consistent with equilibrium in the goods, money, and bond markets. The aggregate demand schedule slopes downward.

An obvious question to ask is this; what, if anything, is different from the closed-economy case? The answer is that the aggregate demand schedule in the open economy case is more price-elastic than it is in the closed economy case. A given increase in the supply of real

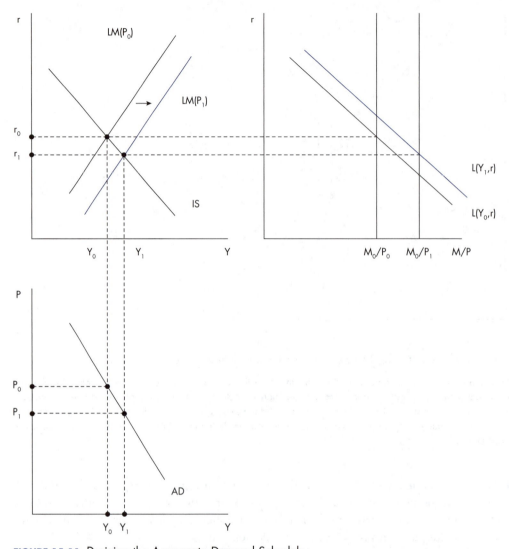

FIGURE 15.11 Deriving the Aggregate Demand Schedule

The aggregate demand curve is obtained by observing how a change in the price level affects equilibrium in the goods, money, and bond markets. The level of real money balances supplied rises with a fall in the price level ($P_0 > P_1$). This causes a decline in the interest rate clearing the money market, causing the LM curve to shift right. A lower real interest rate raises the investment and net export demand for goods. A lower price level results in a higher demand for goods.

balances (generated by a decline in the price level), and induced decline in the interest rate, causes a larger increase in output because both investment and net exports rise (only investment rises in the closed-economy case). So even though the aggregate demand schedule looks the same as in the closed economy case, it now is more price-elastic than it was previously. But this means that we can carry out policy exercises in much the same way as we did in the closed-economy case.

This also means that all of those factors that could shift the aggregate demand schedule in the closed economy case will also shift this schedule in the open economy model. Table 15.4 lists these factors and there are two additions in the closed-economy case. The foreign real interest rate and foreign income will also shift the AD schedule because shifts in these magnitudes affect net exports.

An increase in the foreign real interest rate makes foreign assets more attractive to U.S. investors and foreign residents. As a result, there is an increased supply of dollars in the foreign exchange markets by U.S. residents wanting to purchase more foreign assets and fewer U.S. assets. There will also be a reduced demand for dollars by foreign residents who will plan to buy fewer U.S. assets and more foreign assets. These actions will cause a nominal and **real depreciation** of the dollar. Since there is an inverse relationship between the real exchange rate and net exports, the decline in the real exchange rate causes an increase in net exports and thus a shift rightward in the AD schedule. The depreciation of the dollar raises the exports of the U.S. as U.S. goods become cheaper abroad. Imports decline as foreign goods become more expensive in the U.S. If foreign real incomes rise, U.S. exports rise at any level of prices, thus shifting the AD schedule to the right.

15.7 THE OPEN ECONOMY MACROECONOMIC MODEL

The model of the open economy combines the AD schedule just derived and one of the supply-side models developed in Chapter 12. Here we use the menu cost model that assumes fixed output prices in the short run. We indicate later how our analysis will differ under alternative supply-side models of the economy.

TABLE 15.4 Factors That Shift the Aggregate Demand Schedule in the Open Economy

Shift Variable	Response of Aggregate Demand
Government Expenditures ↑	AD shifts →
Lump-Sum Taxes ↓	
Ricardian Consumers	AD Unaffected
Non-Ricardian Consumers	AD shifts →
Nominal Money Supply ↑	AD shifts →
Investment ↑	AD shifts →
Private Saving ↑	AD shifts ←
Household Consumption ↑	AD shifts →
Foreign Real Interest Rate ↑	AD shifts →
Foreign Real Income ↑	AD shifts →

Figure 15.12 illustrates how domestic and foreign economies will be tied together when an exogenous event generates a recession in the domestic economy. Suppose there is an exogenous decline in investment spending in the U.S. caused by business perceptions of declining investment productivity in the future. The AD schedule in the U.S. shifts to the left, firms observe declining output demand and inventories increasing, so they cut production and lay off workers. The U.S. has entered a recession. Because U.S. incomes fall, so do U.S. imports. These imports are produced, say, in the UK and so exports from the UK decline. This causes a leftward shift in the UK AD schedule so Figure 15.12 qualitatively portrays events in the U.S. and the UK. Each country experiences a recession. Thus in the open economy model, economies are linked through their trade balances and recessions can be transmitted from one economy to another.

The effects on the trade balances of each country are uncertain. In the U.S., declining income reduces imports causing, ceteris paribus, a trade surplus. But U.S. exports also decline since income in the UK falls. So the end result is an ambiguous response of the trade balance to the shock to the AD schedule resulting in a recession. The UK trade balance also responds ambiguously to the U.S. recession since exports fall as do imports since UK incomes decline.

Alternative models of the economy's supply-side generate results that are very similar to the menu cost model. Suppose that we were to use the new classical model of the supply-side of the economy. This model, discussed in Chapter 12, uses incomplete information in labor

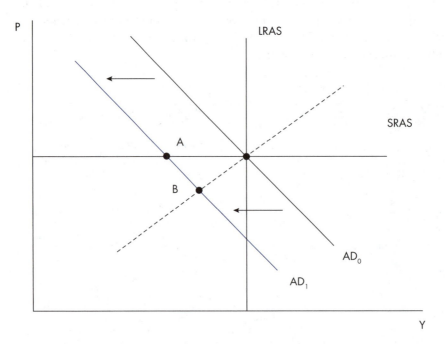

FIGURE 15.12 A Recession in the Open Economy Menu Cost Model

A recession occurs in the U.S. economy due to a shift in the AD schedule from AD_0 to AD_1. This causes a decline in domestic income and imports, given by point A. The foreign economy, say the UK, also experiences a recession because its exports fall; UK exports depend upon incomes in the U.S. If the economy has a new classical short-run supply schedule, the short-run equilibrium will be at point B.

supply to motivate departures of output from Potential GDP. This model generates a short-run aggregate supply curve that is increasing in the price level. For given price expectations, a higher price level fools labor suppliers into thinking that real wages have risen when, in fact, they have declined. With lower real wages, firms use more labor to produce more output so output supply increases. The important difference between this model of the supply side and the menu cost model is that the new classical model leads to price changes during the recession. Figure 15.12 illustrates the story for this case as well.

The shock to U.S. aggregate demand causes a decline in both price and output for given price expectations held by the U.S. public. The shift in AD causes an excess supply of goods which accounts for the decline in the U.S. price level. Since U.S. incomes fall as in the menu cost model, U.S. imports decline and so do exports from the UK. The decline in exports causes a recession in the UK and the UK price level declines. So the recessions in each country are linked, just as in the menu cost model, but now the price levels in each country decline unlike the menu cost model where the price level was fixed in each country in the very short run.

It should also be noted that the linkage between countries, arising from trade in goods and services, need not generate a substantial recession in the country where the shock to aggregate demand does not originate. For a country where trade is a small fraction of GDP, such as the U.S., a shock to aggregate demand in a trading partner will only change exports by a very small amount relative to GDP. So even though the U.S. will experience a negative shock to aggregate demand originating in a trading partner, the effect in the U.S. will be a recession of minimal size. In a country where net exports are a large share of GDP, a recession in a foreign country will have a much larger impact on domestic GDP.

Now we investigate the consequences of fiscal and monetary policy changes that cause output in the domestic economy to depart from Potential GDP. We continue to use the menu cost model of aggregate supply as our description of the short-run supply side of the aggregate economy but we will trace out the effects of policy changes in both the short and long runs.

A Policy Exercise in the Open Economy Model: Fiscal Policy

Changes in government spending can be either permanent or transitory. First consider a transitory increase in government spending, financed by government debt issue. In our discussion of government in Chapter 6, we established that transitory government spending does not imply any changes in the present value of taxes incurred by the public. As a result, there will be no changes in labor supply associated with the increase in government spending. Potential GDP remains fixed in this case. Figure 15.13 illustrates the effects of this policy change.

The increase in government spending shifts the AD schedule to the right. With prices fixed in the short run, there will only be an output response to the shift in aggregate demand. Firms will observe declining inventories and will raise output to replenish depleted inventory stocks. Our analysis of the IS-LM model shows that the real interest rate will go up as the public demands more money to carry out higher spending plans.

A change in government spending has an ambiguous effect upon the real exchange rate. Higher income increases imports and so the domestic economy runs a trade deficit. The trade

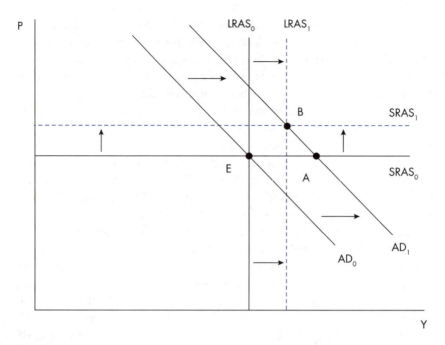

FIGURE 15.13 Fiscal Expansions in the Open Economy Model – Domestic Economy Effects

A transitory increase in government expenditures moves the economy from point E to point A. Output rises above Potential GDP. The real interest rate rises, reducing investment, and imports rise with domestic income. The economy runs a trade deficit. If government spending rises permanently, there will be an increase in Potential GDP because labor supply rises. The new long-run equilibrium is at point B where price and output rise.

deficit causes a depreciation of the dollar as domestic residents must supply more dollars to buy additional imported goods. But the higher domestic interest rate makes U.S. assets more attractive to domestic and foreign residents and so U.S. residents buy fewer foreign assets and foreign residents wish to buy more U.S. assets. These plans cause the dollar to appreciate so that the end result is that the real exchange rate responds ambiguously to the additional government spending. Since the government now is running a deficit and there is a trade deficit as well (assuming that the real exchange rate effects are minimal), the domestic economy has what are sometimes called the **twin deficits**.

Figure 15.14 shows how the temporary increase in government expenditures in the domestic economy affects the foreign country. Because imports in the domestic economy rise, exports in the foreign country increase, shifting the aggregate demand schedule to the right. Prices are fixed in the short run; suppliers replenish declining inventories by increasing output. Incomes rise in the foreign country and money demand increases, raising the foreign interest rate.

Now suppose that the increase in government expenditures is permanent. In the domestic economy displayed in Figure 15.13, there will be an increase in labor supply because households observe an increase in the present value of taxes that they will pay to finance government spending. This implies an increase in Potential GDP. The permanent increase in government spending causes a rightward shift in the AD schedule, just as in the transitory case. The increase in the demand for goods will eventually cause output suppliers to raise prices so

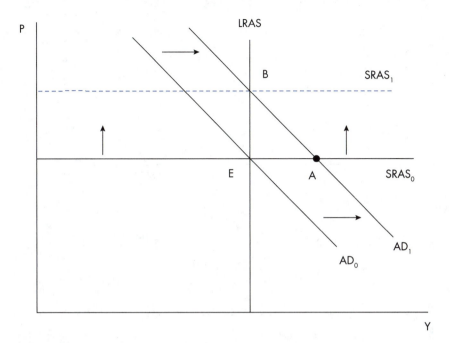

FIGURE 15.14 Fiscal Expansions in the Open Economy Model – Foreign Economy Effects

In the foreign country, a transitory increase in government expenditures in the domestic economy moves the economy from point E to Point A. Output rises above Potential GDP because exports increase. The real interest rate rises, reducing investment, and imports rise with domestic income. If government spending rises permanently in the domestic economy, the new long-run equilibrium is at point B where price rises and output returns to its original full-employment level.

that the price level will be higher in the new long-run equilibrium. Since the nominal supply of money is constant, a higher price level leads to a reduced real supply of money, requiring a higher real interest rate in the new long-run equilibrium to reduce money demand in line with this reduced supply of real money balances.

In the foreign economy in Figure 15.14, Potential GDP is unchanged because there has been no change in government spending or taxes as in the domestic economy. Output suppliers will eventually begin to raise prices in response to the increase in aggregate demand. Higher prices will also pass through to higher money wages. A higher price level reduces the level of the real money supply, requiring a higher real interest rate to reduce household money demand.

A Policy Exercise in the Open Economy Model: Monetary Policy

Now we examine the effects of a domestic monetary contraction. As in our fiscal policy exercises, we study the domestic and foreign economies since they are linked through the trade balance. Figure 15.15 illustrates the short-run and long-run effects in the domestic economy.

In the short run, the decline in the nominal money stock results in an increase in the real interest rate and a consequent decline in investment. The leftward shift in aggregate demand

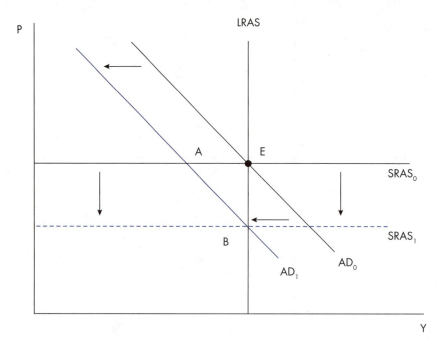

FIGURE 15.15 Monetary Contraction in the Open Economy Model – Domestic Economy Effects

In the domestic economy, a permanent decline in the nominal money stock moves the economy from point E to point A. Output falls below Potential GDP as the economy enters a recession. The real interest rate rises, reducing investment, and imports fall with domestic income. The new long-run equilibrium is at point B where the price level falls and output returns to its original full-employment level.

causes inventories to pile up and suppliers reduce output and lay off workers. The domestic economy has entered a recession. The decline in output reduces imports, causing an increase in the trade balance, but the higher real interest rate causes a decline in net exports. As domestic assets become more attractive, domestic residents buy fewer foreign assets and so supply fewer dollars in the foreign exchange markets. Foreign residents want to buy more domestic assets and so demand more dollars. These actions cause the nominal and real exchange rates to rise. Domestic exports fall and imports into the domestic economy rise. The end result is that the trade balance response to the decline in the money stock is uncertain.

In the foreign country, the effects of the reduction in the domestic money stock are contingent on the behavior of the trade balance in the domestic economy. One possible scenario is illustrated in Figure 15.16. In this case, we assume that the domestic economy trade balance rises in response to the reduction in the domestic money stock. Thus we are assuming that the effect on the trade balance of declining income is larger than the effect on the trade balance of an exchange rate appreciation. Here we observe a leftward shift in the aggregate demand schedule in the foreign economy because a rising trade balance in the domestic economy corresponds to a declining trade balance in the foreign country. Since there is a declining trade balance, there is a leftward shift in the aggregate demand schedule. Output suppliers observe rising inventories as the demand for goods falls, cut production, and lay off workers. The economy is in a recession.

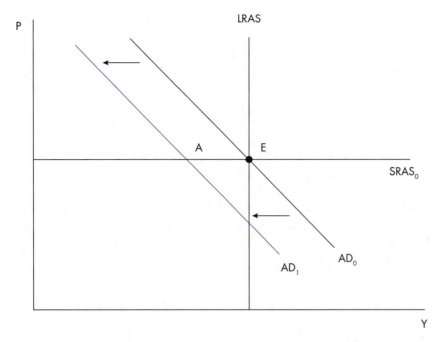

FIGURE 15.16 Monetary Contraction in the Open Economy Model – Foreign Economy Effects

In the foreign economy, a permanent decline in the nominal money stock in the domestic economy moves the economy from point E to point A if the trade balance in the domestic economy declines. Output falls below potential GDP as the foreign economy enters a recession. The new long-run equilibrium is at point E where the price level and output return to their original full-employment levels.

In the long run, the domestic economy returns to Potential GDP. Money is neutral so all real magnitudes are back at their original levels in the domestic and foreign economies. The price level and other nominal magnitudes are lower in the long run in the domestic economy. In the foreign economy, there has been no change in the money supply; all nominal variables are at their initial levels. But the nominal exchange rate rises by the same percentage as the price level falls in the domestic economy. Thus with a constant real exchange rate in the long run, PPP must hold so a decline in the domestic price level must be matched by an appreciation of the domestic currency.

15.8 CONCLUDING REMARKS

This chapter has introduced you to macroeconomics applied to the open economy. Much of the media discussion about globalization centers on the linkages between economies that arise because of trade in goods and financial assets between countries. The discussion in this chapter provides a foundation for understanding these links between economies.

The first part of the chapter described the double-entry bookkeeping system used to record the transactions that occur between trading countries. We then discussed the market for foreign exchange, describing the various institutional arrangements that have been used in foreign exchange markets. We discussed two theories of exchange rate determination, one focused on goods markets, the other concerned with financial markets. We used these economic theories to show how relative inflation rates and interest rates affect nominal exchange rates.

We then went on to develop aggregate macroeconomic models of the open economy. This extended our discussion of the closed-economy model by including the trade balance (exports less imports) into the aggregate demand relationship. We showed that the trade balance was dependent upon real interest rates and real incomes in domestic and foreign economies. In carrying out several exercises using this model with either menu costs or a new classical supply schedule, we observed how business cycles could be transmitted across borders through the trade balances of domestic and foreign economies. This international transmission of business cycles is the important insight that we obtained from our open-economy model.

This chapter should best be viewed as an introduction to the issues that surround trade and investment in the global economy. No single chapter can do justice to all of the economic issues that arise in a global setting. You can learn more about these issues by study in the fields of international trade and finance using this chapter as the foundation for this further study.

Key Ideas

- The Balance of Payments (BOP) is a double-entry bookkeeping system that records economic transactions that occur between trading countries.
- The Current Account is that part of the BOP that measures trade in goods and services between countries.
- The Capital and Financial Account is that part of the BOP that measures portfolio investment in financial and physical assets between countries.
- The nominal exchange rate is a trading ratio for two currencies.
- The foreign exchange market arises from the needs for currencies that are derived from the economic activities measured in the BOP.
- Flexible exchange rate systems allow the exchange rate to be determined by the actions of private traders in the foreign exchange market.
- Fixed exchange rate systems require the central bank of a country to buy and sell currencies so as to keep the nominal exchange rate at a fixed value.
- Absolute Purchasing Power Parity indicates that the foreign price level equals the product of the nominal exchange rate and domestic price level.
- Relative Purchasing Power Parity is an economic theory of nominal exchange rates that shows that relative inflation rates between countries will determine the nominal exchange rate between the currencies of trading countries.
- Uncovered Interest Parity is an economic theory showing that interest rates on comparable securities in two countries are tied together by current and future nominal exchange rates.
- The real exchange rate is defined as the product of the nominal exchange rate and the ratio of domestic to foreign price levels.
- Net exports are inversely related to the real exchange rate.
- The real exchange rate is dependent upon real interest rates in the domestic and foreign economies. The real exchange rate rises with the domestic real interest rate and falls with an increase in the foreign interest rate.

- In the open economy macroeconomic model, the trade balance is a function of real interest rates and incomes in the domestic and foreign economies.
- The trade balance rises (falls) with rising foreign (domestic) incomes.
- The trade balance falls (rises) with rising domestic (foreign) real interest rates.
- Business cycles are transmitted through the trade balance from the originating country to the economies of its trading partners.

Key Words

Balance of Payments	Uncovered Interest Parity	Speculative Attack	Flexible Exchange Rate
Exports	Capital and Financial Accounts	Absolute Purchasing Power Parity	Capital Controls
Appreciation	Current Account	Twin Deficits	Relative Purchasing Power Parity
Nominal Exchange Rate	Imports	Arbitrage	Marginal Propensity to Import (MPI)
Real Appreciation	Depreciation	Capital and Financial Account	Trade Surplus
Fixed Exchange Rate	Real Exchange Rate	Net Exports	Dirty Float
Currency Union	Real Depreciation	Overvalued Currency	Trade Deficit

Questions for Study and Review

Review Questions

1. Describe how a central bank must deal with maintaining a fixed exchange rate when its currency is overvalued.
2. Explain the difference between absolute and relative Purchasing Power Parity.
3. Suppose that the U.S. has an inflation rate which exceeds the inflation rate in the UK. What should happen to the nominal dollar–pound exchange rate according to the theory of Relative Purchasing Power Parity?
4. Explain the relationship between the real exchange rate and net exports. That is, explain how a change in each component of the real exchange rate will affect net exports.
5. Why does a recession originating in a country cause a recession in other economies?
6. How does a monetary contraction in the home country affect the economies of countries that trade with the home country?

Thought Questions

1. Suppose you observe that the return on a 20-year government bond in the U.S. exceeds the yield on the same type of security in France. Does this imply that you should buy the U.S. asset?

2. Suppose a foreign country experiences technical progress that increases the level of Potential GDP. How will this affect economic activity in the home country?
3. Imagine that the home country experiences a transitory negative supply shock. How will this affect economic activity in the home and foreign economies?
4. Suppose that an economy operates in a flexible exchange rate system and that its currency has been depreciating. What policy must the central bank pursue to prevent a further depreciation of its currency?

Numerical Questions

1. Consider the following classical model of the open economy where r denotes the real interest rate. Consumption: $C = 505 - 200 \cdot r$, Investment: $I = 410 - 450 \cdot r$, Government Spending: $G = 150$, Net Exports: $NX = 50 - .5 \cdot e_r$, Real Exchange Rate: $e_r = 50 + 500 \cdot r$, Potential GDP: $Y^P = 1,000$.

    a) Solve for the equilibrium levels of the real interest rate, consumption, investment, net exports, and the real exchange rate.
    b) Suppose that there is a five-unit increase in government expenditures. Solve for the equilibrium levels of the real interest rate, consumption, investment, net exports, and the real exchange rate.

2. Consider the following model of an aggregate economy. $C = 50 + .75 \cdot (Y - T) - 750 \cdot r$, Investment: $I = 100 - 500 \cdot r$, Government Spending: $G = 100$, Taxes: $T = -10 + .2 \cdot Y$, Net Exports: $NX = 160 - .25 \cdot Y - 750 \cdot r$, Potential GDP: $Y^P = 550$, Money Demand: $M^D/P = 10 + .5 \cdot Y - 400 \cdot r$, $M^S = 300$. *Definitions*: $r =$ Real Interest Rate, $P =$ Price Level.

    a) Using the above information, solve for the general equilibrium levels of output, the price level, the real interest rate, consumption, investment, the government deficit(surplus), net exports.
    b) Suppose the economy is characterized by the menu cost model of aggregate supply. If the price level is given at the level you derived above, find the temporary equilibrium levels of output, the real interest rate, consumption, investment, the government deficit (surplus), and net exports when government spending rises by thirty units.
    c) Derive the aggregate demand schedule for the economy using the original information provided in this question.

Data Questions

1. Collect data on the nominal exchange rate for the U.S. and Canada and CPI inflation rates for these two countries. Draw a time series graph of the three series and see how the graph compares to the predictions of Purchasing Power Parity theory.
2. Collect data on government bond yields in the U.S. and the UK, being careful to use bonds that are identical regarding time to maturity. Draw a time series graph of each series and check to see if the series are related as predicted by the theory of Interest Parity.
3. Construct a measure of the real exchange rate for the U.S. and Canada using the CPI for each country and the nominal exchange rate between the U.S. and Canadian dollar.

Next collect data on the constant-dollar level of net exports for the U.S. and plot the real exchange rate and net exports in a time series graph. Does the data confirm the theory in this chapter regarding the two series in the graph? If you use net exports as a share of GDP in the graph in place of net exports, does the theory predict the patterns in the graph?

For further questions, multiple choice quizzes, and weblinks related to this chapter, visit www.routledge.com/textbooks/rossana

Reference

Haskel, J. and Wolf, H. (2001) "The Law of One Price – A Case Study," *Scandinavian Journal of Economics* 103 (4): 545–58.

APPENDIX A: UNCOVERED INTEREST PARITY

Uncovered interest parity arises from the following equilibrium return comparison.

$$(1 + i) = (1 + i^{\text{Foreign}}) \cdot (e/e^*)$$

This expression can be manipulated into another more intuitive form. Since

$$\frac{e^*}{e} = \left[1 + \frac{e^* - e}{e}\right],$$

we can rewrite the equilibrium condition as

$$(1+i)\frac{e^*}{e} = (1+i) \cdot \left[1 + \frac{e^* - e}{e}\right] = (1 + i^{\text{Foreign}}).$$

Now simplify this last expression using

$$(1+i) \cdot \left[1 + \frac{e^* - e}{e}\right] \cong 1 + i + \frac{e^* - e}{e}$$

where "$\cong$" means "approximately." This expression yields

$$1 + i + \frac{e^* - e}{e} = 1 + i^{\text{Foreign}}.$$

Finally, rearranging this last expression gives

$$(1+i) = (1+i^{\text{Foreign}}) - \frac{e^* - e}{e}.$$

This last expression reveals that uncovered interest parity leads to net returns on assets being equalized as long as returns include possible capital gains or losses on foreign exchange.

APPENDIX B: THE OPEN ECONOMY AGGREGATE DEMAND SCHEDULE

In this appendix, an algebraic derivation of the aggregate demand schedule for the open economy is presented. The behavioral relationships will be assumed linear. We use lump-sum taxes and there is no inflation. Thus there is no difference between the real and nominal interest rate. It is assumed, for simplicity, that net exports (NX) depend only upon the domestic real interest rate.

The IS Schedule

Here are the components of the IS schedule.

Consumption: $C = c_0 + c_1 \cdot (Y - T)$, $0 < c_1 < 1$ Disposable Income: $Y^D = Y - T$

Investment: $I = i_0 - i_1 \cdot r$, $i_0 > 0$, $i_1 > 0$ Government Expenditures: $G = G_0$,

Tax Receipts: $T = T_0$ Government Surplus (Deficit): $T - G$

Net Exports: $NX = x_0 - x_1 \cdot r$, $x_0 > 0$, $x_1 > 0$

Definitions: Y = Output, r = Interest Rate, T = Tax Revenues, I = Investment,

G = Government Expenditures, NX = Net Exports, C = Consumption

The LM Schedule

The LM schedule requires the following information.

Money Demand: $\dfrac{M^D}{P} = k_0 + k_1 \cdot Y - k_2 \cdot r$ Money Supply: $M^s = M_0$

Definitions: M = Money Stock, P = Price Level

To derive the IS schedule, form the NIPA relationship $Y = C + I + G + NX$ and, into this expression, substitute the assumptions we are making about each of its components. The result of these substitutions is given below.

$$Y = c_0 + c_1 \cdot (Y - T_0) + i_0 - i_1 \cdot r + G_0 + x_0 - x_1 \cdot r$$

Now solve this for the interest rate to obtain the IS curve.

$$IS : r = \frac{c_0 - c_1 \cdot T_0 + i_0 + G_0 + x_0}{i_1 + x_1} - \left[\frac{1 - c_1}{i_1 + x_1} \right] \cdot Y$$

The slope of this curve is given by $-(1 - c_1)/(i_1 + x_1) < 0$. Note that $(1 - c_1)/(i_1 + x_1) < (1 - c_1)/i_1$ and the curve will shift if taxes or government expenditures change. To obtain the LM schedule, set the supply of money equal to money demand to obtain

$$\frac{M_0}{P} = k_0 + k_1 \cdot Y - k_2 \cdot r$$

Solve this for the interest rate to get

$$r = \frac{k_0 + k_1 \cdot Y}{k_2} - \frac{1}{k_2} \frac{M_0}{P}.$$

The slope of this schedule is $k_1/k_2 > 0$ and it shifts with a change in the money supply.

To derive the AD schedule, eliminate the interest rate from the IS and LM schedules in the following way.

$$\frac{k_0 + k_1 \cdot Y}{k_2} - \frac{1}{k_2} \frac{M_0}{P} = \frac{c_0 - c_1 \cdot T_0 + i_0 + G_0 + x_0}{i_1 + x_1} - \left[\frac{1 - c_1}{i_1 + x_1} \right] \cdot Y$$

Now solve this last expression for the level of real output Y. Some algebra gives

$$AD : Y = \frac{k_2 (c_0 - c_1 \cdot T_0 + i_0 + G_0 + x_0) - k_0 (i_1 + x_1)}{(1 - c_1) \cdot k_2 + k_1 (i_1 + x_1)} + \left[\frac{i_1 + x_1}{(1 - c_1) \cdot k_2 + k_1 (i_1 + x_1)} \right] \cdot \frac{M_0}{P}.$$

The first term to the right of the equal sign captures the effects of magnitudes associated with fiscal policy (government expenditures and taxes), among other things, that can shift the AD schedule. The last term captures the effect of the money supply on the AD schedule (it shifts the curve) and it enables us to compute the slope of the AD schedule. The coefficient preceding the level of real money balances is positive. This implies two things; it shows that an increase in the nominal money supply shifts aggregate demand rightward. It also shows that the slope of the aggregate demand schedule is negative. It may also be shown that

$$\left[\frac{i_1 + x_1}{(1 - c_1) \cdot k_2 + k_1 \cdot (i_1 + x_1)} \right] > \left[\frac{i_1}{(1 - c_1) \cdot k_2 + k_1 \cdot i_1} \right]$$

where the second term in the last expression is the coefficient preceding the stock of real balances when net exports are ignored in the aggregate demand schedule.

Glossary

Absolute convergence A tendency for underdeveloped economies to grow faster than developed economies.

Accelerationist hypothesis The expectations-augmented Phillips Curve implies that an attempt to keep the unemployment rate below its natural rate requires continual accelerating inflation.

Acyclical An economic time series is acyclical if it is neither procyclical nor countercyclical.

Adjustment costs The costs of changing the stock of capital goods held by firms.

After-tax income (or disposable income) Personal income minus tax payments.

After-tax user cost of capital The factor input price of capital goods adjusted by the corporate tax rate.

Amplitude The amplitude of the business cycle measures the distance between a peak or a trough and the trend in real GDP.

Anticipated price change A change in the price level recognized by labor suppliers.

Autonomous components The components of consumption and investment unrelated to real income and the real interest rate.

Average q The stock market value of the firm relative to the replacement cost of the firm's capital stock.

Average tax The average tax is the ratio of tax payments to before-tax real income.

Balance of Payments (BOP) An accounting statement of the economic transactions by residents of a country with the rest of the world in a given time period.

Bank run (or bank panic) Information spreads among depositors that the bank is having trouble meeting currency demands, causing even more depositors to show up on the bank's doorstep demanding currency.

Barter system In a barter system, individuals acquire goods and services by trading goods that they own or by offering to perform services in return for goods and services.

Base year The year in which an economic magnitude has its value set to 100. This year is an arbitrary choice.

Boom An expansion (sometimes called a boom) is the period of time where real output is expanding, rising from a trough to a peak.

Budget deficit If government outlays exceed tax revenues, the government is running a budget deficit.

Budget surplus If tax receipts exceed government outlays, there is a government budget surplus.

Buffer stock Firms face unpredictable demand fluctuations and so they meet the demand for their product by selling output from a stock of finished goods thus buffering fluctuations in the demand for the firm's goods.

Capital and Financial Accounts The Capital and Financial Accounts are sections of the Balance of Payments that record capital and financial flows between countries.

Capital controls These are an example of a government policy that would prevent people from buying foreign exchange for some purposes.

Ceteris Paribus All else the same.

Chain-weighted GDP deflator The ratio of nominal GDP to chain-weighted real GDP.

Chain-Weighted Real GDP The real growth rate of an economy can be distorted when there is rapid structural change. This distortion is avoided by constructing chain-weighted real GDP. An average of two real growth rates is constructed. Real GDP, and its implied growth rate, for two consecutive years is constructed using prices for each year as the base year.

Closed economy A closed economy is one where there is no trade in goods and services or financial transactions with other countries.

Cobb-Douglas A production function with a particular functional form consisting of the product of a constant and each input in production raised to a power. Example: $Y = 100 \cdot K^{.4} \cdot L^{.3}$.

Coincident indicator A coincident indicator is an index number whose behavior suggests a current recession or boom.

Coincident series A coincident series is one that moves above or below trend at the same time that real output moves above or below trend.

Commodity money A commodity money standard is a system where commodities, such as gold or silver, circulate as exchange media.

Comovement Comparison between the pattern in one economic time series to the pattern in real GDP. See *acyclical, countercyclical* and *procyclical*.

Comparative statics Comparing equilibrium positions in the economy as a result of changes in exogenous variables.

Composite commodity A device used to represent a group of goods and services consumed by a household.

Constant-Dollar (Real) GDP Measures output in base year prices.

Constant Returns to Scale A technology displays constant returns to scale if it has the property that changing all inputs in production by the same proportion causes output to rise by the same proportion. That is, $z \cdot Y = F(z \cdot K, z \cdot L)$.

Constraints Households are constrained, in a static context, by their incomes; when they optimize over time, we will assume that there is an intertemporal budget constraint or wealth constraint that binds consumer choices over time.

Consumer Price Index The CPI is a Laspeyres price index, that includes the prices of many goods and services consumed by households. It is a ratio of expenditures on a base-year basket of goods using current prices to expenditures on a base-year basket of goods using base-year prices. It is an important statistic in our society because so many decisions are tied to the value of the CPI, e.g. wage rates and Social Security payments.

Consumption smoothing The idea that consumers find it in their interest for their consumption spending to be less variable than their income over time.

Contraction A recession (or a contraction) is the time period where real output is declining, falling from a peak to a trough in real output.

Countercyclical An economic time series is countercyclical if it tends to be below (above) trend when real GDP is above (below) trend.

Currency unions An example is the EU; these are an alternative to fixed exchange rate systems where a group of countries agree to use a common currency in all transactions.

Current account balance The sum of the value of exports of goods and services minus the value of imports of goods and services plus income receipts derived from the ownership of assets, and unilateral transfers such as foreign aid payments.

Deflating Deflating a nominal economic magnitude is the act of dividing the magnitude by the price level, giving a ratio measured in units of output.

Deflation Deflation is a decline in the price level.

Demand for goods The demand for goods is a relationship between real output and the real interest rate showing how much output will be demanded by households, firms, and the government at any level of the real interest rate.

Deposit An account that is a liability of a bank and an asset of the public such as checkable deposits.

Depreciation The decline in value of durable assets over time.

Desired stock of capital The desired capital stock of the firm is that level of the capital stock consistent with profit maximization by the firm.

Deterministic trend A deterministic trend is one that can be represented in the following way.

$$\text{Trend} = a_0 + a_1 \cdot \text{Time}$$

So a trend in this case is just a linear function of time.

Diminishing marginal utility Consumer preferences have the property of diminishing marginal utility; as consumption of a commodity increases, the consumption of all other goods fixed, the extra utility given to the household from consuming the commodity declines.

Diminishing returns in production A production function displays diminishing returns in production when the Marginal Product (MP) of an input declines as the level of the input increases, the quantities of all other inputs held fixed.

Dirty float In a dirty float, private citizens buy and sell currencies, just as in the floating exchange rate case, but in addition, central banks purchase or sell currencies, often in an attempt to change the equilibrium exchange rate.

Discount rate The number used to translate a future payment stream into its present equivalent. In the case of monetary policy, this is the rate paid by banks to borrow from the Federal Reserve.

Discount window The Federal Reserve lends to banks through thediscount window.

Discouraged workers If a person is not actively searching for work, they are considered to have withdrawn from the labor force. Sometimes these individuals are referred to as discouraged workers since people may give up looking for work if they have been unsuccessful in finding work after a substantial period of job search.

Discretion Discretion is a manner of carrying out economic policy that does not use explicit rules that determine economic policies.

Disposable income (or after-tax income) Personal income minus tax.

Double coincidence of wants When people trade goods for other goods, they must find others who are willing to trade.

Double-counting The faulty practice of counting the value of a nation's goods more than once.

Duration The duration of a cycle just refers to the length of time that the economy experiences an expansion or contraction in economic activity.

Duration of unemployment The time in weeks that the individual has been without work and looking for a job.

Dynamic adjustment path If the economy is not in steady-state equilibrium, there are forces in the economy that will cause it to move towards this equilibrium. The path to equilibrium is known as the dynamic adjustment path.

Dynamic inefficiency A growing economy is dynamically inefficient if it has a capital–labor ratio that is above the level of the capital–labor ratio consistent with the Golden Rule.

Economic agents A phrase used to describe both households and firms. Agents are always trying to maximize something. In the case of households, we will assume that they are trying to maximize their economic welfare. Regarding firms, we will assume they are trying to maximize their profits.

Economic models Abstractions that are meant to represent the structure of actual economies or to represent the behavior of households and firms.

Efficiency units A measure of factor inputs in production that incorporates the quality of these inputs.

Elasticity The **elasticity** of a variable y with respect to another variable x is given by the percentage change in y with respect to a percentage change in x. That is, the elasticity between y and x is measured by the ratio $(\Delta y/y)/(\Delta x/x)$.

Empirical research Testing the predictions of economic theories by using actual economic data.

Endogenous economic variables Variables that are determined within the general equilibrium system.

Endogenous growth model Where the growth rate of the economy is determined endogenously (within the model) rather than being given by exogenous forces.

Exchange rate An exchange rate is the rate at which one currency trades for another in foreign exchange markets.

Excess demand A situation where the quantity demanded by economic agents exceeds the quantity of it supplied.

Excess supply A situation where the quantity demanded by economic agents is less than the quantity of it supplied.

Exogenous economic variables Variables that are determined outside of the general equilibrium system.

Expansion An **expansion** (sometimes called a **boom**) is the period of time where real output is expanding, rising from a trough to a peak.

Expectations Households and firms may need to form expectations about economic magnitudes when they optimize.

Exports These measure goods and services produced domestically that are consumed by foreign residents. Domestic residents consume goods produced domestically and abroad.

Externalities An externality refers to the activity of one individual that affects the welfare of others, e.g. pollution by firms.

Factors of production Inputs in the production process, such as labor and capital goods, which are used to produce goods and services.

Feasible set The set of resource allocations which satisfies all constraints in an economic model.

Federal Funds interest rate The interest rate on interbank loans made in the Federal Funds market.

Federal Open Market Committee (FOMC) The FOMC makes decisions regarding open market operations carried out by the Fed.

Fiat money The paper currency that we use each day is an example of a fiat money; it is money because of government decree or fiat.

Financial intermediaries An intermediary brings parties together to facilitate a transaction. In the case of a financial intermediary, lenders and borrowers are brought together by banks to facilitate loan transactions.

Fisher effect The Fisher effect, developed by the economist Irving Fisher, states that a rise in the inflation rate will increase the nominal interest rate so as to keep the real interest rate fixed.

Fixed exchange rate In a fixed exchange rate system, the exchange rate is pegged at a fixed value and it is the responsibility of the central bank to maintain this fixed value.

Flat tax A flat tax is a tax system with a constant tax rate. There is just one tax bracket.

Flexible accelerator The firm is presumed to maximize its profits in choosing the level of inventories to hold. The results of this profit maximization lead to an inventory investment relationship which is called the flexible accelerator model of inventory investment.

Flexible exchange rate In a flexible exchange rate system, there is no intervention by central banks and thus the market is permitted to set the exchange rate through the actions of all of the participants in the market.

Flow Flows are economic variables measured relative to a time period.

Fractional-reserve banking system In such a system, banks lend out part of their depositor's funds. Fractional reserve banking is attractive to bankers because there are profit opportunities available that the bank can exploit when it needs to keep only a fraction of its depositor's funds in reserve.

Free riders Free riders will not voluntarily pay for goods provided by the government, preferring instead to obtain the benefits of those goods when they are purchased by others.

Frictional unemployment This refers to the fact that firms and workers operate in labor markets under incomplete information about the characteristics of jobs and workers, and so it takes time for appropriate job matches to occur.

Full-employment deficit (surplus) This is a measure of the government's surplus or deficit when the economy is operating at full employment or Potential GDP.

General equilibrium An economy is in general equilibrium when there are no excess demands or supplies for goods and financial assets in the economy and when expectations are correct.

General Equilibrium System A complete model of the aggregate economy including all markets and the connections between them.

Golden Rule The condition that must hold if steady-state consumption, and thus economic welfare, is to be at a maximum.

Government Budget Constraint (GBC) An accounting relationship listing, in tabular or equation form, the sources and uses of funds by the government.

Government investment Durable capital goods purchased by governments.

Government outlays The sum of net transfers (TR), interest payments on government bonds (INT), and government spending (G) is defined as government outlays.

Government purchases This refer to the goods and services purchased by governments at all levels.

Gross Domestic Product Measures the market value in current dollars of final goods and services produced within a given time period by labor and property located within the borders of the U.S.

Gross investment Measures additions to the stock of capital goods held by firms.

Gross production function The production function used by the firm that does not include the planning and installation costs of net investment carried out by the firm.

Growth Accounting An empirical method, designed to quantitatively assess how much of the growth rate in output is contributed by each source of growth.

Harrod-Neutral Technical Progress This is the technical progress associated with the labor used in production.

Hicks-Neutral Technical Progress The idea that more output can be produced from the same resource base and technology.

High-powered money The total amount of bank reserves plus currency.

Household wealth Household wealth is defined to be the present value of household income.

$$\text{Wealth} = Y_0 + \frac{Y_1}{1+r}$$

Human capital The stock of knowledge acquired by individuals that they use in their work.

Hyperinflation An extremely high inflation is called a hyperinflation.

Implicit GDP deflator Another measure of prices in the economy that can be useful because it is a broader measure of prices in the economy compared to the CPI. Its construction is quite easy, given our discussion of nominal and real GDP. The formula below shows how to construct this measure of the price level.

$$\text{Implicit GDP Deflator} = (\text{Nominal GDP/Real GDP}) * 100$$

Imports Measure foreign-produced goods consumed by U.S. households.

Income effect Change in consumption and leisure as a result of rise in income ceteris paribus

Indifference curves A graph showing different bundles of commodities, each measured as to quantity, between which a consumer is *indifferent*. That is, at each point on the curve, the consumer has no preference for one bundle over another. In other words, they are all equally preferred.

Indifference map Consumer preferences will be represented by a concept called an indifference map which is simply a collection of indifference curves. This will describe the way that consumers rank bundles of commodities in terms of the welfare provided to them by these goods and services.

Indifference principle If a household consumes less of one commodity, it can be compensated for this loss in welfare by consuming more of another commodity. This is referred to as the indifference principle.

Inflation Inflation is an increase in the level of all prices in the economy, an ongoing or continuing process that can last indefinitely.

Informational advantage An informational advantage refers to a situation where one group of individuals has more information about the true state of the economy as compared to other groups.

Intermediate goods and services Intermediate goods are products produced by firms in the economy, and used by other firms in the production of their products. To count these in GDP would result in double-counting because the value of intermediate goods is already included in the prices of the goods produced by using these intermediate goods and services.

Intertemporal or **dynamic** In studying the behavior of the household and firm, if multiple periods of time are chosen for analysis, the economic theory developed is called intertemporal or dynamic.

Intertemporal budget constraint All households are constrained over time by their financial resources and this constraint limits the bundles of goods that households may buy. This constraint will be called the constraint faced by the household.

Intertemporal efficiency An economy is intertemporally efficient if it is producing on the frontier of the intertemporal production possibility surface.

Job searcher To be unemployed, a person must be without work and actively seeking employment, i.e. searching for a job.

K-percent rule A k-percent rule is a policy prescription stating that the money supply should grow at a constant rate.

Knowledge externality The knowledge created by one firm has a positive productivity effect upon all other firms.

Knowledge spillovers Research and development (R&D) carried out by one firm will increase the aggregate stock of knowledge in the economy and the new knowledge, created by one firm, will spill over to other firms who will be able to use this new knowledge within their own production processes.

Labor force The **labor force** is the sum of individuals who are working plus those searching for a job.

Labor force participation rate The **labor force participation rate** is the ratio of the labor force to the civilian population.

Lagging indicators A **lagging indicator** is an index number whose behavior suggests a past recession or boom.

Lagging series A lagging series is one that moves above or below trend after the time that real output moves above or below trend.

Lags Lags are the time it takes for policymakers to recognize the need for a policy change, the time it takes to carry out the new policy, and the time it takes for the new policy to affect the economy.

Laspeyres CPI Index A Laspeyres CPI price index measures the current cost of a fixed market basket of goods and services relative to the cost of the market basket in a base year.

Layoff unemployment When demand declines for the goods produced by firms, they will often cut the size of their workforce, planning to re-employ laid-off workers when output demand increases in the future.

Leading indicator A leading indicator is an index number whose behavior suggests a future recession or boom.

Leading series A leading series is one that moves above or below trend prior to the time that real output moves above or below trend.

Learning-by-doing The idea that as time passes the managers of firms learn their production techniques more thoroughly, thus learning how to produce more efficiently.

Life cycle hypothesis This theory stresses the fact that demographic factors, such as the age of the workers in households, should be an important factor explaining the consumption and saving behavior observed in aggregate economies.

Liquidity Generally refers to the ease with which an asset can be converted into another asset or into goods and services.

Lump-sum taxes A lump-sum tax is a tax that is a fixed amount no matter what the change in circumstance of the taxed entity.

M1 The monetary aggregate that comprises currency, demand and checkable deposits, and travelers' checks.

M2 M1 plus savings deposits, small time deposits and retail money market funds.

Marginal q Tobin's marginal q is one plus the marginal adjustment cost of net investment.

Marginal Product of Capital The Marginal Product of Capital (MP_K) measures the extra output produced by an additional unit of capital used in production when the quantities of all other inputs are held fixed.

Marginal Propensity to Import (MPI) The Marginal Propensity to Import is the additional imports into a country as a result of a unit increase in domestic income.

Marginal Rate of Substitution The Marginal Rate of Substitution (MRS) between present and future consumption measures the extra current consumption that must be consumed by the household to compensate it for the loss of a given amount of future consumption.

Marginal Rate of Transformation (MRT) The slope of the intertemporal production possibility frontier is known as the economy's Marginal Rate of Transformation (MRT) in production. The MRT is the measure of the opportunity cost of goods in production.

Marginal revenue The extra revenue that an additional unit of product will bring.

Marginal tax rate If you earn an extra dollar of income, the additional tax that you pay on this extra income is called the marginal tax rate.

Marginal utility The marginal utility of a good measures the change in welfare associated with a change in the consumption of that good, the quantities of all other goods held constant.

Market Economic models use the concept of a market to describe how prices and quantities are determined by the interactions of buyers and sellers.

Market equilibrium In a model where expectations must be formed by economic agents (households and firms), equilibrium in a market is defined to be a situation where there is no excess supply or demand in the market and price expectations are correct.

Mean-reverting If something were to cause a series to deviate from its mean, it will return to its mean if enough time passes.

Medium of exchange The first use of money, its medium of exchange function, means that people trade items called money for the goods and services that they want to consume.

Menu costs The cost of changing the prices of the output produced by firms.

Microeconomic foundations The choices made by individual households and firms at the individual level which allow important insights into the behavior of aggregate economies.

Modified Golden Rule In an economy that has optimizing households whose preferences display time preference, the optimal savings rate should obey the Modified Golden Rule.

Monetarists Monetarists are economists who argue that inflation is caused by the growth rate of the money supply.

Monetary Base **Monetary base** = Currency + Bank Reserves.

Monetized Use money.

Money illusion Economic agents are assumed to know the difference between economic magnitudes measured in dollar units or in real terms (units of goods). If they do not recognize this difference, they are said to suffer from money illusion.

Money multiplier Let k = The Currency/Checkeckable Deposit Ratio and rr = The Required Reserve Ratio. Then the money multiplier is $(1 + k)/(k + rr)$.

MPC out of current income The marginal propensity to consume (MPC) out of current income measures the change in current consumption associated with a one unit increase in current household disposable income, Y.

MPC out of permanent income The marginal propensity to consume (MPC) out of permanent income measures the additional consumption that occurs in response to a one unit increase in permanent income.

MPS out of current income: The marginal propensity to save (MPS) out of current income measures the change in current saving associated with a one unit increase in current household disposable income, Y.

NBER In the U.S., a nonprofit corporation called the National Bureau of Economic Research (NBER) is an organization of economists that, among other things, dates business cycles.

Negative income tax If taxable income is below a certain level, the household receives a payment from the government rather than making a tax payment to the government.

Net Domestic Product This deducts the value of depreciation from GDP. Thus Net Domestic Product measures goods and services produced which may be consumed or added to the stock of physical assets in the economy.

Net exports The difference between exports and imports.

Net investment This deducts from gross investment the amount of investment needed to replace worn-out capital goods so it measures net additions to the stock of capital.

Net production function The production function of the firm that includes the output lost by carrying out net investment.

Neoclassical theory of investment Theory of investment built upon optimizing (or profit-maximizing) behavior by the firm.

Nominal GDP Measures the output produced in the economy in current-dollar units.

Nominal user cost of capital The product of the nominal purchase price of capital goods and the sum of the real interest rate and the depreciation rate.

Nonexcludability Nonexcludable goods are those which once made available to one person become available to all.

Nonrivalry A good is nonrival when its usage by one person does not detract from others' usage.

Nonstationary An economic time series is nonstationary if its average value is not constant over time.

Normal goods Any goods for which demand increases when income increases and falls when income decreases all else the same.

Normative policy evaluation An assessment where we try to decide if a particular policy intervention is desirable for an economy.

Open economy An open economy is one where there is trade in goods and services and financial assets with other countries.

Open market operations The means of implementing monetary policy by the purchase or sale of bonds with the goal of affecting the interest rate and the money stock.

Opportunity costs Opportunity cost is the value of the next best choice that one gives up when making an economic choice.

Pareto-efficient If by a reallocation of goods one person gains welfare, and no other person has a welfare loss, that reallocation unambiguously raises overall welfare in the economy; such a reallocation is said to be Pareto-efficient.

Pareto Optimality An allocation of goods is Pareto Optimal if it is not possible to reallocate goods, making one person better off, without making another person in the economy worse off.

Partial adjustment The firm will only adjust its capital stock part of the way towards its desired level in each period of time if there are costs of adjustment attached to net investment.

Patent protection Governments give patent protection to new ideas. The patent is an attempt to exclude others for a period of time from using the new ideas generated by a firm.

Peak A peak is when real output stops rising and begins to decline.

Perfect markets It is assumed that the firm is a price-taker in output and input markets. This means that the price of the firm's output, P, and the nominal factor input prices (W and U_K) that it pays for its productive inputs are fixed and unaffected by the firm's actions. This is sometimes known as the assumption of perfect markets: prices are simply fixed parameters faced by the firm.

Permanent income Permanent income is the constant amount of income with the property that the household's wealth is the same whether it is measured by permanent or actual income.

Permanent Income Hypothesis Milton Friedman's important theory of consumer behavior which revolves around a distinction between transitory income and permanent income. This theory asserts that consumption is proportional to Permanent Income.

Permanent shock If a time series experiences permanent changes to its level, we will describe this by saying that the series is subject to permanent shocks.

Phillips Curve The original Phillips Curve was an observed negative relationship between the unemployment rate and the inflation rate.

Planning and installation (adjustment) costs The costs attached to changing the capital stock, e.g. shutting down the plant while new equipment is installed.

Policy Ineffectiveness Proposition In a New Classical model of the aggregate economy, only the unanticipated portion of the money supply will have an impact upon the real economic magnitudes in an economy where the public has rational expectations.

Policy Invariance Principle or **Lucas Critique** The decisions rules obeyed by households and firms will contain parameters that are functions of (or depend upon) the parameters of the policy rules used by policymakers. To predict the effects of a change in a policy rule requires that we know the relationship between the parameters in the decision rules used by the public and the parameters of policy rules used by policymakers.

Positive policy evaluation An assessment where we simply determine the effects of a policy without judging the desirability of that policy.

Potential GDP Potential GDP is the level of real output produced when the economy is in a general equilibrium.

Present value A method of translating future benefits into their present equivalent.

Price-taker It is assumed that the firm is a price-taker in output and input markets. This means that the price of the firm's output, P, and the nominal factor input prices (W and U_K) that it pays for its productive inputs are fixed and unaffected by the firm's actions. This is sometimes known as the assumption of perfect markets: prices are simply fixed parameters faced by the firm.

Principal Loan contracts are written using the nominal interest rate; the lender agrees to lend an amount, called the principal, and requires the payment of a dollar amount each year expressed as a fraction of the principal.

Procyclical An economic time series is procyclical if it tends to be above trend when real GDP is above trend.

Produce to order Firms sometimes do not hold inventories of finished goods. Rather they produce goods in response to customer orders, producing output and delivering it to their customers with a substantial delay from the time that a new order is placed. Firms of this type are said to produce to order.

Producing to stock Firms that hold inventories of finished goods are described as producing to stock.

Production function Firms will have a technology, known as a production function, which represents the technical relationship between inputs in production, such as labor and raw materials, and the output that these inputs can produce.

Production-smoothing It is costly for firms to change production because the marginal cost of production rises. So avoiding large changes in production is called production smoothing.

Productivity slowdown A reduction in the rate of growth of output per worker.

Progressive There is more than one marginal tax rate in many countries because income tax codes are frequently progressive, meaning that the higher your income, the higher is your marginal tax rate.

Progressive tax system The tax rate on before-tax income rises with the level of before-tax income.

Public goods Goods and services provided free of charge to the public. The consumption of these by one person does not prevent the consumption by another person, e.g. national defense.

Purchasing Power Parity Purchasing Power Parity is a theory of exchange rates stating that the foreign price level must equal the product of the exchange rate and the domestic price level.

Quality bias Over time, quality changes occur in the production of goods and services in an economy, distorting the information provided by the CPI. This problem is referred to as quality bias.

Rational expectation A rational expectation of an economic magnitude is an expectation with the property that there are no systematic errors made in forecasting the economic variable of interest.

Real exchange rate The real exchange rate is defined as $e_r = e \cdot [P/P^{Foreign}]$ where P denotes the domestic price level, e is the nominal exchange rate, and $P^{Foreign}$ is the price level in the foreign country. It measures the rate at which goods can be exchanged between the two countries.

Real interest rate The real interest rate is the nominal interest rate minus the expected rate of inflation.

Real user cost of capital The ratio of the nominal user cost of capital to the price of the output produced by the firm.

Real wage Wages that have been adjusted by the price level.

Recession The time period where real output is declining, falling from a peak to a trough in real output.

Redistribute income Government may redistribute income to those at the lower end of the income distribution. This can take the form of lower (or even no) taxes for some individuals or perhaps the direct provision of goods.

Relative prices When the price of one commodity rises or falls relative to the prices of other goods and services, economists refer to this as a change in relative prices.

Rental prices The proper way to measure the services of durable goods is to use rental prices for new and used durable goods presumably taken from samples of rental goods market prices that could be used to value the services of durable goods of all vintages.

Replacement investment We refer to the activity of replacing worn-out capital goods as replacement investment.

Representative household or firm An aggregate relationship, describing the behavior of all households, is exactly like the relationship obtained from the analysis of an individual household.

Ricardian Equivalence David Ricardo, a classical English economist, suggested the idea that the methods used to finance government, taxation or borrowing, would have equivalent effects upon the economy.

Rules Rules are explicit descriptions of the economic magnitudes that determine the policies set by policymakers.

Serial persistence An economic time series displays serial persistence if the series tends to be above or below trend for more than one period of time.

Shoe-leather costs The time and other costs of carrying out transactions.

Solow-neutral technical progress Technical progress associated with the stock of capital goods.

Solow residual In the production function $Y = T \cdot F(K, L)$ where K and L measure, respectively, the services of capital and labor, the parameter T is known as the Solow residual or Total Factor Productivity.

Speed of adjustment The speed of adjustment is that fraction of the gap between desired and actual capital stocks that is made up in each time period.

Square-root rule The square-root rule describes the demand for money as implied by the Baumol-Tobin theory of the demand for money.

Stable equilibrium If the economy is not in steady-state equilibrium, there are forces in the economy that will cause it to move towards this equilibrium. For this reason, the equilibrium in the Solow model is said to be stable.

Standard of deferred payment Money is a standard of deferred payment. Loans are carried out by measuring their terms in units of money.

Static In studying the behavior of the household and firm, if a single period is chosen for analysis, the economic theory developed is called static.

Stationary An economic time series is stationary if its average (or mean) value is constant over time.

Stationary economy One where Potential GDP is unchanging over time.

Steady-state equilibrium A steady-state equilibrium in a growing economy is a situation where per capita economic magnitudes remain constant over time.

Stock Stocks are economic variables measured at a point in time.

Stock-outs A stock-out occurs when a firm has no units of output in inventory.

Store of value Any form of commodity, asset, or money that has value and can be stored and retrieved over time, e.g. bonds, ownership of capital.

Structural unemployment One characteristic of industrialized economies is that firms cease operation and new ones form to produce new goods and services. These activities can cause structural unemployment.

Substitution bias The CPI is known to overstate inflation because consumers do not consume constant quantities of goods. As the relative prices of goods and services change, so will the quantities of goods purchased by consumers. This problem is sometimes called substitution bias in the CPI.

Substitution effect The substitution effect measures the response of consumption in each period to a shift in the real interest rate measured along the original indifference curve.

Superneutral If the real equilibrium of an aggregate economy is independent of variations in the growth rate of the money stock, the money stock is said to be superneutral.

Tax smoothing The idea that governments do not change tax rates in response to temporary causes of budget deficits.

Temporary equilibrium An economy is in a temporary equilibrium when excess demands and supplies for goods and financial assets in the economy are zero and when expectations are incorrect.

Time preference The idea that households prefer to consume now, rather than later when making their consumption decisions. The rate of time preference is that amount that must compensate people for waiting to consume goods and services.

Total Factor Productivity In the production function $Y = T \cdot F(K, L)$ where K and L measure, respectively, the services of capital and labor, the parameter T is known as the Solow residual or Total Factor Productivity.

Trade deficit If exports are less than imports, a country has a trade deficit.

Trade surplus If a country's exports exceed its imports, that country is said to have a trade surplus.

Transactions costs The notion of transactions costs generally refers to the costs of carrying out a transaction.

Transfer payments Payments made by the government to individuals, using funds received from other individuals, such as Social Security payments.

Transitory income Unpredictable earnings e.g. overtime pay.

Transitory shocks Shocks that occur for a time and then disappear.

Trend line Output (real GDP) has a general direction of change, described by a trend line. Output will fluctuate about this trend line and it is these fluctuations that are what we mean by the business cycle.

Trough A trough is when output stops declining and begins to rise.

Turning point The fluctuations in economic activity involve turning points. These are called peaks and troughs.

Unanticipated price change A change in the price level that is not recognized by labor suppliers.

Uncovered Interest Parity A theory that we can use to explain the connection between interest rates across countries.

Underground economy Transactions that are carried out "off the books" (part of the underground economy) because they are illegal or because people are trying to avoid taxes on these transactions. These activities are not measured in GDP.

Unemployment rate Unemployment rate = Stock of unemployed workers/Labor force (expressed as a percentage).

Unexpected money supply The unexpected money supply is the component of the monetary policy rule that cannot be predicted by the public or even controlled by the Fed.

Unit of account Money is used as a unit of account, meaning that we measure prices in terms of money.

Unstable equilibrium If the equilibrium were unstable, the economy would not again reach an equilibrium if an event occurred that caused the economy to move away from its equilibrium.

User cost of capital The user cost of capital is the factor input price of the firm's capital stock.

Value-added The value-added of a firm is the difference between the value of a firm's output and its purchases of intermediate goods used in production.

Value of the marginal product of capital The product of the firm's ouput price and the additional output resulting from the use of an additional unit of capital.

Vault cash Cash held by the bank.

Velocity of money The velocity of money is defined as the ratio of nominal income to the money stock.

Wage–rental ratio The ratio of the wage rate to the user cost of capital.

Walras' law of markets In an economy with an arbitrary number of markets, the sum of all the excess demands in the economy must be zero.

Warranted rate of growth The warranted rate of growth of the economy is equal to the population growth rate. In equilibrium, output and the capital stock grow at the warranted rate of growth.

Wealth effect The wealth effect measures the change in consumption associated with a change in wealth at the new real interest rates.

Index